FRATERNAL BENEFITS
AND FINANCIAL SECURITY
FOR LUTHERANS

Kitchen Favorites

Compiled by

AAL Branch 3107
Loveland, Colorado

Expression
of
Appreciation

We wish to express sincere appreciation to all the AAL branch members who so graciously donated their favorite recipes and participated in this project. If the same or similar recipe was submitted by a number of people, one was selected and credit given to all who submitted the recipe.

A very special thanks to all those individuals who helped with the compiling, editing, distribution, and the selling or in any other way contributed to the publication of this delightful cookbook.

Sincere Thanks From,

The Cookbook Committee
AAL Branch 3107
Loveland, Colorado

All the recipes in this book were submitted by various AAL branches across the U.S. and compiled and distributed by the officers and members of AAL Branch 3107 of Loveland, Colorado.

Published By
Cookbook Publishers, Inc.
P.O. Box 1260
2101 Kansas City Road
Olathe, Kansas 66061-1260

R3-112-89

1st printing	April 1989	12,000 books
2nd printing	July 1989	10,000 books
3rd printing	Oct. 1989	20,000 books
4th printing	Jan. 1990	20,000 books

A recipe that is not shared with others
will soon be forgotten,
but when it is shared,
it will be enjoyed by future generations.

TABLE OF CONTENTS

FAVORITE RECIPES
FROM MY COOKBOOK

Recipe Name	Page Number

Appetizers,
Snacks,
Beverages

A HANDY SPICE AND HERB GUIDE

ALLSPICE—a pea-sized fruit that grows in Mexico, Jamaica, Central and South America. Its delicate flavor resembles a blend of cloves, cinnamon and nutmeg. USES: (Whole) Pickles, meats, boiled fish, gravies. (Ground) Puddings, relishes, fruit preserves, baking.

BASIL—the dried leaves and stems of an herb grown in the United States and North Mediterranean area. Has an aromatic, leafy flavor. USES: For flavoring tomato dishes and tomato paste, turtle soup; also use in cooked peas, squash, snap beans; sprinkle chopped over lamb chops and poultry.

BAY LEAVES—the dried leaves of an evergreen grown in the eastern Mediterranean countries. Has a sweet, herbaceous floral spice note. USES: For pickling, stews, for spicing sauces and soup. Also use with a variety of meats and fish.

CARAWAY—the seed of a plant grown in the Netherlands. Flavor that combines the tastes of Anise and Dill. USES: For the cordial Kummel, baking breads; often added to sauerkraut, noodles, cheese spreads. Also adds zest to French fried potatoes, liver, canned asparagus.

CURRY POWDER—a ground blend of ginger, turmeric, fenugreek seed, as many as 16 to 20 spices. USES: For all Indian curry recipes such as lamb, chicken, and rice, eggs, vegetables, and curry puffs.

DILL—the small, dark seed of the dill plant grown in India, having a clean, aromatic taste. USES: Dill is a predominant seasoning in pickling recipes; also adds pleasing flavor to sauerkraut, potato salad, cooked macaroni, and green apple pie.

MACE—the dried covering around the nutmeg seed. Its flavor is similar to nutmeg, but with a fragrant, delicate difference. USES: (Whole) For pickling, fish, fish sauce, stewed fruit. (Ground) Delicious in baked goods, pastries and doughnuts, adds unusual flavor to chocolate desserts.

MARJORAM—an herb of the mint family, grown in France and Chile. Has a minty-sweet flavor. USES: In beverages, jellies and to flavor soups, stews, fish, sauces. Also excellent to sprinkle on lamb while roasting.

MSG (MONOSODIUM GLUTAMATE)—is a vegetable protein derivative for raising the effectiveness of natural food flavors. USES: Small amounts, adjusted to individual taste, can be added to steaks, roasts, chops, seafoods, stews, soups, chowder, chop suey and cooked vegetables.

OREGANO—a plant of the mint family and a species of marjoram of which the dried leaves are used to make an herb seasoning. USES: An excellent flavoring for any tomato dish, especially pizza, chili con carne, and Italian specialties.

PAPRIKA—a mild, sweet red pepper growing in Spain, Central Europe and the United States. Slightly aromatic and prized for brilliant red color. USES: A colorful garnish for pale foods, and for seasoning Chicken Paprika, Hungarian Goulash, salad dressings.

POPPY—the seed of a flower grown in Holland. Has a rich fragrance and crunchy, nut-like flavor. USES: Excellent as a topping for breads, rolls and cookies. Also delicious in buttered noodles.

ROSEMARY—an herb (like a curved pine needle) grown in France, Spain, and Portugal, and having a sweet, fresh taste. USES: In lamb dishes, in soups, stews and to sprinkle on beef before roasting.

SAGE—the leaf of a shrub grown in Greece, Yugoslavia and Albania. Flavor is camphoraceous and minty. USES: For meat and poultry stuffing, sausages, meat loaf, hamburgers, stews and salads.

THYME—the leaves and stems of a shrub grown in France and Spain. Has a strong, distinctive flavor. USES: For poultry seasoning, in croquettes, fricassees and fish dishes. Also tasty on fresh sliced tomatoes.

TURMERIC—a root of the ginger family, grown in India, Haiti, Jamaica and Peru, having a mild, ginger-pepper flavor. USES: As a flavoring and coloring in prepared mustard and in combination with mustard as a flavoring for meats, dressings, salads.

CHEESY ARTICHOKES

1 large can artichoke hearts, drained
1 small jar *marinated* artichoke hearts (drain ½ liquid oil)
1 (4 oz.) can diced green chiles
6 Tbsp. mayonnaise
1½ c. shredded Cheddar cheese

Cut up artichoke hearts in 1 quart microwavable dish. Add green chiles and mayonnaise. Microwave on HIGH for 1 to 2 minutes till heated through. (Can stir halfway through time.) Top with Cheddar cheese. Microwave again just till cheese melts. Serve with crackers or chips.

Marilyn Vogel, Loveland, CO

HANKIE PANKIES

1 lb. hamburger
1 lb. Velveeta cheese
1 lb. pork or pizza sausage
½ tsp. red pepper flakes
½ tsp. oregano
½ tsp. garlic salt
1 loaf of cocktail rye

Fry sausage and drain. Fry hamburger and drain. Mix hamburger, sausage and spices; simmer. Add Velveeta cheese and heat until melted. Spread on cocktail rye and broil for 1 minute.

Audrey Partika, Branch No. 1036, New Londen, WI

HANKIE PANKIES

1 lb. ground beef
1 lb. sausage
½ tsp. oregano
½ tsp. garlic salt
1 lb. Velveeta cheese
1½ loaves cocktail rye bread

Brown beef and sausage together. Drain. Add spices and cheese. Spread on rye bread. Preheat oven to 400° and place slices on cookie sheet. Heat for 12 minutes or until heated through. Serve warm.

Greg West, Branch No. 6399, Orange City, IA

MEXICAN PARTY DIP

1 (10.5 oz.) can bean dip
1 (8 oz.) cream cheese
1 (8 oz.) sour cream
1 pkg. taco mix
5 to 6 green onions, chopped
8 oz. shredded cheese (Cheddar and Monterey Jack)

Mix first 5 ingredients. Pour and spread in 9 inch pie plate. Top with shredded cheese. Bake for 30 minutes at 350°. Serve warm with favorite variety of chips for dipping.

Deric Garnell, Branch No. 4843, Hancock, MI

LAYERED MEXICAN DIP

1 pkg. taco seasoning
1 (8 oz.) ctn. sour cream
1 (16 oz.) can refried beans
½ c. chopped green onion
¼ c. green olives, chopped

1 ctn. avocado dip (optional)
1 medium size tomato, chopped
1 small can chopped green chilies
1 pkg. Monterey Jack cheese,
  grated

Mix taco seasoning envelope with the sour cream. On platter, spread the refried beans, then the sour cream mixture. Continue making layers with the rest of the ingredients as they are listed preceding. Serve with taco style chips. Refrigerate leftovers.

Mrs. Barbara (Rev. David) Splett, St. John's Lutheran,
Branch No. 5488, Fayetteville, AR

LAYERED NACHO DIP

1 (16 oz.) can refried beans
½ pkg. taco seasoning mix
1 (6 oz.) ctn. avocado dip
1 (8 oz.) sour cream
1 (4½ oz.) can chopped ripe olives

2 large tomatoes, diced
1 small onion, finely chopped
1 (4 oz.) can chopped green chiles
1½ c. shredded Monterey Jack
  cheese

Combine beans and seasoning mix; spread bean mixture in 12x8x2 inch serving dish. Layer all other ingredients in order given, topping with cheese. Chill. Serve with nacho chips.

Norma McKinnis, Branch No. 2568, Fredericktown, MO

CHEESE BALL

2 (8 oz.) pkg. cream cheese (room
  temperature)
1 tsp. Lawry's seasoned salt
2 tsp. finely chopped onions
¼ c. finely chopped green peppers

1 (8¼ oz.) can drained crushed
  pineapple
2 c. chopped pecans (save 1 c.
  pecans to roll cheese ball in)

Mix ingredients and chill. Roll cheese ball in remaining pecans.

Opal Sroufe, Branch No. 1743, Garden City, KS

DELICIOUS CHEESE BALL

2 (8 oz.) pkg. cream cheese,
  softened
1 small onion, diced fine
1 small can crushed pineapple,
  drained well

1 small green pepper, diced fine
1 Tbsp. seasoning salt

Mix well. Chill. Roll in crushed nuts or chopped parsley.

Variations: Add chopped pimento, crabmeat, deviled ham, diced jalapeno chilies, and grated Cheddar cheese.

Barbara Ettner, Branch No. 2085, Atwater, CA

VEGETABLE PIZZA

Spread 1 package crescent rolls on pizza pan; bake according to directions on can and cool.

Mix:

1 (3 oz.) Philly cream cheese	1 tsp. seasoned salt
½ c. sour cream	1 tsp. garlic salt
½ c. Miracle Whip	1 tsp. onion powder
1 tsp. dill weed	

Spread over cooled rolls. Arrange cleaned vegetables, as desired, over creamed mixture. I used green onions, peppers, radishes, carrots, parsley, and cauliflower. Put ½ cup shredded Cheddar cheese and ½ cup Mozzarella cheese over vegetables. Sprinkle Parmesan cheese on top. Refrigerate for at least 1 hour before serving.

Miss Tracy Redeker, Branch No. 3837, Champaign, IL

VEGETABLE PIZZA

2 pkg. Pillsbury crescent rolls	Broccoli
2 (8 oz.) pkg. cream cheese	Cauliflower
¾ c. mayonnaise	Chopped black olives
1 pkg. Hidden Valley Ranch dressing	Fresh tomatoes
	Shredded Mozzarella cheese
Diced mushrooms	Shredded Cheddar cheese

Crust: Pat crescent rolls onto ungreased cookie sheet. Bake as directed. Cool.

Mix cream cheese, dressing and mayonnaise; spread on cooled crust. Spread diced and chopped vegetables thinly on cream cheese mixture. Garnish with shredded cheese. Cut into bite-size squares. *Delicious!*

Betty Lou Hencke, Branch No. 3868, Highland Heights, OH

GARDEN VEGETABLE PIZZA

2 pkg. crescent rolls in tube	Chopped vegetables (chopped
¾ c. mayonnaise or Miracle Whip	broccoli, cauliflower, onion,
½ tsp. dill weed	green pepper, tomatoes, ripe
½ tsp. dry onion	olives, and curled carrots)
8 oz. cream cheese	Grated cheese (Cheddar) on top

Prepare crescent rolls according to directions on package. Use flat pan or pizza pan. Prick with fork. *Cool* and top with the following mixture.

Mix ¾ cup mayonnaise or Miracle Whip with the 8 ounces cream cheese, dill weed, and dry onion; spread over crescent rolls. On top of this, put all of the chopped vegetables on with the grated cheese on top. *Eat and enjoy!*

Lillian Generotzke, Branch No. 840, Franklin, WI

VEGGIE PIZZA

1 large pkg. crescent roll
8 oz. cream cheese
½ c. mayonnaise
1 tsp. dill weed
1 tsp. onion salt (optional)

Assorted raw vegetables (black olives, tomatoes, broccoli, mushrooms, cauliflower, shredded carrots, cucumbers, and green pepper)

Spread crescent roll dough on round cookie sheet. Prick with fork. Bake at 425° for 6 to 8 minutes. Allow to cool.

Combine softened cream cheese, mayonnaise, dill weed, and onion salt. Spread mixture on cooled crust. Top with vegetables of your choice.

Marlene Duerr, Branch No. 3289, Milwaukee, WI

VEGETABLE PIZZA

2 pkg. Pillsbury crescent rolls
1 c. Miracle Whip
1 (8 oz.) cream cheese
1 Tbsp. dill weed
1 Tbsp. minced onion

1 Tbsp. parsley flakes
1 Tbsp. Accent flavor enhancer
1 tsp. Lawry's salt
Cheese, grated

Vegetable suggestions:

Celery, diced
Peppers, diced
Carrots, shredded
Radishes, sliced

Green olives, sliced
Cauliflower
Broccoli
Alfalfa sprouts

Press the 2 packages of refrigerator rolls on a 10 x 15½ inch cookie sheet. Bake at 350° for 8 to 10 minutes. Cool.

Cream together Miracle Whip, cream cheese, dill weed, minced onion, parsley, Accent, and Lawry's salt. Spread on cooled crust. Put fresh vegetables on top. Grate cheese on top. Refrigerate.

Patricia Schaefer, Branch No. 192, Hilbert, WI

VEGETABLE PIZZA

Crust:

1 (8 oz.) pkg. crescent dinner rolls   1 (4 oz.) pkg. crescent dinner rolls

Press crescent rolls into 10x14 inch jelly roll pan. Bake at 350° for 8 to 10 minutes or until brown. Cool.

Dressing:

4 oz. cream cheese
¼ Tbsp. seasoned salt
½ Tbsp. parsley flakes

½ Tbsp. dry onion
½ Tbsp. dill weed
½ c. salad dressing

Mix dressing. Spread over baked, cooled crust. Top with small pieces of raw vegetables (broccoli, cauliflower, carrots, onions, tomatoes, etc.). Sprinkle with shredded Cheddar cheese.

Jan Spurlock, Branch No. 1581, Racine, WI

SHRIMP DIP

12 oz. cream cheese	Dash of garlic salt
1 small diced onion	1 bottle chili sauce
2 Tbsp. mayonnaise	1 can shrimp (or crabmeat)
2 Tbsp. lemon juice	Parsley
2 Tbsp. Worcestershire sauce	Ritz crackers

Cream together cream cheese, onion, mayonnaise, lemon juice, Worcestershire sauce, and garlic salt. Spread over a large tray or 2 small trays. Spread chili sauce over bottom layer. Top with shrimp (may mash to go farther) or shredded crabmeat. Sprinkle with parsley. Serve with Ritz crackers.

Note: This dip freezes well and may be made up well ahead of time.

Karen Meenen, Longmont, CO

SHRIMP MOLD

1 (10½ oz.) can cream of	2 green onions, finely chopped
mushroom soup	1 c. celery, finely chopped
3 Tbsp. water	1 c. mayonnaise
1 env. Knox gelatine	2 cans tiny shrimp, well drained
1 (8 oz.) pkg. cream cheese	

In a large saucepan, heat soup, water and gelatine until dissolved. Add cream cheese to soup mixture until smooth. Add green onions, celery, mayonnaise, and shrimp to mixture. Pour entire mixture into a 1 quart mold. Chill overnight. Serve with crackers.

Elaine Behnke, Branch No. 952, Dolton, IL

QUICK SAUSAGE SUPREME

2 lb. good lean sausage (country,	1 onion, sliced
mild or hot Italian)	8 oz. sliced Mozzarella cheese
1 large green pepper, sliced	1 to 2 c. favorite spaghetti sauce

Cover, pressing flat, a 15½ x 10 x 1 inch cookie sheet with sausage. Bake at 350° for 20 to 30 minutes; drain grease. Take from oven. Cover with sliced pepper and onion, then cheese and sauce. Return to oven for 30 minutes. Cut into pieces with pizza cutter.

Russ Inglis, Branch No. 4845, Youngstown, OH

SPINACH BALLS

2 pkg. frozen chopped spinach
2 c. (ground) seasoned stuffing
   cubes
¾ c. butter, softened

1 c. Parmesan cheese
4 eggs, beaten
Salt to taste

Cook spinach according to package and drain well. (Squeeze out excess water.) Mix remaining ingredients together with spinach. Form into walnut size balls. Freeze. To bake, place frozen balls on ungreased cookie sheet. Bake frozen balls in preheated 350° oven for 10 to 15 minutes or till edges begin to brown. Makes approximately 50 balls.

Darlene Specht, Branch No. 4928, Kenosha, WI

CRABMEAT PIZZA

11 oz. cream cheese
1 Tbsp. grated onion
1 Tbsp. lemon juice

2 tsp. Worcestershire sauce
2 Tbsp. mayonnaise
¾ c. chilli sauce

Blend together and spread in 9 inch round plate or tin pie tin. Top with chilli sauce. Chill.

Just before serving, spread a layer of 6½ ounces of crabmeat flakes and chopped fresh parsley on top. Serve with crackers.

Vera Besser, Branch No. 2343, Ogilvie, MN

COLD PIZZA

2 cans crescent rolls
3 (8 oz.) pkg. cream cheese
1 c. mayonnaise
1½ tsp. dill weed
Shredded Cheddar cheese

Assorted finely chopped
   vegetables (onions, celery,
   green peppers, broccoli, green
   and black olives, and
   cauliflower)

Spread crescent rolls in an 11x17 inch pan. Pinch seams together. Bake at 400° for 10 minutes. Cool. Whip mayonnaise and cream cheese; add dill weed and top with chopped vegetables. Chill.

Laura Johnson, Branch No. 2049, Emporia, KS

EASY CHEESE BALL

2 large (8 oz.) cream cheese
2 pkg. chipped beef, chopped fine
2 green onions, chopped

1 Tbsp. chopped ripe olives
2 Tbsp. Miracle Whip
1 tsp. Worcestershire sauce

Mix together all ingredients and shape to size desired or to fit your container. Refrigerate overnight for best results and taste. Let set out for a little while before serving. Serve with crackers.

Linda Bura, Branch No. 2049, Emporia, KS

FANCY CHICKEN LOG

2 (8 oz.) cream cheese, softened
1 Tbsp. Worcestershire sauce
½ tsp. curry powder
1½ c. minced, cooked chicken

½ c. minced celery
¼ c. chopped parsley
¼ c. chopped almonds
Ritz crackers

Beat together cream cheese, sauce and curry powder. Blend in celery, chicken and 2 tablespoons parsley. Refrigerate remaining parsley. Shape mixture into 9 inch log. Wrap in plastic wrap and chill for 4 hours or overnight. Toss together remaining parsley and almonds; use to coat log. Serve with Ritz crackers. Makes about 3 cups spread.

Norma McKinnis, Branch No. 2568, Fredericktown, MO

LITTLE MEATBALLS

1 lb. lean ground beef
1 pkg. dry onion soup mix
1 (6 oz.) can evaporated milk

1 to 2 Tbsp. Worcestershire sauce
¼ to ½ c. dry bread crumbs

Mix together and shape into small meatballs. (Use about 1 teaspoon of mixture for each meatball.) Brown meatballs in a 350° oven until done. Better made the day before and then pour heated sauce over them. Serve. Use little toothpicks to serve.

Sauce:

2 c. ketchup
1 c. brown sugar

1 Tbsp. Worcestershire sauce

Cook thoroughly on top of stove. Cool thoroughly.

Dolores P. Schultz, Branch No. 840, Franklin, WI

COCKTAIL MEAT BALLS

Meat Balls:

1 lb. lean ground beef
⅓ c. dry bread crumbs
¼ c. ground onion
⅓ c. skim milk

1 egg white, beaten
¼ tsp. salt
¼ tsp. allspice
⅛ tsp. pepper

In a medium bowl, mix beef, bread crumbs, onion, milk, egg white, salt, allspice, and pepper. Shape into tiny balls and place on jelly roll pan or baking sheet with sides. Bake until brown at 400° for 12 to 15 minutes. Can be frozen till ready to use.

Yogurt Sauce:

3 tsp. low sodium beef flavored
   bouillon granules
1½ c. water

1 Tbsp. cornstarch
½ c. plain lowfat yogurt

Shortly before serving, dissolve bouillon granules in water. Mix cornstarch with 1 tablespoon yogurt and stir into remaining yogurt. Add yogurt to bouillon. Add meat balls and heat gently

The yogurt mixture may look curdled at first, but it will become creamy as it simmers.

One meat ball equals 20 calories, 0.8 g fat, 5 mg cholesterol, and 24 mg sodium.

Sharon Ziegler, Branch No. 1616, Green Isle, MN

COCKTAIL MEATBALLS

3 eggs, beaten
1 c. fine saltine cracker crumbs
2 Tbsp. soy sauce
1 tsp. dry mustard
⅓ c. catsup
⅔ c. milk

1 tsp. crushed basil
½ tsp. garlic powder
2 Tbsp. parsley flakes
2½ lb. lean ground meat (beef, veal, turkey, or venison)
1 lb. pork sausage

Combine first 9 ingredients. Add ground meat and sausage; mix well. Shape into small balls. Bake at 350° for 20 minutes. Makes about 200.

Sauce:

2 c. chili sauce
¾ c. grape jelly

⅓ c. catsup

Combine sauce ingredients and heat until jelly is melted. Pour over meatballs. Serve hot.

Agnes Daniels, Branch No. 224, Grand Haven, MI

BEEF JERKY

Flank steak
A.1. meat sauce
Worcestershire sauce
Soy sauce
Tabasco sauce (small amount)

Seasoning salt
Onion salt
Garlic salt
Hickory salt

Freeze flank steak. When partially thawed, cut steak into thin strips along the grain of the meat. In shallow baking pan, place one layer of meat strips. Brush on marinade. Sprinkle with salts. (It is better to use salts conservatively the first few times.) On top of first layer of meat strips, place a second layer of meat strips the opposite direction of previous row. Brush on marinade and sprinkle with salts. Continue layering meat strips until all of the meat has been marinated and sprinkled. Cover with wax paper and refrigerate for 24 hours.

Indoor processing: Place drip pan in bottom of oven or line bottom of oven. Place single layer of meat strips on cookie cooling racks or place on oven racks. Set at no more than 140° and leave oven door slightly ajar to allow moisture to escape. Jerky will take several hours to dry.

Outdoor processing: Place single layer of meat strips on racks of a smoker. Smoke with hickory chips. Alternate cooking racks to help jerky dry evenly.

Jerky is done when it is chewy, but not so brittle that it breaks when you bend it. Jerky is best kept in containers which allow air to circulate.

Marcia Drake, Branch No. 6223, Convoy, OH

NACHOS DELUXE

1 pkg. nacho chips
1 lb. ground beef
1 pkg. taco seasoning
1 c. refried beans
2 c. shredded Co-Jack cheese

1 c. salsa
1 c. chopped tomatoes
1/4 c. chopped green onion
1/4 c. sliced black olives
1 c. sour cream

Brown ground beef and drain off fat. Mix taco seasoning and meat together according to package instructions. Add refried beans to mixture and simmer for 10 minutes.

In a large baking dish, cover bottom with layer of chips. Spoon 1/2 meat mixture over chips, then 1/3 salsa over meat and chips, then sprinkle 1/2 cup cheese. Repeat layers and cover with last layer of chips. Sprinkle remaining salsa and cheese over top. Bake for 10 to 15 minutes at 325°. Remove from oven and sprinkle tomatoes, green onions, and black olives over top. Scoop sour cream onto center of Nacho dish for dipping.

Debbie Goebig, New Lenox, IL

CHEESE BOWL

2 c. sour cream
1½ c. shredded cheese (Edam,
    Cheddar or Monterey Jack)

1 (8 oz.) pkg. cream cheese
2 Tbsp. minced onion
2 tsp. Dijon style mustard

Blend all ingredients. Cover and refrigerate overnight. Serve with fresh vegetables or crackers. Makes 5 cups.

Vicki Fredericksen, Branch No. 1068, Murdo, SD

SPINACH BREAD

1 round whole sourdough French
    bread
2 bags sourdough bagettes
2 boxes frozen chopped spinach
1 large and 1 small container sour
    cream

1 bunch green onions
1 box Knorr leek soup mix
5 Tbsp. mayonnaise
4 stalks celery

1. Defrost spinach; drain well.
2. Slice top off of round French bread. Cut out center of bread, leaving 1/2 inch all around.
3. Mix together leek soup mix, sour cream and mayonnaise.
4. Chop green onions and celery. Add to sour cream mixture. Add drained, chopped spinach. Mix thoroughly.

5. Put spinach mixture into round French bread.

6. Slice bagettes and place around French bread or serve in a basket next to dip.

Patricia Rhodes, Branch No. 2085, Atwater, CA

CHEESE-STUFFED MUSHROOMS

About 24 fresh mushrooms (or 2 cans whole mushrooms)
1 Tbsp. grated onion
2 Tbsp. grated sharp Cheddar cheese
2 Tbsp. grated Swiss cheese
½ Tbsp. parsley flakes
¼ tsp. garlic salt

Salt and pepper to taste
2 Tbsp. finely chopped salami
2 Tbsp. bread crumbs
Chopped stems of mushrooms
1 egg yolk (little cream if needed)
3 Tbsp. butter, melted
1 Tbsp. white wine (or more)

Drain mushrooms (if canned). Hollow out crowns and chop the stems into pieces. If using fresh mushrooms, just wash, remove stems and chop. Add all of the remainder of ingredients to the chopped items and mix well. Fill mushroom crowns with stuffing and place in baking dish with 3 tablespoons melted butter. Sprinkle with wine. Bake for 25 minutes at 350°. Serve warm with toothpicks. Serves 4 to 6.

This also makes a nice side dish for dinner.

Beverly Sironen, Branch No. 5754, Boulder, CO

CHEESE SQUARES

1 loaf white bread or Texas toast
8 oz. cream cheese
½ c. oleo or butter

2 egg whites
¼ lb. sharp Cheddar cheese

Remove crust from bread and cut each slice into 4 or 6 squares. Melt cream cheese, oleo and Cheddar cheese in top of double boiler. Cool. Beat egg whites stiff. Fold into cheese mixture. Dip or spread bread squares with mixture. Place on cookie sheet. Bake at 350° for 15 to 20 minutes or till light brown. Makes about 40 squares.

Cheese Squares can be kept in freezer as long as a month. Put on cookie sheet, freeze, and then wrap in foil. When ready to use, remove foil. Do not thaw. Bake for about 20 minutes.

Bernice Isern, Branch No. 1351, Ellinwood, KS

APPETIZER MEATBALLS

Meatballs:

1½ c. ground chuck
½ c. crackers, crushed

⅛ tsp. garlic powder
Salt and pepper to taste

Form meatball mixture into small balls and fry in margarine.

10

Sauce:

1 c. catsup	2 tsp. vinegar
1 tsp. salt	2 tsp. sugar
⅛ tsp. garlic powder	2 tsp. flour
1 tsp. minced onion (dried)	2 tsp. Worcestershire sauce
2 tsp. prepared mustard	2 tsp. liquid smoke

Combine sauce ingredients and simmer meatballs in sauce. This works well in a crock pot. Makes 50 to 60 meatballs.

Nancy Heine, Branch No. 1351, Chase, KS

CHEESE NUGGETS

1 c. (¼ lb.) shredded Cheddar cheese	⅛ tsp. salt
¼ c. soft butter or oleo	½ tsp. paprika
¾ c. flour	Stuffed olives (medium)

Blend cheese and butter. Add flour, salt and paprika. Mix. Shape dough (teaspoonful) around a medium size stuffed olive. Bake at 400° for 12 to 15 minutes.

Roberta Rebiskie, Branch No. 2801, McFarland, KS

CHEESE DUMPLINGS

Dough:

2 c. flour	3 large eggs

Make a large well in center of flour and drop in eggs. Work flour into eggs. You should have a fairly stiff dough. You may have a little flour left in bowl, but this is okay. Set aside to rest while you make filling.

Filling:

1 (24 oz.) ctn. cottage cheese, drained	2 eggs

Mix cottage cheese with eggs.

Topping:

1 lb. thick sliced bacon, diced	6 large onions, sliced

Fry bacon till crisp. Lift out bacon bits with a slotted spoon. Pour off and reserve about ½ of the grease. Fry onions in bacon grease until soft and clear. Do not brown. Use reserved bacon grease only if onions seem too dry. Add bacon bits to onions before serving.

Bring a large pot of salted water to a boil. Divide dough into 2 or 3 portions for easy handling. Roll each portion ⅛ inch thick. Cut into 2 inch squares. Put a spoonful of filling on square and fold over into 3 corner package. Dampen edges of dough and seal with fingers or fork.

11

Drop 12 at a time into boiling water and cook until done, a few minutes after they float to the top. Cook until dough is "al dente." Remove and keep warm. Top with onion-bacon topping and serve.

Jeannette Mathies, Branch No. 2801, McFarland, KS

LOREN'S COWBOYBURGER

2 lb. extra lean ground beef
1 (20 oz.) jar pimentos
2 tsp. minced garlic
2 tsp. red pepper
1 small green bell pepper

4 tsp. black pepper (to taste)
2 Tbsp. salt (to taste)
½ tomato
2 small bunches green onions
¼ white onion

Clean bell pepper and cut into strips. Cut tops off green onions and peel. Peel white onion and cut into strips; peel and quarter tomato. Mix all ingredients, except beef, in blender. Add meat and mix thoroughly. Chill for 2 to 4 hours. Serve on soda crackers.

Loren Pearson, Branch No. 4453, Hays, KS

EGGPLANT CAVIAR

1 (1 lb.) eggplant
2 cloves minced garlic
1 chopped onion
2 chopped tomatoes
1 chopped green pepper
¼ c. tomato sauce

2 Tbsp. vinegar
½ Tbsp. oregano
½ Tbsp. basil
½ Tbsp. salt
⅛ tsp. sugar
¼ tsp. black pepper

Bake the eggplant whole at 375° until tender, about 30 to 45 minutes. Peel the eggplant and dice the meat. Combine tomatoes, garlic, onion, and green pepper in a saucepan. Cover and simmer for 10 minutes. Add cooked eggplant and remaining ingredients. Simmer, uncovered, until soft and almost dry. Chill and use as a spread or dip.

For very low sodium, omit salt and use unsalted tomato sauce.

Winnie Kleist, Branch No. 5680, Cahokia, IL

GOLDEN MUSHROOM FRITTERS

1 c. biscuit mix
1 c. fresh mushrooms
1 Tbsp. ground onion
1 Tbsp. chopped pimento
¼ tsp. salt

¼ tsp. celery seed
1 beaten egg yolk
¼ c. sour cream
1 egg white

Mix mushrooms, onion, pimento, salt, and celery seed with biscuit mix. Mix together the egg yolk and sour cream; add to the dry mixture. Stir until moist. Beat the egg white till stiff and fold into the mushroom mixture. Drop by teaspoons into hot fat (FryBaby) for 2 minutes or until delicately browned. Makes about 12.

Clara Schultz, Branch No. 736, Essexville, MI

CHICKEN WINGS

2 lb. chicken wings (tips cut off)   Cornstarch
1 beaten egg

Sauce:

¼ c. vinegar   3 Tbsp. soy sauce
¼ c. sugar   Little Accent
3 Tbsp. catsup

Dip wings in the beaten egg, then the cornstarch. Brown lightly in oil. Place in a baking pan (heavy pan). Pour the sauce over and bake for ½ hour at 350°, turning a couple of times so that they don't get too brown.

These are good cold or warm.

Darleen Mensing, Branch No. 4560, Rochester, MN

SHRIMP MOUSSE

1 small can shrimp, drained   1 c. mayonnaise (not Miracle
1 can cream of mushroom soup   Whip)
1 (8 oz.) pkg. cream cheese   ⅓ c. celery, chopped
1 env. Knox gelatine   ⅓ c. onion, chopped
¼ c. water

Melt soup and cream cheese together over low heat. Remove from heat. Dissolve gelatine in water. Add gelatine and mayonnaise to soup mixture. Stir well, then fold in remaining ingredients. Put in 4 cup mold and chill to set. Serve with party pumpernickel.

Carol Klosterman, Branch No. 504, Manchester, MO

PIZZA CRACKERS

1 (3 oz.) pkg. smoked beef   ½ Tbsp. oregano
8 oz. grated Cheddar cheese   ½ tsp. garlic powder
10 to 12 black olives, chopped   1½ Tbsp. minced onion

Mix with Miracle Whip till sticky. Spread on cocktail bread. Broil for 5 to 7 minutes.

Velma Young, Branch No. 4534, Litchfield, MN

EGGHEADS

1 lb. turkey sausage (frozen tube), 2 beaten eggs
    thawed   ⅔ c. cheese crackers
8 boiled eggs   Chili sauce

1. Divide sausage into eight 4 inch patties.
2. Wrap patty around boiled egg.
3. Dip egg-sausage patty in beaten egg.
4. Dip in crushed crackers.

5. Bake at 375° on greased pan for 25 to 30 minutes (golden brown). Cut in halves.

6. Serve warm or cold with chili sauce if desired.

Janette McCann, Branch No. 2232, Midland, MI

WHAT IS IT?

1 lb. American cheese, grated
1 large can sauerkraut, well
    drained and chopped
3 Tbsp. minced onion
3 Tbsp. green pepper
3 Tbsp. pimento

2 Tbsp. sugar
½ tsp. salt
1 jalapeno pepper
1 boiled egg
¼ c. mayonnaise

Mix all together. Top with mixture of 4 ounces cream cheese and ¼ small carton sour cream. Sprinkle nuts on top.

Lee Ann Ahlschwede, Branch No. 2630, Greeley, CO

PIZZA TYPE APPETIZER

1 lb. medium pork sausage
1 lb. Velveeta cheese
2 tsp. oregano

2 Tbsp. catsup
Party rye bread

Brown pork sausage; drain off grease. Add cheese until melted. Take off heat. Add oregano and catsup. Put on rye bread. Bake at 350° for 5 to 10 minutes.

You may make the pork sausage mixture ahead of time. Keep it in the refrigerator until ready to use, then put it on rye bread after heating it on the stove.

Doris Seevers, Branch No. 382, St. Louis, MO

HOT MUSHROOM TURNOVERS

1 (8 oz.) pkg. cream cheese,
    softened
1½ c. flour
½ c. butter or margarine
½ lb. fresh mushrooms, minced

1 large onion, minced
¼ c. sour cream
1 tsp. salt
¼ tsp. thyme leaves
1 egg, beaten

About 2 hours before serving: In large bowl with mixer at medium speed, beat cream cheese, 1½ cups flour, and ½ cup butter or margarine until smooth; shape into ball. Wrap and refrigerate for 1 hour.

Meanwhile, in 10 inch skillet over medium heat, in 3 tablespoons hot butter or margarine, cook mushrooms and onion until tender, stirring occasionally. Stir in sour cream, salt, thyme, and 2 tablespoons flour. Set aside.

On floured surface with floured rolling pin, roll half of the dough ⅛ inch thick. With floured 2¼ inch round cookie cutter, cut as many circles as possible. Repeat.

14

Preheat oven to 450°. Onto one half of each dough circle, place a teaspoon of mushroom mixture. Brush edges of circles with some egg. Fold dough over filling. With fork, firmly press edges together to seal and prick tops. Place turnovers on ungreased cookie sheet; brush top with remaining egg. Bake for 12 to 14 minutes until golden. Makes about 3½ dozen (about 65 calories per turnover).

Note: Can be prepared ahead and frozen unbaked. Put in the oven frozen - just bake a bit longer!

Jane Malison, Branch No. 3064, Millbrae, CA

SAUERKRAUT MEATBALLS

½ lb. pork sausage
½ c. chopped onion
14 oz. sauerkraut, snipped,
    drained and squeezed
2 Tbsp. fine bread crumbs

4 oz. cream cheese
2 Tbsp. parsley
1 tsp. mustard
¼ tsp. garlic salt
⅛ tsp. pepper

    Sauce for dipping:

Mustard

Mayonnaise

Brown pork sausage with onion. Add sauerkraut and bread crumbs. Combine cream cheese, parsley, mustard, garlic salt, and pepper; mix all together and chill. Form small balls and roll into flour, then egg and milk and fine cracker crumbs. Fondue or deep-fry.

Judy Lips, The Lutheran Church of the Living Christ,
Branch No. 5473, Chanhassen, MN

OLIVE SPREAD

8 oz. cream cheese, softened
½ lb. bacon, fried and crumbled
½ c. sour cream

½ c. chopped onion
2 tsp. horseradish
2 Tbsp. chopped onion

Combine all ingredients. Use as a party spread.

This is especially good on party rye bread.

Ronda Tucker, Branch No. 2512, Ord, NE

SALMON LOG

8 oz. soft cream cheese
1 (1 lb.) can red salmon
1 Tbsp. grated onion

1 Tbsp. lemon juice
1 tsp. horseradish
1 tsp. liquid smoke

    Topping:

½ c. chopped nuts

2 Tbsp. parsley flakes

Drain salmon well. Combine all ingredients. Chill for several hours or overnight. Shape into a log on wax paper. Roll in topping. Roll tight in plastic wrap. Refrigerate.

Rose Borck, Branch No. 1098, Fremont, NE

PIZZA RYES

1 lb. ground beef
1 lb. hot pork sausage
1 lb. Velveeta cheese

1 tsp. oregano
1 tsp. Worcestershire sauce
¼ tsp. garlic powder

Cook meat till color is gone and drain. Add Velveeta cheese and rest of ingredients. Spread on party rye bread while warm. Just before serving, broil till bubbly.

Can be made ahead and frozen, then put in broiler.

Velma Hornickel, Branch No. 2512, Ord, NE

SAUSAGE BALLS

1 lb. sausage
½ c. Bisquick

4 oz. sharp cheese

Mix ingredients together. Shape into balls. Bake at 350° for 10 minutes.

Suzette McCarty, Branch No. 5776, Mount Joy, PA

VELVEETA FUDGE

½ lb. butter
½ lb. Velveeta cheese, cubed
½ c. unsweetened cocoa

2 lb. powdered sugar
2 tsp. vanilla

Melt butter and cheese in microwave or double boiler. Add cocoa. Use mixer to blend in powdered sugar, ⅓ at a time. Beat until smooth and place in buttered 13x9 inch pan. Chill for 24 hours.

Vicki Schultz, Branch No. 1612, Rothsay, MN

MEAT AND VEGETABLE BARS

1 c. flour
1 tsp. salt
3 eggs, beaten
½ c. margarine
1 c. milk

½ c. chopped onion
1 c. cooked vegetable
1 c. cooked and shredded (or finely
    diced) meat
1 c. shredded cheese

Combine first 6 ingredients and mix well. Add remaining ingredients. Spoon into greased 9x13 inch pan. Bake at 350° for 35 minutes or until set. Cool and cut into small bite-size squares.

Can be made ahead and reheated in microwave for 1 to 2 minutes on REHEAT. Can also be served at room temperature or cold.

Ellie Ennis, Branch No. 3086, Fair Oaks, CA
(Citrus Heights, CA - Branch address)

SPINACH SQUARES

2 Tbsp. butter or margarine
3 eggs
1 c. unsifted flour
1 tsp. salt
1 tsp. baking powder
1 c. milk

1 lb. shredded Cheddar cheese
2 (10 oz.) pkg. frozen chopped
   spinach, thawed and
   thoroughly drained by
   squeezing in hands
Paprika

Preheat oven to 350°. Melt butter in a 9x13 inch pan as the oven preheats. When melted, remove from oven and tilt the pan to thoroughly coat the bottom. Let stand at room temperature as you prepare the following.

In a large bowl, beat eggs thoroughly. Add flour, salt and baking powder. Mix well. Thoroughly mix in milk, cheese and spinach. Spread mixture evenly in the buttered dish. Sprinkle with paprika.

Bake for about 30 minutes, or until slightly browned on top and knife inserted comes out clean. Remove from oven. Let stand at room temperature for about 30 minutes. Cut into 1 inch squares.

Can be frozen, defrosted and reheated in a moderate oven.
Linda Johnson, Branch No. 2716, Northglenn, CO

PIZZA CRAB SPREAD (OR SHRIMP)

12 oz. cream cheese
2 Tbsp. Worcestershire
2 Tbsp. mayonnaise
1 Tbsp. lemon juice

6 oz. Heinz chili sauce
1 can crabmeat or tiny shrimp,
   well drained

Mix first 4 ingredients and spread in pan. Add chili sauce on top of the first 4 ingredients and spread. Next, add crabmeat or shrimp on top of that. Sprinkle with parsley flakes.

When using crabmeat, squeeze well to remove liquid and shred over top. If you use shrimp, rinse in warm water and drain well.
Donna Phillips, Branch No. 2512, Ord, NE

CHEESEBALL

1 (8 oz.) pkg. cream cheese
1 (4 oz.) pkg. crumbled Blue
   cheese
1 (6 oz.) jar Kraft Old English
   cheese spread
1 tsp. lemon juice

1 Tbsp. minced onions
1 Tbsp. Worcestershire sauce
½ c. chopped walnuts
1 tsp. parsley flakes
1 cherry

Allow cheeses to come to room temperature. Put all cheeses in a bowl; mix with fork and blend in 1 teaspoon lemon juice, 1 tablespoon minced onions, 1 tablespoon Worcestershire sauce, and 1 teaspoon parsley flakes.

When all ingredients are mixed together uniformly, scoop up and make a ball, then roll the cheese into a snowball. Roll over chopped walnuts until fully covered. Place in refrigerator for several hours (preferably overnight).

Kathleen Fryer, Loveland, CO

PARTY CHEESE BALL
(Serves a group)

1 lb. cream cheese, softened
½ lb. sharp Cheddar cheese, grated
¼ bell pepper, minced
¼ small onion, minced
1 tsp. fresh lemon juice

2 tsp. Worcestershire sauce
Dash of pepper
Dash of salt
1 small jar pimentos, chopped
Pecans, chopped

Blend together the cream cheese, Cheddar cheese, pepper, onion, lemon juice, Worcestershire sauce, salt, and pepper. Add pimentos after other ingredients are thoroughly blended. Put in refrigerator to chill overnight.

Using hands, form the mixture into a ball. Roll in chopped pecans. Serve with crackers. Serves easier if room temperature.

Carol Ellis, Branch No. 2890, Glendora, CA

SMOKY CHEESE BALL

1 (8 oz.) cream cheese (room temperature)
4 oz. Cheddar cheese, shredded
1 Tbsp. milk or cream

1 Tbsp. steak sauce
¼ c. butter
½ tsp. liquid smoke
¼ c. bacon bits

Mix all ingredients together until light and fluffy. Form mixture into a ball or holiday log. Chill for a couple of hours or overnight. Serve with a variety of snack crackers.

Variation: Substitute 1 teaspoon garlic powder for liquid smoke and add crushed walnuts or pecans in place of bacon bits.

Jeri Manke, Branch No. 5985, Midland, SD

CHIPPED BEEF CHEESE SPREAD

1 tsp. dried minced onion flakes
1 (8 oz.) pkg. cream cheese, softened
2 Tbsp. mayonnaise

1 to 3 Tbsp. milk
1 (3 oz.) pkg. dried chipped beef, chopped up
¼ c. chopped green olives

Mix softened cream cheese with dried minced onion flakes. Add mayonnaise to the cream cheese and minced onion flakes; mix well. Add 1 to 3 tablespoons milk to the cream cheese mixture to give it a smooth texture, but not to make soupy. Add the dried chopped chipped beef and chopped green olives to the cream cheese mixture. Refrigerate for 3 to 4 hours. Serve with variety of crackers.

Marge Spencer, Trinity Lutheran Church, Branch No. 796, Jackson, MI

IRIS CHEDDAR CHEESE BALL

3 c. grated Cheddar cheese
1 (8 oz.) pkg. cream cheese
1 small onion, chopped
1 small can pimento
1 Tbsp. Worcestershire sauce

Dash of garlic salt
Dash of onion salt
2 Tbsp. mayonnaise
1/3 c. chopped olives

Mix all ingredients together and chill. Form into a ball and roll in chopped pecans.

Mrs. Iris Kluever, Branch No. 1131, Worthington, MN

VEGETABLE PIZZA

2 pkg. crescent rolls
1 (8 oz.) pkg. cream cheese
1/3 c. Miracle Whip or mayonnaise

1 tsp. dill weed
1/2 tsp. garlic powder

Roll out crescent rolls and bake at 400° for 10 minutes. Cool. Mix cream cheese, Miracle Whip and spices; spread over crust. Top with raw vegetables (broccoli, cauliflower, carrots, celery, green pepper, and sliced ripe olives). Over this, add grated cheese. Refrigerate.

Mrs. Elmer Olson, Branch No. 6896, Mahnomen, MN

VEGGIE WEDGIES

Roll out 2 packages Pillsbury crescent rolls (found in fridge case) by hand onto *large* cookie sheet. Pat seams together. Bake according to directions on package. Let cool thoroughly.

1 (8 oz.) Philadelphia cream
cheese
1 c. Hellmann's mayonnaise

1 pkg. Hidden Valley Ranch mix
(regular)

Blend till smooth and spread over cooled crust with spatula. Top with desired fresh vegetables (shredded, sliced or small pieces).

Irene M. Perrigo, Branch No. 5124, Alma, MI

MINI PIZZAS

1 lb. ground beef
1 lb. pork sausage
1 lb. Velveeta cheese

3/4 tsp. oregano
Dash of garlic
2 loaves cocktail rye bread

Brown 1 pound ground beef with 1 pound pork sausage. Drain grease. Stir in 1 pound Velveeta cheese, 3/4 teaspoon oregano, and dash of garlic. When cheese is melted, spread on cocktail rye bread. Freeze on cookie sheets. Place in a plastic bag to keep in freezer. Bake at 400° for 10 minutes.

Jeanie Coleman, Loveland, CO

STUFFED SPINACH-CHEESE BREAD

1 large loaf unsliced French bread
1 stick butter (margarine)
¼ c. olive oil
10 cloves garlic, coarsely chopped
1 pkg. frozen chopped spinach,
   thawed and squeezed dry

1 c. grated Swiss cheese
½ c. grated Mozzarella cheese
½ tsp. dried basil
½ tsp. thyme
½ tsp. garlic salt
¼ tsp. coarse black pepper

Cut top from bread; carefully scoop out bread from both halves, leaving crust intact. In large mixing bowl, tear inside bread into small pieces and combine with spinach. Heat butter and olive oil together in skillet until slightly bubbly. Add garlic and stir over heat for 30 seconds.

Remove from heat and add to bread mixture, stirring until well combined. Add cheeses and seasoning; mix well. Mound mixture in bottom crust. Replace top crust and wrap loaf tightly in foil. Bake for 35 minutes at 350°. Serve warm.

For cookout, bake ahead, leave wrapped and reheat on grill rack for about 15 minutes just before serving.

Lorraine Count, Branch No. 64, Elkhorn, WI

CHILI-CHEESE LOG

¾ lb. grated natural American
   cheese
1 (3 oz.) pkg. soft cream cheese
¼ tsp. salt

⅛ tsp. pepper
⅛ tsp. garlic salt
1½ tsp. Worcestershire sauce
Chili powder

Thoroughly combine cheeses, salt, pepper, garlic salt, and Worcestershire sauce 3 or 4 days ahead. To mix easily, use electric mixer. Shape into 2 thin logs.

On waxed paper sprinkled with chili powder, roll each cheese log, coating thoroughly with chili powder. Wrap and let ripen in refrigerator. Arrange log on board; slice and serve with assorted crackers. Leftovers keep well. Makes about 1 pound.

Best if made 3 to 5 days before serving.

Brenda Woelfel, Branch No. 4899, Giddings, TX

HOT CHEESE PUFFS

2 c. Bisquick baking mix
2 eggs, beaten
6 oz. Jimmy Dean *hot* sausage
2 Tbsp. salsa (or to taste)

Milk
⅓ lb. sharp Cheddar cheese,
   grated

Cook sausage (crumbled) until no longer pink. Set aside. Mix Bisquick baking mix with grated cheese. Add drained sausage, salsa, and beaten eggs to baking mix; mix thoroughly, but gently. If too dry, add a little milk. Make 1 small walnut size ball and bake on a piece of greased foil at 450° for 10 to 12 minutes until golden. If not spicy enough, add a little more salsa. Make the rest of the dough into walnut size balls and bake for 10 to 12 minutes at 450° until golden on a greased cookie sheet.

Joan S. Wray, Branch No. 1927, Porterville, CA

STUFFED MUSHROOMS

3 lb. fresh mushrooms
1 lb. hot pork sausage
3 (8 oz.) cans tomato sauce

⅓ c. vermouth
1 tsp. oregano

In saucepan, simmer tomato sauce, vermouth and oregano. Remove stems from mushrooms (freeze for later use). Stuff caps with sausage. Bake on cookie sheet at 350° for ½ hour. Baked mushrooms are then added to sauce. Best if allowed to marinate for a few hours. Serve hot. Can be frozen.

Pam Belt, Branch No. 4806, Sheffield, OH

CLAM DIP

The best you have ever tasted!

1 pkg. cream cheese

1 can clams

Drain clam juice into a cup. Mix cream cheese and clams together; add small amounts of clam juice at a time until you have the consistency you want. Serve with chips or vegetables.

Margie (Dias) Benes, Branch No. 3107, Loveland, CO

SEAFOOD DIP

1 (8 oz.) pkg. cream cheese, softened
1 small jar cocktail sauce

1 can small shrimp, drained
1 can white crabmeat, drained

Mix cheese and cocktail sauce until blended well. Spread in pie plate. Around outer edge of dish, arrange tiny shrimp. Fill in the top with crabmeat. Serve with crackers.

If prepared ahead of serving time, be sure to cover and refrigerate until ready to serve.

Branch No. 628, Farmington, MO

BACON CHEESE DIP

4 slices bacon
2 Tbsp. flour
1 c. milk
1 garlic clove
8 oz. Monterey Jack cheese, shredded (2 c.)

4 oz. Cheddar Cheese, shredded (1 c.)
1 tsp. dry or prepared mustard
½ tsp. Worcestershire sauce
Dash of hot pepper sauce

Fry bacon; crumble and set aside. In bacon drippings, stir flour. Add milk and garlic; stir until smooth. Cook on HIGH in microwave for 3 to 4 minutes until thickened, stirring once. Discard garlic. Stir cheeses into mixture. Cook on MEDIUM for 4 to 6 minutes until smooth, stirring once. Stir in mustard, Worcestershire sauce, pepper sauce, and bacon bits. Mixture will thicken as it stands.

To reheat and thin slightly, cook on MEDIUM for 1 to 2 minutes. Stir once.

Mrs. Glenn Peters, Branch No. 3146, Independence, MO

MEXICAN CHEESE DIP

8 oz. cream cheese
1 lb. Velveeta or Cheddar cheese
    soup
2 Tbsp. butter

2 (5 oz.) cans whole tomatoes
¼ c. chopped chili peppers
    (optional)

Melt cream cheese and butter in slow cooker. Add Velveeta cheese and melt. Add tomatoes and peppers. Heat thoroughly. Serve with chips or crackers.

Wanda Burrer, Branch No. 5616, Wing, ND

LUSCIOUS LEMON CREAM FRUIT DIP

2 eggs
1 c. sugar
⅓ c. lemon juice concentrate
1 Tbsp. cornstarch

½ c. water
1 tsp. vanilla extract
1 c. (½ pt.) whipping cream,
    whipped

In bowl, beat together eggs, ½ cup sugar and lemon juice. In saucepan, combine remaining sugar and cornstarch; stir in water. Cook and stir until thickened; remove from heat. Gradually beat in egg mixture. Over low heat, cook and stir until slightly thickened. Add vanilla. Cool and fold in whipped cream. Serve with fresh fruit. Refrigerate leftovers.

Adele Hogue, Branch No. 952, Dolton, IL

MEATY CHEESE DIP

1 lb. ground beef
1 clove garlic, minced
2 lb. Velveeta

1 (10 oz.) Ro-Tel (hot)
2 Tbsp. chili seasoning mix

Cook ground beef and garlic until brown. Drain well. Place browned ground beef and garlic in crock pot; add cubed Velveeta, Ro-Tel and chili seasoning mix. Bring to simmer. Serve warm with taco chips.

Norma McKinnis, Branch No. 2568, Fredericktown, MO

VEGETABLE DIP

1 c. mayonnaise (genuine)
½ tsp. lemon juice
1 tsp. grated onion
1 tsp. chives
½ tsp. Worcestershire sauce

¼ tsp. paprika
1 tsp. salad herbs
1 tsp. garlic salt
½ tsp. curry powder
½ c. sour cream

Blend all together and let stand overnight.

Great for dipping cucumber slices, celery sticks, green pepper sticks, carrot sticks, raw cauliflower, etc.

St. Peter's Ev. Lutheran Church, Routel Moltke Township, Gibbon, MN

RAW VEGETABLE DIP

⅔ c. sour cream
⅔ c. Best Foods mayonnaise
1 tsp. Beau Monde

1 tsp. dill weed
1 tsp. parsley
Pinch of grated onion

Mix together in bowl and refrigerate overnight or for several hours. Dip with a variety of fresh vegetables.

Julie Padilla, Branch No. 3107, Loveland, CO

VEGETABLE DIP

1 qt. real mayo
4 Tbsp. Parmesan cheese
4 Tbsp. Romano cheese

2 Tbsp. catsup
1 tsp. garlic powder
1 Tbsp. Salad Supreme

Mix and refrigerate overnight. Serve with raw vegetables.

Tracy J. Buchholz, Branch No. 1612, Rothsay, MN

VEGETABLE DIP

1 pt. Hellmann's mayonnaise
8 oz. Kraft French dressing
1 (3 oz.) can Parmesan cheese

¼ tsp. celery salt
¼ tsp. onion salt
¼ tsp. garlic salt

Beat all ingredients well with a mixer.

Barb Koch, Branch No. 6470, Kiron, IA

VEGETABLE DIP

1 (4¼ oz.) can deviled ham
1 (3 oz.) jar pimento cheese spread
2 Tbsp. chopped onion

½ c. mayonnaise or Miracle Whip
Bite-size vegetables of your choice

Mix together all ingredients, except vegetables, in a small bowl. Chill for several hours or overnight. When ready to serve, stir dip with a spoon and place bowl in center of serving tray with bite-size vegetables all around.

Suggested vegetables: Cauliflowerets, carrot sticks, celery sticks, mushrooms, green pepper strips, cherry tomatoes, scallions, broccoli flowerets, and jicama strips.

Ellie Ennis, Branch No. 3086, Fair Oaks, CA
(Citrus Heights, CA - Branch address)

VEGETABLE DIP

1 large can deviled ham
3 oz. cream cheese

2 Tbsp. Miracle Whip
Chopped pickles or olives

Soften cream cheese, then mix ingredients and serve with raw carrots, celery, cauliflower, etc.

Mrs. Margaret Greiner, Branch No. 2838, Wilmot, SD

PEPPERONI PIZZA DIP

1 (8 oz.) cream cheese, softened
½ c. dairy sour cream
1 tsp. crushed oregano
⅛ tsp. garlic powder
⅛ tsp. crushed red pepper
   (optional)

½ c. pizza sauce
½ c. chopped pepperoni
¼ c. sliced green onion
¼ c. chopped green pepper
½ c. shredded Mozzarella cheese

In small mixer bowl, beat together cream cheese, sour cream, oregano, garlic powder, and red pepper. Spread evenly in a 9 to 10 inch quiche dish or pie plate. Spread pizza sauce over the top. Sprinkle with pepperoni, onion and green pepper. Bake at 350° for 10 minutes. Top with cheese. Bake for 5 minutes more or until cheese is melted and mixture is heated through. Serve with pepper strips, broccoli flowerets, carrot strips, or crackers. Makes 1½ cups (138 calories).

Ann Engelbert, Branch No. 2288, Hilton, NY

TACO DIP

1 lb. hamburger
1 medium onion, chopped
1 small green pepper, chopped
1 lb. Velveeta cheese

1 can Cheddar cheese soup
1 (8 oz.) jar hot taco sauce
1 can refried beans

Brown hamburger, onion and green pepper. Drain. Melt Velveeta and soup; add taco sauce and refried beans. Stir in hamburger mixture (takes a big pan or electric skillet). Simmer till all is mixed. I then serve this hot from the crock pot with plain nacho chips.

This can be made ahead and frozen for later use.

Linda Spiegel, Branch No. 3558, Charter Oak, IA

TACO DIP

   Layer 1

1 lb. ground beef, cooked and
   drained
1 pkg. taco seasoning mix (no
   water)

1 small (8½ oz.) can refried beans

   Layer 2

½ bottle green taco sauce

1 c. sour cream

Place in buttered quiche dish or pie plate. For layer 3, sprinkle grated Cheddar cheese. Bake at 350° for 25 to 30 minutes. Serve with corn chips/Nachos.

Branch 5684, Lafayette, IN

DELICIOUS DIP OR SPREAD

½ lb. Braunschweiger, smoked
½ c. butter or margarine
2 tsp. finely chopped onion
2 Tbsp. finely chopped chives
2 Tbsp. finely chopped parsley
2 Tbsp. country style dressing

Have Braunschweiger and oleo at room temperature. Combine all ingredients well. Use as a dip on crackers or a sandwich spread.

Donna Giermann, Branch No. 6470, Kiron, IA

HOT TACO DIP

1 lb. ground chuck
1 lb. Old English cheese (only)
4 (4 oz.) cans mild taco sauce (or 2 (7½ oz.) cans)

Brown ground beef; drain any grease. Dice cheese. Add to meat and sauce. Stir till cheese melts. Serve with taco chips.

Marsha Ruesch, Branch No. 5844, Columbia City, IN

LINDA'S DIP

8 avocados
1 bunch green onions
1 small can black olives
1 small can green olives
1 c. mayonnaise
2 large cans refried beans
32 oz. sour cream
1½ tsp. lemon juice
6 tomatoes
2 packs taco seasoning mix
1½ lb. Cheddar cheese
3 bags tortilla chips

Spread layer of beans in a flat casserole dish. Smash avocados in bowl; add lemon juice and mayonnaise. Spread this layer on top of beans. Mix sour cream, taco seasoning and chopped green onions. Spread this over avocados. Slice olives, grate cheese and dice tomatoes. Sprinkle grated cheese over entire layer. Add olives and tomatoes. Will serve at least 25. Cut in half for smaller gathering. *Serve cold.*

Ruth Flowers, Branch No. 3436, Pico Rivera, CA

SOMBRERO DIP

1 lb. ground beef
¼ c. chopped onion
1 medium clove garlic, minced
1 (7 oz.) can Ortega green chile salsa
1 (16 oz.) can refried beans
1 (4 oz.) can Ortega diced green chiles
1 tsp. salt
Tortilla chips

Garnish:

½ c. shredded Cheddar cheese
¼ c. sliced ripe olives
¼ c. chopped onion

In a 10 inch skillet, brown beef until crumbly. Drain. Add onion and garlic. Cook until onion is soft. Add remaining ingredients. Cook until hot and bubbly. Spoon into chafing dish to keep hot. Garnish with cheese, olives and onion. Serve with tortilla chips. Serves 8.

This dip also makes a delicious filling for burritos!

Leona Metcalfe, Branch No. 3107, Loveland, CO

TEX MEX DIP

2 cans bean dip (mild)
1 c. real mayonnaise
1 c. sour cream
1 pkg. taco mix seasoning
3 avocados
1 Tbsp. lemon juice

¼ c. salsa
Grated cheese
Chopped tomatoes
Chopped olives
Chips

Layer in 9x13 inch dish.

Layer 1: Spread the bean dip on the bottom.

Layer 2: Mix together the mayonnaise, sour cream and taco seasonings.

Layer 3: Mix together avocados, lemon juice and salsa. Top with cheese, tomatoes and olives.

Sharon Verville, Branch No. 3107, Loveland, CO

SHRIMP DIP

1 ctn. Top the Tator cream-chive
    dressing
2 drops of Tabasco sauce

½ c. Western French salad
    dressing
1 can shrimp, rinsed and drained

Mix together. Chill. Serve with chips, crackers or vegetables.

Judy Mielke, Branch No. 286, Bloomer, WI

SUPER CHALUPA DIP

1 lb. ground beef
1 large onion, chopped
1 tsp. salt
¼ tsp. pepper
1 Tbsp. chili powder
1 to 2 (1 lb.) cans refried beans
Hot sauce (desired amount for
    spicing up)

1 to 2 (4 oz.) cans diced green
    chilies
3 c. shredded Cheddar cheese
1 (7 oz.) can green chili salsa
¼ c. chopped green onion
1 can chopped black olives
Guacamole dip
1 c. sour cream

Brown meat and onion in large skillet; drain. Add salt, pepper, chili powder, refried beans, hot sauce, and half of the green chilies. Mix well. Pour meat mixture into large baking dish. Top with layers of remaining green chilies, cheese and salsa.

Cover and chill if made ahead. Bake, uncovered, in a 400° oven for 20 to 30 minutes or until very hot throughout. Remove from oven and quickly garnish with some or all of the green onion and black olives.

In the center, mound guacamole dip and top with sour cream. Serve with tortilla chips. (Stand extra chips around the edges of baking dish for looks.)

Connie Davis, Branch No. 3107, Loveland, CO

MEXICAN DIP

1 (8 oz.) pkg. cream cheese
1 (6 to 7 oz.) can chili salsa

1 (4 oz.) can chopped green chilies

Blend ingredients well. Refrigerate. Serve with tortilla chips.

Connie Davis, Branch No. 3107, Loveland, CO

DILL DIP

½ pt. sour cream
1 tsp. dill weed
1 tsp. garlic salt

1 tsp. Beau Monde seasoning
½ c. Miracle Whip

Mix and serve with raw vegetables.

Tracy J. Buchholz, Branch No. 1612, Rothsay, MN

DRIED BEEF DIP

1 (8 oz.) pkg. cream cheese,
  softened
1 (8 oz.) sour cream
2 Tbsp. milk
3 Tbsp. finely chopped green
  pepper

3 Tbsp. instant minced onion
1 (5 oz.) jar dried beef, chopped
  fine
½ c. chopped pecans

Mix cream cheese, sour cream and milk in small mixing bowl till smooth. Add chopped green pepper, onion and dried beef. Place in a pie plate and sprinkle with chopped pecans. Bake in a 350° oven for 15 minutes. Serve with your favorite crackers.

Lois Hauschild, Branch No. 6084, Anoka, MN

NOTABLE CHEESE DIP

½ lb. Velveeta cheese, cubed
2 Tbsp. milk
⅓ c. sour cream

2 Tbsp. chopped green or red
  peppers
1 Tbsp. chopped onions

Heat cheese and milk over low heat until smooth. Add remaining ingredients and mix well. Makes 1⅔ cups.

This is a good dip to serve with raw vegetables, especially broccoli and cauliflower.

Faye Schriver, Branch No. 5511, Dover, PA

SPINACH DIP

1 pkg. frozen chopped spinach
1 c. sour cream
1 c. mayonnaise
½ c. parsley
½ c. green onion, chopped

1 tsp. salt
1 tsp. Beau Monde (Spice Islands
    brand)
½ tsp. dill weed
Juice of 1 lemon

Thaw, drain and blot spinach. Mix all ingredients thoroughly. Refrigerate for several hours. Serve with potato chips.

Mrs. Margaret T. Sandifer, Branch No. 5968, Greensboro, NC

SALMON DIP

1 (1 lb.) can salmon, drained and
    cleaned
1 (8 oz.) pkg. cream cheese,
    softened
1 golf ball size onion, minced

2 Tbsp. horseradish
⅛ to ¼ tsp. liquid smoke
¼ tsp. cayenne pepper
Few shakes of salt
½ tsp. lemon juice

Mix well with fork. Make ahead, cover and chill.

Eleanor Miller, Branch No. 2295, Allen Park, MI

POTTED MEAT DIP

1 large (5½ oz.) can potted meat
1 large (8 oz.) pkg. Philadelphia
    cream cheese

Catsup (to taste)

Let the cream cheese soften. Add the potted meat to cream cheese and stir until thoroughly mixed. Add the catsup. Start with 2 tablespoons and add a bit more if you think it needs a bit more flavor.

Nancy Gremel, Branch No. 5754, Boulder, CO

PINEAPPLE-CHEESE DIP

2 (8 oz.) cans Dole crushed
    pineapple
1 (8 oz.) pkg. cream cheese,
    softened
4 c. shredded Cheddar cheese
½ c. mayonnaise

1 Tbsp. soy sauce
1 c. chopped almonds, toasted
½ c. finely chopped green pepper
¼ c. minced green onion or chives
1 loaf round sourdough bread (or
    crackers)

Cut top off of bread. Tear out insides and break into bite-size pieces, leaving bread in bowl shape. Cover loaf and bread pieces to prevent drying out.

Drain pineapple. In large bowl, beat cream cheese until smooth; beat in Cheddar cheese, mayonnaise, and soy sauce until smooth. Stir in pineapple, almonds, green pepper, and onion. Refrigerate, covered. When ready to serve, spoon into bread bowl. Serve at room temperature.

Cheryl O'Brien, Branch No. 4718, New Lenox, IL

NACHO DIP

1 lb. Velveeta cheese
1 bottle mild taco sauce

1 (9 oz.) can Nacho cheese sauce
Ground red pepper

Melt together. Sprinkle in ground red pepper spice to taste. Serve warm. *Works well in crock pot.*

Sally Kraayenbrink, Branch No. 559, Fort Dodge, IA

ONION APPETIZER MEATBALLS

Meatballs:

2 eggs, slightly beaten
1 tsp. onion powder
1 tsp. seasoned salt
2 tsp. Worcestershire sauce

2 Tbsp. snipped parsley
2 Tbsp. barbecue sauce
1 c. finely crushed Wheat Chex
1 lb. lean ground beef

Combine meatball ingredients and shape into 1¼ inch meatballs. Place on baking sheet. Cover with wax paper and microwave on HIGH for 8 minutes, turning meatballs once after 4 minutes. Place in chafing dish.

Sauce:

1 (10½ oz.) can condensed cream
   of onion soup

½ c. dairy sour cream
1 tsp. Worcestershire sauce

Combine sauce ingredients. Cover and microwave on HIGH for 2 to 6 minutes, just to boiling. Pour over meatballs. Serve hot.

Vicki Pflughaupt, Branch No. 6569, Seward, NE

DILL DIP

1 c. sour cream
1 c. mayonnaise
1 Tbsp. parsley

1 tsp. dill weed
2 tsp. minced onions

Blend and serve with vegetables or chips.

Myrtle Callies, Branch 53, Hartford, WI

TACO DIP

2 (8 oz.) pkg. cream cheese

1 (12 oz.) jar picante sauce

Whip together and spread on a pizza pan or other 12 inch tray. Top with shredded lettuce, cherry tomatoes and shredded cheese. Serve with Tostitos.

Kay Steinberg, Branch 4122, Spearfish, SD

HOT CHEESE DIP

1 lb. Velveeta cheese
1 can Hormel chili (no beans)

1 medium onion, diced
2 to 4 jalapenos diced

Combine all ingredients and heat in oven at 350° for ½ hour. Stir and serve with taco chips.

Alternative method: Combine all ingredients in crock-pot and heat on LOW for several hours.

Marti Conrad, Loveland, CO

CRAB DIP

12 oz. cream cheese (4 (3 oz.) pkg.)
½ lb. white lump crabmeat

6 Tbsp. mayonnaise
3 Tbsp. white wine
Dash of garlic salt

Mix crabmeat, mayonnaise, and wine into softened cream cheese. Stir in garlic salt. Serve with crackers.

Estelle Krist, Branch 1221

CRAB DIP

1 (12 oz.) pkg. cream cheese
1 large bottle seafood sauce (Crosse & Blackwell)

1 (6 oz.) pkg. frozen crabmeat or canned crab

Mix crab and sauce. Press cream cheese in 9 inch pan. Pour sauce over cream cheese. Serve with crackers.

Marti Conrad, Loveland, CO

SAUSAGE DIP

1 lb. sausage
1 (8 oz.) pkg. cream cheese
1 large sour cream
1 (4 oz.) can chopped green chilies
1 qt. canned tomatoes

Corn starch (about 1 heaping Tbsp.)
French bread hunks or tortilla chips (to serve)

Crumble and fry sausage. Drain. Stir in remaining ingredients (except for corn starch). Heat through. It should be the consistency of a heavy gravy. If not, mix some corn starch with water and stir in to thicken.

Serve over hunks of torn French bread or tortilla chips.

Linda Sedlacek, Branch No. 3107, Loveland, CO

CILE'S CINCHIE HOT DIP

1 lb. Velveeta cheese
1 can Hormel chili with meat (no beans)

1 small can chopped Ortega chilies

Heat over low heat in saucepan until melted. Serve with tortilla type chips.

Can be made day before and heated in microwave when needed.

Luann Mathev, Loveland, CO

CHEESE-HAMBURGER DIP

1 lb. ground beef
1 Tbsp. Worcestershire sauce
1 can El Paso tomatoes and green
    chiles

Chili powder (if desired)
1 (2 lb.) box Velveeta, cut in
    chunks

Brown 1 pound ground beef; drain well. Stir in Worcestershire sauce and tomatoes and green chilies. Place ground beef mixture in bottom of crock pot. Add Velveeta chunks on top. Stir occasionally until melted.

Serve warm as a dip for tortilla chips.

Jan McLaughlin, Branch No. 3107, Loveland, CO

CHILLI DIP

2 lb. ground beef, browned and
    drained
2 lb. Velveeta

1 to 1½ lb. Armour chilli (no
    beans)

Add to crock pot. Stir occasionally until melted. Serve with chips, etc.

Ruth Neeley, Branch 2254

ARTICHOKE/CHEESE DIP
(Microwave)

1 can artichoke hearts
1 jar marinated artichoke hearts
1 can mild diced green chilies, well
    rinsed

Grated cheese
Mayonnaise

Cut artichokes into bite-size pieces. Layer the can of artichoke hearts on bottom of dish. Next, layer the jar of marinated artichoke hearts. For third layer, spread green chilies. Sprinkle grated cheese to cover for fourth layer. Add 5 "blobs" of mayonnaise for the top layer. Heat in microwave for about 7 or 8 minutes and stir. Serve warm with crackers.

Julie Padilla, Branch No. 3107, Loveland, CO

CRABMEAT DIP

8 oz. Philadelphia cream cheese
Chili sauce

10 oz. crabmeat (or imitation)

Spread cream cheese on a plate or tray. Top with desired amount of chili sauce Or top of that, put crabmeat. Serve with crackers.

Renae Tegtmeier, Branch No. 2049 Emporia, KS

ROYAL BEAN DIP

1 can Fritos bean dip
1 Tbsp. sour cream
4 baby green onions, cut in halves

½ can Ro-Tel tomatoes
Grated Cheddar cheese
Grated Monterey Jack cheese

Mix together first 4 ingredients. Place in large Pyrex baking dish. Top with both cheeses. Bake at 350° for approximately ½ hour. Serve with chips or Doritos.

Linda Bura, Branch No. 2049, Emporia, KS

FRUIT PIZZA

¾ c. butter or margarine
½ c. sugar
1½ c. flour
11 oz. cream cheese

½ c. powdered sugar
1 tsp. vanilla
Any kind of fruit

Crust: Combine butter, sugar and flour. Pat into round pizza pan (or square cookie sheet or cake pan). Bake crust only at 350° for 15 to 20 minutes. Cool for a few minutes.

Topping: Soften cream cheese. Beat in powdered sugar and vanilla. Spread on cooled crust. Arrange fruit on cheese. Chill. Cut like a pizza.

Tiffanie Sedlacek, Branch No. 3107, Loveland, CO

FRUIT PIZZA

½ c. butter
¼ c. powdered sugar
1 (8 oz.) pkg. cream cheese
⅓ c. sugar
1 tsp. vanilla
Fruit of your choice (strawberries, melon, pineapple, kiwi,

blueberries, mandarin oranges, apples, etc.)
2 Tbsp. cornstarch
¼ c. sugar
1 tsp. lemon juice
1 c. fruit juice and water

Crumb crust: Mix together ½ cup butter, 1 cup flour, and ¼ cup powdered sugar. Press into small pizza pan or 13x9 inch pan to form crust. Bake for 15 minutes at 350°.

Combine one 8 ounce package cream cheese, ⅓ cup sugar, and 1 teaspoon vanilla. Spread on cooled crust. Layer fruit of your choice in artistic pattern over cream cheese layer.

Sauce: Combine 2 tablespoons cornstarch, ¼ cup sugar, 1 teaspoon lemon juice, and fruit juice and water to equal 1 cup. Cook until clear. Cool and pour over fruit. Refrigerate.

Mrs. Elizabeth Buck, Branch No. 102, Zumbrota, MN

PUPPY CHOW

1 (12 oz.) pkg. chocolate chips
1 c. peanut butter
1 stick oleo

12½ oz. Crispix cereal
Scant 1 lb. powdered sugar, sifted

Melt in microwave on HIGH the chocolate chips, peanut butter and oleo. Mix well. Pour over cereal and mix to coat. Into a clean, large grocery sack, pour some powdered sugar (enough just to cover the bottom). Pour coated cereal into sack. Sprinkle almost all of the remaining powdered sugar onto cereal. Close bag and shake to cover cereal. (Best to do this step outside if possible!) If necessary, add the remaining powdered sugar. Be careful to add only enough to make the cereal white without excess powdered sugar.

This snack is easy and quick to make and always a hit.

Holly Wietfeldt, Branch No. 5454, Auburn, IL

PUPPY CHOW

12 oz. chocolate chips
½ c. peanut butter
1 stick oleo

9 c. Rice Chex
2½ c. powdered sugar

Melt first 3 items together. Pour over Rice Chex, which have been put in large bowl. While still hot, put on the sugar. With a large spoon, stir until everything is covered. Stir occasionally until cool. Store in covered containers.

Phyllis Vogtmann, Branch No. 2232, Auburn, MI

PUPPY CHOW

1 stick butter or margarine
1 c. *milk* chocolate chips
1 c. creamy peanut butter

8 c. Rice Chex
2½ c. powdered sugar

Mix first 3 ingredients together and microwave on HIGH for 1 minute. Stir thoroughly. Microwave on HIGH for 1 more minute. Pour over 8 cups of Rice Chex. Stir until covered completely. Put 1½ cups powdered sugar in a large Ziploc bag. Add Chex mixture; close and shake well. Add another cup of powdered sugar and shake again. Chill.

Marlyss Smith, Branch No. 5844, Columbia City, IN

PEANUT BUTTER POPCORN

3 qt. popped popcorn
1 c. sugar
½ c. light corn syrup
1 tsp. vanilla

1½ c. almonds (whole)
½ c. honey
1 c. peanut butter

In a large roasting pan, combine popcorn and almonds. Keep warm in a 250° oven. In a saucepan, combine sugar, honey and corn syrup. Bring to a boil, stirring constantly. Boil hard for 2 minutes and remove from heat. Stir in peanut butter and vanilla till blended. Immediately pour over popcorn mixture. Stir to coat well. Cool and break into bite-size pieces.

Emlyn Larson, Branch 5325, Stratford, IA

FINGER JELLO

4 env. Knox gelatine
4 c. boiling water

3 (3 oz.) pkg. jello (your choice of
flavor)

In a large bowl, combine the gelatine and jello. Add boiling water; stir until all gelatine dissolves. Pour into a 9x13 inch pan to set. Cut into shapes. *Enjoy!*

Doris Ruhs, Branch No. 3107, Loveland, CO

BEER NUTS

1 lb. raw peanuts
¾ c. sugar

½ c. water

Put in fry pan and cook until water is gone. Put on a buttered cookie sheet. Sprinkle with salt and put in a 300° oven for 30 minutes. Stir after first 15 minutes. Let cool and store in glass jar.

Branch No. 1068, Murdo, SD

ORIGINAL CEREAL MIX

1 box Rice Chex
1 box Corn Chex
1 box Crispix

1 box pretzel sticks
1 can nuts

Blend:

2 c. oil
3 Tbsp. Worcestershire sauce

1 Tbsp. celery salt
1 Tbsp. garlic salt

Mix cereals, nuts and pretzels. Pour oil mixture over cereal mix. Put in large flat pans. Bake for 2 hours at 250°. Stir every half hour.

Mrs. LeRoy Miller, Branch No. 557, Hampton, IA

MUNCHIE MIX

⅓ c. butter
1 Tbsp. Worcestershire sauce
½ tsp. garlic powder
½ tsp. celery salt

2 c. Crispix
2 c. Cheerios
2 c. pretzels
1½ c. mixed nuts

Mix butter, sauce, garlic powder, and celery salt. Heat till butter is melted. Pour over remaining ingredients and mix. Pour in cookie sheet. Bake at 250° for 30 minutes. Stir after 15 minutes.

Ronda Tucker, Branch No. 2512, Ord, NE

CHICKEN SNACKS

2 lb. chicken wings
½ c. soy sauce
½ c. water

¼ tsp. garlic powder
2 Tbsp. brown sugar

Wash chicken wings and cut at joints. Place in casserole dish. Mix and pour remaining ingredients over wings. Refrigerate for 8 hours or overnight. Bake for 2 hours at 325°.

Marlene Duerr, Branch No. 3289, Milwaukee, WI

CORNED BEEF HORS D'OEUVRES

1 (8 oz.) cream cheese
½ c. sour cream
1 Tbsp. chopped onion

2 Tbsp. milk or half & half
1 jar corned beef

Brown nuts in butter and put on top. Bake in a 350° oven to heat through.

Debbie Meisel, Zion Lutheran, Branch 2232, Auburn, MI

TRADITIONAL CHEX PARTY MIX

½ c. (1 stick) butter or margarine
1¼ tsp. seasoned salt
4½ tsp. Worcestershire sauce
2⅔ c. Corn Chex cereal

2⅔ c. Rice Chex cereal
2⅔ c. Wheat Chex cereal
1 c. salted mixed nuts

Preheat oven to 250°. Melt butter in large shallow roasting pan (about 15x10x2 inches) in oven. Remove. Stir in seasoned salt and Worcestershire sauce. Add cereal and nuts. Mix until all pieces are coated and then allow to cool.

Microwave instructions: In large bowl, melt butter on HIGH for 1 minute. Stir in seasoned salt and Worcestershire sauce. Add Chex and nuts. Mix until all pieces are coated. Microwave on HIGH for 6 to 7 minutes, stirring every 2 minutes. Makes about 9 cups.

CANDIED WALNUTS

¼ c. butter, melted (½ stick)
1 egg *white*
½ c. granulated sugar

¼ tsp. salt
½ lb. shelled walnuts

Preheat oven to 300°. Place melted butter in 13x9 inch pan. In small bowl with mixer at high speed, beat egg white, gradually adding sugar and salt. Beat until stiff peaks form. Fold in nuts. Spread mixture in buttered pan. Bake for 30 to 40 minutes, turning nuts and shaking pan frequently until nuts are slightly browned and crisp. Cool nuts in pan on wire rack for a few minutes. Turn out on heavy brown paper to cool completely.

Bertha Lang, Branch No. 4633, Stockton CA

FRESH FRUIT TOPPING

1 (6 oz.) can frozen orange juice
concentrate
1¼ c. cold milk

1 small pkg. instant vanilla
pudding
¼ c. sour cream

Mix juice and milk together well in bowl. Beat in pudding and stir in sour cream. Refrigerate. Serve chilled with a variety of fresh fruit for dipping.

Julie Padilla, Branch No. 3107, Loveland, CO

SWEDISH FRUIT SOUP

2 Tbsp. tapioca
2 c. pineapple juice
1 Tbsp. sugar

1 Tbsp. lemon juice
1 (11 oz.) can mandarin oranges
1 (10 oz.) pkg. frozen raspberries

Soak tapioca in 1 cup pineapple juice for 5 minutes. Bring to a boil. Add remaining juice, sugar and lemon juice. Chill. Fold in oranges and raspberries.

Great as supplement to brunch.

Cheryl Schultz, Branch No. 3107, Loveland, CO

CARAMEL DIP FOR APPLES OR BANANAS

8 oz. cream cheese
¼ c. brown sugar
¾ c. butterscotch topping or
caramel topping (any brand is
good)

½ tsp. vanilla flavoring
Chopped peanuts (optional)

Mix preceding ingredients together and serve with fruit.

A dish of chopped peanuts may be served on same fruit plate. Tastes like caramel apples. Can be used as a separate snack also.

Sue Morack, Branch No. 31, Weyauwega, WI

BAKED APPLES FOR TWO
(Microwave)

2 tart baking apples
2 tsp. brown sugar
2 tsp. butter

Lemon juice
Brandy (optional)
Cinnamon

Core the apples; cut away peels halfway down each. Place each in its own small, microwavesafe baking dish. Spoon 1 teaspoon brown sugar and 1 teaspoon butter into the center of each apple; splash each with lemon juice and brandy if desired. Dust with cinnamon. Cover each with microwavesafe plastic wrap. Place in oven 1 inch apart. Bake on HIGH for 3 minutes. Rotate ¼ turn and bake until apples are soft, but not mushy, 2 to 3 minutes

Julie Padilla, Branch No. 3107, Loveland, CO

MICROWAVE CARAMEL CORN

1 c. brown sugar
1 stick margarine
¼ c. white corn syrup

½ tsp. baking soda
½ tsp. salt
5 to 6 qt. popped corn

Combine all ingredients, "except" baking soda and popped corn, in a 2 quart microwavesafe bowl. Bring to a boil by cooking on FULL microwave power for 2 minutes and 30 seconds. Remove bowl from microwave and stir in baking soda. Put popped corn in a brown grocery bag and pour syrup over corn. Stir with a large spoon. Close bag and shake. Cook on HIGH for 1 minute and 30 seconds. Shake and turn sack over to other side for 1 minute and 30 seconds on HIGH power. Shake sack and turn over again. Microwave on HIGH power for 1 minute and 30 seconds.

Mrs. Kenneth (Elda) Siebert, Branch No. 1374, Jackson, MO

MICROWAVE KARMEL KORN

1 c. brown sugar
¾ c. margarine
¼ c. light corn syrup

½ tsp. salt
½ tsp. soda
6 qt. popped popcorn

Combine brown sugar, margarine and corn syrup in microwave bowl. Cook on HIGH for 2 minutes. Add ½ teaspoon soda and mix well. Pour over 6 quarts popped popcorn in large paper grocery bag and shake well. Cook for 1½ minutes on HIGH; shake well and cook for 1½ minutes more. Shake well and pour on cookie sheet to cool.

Optional: Add roasted peanuts.

Beatrice Kampfe, Branch No. 6706, Brule, NE

MICROWAVE CARAMEL CORN

16 c. popped popcorn, put in
    brown paper bag
½ c. butter

1 c. brown sugar
¼ c. light corn syrup
½ tsp. baking soda

In large glass bowl, melt butter. Add brown sugar and Karo syrup. Microwave for 3 minutes. Stir every 1 minute. Microwave for another 3 minutes; stir every 45 seconds. After last 45 seconds, add baking soda and stir until foamy.

Add to popcorn in brown paper bag. Mix well. Microwave for another 3 minutes, stopping every minute to take bag out and shake. Cool on wax paper. (If nuts are desired, add with baking soda.)

Lori Ann Peterson, Branch No. 2412, Green Bay, WI

MICROWAVE CARAMEL CORN

16 c. popped popcorn
½ c. butter
¼ c. dark corn syrup

1 c. packed light brown sugar
1 tsp. vanilla
½ tsp. baking soda

Place popped corn in large, heavy brown paper grocery bag. Microwave butter, corn syrup and sugar in 8 cup glass measure, uncovered, at HIGH for 5 minutes, stirring every 2 minutes. Stir in vanilla and baking soda. Pour syrup mixture over popped corn in bag. Close bag, folding top of bag down twice to close securely. Shake well. Microwave at HIGH for 2 minutes, shaking bag every minute. Microwave at HIGH for 30 seconds; shake bag and pour mixture into serving bowl. Let cool.

Arleen Heidenreich, Branch No. 2560, Mansfield, SD

MICROWAVE CARAMEL CORN

3 qt. popped corn
1 c. brown sugar
¼ c. corn syrup
½ stick oleo or butter

Dash of salt
½ tsp. vanilla
½ tsp. soda

Spray inside of large grocery sack with vegetable spray. Add popped corn. In 1 ½ quart casserole, combine brown sugar, syrup, oleo (butter), salt, and vanilla. Microwave on HIGH for 2 minutes, uncovered. Stir. Microwave on HIGH for 1¼ to 1½ minutes or till boiling. Stir in soda until frothy. Pour over popcorn in bag. Roll up bag and shake. Microwave on HIGH for 1½ minutes, then shake. Microwave for 1½ minutes, then shake. Microwave for ½ minute, then shake. Microwave for ½ minute, then shake. Pour out onto large cooky sheet; let cool and break apart.

Nancy Sorensen, Branch No. 5992, Franklin, WI

MICROWAVE CARAMEL CORN

1 c. brown sugar
½ c. margarine
¼ c. honey
½ tsp. salt

½ tsp. baking soda
½ tsp. vanilla
3 to 4 qt. popped corn (air popper works)

Combine all ingredients, except soda, vanilla and corn in 2 quart bowl. Bring to a boil. Let boil on FULL power for 1½ minutes. Remove from microwave. Stir in soda and vanilla. Put popped corn in brown grocery bag and microwave for 1½ minutes on HIGH. Shake and cook for 1 minute longer. Pour onto cookie sheet and allow to cool. Store in airtight container.

MICROWAVE CARAMEL CORN

4 qt. popped corn
1 c. brown sugar
¼ c. corn syrup

1 stick margarine
½ tsp. baking soda

Combine sugar, syrup and margarine in a 4 cup Pyrex measuring cup. Cook for 3 to 4 minutes on HIGH until boiling. Stir in soda. Put popped corn into grocery bag and pour over corn and shake. Microwave on HIGH for 1½ minutes. Shake bag well. Microwave on HIGH for 45 seconds and shake well. Microwave once more on HIGH for 30 seconds. Cool and eat.

Kathy Busch

CARAMEL CORN

⅔ c. brown sugar
⅔ stick oleo

8 large marshmallows
2 c. popped corn

Carefully melt brown sugar, oleo and marshmallows in microwave oven. Pour over popped corn and mix very well.

Doris Ruhs, Branch No. 3107, Loveland, CO

CARAMEL POPCORN

Cook for 5 minutes:

2 c. brown sugar
½ c. white corn syrup

2 sticks margarine

Add:

1 tsp. baking soda
1 tsp. vanilla

½ tsp. salt

Pour over 5 or 6 quarts of popped corn. Stir until well mixed and bake for 1 hour at 250°, stirring every 15 minutes. Use a big roaster pan or whatever that is not too deep.

Connie Davis, Branch No. 3107, Loveland, CO

CARAMEL POPCORN

20 c. popcorn
½ c. pecans
2 c. brown sugar
2 sticks margarine
½ c. Karo syrup

½ tsp. salt
1 tsp. vanilla
½ tsp. soda
Pinch of cream of tartar

Combine brown sugar, margarine, and syrup; boil for 5 minutes. Add salt, vanilla, soda, and cream of tartar (it should foam up). Pour over popcorn and nuts. Put in dish and bake at 250° to 275° for 1 hour, stirring every 15 minutes. Spread out after removing from oven.

Doris Wohlschlegel, Branch No. 5425, Louisville, KY

TOMATO JUICE COCKTAIL

6 qt. tomatoes, cut up (no need to
    skin)
6 c. water
6 small onions, cut up
3 stalks celery, cut up
1½ green peppers, cut up

24 whole cloves
6 Tbsp. sugar
3 Tbsp. salt
1 tsp. pepper
1 bay leaf

Put all ingredients in a kettle. Bring to a boil. Boil for 45 minutes or until tomatoes, celery and green peppers are soft. Push through a food mill or strain. Add ¾ cup cider vinegar. Bring up to heat and seal in jars. Yield: 7 pints or 5 quarts.

Lynn and Bill Swift, Branch No. 1359, Milwaukee WI

EGGNOG

2 eggs
¾ tsp. vanilla
2½ c. milk

4 tsp. sugar
¼ tsp. nutmeg

Beat eggs and sugar. Add vanilla and nutmeg; mix well. Stir milk into this.

This is a very good drink.

Doris Ruhs, Branch No. 3107, Loveland, CO

SPICY-HOT BEVERAGE

1½ qt. cranberry juice
2 qt. apple juice or cider
½ c. brown sugar

½ tsp. salt
4 sticks cinnamon
1½ tsp. whole cloves

Pour juice/cider into percolator. Place remaining ingredients into basket of percolator and allow to perk through. Serve hot. Makes 25 (½ cup) servings.

Sally Mueller, Branch No. 3107, Loveland, CO

STRAWBERRY SLUSH

9 c. water

2 c. sugar

Boil until sugar dissolves and let cool.

Add:

1 (12 oz.) can orange juice
   concentrate
2 regular size strawberry Kool-Aid
   (or 2 c. strawberry puree)

1½ c. vodka (can be omitted)

Mix all ingredients together. Pour into 5 quart ice cream pail and freeze until it gets to be slush. Serve. Put one ice cream scoop slush in glass with 7-Up and slice of lemon with mint leaf for garnish.

Florence Lisko, Branch No. 1400, Arbor Vitae, WI

SLUSH

3 c. water
1 c. sugar
½ c. water
1 tea bag

1 (6 oz.) can orange juice
1 (6 oz.) can lemonade
1 c. vodka

Boil 3 cups of water with 1 cup of sugar. Add another ½ cup of boiling water and 1 tea bag; steep well. Let this mixture cool. Add the orange juice, lemonade and vodka. Freeze.

Serve by adding a half of glass of 7-Up to ½ glass of slush. (Keep the slush frozen - once it melts, it is not nearly as good.)

This keeps for a long time in the freezer.

Dawn Benedict, Branch No. 5331 Toledo, OH

PUNCH

1 qt. pineapple juice
1 qt. apple juice
1 large can frozen orange juice,
    prepared as directed on label

1 small can lemonade (undiluted -
    frozen)
3 qt. ginger ale (sugar free
    preferred)

Mix fruit juices together and let stand to blend flavors at least 3 hours. Pour over ice block or ring into punch bowl; add ginger ale. Float sherbet (orange, lemon or pineapple) if desired. Makes 50 cups.

Helen Ouzman, Branch No. 5865, Sun City/Ruskin

TANGY PUNCH
(Slush)

1⅓ c. Tang
1 c. sugar
6 c. water

4 c. pineapple juice or cranberry
    juice
½ tsp. almond extract

Mix together and freeze until slushy. Put into glasses and fill with ginger ale to cover.

This is a very good festive punch!

Mrs. Margaret Greiner, Branch No. 2838, Wilmot, SD

CHRISTMAS PUNCH

Ice cream
Milk

White soda (7-Up, etc.)
Eggnog

Mix ice cream with milk; add soda and eggnog. If you have no preferences, use 1 quart ice cream (vanilla if using eggnog - flavored if no eggnog), 2 cups milk, and 2 liter soda. Adjust amount according to liking. Larger amounts can be used.

Great for family parties as you can use their favorite flavor of ice cream. Adjust amounts to family likings or item on hand.

Darlene Strack, Branch No. 235, Colby, WI

GRADUATION PUNCH

4 pkg. strawberry drink mix
    (Kool-Aid)
2 c. sugar
8 qt. water

3 (6 oz.) cans frozen lemonade
3 (6 oz.) cans frozen orange juice
2 (46 oz.) cans pineapple juice
2 qt. ginger ale

Combine sugar and 1 quart water; boil for 5 minutes. Cool. Combine ingredients. When ready to serve, add ginger ale.

These ingredients may be refrigerated and used later. Just add ginger ale when ready to serve. Serves 50.

Doris Seevers, Branch No. 382, St. Louis, MO

HOT APPLE CIDER

1 qt. apple cider
1 c. orange juice
½ c. pineapple juice
½ c. lemon juice

½ c. sugar
2 (2 inch) sticks cinnamon
1 tsp. whole cloves

Combine all ingredients in 2 quart microwaveable pitcher. Microwave on HIGH for 10 minutes. Let cider stand for 5 minutes. Microwave on HIGH for an additional 3 to 4 minutes. Yield: 6 to 8 servings.

Judy Eggers, Branch No. 1589, Wisner, NE

PINK CRANBERRY SLUSH

48 oz. cranberry juice
12 oz. frozen lemonade
12 oz. frozen limeade

16 oz. 7-Up
2½ c. water
2 c. vodka

Mix ingredients and freeze in a large container. Stir 2 or 3 times the first 24 hours. Scoop into a glass and fill approximately ⅔ full. Fill the glass with lemon sour, ginger ale or 7-Up. Stir until slushy.

Mrs. Elizabeth Buck, Branch No. 102, Zumbrota, MN

RHUBARB WINE

12 lb. rhubarb, cut into 1 inch
    pieces (fresh, moist)
12 qt. boiling water
12 lb. white sugar

3 lemons, sliced
3 c. raisins
1 pkg. dry yeast

Place cut up rhubarb in a stone crock or glass jar (not plastic). Add boiling water; cover with cloth and let stand for 3 days. Remove pulp without crushing. Add 1 pound sugar to each quart of juice, also add lemons, raisins, and yeast. (Note: For especially sweet rhubarb, cut back on amount of sugar by 10% to 20%.) Let stand in crock for 9 days in a warm place.

Remove all pulp. Leave juice in covered crock for 2 months in warm place. Without stirring, siphon juice into bottles and cork. Place in cooler temperature. Useable after 30 days.

Norma Doering, Branch 4534, Litchfield, MN

HOT BUTTERED RUM

1 lb. butter
1 lb. brown sugar
1 lb. powdered sugar
1 tsp. cinnamon

1 tsp. nutmeg
1 tsp. salt
1 qt. vanilla ice cream

Soften butter and mix all ingredients at high speed with mixer. Heat water to boiling. Put rum in cup and add heaping tablespoonful of mixture and fill with hot water.

Esther Meston, Branch No. 7063, Albany, OR

TOPAZ PUNCH WITH SHERBET RING

Punch:

6 oz. frozen orange juice
6 oz. frozen lemonade
¼ c. sugar

¼ c. water
48 oz. Welch's white grape juice
1 qt. ginger ale

Mix concentrates, sugar and water. Add grape juice and ginger ale. Serve in large bowl and float a frozen ring of sherbet. Serves 20 (5 ounce) cups.

Sherbet Ring:

1 pt. lemon sherbet
8 red maraschino cherries

4 green maraschino cherries

Cut red cherries in halves. Cut green cherries in fourths. Pour small amount of water in bottom of 8 inch ring mold and set cherries decoratively in place like a holly wreath. Freeze, then spoon softened sherbet in mold. Smooth surface and freeze again. Unmold and slide into filled punch bowl.

Wilma Benz, Branch No. 1048, Muskego, WI

HOT SPICED PERCOLATOR PUNCH

9 c. pineapple juice
9 c. cranberry juice
4½ c. water
1 c. brown sugar

¼ tsp. salt
4½ tsp. whole cloves
4 cinnamon sticks

Place in percolator. Put the whole cloves and cinnamon sticks in the basket. Use a 36 cup percolator. Brew as for coffee. When the cycle is completed, stir the basket to allow the liquid to finish flowing through.

Sally Harms, Branch No. 5331, Toledo, OH

ORANGE JULIUS

⅓ c. frozen orange juice
  concentrate
½ c. water
½ tsp. vanilla

½ c. milk
¼ c. sugar
Ice cubes

Put the preceding ingredients in blender. Drop 5 to 6 ice cubes in. Blend until ice cubes are crushed. *Delicious beverage!*

Rev. Gene R. Kangas, Branch No. 192, Hilbert, WI

ORANGE SLUSH

12 c. water
1 fifth (25.4 oz.) vodka
12 oz. frozen orange juice

12 oz. frozen lemon juice
1 c. sugar

Bring water and sugar to boil. Heat until sugar is melted, then add the vodka, frozen orange juice and frozen lemon juice. Freeze.

Mrs. Iris Kluever, Branch No. 1131, Worthington, MN

RHUBARB PUNCH

20 c. cut up rhubarb
15 c. water (or at least to cover)
2 (6 oz.) cans frozen lemonade
   concentrate

2 (6 oz.) cans frozen orange juice
   concentrate (do not dilute)
2 c. sugar
1 (6 oz.) pkg. red jello

Cook rhubarb and water until rhubarb is tender; drain. Use the juice for the punch, not the pieces of rhubarb. Boil concentrates, sugar and red jello with rhubarb juice and seal. When ready to use, chill well. Makes 6 quarts. *Enjoy!*

Tricia Schellen, Branch No. 1957, Creighton, NE

SLUSH PUNCH FOR FIFTY

2 c. sugar
1 (6 oz.) pkg. gelatin (any flavor)
6 c. boiling water

2 (46 oz.) cans pineapple juice
4 (28 oz.) bottles chilled ginger ale

Mix sugar and gelatin together in large 4 quart container. Add boiling water and stir until dissolved. Add pineapple juice and mix well. Pour into plastic containers and freeze for at least 24 hours.

Set out containers about an hour before you wish to serve. Empty containers into large punch bowl and break into chunks with wooden spoon. Pour the 4 bottles of ginger ale over this and mix to slushy consistency. Makes 50 punch cup servings.

This punch will vary in color and flavor, depending on the flavor of gelatin used.

Nellie Rathke, Branch No. 2049, Emporia, KS

Notes

Notes

Salads

FOOD QUANTITIES FOR 25, 50, AND 100 SERVINGS

FOOD	25 SERVINGS	50 SERVINGS	100 SERVINGS
Rolls	4 doz.	8 doz.	16 doz.
Bread	50 slices or 3 1-lb. loaves	100 slices or 6 1-lb. loaves	200 slices or 12 1-lb. loaves
Butter	½ pound	¾ to 1 pound	1½ pounds
Mayonnaise	1 cup	2 to 3 cups	4 to 6 cups
Mixed Filling for Sandwiches (meat, eggs, fish)	1½ quarts	2½ to 3 quarts	5 to 6 quarts
Mixed Filling (sweet-fruit)	1 quart	1¾ to 2 quarts	2½ to 4 quarts
Jams & Preserves	1½ lb.	3 lb.	6 lb.
Crackers	1½ lb.	3 lb.	6 lb.
Cheese (2 oz. per serving)	3 lb.	6 lb.	12 lb.
Soup	1½ gal.	3 gal.	6 gal.
Salad Dressings	1 pt.	2½ pt.	½ gal.
Meat, Poultry or Fish:			
Wieners (beef)	6½ pounds	13 pounds	25 pounds
Hamburger	9 pounds	18 pounds	35 pounds
Turkey or chicken	13 pounds	25 to 35 pounds	50 to 75 pounds
Fish, large whole (round)	13 pounds	25 pounds	50 pounds
Fish, fillets or steaks	7½ pounds	15 pounds	30 pounds
Salads, Casseroles, Vegetables:			
Potato Salad	4¼ quarts	2¼ gallons	4½ gallons
Scalloped Potatoes	4½ quarts or 1 12x20" pan	8½ quarts	17 quarts
Mashed Potatoes	9 lb.	18-20 lb.	25-35 lb.
Spaghetti	1¼ gallons	2½ gallons	5 gallons
Baked Beans	¾ gallon	1¼ gallons	2½ gallons
Jello Salad	¾ gallon	1¼ gallons	2½ gallons
Canned Vegetables	1 #10 can	2½ #10 cans	4 #10 cans
Fresh Vegetables:			
Lettuce (for salads)	4 heads	8 heads	15 heads
Carrots (3 oz. or ½ c.)	6¼ lb.	12½ lb.	25 lb.
Tomatoes	3-5 lb.	7-10 lb.	14-20 lb.
Desserts:			
Watermelon	37½ pounds	75 pounds	150 pounds
Fruit Cup (½ c. per serving)	3 qt.	6 qt.	12 qt.
Cake	1 10x12" sheet cake 1½ 10" layer cakes	1 12x20" sheet cake 3 10" layer cakes	2 12x20" sheet cakes 6 10" layer cakes
Whipping Cream	¾ pint	1½ to 2 pints	3 pints
Ice Cream:			
Brick	3¼ quarts	6½ quarts	12½ quarts
Bulk	2¼ quarts	4½ quarts or 1¼ gallons	9 quarts or 2½ gallons
Beverages:			
Coffee	½ pound and 1½ gal. water	1 pound and 3 gal. water	2 pounds and 6 gal. water
Tea	1/12 pound and 1½ gal. water	1/6 pound and 3 gal. water	1/3 pound and 6 gal. water
Lemonade	10 to 15 lemons, 1½ gal. water	20 to 30 lemons, 3 gal. water	40 to 60 lemons, 6 gal. water

SALADS

BAKED PINEAPPLE

1 (1 lb.) can chunk pineapple
1 c. grated Cheddar cheese
2 Tbsp. flour

1 c. sugar
1 c. dried bread crumbs
2 Tbsp. margarine

Drain pineapple and save juice. Toss pineapple with cheese and place in 8x8 inch pan. Blend flour and sugar with pineapple juice; heat until thickened. Pour over pineapple and cheese. Top with bread crumbs and dot with margarine. Bake at 350° for 25 minutes.

SPAGHETTI SALAD

1 lb. cooked spaghetti noodles
1 green pepper, cut up
1 cucumber, cut up
1 red onion, cut up

1 tomato, cut up
1 bottle Italian dressing
Salad Supreme seasoning

Combine cut up vegetables with cooked noodles. Pour dressing over all and toss. Sprinkle several tablespoons "Salad Supreme" seasoning. Toss again and let set for 1 hour before serving.

Marilyn Vogel, Loveland, CO

SHOE PEG CORN SALAD

1 can shoe peg corn
1/4 c. chopped green pepper
2 Tbsp. chopped pimento

1/2 c. chopped celery
1 c. thinly sliced cucumbers
1/4 c. thinly sliced red onions

Dressing:

1/3 c. oil
1 1/2 tsp. salt

3 Tbsp. sugar
3 Tbsp. wine vinegar

Mix all ingredients and marinate overnight. Drain before serving if desired.
Jeanie Coleman, Loveland, CO

CHERRY SALAD

1 (6 oz.) box cherry jello
2 c. boiling water

1 (30 oz.) can cherry pie filling

Topping:

2 oz. cream cheese (room
    temperature)
Pineapple juice and cream (to thin
    cream cheese)

3 c. Cool Whip

Dissolve jello in boiling water and add pie filling. Put in dish and when firm, spread on topping.

Other fruit and flavors of jello may be used.

Jerrene Braisted, Branch No. 2678, Laramie, WY

ORIENTAL SALAD

3 oz. chicken flavored Top Ramen
4 c. cabbage, shredded
4 green onions, chopped
2 Tbsp. sesame seeds
3 Tbsp. vinegar
2 Tbsp. sugar

2 Tbsp. oil
½ tsp. pepper
¼ tsp. salt
Chicken packet
½ c. almonds, slivered

Pour hot water over Top Ramen noodles. Omit chicken packet. Let set for 5 minutes and drain thoroughly. Place in large mixer bowl and add shredded cabbage, onion and sesame seed. Set aside.

In jar, shake together the vinegar, sugar, oil, salt, pepper, and chicken packet. Pour over the noodle mixture and mix thoroughly. Refrigerate overnight, then add slivered almonds. Refrigerate for at least 4 hours for best flavor if you need faster than overnight. *Delicious!*

Holly Brantz, Branch No. 2678, Laramie, WY

MACARONI SALAD

1 (1½ lb.) pkg. curly or shell
  macaroni
1 onion, chopped

1 green pepper, diced
2 c. grated carrots

Cook macaroni until done; cool, then add the vegetables.

Dressing:

1 c. Eagle Brand sweetened
  condensed milk
1 c. cider vinegar (mild)

2 c. mayonnaise
1 tsp. sugar

Mix and chill.

Edna Frerichs, Branch No. 2121, Chico, CA

BETTY'S MACARONI SALAD

2 c. mayonnaise
1 c. Eagle Brand milk
½ c. sugar
¼ c. vinegar

2 (8 oz.) pkg. rotini macaroni
Carrots
Peppers
Onions

Cut up vegetables. Cook macaroni until tender. Drain. Mix remaining ingredients; pour over cooked macaroni and vegetables.

Betty Eilers, Branch No. 1128, Webster City, IA

SEVEN-UP SALAD

1 large (6 oz.) box lemon gelatin
2 c. boiling water
2 c. 7-Up
1 large (20 oz.) can pineapple
    tidbits, drained

1 c. miniature marshmallows
2 bananas, sliced thin

Dissolve gelatin and cool; add 7-Up slowly and carefully to preserve the carbonation. Add pineapple, marshmallows and banana slices after gelatin begins to thicken.

Combine drained pineapple juice (add water, if necessary, to make 1 cup), ½ cup sugar, and 1 beaten egg. Cook mixture until it thickens. Add 2 tablespoons margarine. Cool.

Fold into the cooled mixture 1 cup whipped cream or prepared Dream Whip or Cool Whip; spread over set gelatin mixture. Sprinkle with crushed nutmeats or ¼ cup grated Longhorn cheese.

Ruth Rogers, Branch No. 885, Sadorus, IL

PEACH SALAD

1 (16 to 17 oz.) can crushed
    pineapple with juice
2 small boxes peach jello
1 (8 oz.) pkg. cream cheese
¾ c. sugar

1 junior size jar peach baby food
1 (8 oz.) Cool Whip
½ c. walnuts, broken into small
    pieces

Pour jello into pineapple with juice in a pan. Bring to a boil; let cool. Mix cream cheese and sugar together in bowl with a mixer. Add baby food. Mix into cooled jello. Fold in Cool Whip and nuts. Chill.

Jan McLaughlin, Branch No. 3107, Loveland, CO

TACO SAUCE

1 can stewed tomatoes
1 small green pepper, cut up
1 small onion, cut up
½ tsp. comino

½ tsp. crushed red pepper
½ tsp. coarse black pepper
½ tsp. salt
½ stalk celery, cut up

Place all ingredients in blender. Blend. Serve on tacos.

Also may be used as a dip for tortilla chips and may be added to chili for extra seasoning.

Jan McLaughlin, Branch No. 3107, Loveland, CO

MACARONI SALAD

1 c. salad macaroni, cooked and
    drained (can add a little
    cooking oil when cooking)
1 Tbsp. chopped onion

1 c. diced celery
1 c. diced ham
½ c. grated cheese
½ c. black olives

Dressing:

½ c. Miracle Whip
1 Tbsp. vinegar

½ tsp. prepared mustard
½ tsp. salt

Mix dressing ingredients together and pour over the salad.

Loraine Grootheius, Branch No. 2714, Ogden, UT

BAR-B-Q MACARONI SALAD

1 lb. salad macaroni
1 can marinara sauce
1½ c. chopped celery
1½ c. chopped sweet pickle
2 Tbsp. sweet pickle juice

1 (4½ oz.) chopped ripe olives
½ tsp. chilli powder
1 finely chopped small onion
1 c. mayonnaise

Bring 4 quarts water and 2 tablespoons salt to a rapid boil. Add macaroni and cook for 10 minutes, stirring often. Drain and blanch. Mix all ingredients, except mayonnaise and onion. Chill. Before serving, add mayonnaise, onion, and salt and pepper to taste. Garnish with hard cooked egg and tomato wedges. Serves 6 to 8.

Will keep well in refrigerator for 1 week.

Ruth Maas, Branch No. 3436, Pico Rivera, CA

THE "ORIGINAL PANTRY" COLESLAW RECIPE

1½ c. plus 2 Tbsp. mayonnaise
6 Tbsp. plus 1 tsp. sugar
3 Tbsp. plus ½ tsp. wine vinegar
¾ c. plus 1 Tbsp. oil
⅛ tsp. garlic powder
⅛ tsp. onion powder
⅛ tsp. mustard powder

⅛ tsp. celery powder
Dash of black pepper
1 Tbsp. plus 2 tsp. lemon juice
¾ c. plus 1 Tbsp. half & half
½ tsp. salt
2 heads cabbage, very finely
   shredded

Blend together mayonnaise, sugar, vinegar, and oil. Add spice powders, pepper, lemon juice, half & half, and salt. Stir until smooth. Pour over coleslaw in a large bowl and toss until cabbage is well coated. If wished, use only half the dressing to a head of cabbage and save remaining to dress fruit salad or other salads. Dressing keeps well, covered tightly, in the refrigerator for several days. Makes about 1 quart dressing.

The Avedissian Family, Branch No. 2785, Santa Maria, CA

GRACE LUTHERAN'S COLE SLAW
(Serves 300)

Approx. 50 lb. cabbage (13 heads)
1 tsp. salt (per head)
4 lb. carrots, grated
3 medium size green peppers,
   grated

1 c. white vinegar (per head)
¼ c. water (per head)
1 tsp. mustard seed (per head)
1 tsp. celery seed (per head)
2 c. sugar (per head)

Chop cabbage and add salt. Let stand for 1 hour. Squeeze liquid from cabbage. Add all other vegetables.

Mix together sugar, vinegar, water, mustard, and celery seed; boil for 1 minute. Cool and pour over cabbage. Mix well and store in refrigerator. Freezes well if made ahead of time.

Grace Lutheran Church, Branch No. 4788, Denison, TX

FAVORITE COLESLAW

1 medium head cabbage,
   shredded
1 medium onion, finely chopped
1 green pepper, finely chopped
1 (2 oz.) jar pimento, finely
   chopped

⅔ c. salad oil
½ c. honey
2 tsp. sugar
2 tsp. salt
1 c. cider vinegar

Toss cabbage, onion, green pepper, and pimento in large serving bowl. Combine oil, honey, sugar, salt, and vinegar in saucepan. Heat to boil, stirring constantly. Immediately pour over vegetables. Do not stir. Refrigerate for 2 days.

MOLDED SPINACH SALAD

1 (3 oz.) pkg. lemon jello
1 c. boiling water
½ c. cold water
1½ Tbsp. vinegar
½ c. mayonnaise

¾ c. cottage cheese
1 c. fresh chopped spinach
⅓ c. finely chopped celery
1 tsp. grated onion

Dissolve jello in boiling water; add cold water, vinegar, and mayonnaise. Blend. Put into refrigerator for 15 minutes, until it slightly jells. Remove and beat with electric beater until fluffy. Fold in the remaining ingredients and return to refrigerator until set.

Best if made the day before, but may be made 5 hours before meal.

Mrs. David Pease, Branch No. 4896, Kalamazoo, MI

SPINACH SALAD

Dressing:

⅓ c. vegetable oil
⅓ c. vinegar
⅔ c. sugar
3 tsp. prepared mustard

1 tsp. salt
⅛ tsp. pepper
1 medium onion

Salad:

2 (10 oz.) fresh spinach
½ lb. bacon
6 eggs

½ pkg. Pepperidge Farm dressing
   mix

Mix dressing and let stand overnight. Wash spinach. Fry bacon crisp and crumble. Boil and chop the eggs. Add Pepperidge Farm dressing mix. Add the dressing just before serving.

Barbara Lester, Branch No. 1846, Cylinder, IA

FRESH SPINACH SALAD

1 lb. fresh spinach
1 onion, finely chopped
½ can water chestnuts, finely
    chopped

2 hard-boiled eggs, finely chopped
Bacon chips

Dressing:

1 c. oil
¼ c. sugar

2 Tbsp. Worcestershire sauce
⅓ c. catsup

Blend all dressing ingredients.

SPINACH SALAD

1 (10 oz.) bag spinach
1 can sliced, drained water
    chestnuts

1 can bean sprouts
½ lb. bacon, minced and rendered

Salad Dressing:

½ c. vegetable oil
¼ c. vinegar
½ to 2 tsp. salt (or none!)
¾ c. sugar or honey

1 tsp. Worcestershire sauce
⅓ c. catsup
1 medium onion, grated

Blend all of the salad dressing ingredients together. Pour over tossed salad ingredients.

Mrs. Arthur L. Harley, Branch No. 1052, South Whitley, IN

MOM'S FRESH SPINACH SALAD

1 large bunch fresh spinach,
    washed, patted dry, and cut or
    broken into pieces
5 slices bacon, fried and crumbled
4 hard-boiled eggs, chopped
½ large head lettuce, shredded
1 bunch green onions, chopped
1 box frozen peas, thawed and
    drained (do not cook)

⅔ c. mayonnaise, mixed with ⅔ c.
    salad dressing (spread over
    peas)
1 chunk Swiss cheese, grated
    (spread over mayonnaise
    mixture)

Layer in order given in 8x12 inch Pyrex dish and lightly salt each layer. Cover and refrigerate for 24 hours.

Connie Davis, Branch No. 3107, Loveland, CO

HOT GERMAN POTATO SALAD

½ lb. bacon, fried and crumbled
6 c. raw peeled, sliced potatoes
1 diced onion

½ c. apple cider vinegar
⅓ c. sugar

Put potatoes in bacon grease. Pour vinegar, sugar and 1 cup water over potatoes. Salt and pepper. Bring to a boil; cover and simmer for 20 minutes or until potatoes are soft. Put bacon crumbs over top of potatoes and serve.

Alice Martin, Branch No. 1455, Great Falls, MT

BAKED GERMAN POTATO SALAD

1 c. diced bacon	3 Tbsp. flour
1 c. diced celery	1/3 c. sugar
1 c. chopped onion	2/3 c. vinegar
3 tsp. salt	1 1/3 c. water
1/2 tsp. pepper	8 c. sliced, cooked potatoes

Fry bacon and drain; return 4 tablespoons of fat to skillet. Add celery, onion, salt, and flour. Cook gently. Add sugar, vinegar, pepper, and water. Bring to a boil. Pour over potatoes and bacon. Put in a 3 quart baking dish. Cover and bake at 350° for 30 minutes.

St. Peter's Ev. Lutheran Church, Moltke Township, Gibbon, MN

GERMAN POTATO SALAD

1 c. diced bacon	2/3 c. sugar
1 c. sliced celery	1/2 c. vinegar
1 c. chopped onion	1/2 tsp. pepper
3 tsp. salt	1 1/3 c. water
3 Tbsp. flour	8 c. sliced, cooked potatoes

Fry bacon; drain on paper towels. Return 4 tablespoons fat to skillet. Add celery, onion, salt, and pepper. Cook gently. Add flour, sugar, vinegar, and water; bring to a boil. Pour over potatoes and bacon in 3 quart baking dish. Cover and bake in a 350° oven for 30 minutes. Serves 12.

Marnell Nichols, Branch No. 1872, Ogallala, NE

GERMAN POTATO SALAD

12 medium size potatoes	1/2 c. green pepper
3 hard-boiled eggs	1 small raw carrot

Boil potatoes and cut up in small pieces. Add pepper, cut up carrot and boiled eggs. Salt potatoes.

Dressing:

1/2 lb. bacon, cut up small	1 c. cider vinegar
1 large onion	1 1/2 c. water
1 Tbsp. salad mustard	2 Tbsp. corn starch
2/3 c. sugar	1/4 c. water

Fry bacon until slightly browned. Cut up onion small and add to bacon. When onion is browned, add mustard, sugar, vinegar, and 1 1/2 cups water; simmer for 5 minutes. Mix corn starch with 1/4 cup of water. Add to bacon mixture to thicken. Cook for a couple minutes longer. Pour over potatoes.

Mrs. Russell Bruemmer, Branch No. 362, Michigan City, IN

51

GERMAN POTATO SALAD

5 lb. potatoes, cooked in salted
    water, peeled and sliced
8 to 10 slices bacon, chopped into
    1 inch pieces
2 large onions, chopped
1⅓ c. water

2 Tbsp. flour
⅔ c. sugar
⅔ c. vinegar
1 tsp. dry mustard
1 tsp. salt

Brown onions and bacon. Add flour to thicken. Add water, sugar, vinegar, dry mustard, and salt. Bring to a boil. Simmer vigorously for 15 minutes. Pour over sliced potatoes. May add additional salt or pepper after tasting. Serve warm.

Marlene Haegele, Branch No. 3775, Utica, MI

GERMAN POTATO SALAD

Red potatoes (about 14)
¾ lb. bacon
1 c. water
1 c. cider vinegar
½ c. sugar

2 Tbsp. cornstarch, mixed with
    cold water
1 c. celery, chopped
1 c. onion, chopped
1 Tbsp. parsley

Boil potatoes slowly for 20 to 30 minutes with skins on. Dice and fry bacon. Pour out all but 2 tablespoons fat. Add water, vinegar and sugar. Cook and boil. Add cornstarch. Stir. Add celery, onion, parsley, and bacon. Cook for a couple of minutes. Pour over diced potatoes. Serve warm.

Beverly C. Gemeinhardt, Branch No. 2189, Oregon City, OR

GERMAN POTATO SALAD

6 slices bacon
½ c. sugar
¼ tsp. pepper
1 c. water (or more)
8 c. potatoes, diced

2 Tbsp. flour
½ c. vinegar
2 large onions, finely cut
½ tsp. salt

Fry bacon. Add onions to fat and fry until light golden brown. Stir in flour and blend well. Add sugar, salt, pepper, vinegar, and water. Cook until clear, stirring. Pour over hot potatoes. Let stand, closed, to bring out flavor.

Janis Radies, Branch No. 2323, Caroline, WI

GERMAN POTATO SALAD

½ lb. bacon
¾ c. chopped onion
3 Tbsp. sugar
3 Tbsp. flour
1½ tsp. salt
1 tsp. celery seed

¾ c. cider vinegar
1½ c. water
6 c. sliced, cooked potatoes
2 hard cooked eggs, peeled and
    chopped
Parsley (for garnish)

Fry bacon until crisp; drain and crumble. Saute onion in ⅓ cup bacon drippings until tender. Add flour, sugar, salt, and celery seed. Stir in vinegar and water. Cook until thick. Combine with bacon, potatoes, and eggs. Turn into a greased 3 quart casserole. Bake, covered, at 350° for 20 minutes or until heated through. Garnish with parsley.

Janet Schave, Branch No. 2209, Port Hope, MI

GERMAN POTATO SALAD

12 lb. potatoes	1 c. vinegar
⅓ lb. bacon	½ tsp. pepper
2¼ c. sugar	⅛ c. salt
⅓ c. flour	3 sticks celery
1½ c. water	1 onion

Cut up bacon and brown; set aside. Mix dry ingredients, then add vinegar and water. Let it come to a boil. Keep some bacon piece for garnish on top of potatoes. Add remaining bacon and grease to mixture. Makes enough for 12 pounds potatoes.

Marie Rode, Salem Lutheran Church, Branch No. 389, Affton, MO

CRANBERRY ORANGE RELISH

4 c. cranberries	2 c. sugar
2 oranges	

Put cranberries through food grinder. Quarter whole oranges; remove seeds and put through grinder. Add sugar and mix well. Chill in refrigerator for a few hours before serving. Makes 1 quart.

Mixture will keep for several days in refrigerator.

Guy and Marian Orton, Branch No. 5076, Topeka, KS

CRANBERRY ORANGE MOLD

2 (3 oz.) pkg. jello (any red flavor)	1 (16 oz.) can whole or jellied
2 c. boiling water	cranberry sauce
¼ tsp. cinnamon	2 c. diced orange sections*
¼ tsp. cloves	

Dissolve gelatin in water until dissolved well. Add spices and sauce. Chill until it starts to thicken. Fold in oranges and/or apple. Pour into 6 cup mold or bowl. Serve as salad or relish. Makes 5 cups or 10 side salads or 14 relish servings.

* Or, use 1 cup diced oranges or 1 cup chopped apple or 1½ cups chopped apple and ½ cup chopped celery.

Carlene Cay Knutson, Branch No. 5616, Tuttle, ND

CRANBERRY SALAD

1 pkg. fresh cranberries
2 oranges, peeled
2 small apples, peeled

1¼ c. sugar
1 large pkg. red jello
2 c. boiling water

Dissolve jello in boiling water. Grind cranberries, oranges and apples together. Drain off all juice and discard. Add sugar. When jello is cool and just beginning to set, add to cranberry mixture. Put in large jello mold. May be served on lettuce.

Mrs. Mildred Foreman, Branch 2090, Dowagiac, MI

CRANBERRY SALAD

1 lb. cranberries
2 c. sugar
1 pt. cream (must be whipping
cream)

½ lb. marshmallows
½ c. nutmeats

Grind cranberries and mix with sugar. Let stand for 2 hours. Add the cream which has been whipped. Add the marshmallows which have been cut into small pieces. Add the nuts. Refrigerate overnight.

Sherry Battke, Branch No. 286, Bloomer, WI

RASPBERRY CRANBERRY SALAD

1 large size pkg. raspberry Jell-O
1½ c. boiling water

1 can whole cranberry sauce
1 c. crushed pineapple, drained

Dissolve Jell-O in hot water. Add cranberry sauce and pineapple. Mix well. Refrigerate until firm.

Martha Kreutz, Branch No. 3107, Loveland, CO

CRANBERRY SALAD

2 c. raw cranberries
1½ c. water
1 c. sugar
1 (3 oz.) pkg. cherry jello

½ c. crushed pineapple, drained
9 apples, peeled
1½ c. walnuts, chopped

Simmer cranberries and water for 10 minutes. While still hot, add sugar and jello. Cool. Add pineapple, apples and finally chopped nuts. Mix well. Let set in refrigerator to set and cool.

Ella Riebe, Branch No. 5616, Wilton, ND

CRANBERRY SALAD

3 env. unflavored gelatin
1 c. boiling orange juice
2 c. sugar
1 qt. ground cranberries

2 Delicious apples, ground
2 large oranges, sliced
2 c. chopped pecans
¾ c. cold water

54

Soften gelatin in cold water. Dissolve gelatin mixture in the boiling orange juice. Add sugar and stir until sugar is dissolved. Cool. Combine fruit and pecans; fold into gelatin mixture. Chill until firm.

This may be frozen. One may substitute 2 cans of drained mandarin oranges for the fresh oranges and use the juice for the orange juice.

Edna Lange, Branch No. 1995, Hudson, CO

CRANBERRY SALAD

2 c. or 1 bag cranberries
3 c. mini marshmallows
¾ c. sugar
2 c. diced, unpeeled red apples
½ c. grapes

1 c. diced pineapple
½ c. nuts
1 c. Cool Whip
¼ c. salad dressing

Put cranberries through grinder. Use coarse blade or may use blender. Add marshmallows and sugar; stir. Let stand overnight (refrigerate). The next day, add the rest of the ingredients. Mix Cool Whip with salad dressing and combine with all ingredients.

Barb Koch, Branch No. 6470, Kiron, IA

CRANBERRY SALAD

1 (8 oz.) pkg. cream cheese
2 Tbsp. mayonnaise
2 Tbsp. powdered sugar
1 (1 lb.) whole cranberry sauce

1 (15 oz.) can crushed pineapple, drained
1½ c. cream, whipped, or Cool Whip

Using electric mixer, soften cheese. Blend in sugar and mayonnaise. Beat till smooth. Add whole cranberry sauce and pineapple (drained). Add whipped cream or Cool Whip. Place in lightly greased loaf pan and freeze for 8 hours. Slice and serve frozen.

Myrtle Prestebak, Branch No. 341, Dorchester, WI

BAKED TURKEY SALAD
(Can use chicken)

2 c. turkey or chicken, cut up
2 c. celery, cut up
1 Tbsp. onion (can use more)
2 Tbsp. lemon juice
½ tsp. salt
¼ tsp. pepper

½ c. nuts
1 c. mayonnaise
2 c. uncooked rice, cooked
½ c. grated cheese (for top)
Crushed potato chips (for top)

Have the turkey or chicken roasted until done. Have the rice cooked or steamed. Grate the cheese. Crush the potato chips. Mix all together, except cheese and chips. Pour into 9x13 inch pan. Top with cheese and potato chips. Bake for 20 to 30 minutes at 350°. Serve hot. *Great for lunch!*

Wilma B. Schmidt, Branch No. 3086, Roseville, CA

ELEGANT TURKEY SALAD

2 qt. cooked turkey breast
1 (20 oz.) can sliced water
   chestnuts
2 lb. seedless grapes or well
   drained pineapple tidbits
2 c. sliced celery
2/3 c. toasted almonds, slivered

2 c. mayonnaise
2 Tbsp. soy sauce
1 Tbsp. curry powder
2 Tbsp. fresh lemon juice
Paprika and parsley flakes (for
   garnish)

Coarsely cut up the turkey breast. Make dressing by combining mayonnaise, soy sauce, curry powder, and lemon juice in a small bowl. Combine remaining ingredients and toss with dressing. Chill for several hours. Spoon into nest of lettuce. Garnish with additional toasted almonds and pineapple chunks. This will serve 12 generously.

Lil Walton, Branch No. 2343, Ogilvie, MN

HOT CHICKEN SALAD

2 c. cooked chicken, cut up
1½ c. diced celery
½ c. diced, toasted nuts (not too
   small)
¼ c. diced green pepper

2 Tbsp. diced pimiento
1 Tbsp. diced onion
2 Tbsp. lemon juice
½ tsp. salt

White Sauce:

2 Tbsp. butter
2 Tbsp. flour

1 c. chicken stock
½ c. mayonnaise

Prepare White Sauce of 2 tablespoons butter, 2 tablespoons flour, and 1 cup chicken stock. Add ½ cup mayonnaise. Mix all ingredients together. Put in an 8x10 inch casserole. Top with 2 cups crushed potato chips and ½ cup grated Cheddar cheese. Bake for 20 minutes in a 350° oven.

Myrtle Schappert, Branch No. 3197, Skokie, IL

BAKED CHICKEN SALAD

1 chicken, baked, deboned and cut
   up
1 can cream of chicken soup
1 c. sour cream
1 c. mayonnaise

1 can water chestnuts, sliced and
   drained
1 tsp. lemon juice
Salt and pepper

Mix chicken, soup, sour cream, mayonnaise, water chestnuts, lemon juice, and seasonings. Place in 9x13 inch baking dish and top with 1 stack Ritz crackers (crushed) and 1 stick melted margarine. Bake at 350° for 25 minutes.

Rhonda Steinert, Branch No. 0714, Fairmont, OK

DELICIOUS CHICKEN SALAD

1 can peas, drained
3 boiled eggs, chopped fine
1 small can crushed pineapple
½ env. Lipton onion soup mix
1 c. diced celery

4 c. diced, cooked chicken
¼ c. diced green pepper (optional)
Miracle Whip salad dressing
   (amount to suit your taste)

Mix with spoon and serve on a leaf of lettuce.

I like to add shoestring potatoes just before serving - adds a crunchy texture. Water chestnuts may be added too.

Betty Rennau, Branch No. 615, Grand Island, NE

MANDARIN CHICKEN SALAD

4 c. cooked chicken or turkey
2 Tbsp. minced onion
2 tsp. salt
2 c. grapes
2 c. chopped celery

2 c. mandarin oranges
¾ c. slivered almonds
2 c. macaroni rings
2 c. salad dressing

Combine chicken, onion and salt. Refrigerate for several hours. Add grapes, celery, mandarin oranges, almonds, macaroni, and dressing. Mix all together and refrigerate until ready to serve.

Frances Huebner, Branch No. 429, Goodhue, MN

BOMBAY CHICKEN SALAD

1 c. cooked rice
1 Tbsp. minced onion
½ Tbsp. cider vinegar
½ tsp. curry powder
1 Tbsp. salad oil
2 c. cubed chicken, cooked

½ c. chopped celery
1 c. mandarin oranges, drained
   and diced
⅔ c. mayonnaise
2 Tbsp. French dressing
½ c. broken walnuts

Combine rice, onion, vinegar, curry powder, and salad oil; chill. Add cubed chicken, celery, mandarin oranges, mayonnaise, French dressing, and walnuts. Salt and pepper to taste. Chill.

Alice Ellis, Branch No. 0207, Ashland, WI

ORIENTAL CHICKEN SALAD

1 chicken breast, cooked and cut
   up
2 Tbsp. toasted sesame seeds
3 Tbsp. toasted, slivered almonds

½ head cabbage, thinly sliced
2 green onions, chopped
1 pkg. Ramen noodles, crumbled

Dressing:

2 Tbsp. sugar
1 tsp. salt
¼ tsp. pepper

½ c. salad oil
3 Tbsp. white vinegar
½ pkg. Ramen noodle seasoning

Mix dressing ingredients well and pour over salad. Toss.

Irma Martens, Branch No. 1643, Eden, ID

CHICKEN SALAD

3 to 3½ lb. fryer or 6 breasts of
   chicken, cooked
1½ c. celery
2 cans Dole pineapple tidbits,
   drained
¼ to ½ tsp. garlic salt

Salt and pepper to taste
¼ to ½ c. minced onion
¼ to ½ c. slivered almonds
1 pt. mayonnaise
1 large can Chinese noodles

Cut up chicken in bite-sizes and toss rest of ingredients together, except the Chinese noodles. Chill. Just before serving, mix with Chinese noodles and serve.

Connie Krueger, Branch No. 6274, Lafayette, IN

HOT CHICKEN SALAD

4 whole chicken breasts, cooked
   and cut up
3 hard-boiled eggs, chopped
1 can cream of chicken soup
1 (4 oz.) can sliced mushrooms
1 c. sour cream
2 cans (4 oz.) sliced water
   chestnuts

1 tsp. salt
½ c. slivered almonds
2 c. diced celery
2 Tbsp. minced onions
1 c. mayonnaise
2 Tbsp. lemon juice
¼ tsp. pepper
1 c. grated Cheddar cheese

Mix all ingredients together and bake in 9x13 inch pan at 350° for 45 minutes. You may add the slivered almonds and Cheddar cheese on top, or mix with other ingredients.

This dish and a tossed salad is all that is needed for a luncheon.

Bertha Lang, Lamplighter, Branch No. 4633, Stockton, CA

CAULIFLOWER CRUNCH SALAD

1 medium head cauliflower
1 c. finely chopped celery
⅔ c. dill pickles, chopped fine
1 c. Cheddar cheese, grated

½ c. cole slaw dressing, thinned
   with 2 Tbsp. Italian dressing
½ c. chopped onions
Salt and pepper to taste

Remove flowerets from stems; wash and drain cauliflower. Slice or chop finely. Add other ingredients. Blend in dressing and seasonings.

Jean Landgraf, Branch No. 2568, Fredericktown, MO

58

BROCCOLI SALAD

1 bunch broccoli
3 green onions, chopped
¾ lb. bacon, cooked and crumbled
⅔ c. raisins

1 (3¾ oz.) pkg. sunflower seeds
6 hard cooked eggs, coarsely
   chopped

Dressing:

1 c. mayonnaise
2 Tbsp. sugar

1 Tbsp. white vinegar

Combine salad ingredients. May reserve 1 egg for garnish. Mix dressing and pour over salad shortly before serving. Garnish as desired.

Pat Westrum, Branch No. 5325, Stratford, IA

BROCCOLI DELIGHT SALAD

1 large bunch broccoli, cut in
   pieces
1 c. raisins
¼ c. diced red onion

10 strips bacon, fried and
   crumbled
1 c. sunflower seeds

Dressing:

3 to 4 Tbsp. sugar
½ c. lite mayo

1 Tbsp. vinegar

Toss first 5 ingredients together. Mix dressing and pour over salad. Lightly toss to coat salad.

Carol Riedel, Branch No. 3999, Centralia, MO

BROCCOLI SALAD

1 bunch broccoli (approx. 1½ lb.)
1 c. raisins
1 c. sunflower seeds

8 slices bacon, fried crisp and
   crumbled

Dressing:

1 c. mayonnaise
¼ c. sugar

1 Tbsp. vinegar

Wash broccoli and cut into bite-size pieces. Use stems also, peeling larger ones. Mix together at least 2 hours before serving.

Ruby Swanson, Branch No. 1122, Brighton, CO

ROYAL OAK BROCCOLI SALAD

1 bunch broccoli (using 3 inches of
   stems and flowerets)
12 strips bacon, cooked crisp and
   crushed

½ c. sunflower seeds (unsalted)
½ c. raisins
1 small red onion, sliced thin

Dressing:

1 c. mayonnaise
½ c. sugar

2 Tbsp. vinegar

Wash and drain broccoli, then coarsely chop. Place in bowl. Add bacon, raisins, sunflower seeds, and onion. Combine dressing ingredients in bowl, then toss with salad. Serves 6 to 8.

Phyllis Kivitrud, Branch No. 5943, New Brighton, MN

COLD BROCCOLI SALAD

10 oz. frozen broccoli
10 oz. frozen green peas
3 stalks celery
1 small onion, finely chopped
1 carrot, sliced
1 c. cauliflowerets
3 hard cooked eggs, chopped

Dash of lemon juice
⅔ to 1 c. Miracle Whip
⅓ to ½ c. sour cream
Salt and pepper to taste
1 (4 oz.) can sliced mushrooms
Lettuce, broken in pieces
8 oz. bacon, broiled and crumbled

Thaw broccoli. Drain on paper towel and press out as much moisture as possible. Thaw peas on paper towel. Combine broccoli and peas; sprinkle with lemon juice. Add celery, onion, carrot, cauliflower, lettuce, bacon, mushrooms, and salt and pepper to taste. Combine Miracle Whip and sour cream. Stir into vegetables until moistened. Add chopped eggs and mix lightly. Adjust seasonings to taste. Serve in lettuce lined bowl or as individual salads.

In memory of Orilla Rosendale, AAL Branch member,
by Lisa Rosendale, Augusta, IL

BROCCOLI SALAD

2 bunches broccoli, diced
1 c. raisins

½ medium onion, chopped
½ c. bacon, fried crisp

Dressing:

1 c. mayonnaise
½ c. sugar

2 Tbsp. vinegar

Mix and serve.

Freada Reinhardt, Branch No. 2014, Stillwater, OK

BROCCOLI SALAD

1 head broccoli
¾ lb. bacon
8 oz. (1 c.) grated Cheddar cheese
1 large sweet white onion

½ c. salad dressing
¼ c. sugar
1 Tbsp. vinegar

Wash and break broccoli into bite-size pieces. Brown and crisp the bacon. Grate the Cheddar cheese. Slice the onion into slices and cut into halves. Separate. Make the dressing of the ½ cup salad dressing, ¼ cup sugar and 1 tablespoon vinegar. Toss all ingredients. Chill.

Caroline Geisert, Branch No. 1412, Corvallis, OR

RAW BROCCOLI SALAD

1 head broccoli
½ lb. bacon
1 medium onion
½ c. walnuts, chopped

⅓ c. sugar
1 c. mayonnaise
3 Tbsp. vinegar

Cut up broccoli in small pieces; dice bacon and fry crispy. Cut up onion. Mix all together with walnuts. Prepare dressing with sugar, mayonnaise and vinegar.

Joanne Weber, Branch No. 1048, Muskego, WI

RAW CAULIFLOWER AND BROCCOLI SALAD

In bowl, put:

1 large head cauliflower
1 large bunch broccoli
1 small box frozen peas

1 c. chopped celery
1 c. chopped onion

Dressing:

2 c. Miracle Whip
1 c. sour cream
⅓ c. sugar
1 tsp. garlic salt

1 tsp. Bonne Saveur spice (by Durkee)
1 tsp. black pepper

Cut cauliflower and broccoli into bite-size pieces. Lightly toss all vegetables together. *Do not thaw* frozen peas, as they dilute the dressing ingredients. Blend well all dressing ingredients. Pour over vegetables. Toss lightly till all vegetables are coated.

Goodie Olson Gervais, Branch No. 4693, Gleason, WI

BROCCOLI-CAULIFLOWER SALAD

1 head fresh cauliflower
1 bunch fresh broccoli

1 (10 oz.) pkg. frozen peas
3 green onions

Dressing:

1 c. sour cream (may use half plain yogurt)
2 c. mayonnaise
1 Tbsp. Worcestershire sauce

Dash of Tabasco
1 tsp. garlic powder
1 Tbsp. lemon juice
Salt and pepper

Cut vegetables into bite-size pieces. Add frozen peas. Mix dressing together and mix through salad.

Makes a large salad and will keep for several days in the refrigerator.

Ramona Thompson, Branch No. 3879, Billings, MT

CAULIFLOWER-BROCCOLI SALAD

Salad:

2 to 2½ c. raw chopped
   cauliflower
2 to 2½ c. raw chopped broccoli
1 small can sliced mushrooms

1 small can sliced water chestnuts
½ c. finely chopped carrots
1 c. chopped celery

Dressing:

⅔ c. sugar
1 tsp. garlic salt
1 tsp. dry mustard
2 tsp. grated onion

⅓ c. vinegar
1 c. oil
½ to 1½ tsp. celery seed

Mix vegetables together. In blender on high speed, blend sugar, salt, mustard, onion, vinegar, and celery seed; slowly add oil until homogenized. Pour over vegetables and let stand for a couple of hours. Stir again before serving.

Lynn Vecsernyes, Branch No. 2295, Allen Pard, MI

TWENTY-FOUR (24) HOUR SALAD

2 c. white cherries, pitted and
   halved
2 c. diced pineapple
2 c. orange sections (mandarin
   can be used)
2 c. miniature marshmallows
4 oz. almonds, blanched and
   chopped

2 eggs
2 Tbsp. sugar
¼ c. half & half
Juice of 1 lemon (or 3 Tbsp.)
1 c. heavy cream, whipped

Combine well drained fruits. Add marshmallows and nuts. Beat eggs until light; gradually add sugar, half & half and lemon juice. Mix. Cook in double boiler until smooth and thick. Stir constantly. Cool. Pour over fruit mixture. *Mix* gently. Chill for 24 hours (do not freeze).

If adding fresh fruits such as apples or bananas, dip them in lemon juice first, then drain. It is best to add the bananas an hour or so before serving so they do not become mushy. Makes 10 to 12 servings.

Can substitute apples, bananas, maraschino cherries, etc., for fruits.

Donna Krug, Branch No. 3035, Ft. Collins, CO

OVERNIGHT SALAD

Lemon Sauce:

1 egg
2 Tbsp. lemon juice

2 Tbsp. sugar

Beat the egg until light and lemon colored. Add lemon juice and sugar. Cook in the top of double boiler over hot water until thick and smooth, stirring constantly. Remove from heat and cool.

1 large can mandarin oranges
1 can white cherries
1 can diced pineapple

8 oz. quartered marshmallows
½ c. heavy cream

Quarter marshmallows in large bowl. Add just enough pineapple juice to separate the pieces of marshmallows. Add drained fruit. Whip cream. Add cooled Lemon Sauce, folding gently. Pour over fruit in big bowl with folding motion.

Harriet Wahlstedt, Branch No. 64, Elkhorn, WI

LAYERED SALAD

1 head lettuce
1 lb. bacon, crumbled

1 onion, chopped
1 head cauliflower, finely chopped

Dressing:

2 c. Miracle Whip
¼ c. sugar

⅓ c. Parmesan cheese
Salt and pepper to taste

Layer ingredients, starting with lettuce. Break up lettuce for the first layer. Next, add the onion, cauliflower and the bacon.

Mix together Miracle Whip, sugar, Parmesan cheese, and salt and pepper to taste. Spread the dressing over salad. Cover tightly. Refrigerate overnight. Toss before serving.

Ann Paulsen, Branch No. 04930, Kenosha, WI

TWENTY-FOUR HOUR SALAD

1 medium size head lettuce,
    shredded
1 c. thinly sliced celery
1 (8 oz.) can drained, sliced water
    chestnuts
½ c. sliced green onions
1 (10 oz.) pkg. frozen peas
2 c. mayonnaise
2 tsp. sugar

½ c. grated Parmesan cheese
¼ tsp. garlic powder
1 tsp. Lawry's garlic salt
3 hard-boiled eggs
¾ lb. bacon, chopped and fried
    crisp
Tomatoes, cut in wedges
Avocado slices

Put shredded lettuce in 9x13 inch pan. Top with celery, water chestnuts, and green onions in layers. Sprinkle peas over top. Top with mayonnaise and sprinkle with sugar. Combine Parmesan cheese, garlic powder, and Lawry's garlic salt. Sprinkle over top. Chop eggs and sprinkle over top. Top with bacon. Decorate with tomatoes and avocado slices.

Eleanor E. Kreidt, Branch No. 3436, Pico Rivera, CA

LAYERED SALAD

2 qt. lettuce
½ c. celery, finely chopped
½ c. green pepper, chopped
½ c. chopped onion

1½ c. Miracle Whip, mixed with 3
Tbsp. sugar
6 oz. shredded Cheddar cheese
½ c. bacon bits (Bac-Os chips)

Layer ingredients in a 9x13 inch dish in the order listed. Cover and chill for 8 hours before serving. Yield: 12 servings.

Frances Kirk, Branch No. 3383, Indianapolis, IN

SEVEN-LAYERED SALAD

1 head lettuce
½ c. green peppers, diced
½ c. diced celery
½ c. diced onion (or less)
1 pkg. frozen peas, thawed
2 c. mayonnaise

2 Tbsp. sugar
1 c. Cheddar cheese, shredded
6 to 8 slices bacon, fried crisp and
crumbled in small pieces
Boiled eggs (optional)

Tear lettuce in pieces. Layer in 9x13 inch oblong Pyrex dish in order: Lettuce, green peppers, celery, onion, peas, mayonnaise, sugar, cheese, and bacon. May add boiled eggs. Chill for 4 hours.

Doris Seevers, Branch No. 382, St. Louis, MO

SEVEN LAYER SALAD

1 head lettuce, broken up
½ c. celery, chopped in small
pieces
1 (10 oz.) pkg. frozen peas, cooked
and cooled

Dressing:

2 c. mayonnaise
2 Tbsp. sugar

½ c. green pepper, chopped in
small pieces
2 Tbsp. chopped onions
2 hard-boiled eggs, chopped
Bac-Os (to cover)

4 oz. grated cheese

Layer in 9x13 inch pan as listed (except dressing). Top with 2 cups mayonnaise, mixed with 2 tablespoons sugar and 4 ounces cheese on top.

Rebecca Schroeder, Branch No. 647, Carrington, ND

64

LAYERED LETTUCE SALAD

1 head lettuce, broken in bite-sizes
½ c. chopped red onion
½ c. strips green pepper
½ c. chopped celery
1 can sliced water chestnuts
1 pkg. uncooked frozen green peas
1 pt. mayonnaise
1 Tbsp. sugar
4 oz. grated Cheddar cheese
¼ c. bacon bits

Arrange in salad bowl or 9x13 inch glass pan in the order given. Stick a knife through to the bottom in several places to allow dressing to drip through. Cover and refrigerate overnight. Will keep for 2 or 3 days.

Connie Davis, Branch No. 3107, Loveland, CO

SEVEN LAYERS LETTUCE SALAD

½ head chopped lettuce
½ c. green peppers, diced
½ c. raw carrots, diced
½ c. celery, diced
1 c. sweet peas, drained
½ c. crumbled bacon *or* cooked
   bacon
6 hard-boiled eggs, sliced
Miracle Whip salad dressing
Shredded cheese

Put a layer of chopped lettuce in a glass pan. Add a layer of peppers, carrots, celery, peas, bacon, and hard-boiled eggs. Spread top with Miracle Whip salad dressing. (You may add a little sugar to get a sweet tasting dressing or if you prefer a spice taste, add some Hidden Valley or Ranch dressing in place of sugar.) Make sure to spread dressing to edges of pan so air won't reach vegetables. Shred cheese for top of dressing. Set in refrigerator to keep cool. *Ideal summer time salad.*

Jeri Manke, Branch No. 5985, Midland, SD

ORIENTAL SALAD

2 c. cooked rice
2 c. frozen peas (uncooked)
1 can sliced water chestnuts
½ c. celery
1 Tbsp. onion (optional)
1 c. mushrooms (fresh)
1 can chow mein noodles

Mix first 6 ingredients together. Add dressing and toss. Before serving, add chow mein noodles.

Dressing:

3 Tbsp. white vinegar
½ c. oil
3 Tbsp. soy sauce

Cook until mixture boils. Cool to room temperature.

Rhonda Redeker, Branch No. 3837, Nokomis, IL

65

ORIENTAL SALAD

1 (3 oz.) pkg. chicken flavored
   Ramen noodles
6 to 8 c. chopped cabbage
4 green onions, chopped
½ c. salted sunflower kernels

½ c. vegetable oil
3 Tbsp. vinegar
2 tsp. sugar
½ tsp. salt
½ tsp. pepper

Crush noodles between your hands. Combine noodles, cabbage, onions, and sunflower seeds. Combine seasoning packet from Ramen noodles with remaining ingredients. Mix well. Pour over cabbage mixture. Cover and chill for 2 hours or more. Serves 6.

Mrs. Barbara (Rev. David) Splett, St. John's Lutheran,
Branch No. 5488, Fayetteville, AR

ORIENTAL SALAD

2 (1 lb.) bags fresh spinach
2 cans water chestnuts, thinly
   sliced

4 hard cooked eggs, chopped
1 can bean sprouts, drained
½ lb. bacon, fried crisp

Clean fresh spinach and tear into bite-size pieces and place into large bowl. Add all the other ingredients, crumbling the bacon and sprinkling onto the salad just before serving. Add the dressing and toss all ingredients or let each person add their own dressing.

Dressing:

1 c. salad oil
¾ c. white granulated sugar
⅓ c. catsup
¼ c. vinegar (any type)

2 tsp. salt
1 Tbsp. Worcestershire sauce
1 medium onion, chopped

Blend all ingredients (onion may be blended or left chopped and added at the end) in a blender until smooth. Store in container in refrigerator. Shake well before pouring on salad. Dressing is great for any lettuce salad!

Mrs. David Pease, Branch No. 4896, Kalamazoo, MI

MEATLESS TACO SALAD

8 oz. cream cheese
16 oz. sour cream
1 pkg. taco seasoning mix
½ to 1 head lettuce, shredded
2 to 3 tomatoes, cubed

2 medium onions, chopped
Black olives, sliced
Cheddar cheese, shredded
Round nacho chips

Mix together cream cheese, sour cream and taco seasoning mix. On a large (round) platter, layer lettuce, then tomatoes, onions, black olives, and cream cheese mixture. Top with Cheddar cheese. Arrange nacho chips around the outside, putting some slightly under lettuce. (Some of the cream cheese mixture could be spread on the platter before putting on the lettuce.)

This can be used as a salad or an appetizer.

Sue Maxey, Branch No. 4928, Kenosha, WI

TACO SALAD

1 lb. hamburger
1 medium head lettuce
1 pkg. taco seasoning
1 small onion, chopped
1 small can kidney beans, drained and washed

8 oz. shredded Cheddar cheese
8 oz. Thousand Island dressing
⅓ c. sugar
1 large pkg. Nacho cheese chips
4 tomatoes, chopped

Brown hamburger with taco seasoning minus 1 tablespoon. Meanwhile, mix together lettuce, onion, kidney beans, Cheddar cheese, and tomatoes. Before serving, mix Thousand Island dressing, 1 tablespoon taco seasoning, and sugar. Add Nacho cheese chips and dressing. Mix well and serve.

Mrs. Esther Roth, Branch No. 547, St. Louis, MO

TACO SALAD

1 head lettuce, chopped or shredded
1 (15 oz.) can kidney beans, drained
3 small tomatoes, cut in small pieces
1 green pepper, chopped
1 medium onion, chopped fine

8 oz. Cheddar cheese, grated
1 medium bag taco flavored tortilla chips
1 lb. pork sausage (like Jimmy Dean regular), browned, drained and cooled
1 (8 oz.) bottle Western dressing

Toss all ingredients in a large bowl just before serving.

Twyla Zaske, Branch No. 1784, Renville, MN

TACO SALAD

1½ lb. hamburger meat
½ to ¾ c. chopped onion
1 large and 1 (No. 1) can Ranch Style beans
2 Tbsp. Taco Seasoning Master Mix

1 head lettuce, cut up
1 (1 lb.) bag regular Fritos corn chips
1 lb. shredded Cheddar cheese
1 large bottle Catalina dressing

Brown meat. Add onion, beans and seasoning mix. Simmer for about 15 minutes. (Can be left in crock pot on LOW for quite awhile.) Cool mixture before adding to lettuce, chips and cheese. Pour Catalina dressing over all and stir.

This makes a large amount, so you may want to adjust for family serving.

Taco Seasoning Master Mix:

4 Tbsp. instant minced onion
2 Tbsp. salt
2 Tbsp. chili powder
1 Tbsp. cornstarch

1½ tsp. oregano
1 Tbsp. crushed dried red peppers
1 Tbsp. instant minced garlic
1 Tbsp. cumin

Mix. Store in airtight jar. Two tablespoons equal one package. Makes 6 packages of store bought.

Bonnie Schulze, Branch No. 4477, Claremore, OK

TACO SALAD

1 medium head lettuce
3 medium tomatoes, diced
1½ c. grated Cheddar cheese
1 small diced onion
1 c. sliced, pitted ripe olives
1½ lb. hamburger

1 c. crushed taco chips
1 c. Western dressing
½ c. mild taco sauce
½ tsp. chili powder
½ tsp. ground cumin

Fry hamburger, cumin and chili powder together until meat is browned. Drain off fat and set aside to cool. Shred lettuce. Toss lettuce, tomatoes, onion, olives, cheese, chips, and hamburger together. Combine the taco sauce and the Western dressing. Pour over the salad and serve.

Darla Springer, Peshtigo, WI, Branch No. 5515, Marinette, WI

HEAVENLY FOOD SALAD

6 to 8 oranges
½ c. sugar
6 bananas

1 large ctn. Cool Whip
Nuts

Cake Base:

2 eggs, beaten
4 Tbsp. flour
½ lb. chopped dates

1 c. sugar
1 tsp. baking powder
½ lb. nuts

Mix thoroughly. Bake for 30 minutes at 350°. When cool, crumble ½ of the cake. Peel and slice 6 to 8 oranges. Add ½ cup sugar and let stand for 15 minutes or more. Combine cake, oranges, and 6 bananas (sliced). Top with 1 large carton Cool Whip. Sprinkle with a few nuts.

Remaining cake may be frozen for another salad.

Betty Rufledt, Branch No. 286, Bloomer, WI

GREEN PEA SALAD

2 (16 oz.) cans drained peas
¾ c. diced celery
¼ c. green onion, chopped fine
1 small jar pimento, drained well
1 tsp. lemon juice

¼ c. sugar
1 c. light Miracle Whip
1 c. Spanish salted skin on
  peanuts

Mix together 2 cans peas, ¾ cup diced celery, ¼ cup green onion, and small jar pimento.

For dressing, mix together 1 teaspoon lemon juice, ¼ cup sugar and 1 cup light Miracle Whip. Pour this over vegetable mixture and mix. Just before serving, add 1 cup Spanish salted skin on peanuts.

Mrs. Leo Schmidt, Branch No. 1836, Watertown, MN

ROMAN SALAD

½ head lettuce, chopped
¾ c. celery, chopped
½ (10 oz.) pkg. frozen peas,
    thawed (not cooked)
¼ c. onions, chopped
2 tsp. McCormick Salad Supreme
    seasoning or similar salad
    seasoning

⅓ lb. bacon, cooked crisp and
    crumbled
¾ c. Miracle Whip
⅓ c. Parmesan cheese

1. Layer the first 6 ingredients in pan as listed.
2. Spread top with Miracle Whip dressing.
3. Sprinkle Parmesan cheese over Miracle Whip. Chill or let stand overnight.
Yield: 6 to 8 servings.

This may be prepared in morning for evening. Toss before serving. Do not toss too far ahead.

Ms. Maxine Wilson, Branch No. 4734, West Lafayette, IN

MOLDED BING CHERRY SALAD

1 (3 oz.) pkg. raspberry or cherry
    gelatin
1 c. hot water
⅞ c. cold water and juice

1 (16 oz.) can pitted Bing cherries,
    drained
¼ c. nuts, chopped

1. Stir hot water into gelatin until thoroughly dissolved.
2. Add cold water and juice. Chill until partially congealed.
3. Add drained cherries and nuts. Let set. Yield: 10 servings.

Note: If desired, you may add cream cheese balls before the mixture is set.

Maxine Wilson, Branch No. 4734, West Lafayette, IN

CIRCUS PEANUT SALAD

30 orange candy peanuts
1 (6 oz.) orange jello
1 large Cool Whip
1 (No. 2) crushed pineapple,
    drained

2 c. hot water
Pineapple juice and cold water to
    equal 2 c.

Cut candy into small pieces. Mix jello with 2 cups hot water and dissolve the candy in hot mixture. Add 2 cups cold water (part of pineapple juice). Let cool until jelly consistency. Add Cool Whip and pineapple. Beat on slow speed until Cool Whip is dissolved. Chill in 9x13 inch pan.

Mary Werling, Branch No. 1496, New Haven, IN

STRAWBERRY JELLO SALAD

2 (6 oz.) pkg. strawberry jello
2 c. hot water
1 lb. frozen strawberries

1 (16 oz.) can crushed pineapple
with juice
2 mashed bananas

Combine 2 packages jello and 2 cups hot water. Add strawberries, pineapple with juice and bananas. Chill.

Betty Zych, Branch No. 545, Mosinee, WI

COTTAGE CHEESE SALAD

9 oz. Cool Whip
1 (3 oz.) pkg. jello
1 small ctn. cottage cheese

1 small can pineapple tidbits
1 can mandarin oranges
1 c. miniature marshmallows

Fold dry jello (any flavor) into Cool Whip. Add cottage cheese and mix. Drain pineapple and mandarin oranges. Add these and the marshmallows to jello mixture. Salad is ready to serve and keeps well.

Helen Shannon, Branch No. 1612, Rothsay, MN

YOGURT CRANBERRY SALAD

1 (3 oz.) pkg. jello (raspberry)
1 c. boiling water
1 (16 oz.) can whole cranberry
    sauce
1 (3 oz.) pkg. lemon jello

1 c. boiling water
3 oz. softened cream chese
1 (8 oz.) can crushed pineapple
1 (8 oz.) plain or lemon yogurt
1 c. miniature marshmallows

Dissolve raspberry jello in 1 cup hot water. Stir in cranberry sauce. Pour into 9x9 inch baking pan. Chill until almost firm. Meanwhile, dissolve lemon jello in 1 cup hot water; set aside.

In bowl, using mixer at medium speed, beat together cream cheese and yogurt. Add lemon jello gradually and beat. Stir in undrained pineapple. Chill until partially set. Stir in marshmallows and pour on top of red layer. Chill until firm.

Ida Aaberg, Branch No. 1612, Rothsay, MN

CHERRY SALAD-DESSERT

1 (14 oz.) can sweetened
    condensed milk
1 (21 oz.) can cherry pie filling
2 Tbsp. lemon juice
1 (13 oz.) can crushed pineapple,
    drained (optional)

1 c. small marshmallows
½ c. chopped nuts (optional)
1 (9 oz.) ctn. whipped topping

Mix ingredients together, one at a time. Pour into a 9 inch square pan and freeze. Let set at room temperature for about 20 minutes before serving. Makes 10 servings.

Shirley Welp, Branch No. 6973, Strasburg, CO

FROZEN FRUIT SALAD

Beat:

8 oz. cream cheese   ½ c. sugar

Add:

1 tall can pineapple tidbits,   2 bananas, sliced
   drained   1 large Cool Whip
1 (16 oz.) frozen strawberries

Mix together and freeze. Will serve 6 or 8.

AMBROSIA

3 medium size oranges   ½ c. coconut
1 banana   1 Tbsp. sugar (if needed)

Peel the oranges. Remove the skin from each section as much as you can. You may need a knife to do this. Work over a bowl and save the juice. Slice the banana into the bowl with the orange pieces. Stir so the orange juice gets over the banana pieces so the banana won't get brown. Add the sugar if the oranges are sour. Add the coconut and mix lightly. Chill in refrigerator for 15 to 20 minutes before serving.

Doris Ruhs, Branch 3107, Loveland, CO

BAKED FRUIT

1 (21 oz.) can cherry pie filling   1 (6 oz.) pkg. dried apricots
1 (20 oz.) can pineapple chunks,   1 (12 oz.) pkg. dried prunes
   drained   2 (11 oz.) cans mandarin oranges

Mix all, except mandarin oranges, in a large bowl. Pour into a large flat baking dish, then place mandarin oranges in and around other fruit (careful not to break oranges). Cover with foil and bake for 1 hour at 325° to 350°

This is a very attractive dish and delicious.

Cheryl Jordan, Branch No. 2150, Tomball, TX

FRESH VEGETABLE SALAD

½ lb. broccoli, cut into flowerets   1 medium red onion, sliced
½ lb. cauliflower, cut into   1 medium tomato, cut up
   flowerets   1 small bottle Wish-Bone Italian
1 carrot, thinly sliced with potato   dressing
   peeler   1 pkg. (dry) Good Seasons Italian
½ to 1 green pepper, diced   dressing
4 to 5 ribs celery, cut up   Fresh mushrooms

Mix preceding ingredients with salad dressings. Marinate for 8 hours or overnight. Add sliced fresh mushrooms 1 hour before serving.

Connie Krueger, Branch No. 6274, Lafayette, IN

HOLIDAY RIBBON RING

2 (4 serving size) pkg. strawberry
   jello
5 c. boiling water

⅔ c. sour cream *or* vanilla yogurt
2 (4 serving size) pkg. lime jello

Dissolve strawberry jello in 2½ cups boiling water. Pour 1½ cups into 6 cup mold. Chill until set, but not firm (about 15 to 20 minutes). Chill remaining jello in bowl. Gradually blend in ⅓ cup of sour cream and *spoon over* gelatin in mold. Chill until set, but not firm, about 15 minutes. Repeat with lime jello, remaining 2½ cups water and ⅓ cup sour cream, chilling dissolved jello before measuring and pouring into mold. Chill for at least 2 hours. Unmold. Makes about 12 servings.

Jackie Neuman, Branch 2525, Larsen, WI

LEMON SHRIMP SALAD

2 small pkg. lemon jello
2 c. boiling water
2 c. Cool Whip
1 c. salad dressing
1 can shrimp

⅔ c. grated Longhorn cheese
1 tsp. grated onion
1 c. chopped celery
3 hard-boiled eggs, chopped

Mix jello with boiling water. Cool until slightly thick. Fold in Cool Whip, salad dressing, cheese, onion, celery, eggs, and shrimp. Serve on a bed of lettuce with additional salad dressing if desired.

Jean Schulz, Branch No. 1292, Akaska, SD

TRI-COLOR MOLDED SALAD

2 (1 lb. 1 oz.) cans fruit cocktail
1 (3 oz.) pkg. raspberry flavored
   gelatin
1 c. boiling water
1 (3 oz.) pkg. lemon flavored
   gelatin

1 c. boiling water
1 c. Miracle Whip
½ c. heavy cream, whipped
1 (3 oz.) pkg. lime flavored gelatin
1 c. boiling water

Drain fruit cocktail, reserving 1 cup syrup. Dissolve raspberry gelatin in boiling water. Add ½ cup syrup and 1⅓ cups fruit cocktail. Pour into greased 2 quart mold. Chill until almost firm.

Dissolve lemon gelatin in boiling water; cool. Gradually add to salad dressing, mixing until well blended. Fold in whipped cream. Pour over raspberry layer. Chill until almost firm.

Dissolve lime gelatin in boiling water. Add ½ cup syrup and remaining fruit cocktail. Pour over lemon layer. Chill until firm. Unmold on serving platter. Makes 10 to 12 servings.

Mary Mueller, Branch No. 6902, El Paso, TX

RASPBERRY OR STRAWBERRY SALAD

First layer:

1½ c. crushed pretzels   2 Tbsp. sugar
¾ c. melted butter

Mix together and bake for 8 to 10 minutes at 350°.

Second layer:

1 (6 oz.) pkg. raspberry or   2 c. boiling water
  strawberry jello

Mix jello and water; add 1 package of frozen berries. Mix gently until the berries have thawed and mixture jells.

Third layer:

1 (8 oz.) pkg. cream cheese   1 (8 oz.) container Cool Whip
1 c. sugar

Mix together.

Put most of the pretzel mixture on bottom of 9x13 inch pan. (Some of the crumb can be put on top), then the layer of berries and jello. Top with cheese mixture and few of pretzel crumbs on top.

I've also put in deep glass bowl in alternate layers (very pretty).
Carolyn Olson, Branch No. 1094, Knapp, WI

KOREAN SALAD

1 pkg. raw spinach, cleaned and   1 can bean sprouts, drained
  broken   3 or 4 hard-boiled eggs, sliced
1 can sliced water chestnuts,   6 to 8 slices cooked bacon,
  drained   crumbled

Combine salad ingredients and dressing. Let stand for at least ½ hour before serving.

Dressing:

1 c. oil   1 Tbsp. Worcestershire sauce
¾ c. sugar   1 medium onion, chopped

Blend oil, sugar, Worcestershire sauce, and onion with ⅓ cup ketchup and ¼ cup vinegar.

Dressing also good on fruit salad (without ketchup and vinegar).
Clara Martin, Branch No. 366, Pittsburgh, PA

NO. 7 CONFETTI RICE SALAD

2½ c. cooked rice
1 carrot, diced (⅓ c.)
¼ c. thinly sliced green onions
¼ c. diced green pepper
¼ c. diced red pepper

¼ c. diced black olives
3 Tbsp. corn oil
3 Tbsp. tarragon wine vinegar
½ tsp. salt
⅛ tsp. pepper

In medium bowl, toss together rice, carrot, onion, green pepper, red pepper, olives, corn oil, vinegar, salt, and pepper until well mixed. Cover and refrigerate for several hours. Makes 6 (½ cup) servings.

Wilma Bauschlicher, St. Matthew Lutheran Church, AAL Branch 1936, Corning, AR

MARINATED VEGETABLE-RICE SALAD

1 (8 oz.) can water chestnuts,
   sliced
1 (16 oz.) can whole kernel corn
1 (2 oz.) can diced pimento
1 (16 oz.) can sliced carrots
1 (17 oz.) can English peas
1 c. chopped celery
½ c. seeded and chopped green
   pepper

½ c. chopped onion
4 c. cooked, cooled rice
½ c. water
½ c. vegetable oil
1 c. vinegar
1½ c. sugar
2 tsp. salt

Drain all canned vegetables. Combine all vegetables and rice in a large container. In a saucepan, combine water, oil, vinegar, sugar, and salt. Heat almost to boiling. Allow to cool slightly and pour over vegetables. Cover and refrigerate for several hours or overnight. Serves 12 to 15.

Luanna Bauschlicher, Corning AR

STRAWBERRY SPINACH SALAD

Salad:

2 bunches spinach

1 pt. fresh strawberries

Dressing:

½ c. sugar
2 Tbsp. sesame seeds
1½ tsp. minced onions
¼ tsp. Worcestershire sauce

1¼ tsp. paprika
⅓ c. oil
¼ c. vinegar

Mix ingredients for dressing and pour over salad. Do not pour on dressing prior to 1 hour before serving.

Deb Austin, Branch No. 3887, Greeley, CO

STRAWBERRY-RHUBARB SALAD

4 c. diced raw rhubarb
1½ c. water
½ c. sugar
2 (3 oz.) pkg. strawberry gelatin

1 c. orange juice
1 Tbsp. grated orange rind
2 c. fresh strawberries, sliced
Strawberries (for garnish)

Combine rhubarb, water and sugar in saucepan; cook until tender. Pour hot rhubarb mixture over gelatin and stir until completely dissolved. Add orange juice and rind. Chill until syrupy; fold in strawberries. Pour into a 1 quart mold. Chill until set. Garnish with whole strawberries with hulls. Yield: 8 servings.

Karen Frederking, Branch No. 1038, Nashville, IL

CHERRY RICE SALAD

1 can cherry pie filling
1 qt. milk
⅔ c. regular uncooked rice
1 Tbsp. butter
½ c. cold water
1 Tbsp. vanilla

1¼ qt. hot water
¾ c. sugar
1 tsp. salt
3 env. unflavored gelatin
1 pt. whipping cream, whipped

Pour rice in hot water. Boil for 2 minutes; drain in cold water. Put rice into 2 cups milk, 1 tablespoon sugar, and 1 teaspoon salt. Bring to a boil; add butter. Cover and simmer for 20 minutes. Pour into a big bowl. Add 2 cups milk, sugar and gelatin that has been softened in cold water. Chill until thick, stirring occasionally. Fold in whipped cream and vanilla. Top with cherry pie mix.

Twyla Zaske, Branch No. 1784, Renville, MN

BELGIUM TOSSED SALAD

1 (10 oz.) pkg. Brussels sprouts
½ c. salad oil
¼ c. vinegar
1 clove garlic, crushed
1 tsp. dried parsley
½ tsp. salt

¼ tsp. basil
⅛ tsp. pepper
2 qt. salad greens
½ medium red onion, cut in rings
6 slices bacon, crisp cooked and
    crumbled

Cook Brussels sprouts until tender. Cut in halves lengthwise. Combine oil, vinegar, garlic, parsley, salt, basil, and pepper. Blend well. Add sprouts. Marinate for at least 1 hour. Chill. Toss sprouts and marinate with greens and onion. Sprinkle bacon on top.

Marlene Klukken, Branch No. 4665, Knoxville, TN

VEGETABLE PIZZA

2 pkg. Pillsbury crescent rolls
    (refrigerated)
1 c. *salad dressing*
1 Tbsp. parsley flakes
1 Tbsp. dill weed
1 (8 oz.) cream cheese

1 Tbsp. Accent
1 Tbsp. minced dry onion
1 tsp. salt
2 c. shredded cheese (process or
    Cheddar)

Pat crescent rolls into slightly greased cookie sheet pan. Bake at 350° to 375° for 8 to 10 minutes or until lightly browned. Cool. Combine cream cheese, salad dressing and seasonings in small mixer bowl; beat until creamy. Spread on cooled crust. Chop or shred onions, green peppers, carrots, cauliflower, or broccoli. Slice green and black olives. Sprinkle all of these items over creamed mixture. Chill. Cut into serving pieces. Serves 36 to 40.

You may vary vegetables to suit your own personal taste.

Caroline Behnke, Branch No. 432, Manawa, WI

CHAMPAGNE SALAD

8 oz. cream cheese, softened
¾ c. sugar
½ c. nuts, chopped
8 oz. Cool Whip

1 can crushed pineapple, drained
2 bananas, sliced
1 (10 oz.) pkg. strawberries,
    thawed

Mix the softened cream cheese with the sugar. Add all of the other ingredients. Stir gently together. Put in small cake pan and freeze. To use, take out of freezer and let stand for 10 minutes. Cut and place on plates to serve.

Or, you could freeze the salad in individual small plastic souffle cups and serve the cup at the table.

Dennis Hugdahl, Branch No. 6872, Bricelyn, MN

MANDARIN ORANGE SALAD

1 head lettuce
1 (11 oz.) can mandarin oranges,
    drained, or cantaloupe

¼ c. celery
Sliced almonds

Poppy Seed Dressing:

½ c. sugar
⅔ c. vegetable oil
1 tsp. prepared mustard

¼ c. vinegar
1 to 2 tsp. poppy seed
1 tsp. salt

Combine all ingredients in a jar and shake vigorously. Pour over lettuce, celery, mandarin oranges, and almonds. Toss lightly.

Mrs. Esther Roth, Branch No. 547, St. Louis, MO
Mrs. Florence Hempel, Branch No. 547, St. Louis, MO

FROZEN CABBAGE SALAD

1 head cabbage, chopped
1 carrot, grated
1 green pepper, chopped

1 tsp. salt
Chopped onion to suit taste

Mix salt with cabbage and let stand for 1 hour. Squeeze the moisture out. Add the vegetables.

Dressing:

1 c. vinegar
¼ c. water
1 tsp. whole mustard seed

1 tsp. celery seed
2 c. sugar

Combine dressing ingredients and bring to a boil. Boil for 1 minute. Cool to lukewarm. Cover vegetable mixture with dressing. Pack into freezer containers and freeze.

Excellent flavor, fresh as well as after freezing.
Elaine Christison, Branch No. 64, Elkhorn, WI

FROZEN CUCUMBERS

5 to 6 medium cucumbers
1 to 2 onions

Black pepper (optional)
Salt

Dressing:

1 c. white vinegar
¼ c. water

2 scant c. sugar

Combine dressing ingredients and bring to a boil. Boil for 1 minute and then cool.

Peel and slice the cucumbers; sprinkle with salt. Let stand for 1 hour, then drain off the juice. Slice onions in with the cucumbers. Add black pepper if desired. Cover with dressing and mix. Pack into freezer containers and freeze.

Excellent flavor, fresh as well as after freezing.
Elaine Christison, Branch No. 64, Elkhorn, WI

HIDDEN VALLEY SALAD

1 head lettuce
1 bunch spinach
1 lb. bacon, fried and crumbled
1 bunch green onions, chopped

1 green pepper, chopped
1 small pkg. fresh mushrooms, sliced
5 hard-boiled eggs, chopped

Tear spinach and lettuce into bite-size pieces. Layer lettuce, spinach, green pepper, bacon, mushrooms, green onions, and eggs in large bowl.

Dressing:

1 pkg. Hidden Valley Dressing
1 c. sour cream

2 c. mayonnaise

Mix dressing ingredients together and spread over top of salad like frosting. Cover and refrigerate all day or overnight. Toss before serving.
Janis Boyd, Branch No. 1717, Belleville, IL

PERSIMMON SALAD

1 small pkg. jello (orange or lemon flavor)
1 c. boiling water

Topping:

1 small (4 oz.) pkg. cream cheese
Several Tbsp. half & half
1 Tbsp. mayonnaise

1 c. very soft persimmon pulp
1 small can crushed pineapple
1 dash of salt

1 dash of salt
Some ground nuts

Dissolve jello in boiling water. Put the persimmon through a sieve and add to jello, then add the crushed pineapple and salt. After the mixture has jelled, make a topping of cream cheese; soften it by mixing in half & half and the mayonnaise (according to taste). Spread over jello and add nuts to topping.

Agnelsa M. Teachenor, Branch No. 1540, Berkeley, CA

MOLDED SHRIMP COCKTAIL

1 large pkg. lemon jello
2 c. boiling water
1 (12 oz.) bottle cocktail sauce
1/4 c. vinegar
1 can shrimp or crab (or fresh)

3 Tbsp. chopped onion
1 c. celery
1/3 c. olives
1/3 c. peppers or pimento

Dissolve jello in boiling water. Add cocktail sauce and vinegar. When starting to set, add other ingredients.

Paula Cowley, Branch No. 7063, Albany, OR

ORIENTAL COLE SLAW

Note: All ingredients are approximate measures.

1/2 head cabbage, shredded
2 to 3 green onions, chopped
1 c. shredded chicken, turkey, ham, or beef (optional)
1 or 2 pkg. Ramen noodles, broken up (do not cook - do not use sauce mix)

Something crunchy (sunflower seeds, water chestnuts, walnuts, almonds)
1 c. chopped celery

Mix everything together and pour dressing over; mix well. Refrigerate for an hour or more.

Dressing:

2/3 c. salad oil
4 Tbsp. sugar

1/4 tsp. pepper
5 Tbsp. red wine vinegar

Mix together well.

Marilyn Pykkonen, Branch No. 3339, Esko, MN

78

PEG CORN SALAD

1 can French green beans, drained
1 can white whole kernel corn, drained
1 can peas, drained
1 c. celery, cut up
½ c. chopped onion
1 c. chopped green pepper
1 small jar chopped pimiento
Salt and garlic salt to taste
1 c. sugar
¾ c. vinegar
½ c. salad oil

Drain the vegetables; mix with salt and garlic salt. Boil together sugar, vinegar and salad oil. Cool and pour over vegetables. Chill before serving.

Mrs. Hilda Bodendieck, Branch No. 5680, Cahokia, IL

BLUEBERRY SALAD

2 (3 oz.) pkg. blackberry gelatin
2 c. boiling water
1 (15 oz.) can blueberries, drained (save juice)
1 (8 oz.) pkg. cream cheese
1 small can crushed pineapple
½ c. sugar
½ tsp. vanilla
1 c. sour cream
½ c. chopped pecans

Dissolve gelatin in boiling water. Drain blueberries and pineapple; measure liquid. Add enough water to make 1 cup. Add gelatin mixture. Stir in blueberries and pineapple. Pour in a 2 quart flat pan and refrigerate until firm. Blend softened cream cheese, sugar, sour cream, and vanilla; spread over congealed salad. Sprinkle with nuts. Makes 10 to 12 servings.

Doris Wohlschlegel, Branch No. 5425, Louisville, KY

PASTA-BEAN SALAD

1 can garbanzo beans, drained
1 can green beans, drained
1 small can or jar pimentos, drained
2 c. cooked 3 color rotini
Sliced onion (desired amounts)
Chopped celery (desired amounts)
Chopped carrots (desired amounts)
½ c. sugar
½ c. vinegar
½ c. vegetable oil
1 tsp. salt
Dash of pepper
Dash of minced garlic

Combine vegetables in large bowl. Mix remaining ingredients well and pour over vegetables. Cover bowl and chill for at least 4 hours or overnight. Stir occasionally. Refrigerate tightly.

Jane Helton, Branch No. 5844, Columbia City, IN

RAW CAULIFLOWER SALAD

1 head fresh cauliflower
1 small can pitted ripe olives
1 red onion, sliced thin

1 bottle Seven Seas Italian salad
  dressing

Break cauliflower into bite-size flowerets. Slice olives and add to cauliflower with onion. Toss with dressing. Let marinate overnight, tossing occasionally.

Marsha Ruesch, Branch No. 5844, Columbia City, IN

RICH AND GOOD SALAD

1 (1 lb.) pkg. marshmallows
½ c. milk
1 (8 oz.) pkg. cream cheese
1 pt. cottage cheese
1 can pineapple tidbits, drained

1 can mandarin oranges, drained
1 large ctn. Cool Whip
½ c. maraschino cherries, halved
½ c. chopped nuts

Heat marshmallows and milk over low heat until melted. Remove from heat and stir in cream cheese until melted. Add cottage cheese, pineapple, cherries, and oranges. Add nuts and fold in Cool Whip. Pour out in dish and refrigerate overnight.

Bernice Sheets, Branch No. 5844, Columbia City, IN

RICE SALAD SUPREME

1 box chicken flavored
  Rice-A-Roni
1 c. sliced onions
½ c. sliced green peppers
1 c. sliced black olives
1 small jar chopped pimentos

2 (6 oz.) jars marinated artichoke
  hearts, chopped (save
  marinade from 1 jar)
¾ tsp. curry powder
½ c. mayonnaise

Cook Rice-A-Roni as directed on package. Add all other ingredients, except marinade. Mix ¾ teaspoon curry powder, ½ cup mayonnaise and marinade from artichoke hearts. Stir into salad and chill several hours. Serves 8 to 10.

Lloyd Williams, Branch No. 5844, Columbia City, IN

MANDARIN ORANGE SALAD

60 Ritz crackers, crushed
1 stick oleo, melted
¼ c. sugar
1 (6 oz.) can frozen orange juice,
  thawed

1 can Eagle Brand milk
1 (8 oz.) Cool Whip
2 small cans mandarin oranges,
  drained

Crush crackers. Add melted oleo and sugar; press in a 9x13 inch pan. Save some for garnish. Blend orange juice and milk; stir in Cool Whip and oranges. Fold in; do not beat. Pour over crumb crust. Top with reserved crumbs. Refrigerate or freeze.

Phyllis Vogtmann, Branch No. 2232, Auburn, MI

STRAWBERRY SALAD

1 (6 oz.) box strawberry jello
1 c. hot water
1 c. cold water
1 (10 oz.) box frozen strawberries,
 thawed

1 (8¼ oz.) can crushed pineapple,
 drained
2 to 3 bananas, mashed
1 c. sour cream

Dissolve jello in hot water. Add cold water and mix. Add strawberries, bananas, and pineapple. Stir. Put ½ of mixture in 9x13 inch glass pan and refrigerate to jell. Cover remaining mixture, but do not refrigerate. When first layer jells, cover with a layer of sour cream and add remaining strawberry mixture. Refrigerate to jell.

Judy Smith, Branch No. 2630, Greeley, CO

PASTA SALAD

1 (8 oz.) bottle Italian dressing
2 c. spiral macaroni
1½ c. cherry tomato halves
1 c. zucchini slices
1 c. radish slices
½ c. chopped green pepper

¼ c. green onion slices
¾ c. mayonnaise
1 (3 oz.) canister grated Parmesan
 cheese
1 garlic clove, minced
½ c. shredded carrot

Pour dressing over macaroni and vegetables. Cover. Marinate for several hours or overnight. Drain well. Combine mayonnaise, cheese and garlic. Mix well. Add to macaroni mixture. Toss lightly. Garnish with shredded carrot. Makes 6 servings.

Delyte Ahlschwede, Branch No. 2630, Greeley, CO

RASPBERRY SALAD

1 (10 oz.) pkg. frozen raspberries
1 (3 oz.) pkg. raspberry gelatin
1 c. boiling water
1 c. vanilla ice cream

2 Tbsp. lemon juice
½ c. raspberry juice
¼ c. nuts, chopped

Thaw raspberries; drain and measure syrup. Dissolve gelatin in boiling water. Add ice cream, stirring until well blended. Add raspberry juice up to ½ cup (no more). Stir in lemon juice and chill until syrupy. Beat until light and spongy. Fold in raspberries and nuts. Pour into a salad mold. Serve with whipped topping mixed with a little salad dressing.

Ruth Peters, Branch No. 2630, Greeley, CO

PINEAPPLE LEMON SALAD

1 (15 oz.) can crushed pineapple
½ c. water
½ c. sugar
1 (3 oz.) pkg. lemon jello

½ c. Cheddar cheese, grated
½ c. pecans, chopped
1 (8 oz.) ctn. Cool Whip

Combine pineapple plus juice, water, and sugar in a saucepan; bring to a boil. Add dry jello and stir until dissolved. Cool. When thickened, add cheese, pecans and Cool Whip. Refrigerate.

Clara Riedel, Branch No. 1250, Vernon, TX

CHERRY SALAD

1 can cherry pie filling
1 (9 oz.) can crushed pineapple, drained
1 can Eagle Brand sweetened condensed milk

1½ c. miniature marshmallows
1 (9 oz.) Cool Whip
½ c. chopped pecans

Mix in order given. You can freeze or refrigerate. *Good, sweet and easy!*

Sharon Rohloff, Branch No. 5590, Casselberry, FL

RED, WHITE AND GREEN SALAD

2 bunches broccoli (5 c.), broken into flowerets
1 head cauliflower (2½ c.), broken into flowerets
1 bunch green onions, sliced
2 c. cherry tomatoes

1 c. mayonnaise
½ c. sour cream
1 Tbsp. vinegar
2 Tbsp. sugar
Salt and pepper to taste

Combine broccoli, cauliflower, onion, and tomatoes in salad bowl. Mix mayonnaise, sour cream, vinegar, sugar, salt, and pepper. Pour over salad and toss gently to coat vegetables. Cover and refrigerate for 4 hours or more. Serves 12. Makes about 1½ cups dressing.

Marcia Strickler, Branch No. 2334, Pasadena, TX

RASPBERRY MOLDED SALAD

3 small boxes raspberry jello
2 pkg. frozen raspberries
1 (16 oz.) can crushed pineapple

3 c. liquid (water and drained pineapple juice)
1 small sour cream

Drain pineapple and boil juice with water to make 3 cups. Mix boiling liquid with raspberry jello. Add 2 packages frozen raspberries and pineapple. Pour ½ mixture into mold. Chill until it sets. Spread sour cream and add rest of mixture.

Mildred Alexander, Branch No. 3064, San Bruno, CA

WILMA'S DELIGHT

½ c. acini de pepe
1 tsp. salt
1 Tbsp. cooking oil
1 (15¼ oz.) can crushed pineapple
¼ c. powdered sugar
1 c. miniature marshmallows

20 maraschino cherries, chopped
1 (3½ oz.) pkg. instant French vanilla pudding
2 c. thawed non-dairy whipped topping
1 c. coconut (optional)

Place acini de pepe, salt and oil in boiling water; cook until tender, about 10 to 12 minutes. Drain acini de pepe; rinse with water and drain. Cool to room temperature.

Add pineapple and juice, powdered sugar, marshmallows, cherries, and coconut. Blend in instant pudding, followed with whipped topping. Mix lightly, but thoroughly. Refrigerate until chilled, about 2 hours or overnight.

If desired, garnish with chopped nuts and maraschino cherries.

Wilma Kahre, Coffeyville, KS

PINEAPPLE WHEAT SALAD

3 c. cooked whole wheat
1½ c. crushed pineapple, drained
8 oz. cream cheese
2 small pkg. instant vanilla
    pudding (or 1 large pkg.)

3 Tbsp. lemon juice
1 large container Cool Whip
1 tsp. vanilla

To make wheat: Pour 2 cups boiling water over 1 cup whole wheat. Soak overnight. In the morning, simmer wheat for 30 minutes.

To mix salad: Add softened cream cheese to pudding mix and lemon juice. Mix, then stir in Cool Whip and vanilla. Fold in pineapple and cooked wheat. (I add juice and all.)

Nancy Morast, Lamplighter, Branch No. 1393, Kalispell, MT

FROG EYE SALAD

1 c. sugar
2 Tbsp. flour
2½ tsp. salt
1¾ c. pineapple juice
2 eggs, beaten
1 Tbsp. lemon juice
3 qt. water
1 Tbsp. cooking oil
3 (11 oz.) cans mandarin oranges, drained
2 (20 oz.) cans pineapple chunks, drained

1 (20 oz.) can crushed pineapple, drained
1 (9 oz.) Cool Whip
1 (4½ oz.) Cool Whip
1 c. miniature marshmallows (optional)
1 c. coconut (optional)
1 (16 oz.) pkg. acini de pepe (a macaroni product about BB size)

Combine sugar, flour and ½ teaspoon of the salt. Gradually stir in pineapple juice and eggs. Cook over moderate heat, stirring until thickened. Add lemon juice. Cool mixture to room temperature.

Bring water, rest of salt and oil to a boil. Add acini de pepe and cook at a rolling boil until acini de pepe is done. Drain and rinse with water; drain again and cool to room temperature. Combine egg mixture and acini de pepe; mix lightly, but thoroughly. Refrigerate overnight in airtight container. Add the remaining ingredients. Mix lightly, but thoroughly. Refrigerate until chilled. Yield: 25 servings.

Salad may be refrigerated up to a week in airtight container. It also may be frozen, though freezing somewhat changes the texture.

Elinor Fuhrman, Branch No. 0207, Ashland, WI

CRANBERRY-TOKAY SALAD

2 c. fresh or frozen cranberries
1 c. sugar
1 c. Tokay or red seedless grapes

¼ c. walnuts
½ c. whipped cream

Put cranberries through food chopper. Use coarse blade. Stir in sugar and let set in refrigerator overnight. Let drain and press lightly to release juice. Cut grapes in halves to remove seeds. Add grapes and nuts to cranberry mixture. Fold in whipped cream. Makes 4 to 5 servings.

May be served immediately. It will keep for a week in refrigerator.

Ruth Gertz, Branch No. 2876, Gladwin, MI

FAVORITE SALAD

1 bunch broccoli (mostly
    flowerets)
1 head cauliflower
1 bunch green onions, chopped
1 pkg. frozen peas

1 c. Miracle Whip
½ c. sour cream
2 tsp. garlic powder
Salt and pepper

Wash vegetables. Separate broccoli and cauliflower into small pieces. Add chopped onion and frozen peas. Mix remaining ingredients and add to vegetables. Mix well. Keeps well for 3 days in the refrigerator.

Mrs. ElVera Schultz, Branch No. 341, Curtiss, WI

BROCCOLI AND CAULIFLOWER SALAD

1 bunch broccoli ends

1 head cauliflower ends

Dressing or Dip:

¾ c. light salad dressing
½ c. sour cream
1 Tbsp. lemon juice
1 tsp. prepared mustard

½ tsp. salt
2 Tbsp. chopped green onion and
    tops
2 tsp. chopped fresh parsley

Combine all ingredients. Mix about ½ dressing with broccoli and cauliflower for salad or place all in container at side of vegetable tray for dip.

Mrs. Howard (Margaret) Loveless, Branch No. 1648, Eden, TX

ANGEL SALAD

2 small pkg. lemon jello
1 (8 oz.) cream cheese
½ c. celery, finely diced
1 (15½ oz.) can crushed
  pineapple, drained

½ c. chopped nuts (pecans)
1 c. whipped cream
1 small can or jar chopped
  pimento

When jello congeals, add the other chopped ingredients with the exception of the cream which needs to be whipped separately to the right consistency before adding so it will not separate. Don't let jello get really hard, only softly congealed so ingredients will blend in smoothly.

Mrs. Anton (Frances) Lubke, Branch No. 1648, Eden, TX

LAYERED WALNUT SALAD

1 c. walnuts
1 tsp. oil
¼ tsp. garlic salt
⅛ tsp. dill weed
2 c. finely shredded lettuce
6 to 8 cherry tomatoes, cut in
  halves
1 c. shredded Cheddar cheese
1 (10 oz.) pkg. frozen peas, cooked
2 c. finely shredded lettuce

¾ c. light salad dressing
½ c. sour cream
1 Tbsp. lemon juice
1 tsp. prepared mustard
½ tsp. salt
2 Tbsp. chopped onion (include
  green tops)
2 tsp. chopped parsley
Paprika (if desired)

Place walnuts in rapidly boiling water in saucepan. Boil for 3 minutes; drain well. Mix with oil, garlic salt and dill weed; spread in shallow baking pan. Toast at 350° for 10 to 12 minutes, stirring once; cool.

Place 2 cups lettuce in straight sided glass bowl. Arrange tomatoes around bowl with cut sides against the glass. Add layers of cheese, peas, ¾ cup toasted walnuts, and 2 cups lettuce. Combine remaining ingredients in bowl, mixing well. Spread 1 cup salad dressing mixture over salad, sealing to edge. Chill, covered, for several hours. Top with remaining dressing and walnuts just before serving. Garnish with onion tops and paprika. Yields 6 servings.

Karen Loveless, Branch No. 1648, Eden, TX

PRETZEL SALAD

1 (6 oz.) pkg. strawberry gelatin
2 (10 oz.) pkg. frozen strawberries,
  partially defrosted
3 Tbsp. sugar
1½ sticks margarine
2 c. boiling water

½ c. cold water
2 c. coarse crushed pretzels
1 (8 oz.) pkg. cream cheese
¾ c. powdered sugar
1 small container whipped topping

Dissolve gelatin in boiling water. Add cold water. Add strawberries and set aside to cool. Do not refrigerate. Cream 3 tablespoons sugar with margarine. Add pretzels. Press in 9x13 inch pan. Bake for 10 minutes at 350°. Cool.

Blend cream cheese with powdered sugar. Add whipped topping. Spread cream cheese mixture over cooled crust and let firm up in refrigerator. When cream cheese mixture firms, top with strawberry mixture and refrigerate overnight.

Delores Procknow, Branch No. 1683, Merrill, WI

PRETZEL SALAD

2⅓ c. crushed pretzels
¾ c. melted margarine
4 Tbsp. sugar
8 oz. cream cheese
1 c. sugar

1 c. Cool Whip
1 large pkg. strawberry jello
1 small pkg. strawberry jello
2½ c. boiling water
2 (10 oz.) pkg. frozen strawberries

Combine first 3 ingredients and press in a 9x13 inch pan. Bake at 350° for 10 minutes.

Combine next 3 ingredients and spread on crust. Dissolve jello in boiling water and add strawberries. Let mixture cool until it thickens, then pour over cheese mixture.

Mollie Hanneman, Branch No. 1743, Garden City, KS

CRANBERRY SOUFFLE

2½ c. orange juice
1 (16 oz.) can jellied cranberry
   sauce

1 (6 oz.) pkg. raspberry flavored
   gelatin
1½ c. whipping cream

In saucepan, combine 1¼ cups orange juice, cranberry sauce and gelatin. Cook and stir on medium heat until gelatin dissolves. Stir in remaining orange juice. Transfer to medium mixing bowl. Cover and chill until partially set.

In small mixing bowl, beat whipping cream to soft peaks. Fold into gelatin mixture and pour into mold. Chill for 4 to 6 hours, or overnight.

Marty Tews, Branch 1221

PISTACHIO SALAD

1 pkg. instant pistachio pudding
1 can crushed pineapple, drained
1 large Cool Whip

½ to ¾ bag miniature
   marshmallows (as desired)

Prepare pudding according to package. Stir in pineapple, Cool Whip and marshmallows gently. Top with chopped nuts and/or cherries if desired. Refrigerate.

Angela Miller, Branch No. 932, Minneapolis, MN

MEXICAN SALAD

1 can Ranch Style beans
1 lb. Cheddar cheese
1 small onion
1 (8 oz.) bottle Kraft Catalina
    dressing

1 large head lettuce
2 large tomatoes
1 pkg. Fritos (medium size)

Mix chopped onion, tomatoes, lettuce, shredded cheese, and drained beans. Pour dressing over this mixture. Let stand in refrigerator for 1 hour. Just before serving, add crushed Fritos. Serves 10 to 12.

Janet M. Pusey, Branch No. 3802, Fort Worth, TX

KUNTRY KITCHEN POTATO SALAD

4 c. cooked, diced potatoes
4 c. hard-boiled eggs, diced
1/4 medium onion, diced
3/4 c. celery, diced
1 c. salad dressing

1 1/4 tsp. salt
1 Tbsp. prepared mustard
3/4 c. sugar
1 1/4 Tbsp. vinegar
Dab of milk

Combine potatoes, eggs, onion, and celery. Mix together salad dressing, salt, mustard, sugar, vinegar, and milk. Add to potato mixture, mixing just enough to cover.

Tricia Schellen, Branch No. 1957, Creighton, NE

PASTA SALAD

1 lb. vermicelli
1 green pepper, chopped
1 small purple onion, chopped
3 large tomatoes, diced
1 small cucumber or zucchini,
    diced

1/2 bottle McCormick Salad
    Supreme
1 1/2 c. Italian dressing

Cook vermicelli according to package directions; drain and chill. Add rest of ingredients in a large bowl. Chill overnight. Serves many.

Jill Nagel, Branch No. 224, Grand Haven, MI

BROCCOLI BACON SALAD

1 bunch broccoli (3 stems)
12 slices bacon
1 small red onion, sliced

1 c. sunflower seeds, roasted and
    salted
1/2 c. raisins

Dressing:

1/2 c. mayonnaise
2 Tbsp. vinegar

1/4 c. sugar

Slice broccoli into bite-size pieces. Fry bacon and crumble or cut into pieces. Mix all ingredients together. Add dressing and let stand for 3 hours. Serves 12.

Marjorie Tjepkema, Branch No. 767, Norwood, MN

CHERRY SALAD

1 (6 oz.) pkg. cherry flavored
   gelatin
3 c. boiling water
1 can cherry pie filling

½ c. celery, chopped
1 c. apples, chopped
¼ c. nuts, chopped

Dissolve gelatin in water. Add pie filling. Cool until slightly thickened; add remaining ingredients. Chill until firm.

Arlene Twardokus, AAL Branch No. 1400, Hartford, WI

COOKIE SALAD

2 pkg. instant vanilla coconut
   cream pudding
1½ c. half & half
1 pkg. fudge striped cookies

1 (11 oz.) can mandarin oranges
1 (8 oz.) can pineapple tidbits
1 (10 oz.) container whipped
   topping

Beat pudding and half & half. Fold in whipped topping. Add well drained fruit. Break cookies into small pieces. Fold half of the cookies into the mixture. Put the rest on top. Cool for 4 hours.

Marlene Martin, Branch No. 1581, Racine, WI

CHINESE SALAD

½ head cabbage
3 Tbsp. toasted almonds
3 Tbsp. sunflower seeds
1 can shrimp or diced pork
1 Tbsp. sugar
1 tsp. Accent
½ c. oil

6 to 8 green onions
3 Tbsp. sesame seeds
1 pkg. pork Top Ramen
½ tsp. salt
½ tsp. pepper
1 Tbsp. vinegar

Slice or grate cabbage into large bowl. Dice onion and add along with nuts, seeds, and shrimp or pork. Break up Top Ramen noodles and toss in salad. Sprinkle with Top Ramen seasoning. Combine oil, vinegar, sugar, salt, pepper, and Accent. Pour over salad and mix well.

Angela Gangelhoff, Branch No. 1737, Sandstone, MN

RED, WHITE AND BLUE SALAD

2 (3 oz.) pkg. raspberry jello
1 c. Coffee Rich
¾ c. sugar
1 env. Knox gelatine
½ c. cold water

8 oz. cream cheese
1 tsp. vanilla
1½ c. boiling water
2 c. blueberries

First layer: Make 1 package of raspberry jello as package directs and let set in a 9x13 inch cake pan.

Second layer: Heat Coffee Rich and sugar in saucepan. Dissolve Knox gelatine in cold water and add to Coffee Rich mixture. Cream the cream cheese and vanilla. Gradually add hot Coffee Rich mixture to cream cheese mixture. Pour over first layer and allow to set.

Third layer: Add boiling water to the second package of jello and then add blueberries. (If the blueberries are frozen, the jello sets faster, but the third layer may not adhere to the second layer.) Pour over second layer. Serve when set.

Ginger Roney, Branch No. 3725, Urbana, IL

SPINACH AND PEANUT SALAD

8 c. torn spinach or mixed greens
3 red apples, diced (with peel)
⅔ c. Spanish peanuts

½ c. raisins
⅓ c. sliced green onions
2 Tbsp. toasted sesame seeds

Chutney Dressing:

½ c. white wine vinegar
⅔ c. salad oil
2 Tbsp. chopped chutney
1 tsp. salt

1 tsp. curry powder
1 tsp. dry mustard
½ tsp. sugar
¼ tsp. Tabasco sauce

Mix dressing ingredients and let stand for 2 hours to blend flavors. Arrange greens on salad plates and scatter other ingredients on top. Serve with Chutney Dressing. Serves 8.

Lorene Buescher, Branch No. 3017, Portland, OR

RASPBERRY JELLO SALAD

1 small box raspberry jello
1 c. boiling water

1 c. applesauce
1 small pkg. frozen raspberries

Dissolve jello in boiling water. Add applesauce and unthawed raspberries. After berries are thawed, stir well and put in mold to set.

Marguerite Boerger, Branch No. 4734, Delphi, IN

SPAGHETTI SALAD

1 doz. hard-boiled eggs, diced
1 large onion, diced
1 large cucumber, diced
1 lb. cooked spaghetti noodles

Miracle Whip salad dressing
Milk
1 large tomato, diced
Salt

Toss first 4 ingredients together. Mix Miracle Whip salad dressing with milk until *slightly* runny. Pour over mixture. Add diced tomatoes to salad. Toss lightly. Salt to taste.

Julie Smith, Branch No. 0916, Molalla, OR

FRUIT SALAD

2 large cans chunk pineapple
2 cans mandarin oranges
1 can fruit cocktail

6 to 8 bananas
1 pkg. regular vanilla pudding mix
1 pkg. tapioca pudding mix

Drain juice from fruits. Save 3 cans of juice (different kinds). Cook the 2 mixes with the 3 cans of juice. Cool and mix in the fruits. Serves many.

Lillian Nickademus, Branch No. 0916, Mt. Angel, OR

JELLED VEGETABLE SALADE
(Low calorie)

1 env. unflavored gelatin
¼ c. water
1½ c. boiling water
2 Tbsp. tarragon vinegar
¼ tsp. salt
½ Tbsp. honey

¾ c. finely chopped carrots
¼ c. chopped celery
½ c. cucumbers, pared and diced
1 Tbsp. chopped green onion
1 Tbsp. finely chopped pimiento
Salad greens

Soften gelatin in ¼ cup water for 5 minutes. Add softened gelatin to boiling water. Stir until gelatin is dissolved. Stir in vinegar, salt and honey. Chill until mixture begins to thicken. Fold in remaining ingredients, except greens.

Pour into a 1 quart mold or 8 inch square pan. Chill until set. Unmold and serve on crisp salad greens. Yield: 4 (⅔ cup) servings.

For low sodium diets, omit salt. Contains 30 calories, 0 g saturated fat, and 0 mg cholesterol.

Annabell Meyer, Branch No. 0714, Fairmont, OK

CRANBERRY FLUFF

2 c. raw cranberries, ground
3 c. miniature marshmallows
1 can crushed pineapple
¾ c. sugar

½ c. walnuts, chopped
1 c. whipping cream
2 c. apples, chopped (optional)

Combine cranberries, sugar and marshmallows. Chill overnight. Add walnuts and pineapple (and apple). Fold in whipped cream. Chill before serving.

Barbara Blombach, Branch No. 5585, LaGrange, KY

SEA SHELL SALAD

1 (1 lb.) box pasta shells (medium
    or large)
3 stalks celery, chopped
2 green peppers, chopped
1 can black olives, sliced

1 jar green olives, sliced
3 green onions, chopped
½ lb. Provolone cheese, chopped
¼ lb. hard salami, cubed
2 tomatoes

Cook pasta according to package directions. Drain and toss with dressing while hot. Cool. Add remaining ingredients. Make 12 to 24 hours before you plan to serve. Add tomatoes just before serving.

Dressing:

1 c. oil
¼ c. vinegar
2 to 3 tsp. oregano

1 tsp. salt
Pepper to taste

Mix together and shake well.

Barbara Blombach, Branch No. 5585, LaGrange KY

CRANBERRY CRIMSON MOLD

2 (3 oz.) pkg. strawberry jello
1½ c. boiling water
1 c. Hellmann's mayonnaise

1½ c. cranberry-orange relish
1½ c. applesauce

Dissolve the jello in the boiling water; gradually add the mayonnaise, mixing until well blended. Chill until slightly thickened. Fold in the relish and applesauce. Pour into a 5 cup mold. Chill until firm. Unmold and garnish as desired.

Doris Jansen, Branch No. 3678, Suring, WI

TURKEY CASHEW SALAD

½ head lettuce
1 large red apple
⅔ c. diced celery
⅔ c. diced smoked turkey

½ c. halved cashew nuts
½ c. mayonnaise
Milk

Cut lettuce into bite-size pieces. Add diced apple, celery, turkey, and cashew nuts. Toss. Thin mayonnaise with a little milk and toss again.

Maxine Rodgers, Branch No. 1412, Corvallis, OR

FROSTED SALAD

2 (3 oz.) pkg. lemon jello
1¾ c. boiling water
2 c. cold water or Canada Dry
    ginger ale

1 (20 oz.) can crushed pineapple,
    drained
2 to 3 large bananas, sliced

Dissolve jello in boiling water and stir in water or ginger ale. Chill till partially set. Fold in pineapple and bananas; pour in 7x12 or 9x13 inch pan. Chill until firm and add topping. Chill overnight.

Whipped Cream Topping:

½ c. sugar
2 Tbsp. flour
1 c. pineapple juice, drained from
    fruit
1 egg, slightly beaten

2 Tbsp. butter
1 c. whipping cream, whipped
¼ c. shredded American cheese
    (optional)

Combine sugar and flour in saucepan. Stir in pineapple juice and egg. Cook over low heat until thickened. Remove from heat. Add butter. Chill. When cool, fold into whipped cream. Frost gelatin mixture and sprinkle with cheese.

Marge Milz, Branch No. 2295, Detroit, MI

GOLDEN FRUIT SALAD

2 Golden Delicious apples, diced
2 Red Delicious apples, diced
4 bananas, sliced
2 (20 oz.) cans pineapple chunks,
   drained

2 (16 oz.) cans mandarin oranges,
   drained (discard juice)
Whole green grapes (optional)

Dressing:

1 c. sugar
4 Tbsp. cornstarch
Reserved pineapple juice

2 Tbsp. lemon juice
2/3 c. orange juice

Combine fruits; reserve pineapple juice. Combine sugar and cornstarch. Gradually add fruit juices and cook, stirring constantly, until thickened. Pour hot dressing over fruits and combine well. Let stand, uncovered, until cool. Cover and refrigerate overnight. Keeps well.

This is a large recipe serving 12 to 14. It may be cut in half easily.
Marjorie M. Anderson, Branch No. 5325, Stratford, IA

RAINBOW RIBBON SALAD

Layer 1:

1 (3 oz.) pkg. black cherry jello
1 c. boiling water

1/2 c. ice water

Layer 2:

1 (3 oz.) pkg. cherry jello
1 c. boiling water

1/3 c. sweetened condensed milk

Layer 3:

1 (3 oz.) pkg. lime jello
1 c. boiling water

1/2 c. ice water

Layer 4:

1 (3 oz.) pkg. lemon jello
1 c. boiling water

1/3 c. sweetened condensed milk

Layer 5:

1 (3 oz.) pkg. orange jello
1 c. boiling water

1/2 c. ice water

Layer 6:

1 (3 oz.) pkg. pineapple jello
1 c. boiling water

1/3 c. sweetened condensed milk

Layer 7:

1 (3 oz.) pkg. strawberry jello
1 c. boiling water

1/2 c. ice water

Dissolve the black cherry jello in 1 cup boiling water; add ½ cup ice water. Pour into a 9x13 inch pan. Refrigerate to set. While it is setting, dissolve the cherry jello in 1 cup boiling water; let set at room temperature. After the first layer is firm, add ⅓ cup sweetened condensed milk to the cherry jello. Pour it over the first layer and refrigerate until firm. Add the third layer of lime jello dissolved in 1 cup boiling water and ½ cup ice water.

When it is firm, add the fourth layer of lemon jello, water and sweetened condensed milk. Repeat the process for the remaining layers. Layers 1, 3, 5, and 7 use 1 cup boiling water and ½ cup ice water. Layers 2, 4, and 6 use 1 cup boiling water and ⅓ cup sweetened condensed milk. While one layer is setting up, the next layer can be dissolved in the boiling water and left at room temperature to cool. Add the ice water or sweetened condensed milk to the jello just before pouring it in the pan.

A low calorie version can be made by using low calorie jello and using either condensed skim milk or regular 1% or 2% milk. Adding these types of milk may make the jello look curdled, but it looks fine in the salad and reduces the calories.

Joan Gloystein (recipe of Ruth Gloystein), Branch No. 0769, Utica, NE

SEVEN LAYERED GELATIN SALAD

Have on hand 1 large can evaporated milk.

1 (3 oz.) box black cherry gelatin, dissolved in 1½ c. hot boiling water

1 (3 oz.) box cherry gelatin, dissolved in 1 c. hot water, then ½ c. evaporated milk added

1 (3 oz.) box lime gelatin, dissolved in 1½ c. hot water

1 (3 oz.) box lemon gelatin, dissolved in 1 c. hot water,

then ½ c. evaporated milk added

1 (3 oz.) box orange gelatin, dissolved in 1½ c. hot water

1 (3 oz.) box orange pineapple or apricot gelatin, dissolved in 1 c. hot water, then ½ c. evaporated milk added

1 (3 oz.) box strawberry gelatin, dissolved in 1½ c. hot water

Use a 9x13 inch pan (Tupperware works best). Start with black cherry. Put in pan. Chill till set. While it chills, mix cherry gelatin. Let cool, then pour slowly over black cherry. Chill till set. Make each box in order and cool. Pour over layers, allowing each to set.

Shirley Ege, Branch No. 771, Elizabeth, IL

APRICOT DELIGHT

8 oz. cream cheese (soft)
3 oz. apricot gelatin
16 oz. Cool Whip
15½ oz. crushed pineapple, drained

17 oz. apricots, drained
Pecans (optional)

Mix very soft cream cheese with gelatin. Add Cool Whip, pineapple, mashed apricots, and chopped pecans. If the mixture is too stiff, add a small amount of pineapple juice and chill.

This will keep for a few days in the refrigerator.

Sally Lundberg, Branch No. 5325, Stratford, IA

BEAN SALAD

1 can red kidney beans	1 onion*
1 can cut green beans	Celery (optional)
1 can cut wax beans	Green pepper (optional)
1 can small lima beans	

Marinade:

¾ c. sugar	½ c. salad oil
1 tsp. salt	⅔ c. vinegar
½ tsp. pepper	

Wash and drain all beans. Mix marinade ingredients and pour over beans. Mix well and let marinate for 24 hours.

* Add onion about 1 hour before serving. Celery and green pepper may be added also.

Eleanor Schmude, Branch No. 2408, Port Huron, MI

LEMON JELLO MOLD

2 (3 oz.) pkg. lemon jello, dissolved in 2 c. boiling water	1 (6 oz.) frozen lemonade 1 (9 oz.) container Cool Whip

Add lemonade to lemon jello. Refrigerate until it starts to gel. Beat until foamy with electric mixer and beat in one 9 ounce Cool Whip. Pour into mold and chill.

Betty Juern, Branch No. 3197, Skokie, IL

LIME PARTY SALAD

¼ lb. marshmallows (about 16)	1 (No. 2) can crushed pineapple
1 c. milk	1 c. whipping cream
1 pkg. lime gelatin	⅔ c. mayonnaise
2 (3 oz.) pkg. cream cheese	

Melt in top of double boiler ¼ pound marshmallows (about 16) and 1 cup milk. Pour hot mixture over 1 package lime flavored gelatin. Stir until dissolved, then stir in two 3 ounce packages cream cheese. Stir until cheese dissolves. Add one No. 2 can undrained crushed pineapple. Cool. Blend in 1 cup whipping cream, whipped, and ⅔ cup mayonnaise. Chill until firm. Makes 12 servings.

Wilferd Deke, Branch No. 445, Beatrice, NE

BLACK CHERRY SALAD

1 large box black cherry Jell-O
2 c. boiling water
1 can pitted dark cherries
1 c. whipped cream

2 Tbsp. sugar
1 (3 oz.) pkg. cream cheese
1 c. small marshmallows

Dissolve Jell-O in boiling water and add can of cherries with juice. Let stand until set. Whip cream and beat in sugar and cream cheese. Stir in marshmallows. Frost top of salad with this mixture and refrigerate.

Dorothy Davis, Branch No. 2568, Fredericktown, MO

CABBAGE SALAD

3½ lb. cabbage, shredded
3 c. celery, cut up
3 c. onions, sliced
1 green pepper
1 red pepper
2 c. white vinegar

1 c. water
2½ c. sugar
1 Tbsp. salt
1 Tbsp. celery seed
1 Tbsp. turmeric
2 Tbsp. mustard seed

Mix all preceding ingredients and put in jar or crock. Bring to boil the vinegar, water, sugar, salt, celery seed, turmeric, and mustard seed. Pour when hot over vegetables. Stir 2 or 3 times. Let stand a day before eating. Will keep for about a month in refrigerator.

Ella Riebe, Branch No. 5616, Wilton, ND

FROZEN SALAD

1 (8 oz.) cream cheese
¾ c. sugar
10 oz. frozen strawberries
8 oz. Cool Whip

20 oz. blueberries
2 or 3 bananas, cut up
½ c. chopped nuts

Thoroughly mix together cream cheese and sugar; combine other ingredients and freeze. Set out 1 or 2 hours before serving.

Monica Bienz, Branch No. 896, New Haven, IN

TAFFY APPLE SALAD

4 c. cubed apples
1 (8¼ oz.) can pineapple chunks
  (save juice)
1 c. salted peanuts (no skins)
1 egg

1 Tbsp. flour
2 Tbsp. cider vinegar
1 (8 oz.) Cool Whip
½ c. sugar

Bring pineapple juice to a boil. Beat egg, sugar, vinegar, and flour together. Add juice till thick, then add Cool Whip. Add peanuts and pineapple. Mix and refrigerate.

Adele Hogue, Branch No. 952, Dolton, IL

LEMON COCONUT SALAD

1 (8 oz.) pkg. cream cheese
1 can Eagle Brand milk
1 medium can crushed pineapple,
    drained

1 can lemon pie filling
1 (9 oz.) ctn. Cool Whip
½ c. coconut

Cream the cream cheese. Add milk and mix well. Add pineapple and pie filling. Mix lightly. Add Cool Whip and coconut. Mix well. Chill.

Ione Bentz, Branch No. 1552, Breckinridge, OK

COLE SLAW DRESSING

1 c. water
½ c. white vinegar
1 c. salad oil

1 tsp. salt
1 tsp. celery salt
1 medium onion, grated

Put all together in blender until well blended. Makes 1 pint.

St. Peter's Lutheran Church Mission Circle, Branch No. 2379, Easton, MN

POTATO SALAD DRESSING

½ c. vinegar, heated
4 beaten eggs
1 c. sugar
2 Tbsp. butter
1 tsp. mustard

½ tsp. pepper
Pinch of salt
1 Tbsp. flour, mixed in with the
    sugar

Cook until thick. Store in covered container in refrigerator. Makes about 2 cups.

When using, mix one half of this dressing with one half of mayonnaise. (Miracle Whip is very good.) Thin with cream.

Mrs. Lawrence Greiner, Branch No. 2838, Wilmot, SD

MY FAVORITE SALAD DRESSING
(Used for 30 years)

1 c. white sugar (or less)
½ c. Wesson or Mazola oil
¼ c. vinegar
⅓ c. catsup

Juice of 1 lemon
1 small onion, grated fine
Salt and pepper to taste
Dash of paprika

Mix well before using.

You may keep a piece of garlic in the bottle. Also, may be mixed with Blue cheese or sour cream.

Jeanne Brown, Branch No. 03064, Millbrac, CA

DRESSING FOR COLE SLAW

1 c. salad oil
½ c. vinegar
½ c. cold water
1 c. sugar

1 Tbsp. salt
1 large carrot, grated
1 green pepper, chopped
1 onion, grated

Mix thoroughly. Put in container and keep in refrigerator. Keeps indefinitely.
Marlis Glamann, Branch No. 3725, Urbana, IL

KNOTT'S BERRY FRENCH DRESSING

¾ c. sugar or honey
⅓ c. vinegar
1 small onion
1 tsp. celery seed
1 tsp. parsley
1 tsp. paprika

1 tsp. salt
1 tsp. dry mustard
1 Tbsp. lemon juice
2 Tbsp. catsup
1 c. oil

Cook sugar and vinegar to dissolve sugar. Set aside. Put into blender the next 8 ingredients. Gradually add oil, then add the sugar and vinegar. Mix and beat until creamy. Refrigerate. Will keep a long time.
Vi White, Branch No. 2568, Fredericktown, MO

HORSERADISH SAUCE-PEAS
(Served cold)

1 (10 oz.) pkg. frozen peas
½ c. plain lowfat yogurt
¼ c. lite mayonnaise (or salad
   dressing)
1 Tbsp. skim milk

1 tsp. dry mustard
1 tsp. prepared horseradish
¼ tsp. pepper
1 (4 oz.) can sliced mushrooms,
   drained

Cook peas according to package directions; drain. In mixing bowl, stir together yogurt, mayonnaise, milk, mustard, horseradish, and pepper. Stir in peas and mushrooms. Cover and chill before serving. Chill to store. Makes 2 cups (16 servings).

Nutrition information per serving: 44 calories, 1 gram protein, 3 grams fat, 3 milligrams cholesterol, 66 milligrams sodium, and 22 milligrams calcium.
Lillian Fairman, Loveland, CO

ORANGE-CREAM FRUIT SALAD

1 (20 oz.) can pineapple tidbits,
   drained
1 (16 oz.) can peach slices,
   drained, or use fruit cocktail
1 (11 oz.) can mandarin oranges,
   drained
2 medium apples, cored and
   chopped

3 medium bananas, sliced
1 (3¾ oz.) pkg. instant vanilla
   pudding mix
1½ c. milk
⅓ c. frozen orange juice
   concentrate, thawed
¾ c. sour cream
Lettuce cups

In a large bowl, combine fruits; set aside. In a small bowl, combine dry pudding mix, milk and orange juice concentrate. Beat until blended, 1 to 2 minutes. Beat in sour cream. Fold into fruit mixture. Cover and chill. Serve in lettuce cups. Garnish with additional mandarin oranges if desired.

Connie Davis, Branch No. 3107, Loveland, CO

ORANGE SHERBET JELL-O SALAD

1 large box orange Jell-O
1 pt. (2 c.) orange sherbet ice
  cream

½ pt. whipping cream
1 can mandarin oranges

Boil 2 cups water. Pour water into glass square pan and stir in Jell-O. Dissolve thoroughly. Stir in ice cream until it all melts. Refrigerate until partially set and remove from refrigerator. Stir in whipping cream (whip cream first) until mixed thoroughly. Add mandarin oranges. Refrigerate.

Connie Davis, Branch No. 3107, Loveland, CO

COLD SPAGHETTI SALAD

1 lb. spaghetti
1 chopped bell pepper
1 chopped red onion
1 large tomato, chopped

1 bottle Italian dressing
½ bottle Salad Supreme
  (seasoning)

Cook spaghetti. Add vegetables. (Other raw vegetables such as cucumbers, mushrooms, etc., may be used.) Pour dressing over all. Add Salad Supreme. Stir. Keep refrigerated. Keeps well.

Connie Davis, Branch 3107, Loveland, CO

ICE CREAM SALAD

1 large box raspberry jello
1 c. boiling water
1 small can crushed pineapple
  (with juice)

1 c. chopped celery, cut fine
1 c. finely chopped nuts
1 pt. vanilla ice cream, slightly
  softened

Dissolve jello in boiling water in 8x8 inch glass dish. Add all other ingredients. Blend well after ice cream is added until smooth. Let set in fridge overnight.

Use lime jello for alternate recipe.

Julie Padilla, Branch No. 3107, Loveland, CO

COLD PEA SALAD

1 (16 oz.) can tiny LeSueur peas, drained
1 (16 oz.) can shoe peg "white" corn, drained
1 (16 oz.) can French style green beans, drained
1 c. celery, chopped fine
¼ to ½ c. chopped onions (fine)

1 green pepper, chopped fine
1 small jar pimento, chopped
1 tsp. salt
1 c. sugar
¾ c. vinegar
½ c. salad oil
1 tsp. celery seed

Make day before serving for flavors to blend. Add all ingredients together and mix well. Set in fridge and stir once in awhile. Drain liquid off the last minute before serving. Serves 8 to 12.

Julie Padilla, Branch No. 3107, Loveland, CO

TACO SALAD

1 lb. ground beef, browned and drained
1 head lettuce, torn in bits
2 diced tomatoes

1 diced cucumber
2 green onions, chopped
Corn chips or tortilla chips, crushed

Spicy Dressing:

1 c. Miracle Whip
⅓ c. catsup

3 to 4 drops of Tabasco sauce

Toss all ingredients, except corn chips. Add chips and dressing just before serving.

Mary Schaffer, Loveland, CO

FRUIT BASKET UPSET

1 (8 oz.) can fruit cocktail, drained
2 bananas, peeled and sliced
1 apple, cut into small pieces
½ c. halved seedless grapes
½ c. sliced strawberries

5 maraschino cherries, cut up
¼ c. mini marshmallows
Whipping cream
Red food coloring

Place all of the fruit and the marshmallows in a large bowl. Fold in whipping cream. Add 2 teaspoons maraschino juice and 1 to 2 drops of food coloring; carefully toss. Refrigerate until serving. Makes 4 to 6 servings.

Sharon Verville, Branch No. 3107, Loveland, CO

TACO SALAD

1 lb. lean ground beef
½ bottle taco sauce (mild is best if others will be eating it)
Salt and pepper to taste
Chopped tomatoes
1 chopped onion

1 can kidney beans
1 lb. grated cheese
1 head grated or torn iceberg lettuce
1 bag Doritos chips
French or Catalina dressing

Brown beef and onion; season with salt and pepper. Stir in beans and taco sauce. *Cool* completely. Combine all but the chips and dressing in a large bowl. Fold in chips just before serving. Pass dressing with salad.

This does not hold over well. Put together just before serving.

Sharon Verville, Branch No. 3107, Loveland, CO

BROCCOLI-RAISIN SALAD

4 stalks broccoli flowerets
½ c. green onion, sliced

½ c. raisins
8 slices bacon, crumbled

Dressing:

1 c. Miracle Whip
¼ c. sugar

2 Tbsp. vinegar

Combine the broccoli, onion, raisins, and bacon. Mix together the dressing and add to the vegetables just before serving.

Linda Moersen, Loveland, CO

FROZEN CHRISTMAS SALAD

1 (3 oz.) pkg. cream cheese
1 c. canned sweet cherries
¼ c. cut up green maraschino
    cherries
¼ c. orange sections, cut up

1 c. crushed pineapple, drained
1 c. chopped nuts
1 Tbsp. mayonnaise
½ c. red maraschino cherries
1 c. heavy cream, whipped

Soften cheese. Blend with mayonnaise, cherries, remaining fruit, and nuts. Fold whipped cream into mixture and spoon in loaf pan. Cover tightly and freeze. To serve, unmold and slice.

Sharon Walters, Branch No. 3107, Loveland, CO

BEST EVER SALAD

1 pkg. lime jello
1 (8 oz.) pkg. cream cheese
2 c. boiling water

1 c. whipped topping
9 marshmallows, cut up
1 c. drained crushed pineapple

Prepare jello as usual. Add marshmallows and cream cheese. Cool. Add pineapple and fold in topping. Garnish with chopped nuts. Refrigerate.

Roberta Kallsen, Branch No. 3107, Loveland, CO

FLUFFY SALAD

1⅓ c. cottage cheese
1 small pkg. sugar free jello
½ c. crushed pineapple
    (unsweetened)

2 c. whipped topping

Mix topping with dry jello, then add cottage cheese and pineapple. Chill.

Color of jello determines color of salad. For less calories, use only 1 cup whipped topping.

Bev McVay, St. John's AAL, Branch No. 3806, Center Point, IA

MICROWAVE FRUIT SALAD

1 (3 oz.) pkg. tapioca pudding
1 (3 oz.) pkg. vanilla pudding (not instant)
1 (20 oz.) can chunk pineapple

1 (20 oz.) can mandarin oranges
1 (20 oz.) can peaches, chunked
2 large bananas, cut into chunks

Drain juice from fruits into large glass casserole. Add enough water to juice until it measures 3 cups. Add juice to both pudding mixes and microwave on HIGH for 8 to 10 minutes or until bubbly and thick, stirring occasionally. Add drained fruits and bananas. You may also add other fruits if desired. Stir and chill.

Louise Tippett, Branch No. 1781, Elizabeth, IL

ZERO CALORIE DRESSING

½ c. tomato juice
2 Tbsp. lemon juice
1 tsp. salt
1 tsp. grated onion

1 clove minced garlic
½ tsp. mustard
½ tsp. Worcestershire sauce
Sweetener to taste

Shake ingredients in jar. Store in refrigerator.

DIABETIC VINEGAR DRESSING

1 Tbsp. liquid artificial sweetener
1 c. vinegar (choose cider, tarragon, or wine as preferred)

¼ to ¾ c. water (according to strength of vinegar)
Salt and pepper (as diet permits)
Herbs (as diet permits)

Mix all ingredients. May be stored indefinitely. May be used to pickle beets, on cabbage slaw, on a bean salad, on tossed salad, etc.

Mrs. Arthur L. Harley, Branch No. 1052, South Whitley, IN

KOREAN SPINACH SALAD

1 lb. fresh washed and dried spinach
4 hard cooked eggs, peeled and sliced

½ lb. bacon, fried crisp and crumbled
1 can sliced water chestnuts, drained

Place into salad bowl in order.

Dressing - Blend and chill:

1 c. salad oil
½ c. cider vinegar
1 Tbsp. Worcestershire sauce
⅓ c. catsup

1 Tbsp. minced onion
¾ c. sugar
1 tsp. salt

Add dressing just before serving.

Carol Simerman, Branch No. 5844, Columbia City, IN

MARSHMALLOW SALAD

1 lb. marshmallows, cut in fourths
½ lb. cheese
1 can pineapple

½ pt. whipping cream
1 or 2 Tbsp. salad dressing

Dice pineapple and drain well. Grate cheese. Add pineapple and cheese to marshmallows. Whip cream and mix salad dressing with whipped cream. Pour and mix with first mixture.

Frieda Augenstein, Branch No. 5844, Columbia City, IN

PASTA SALAD

½ green pepper, chopped
½ red pepper, chopped
1 onion, chopped fine

1 cucumber, chopped fine
1 pkg. colored pasta
¼ c. oil

Cook pasta according to the package directions. Add the ¼ cup oil to keep the pasta from sticking together. Add the green and red peppers, onion and cucumbers. Mix well.

Dressing:

1 tsp. prepared mustard
1 tsp. salt
1 tsp. garlic salt

½ c. sugar
1 c. vinegar

Mix dressing ingredients of mustard, salt, pepper, garlic salt, sugar, and vinegar. Pour over pasta and mix well.

Dee Frantz, Branch No. 2049, Emporia, KS

LAYERED LETTUCE SALAD

1 head lettuce
1 c. celery, chopped
Onion to taste
8 strips bacon, cooked crisp
2 c. mayonnaise

4 oz. shredded Cheddar cheese
4 boiled eggs
1 (10 oz.) box frozen peas, thawed
2 Tbsp. sugar

Tear lettuce into bite-size pieces and place in 9x13 inch pan. Make layers of the remaining ingredients of celery, onion, bacon, eggs, and peas. Add sugar to mayonnaise; mix well. Spread over top of lettuce layers. Top with shredded Cheddar cheese. Refrigerate for at least 12 hours.

Dee Frantz, Branch No. 2049, Emporia, KS

SPINACH SALAD

¾ c. boiling water
1 small pkg. lemon jello
1 c. cottage cheese
½ c. chopped celery

½ c. chopped onion
½ c. Miracle Whip
1 pkg. frozen spinach, thawed and
   slightly cooked

Topping:

½ c. Miracle Whip
½ c. sour cream

Shredded Cheddar cheese

Dissolve the jello in the ¾ cup boiling water. Let cool. Add the cottage cheese, chopped celery, chopped onion, Miracle Whip, and the spinach. Let set until firm. Top with the mixture of Miracle Whip and sour cream. Sprinkle with desired Cheddar cheese.

Laura Johnson, Branch No. 2049, Emporia, KS

CRANBERRY DELIGHT

1 pkg. cranberries
2 c. sugar
1 small can crushed pineapple

1 small pkg. small marshmallows
1 large Cool Whip

Grind the package of cranberries; add the sugar and pineapple. Mix well and let stand for 1 hour. Add the package of marshmallows and Cool Whip. Mix well. This freezes well.

Dee Frantz, Branch No. 2049, Emporia, KS

Notes

Soups,
Sandwiches,
Sauces

UNUSUAL HERBS

Angelica—bienniel, homegrown herb. Leaves, seeds and root used.

Bergamots—used in these recipes are the orange-scented mint and Napaka (Monarda austromonta) or mountain oregano.

Borage—hairy annual, self-seeds, leaves and flowers used, cucumber flavor.

Burdock—root vegetable or pot herb, in Japanese produce section as "Gobo".

Burnet—pretty leafy perennial, leaves have cucumber flavor.

Chervil—annual, taste similar to parsley, but milder with slight anise taste.

Chia—is the seed of a sage, high in protein.

Cilantro—Mexican name for fresh leaf of coriander. Also called Chinese Parsley.

Chuchupate—root of a celery flavored plant. Robust in flavor. Use sparingly.

Coltsfoot—used in Japanese cooking, bought in cans, grows wild all over England.

Damiana (Turnera diffusa)—aphrodisiac herb used by Aztecs in their rites.

Epasote—Mexican herb (Chenopodium ambrosidies) used with pork and fish.

Jamica Roselle Hibiscus (Hibiscus Sabdariffa)—makes a pink lemonade tea.

Lemon Balm—perennial, lemon flavored used for flavoring.

Lemon Grass—lemon flavored grass, used in cooking and teas.

Lemon Eucalyptus (Eucalyptus citriodora)—30 foot tree with lemon scented leaves.

Lemon Thyme—very fragrant, lemon scented.

Mate—a South American tea, containing large amount of caffeine.

Mints—orange, apple, pineapple scented, use interchangeably in any mint recipe.

Oriental Garlic—looks like a wide leaf chive. Just leaves are used.

Perilla—annual called "Sisho" by Japanese. Resembles purple coleus. Perilla can be used in salads.

Pineapple Sage—pineapple fragrance, much used with fruit recipes.

Purslane—fleshy weed common in gardens, good cooked or raw, high in Vitamin C.

Quelites (Chenopodium album)—Indian pot herb, a variety of lambsquarters.

Saffron—stamens of Corcus Sativus, most expensive spice in the world.

Shallots—bulbs are small, lavender, mild onion flavor.

Skirret—roots and leaves used in salad, also good cooked, green leafy plant.

Tarragon—mild licorice taste. Do not start from seed, get divisions from nursery.

Woodruff—coumarin scented when dry, good in wine or jelly.

Yerbanis (Pericon, Tagetes Lucida)—marigold leaves, tarragon type flavor —Mexico.

SOUPS, SANDWICHES, SAUCES

POTATO SOUP

2 Tbsp. butter or oleo
2 Tbsp. chopped onion
2½ tsp. salt
⅛ tsp. pepper
1 Tbsp. flour

1 Tbsp. parsley flakes
½ c. celery, chopped
2 c. sliced potatoes
2 c. water
3 c. milk

Heat butter in large saucepan. Add onion and fry slowly till tender. Add salt, pepper and flour. Blend. Add parsley, celery, potatoes, and water. Mix thoroughly. Cover and cook until potatoes are tender, about 20 minutes. Add milk. Heat thoroughly. Serves 6.

Coyladean (Dee) Yager, Branch No. 2935, Torrington, WY

CLAM CHOWDER SOUP

8 slices bacon, chopped
3 potatoes, peeled and diced
¼ c. finely chopped onion
5 Tbsp. flour
1 tsp. salt (optional)

¼ tsp. dried thyme leaves
  (optional)
⅛ tsp. pepper
1 (6½ oz.) can minced clams
3 c. milk

Place bacon in a large casserole. Microwave on HIGH for 4 minutes or until crisp. Remove bacon, reserving drippings. Drain bacon on paper towel and set aside. Stir in potatoes and onion into bacon drippings. Cover and microwave on HIGH for 7 minutes or until potatoes are tender, stirring every 3 minutes. Stir in flour, salt, thyme, and pepper. Drain clams, reserving juice. Blend clam juice and milk into potato mixture. Microwave on HIGH for 7 minutes, or until mixture thickens, stirring every 2 minutes. Crumble bacon into mixture. Stir in clams.

Charlotte Holm, Branch No. 429, Goodhue, MN

CHILI WITH YELLOW BEANS
(Low calorie)

1 lb. lean ground beef
16 oz. tomatoes
1 can tomato soup
1 tsp. salt

1 tsp. chili powder
¼ c. chopped onion
1 can wax beans, drained
¼ tsp. pepper

Brown beef and onion in large skillet. Drain fat. Stir in rest of ingredients and heat to a boil. Reduce heat; cover and simmer for 25 to 30 minutes. Makes 6 (1 cup) servings (190 calories each).

Sharon Verville, Branch No. 3107, Loveland, CO

105

SPECIAL BROCCOLI SOUP

1 (10 oz.) pkg. frozen chopped
   broccoli
1 c. chicken broth or bouillon
1 medium chopped onion
½ tsp. nutmeg

1 can condensed cream of
   mushroom soup
1 Tbsp. margarine or butter
1 c. sour cream
¼ tsp. pepper

Blend for 15 seconds 1 cup sour cream and ¼ teaspoon pepper together. Cook for 5 minutes until boiling the broccoli, broth, onion, and nutmeg. Cover and simmer for 5 minutes or until broccoli is tender. Add mushroom soup and butter to broccoli mixture. Blend in blender for 15 seconds until smooth. Add sour cream and blend for 15 seconds till smooth. Sprinkle with pepper. Serve hot or cold.

Diane Robertson, Branch No. 3253, East Meadow, NY

LIMA BEAN SOUP

1 lb. dry baby lima beans
1 pkg. ham hocks
1 large can tomatoes
1 onion

1 small green pepper
3 stalks celery
A little pepper and parsley

Soak lima beans overnight; drain and rinse. Put into crock pot with ham hocks and tomatoes. Cut onion, green pepper and celery into small pieces; add to the crock pot. Also add water as you see fit. Cook on LOW for 8 hours or more.

Hertha Beisel, Branch No. 3107, Loveland, CO

FRENCH VEGETABLE BEEF SOUP

1 lb. beef stew meat, cut into ½
   inch cubes
¼ c. salad oil
1 can condensed French onion
   soup
1 (6 oz.) can tomato paste
1 Tbsp. basil

1½ tsp. salt
¼ tsp. pepper
4 carrots, sliced
2 c. sliced celery
1 can wax beans
1 can kidney beans

In Dutch oven, over medium heat, brown meat in hot oil. Reduce heat to medium; stir in undiluted soup, 5 soup cans of water, tomato paste, basil, salt, and pepper. Simmer, covered, for 1½ hours. Add vegetables. Reheat to boiling. Simmer, covered, for 30 minutes or until meat and vegetables are fork tender.

Sally Mueller, Branch No. 3107, Loveland, CO

POTATO CHOWDER
(Can use microwave)

3 Tbsp. butter
1½ c. onions, diced
¼ c. green pepper, diced
1½ c. celery, cut
½ c. carrots, julienne cut
1 garlic clove, grated (powder to taste substituted)

6 c. chicken bouillon
4 c. unpared potatoes, cubed
1½ Tbsp. soy sauce
1½ tsp. thyme
1 tsp. basil
Salt and pepper to taste

Melt butter in microwave. Saute onion until golden brown. Microcook vegetables until tender crisp on HIGH power in large microwave kettle. Add bouillon and all seasonings. Cook all ingredients on HIGH until mixture starts to boil. Program microwave on LOW power for balance of cooking, about 10 minutes total. Let stand for 6 minutes. Garnish with parsley. Serves 6 to 8.

Florence Lisko, Branch 1400, Arbor Vitae, WI

FRENCH ONION SOUP

4 large onions, sliced
½ stick butter or margarine
2 Tbsp. flour
7 c. beef broth (use instant crystals, dissolved in boiling water)

Pepper to taste
6 slices French bread (optional)
¾ c. Swiss cheese, grated

Slice peeled onions thinly. Separate into rings. Saute rings in hot butter until softened and lightly browned. Stir in flour; add onions and pepper to hot broth. Cover and simmer for 20 minutes. May place slice of bread in bottom of individual ovenproof dishes. Ladle soup into bowls. Sprinkle generously with shredded cheese. (Using bread is optional. Bread may also be toasted before using in soup if desired.)

Place dishes on a cookie sheet and place under broiler for 3 minutes until cheese is melted and slightly browned.

Jan McLaughlin, Branch No. 3107, Loveland, CO

DAVE'S WILD RICE SOUP

6 Tbsp. butter
1 Tbsp. minced onion
½ c. flour
3 c. chicken broth
2 c. cooked Wild Rice
⅓ c. minced ham

½ c. finely grated carrots
3 Tbsp. chopped, slivered almonds
½ tsp. salt
1 c. half & half
2 Tbsp. dry sherry (optional)
Minced parsley or chives

Melt butter in saucepan; saute onion until tender. Blend in flour; gradually add broth. Cook, stirring constantly, until mixture comes to a boil; boil for 1 minute. Stir in rice, ham, carrots, almonds, and salt; simmer for 5 minutes. Blend in half & half and sherry; heat to serving temperature. Garnish with minced parsley or chives. Makes about 6 cups.

Cooking method for Wild Rice:

½ c. wild rice   ½ tsp. salt
2 c. water

Rinse wild rice under running water, using a strainer, or in a bowl of water; drain. Place wild rice in a heavy saucepan with salt and water. Bring to a boil. Simmer, covered, until kernels are open and tender, but not mushy (45 to 55 minutes). Drain excess liquid. (Wild rice arithmetic: ½ cup uncooked rice equals 2 cups cooked.)

Deborah Chellew, Branch No. 3107, Loveland, CO

DAD'S GREEN CHILI

4 to 5 c. lean pork, diced small   20 oz. diced green chilies
2 medium onions, chopped fine   Salt to taste
6 cloves minced garlic
3 to 4 (14 oz.) cans tomatoes,
    chopped

Brown pork in oil. Saute onions and garlic till transparent and add to pork. Add tomatoes with juice, green chilies, and salt. Simmer for 4 or 5 hours. Let it cool overnight. Taste in the morning and add another can or two of green chilies if it's too mild. Let it simmer for another 5 or 6 hours, tasting occasionally. If it is still too mild, add jalapeno peppers, 1 tablespoon at a time, and let simmer for an hour or so before adding more because the flavor develops slowly and it's easy to get it too hot. It will be thick by the time it's done.

You can eat as a soup or as a sauce over chili rellenos. You will need to add water and thicken with flour for sauce.

Lynn Schmidt, Branch No. 3107, Loveland, CO

GREEN BEAN SOUP

2 lb. meaty ham bone   ¼ tsp. savory
2 qt. water   ¼ tsp. pepper
4 c. green beans   1 tsp. salt
3 c. potatoes, cubed   ¼ c. parsley
2 medium onions   1 c. light cream (optional)

Cook the bone in the 2 quarts of water in a Dutch oven until tender (1½ hours or so). Debone the meat. Add everything else, *except* the cream. Bring to a boil; reduce heat and simmer, covered, for about 20 minutes, or until veggies are tender. Skim off fat. Just before serving, add cream and stir in if you choose to use it.

Sharon Verville, Branch No. 3107, Loveland, CO

CHERRY SOUP

1 qt. pitted cherries and juice   ½ to ¾ c. sugar
4 to 6 c. water   1 pinch of salt
1 stick cinnamon

Put cherries in a 6 quart kettle and add about 2 cups water; bring to a boil. Simmer for 15 to 20 minutes, then add sugar to taste. Bring to a boil and add the following Dumplings.

Dumplings:

1 large egg	**½ c. milk**
½ tsp. salt	**½ tsp. baking powder**
¾ Tbsp. cooking oil	**1 to 2 c. flour**

Mix all ingredients together and add flour to make a stiff paste. Add a teaspoonful at a time to soup mixture and simmer for 15 to 20 minutes. Serve.

This is also a good soup for hot weather served cool.

Arlene Twardokus, AAL Branch 1400, Hartford, WI

CREAMY VEGETABLE SOUP

½ c. grated onion	**¼ c. butter**
2 Tbsp. oil	**¾ c. flour**
1 c. chopped celery	**2 c. milk**
2 (only) grated carrots	**1 c. half & half**
½ medium head cauliflower	**Salt to taste**
2 Tbsp. minced parsley	**1 c. cream**
6 c. chicken broth	

Bouquet garni - Tie in cheesecloth bag:

2 bay leaves	**½ tsp. peppercorn**
1 tsp. tarragon	

Saute onion in oil. Add celery and carrots. Cook over low heat for 2 minutes. Stir in cauliflower and parsley. Simmer for 12 minutes. Add chicken broth and bouquet garni. Bring to a boil; reduce to low heat and simmer for 5 minutes.

Meanwhile, melt butter in heavy pan; add flour to make a roux. Gradually add milk; stir with a whisk so mixture is smooth. Remove and add half & half. Stir white sauce into simmering soup. Simmer until cauliflower is tender, about 10 minutes.

Remove bouquet garni; mix some hot soup into cream, then add into the rest of the soup. Serve. Garnish with sprig of parsley.

This recipe may be doubled or tripled and some frozen. Only 1 "bouquet garni" need be added.

Verona Gehring, Branch No. 1810, Platte Center, NE

MEAT BALL CHOWDER

2 lb. ground beef
2 tsp. seasoned salt
1/8 tsp. pepper
2 eggs, slightly beaten
1/4 c. parsley
1/4 c. fine cracker crumbs
2 Tbsp. milk
3 Tbsp. flour
1 Tbsp. salad oil
4 to 6 onions, cut in eighths

6 c. tomato juice
6 beef bouillon cubes
6 carrots, sliced (3 c.)
3 to 4 potatoes, diced (2 to 3 c.)
1/4 c. long grain rice
1 Tbsp. sugar
2 tsp. salt
2 bay leaves
1/2 to 1 tsp. marjoram (optional)
1 (12 oz.) can Mexicorn

Combine meat, seasoned salt, pepper, eggs, parsley, cracker crumbs, and milk. Mix thoroughly. Form into balls about the size of a walnut. Makes about 40.

Dip in flour. Heat oil in 8 to 10 quart kettle. Lightly brown meat balls on all sides (or drop unbrowned into boiling vegetables). Add remaining ingredients (except add corn last 10 minutes of cooking). Bring to slow boil for 30 minutes or until vegetables are tender. (If dinner must wait, turn off heat at this point.) Makes 6 to 7 quarts.

Genevieve Johnson, Branch No. 5915, Grassflat, PA

MOM'S CHICKEN VEGETABLE SOUP

1 cut up chicken
1/2 c. rice
1 small head cabbage
1 small sliced onion
2 cubes chicken bouillon

1 large can or pkg. mixed
    vegetables
1 can tomato soup or 1 pt. home
    canned tomatoes with juice

Cook chicken until almost tender in 3 quart kettle filled with water. Add rice and onion; cook a little longer. Add cabbage and chicken bouillon. Cook until cabbage is almost tender. Add vegetables and cook until almost tender. Add tomato soup or canned tomatoes and cook for an additional 15 to 20 minutes on low heat. Season to taste.

Paulette Gross, Branch No. 2471, Yankton, SD

CHEESE SOUP

5 chicken cubes
1 1/2 qt. water

1 c. diced celery
1 c. diced onion

Boil until tender.

Add:

1 (8 oz.) broccoli
1 (8 oz.) cauliflower

2 cans cream of chicken soup
1 lb. Velveeta cheese

I usually add some hot Velveeta cheese. Simmer slowly. *Enjoy!*

Florence Maki, Branch No. 3339, Esko, MN

110

BEER CHEESE SOUP

½ c. butter
1 c. flour
4 cans chicken broth soup
1½ c. half & half cream
1 (16 oz.) jar Cheez Whiz

1 can beer
1 Tbsp. Worcestershire sauce
½ tsp. yellow food coloring
¼ c. chives

Melt butter and mix in flour. Stir over low heat and make sure lumps are gone. Add chicken broth and half & half. Heat on low for 5 minutes. Add Cheez Whiz, beer, Worcestershire sauce, food coloring, and chives. Heat on low for 15 minutes, stirring occasionally.

Debbie Link, Branch No. 3984, Washburn, ND

CANADIAN CHEESE SOUP

½ c. butter or oleo
½ c. flour
½ tsp. salt
1½ pt. (3 c.) milk
7 oz. (scant 2 c.) cheese, grated
(use about ¾ American and
¼ Cheddar)

¼ c. celery
¼ c. onion
¼ c. green peppers
¼ c. carrots
1 pt. (2 c.) chicken broth (may be
canned)

1. Melt butter or oleo and blend in flour. Cook for about 5 minutes on low heat. Add salt and milk; cook until thick.
2. Turn down heat and add grated cheese. Stir until melted, keeping heat low.
3. Parboil vegetables in chicken stock and add to cheese and milk.
4. Bring to simmering stage, but *do not boil* or cheese will curdle.
5. Check for salt. Add if needed.
6. Add paprika to give a delicate flavor. Yield: 8 servings.

Maxine Wilson, Branch No. 4734, West Lafayette, IN

CHEDDAR CHOWDER

2 c. boiling water
2 c. diced potatoes
½ c. sliced carrots
½ c. sliced celery
¼ c. chopped onion
1½ tsp. salt
¼ tsp. pepper

¼ c. margarine
¼ c. flour
2 c. milk
2 c. (8 oz.) shredded Cracker
Barrel brand sharp natural
Cheddar cheese
1 c. cubed, cooked ham

Add water to potatoes, carrots, celery, onion, salt, and pepper. Cover and simmer for 10 minutes. Do not drain. Make white sauce with the margarine, flour and milk. Add cheese; stir until melted. Add ham and undrained vegetables. Heat. Do not boil. Serves 6 to 8.

Varsity Chowder: Omit ham. Add 8 slices crisp bacon, crumbled.

School Day Chowder: Omit ham. Add ½ pound sliced frankfurters.

Midwest Chowder: Omit ham. Add 2 cups (one 1 pound can) cream style corn.

Eileen Ritter, Branch No. 224, Grand Haven, MI

MUSHROOM SOUP
(Slovak style)

3 Tbsp. butter
2 small onions, chopped
⅛ c. flour
½ lb. fresh chopped mushrooms

4 beef boulllon cubes
10 c. hot water
Salt to taste

Optional:

1 (10 oz.) pkg. sq. noodles

Sauerkraut juice to taste

Melt butter. Add onion and brown slightly. Add flour and brown. When flour is brown, add water, slowing stirring slowly to dissolve flour mixture. Add all of the water. Add fresh, clean chopped mushrooms and simmer for 20 minutes. Add bouillon cubes and salt. Taste. Simmer till mushrooms are tender, about 10 minutes more. Cook noodles and serve with sauerkraut juice on the side. Add to each persons taste.

Shirley McCowan, Branch No. 4806, Sheffield, OH

CHILI

4 lb. ground beef, browned
1 large onion, sauteed and
   chopped
2 cloves garlic, crushed
6 cans tomato sauce (16 oz.)

8 stalks celery, sliced
8 Tbsp. chili powder
4 tsp. salt
4 tsp. sugar
4 cans kidney beans (16 oz.)

Cook and stir hamburger, onion and garlic in large pan. Stir in tomatoes, celery, chili powder, salt, sugar, and beans. Cook at 350° for 1½ hours. Serve with crackers or corn chips and shredded cheese.

Anita Nelson, Branch No. 5230, Meckling, SD

CHILI

2 lb. hamburger
3 (2½ c. size) cans red beans or
   kidney beans
1 large onion

2 cans tomato soup or tomato
   juice
3 or 4 tsp. chili powder
Salt and pepper to taste

Brown hamburger and onion. Add remainder and simmer for ½ hour or so.

Edith DeBower, Branch No. 2346, Schuyler, NE

BEST EVER CROCK POT CHILI!

2 lb. ground beef
2 medium onions, chopped
1 tsp. salt
¼ tsp. pepper
4 Tbsp. chili powder
½ tsp. cayenne (red) pepper

2 cans tomato soup
1 can tomatoes, chopped into
    pieces (and juice)
2 cans dark red kidney beans
2 cans chili hot beans
1 c. (or more) tomato juice

Brown ground beef and onions. Drain well. Mix all ingredients together in crock pot and simmer on HIGH temperature for 5 hours or so.

This recipe is for a 5 quart crock pot. You can cut it in half for smaller pot. This is a favorite among the members of St. John's for our annual soup and chili dinner! It's so easy and tastes so *good!*

Mrs. Barbara (Rev. David) Splett, St. John's Lutheran,
Branch No. 5488, Fayetteville, AR

AAL CHILI FOR NESCO

5 lb. ground beef
2 (26 oz.) tomato soup
2 (26 oz.) cans water
2 (46 oz.) tomato juice
2 or 3 c. chopped celery
1 lb. chopped onions

3 (15 oz.) chili beans in their sauce
3 tsp. chili powder
4 Tbsp. salt (or less)
1½ tsp. black pepper
4 to 5 Tbsp. parsley flakes
3 to 4 c. uncooked spaghetti

Brown and fry ground beef. Cook or microwave the celery and onions. Cook spaghetti according to package directions and drain. Mix all ingredients in the Nesco, except spaghetti. Cook together for about 15 minutes or more. Add the spaghetti before serving the chili and heat to almost boiling. Serve with Wisconsin cheese and crackers.

Florence Lisko, Branch No. 1400, Hartford, WI

TEXAS CHILI

1½ lb. ground beef
1 chopped onion
3 cloves garlic, mashed
2 Tbsp. chili powder
1 tsp. cumin
1 tsp. oregano
1 c. hot water
2 beef bouillon cubes

1 or 2 (8 oz.) cans tomato sauce
1 tsp. salt
1 tsp. sugar
½ tsp. white pepper
1 tsp. ground red pepper (optional)
2 large cans small red beans,
    liquid drained off

Brown meat and onion. Add garlic, chili powder, cumin, oregano, bouillon cubes (dissolved in water,) tomato sauce, salt, sugar, peppers, and red beans. Bring to a boil, then simmer for at least 1 hour in a covered pot. To improve flavor, refrigerate for 24 hours and then cook. (Will give spices better chance to enhance.)

Marie Grossnicklaus, Branch No. 1412, Corvallis, OR

KRIS' CHILE

1 lb. ground beef
1 c. chopped onion
1 (1 lb.) can tomatoes
1 (1 lb.) can red kidney beans,
   drained

1 (8 oz.) can tomato sauce
1 tsp. salt
2 tsp. chili powder
1 bay leaf

In heavy skillet, cook meat and onion until meat is browned. Stir in the remaining ingredients. Cover and simmer for 1 hour. Remove bay leaf. Makes 4 servings.

Joe Warren, Branch No. 0207, Ashland, WI

CHILI

5 lb. hamburger
1 (6 lb. 8 oz.) can tomato sauce
   (10 c.)
1 (6 lb. 6 oz.) can crushed
   tomatoes (15 c.)
¾ can (6 lb. 13 oz.) kidney beans
   (12 c.)

2 c. onions, diced
1½ c. celery, diced
5 tsp. salt
4 tsp. chili powder (or more if
   desired)
½ c. sugar

Brown hamburger, celery and onions. Add remaining ingredients and simmer for at least 1 hour.

This is the recipe used at Redeemer Lutheran Church each year for an annual chili supper to benefit a food pantry.

Redeemer Lutheran Church, Branch No. 1568, Waukegan, IL

CHILI FOR A CROWD

½ lb. bacon pieces
2 lb. ground beef
1 small onion, chopped
1 small green pepper, chopped
1 Tbsp. sugar
2 to 3 Tbsp. chili powder

2 tsp. black pepper
1 qt. tomato puree
1 qt. crushed tomatoes
75 to 80 oz. red kidney beans (5
   (15 oz.) cans or 2 (40 oz.)
   cans)

In 6 quart Dutch oven, cook bacon crisp; brown hamburger. Add chopped onion, chopped green pepper and other seasonings. Mix well. Add tomato products and beans. Stir thoroughly. Cover and cook in a 350° oven for 2 hours (no watching or stirring necessary). Makes approximately 5 quarts (25 to 30 servings).

If your crowd is late, no problem. The longer it cooks, the better it gets. Leftovers freeze beautifully.

Mrs. Richard (Mary Ann) Schutt, Branch No. 2013, Gowanda, NY

CALIFORNIA CHILI

Brown together:

3 lb. lean hamburger

2 onions, chopped

Add:

4 tsp. chili powder	1 c. water
1 (8 oz.) can tomato sauce	1 (23 oz.) can Ranch Style beans
1 (6 oz.) can tomato paste	1 (4 oz.) can chopped California
2 (14½ oz.) cans ready cut, peeled	green chilies
tomatoes	

Simmer for 1 hour or longer. If crock pot is used, add browned meat and onion and remaining ingredients to pot. Cook on HIGH for about 1 hour, then keep on LOW. Serve with bowls of chopped onions, chopped tomatoes, chopped olives, grated cheese, Fritos, and salsa. Serves 8.

Gloria Byrd, Santa Maria, CA

CREAM OF BROCCOLI SOUP

2 to 3 medium potatoes	6 c. cold milk
1 c. margarine	1 c. diced ham
½ c. chopped celery	1 pkg. frozen broccoli (or fresh),
½ c. chopped onion	cooked
1 c. flour	1 tsp. Accent
4 tsp. chicken bouillon granules	Salt

Cook potatoes in 2 cups water. Potatoes should be peeled and cubed. Don't overcook (just tender). Set aside.

Melt 1 cup margarine. Add celery and onion. Saute. Add 1 cup flour and bouillon. Stir until blended. Add cold milk. Stir until thick and smooth. Add potato cubes and water, also ham, broccoli, Accent, and salt. Simmer until vegetables are done. Makes enough for 6 people.

Sharon Moenter, Branch No. 4119, Pemberville, OH

BROCCOLI SOUP

Cook for 10 minutes:

2 chicken bouillon cubes	2 c. water
2 pkg. broccoli	

Mix in blender:

2 c. milk	⅓ c. flour
2 c. Velveeta cheese	

Combine all of the preceding and heat. Add 1 cup half & half. Stir in.

Wilma Gast, Branch 1162, Dale, WI

BROCCOLI CHOWDER

1 (10 oz.) pkg. frozen chopped	1 c. milk
broccoli	1 c. shredded Cheddar cheese
1 medium onion, finely chopped	⅛ tsp. ground red pepper
1 (10¾ oz.) can condensed cream	¼ c. peanuts, chopped
of chicken soup	

In a 2 quart saucepan, bring ½ cup water to boiling; add broccoli and onion. Cover and simmer for 5 minutes or till tender. Do not drain. Stir in soup, milk, cheese, and pepper. Cook and stir till heated through. Top each serving with peanuts. Makes 6 side dish servings.

BROCCOLI SOUP

4 c. broccoli, cut in small pieces
1 medium onion
1 carrot, shredded
¼ c. butter or margarine
2 c. milk

1 can cream of chicken soup
    (undiluted)
Pepper
Salt
Paprika

Saute onion, broccoli and carrot until tender in margarine. Stir in milk and soup; cook till heated. Sprinkle with paprika. (Take it easy on the salt as the chicken soup is salted.)

Alice Altman, Branch No. 812, Medina, NY

BROCCOLI SOUP

1 Tbsp. butter
¾ c. chopped onion
6 Tbsp. water
6 bouillon cubes (chicken)
8 oz. thin noodles

2 pkg. (10 oz.) frozen broccoli
⅛ tsp. salt (garlic is good)
1½ lb. Velveeta cheese
Good shake of pepper

Saute onion in butter. Add water and bouillon cubes. Add noodles and cook. Add broccoli and garlic salt. Heat well. Add cheese and pepper. Heat slowly. *Don't* boil. May be frozen.

Verna M. Heitschmidt, Branch 1122, Brighton, CO

LOWFAT CREAM OF BROCCOLI SOUP

1 lb. broccoli, chopped
3 c. water
1 tsp. salt
1 Tbsp. margarine
1 medium to large onion, chopped
¾ tsp. garlic powder

¾ tsp. ginger
¼ tsp. nutmeg
1 c. powdered milk
3 Tbsp. whole wheat flour
    (optional)

1. In a 2½ quart saucepan, heat the margarine and saute onion, stirring in the salt, garlic, ginger, and nutmeg.

2. When onion is soft, but not brown, add chopped broccoli (stalk and all) and cook in 3 cups of water. For extra body, 3 tablespoons of whole wheat flour may be added.

3. When broccoli is tender (after about 10 or 15 minutes), pour the entire contents of the pan into a blender. Add a cup of powdered milk and blend until smooth. Serve while hot. Makes about 4 servings.

Pastor James W. Rehley, Branch No. 1412, Corvallis, OR

BROCCOLI-CHEESE SOUP

1 onion
½ c. margarine
3 cans chicken broth
2 cans water
Salt and pepper

2 (10 oz.) pkg. frozen chopped broccoli
¼ tsp. garlic powder
1 lb. pasteurized process cheese
3 c. half & half

Saute onion in margarine. Add chicken broth, water, and salt and pepper (enough to flavor to taste). Bring to a boil. Add broccoli, garlic powder, and salt and pepper if needed. Cook for 5 minutes. Grate cheese into soup. Add half & half. Heat until cheese is melted and soup is hot enough for taste.

Dee Frantz, Branch No. 2049, Emporia, KS

POTATO SOUP

4 potatoes
1 onion
1 can cream of mushroom soup

½ tsp. salt
1 tsp. soy sauce

Cook potatoes in just enough water to cover potatoes. Saute onion in margarine until light brown. When potatoes are done, add mushroom soup. Do not drain water. Add onion, salt, and soy sauce. Heat. Serves 4 to 6.

Esther Dumler, Branch No. 3107, Loveland, CO

POTATO-CHEESE SOUP

1 qt. pared, diced potatoes
2 c. water
1½ tsp. salt
¼ tsp. pepper
½ c. thinly sliced green onions
    with tops

¼ c. butter
3 Tbsp. flour
3 c. hot milk
1½ c. shredded Cheddar cheese
Paprika

Cook potatoes in water with salt and pepper until tender. Saute onions in butter; blend in flour. Add hot milk, stirring constantly until thick and smooth. Add potatoes with the water and cheese. Heat until cheese is melted. Serve at once. Garnish with paprika. Serves 4 to 6.

Esther Dumler, Branch No. 3107, Loveland, CO

POTATO SOUP

6 medium potatoes (about 2 lb.)
5 c. cold water
1 carrot, washed, scraped and
    pared
1 leek, washed thoroughly (white
    part only)
1 stalk celery, cut into pieces
1 medium onion, sliced

2 tsp. salt
¼ tsp. white pepper
¼ tsp. thyme
¼ tsp. marjoram
1 bay leaf
1 beef bouillon cube
2 Tbsp. butter
3 Tbsp. all-purpose flour

In a heavy saucepan (3 quarts) with a tight cover, place the potatoes, cut into ¼ inch slices, with the water and salt. Cover and bring to a boil. Reduce heat. Add carrot, leek, celery, onion, pepper, thyme, marjoram, and bay leaf. Cover and cook for 1 hour, or until veggies are tender.

With a slotted spoon, remove the carrot, leek, onion, celery, and bay leaf. Discard. Remove 1 cup of the potato broth. With a potato masher, mash the remaining potato mixture until it becomes a fine mush. Dissolve bouillon in the reserved broth. Heat butter over low heat. Mix in flour and stir until bubbly. Add the bouillon mixture gradually to the butter mixture, stirring constantly. Pour the mixture into the soup and mix well. Return to boiling, then simmer gently for 5 to 10 minutes. Makes about 2½ pints of soup.

Donald Fite, Branch 6557, San Antonio, TX

POTATO SOUP

3 c. potatoes, diced
½ c. celery, diced
½ c. onion, diced
½ c. carrots, diced
1½ c. water

2 cubes chicken bouillon
¼ tsp. salt
2 c. milk
1 c. sour cream

In large pot, combine vegetables, water, bouillon cubes, and salt. Cook until tender, about 20 minutes. Mash vegetables; add milk and heat thoroughly. Add sour cream to soup pot just before serving. Serves 6.

Viola White, Branch No. 2568, Fredericktown, MO

POTATO SOUP

5 large potatoes, peeled and diced
5 stalks celery, diced
3 large onions, chopped
1 Tbsp. salt
½ tsp. pepper
1 tsp. dill seed

½ tsp. celery seed
½ tsp. thyme
⅓ c. margarine (⅔ stick)
⅓ c. flour
2 c. milk
1 c. sour cream

Put vegetables into a heavy 4 quart saucepan. Add water to cover. Stir in seasonings. Cook for 15 to 20 minutes until tender. In a medium saucepan, melt the margarine; stir in flour. Gradually add milk. Cook until thickened. Remove from heat. Stir in the sour cream. Stir milk mixture into the soup. Makes 6 servings.

Mrs. Robert Bishop, Branch No. 441, Bloomington, IL

SPECIAL POTATO SOUP

2 stalks celery, sliced
1 medium onion, chopped
2 Tbsp. butter or margarine,
    melted
6 medium potatoes, cubed
2 carrots, sliced
3 c. water
5 chicken flavored bouillon cubes

¾ tsp. seasoned salt
½ tsp. dried whole thyme
½ tsp. rosemary, crushed
Dash of garlic powder
Dash of pepper
2 c. milk
1 c. (4 oz.) shredded Cheddar
    cheese

Saute celery and onion in butter in a large Dutch oven until tender. Add next 9 ingredients; cover and simmer for about 20 minutes or until vegetables are tender. Remove from heat and mash vegetables with a potato masher. Add milk and cheese. Cook, stirring constantly, until cheese is melted. Yield: 10 cups.

Barbara Blombach, Branch No. 5585, LaGrange, KY

COUNTRY POTATO SOUP

3 c. diced raw potatoes
½ c. diced celery
½ c. diced onion
1½ c. water
2 c. chicken bouillon cubes

½ tsp. salt
2 c. milk
2 Tbsp. flour
1 Tbsp. chopped chives (optional)
1 c. sour cream

In a large saucepan, combine potatoes, celery, onion, water, bouillon cubes, and salt. Cover and cook over low heat until vegetables are tender, about 20 minutes. Add 1 cup milk. Stir and heat thoroughly.

In a medium bowl, mix sour cream, flour, chives, and remaining cup of milk. Gradually add this mixture to the soup, stirring constantly over low heat until soup is thickened. Yields 6 cups.

Dee Frantz, Branch No. 2049, Emporia, KS

CABBAGE PATCH SOUP

1 lb. ground beef
3 slices bacon, diced
½ c. diced celery
1 (16 oz.) can tomatoes
¼ c. margarine
1½ c. water

1 onion, thinly sliced
1 can red kidney beans
Salt and pepper to taste
1 tsp. chili powder
2 c. shredded cabbage

Brown beef and bacon; drain. Drain and rinse kidney beans. Combine all ingredients and simmer for 1½ hours. Amounts of bacon, water and cabbage can be varied as desired. Serves 4 to 6.

Esther Dumler, Branch No. 3107, Loveland, CO

119

CABBAGE SOUP

48 oz. tomato juice*
48 oz. water*
1 (2 serving) dry onion soup
3 beef bouillon cubes
1 pt. tomatoes
8 oz. mushrooms

4 to 6 stalks celery
2 to 4 carrots
1 Tbsp. dry parsley
⅛ tsp. garlic powder
Cabbage (as needed)

Slice celery and carrots thinly. Mix with other ingredients in large pot. Add cabbage to make full soup. Bring to a boil. Reduce heat and cook slowly for at least 1 hour. Add seasoned salt to taste.

* Or, use 2 quarts juice and 1 quart water.

Marilyn Schade, Branch No. 1700, Richmond, MI

COLORADO CHILE
(Mexican)

1 lb. cubed stew meat
3 Tbsp. flour
2 tsp. chile powder
1 large onion, chopped
1 clove garlic, minced

¼ tsp. ground comino
1 bay leaf
4 c. water
Salt and pepper to taste

Brown meat in oil. Add flour and brown. Add next 4 ingredients. Cook until onion is tender, then add water slowly. Stir and bring to a boil. Reduce heat. Add bay leaf and simmer until meat is tender, approximately 2 hours. Salt and pepper to taste.

Serve with Mexican Rice (recipe following), Refried Beans (recipe following), and flour tortillas. Can also be used in making burritos.

Jan McLaughlin, Branch No. 3107, Loveland, CO

MEXICAN RICE

2 c. raw rice
2 Tbsp. bacon drippings
⅛ tsp. comino
½ tsp. black pepper
½ tsp. garlic powder

1 c. chicken broth*
2 tomatoes, chopped
Salt to taste
3 c. water

Saute rice and seasonings in bacon drippings for 3 minutes. Add chicken broth, tomatoes, and water. Mix well. Cover and cook for 20 minutes. Serve smothered with Colorado Chile.

* Can use instant crystals dissolved in 1 cup water.

Jan McLaughlin, Branch No. 3107, Loveland, CO

REFRIED BEANS

3 c. dried pinto beans
1 medium onion
1 clove garlic
¼ to ½ tsp. ground comino

1 tsp. sugar
Salt and pepper to taste
Water

Wash beans. Beans are more flavorful if soaked overnight, but may be cooked right away. Put beans in pan with large amount of water. Add whole peeled onion, whole garlic clove and all seasonings. Simmer for at least 2 hours or until beans are soft. Add water, as needed, during cooking. When beans are done, remove onion and garlic.

Mash beans. Add touch of garlic powder and 1 to 2 tablespoons bacon drippings. Salt to taste. Heat until all of bacon drippings are absorbed.

Use on the side with Colorado Chile and Mexican Rice or use in burritos.
Jan McLaughlin, Branch No. 3107, Loveland, CO

SPLIT PEA WITH HAM SOUP

2 c. dried split peas
1½ qt. water
1 ham bone (about 1½ lb.)
1 onion, sliced
1 c. sliced celery
1 c. grated carrots

1½ tsp. salt
1 tsp. crushed basil
¼ c. oleo
¼ c. flour
2 c. milk

In a large saucepan, combine peas, water, bone, onion, celery, carrots, salt, and basil. Bring to boiling; reduce heat and simmer for 1½ to 2 hours. Stir flour into melted oleo in a separate saucepan. Cook until bubbly. Gradually add milk, stirring constantly. Bring to boiling. Cook for 1 minute. Stir white sauce into soup. Serves 8.
Deborah Chellew, Loveland, CO

MEXICAN STEW

2 lb. hamburger
1 large onion
1 qt. plus 1 pt. tomato juice
1 can mushroom soup
2 cans green beans (whole)

5 carrots, sliced
5 potatoes, diced
5 "squirts" of Tabasco sauce
Salt and pepper to taste

Brown hamburger and onion. Add all other ingredients. Bake for 3 hours at 300°. Makes over 3 quarts.

Lori Anderson, Branch 6872, Bricelyn, MN

HAMBURGER SOUP

1 lb. hamburger
4 c. water
2½ c. tomato juice
⅓ c. potatoes or ⅓ c. long
    cooking rice

1 c. onions, chopped
1 c. chopped celery
1 can chopped carrots
Salt to taste
1 can green beans

Brown hamburger. Put all ingredients, except green beans, in large kettle and cook slowly for 2 hours, then add green beans. Simmer for about 15 minutes. Serves 6 to 8.

Esther Dumler, Branch No. 3107, Loveland, CO

HAMBURGER SOUP

2 lb. ground beef (or turkey)
1 large can (5¾ c.) tomato juice
1 c. stewed tomatoes
2 c. chopped celery
1 c. sliced carrots
2 c. French green beans
2 c. sliced cabbage

1 bay leaf
1 Tbsp. garlic powder
2 tsp. basil
2 tsp. oregano
2 tsp. onion flakes
1 Tbsp. Worcestershire sauce
1 c. drained canned mushrooms

In a large saucepan, brown meat. Drain off fat. In a deep kettle, combine all other ingredients and add meat. Simmer for 2 hours. Stir often.

Edna Gawry, Branch No. 258, Buffalo, NY

CROCK POT SPLIT PEA SOUP

1 lb. split peas
2 qt. water
Ham bone and/or ham chunks
½ tsp. pepper
1 tsp. garlic

1 onion, chopped
1½ c. carrots
3 c. cubed potatoes
½ c. chopped celery

Put all ingredients into slow cooker. Cover and cook for 10 to 12 hours. If the cooker is low wattage, it may take longer.

Arlene E. Knutson, Branch No. 5616, Tuttle, ND

SPLIT PEA SOUP

2½ c. green split peas
1 c. diced carrots
1 c. diced celery

½ c. diced onions
1½ lb. pork sausage

Cook peas in 3 quarts of water for 30 minutes in large kettle. Brown sausage in frying pan. Add vegetables and meat to soup, cooking slowly and stirring occasionally until peas are tender (about 2 hours). Add more water if needed.

Leftover soup can be frozen.

Alma Schudde, Branch No. 2189, Oregon City, OR

CREAM OF WILD RICE SOUP

3 c. cooked wild rice
1 large onion, finely diced
1 carrot, finely diced
1 rib celery, finely diced
1 c. finely diced ham

½ c. butter
¾ c. flour
8 c. chicken broth
1 c. half & half

Prepare the wild rice. In a 4 to 5 quart soup kettle, saute the onion, carrot, celery, and ham in butter for about 8 minutes or until the vegetables have softened slightly. Sift in the flour, a little at a time, stirring and cooking until the flour is blended in, but do not let it brown.

Slowly add the chicken broth, stirring until all of the flour-butter-vegetable mixture is blended well. Add the wild rice and adjust seasonings as desired. Heat thoroughly. Add the half & half and reheat gently, but do not boil.

Linda Reiser, Branch No. 615, Grand Island, NE

CREAM OF WILD RICE SOUP

2 c. cooked wild rice (½ c. uncooked)
1 large onion, diced
1½ ribs (from stalk) celery, diced
1 large can mushrooms
½ c. butter
1 c. flour

8 c. hot chicken broth
Salt
Pepper
1 c. light cream or half & half
1 to 2 Tbsp. dry white wine (optional)

Prepare wild rice according to package or basic directions. Saute onion, celery and mushrooms in butter for about 3 minutes or just until vegetables soften. Sprinkle in flour, stirring and cooking until it is mixed in, but do not let it begin to brown.

Slowly add chicken stock, stirring until all flour, butter and vegetable mixture is blended well. Add rice and season to taste with salt and pepper. Heat thoroughly. Stir in cream. Add dry white wine if desired. Heat gently, but do not boil. Serves 12.

Mrs. Catie Belleveau, Branch No. 6085, Bemidji, MN

MINNESOTA WILD RICE SOUP

½ c. wild rice
1½ qt. chicken broth
½ c. chopped onions
½ c. diced celery
1 small stalk broccoli, chopped fine

2 small potatoes, diced
1 heaping Tbsp. bacon bits
1 c. milk, heated

Cook rice and chicken broth with onion and celery. Add broccoli and diced potatoes. Boil until rice is done. Add bacon bits and milk. (Do not add cold milk as it will separate.) Bring to boil. Take off heat and add 6 slices of Velveeta cheese or equal amount of Cheez Whiz. Add more liquid if necessary. Serves 6 to 8 people.

Dennis and Karen Martin, Branch No. 1073, Crookston, MN

WILD RICE SOUP

1 c. wild rice
3 to 4 c. water (or chicken broth)
1 tsp. salt (omit salt if using broth)
2 c. cooked wild rice
1 large onion, finely diced
1 large carrot, finely diced
1 rib celery, finely diced

1 c. finely diced meat (chicken or turkey)
½ c. butter or margarine
4 Tbsp. flour
8 c. chicken broth
Salt and white pepper to taste
1 c. light cream or half & half

Wash wild rice by rinsing well in cold water and draining. Place washed wild rice in heavy saucepan with water. Bring to boil; reduce heat and simmer, covered, for 40 to 50 minutes or until rice is tender and most of the grains have split slightly. Drain any excess liquid and fluff with a fork.

Prepare the wild rice. In a 4 or 5 quart soup kettle, saute onion, carrot, celery, and meat in the margarine or butter for about 3 minutes or until the vegetables have softened slightly. Sift in the flour, a little bit at a time, stirring and cooking until the flour is blended in well, but do not let it brown.

Slowly add the chicken broth, stirring until all the flour-butter mixture is blended well. Add the wild rice. Adjust seasonings as desired. Heat thoroughly. Add the cream or half & half and reheat gently, but do not boil.

Twyla Zaske, Branch No. 1784, Renville, MN

HEARTY TURKEY 'N RICE SOUP

2 chicken bouillon cubes
2 c. boiling water
½ c. celery slices
½ c. carrot slices
¾ lb. Velveeta pasteurized process cheese spread, cubed

1½ c. cooked rice
1½ c. chopped, cooked turkey or chicken
1 (4 oz.) can mushrooms, drained

Dissolve bouillon in water; add celery and carrots. Cover and simmer for 20 to 25 minutes or until vegetables are tender. Add remaining ingredients; stir until process cheese spread is melted. Makes 5 (1 cup) servings.

Mrs. Elizabeth Buck, Branch No. 102, Zumbrota, MN

TURKEY SOUP

3 to 4 lb. turkey legs or drumettes
1 large onion, diced
2 c. diced celery
2½ c. diced carrots
½ tsp. rosemary leaves

1 Tbsp. parsley flakes
1 small bay leaf
4 chicken bouillon cubes
2 c. cooked rice or macaroni

Put turkey in large Dutch oven and cover with water; bring to a boil. Reduce heat and simmer for about 2 hours. Remove turkey and set aside to cool. To broth, add all of the ingredients, except the rice or macaroni. Simmer until the vegetables are done. Remove the turkey from the bones and dice it. Add the turkey and the rice or macaroni to the broth; simmer for 10 minutes longer. Salt and pepper to taste.

Darla Springer, Peshtigo, WI, Branch No. 5515, Marinette, WI

EUROPEAN VEGETABLE SOUP
(Microwave)

1 c. potatoes, diced
2 medium carrots, thinly sliced
3 c. cabbage, coarsely shredded
1 (1 lb.) ham slice (with bone), diced
1 (1 lb.) can kidney beans, drained

1 (8 oz.) can tomato sauce with onion
⅛ tsp. instant minced garlic
1 tsp. salt (less if ham is very salty)
½ tsp. pepper
1 qt. water

Cook first 3 ingredients on HIGH for 6 to 8 minutes until tender. Add remaining ingredients. Cook on HIGH for 10 minutes. Stir. Cook for another 10 minutes until heated through. Yield: 2½ quarts.

Sharon Lee Stewart, Branch No. 4850, Tuscaloosa, AL

ITALIAN MEATBALL MAIN-DISH SOUP

½ lb. ground beef
¼ tsp. salt
Dash of pepper
½ c. sliced celery
¼ c. chopped onion
1 medium clove garlic, minced
¼ tsp. Italian seasoning
1 c. carrots, diced
4 Tbsp. beef stock (if desired)

2 cans bean and bacon soup
2½ cans water
1 c. cooked macaroni (optional)
1 (8 oz.) can kidney beans
1 (8 oz.) can tomatoes
2 Tbsp. chopped parsley
1 can tomato soup
1 c. potatoes, diced

Season meat with salt and pepper; brown with onion. Add rest of ingredients and cook until vegetables are done.

This soup was served in the soup kitchen at Lethbridge, Alberta, Canada in 1987.

Gretchen Wiedman, Branch No. 5844, Columbia City, IN

HAM AND VEGETABLE CHOWDER

1 qt. water
1 (10 oz.) frozen chopped broccoli
2 c. cut up, cooked smoked ham
2 c. thinly sliced carrots
2 c. thinly sliced celery

½ c. chopped onion
½ tsp. salt
2 c. milk
½ c. Bisquick
8 oz. Swiss cheese, cut in cubes

Heat water, broccoli, ham, carrots, celery, onion, and salt to boiling. Reduce heat; cover and simmer for 10 minutes. Gradually stir milk into Bisquick (it will be lumpy). Stir into ham mixture and heat to boiling, stirring constantly. Boil and stir for 1 minute. Remove from heat and add cubed cheese. Cover and let set until cheese is partially melted, about 5 minutes. Stir before serving. Serves 6.

Gladys Koenig, Branch No. 449, Lockport, NY

CLAM CHOWDER

2 c. diced raw potatoes
3 c. water
1 tsp. salt
1 (10½ oz.) can cream of celery
soup

2 c. milk
1 Tbsp. instant minced onion
2 (7 oz.) cans minced clams (do
not drain)

Simmer potatoes in water and salt in saucepan for 15 minutes until tender. Drain. Stir in soup, milk, onion, and clams. Heat thoroughly. Makes 6 servings.

Laura Johnson, Branch No. 2049, Emporia, KS

CHINESE EGG DROP SOUP - DUN FAR TONG

1 egg, beaten
2 drops of vegetable oil
1 qt. chicken stock (may use 4
bouillon cubes in water)
¾ tsp. salt (omit if using bouillon
cubes)

¼ tsp. sugar
Thinly sliced green onion
1 Tbsp. cornstarch, mixed in a
little water

Bring stock to boiling; thicken with cornstarch. Turn heat off. Add egg slowly, stirring constantly. Add seasoning and onion. Serves 4.

This is a favorite in oriental restaurants, but rarely served in a Chinese home. When I was a child, my German mother made it for Sunday dinner, but you won't find it in German cookbooks. It is also called "Egg Flower Soup."

Vivian Merkel, Lamplighter, Branch No. 3984, Washburn, ND

GOLDEN CREAM SOUP

3 c. chopped potatoes
1 c. water
½ c. celery slices
½ c. carrot slices
¼ c. chopped onion
1 tsp. parsley flakes

½ tsp. salt
Dash of pepper
1 chicken bouillon cube
1½ c. milk
2 Tbsp. flour
½ lb. Velveeta, cubed

Combine potatoes, water, celery, carrots, onion, parsley flakes, seasonings, and bouillon cube. Cover and simmer for 15 to 20 minutes till vegetables are tender. Gradually add milk to flour, stirring till well blended. Add milk mixture to vegetables; cook until thickened. Add Velveeta and stir until melted. Makes 4 (¼ cup) servings.

Skipper Lindenmayer, Branch No. 6533, Boulder, CO

SCANDINAVIAN FRUIT SOUP

1½ lb. mixed dried fruit (prunes,
apricots, pears, raisins)
1 stick cinnamon
½ c. tapioca

¼ c. cornstarch
1 c. sugar
2 Tbsp. wine

Rinse fruit. Cover fruit, cinnamon and tapioca with cold water; bring to a boil until fruit is softened. Remove cinnamon. Add sugar and cornstarch mixed with a little cold water. Cook until clear. Remove from heat and add wine. Serve hot or cold.

Karen Pamperin, St. Luke (ELCA), Branch No. 6304, Slinger, WI

FARINA DUMPLINGS

4 eggs, beaten	1 c. farina
4 Tbsp. melted butter	½ tsp. salt

Beat eggs well. Add melted butter (or oleo) and salt. Let stand for 10 minutes. Drop by teaspoon into boiling broth (preferably chicken). To make dumplings, drop from spoon. Dip spoon into hot broth before spooning up dumpling mixture.

Popular soup served at Slovenian weddings.

Olga (Polvanec) Schley, Branch No. 625, Dorset, OH

SCHWEMM CLOESE - VERY LIGHT DUMPLINGS

Butter (about the size of an egg)	1 c. flour
1 c. milk	2 eggs

Add butter the size of an egg to 1 cup of milk and let come to a boil. Dump 1 cup flour into the boiling milk. Remove from the heat and stir until it is very smooth. Separate the eggs. Add the 2 egg yolks to the flour/milk mixture. Beat the egg whites until light and fluffy, then add them to the mixture. Moisten a teaspoon and take off teaspoonfuls of the mixture; add to your soup. Cover the soup and cook for 10 minutes or so. Do not uncover the soup during this time.

These are absolutely delicious light dumplings and go very well in split pea soup or in chicken soup.

The recipe is very old and has been in our family for almost 100 years and continues to be a favorite!!!

Theresa Gremel, Branch No. 5754, Boulder, CO

WIDOWS' STEW

1 lb. venison (or beef stew meat)	1 c. sliced carrots
1 pkg. dry onion soup mix	1 c. sliced potatoes
1 can cream of celery soup	2 Tbsp. margarine
1 (15 oz.) can chili hot beans	Water (as needed)

Flour and brown meat in melted margarine. Add remaining ingredients and ½ cup water (or more as needed). Bring to a boil. Cover and simmer until meat and vegetables are tender, about 2 hours. Stir occasionally and add water, as needed, to prevent burning.

Cooking time can be cut in half by using canned vegetables instead of fresh.

Marlene Duerr, Branch No. 3289, Milwaukee, WI

PHEASANT STEW WITH BAKING POWDER DUMPLINGS

2 boned pheasants
1 c. chopped onion
6 to 8 carrots, sliced

1 c. chopped celery
1 can green beans
Flour with salt and pepper to taste

Brown bite-size pieces of floured pheasant. In cooker, add carrots, onion, celery, and beans. Add enough water to form a thin gravy. Season to taste. Simmer a good 4 hours. When ready, add dumplings. Can add cornstarch mixture to thicken gravy if necessary.

Baking Powder Dumplings:

2 c. flour
1 tsp. salt
2 tsp. baking powder
2 Tbsp. parsley

½ c. chopped green onions
1 egg, beaten
Milk

Beat 1 egg in measuring cup and fill with milk to make 1 cup. Beat into flour mixture. Drop by spoons into boiling stew. Cover tightly and return to boil. Reduce heat (don't lift cover). Simmer for 12 to 15 minutes.

Beth Storlie, Branch No. 6220, Taylor, WI

GROUND BEEF STEW

1½ lb. ground beef
2 ribs celery, sliced
2 large carrots, sliced

5 medium potatoes, cut in eighths
3 c. water
1 pkg. McCormick stew seasoning

Brown meat and drain grease. Add water and seasoning mix. Add celery, carrots and potatoes. Cover and let simmer for 45 minutes to 1 hour, until vegetables are tender. Serves 4.

Gabi Stroud, Branch 1221

STEW FOR TWO (OR THREE)

1 large potato
1 pt. stewed tomatoes
¾ lb. ground beef
½ medium size onion
½ tsp. soup blend seasoning

4 Tbsp. catsup
1 tsp. Worcestershire sauce
1 pinch of salt
Pepper to taste

Break meat into small pieces and dice onion. Fry them both until they start to turn brown. Cut the potato into ½ to ¾ inch pieces and put them into a crock pot on LOW. Add the Worcestershire sauce and the salt. When the stew begins to get warm, add the soup blend and the catsup. Pepper it anytime. Cook on HIGH for 2½ to 3 hours and let simmer on LOW for 1 hour.

Douglas A. Turner, Branch No. 2320, Fowler, MI

OVEN STEW

2 lb. beef stew meat, browned
    without flour
3 Tbsp. quick cooking tapioca
3 to 6 carrots, cut in 1 inch slices
3 to 6 potatoes, cut in small
    chunks

1 medium onion, diced
1 c. celery, diced
1 (8 oz.) tomato sauce
18 oz. water
Salt and pepper to taste

Cover and bake at 250° for 5 hours.

Charlotte Steffens, Branch No. 2386, Potter, NE

RANCH STEW

1 lb. ground beef
Onion (as desired)
Green pepper (as desired)
1 Tbsp. chili powder
1 can stewed tomatoes

1 can whole kernel corn
1 can kidney beans
Salt and pepper to taste
1 Tbsp. oil

Saute onion and green pepper in 1 tablespoon oil. Brown meat and add chili powder, salt and pepper. Add juice from can of tomatoes, corn, and beans. Simmer for 30 minutes or until slightly thickened. Add tomatoes, corn, and beans; heat thoroughly. Serve with corn bread.

Rev. James Witschorke, Branch No. 6196, Marion, TX

ALASKA WHALE STEW

1 (105 ton) blue or sufur bottom
    whale
7326 lb. potatoes
2276 lb. carrots
104 lb. salt

52 gal. Tabasco hot sauce
1896 lb. onions
1908 gal. tomato sauce
927 lb. celery
76 lb. black pepper

Place whale in pot with tomato sauce. Cook at 300° for 4 hours. Add onions, potatoes, carrots, celery, salt, pepper, and hot sauce. Simmer for 36 hours. Serves 347,161. If you care for hare in your stew, add a 2 pound rabbit.

Lord of Life Lutheran, "Heavenly Dishes" Cookbook,
Branch No. 6677, North Pole, Alaska

HEARTY MEATBALL AND VEGETABLE STEW

The steamed cabbage wedges arranged around the edge of the serving platter complement the stew. (Very pretty.)

1 lb. bulk pork sausage
2 Tbsp. oil
1/4 c. flour
1/8 tsp. pepper
1 c. water
1 (10¾ oz.) can condensed
    chicken broth
3 carrots, sliced

2 stalks celery, sliced
1 large (1 c.) onion, sliced
1 (12 oz.) can whole kernel corn
    (undrained)
2 c. water
1 medium head cabbage, cut into
    8 wedges

Shape pork sausage into 25 balls. In large skillet, brown meatballs in oil, carefully turning. Remove meatballs from skillet. Reserve 2 tablespoons meat drippings in skillet; stir in flour and pepper. Gradually add 1 cup water and chicken broth. Cook until mixture boils and thickens, stirring constantly. Add carrots, celery, onion, and meatballs. Simmer, uncovered, for 20 to 30 minutes or until vegetables are tender and stew is thickened, stirring occasionally. Add corn and heat thoroughly.

In large saucepan, heat 2 cups water to boiling; add cabbage. Cover and cook for 8 minutes or until crisp tender. Drain. Arrange cabbage wedges in a ring, cut side down, around edge of serving platter. Spoon stew into center of cabbage ring. Serves 6 to 8.

Viola Pergande, Branch No. 3107, Loveland, CO

SNOW BELT STEW

2 slices bacon
1½ lb. round steak, cubed
1 large onion, diced
1 env. au jus gravy mix
½ c. beer

½ c. water
1 Tbsp. brown sugar
Rice or mashed potatoes
¼ c. grated cheese (optional)

Cook bacon until crisp in large skillet. Remove and crumble. Cook meat and onion in bacon drippings until meat is brown and onion is tender. Stir in contents of envelope of au jus gravy mix, beer, water, and brown sugar. Cover and simmer for 30 to 45 minutes or until tender. Stir in bacon; spoon into serving dish. Serve stew over rice or mashed potatoes. Sprinkle with cheese if desired.

Julie Padilla, Branch No. 3107, Loveland, CO

ELEPHANT STEW

1 elephant
2 c. salt

2 c. pepper

Cut elephant into 1 inch pieces. (Allow approximately 72 hours for this procedure.) Frequently add pinches of salt and pepper. Cook over kerosene fire for about 4 weeks at 465°. If more than 3,800 guests are expected for dinner, 2 rabbits may be added, but do this only if necessary as most people do not like to find "hare" in their stew!!

Connie Davis, Branch No. 3107, Loveland, CO

BAKED STEW

2 lb. stew meat (do not brown)
1 c. canned tomatoes
1 tsp. sugar
6 small carrots, cut up
3 medium potatoes, quartered
1½ tsp. salt

½ c. chopped celery
1 onion
1 slice bread, broken
1 c. water
2 Tbsp. tapioca

Mix all ingredients together in a large baking dish or Dutch oven. Bake, covered. Bake in a 325° oven for 3½ hours.

Doris Seevers, Branch No. 382, St. Louis, MO

CROCK-POT VENISON STEW

2 lb. breast/shoulder venison
2 Tbsp. oil
6 c. boiling water
2 tsp. salt
¼ tsp. pepper
2 Tbsp. seasoned flour

4 medium rutabagas, diced
4 carrots, diced
2 turnips, diced
4 onions, diced
2 celery stalks, chopped
¼ c. green peppers, chopped

Cut the venison into 1 inch cubes. Roll in seasoned flour and brown in a small amount of oil in a heavy skillet. Put the browned venison and boiling water into a crock-pot. Add the salt, pepper and the vegetables. Cook on LOW heat for 8 hours or longer. If the liquid gets low, add additional boiling water. When done, add the remaining seasoned flour moistened with water to thicken the remaining liquid. Yield: 8 servings.

Robert A. Knudsen, Branch No. 5568, Anderson, SC

RUNZA BUNS

1 lb. hamburger
1 medium can sauerkraut
1 box hot roll mix

½ tsp. oregano
2 tsp. dry onion soup mix
1 c. Cheddar cheese

Brown hamburger, oregano and dry soup mix. Prepare roll mix as directed. *Don't* let rise. Roll into squares. Top with hamburger, sauerkraut, and cheese. Fold over and pinch ends to close. Bake at 400° for 20 minutes.

Mary Hohbach, Branch No. 2306, Marcus, IA

131

HOT HAM SANDWICHES

Ham slices
Swiss cheese slices

Sesame seed buns

Mix together:

½ c. butter
2 Tbsp. grated onion

2 Tbsp. mustard
1 Tbsp. poppy seeds

Place ham slice and Swiss cheese slice on sesame seed bun, which has been spread with 1 tablespoon of the preceding mixture. Wrap in foil and refrigerate for 1 hour. Bake at 350° for 20 minutes. Makes enough spread for 12 to 14 buns.

May be frozen, but allow longer baking time at lower temperature.
Verna Borgmann, Branch No. 401, Washington, MO

BENEFIT OX ROAST

100 lb. roast beef
3 lb. onions
3 lb. green peppers
6 lb. apples
6 lb. carrots
3 lb. tomatoes
3 lb. turnips
1½ tsp. nutmeg
5 tsp. mixed pickling spices

1½ tsp. garlic powder
1 tsp. red pepper
5 tsp. paprika
3½ tsp. chili powder
10 bay leaves (less if desired)
4 Tbsp. Worcestershire sauce
½ lb. salt
Cornstarch (till gravy thickens)
½ gal. water

Arrange meat in pans. Put vegetables on meat. Combine spices and sprinkle on top of meat. Add water and Worcestershire sauce. Bake in slow oven (325°) for 8 to 12 hours. Remove bay leaves and discard. Shred meat and mash vegetables. Thicken gravy and mix all together. Serve on buns. Serves about 350, depending on meat fat.

Members Branch No. 1570, Oberlin, KS

HUMMUS

2 c. cooked garbanzo beans
½ c. sesame butter or peanut
    butter
¼ c. lemon juice
2 cloves garlic

1 large onion
¼ tsp. pepper and paprika
⅛ tsp. cayenne pepper
⅓ c. fresh parsley

Blend all ingredients in food processor. Add water if needed. Serve chilled with lettuce, sprouts, and tomato in pita bread.
Lorraine Just, Branch 5865, Sun City/Ruskin

LASAGNA IN A BUN

¾ lb. ground beef
1 (8 oz.) can tomato sauce
¼ tsp. oregano
¼ tsp. basil
½ env. dry onion soup mix

1 egg
¾ c. Ricotta or creamed cottage
  cheese, drained
½ c. shredded Mozzarella cheese
8 hard rolls

Brown ground beef. Add tomato sauce, oregano, basil, and dry soup mix; simmer for 10 minutes. Beat egg with Ricotta or cottage cheese separately; set aside. Split rolls and hollow out some of the bread. Spread some of the meat mixture, then the egg and cheese mixture. Sprinkle on some Mozzarella, then a little more meat sauce. Wrap in aluminum foil and bake for 20 minutes at 400°.

Diane Roberts, Branch No. 5331, Toledo, OH

TUNA PATTIE MELT

½ c. quick cooking or
  old-fashioned oatmeal
1 (6½ oz.) can tuna, drained and
  flaked
⅓ c. shredded carrot
1 egg, beaten

¼ c. mayonnaise
2 Tbsp. green onion slices
⅛ tsp. salt (optional)
Dash of pepper
Cheese
1 to 2 Tbsp. vegetable oil

Combine all ingredients, except oil and cheese. Mix well. Shape to form four 3 ½ inch patties. Brown in oil in 12 inch skillet over medium high heat for 3 to 4 minutes or until golden brown. Turn and continue cooking for 3 to 4 minutes, placing cheese triangles on each patty during last 2 minutes of cooking. Serve on hamburger buns with lettuce and tomato if desired.

Mrs. Ronald (Bea) Schultz, Branch 0743, Truman, MN

CORNED BEEF SANDWICHES

1 can corned beef
Chopped cheese (equal to amount
  of corned beef)
2 Tbsp. chopped onion

1 green pepper, chopped
Catsup (enough for spreading
  consistency)
Hamburger buns

Mix all ingredients and put on hamburger buns. Makes 8 to 10 sandwiches.

May place hamburger buns in foil and place in oven until cheese is melted and sandwich is warm. May put on paper towel or waxed paper in microwave oven until warm. Make sandwiches ahead and put in freezer until needed.

Maxine Pulter, Branch No. 2295, Taylor, MI

PIAZZA SANDWICH

1 lb. lean ground beef
½ c. grated Parmesan cheese
¼ c. finely chopped onion
1 (6 oz.) can tomato paste
1 tsp. salt
½ tsp. oregano
⅛ tsp. pepper

1 loaf French bread, cut in half
  lengthwise
5 slices Cheddar cheese, sliced
  diagonally
¼ c. chopped black olives
  (optional)

Combine all ingredients thoroughly, except bread, Cheddar cheese and olives. Spread beef mixture on each half of bread; place on cookie sheet. Broil 5 inches from heat for 10 to 12 minutes. Remove from oven. Top with cheese and olives. Broil for 1 minute longer or until cheese melts.

Eight hard rolls may be substituted for French bread.

Sharon Anderson, Branch 5325, Stratford, IA

RUNZAS
(Makes 55 to 75 Runzas)

Dough:

1¼ oz. dry yeast
2 qt. warm water
14 oz. sugar
1 oz. (1½ Tbsp.) salt

2 lb. 6 oz. flour
8 eggs
5 oz. melted shortening
5 lb. 8 oz. flour

Sprinkle yeast over water. Let stand for 5 minutes. Add sugar, salt and 2 pounds and 6 ounces flour. Beat on medium speed until smooth. Add eggs and shortening. Continue beating. Add remaining 5 pounds and 8 ounces flour to make a soft dough. Knead for 5 minutes. Cover and let rise until double. Punch down. Divide dough into 4 or 5 balls. Roll out each ball and cut into 4x6 inch rectangle (about 3 ounces of dough). Or, weigh out 3 ounce portions and roll each one out individually. For a smaller Runza, weigh 2½ ounces of dough.

Place ⅔ cup to 1 cup of filling on dough. Fold lengthwise and pinch edges of dough securely to seal. Place on baking sheet with sealed edges down. Bake 25 to 30 minutes at 400°F.

Filling:

15 lb. ground beef
15 lb. cabbage
3 large chopped onions
¼ c. Worcestershire sauce
  (optional)

2 oz. salt
1 tsp. pepper

Brown and drain beef. Steam cabbage and onion until slightly underdone. Add seasonings and vegetables to ground beef. Mix lightly.

Joan Gloystein (recipe of Vickie Conell), Branch No. 769, Utica, NE

BURGER BUNS

1 c. catsup
½ c. water
2 Tbsp. sugar
2 Tbsp. cider vinegar
2 tsp. prepared mustard
2 Tbsp. butter

1 c. chopped onion
2 lb. hamburger
Salt to taste
Pepper to taste
1 can chicken gumbo soup

Make a sauce of catsup, water, sugar, vinegar, and mustard. Mix well and put into small jar. May be stored in refrigerator. Melt butter in pan. Add onion. Cook until done. Add hamburger, salt and pepper. Fry until meat is browned and done. Add chicken gumbo soup (undiluted). Add the sauce or as much as desired (I use about ½ of the sauce for 2 pounds of hamburger). Simmer for at least 15 minutes. Fill between buns. *Enjoy!*

Mrs. Dorothy H. Meyer, Branch No. 5935, Loganville, WI

OPEN-WARM SANDWICH

½ lb. raw bacon
½ lb. Velveeta cheese
1 small onion

1 Tbsp. horseradish or mustard
1 Tbsp. mayonnaise

Grind bacon, cheese and onion together. Mix with the mustard or horseradish and mayonnaise. Spread on halves of hamburger buns or hot dog rolls or bread and broil till top bubbles. Watch closely so they do not burn. Freezes well.

Eleanor Miller, Branch No. 2295, Allen Park, MI

MUSTARD SAUCE FOR HAM

½ c. tomato soup
½ c. French salad mustard
½ c. vinegar

½ c. sugar
2 beaten egg yolks

Mix first 4 ingredients on the stove. Add egg yolks last. Cook until slightly thickened.

Martha H. Kahanak, Branch No. 3107, Loveland, CO

SWEETENED CONDENSED MILK

1 c. powdered milk
⅔ c. sugar

⅓ c. boiling water
3 Tbsp. melted butter

Mix all ingredients till sugar and milk are dissolved. Use in any recipe calling for sweetened condensed milk. *Much more inexpensive.*

Cheryl Schultz, Branch No. 3107, Loveland, CO

CHEEZ WHIZ

½ c. water
¾ c. dry milk
2 Tbsp. margarine

Dash of Worcestershire sauce
½ lb. Velveeta

Put all ingredients in double boiler to melt. Stir and cool. Use as the commercial brand. *A lot more inexpensive!*

Cheryl Schultz, Branch No. 3107, Loveland, CO

SPAGHETTI SAUCE

2 tsp. minced garlic
1 large onion
1 lb. ground beef
2 Tbsp. flour
4 c. tomatoes
1 Tbsp. sugar

1 tsp. salt
½ tsp. pepper
1 tsp. Worcestershire sauce
⅔ c. sliced mushrooms (optional)
½ tsp. garlic salt

Cook onion, garlic and ground beef together until brown (not overly brown - just until pink is gone). Drain. Add flour that's been mixed with sugar to remaining ingredients. Pour over drained hamburger. Simmer for ½ hour or longer. Serve with spaghetti or can be used for lasagne.

Donna Phillips, Branch No. 2512, Ord, NE

BRANDIED FRUIT

1 c. sugar
2 slices pineapple, diced
1 (13 to 16 oz.) can sliced peaches,
    drained

5 maraschino cherries

Put fruit in decanter and let stand for 2 weeks. Add all of the preceding ingredients again. Allow to stand for 10 minutes, then stir well, but gently. Stir twice a week. Repeat process every 2 weeks (adding same group of ingredients). Good on ice cream, cake, baked ham, etc. *Do not refrigerate.*

A little of this goes a long way.

Donna Krug, Branch No. 3035, Ft. Collins, CO

JIFFY MUSTARD SAUCE

1 c. dairy sour cream
2 Tbsp. prepared mustard

1 tsp. prepared horseradish

Combine all ingredients. Chill until ready to serve. Makes about 1 cup sauce.
Katherine Fredericksen, Branch No. 1068, Murdo, SD

136

OCCIDENTAL HOT FUDGE SAUCE

2 c. sugar
⅔ c. cocoa
6 Tbsp. flour
1 tsp. salt

2 c. milk
2 Tbsp. butter
2 tsp. vanilla

Mix sugar, cocoa, flour, and salt in top of double boiler. Add milk. Cook until thickened. Remove from heat; add butter and vanilla.

Karen Shields, Branch No. 224, Grand Haven

SPAGHETTI SAUCE

1 lb. ground beef
½ lb. hot sausage
½ c. chopped onion
3 c. tomato juice
12 oz. tomato paste
2 tsp. sugar

1½ tsp. basil
1½ tsp. salt
1 tsp. garlic powder
1 tsp. oregano
½ tsp. pepper

In large saucepan, brown meat with onion; drain. Stir in remaining ingredients. Simmer, uncovered, stirring occasionally for 20 minutes or until desired thickness. Makes 4 cups (serves 6 to 8).

Lorraine Tucker, Branch No. 4845, Youngstown, OH

CREAM ROYALÉ SPAGHETTI SAUCE

¼ c. butter
1 lb. bacon, diced
1 medium onion, chopped
2 carrots, chopped
2 stalks celery, chopped
1 (6 oz.) can tomato paste
¼ tsp. garlic powder

4 (6 oz.) cans mushroom steak
   sauce
2 bay leaves
1 c. sweet cream
½ c. red wine
1 lb. spaghetti
¼ c. Parmesan cheese

Fry bacon and drain. In saucepan, cook onion in butter until tender. Add bacon, carrots, celery, tomato paste, garlic powder, mushroom steak sauce, and bay leaves. Simmer over low heat for 1½ hours. Add cream and wine; heat for 10 minutes. Serve over spaghetti. Cook spaghetti in salted, boiling water; drain and toss in ¼ cup of Parmesan cheese. Serves 4.

David Roth, Branch 1367, Wapato, WI

SALSA

8 c. peeled, chopped tomatoes
2 c. roasted, seeded and chopped
   long green chili peppers
1 c. roasted, seeded and chopped
   jalapeno peppers

¾ c. chopped onions
1½ tsp. salt
2 garlic cloves, minced
1½ c. cider vinegar
2 to 3 Tbsp. sugar

Combine all ingredients in large pan. Bring mixture to a boil; reduce heat and simmer for about 20 minutes. Pour in hot jars, leaving ½ inch head space. Put on lids and process in boiling water bath for 30 minutes (sea level). Add 2 minutes to process time for each 1,000 feet altitude.

I put all of the vegetables through my food grinder.

Barbara Alsum, Branch No. 3107, Loveland, CO

SPAGHETTI SAUCE

2 (15 oz.) cans tomato paste and 2
   cans water
2 (15 oz.) cans tomato sauce and 2
   cans water
1 pkg. French onion soup mix
3 Tbsp. Worcestershire sauce

1 tsp. Tabasco
1 c. catsup
2 Tbsp. sugar
Couple pinches of oregano
Couple pinches of garlic salt

Add plenty of water while cooking. Stir often. Leave on low for 3 to 4 hours. Season to taste with extra sugar and oregano. Add your favorite recipe of meatballs if you so desire.

Vicki Guolee, Branch No. 4693, Rhinelander, WI

NUGGET'S CREAM SAUCE

1 medium size onion
1 clove garlic
3 slices bacon, chopped fine
½ tsp. Lawry's salt
½ tsp. white pepper

3 Tbsp. butter or margarine
3 Tbsp. flour
1½ c. milk
1 (10 oz.) pkg. chopped spinach or
   broccoli

Saute onion, garlic, bacon, and condiments in butter (or margarine). Add flour and cook until a smooth roux is created. Gradually add milk and cook for several minutes to consistency of a medium cream sauce.

Cook vegetable according to package directions. Squeeze all juice from vegetable. Add vegetable to sauce, bring to a slow boil and cook for 5 minutes.

Lillian Fairman, Loveland, CO

MICROWAVE HOT FUDGE SAUCE

½ c. sugar
3 Tbsp. cocoa
1½ tsp. cornstarch

Dash of salt
½ c. water
1 tsp. vanilla

Mix together the first 4 ingredients in a 1 quart casserole. Add the water and vanilla. Stir until blended. Microwave for 1½ minutes, stirring every 30 seconds. Makes 1 cup of sauce for sundaes.

Jane M. Rottmann, Branch No. 4605, Highland, IL

HOT FUDGE SUNDAE SAUCE

2 c. sugar
4 Tbsp. cocoa
Pinch of salt

½ stick oleo
1 can evaporated milk
1 tsp. vanilla

Heat sugar, cocoa and salt until warm to touch. Add oleo and mix, then add evaporated milk. Bring to a boil and cook for 1 minute. Add vanilla. Put on ice cream!

Marguerite Boerger, Branch No. 4734, Delphi, IN

Notes

Vegetables

TO QUICK-FREEZE VEGETABLES

Vegetables for freezing are prepared as for cooking, then blanched (scalded) and packed dry, or with the brine. The dry pack is less trouble and is satisfactory for all vegetables except green peppers.

Blanching vegetables is important because it minimizes loss of flavor and color. To blanch in boiling water, put about one pound of vegetables in a fine-mesh wire basket with a wire cover to hold food under the water and lower into rapidly boiling water, enough to cover food. Cover the kettle and then COUNT THE TIME RECOMMENDED FOR EACH vegetable. After blanching, chill quickly and thoroughly, plunge the vegetables into ice water, or hold under cold running water. When completely chilled, remove and drain, and PACK AT ONCE.

VEGETABLE	HOW PREPARED	BLANCHING
ASPARAGUS	Wash, cut, sort into groups according to thickness of stalk. Blanch, chill, pack.	3 to 4 minutes in boiling water, depending on size.
BEANS, GREEN AND WAX	Wash, stem, slice, cut or leave whole. Blanch, chill, pack.	Cut: 2 minutes in boiling water. Whole: 2½ minutes in boiling water.
BEANS, LIMA	Shell, wash, blanch, chill. Remove white beans, which may be used for cooking. Pack.	1 to 2 minutes in boiling water, depending on size.
CARROTS	Remove tops, wash, scrape. Slice lengthwise or crosswise as preferred, or leave small carrots whole.	Whole: 4½ minutes in boiling water. Sliced: 3 minutes in boiling water.
CAULIFLOWER	Break heads into flowerets about 1 inch across. Wash, blanch, chill, pack.	3 to 4 minutes in boiling water.
CORN, ON COB	Husk, trim away silk and spots. Wash, blanch, chill, pack.	7 minutes in boiling water for slender ears. 9 for medium, 11 for large.
CORN, KERNELS	Same as corn on cob. After chilling, cut off kernels and pack.	
GREENS Beet, Chard, Kale, Mustard, Spinach, Collards, etc.	Wash, discard bad leaves, tough stems. Blanch, chill, pack.	2 minutes in boiling water.
PEAS	Shell, sort, blanch, chill, pack.	1 to 2 minutes in boiling water, depending on size.
PEPPERS, GREEN	Wash, cut away seeds, slice. Blanch, pack in brine of 1 tsp. salt to 1 c. cold water.	3 minutes in boiling water.

VEGETABLES

MICRO FRIED POTATOES
(Microwave)

2 Tbsp. butter
⅓ c. corn flakes
½ tsp. salt

3 medium potatoes, pared and
sliced ½ inch thick
Paprika

In 1 cup glass measure, heat butter for about 30 seconds. Combine salt and corn flakes in small paper sack. Shake potato slices in sack to coat each slice. Arrange slices in 9 inch glass baking dish. Pour melted butter evenly over top and sprinkle with paprika.

Cook potatoes, covered, for about 6 minutes. Remove cover and rotate dish ½ turn; cook, uncovered, for about 4 to 5 minutes more. Let rest, uncovered, for 5 minutes. Makes 3 to 4 servings.

Sandi Johansen, Branch No. 1400, Arbor Vitae, WI

HOLIDAY POTATO DISH

4 lb. unpared potatoes, cooked,
drained and cooled
1 c. chopped onion
1 c. chopped celery
¼ c. butter
1 can cream of mushroom or
cream of chicken soup

1 pt. sour cream
1½ c. shredded Cheddar cheese
½ c. crushed corn flakes or
crackers
3 Tbsp. melted butter

Cut up potatoes. Saute onion and celery in ¼ cup butter. Remove from heat. Stir in soup and sour cream. Mix together potatoes and cheese; place in greased 9x13 inch pan. Pour soup mixture over all and mix well. Cover and refrigerate overnight. (Do not cover with aluminum foil.)

Next day, sprinkle with corn flake or cracker crumbs; drizzle with 3 tablespoons melted butter. Bake at 350° for 1 hour. Makes 12 servings.

Barbara Schreiner, Branch No. 5124, Alma, MI

CREAMY HASH BROWN POTATOES

2 lb. frozen hash brown potatoes,
slightly thawed
1 cube melted butter
½ tsp. pepper
½ tsp. salt
½ c. onion

1 can cream of chicken soup
1 c. sour cream
1 c. half & half
2 c. grated cheese
1 c. potato chips, crumbled

Grease 9x13 inch baking dish. Mix all ingredients together in large bowl; pour all into greased dish. Top with potato chip crumbs. Bake at 325° for 45 minutes.

Joan Schwarz, Branch No. 2986, Torrance, CA

SCALLOPED POTATOES

3 qt. sliced raw potatoes (15)
4 tsp. salt
½ tsp. pepper

6 Tbsp. flour
½ c. melted butter
4 c. hot milk

Place a layer of potatoes in greased roaster or casserole. Mix together salt, pepper, and flour. Sprinkle part over potatoes along with part melted butter. Repeat layering. Pour over hot milk. Bake, covered, for 2 hours at 350°. Uncover and brown at 400° for ½ hour. You may have to adjust time (may be less).

Myrna Sisel, Branch No. 2412, Green Bay, WI

CHEESE POTATOES

24 oz. frozen hash brown potatoes,
   thawed
1 can cream of chicken soup
¾ can milk (use empty soup can)
3 Tbsp. sour cream

1 small onion, chopped
Salt and pepper to taste
1 stick butter or margarine
2 c. Cheddar cheese, shredded
1 c. corn flakes, crushed

Mix preceding ingredients together and pour into 9x13 inch pan. Melt 1 stick of margarine or butter and set aside. Sprinkle 2 cups of shredded Cheddar cheese over potato mixture. Pour ½ of the melted butter over the cheese. Roll out 1 cup of corn flakes to crush. Drizzle the rest of the butter over the corn flakes. Bake for 35 minutes at 350°.

Luann Behnen, Branch No. 5331, Toledo, OH

CHEESE POTATOES

8 medium potatoes
8 oz. sharp cheese
1 tsp. salt

1 pt. whipping cream
¼ c. bread crumbs
4 Tbsp. butter

Boil potatoes with skins on. Cook overnight if possible. Peel and shred on medium grater. Shred cheese on same. In 2 quart casserole, arrange alternating layers of potatoes and cheese. Add salt and pour cream over the potatoes. Top with buttered crumbs. Bake in 350° oven until heated.

Beverly Bolte, Branch No. 1846, Cylinder, IA

HASH BROWN POTATOES

2 lb. frozen hash browns
½ c. softened oleo
½ tsp. salt
¼ tsp. pepper

¼ c. chopped onion
½ lb. grated Cheddar cheese
1 large ctn. sour cream
1 can cream of chicken soup

Slightly thaw hash browns and mix together with remaining ingredients. Put in a 9x13 inch pan (greased). Bake at 350° for 40 to 50 minutes.

Lu Ann Alleman, Branch No. 1737, Finlayson, MN

GERMAN POTATO SALAD

First Mixture:

8 potatoes, cooked with skins on, cooled, peeled, and diced
1 medium onion, diced

4 stalks celery, diced
1 tsp. salt
¼ tsp. pepper

Place in large bowl.

Second Mixture:

2 eggs, beaten
¾ c. vinegar
¼ c. water
1½ c. sugar

¼ lb. bacon, diced
½ c. Miracle Whip salad dressing
2 Tbsp. flour

Fry bacon and drain off grease, except for 2 tablespoons. Stir in flour. Remove from heat. Add vinegar, water, sugar, and beaten eggs. Cook over medium heat, stirring constantly, until mixture thickens and starts to bubble. Pour over first mixture. Stir in. Add salad dressing and stir in. Best served warm.

Jim Boerger, Branch No. 4734, Delphi, IN

COMPANY POTATOES

8 medium potatoes (unpeeled)
1 bay leaf
¼ c. melted butter
1 can cream of chicken soup
1½ c. sour cream

¼ tsp. pepper
3 green onions with tops, chopped
2 c. grated sharp Cheddar cheese
½ c. corn flakes

Cook unpeeled potatoes with bay leaf until potatoes are almost done. Cool, peel, and grate potatoes. (Discard bay leaf.) Combine butter, soup, sour cream, pepper, onions, and 1½ cups of the grated cheese. Pour over potatoes and stir gently. Put into buttered 2½ quart casserole or a 9x13 inch baking dish. Bake, uncovered, for 30 minutes at 350°. Now, add the following topping.

Topping: Combine the reserved ½ cup cheese and the corn flakes. Sprinkle on top. Bake for 10 to 15 minutes longer. These freeze nicely. Allow to thaw before baking.

Debbie Ehrlich, Branch No. 1995, Hudson, CO

CRUNCH TOP POTATOES
(Microwave)

3 medium potatoes
⅓ c. corn flake crumbs
¼ tsp. salt

3 Tbsp. butter
¾ c. shredded Cheddar cheese
½ tsp. paprika

143

Melt butter in 8x12 inch dish. Slice potatoes ½ inch thick (no need to peel) and coat with butter. Arrange the potatoes in baking dish. Cover with plastic wrap or a glass lid. Cook on HIGH for 8 minutes. Combine the rest of the ingredients and sprinkle them on top of the potatoes. Cook, uncovered, on level 8 for 2 to 4 minutes.

Ardelle Phipps, Branch No. 5325, Stratford, IA

EASY POTATO CASSEROLE

6 to 8 medium size potatoes,
    peeled and sliced
⅓ c. melted butter

1 env. dry onion soup mix
½ c. water

Layer ½ potatoes in baking dish. Pour ½ of the melted butter over the potatoes. Sprinkle ½ of the soup mix over the butter, then layer with remaining potatoes, butter and soup mix. Pour water over all. Cover dish and bake at 350° for 1 hour. (Remove cover after ½ hour.)

Joyce Hischke, Branch No. 3678, Suring, WI

RAW FRIES

2 lb. potatoes (6 medium)
2 Tbsp. oil or shortening
1 large onion, thinly sliced
    (optional)

1½ tsp. salt
Pepper
2 Tbsp. butter or margarine

Thinly slice raw potatoes (measures about 4 cups). Heat oil in 10 inch skillet until melted. Layer ⅓ each of potato and onion slices in skillet. Sprinkle ½ teaspoon salt and dash of pepper. Repeat 2 times. Dot top layer with butter. Cover and cook over medium heat for 20 minutes. Uncover and cook, turning once until potatoes are brown.

Bud Manke, Branch No. 5985, Midland, SD

POTATOES AU GRATIN

1 qt. cooked potatoes
2 Tbsp. butter
2 Tbsp. flour
½ tsp. dry mustard
1 c. milk

1 c. grated Cheddar cheese
Salt (to taste)
½ c. bread crumbs
1 Tbsp. melted butter

Cook potatoes until almost fork tender. Slice ¼ inch pieces into a shallow pan (1 inch). Make cheese sauce with the butter, flour, mustard, milk, and cheese. Cook until thickened, stirring constantly. Pour over the potatoes. Add topping of bread crumbs and melted butter, mixed together. Heat potato dish thoroughly in the oven or broil lightly.

Mrs. Edna Lohmann, Branch No. 102, Zumbrota, MN

OVEN FRIED POTATOES

8 large unpeeled baking potatoes,
  each cut in 8 wedges
½ c. oil
¼ tsp. pepper

1 tsp. salt
½ tsp. garlic powder
½ tsp. paprika
2 Tbsp. grated Parmesan cheese

Arrange potato wedges, peel side down, in 2 shallow baking pans. Mix remaining ingredients and brush over potatoes. Bake in preheated oven at 375° for 45 minutes or until golden brown and tender. Brush occasionally with oil mixture.

Virginia Steward, Branch No. 5285, Madison, WI

SHREDDED POTATOES

8 potatoes, boiled with bay leaf
  and cooled before shredding
1 can cream of chicken soup
½ c. sour cream
¼ c. melted margarine or butter

Chopped onion
Salt
Pepper
½ c. shredded Cheddar cheese

Mix together soup, sour cream, butter, onion, salt, pepper, and cheese in a large bowl. Shred potatoes and add to mixture. Place in 9x13 inch pan. Bake at 350° for 30 to 35 minutes. Top with crushed potato chips and ½ cup shredded cheese. Bake till cheese melts.

Kathie Sybrant, Branch No. 1455, Great Falls, MT

POTATOES AND GREEN CHILIES

6 potatoes
1 pt. sour cream
1 large or small can green chilies

½ lb. Monterey Jack cheese,
  broken in pieces
Salt and pepper

Boil potatoes in jackets and slice thin. Mix with remaining ingredients and place in casserole. Bake at 350° for 45 minutes.

Joyce Gunn, Branch No. 4570, Andrews, TX

BAKED MASH POTATOES

10 to 12 medium size potatoes
3 oz. Philadelphia cream cheese
1 c. sour cream
¼ lb. oleo

Salt
Pepper
Paprika

Cook and mash potatoes. Add Philadelphia cream cheese, sour cream, oleo, and seasonings. Dot with paprika. Store for 1 day or freeze. Partially thaw before baking. Bake for 45 minutes at 350°. Bake when thawed completely at 325° for 30 minutes.

Mary E. Trur, Branch No. 5844, Columbia City, IN

REFRIGERATED MASHED POTATOES

5 lb. potatoes, pared and
   quartered
2 (3 oz.) pkg. cream cheese
1 c. dairy sour cream

2 tsp. onion salt
1 tsp. pepper
2 Tbsp. butter
1 Tbsp. chives (optional)

Cook potatoes in boiling water until tender; drain well. Mash until smooth. Add cream cheese, sour cream, onion salt, salt, pepper, and butter. Beat with potato masher until smooth and fluffy. Place in refrigerator container. Cool, then cover. Recommended storage time is 2 weeks. Place desired amount of potatoes in greased casserole. Dot with butter and microwave until heated through. If using full amount, heat in 2 quart casserole. Makes 8 cups.

A make ahead recipe that makes potatoes taste like a million. This can be doubled for a large group.

Ruby Hartfiel, Branch No. 31, Weyauwega, WI

MASHED POTATOES DELUXE

4 lb. medium size potatoes
1 c. sour cream
1 (8 oz.) pkg. cream cheese
1/8 tsp. pepper
1/4 c. chives, chopped (if desired)

1 tsp. salt
1 Tbsp. butter or margarine
Garlic powder (as desired)
Paprika
Butter (for top)

Cook, peel and mash potatoes. Add sour cream, cream cheese, pepper, salt, butter, chives, and garlic powder. Beat thoroughly. Pour into casserole dish. Sprinkle with paprika and dot with butter. Bake at 350° for about 30 minutes.

These potatoes can be made ahead, refrigerated and baked just before serving.

Doreen Preuss, Branch No. 5016, Laguna Hills, CA

COMPANY POTATOES

Cut up:

9 medium size potatoes, peeled
   and cubed

1/2 c. onions
1 c. chopped ham, cubed

Mix together on stove and heat:

1/2 c. butter
1/2 c. grated Cheddar cheese
1 can cream of chicken soup

1 pt. sour cream
Salt and pepper to taste

Pour over potatoes and stir. Pour into casserole dish and bake at 350°F. for 45 minutes. Take out of oven and cover with chow mein noodles.

Shirley Schutte, Branch No. 1643, Eden, ID

POTATO CASSEROLE

2 lb. frozen hash browns
2 c. sour cream
1 can cream of celery soup
½ c. chopped onion

10 oz. shredded Cheddar cheese
1 stick melted butter
No salt or pepper

Mix all of the preceding in order, adding the butter last. Put in greased 9x13 inch casserole dish. Mix together 2 cups crushed corn flakes and ½ cup milk. Put on top of potatoes. Bake at 350° for 40 minutes.

Bev Braun, Branch No. 6466, Batesville, AR

POTATO CASSEROLE

2 lb. frozen hash browns
½ c. melted butter
1 tsp. salt
¼ tsp. pepper

½ c. chopped onion
8 oz. sour cream
5 oz. grated sharp Cheddar cheese
1 can cream of chicken soup

Mix together and place in 9x13 inch pan.

Topping:

2 c. crushed corn flakes   ¼ c. melted butter

Mix this together and spread on potato mixture. Bake in a 350° oven for 45 minutes. Serves 10 to 12.

Elizabeth Birnschein, Branch No. 817, Sturgeon Bay, WI

CHEESY BUFFET POTATOES

2 lb. frozen hash browned potatoes
1 pt. sour cream
2 cans cream of chicken soup
½ c. onions, chopped
2 c. Cheddar cheese, shredded

½ tsp. salt (optional)
½ tsp. pepper
2 c. crushed corn flakes
½ c. melted butter

Combine first 7 ingredients. Spoon into 2 medium size casseroles. Toss crumbled corn flakes with melted butter and sprinkle over top. Bake at 350°F. for 40 to 45 minutes. Serves 12 to 15.

May be prepared ahead and refrigerated until time to bake.

Ann Maurhoff, Branch No. 366, Pittsburgh, PA

147

HASH BROWN CASSEROLE

1 (2 lb.) bag hash browns, thawed
¼ c. oleo, melted
½ c. chopped onions
1 c. grated Cheddar cheese
1 tsp. salt

¼ tsp. pepper
½ pt. sour cream
1 can cream of chicken or celery
  soup

Save a little of the oleo to pour over the top. Mix the rest together in a 9x13 inch pan. Bake at 375° for 60 to 90 minutes.

Miss Theresa Riechmann, Branch No. 0356, Dubuque, IA

POTATO CASSEROLE

2 lb. frozen hash browns, thawed
½ c. melted margarine
½ tsp. salt and pepper
1 can cream of chicken soup

1 pt. sour cream
2 Tbsp. dried minced onion
2 c. grated cheese (Cheddar)
2 cups corn Flakes

Mix the preceding ingredients and put in buttered (greased) 9x13 inch pan. Mix ¼ cup melted margarine and 2 cups crushed corn flakes. Spread over top and bake at 350° for 45 minutes to 1 hour.

Eileen Entzel, Branch No. 1166, Miles City, MT

HASH BROWN POTATOES DELUXE

1 (2 lb.) bag hash brown potatoes
½ c. melted butter
1 tsp. salt
½ tsp. pepper
½ c. chopped onion
1 can cream of chicken soup

1 pt. sour cream
1 (10 oz.) or 2 c. grated Cheddar
  cheese
½ c. crushed corn flakes
¼ c. melted butter

Defrost potatoes. Coat with ½ cup butter. Add rest of ingredients in order, except corn flakes and last ¼ cup melted butter. Pour into 3 quart greased casserole. Mix corn flakes and butter. Sprinkle on top of potatoes and bake for 45 minutes, uncovered, at 250°. Serves 16.

Shirley Schaefer, Branch No. 2793, Vandalia, IL

LARRUPIN POTATOES

1 (1 lb.) pkg. frozen hash browns
1 (8 oz.) ctn. sour cream
1 c. shredded American cheese
1 can cream of chicken soup

¼ c. melted butter or oleo
1 Tbsp. grated onion
½ tsp. salt

Mix ingredients together. Place in 9x10 or 9x11 inch pan. Sprinkle with extra Cheddar cheese on top if desired. Bake at 350° for 45 minutes.

Linda Bura, Branch No. 2049, Emporia, KS

GERMAN POTATO SALAD

8 cooked potatoes
2 hard-boiled eggs
Onion
Salt and pepper to taste
½ lb. bacon

¾ c. vinegar
1 Tbsp. flour
3 Tbsp. sugar
¼ c. water

Slice potatoes and eggs. Add chopped onions, salt and pepper. Fry bacon and cut in pieces. Add to fat the vinegar and water; boil. Combine flour and sugar to liquid; cook till thick. Pour over potatoes, egg and bacon. Heat oven to 325° and cook for ½ hour.

Carolyn Hurlbutt, Branch No. 2288, Hilton, NY

MAKE AHEAD CREAMED POTATOES

12 large potatoes, cooked and
    diced
8 oz. cream cheese
Diced onion

Bac-Os (if desired)
Salt and pepper
Paprika
1 c. sour cream

Mix together and bake for 1 hour or use slow cooker and bake longer.

CRUNCH-TOP POTATOES

⅓ c. butter
4 large potatoes
¾ c. crushed corn flakes

1½ c. shredded Cheddar cheese
2 tsp. salt
1½ tsp. paprika

Melt butter in large pan. Add single layer of sliced ½ inch potatoes. Turn once in butter. Mix remaining ingredients and sprinkle over. Bake for 45 minutes or until done and tops are crisp.

Ardith Mueller, Branch No. 1775, Columbus, NE

GOLDEN PARMESAN POTATOES

6 large potatoes
¼ c. sifted flour
¼ c. Parmesan cheese
¾ tsp. salt

⅛ tsp. pepper
⅓ c. butter
Parsley

Pare and cut potatoes in quarters. Combine flour, cheese, salt, and pepper in bag. Moisten potatoes and shake, a few at a time, in bag, coating well.

Melt butter in 9x13 inch pan. Place potatoes in single layer in pan. Bake at 375° for 1 hour, turning once during baking. When brown, sprinkle with parsley.

Ardith Mueller, Branch No. 1775, Columbus, NE

HOLIDAY POTATOES

2 lb. frozen hash browns or
    shoestring potatoes
2 Tbsp. minced onion

1 can cream of celery soup
1 pt. sour cream
1½ c. Cheddar cheese, shredded

Mix and put in 9x13 inch pan (not aluminum). Cover and refrigerate overnight. Before baking, crush 1 cup corn flakes and mix with 3 tablespoons melted butter. Put on potatoes. Bake for 1 hour at 350°.

Ann Wind, Caroline Klemz, Branch No. 3650, Lester Prairie, MN

COTTAGE POTATO BAKE

1 qt. thinly sliced potatoes
½ c. butter

Salt and pepper
Onion (optional)

In baking dish, arrange ⅓ of the potatoes in a layer. Dot with ⅓ of butter, salt and pepper. Repeat 2 more times. Cover. Bake at 425° for 45 minutes. To brown, uncover the last 15 minutes.

TWICE GOLDEN POTATOES

Scrub and bake 6 large potatoes. Rub with shortening and bake at 400° for 1 hour. While hot, cut top fourth off and scoop out potatoes into a bowl. Mash.

Add:

¼ c. butter
1 tsp. salt
½ c. hot milk

¼ c. onion, grated
3 egg yolks

Beat until smooth. Beat egg whites until light. Fold into potato mixture. Season with pepper and paprika. Fill shells. To serve, heat in a 350° oven for 15 minutes.

May quick freeze and wrap individually. To serve, heat in a 375° oven for 45 minutes.

SCALLOPED POTATOES

25 lb. potatoes, peeled and sliced
6 pt. half & half
¾ to 1 qt. milk

½ lb. butter
3 lb. ham, diced
Salt and pepper

Bake at 325° until potatoes are tender. Serves 50 people.

Wilma Gast, Branch No. 1162, Dale, WI

HOT POTATO SALAD

1 c. chopped onions
1 Tbsp. margarine
½ c. mayonnaise or Miracle Whip
⅓ c. cider vinegar
1¾ tsp. salt

¼ tsp. pepper
4 medium potatoes (about 4 c.)
1 Tbsp. chopped parsley
1 Tbsp. cooked, crumbled bacon

Cook, peel and slice the potatoes. In large skillet over medium heat, cook onions in margarine for 2 to 3 minutes. Stir in next 4 ingredients. Add potatoes and continue cooking, stirring constantly, for about 2 minutes or until heated through. Garnish with parsley and bacon.

Corry McDowell, Loveland, CO

POTATO DUMPLINGS

4 or 5 large potatoes
1 tsp. salt
½ tsp. soda

Flour (to make a rather stiff dough)

Grate or grind potatoes. Drain off excess liquid. Add salt, soda and flour. Shape into balls with hands (use flour on hands). Drop into boiling broth made with pork hocks or ham shank.

This recipe is submitted by Mrs. Franis Thompson and is a recipe of her mother, Mrs. Emma Klebe, who was Secretary-Treasurer for Branch 1248 for 50 years, so we feel this should be in her honor.

Mrs. Franis Thompson, Branch No. 1248, Willow City, ND;
Mrs. Anna Biberdorf, Branch No. 1248

POTATO CASSEROLE

2 lb. frozen hash browns, thawed
½ c. melted margarine
1 tsp. salt
½ tsp. pepper

2 Tbsp. dried diced onion
1 can cream of chicken soup
1 pt. sour cream
2 c. grated American cheese

Topping:

2 c. crushed corn flakes

¼ c. melted margarine

Mix all ingredients (except topping) together and spread in a 9x13 inch pan. Mix together topping ingredients and spread over casserole. Bake at 350° for 45 to 60 minutes.

Janice Warneke, Ester Finngsmier, Branch 4818, Hastings, NE

MAKE AHEAD POTATOES

12 large potatoes
1 tsp. onion powder
Salt to suit taste
Paprika

8 oz. cream cheese
8 oz. sour cream
¼ c. melted butter or oleo

Boil potatoes until done; drain water. Combine potatoes, cream cheese and sour cream; mash and whip until fluffy. Add a small amount of water, if needed, and the onion powder. Mix well. Spread in 9x13 inch pan and refrigerate or freeze until needed.

When ready to use, drizzle oleo over top and sprinkle with paprika. Bake at 350° for 1 hour. Bake, uncovered, for the last 15 minutes.

Doris Ruhs, Branch No. 3107, Loveland, CO

FAVORITE DINING POTATOES

5 c. potatoes
1 Tbsp. chopped onion
½ tsp. garlic salt
Cheese or chives or paprika

1 c. sour cream
16 oz. small curd cottage cheese
Salt and pepper to taste

Shred potatoes to make 5 cups. Use either cooked or raw potatoes. Add the sour cream, cottage cheese, onion, garlic salt, salt and pepper. Mix and turn into a baking dish. Top with cheese, chives or paprika. Bake in a 350° oven for 40 minutes. If you use raw potatoes, bake for 15 minutes longer.

Doris Ruhs, Branch No. 3107, Loveland, CO

POTATO BOATS

4 potatoes, baked
3 Tbsp. milk
1 c. sour cream
Salt and pepper

1 c. shredded sharp Cheddar
   cheese
4 slices bacon, cooked crisp and
   crumbled

Fix potatoes as for twice baked. Mash potatoes. Beat in milk and sour cream. Fold in other ingredients. Bake at 400° for 20 minutes.

Connie Davis, Branch No. 3107, Loveland, CO

SWEET POTATO CASSEROLE

4 sweet potatoes (about 3 c.)
½ c. sugar
½ c. margarine
2 eggs, beaten
1 tsp. vanilla

⅓ c. milk
⅓ c. butter, melted
½ c. flour
1 c. light brown sugar
1 c. pecans or walnuts

Cook and mash sweet potatoes. Add the sugar, margarine, eggs, vanilla, and milk. Mix the melted butter, flour, brown sugar, and pecans or walnuts together. Cover sweet potato mixture as a topping. Bake at 350° for 25 minutes.

Julie Padilla, Branch No. 3107, Loveland, CO

BROCCOLI CASSEROLE

2 boxes frozen broccoli, chopped
1 c. mayonnaise
1 can cream of mushroom soup

2 eggs
Onion (as desired)
6 oz. Cheddar cheese, shredded

Cook broccoli as on instructions on box; drain and cool. Mix all ingredients together well in casserole. Bake at 350°F. for 30 minutes or microwave for 10 minutes on HIGH.

Susan Fleischmann, Branch No. 366, Pittsburgh, PA

BROCCOLI CASSEROLE

2 (10 oz.) pkg. frozen broccoli
1 can cream of mushroom soup
½ c. corn flake crumbs
½ c. chopped onion*

2 Tbsp. butter
½ c. milk
½ c. grated sharp cheese

Boil broccoli with ¼ cup onion until tender. Drain and place in casserole dish. Mix grated cheese and ¼ cup onion; add soup mixed with ½ cup milk. Pour mixture over broccoli. Mix corn flake crumbs with melted butter; sprinkle on top of casserole. Bake at 350° for 25 to 30 minutes or until brown and bubbly.

* Can use dry minced onion.

Gladys Lohmeyer, Branch No. 401, Washington, MO

BROCCOLI RICE CASSEROLE

1 (20 oz.) bag frozen diced broccoli
1 stick margarine
1 (4 oz.) can mushrooms, drained
    and cut up
1 can cream of mushroom soup

1 soup can milk
1 (7 oz.) jar Cheez Whiz or ⅓ lb.
    Velveeta cheese, cut up
1 soup can Minute rice

Cook broccoli according to package directions. Combine margarine, mushroom soup, milk, and cheese; heat on stove or in microwave until cheese melts. Add broccoli to soup mixture. Add mushrooms and Minute rice. Place in 3 quart casserole and bake, uncovered, in a 350° oven for 30 minutes.

Lorene Biermann, Branch No. 3619, Waverly, IA

BROCCOLI CASSEROLE

20 oz. chopped broccoli
1 stick margarine
½ c. chopped celery
½ c. chopped onion
½ c. water

Cheese Sauce (recipe following)
1 can cream of mushroom soup
1⅓ c. quick cooking rice
    (uncooked)
3 strips crisp bacon

Grease a 9x13 inch pan. Arrange broccoli in bottom of 9x13 inch baking dish. Melt margarine in pan and saute the celery and onion. To that pan, add water, Cheese Sauce, undiluted soup, and uncooked rice. Mix well. Pour mixture over broccoli. Crumble bacon over top. Bake in a 350° oven for 45 to 60 minutes.

Cheese Sauce: Melt ⅓ stick butter or oleo over medium heat; stir in about 4 tablespoons flour to form a paste. Stir in 1 cup milk and shredded American cheese to taste. Stir until melted.

Ella Mae Victor, Branch No. 6537, Emerson, NE

BROCCOLI-RICE CASSEROLE

1 c. instant rice (uncooked)
½ c. chopped celery
½ c. chopped onion
8 oz. Cheez Whiz
1 can cream of mushroom soup

1 can cream of chicken soup
2 pkg. frozen chopped broccoli,
   cooked without salt and
   drained

Mix all ingredients in a 2½ quart casserole. Bake at 300° for 1 hour.

Erma Poole, Branch No. 1717, Belleville, IL

MARINATED BROCCOLI

3 or 4 stalks broccoli (use mostly
   top part)
1 zucchini, sliced
1 medium size head cauliflower
Fresh mushrooms (as many as you
   like)

1 medium onion, cut up
1 green pepper, cut or diced
3 medium carrots, sliced thin
1 can black olives, sliced
Celery, sliced (as much as you
   like)

Dressing:

1 c. oil
4 Tbsp. sugar
1 c. red wine vinegar
2 Tbsp. MSG seasoning

1 Tbsp. dill weed
1 Tbsp. garlic powder
1 Tbsp. salt
1 tsp. pepper (coarse)

Cut all fresh vegetables into small bit size pieces and wash well. Mix all dressing ingredients together in blender. Refrigerate dressing overnight. Pour dressing over vegetables and toss lightly to coat. Let marinate for about 2 to 4 hours before serving. Makes large bowl of salad.

Doris Burns, Branch No. 1061, Saline, MI

BROCCOLI CASSEROLE

1 can cream of mushroom soup
1 can cream of celery soup
1 can cream of chicken soup
1 medium onion, chopped
1 soup can milk

1 stick oleo
2 lb. Velveeta
1 (16 oz.) pkg. shell macaroni
2 large bags frozen broccoli

Mix soups, milk, oleo, and cheese in pan over low heat till melted. Cook macaroni until tender. Pour cheese mixture and macaroni in casserole dish; add broccoli. Bake for 1 hour, uncovered, in a 350° oven.

Ruth Neeley, Branch No. 2254

BROCCOLI SUPREME

1 large head broccoli, cooked and
   drained
1 can cream of mushroom soup
1 c. Miracle Whip
2 eggs, well beaten

1 small onion, chopped
1 c. white cheese, shredded
1 c. Cheddar cheese, shredded
1½ c. herb croutons, crushed

154

In large dish, combine soup, eggs, Miracle Whip, and onion. Mix in ½ of both cheeses and all of the broccoli (cut in small pieces). Sprinkle with remaining cheeses and the crumbs. Bake at 350° for 40 to 45 minutes.

Dawn Gronner, Branch No. 186, Homer, MN

MOM'S COMPANY BROCCOLI

2 pkg. frozen chopped broccoli
1 (5 oz.) can water chestnuts,
    chopped
1 c. grated American cheese

1 can cream of mushroom soup
1 small can (⅔ c.) evaporated milk
1 can French fried onion rings

Cook broccoli for 4 minutes. Drain and place in 2 quart baking dish. Add chestnuts. Sprinkle cheese over broccoli mixture. Combine soup and milk; pour over cheese. This may be mixed together or left in layers.

Bake, uncovered, at 350° for 25 minutes. Take from oven and cover with onion rings. Bake for 8 to 10 minutes longer or until crisp.

Marcia Venzke, Branch No. 3107, Loveland, CO

BROCCOLI QUICHE

1 (10 oz.) pkg. frozen chopped
    broccoli
⅔ c. chopped onion
2 c. shredded Cheddar cheese
4 eggs

2 c. milk
½ tsp. salt
¼ tsp. pepper
1 unbaked pie shell

Thaw broccoli under running cold water. Drain well. Mix broccoli, onion and cheese. Put in pie shell. Beat together eggs, milk, salt, and pepper. Pour over vegetables in shell. Bake for 25 to 35 minutes in a 400° oven until knife inserted in center comes out clean.

Betty L. Mitchell, Branch No. 1014, Avoca, NY

MOM'S BROCCOLI

2 pkg. frozen or fresh bunches
    broccoli
¼ lb. Cheddar cheese
1 c. fresh mushrooms

6 slices bacon, fried crisp and
    crumbled
⅛ lb. slivered almonds

White Sauce:

4 Tbsp. margarine
4 Tbsp. flour

¼ tsp. salt
2 c. milk

If frozen broccoli is used, don't cook first. Cook fresh broccoli till almost done. Mushrooms can be sauteed in butter or used raw. Place all ingredients in baking dish and pour sauce over.

Can be made ahead and refrigerated until 1 hour before cooking. If broccoli is frozen, cook for at least 1 hour until tender (not so long for fresh) at 350°.

Connie Davis, Branch No. 3107, Loveland, CO

SAUSAGE-STUFFED ACORN SQUASH
(Microwave)

2 small acorn squash (about 1 lb. each)
1 lb. bulk pork sausage
½ c. chopped walnuts

¼ c. dry bread crumbs
1 egg
½ tsp. seasoned salt
¼ tsp. dried basil leaves, crushed

Cut each squash in half and scoop out seeds. Wrap individually in plastic wrap. Microwave on HIGH for 8 to 10 minutes or till tender, rearranging once. Remove from oven and let stand for 5 minutes.

Meanwhile, in 2 quart casserole, break up sausage. Cover tightly, turning one edge back. Microwave on HIGH for 5 to 6 minutes, stirring and breaking up meat after 3 minutes. Drain well.

In small bowl, combine walnuts, bread crumbs, egg, salt, and basil. Mix lightly. Stir into sausage. Fill each squash half with stuffing mixture. Arrange in a circle on paper towel in microwave. Heat, uncovered, on HIGH for 2 to 3 minutes or till heated through.

Cheryl Schultz, Branch No. 3107, Loveland, CO

WILTED SPINACH
(Microwave)

6 slices bacon
½ c. sliced green onion
¼ c. vinegar (cider)
¼ c. water
3 to 4 Tbsp. sugar (may use part brown sugar)

½ tsp. salt
6 c. torn fresh spinach*
6 radishes, thinly sliced (optional)

Place bacon slices in large bowl; cover with paper towels. Microwave until bacon is crisp, 4 to 5 minutes. Remove bacon and drain thoroughly, reserving ¼ cup drippings in bowl. Crumble bacon and set aside.

Microwave onion in drippings for 3 minutes. Add vinegar, water, sugar, and salt. Cook, uncovered, until boiling, about 1½ minutes. Stir to dissolve sugar. Place spinach in bowl. Toss to coat well with dressing. Serve in salad bowl. Garnish with bacon and radishes.

* Other greens may be used.

Sandi Johansen, Branch No. 1400, Arbor Vitae, WI

SUPREME BAKED CORN

1 (16 oz.) can creamed corn
1 (16 oz.) can regular corn, drained
1 (8 oz.) pkg. corn muffin mix

3 eggs
½ c. margarine, melted
1 c. sour cream
1 c. shredded cheese (optional)

Mix well and pour in buttered 9x13 inch pan. Bake in a 350° oven for 15 minutes. Sprinkle with 1 cup shredded cheese. Bake for an additional 25 minutes or till knife inserted in center comes out clean.

Marjorie Miller, Branch No. 5433, Newcomerstown, OH

SCALLOPED CORN

2 eggs, well beaten
1 (16½ oz.) cream style corn
1 (16½ oz.) whole kernel corn
1 Tbsp. sugar
½ c. bread crumbs

1 tsp. salt
¼ tsp. pepper
½ c. milk
2 Tbsp. butter

Mix together corn, sugar, salt, pepper, milk, and eggs. Place in greased casserole dish. Add crumbs and dot with butter. Bake for 1 hour until done at 350°.

Mary Johnson, Branch No. 736, Essexville, MI

ELEGANT CORN

1 (16 oz.) can corn
1 c. cracker crumbs
⅓ c. diced celery
¼ c. onion
¾ c. American cheese, diced

1 tsp. salt
2 eggs, well beaten
2 Tbsp. melted butter
¼ tsp. paprika
1 c. milk

Combine all ingredients and pour into a greased casserole. Bake at 350° for 50 minutes. Serves 4 to 6.

Doris Seevers, Branch No. 382, St. Louis, MO

FROZEN CORN
(Very good)

Combine:

4 qt. corn
1 qt. water

1 c. sugar
4 tsp. salt

Cut corn off cob. Mix all together, then *boil* lightly for 10 minutes. Cool for several hours. Put in containers and freeze. Just thaw and heat to serve.

Jenny Bruss, Branch No. 840, Oak Creek, WI

CORN DELIGHT

1 can cream style corn
1 can whole kernel corn, drained
1 stick oleo, melted
1 c. cubed cheese (American)

¼ c. celery, diced
⅛ c. onion, diced
1 c. broken spaghetti

Mix everything together in 3 quart casserole dish. Bake at 350° for ½ hour, uncovered, and stir well. Bake for ½ hour, covered, to finish cooking.

Can also be cooked in microwave for about 12 minutes, uncovered, and 8 to 10 minutes, covered.

Anita Wochner, Branch No. 2143, Bradshaw, NE

CORN DELIGHT

1 can cream style corn
1 can whole kernel corn
   (undrained)
1 c. uncooked spaghetti, cut in 1
   inch pieces

1 c. Velveeta cheese, diced
½ c. margarine, melted
2 Tbsp. onion, chopped

Stir all together in a 2 quart buttered casserole dish. Bake at 375° for ½ hour covered and ½ hour uncovered.

Ronda Tucker, Branch No. 2512, Ord, NE

FANCY CORN

1 pkg. frozen whole kernel corn
1 (8 oz.) pkg. cream cheese

Chives

Put corn (with a little water to keep from going dry) and the cream cheese in crock pot. Melt on LOW. After corn is done, throw in some chives (enough to add color). Serve.

Note: For each package of corn used, put in a package of cream cheese, but add gradually for taste. May not use a whole package each time, for over 1 package of corn as stated in original recipe.

Linda Bura, Branch No. 2049, Emporia, KS

COMPANY'S FAVORITE SIDE DISH

1 pkg. long grain and wild rice
   mix, cooked
10 oz. broccoli, cooked
1 can sliced water chestnuts,
   drained

1 (8 oz.) jar Cheez Whiz
1 (4 oz.) can mushrooms, drained
1 can cream of mushroom soup
1 (6 oz.) pkg. onion garlic croutons
4 Tbsp. butter

Place cooked rice in bottom of casserole. Top with broccoli, mushrooms and water chestnuts. Mix Cheez Whiz and undiluted mushroom soup; pour over. Top with croutons that have been tossed with melted butter. Bake at 350° for 30 minutes. Makes 8 to 10 servings.

Helen Emich, Branch No. 3650, Lester Prairie, MN

YELLOW SQUASH CASSEROLE

2 lb. yellow squash
1 small jar chopped pimento
1 Tbsp. minced onion (dehydrated)
2 large carrots, grated
1 c. sour cream

1 can cream of chicken (or celery)
  soup
¼ lb. margarine
1 pkg. corn bread stuffing mix

Slice squash and cook until tender; drain and mash. Add next 5 ingredients. Melt margarine and mix with corn bread stuffing mix. Line bottom of 9x13 inch baking dish with ½ of the stuffing mixture. Add squash mixture. Top with remaining stuffing mix. Bake for 30 minutes in a 350° oven. Makes 12 to 15 servings.

Hattie Erdman, Branch 1221

VEGETABLE PIZZA

2 pkg. crescent rolls
2 (8 oz.) pkg. cream cheese
1 c. + 2 Tbsp. mayonnaise
1 tsp. onion powder

1 tsp. garlic powder
1 tsp. dill weed
½ tsp. seasoned salt

Spread crescent rolls in cookie sheet and bake for 8 to 10 minutes. Cool. Mix remaining ingredients and spread on crust. Cover with fresh chopped vegetables (cauliflower, broccoli, radishes, carrots, or whatever you like).

Esther Ploog, Branch No. 997, Charlotte, IA

TOMATO CHUTNEY
(Passover)

1 (1 lb. 13 oz.) can tomatoes,
  chopped
½ c. chopped onion
1 clove garlic, minced
2 green apples, pared, cored and
  chopped
¼ tsp. crushed dried red pepper
1 tsp. ground ginger

½ tsp. cumin seed
¼ tsp. ground nutmeg
¼ tsp. mustard seed
⅓ c. raisins, chopped
½ tsp. salt
1 c. vinegar
½ to 1 c. brown sugar, packed

Combine all ingredients in a large heavy saucepan. Cook, uncovered, over medium heat, stirring occasionally, for 20 to 30 minutes or until mixture is thick. Cool and store in refrigerator. This recipe makes about 3½ cups and usual servings are a very small amount.

Mona Geidel, Branch No. 3107, Loveland, CO

SWISS VEGETABLE MEDLEY

1 (16 oz.) bag frozen broccoli,
  carrots and cauliflower
  combination
1 (10¾ oz.) can cream of
  mushroom soup

1 c. shredded Swiss cheese
⅓ c. sour cream
¼ tsp. pepper
1 jar chopped pimiento (optional)
1 can French fried onions

Combine vegetables, soup, ½ cup cheese, sour cream, pepper, and onions. Pour into 1 quart casserole. Bake at 350° for 30 minutes. Top with remaining cheese and onions. Bake, uncovered, for 5 minutes longer. Serves 6.

Variation by Esther Lou Wiedey - Microwave directions: Prepare as before. Cook, covered, on HIGH for 8 minutes. Turn halfway through. Top with remaining cheese and onions. Cook, uncovered, on HIGH for 1 minute or until cheese melts. *Donna Phillips, Branch No. 2512, Ord, NE; Angela Gangelhoff, Branch No. 1737, Sandstone, MN; Esther Lou Wiedey, Branch No. 1387, Carrollton, MO; Lola Mae Spicknall, Branch No. 2248, Akron, CO*

VEGETABLE MEDLEY

10 oz. frozen carrots
10 oz. frozen broccoli
10 oz. frozen cauliflower
10 oz. frozen Brussels sprouts

1 can cream of mushroom soup
1 small jar Cheez Whiz
1 can French fried onion rings

Cook all vegetables ½ the time stated on package directions. Put in a large casserole. In a saucepan, heat and blend condensed soup and cheese. Pour over top of vegetables and carefully mix. Bake at 375° for 30 minutes. Top with onion rings the last 5 minutes.

Mary Vander Top, Loveland, CO

GARDEN PIZZA

Press 1 package crescent dinner rolls in 9x13 inch baking pan *or* 12 inch round pizza pan. Bake for 8 minutes at 375°

1 (8 oz.) pkg. cream cheese
⅓ c. Miracle Whip
1½ tsp. dill weed seed

1½ tsp. oregano
1½ tsp. minced onion

Beat cream cheese with other ingredients. Spread on baked, cooled crust. Cut. Top with chopped vegetables (broccoli, tomatoes, cauliflower, black olives, green peppers, and grated carrots). Sprinkle with seasoned salt and shredded cheese for garnish. Shake a few bacon bits over the top. *Delicious!*
Winnifred Laabs, Branch No. 1162, Hortonville, WI

CALIFORNIA VEGETABLE CASSEROLE

1 bag California frozen vegetables
1 c. Minute rice
1 can cream of chicken soup

½ c. water
¼ c. milk
1 small jar Cheez Whiz

Mix all ingredients together and put in 8x8 inch Pyrex dish. Spread small jar of Cheez Whiz on top. Bake for 40 minutes at 375°.

Jeanie Coleman, Loveland, CO

HOLIDAY YAM CASSEROLE

5 or 6 medium uncooked yams or
    sweet potatoes
¾ c. white sugar
½ c. brown sugar
¼ c. dark syrup
¾ c. butter or margarine
2 or 3 tsp. cinnamon
2 tsp. nutmeg

Pinch of ginger
½ c. orange juice
¼ c. pineapple juice or crushed
    pineapple
Slivered nuts (pecans or walnuts
    as desired or tiny
    marshmallows)

Heat oven to 300° or 350°. Boil uncooked potatoes until tender. Melt butter and stir in both kinds of white and brown sugars and condiments. Add liquid or orange and pineapple juices or crushed pineapple to preceding mixture. Set aside the preceding ingredients until later.

Lightly grease the casserole dish with margarine or butter. Slice cooked potatoes round or lengthwise and place in dish. Pour the complete mixture over layers of yams or sweet potatoes. Top with slivered nuts as desired. Cook for 25 or 30 minutes.

Mary J. Armstead, Branch No. 2262, Alton, IL

SUGARY SAM YAMS

Yam ingredients:

3 c. canned yams, drained
½ c. milk
2 eggs

1 stick margarine
½ c. sugar
1 tsp. vanilla

Mix yam ingredients with electric mixer. Pour into oblong casserole, 12x7 or 13x9 inches.

Topping Ingredients:

1 c. brown sugar, lightly packed
2 Tbsp. flour
1 tsp. vanilla

⅓ c. margarine, softened
1 c. Grape-Nuts

Mix topping with fork. Spread over potato mixture. Bake till bubbly and golden brown for 45 minutes at 350°.

Becky Sadosky, Branch No. 4845, Youngstown, OH

FRENCH ONION CASSEROLE

2 large white sweet onions, peeled
    and sliced ¼ inch thick
3 Tbsp. butter
½ lb. Swiss cheese, grated
1 can cream of chicken soup

½ c. milk
1 tsp. soy sauce
8 slices French bread (¼ inch
    thick), buttered

Saute onions in butter until tender; spoon into 11x7 inch glass dish. Spread cheese over onions. Heat soup, milk and soy sauce together until well blended. Pour over onions and cheese. Mix gently with fork. Place buttered bread slices on top, overlapping if necessary. Bake, uncovered, at 350° for 30 minutes. Yield: 6 to 8 servings.

Julia Riedel, Branch No. 3107, Loveland, CO

ZUCCHINI CRESCENT PIE

4 c. thinly sliced small zucchini
1 c. chopped onion
¼ c. margarine
2 Tbsp. parsley flakes
½ tsp. salt
½ tsp. pepper
¼ tsp. garlic powder

¼ tsp. basil
¼ tsp. crushed oregano leaves
2 beaten eggs
8 oz. (2 c.) shredded Mozzarella
  cheese
1 (8 oz.) pkg. crescent rolls
2 tsp. prepared mustard

Melt margarine in 10 inch skillet. Add zucchini and onion. Cook, stirring occasionally, for 10 minutes. Stir in the seasonings. Combine eggs and cheese. Stir in zucchini mixture. Separate crescent rolls into 8 triangles. Press into ungreased 10 inch pie pan. Spread with the mustard. Pour zucchini mixture into crust. Bake at 375° for 20 minutes or until center is set. Let stand for 10 minutes before serving. Makes 6 servings.

Mrs. Robert Bishop (or Joyce Bishop), Branch No. 441, Bloomington, IL

ZUCCHINI CASSEROLE

3 c. zucchini, grated and drained
1 c. Bisquick
½ c. cooking oil

½ c. chopped onion
1 tsp. salt
5 eggs, beaten

Mix all ingredients together and pour into baking dish. Top with Parmesan cheese. Bake for 30 to 35 minutes at 350°.

Doris Wohlschlegel, Branch No. 5425, Louisville, KY

SUMMER SQUASH CASSEROLE

2 lb. yellow or green summer
  squash, sliced (6 c.)
¼ c. chopped onion
1 can condensed cream of chicken
  soup

1 c. dairy sour cream
1 c. shredded carrots
1 (8 oz.) pkg. herb seasoned
  stuffing mix
½ c. butter or margarine, melted

Cook sliced squash and onion in boiling, salted water for 5 minutes; drain. Combine cream of chicken soup and sour cream. Stir in shredded carrots. Fold in drained squash and onion. Combine stuffing mix and butter or margarine. Spread half of stuffing mixture in bottom of 12 x 7½ x 2 inch baking dish. Spoon vegetable mixture atop. Sprinkle remaining stuffing over vegetables. Bake at 350° for 25 to 30 minutes, or heated through. Serves 6.

Mrs. Lois Meinert, Branch No. 283, Leavenworth, KS

VEGETABLE CHILI

6 Tbsp. olive oil, divided
2 medium or 1 large zucchini (do not peel), cut into ½ inch cubes
2 small onions, sliced
4 cloves garlic, finely chopped
2 large red or green bell peppers, cored and diced
1 (32 oz.) can tomatoes (undrained)
1 lb. fresh tomatoes, cut in 1 inch cubes

2 Tbsp. chili powder
2 tsp. ground cumin
2 tsp. dried basil
2 tsp. ground pepper
½ tsp. salt
¼ c. dried parsley
¼ c. dried dill weed
3 c. canned dark red kidney beans, drained, or hot chili beans
2 Tbsp. lemon juice

Heat 4 tablespoons oil in large skillet over medium heat. Add zucchini. Saute till just tender. Remove zucchini to large heavy pot. Add remaining 2 tablespoons oil to skillet over low heat. Add onions, garlic and peppers; saute until just wilted, about 10 minutes. Transfer mixture, including oil, to large pot.

Place pot over low heat. Add undrained canned tomatoes, fresh tomatoes, chili powder, cumin, basil, pepper, salt, parsley, and dill. Cook, uncovered, stirring often for 30 minutes. Stir in canned beans and lemon juice; cook for 15 minutes. Stir well. Yield: 8 or more servings.

Dorothy Ann Marcrander, Branch No. 3193, St. Louis, MO

VEGETABLES AND RICE

1 (16 oz.) pkg. California Blend vegetables
¾ c. Minute rice

¾ c. water
¼ tsp. salt
¼ lb. Velveeta cheese

Cook vegetables according to package directions; drain. Cook Minute rice in water and salt to a boil and let stand for 5 minutes. Blend with vegetables. Slice cheese. Mix with vegetables and rice until melted. Serve.

Susan Stich, Branch No. 2820, Chanute, KS

VEGETABLE CASSEROLE

½ loaf Swedish limpa bread, cut in 1 inch cubes
2 small zucchini, sliced
2 green peppers, sliced
1 doz. mushrooms, sliced

1 bunch broccoli, chunked
½ head cauliflower, chunked
2 carrots, sliced
4 to 6 large tomatoes
1 to 2 c. grated Cheddar cheese

In a large baking casserole, place bread on the bottom and the rest of the vegetables on top, ending with tomatoes and cheese. Any other vegetable can be added or any subtracted. The tomatoes on top drip the juice through to the bread and the cheese covering (heavy) seals it. Bake for 1 hour at 350°.

Verna Puline, Branch No. 3339, Esko, MN

VEGETABLE HOT DISH

2 (16 oz.) pkg. California Blend
   vegetables (frozen)
1 jar sliced mushrooms
1 can sliced water chestnuts
1 pkg. small frozen onions
2 cans cream of mushroom soup

½ lb. American cheese or
   Velveeta, cubed
1 tsp. Worcestershire sauce
3 Tbsp. white wine (optional)
Buttered croutons (optional)

Mix all ingredients, except the croutons, together. Pour into a 3 quart casserole dish. Bake for 40 minutes at 350°. Add buttered croutons, if desired, and bake for an additional 20 minutes.

Nancy Ziegeldorf, Branch No. 2620, Yale, SD

VEGETABLE CASSEROLE

1 (10 oz.) pkg. frozen broccoli
1 (10 oz.) pkg. frozen cauliflower
1 (10 oz.) pkg. frozen Brussels
   sprouts
1 (10 oz.) pkg. frozen peas with
   pearl onions

1 (10¾ oz.) can cream of
   mushroom soup
1 small jar Cheez Whiz

Parcook vegetables by just bringing them to a boil. Remove from heat and drain. Layer vegetables in a 2 quart casserole which has been buttered. In a saucepan, heat the soup and Cheez Whiz. Pour over vegetables. Top with buttered bread or cracker crumbs. Bake at 350° for about 45 minutes. *Very good!*

Regina Stueber, Branch No. 1478, Clyman, WI

VEGETABLE CASSEROLE

2 (16 oz.) pkg. frozen vegetables
   (carrot, broccoli, cauliflower
   mix)

1 can cream of mushroom soup
1 can golden mushroom soup
1 can Cheddar cheese soup

Mix frozen vegetables and all 3 cans of soup together. Put in a casserole and bake for 1 hour at 350°.

Mrs. Luetta Kluever, Branch No. 1131, Worthington, MN

VEGETABLE CASSEROLE

1 (10 oz.) pkg. cauliflower
1 (10 oz.) pkg. broccoli

1 can Cheddar cheese soup
½ can onion rings

Boil cauliflower and broccoli for about 5 minutes. Drain and add soup. Put in baking dish; cover and bake for 1 hour at 350°. Spread onions over mixture and bake, uncovered, until brown.

SPINACH SOUFFLE

6 eggs
2 pkg. frozen chopped spinach
6 Tbsp. Wondra flour
1½ lb. tiny curd cottage cheese
1 stick (¼ lb.) butter

½ lb. sharp Cheddar cheese,
  shredded
½ lb. Velveeta cheese, grated
Salt and pepper to taste

Beat eggs well. Mix in flour, cottage cheese, Cheddar cheese, Velveeta, and seasoning. (Use mixer or blender.) Pour mix into greased 9x13 inch casserole. Break up spinach into mixture. Dot with butter. Bake at 325° to 350° for about 1 hour until set.

Alyce Hildebrandt, Branch No. 3405, St. Louis, MO

STUFFED PEPPERS WITH ROSA MARINA

1 stick butter or margarine
½ box rosa marina
¾ c. chopped onion
¾ c. sliced mushrooms
2 c. beef bouillon

1 Tbsp. Worcestershire sauce
½ c. soft bread crumbs
½ c. freshly grated Parmesan
  cheese
5 or 6 green peppers, cleaned out

Brown the rosa marina in the butter or margarine. Add the chopped onion and chopped mushrooms. Continue to cook until the mushrooms are slightly soft. Pour the 2 cups of bouillon, which is still hot, over the rosa marina. Add the Worcestershire sauce.

Cover the pan tightly and simmer over a low fire for about ½ hour. Add the bread crumbs and Parmesan cheese. Stuff into 5 to 6 green peppers, which have been scooped out and steamed for 5 minutes. Top with a plain marinara tomato sauce and bake at 350° for 30 minutes.

Mary Spisak, Branch No. 1848, Lorain, OH

SPINACH-CHEESE CASSEROLE

2 slices bacon
½ c. chopped carrot
¼ c. chopped onion
2 (10 oz.) pkg. frozen chopped
  spinach, thawed and drained

1 c. cooked rice
¼ c. milk
1 (11 oz.) can condensed Cheddar
  cheese soup

In a 2 quart saucepan, cook bacon till crisp. Drain, reserving drippings. Crumble bacon and set aside. In reserved drippings, cook carrot and onion till onion is tender. Stir in soup, spinach, rice, and milk. Turn mixture into a 1 quart casserole. Bake, covered, at 375° until heated through, 35 to 40 minutes. Sprinkle with crumbled bacon. Makes 6 to 8 servings.

Mrs. Gertrude Hacker, Branch No. 1182, Perryville, MO

CELERY CASSEROLE

1 bunch (4 c.) celery, cut in ¼ inch
    slices
1 can water chestnuts, sliced
1 can cream of chicken soup

⅓ c. slivered almonds
½ c. unseasoned croutons
5 Tbsp. oleo

Cook celery in small amount of water till crisp tender. Drain. Combine with sliced chestnuts and soup in greased casserole. Saute ⅓ cup slivered almonds and ½ cup unseasoned croutons in 5 tablespoons oleo. Spread over celery mixture. Bake for 45 minutes at 350°.

This makes a nice luncheon dish also by adding 1½ cups cut up chicken and ½ cup chicken broth along with the chestnuts before baking. Serve over noodles. Serves 6.

Laverne Mathay, Branch No. 3868, Highland Heights, OH

CELERY CASSEROLE
(Out of this world)

4 c. celery, sliced
1 (10¾ oz.) can cream of chicken
    soup
½ c. milk
1 tsp. onion salt
1 tsp. curry powder

1 c. slivered almonds
1 (8½ oz.) can water chestnuts,
    chopped and drained
2 Tbsp. margarine
3 Tbsp. flour

Parboil celery until tender crisp (about 10 minutes). Combine cream of chicken soup, milk, onion salt, curry powder, almonds, and water chestnuts in bowl. Melt margarine in saucepan; sprinkle flour over it and mix with wire whisk until thick. Add to chicken soup mixture and stir until blended.

In buttered 2 quart casserole, alternate layers of celery and sauce, ending with sauce. Sprinkle bread crumbs on top. Bake in a 350° oven for 35 minutes. Yield: 8 servings.

Carole Wesche Harrington, Branch No. 2630, Greeley, CO

ROYAL CELERY

8 c. celery, sliced
1 (5 oz.) water chestnuts, sliced
1 can cream of chicken or celery
    soup

2 Tbsp. butter
½ c. slivered almonds, browned
½ c. buttered crumbs

Parboil celery for 3 minutes in a small amount of salted water. Drain. Drain and slice water chestnuts. Brown almonds in butter. Combine celery, water chestnuts, almonds, and soup. Put into a 2 quart casserole and top with crumbs. Bake in a 350° oven for 30 minutes, covered. Bake for 15 minutes more, uncovered.

Joyce Lehmann, Branch No. 1878, Claflin, KS

ASPARAGUS LUNCHEON BAKE

2 (10 oz.) pkg. frozen chopped
asparagus
1 (10 oz.) can condensed cream of
mushroom soup (undiluted)
¼ c. milk
1 can water chestnuts, drained and
sliced

2 (3 oz.) cans sliced mushrooms,
drained
4 hard cooked eggs, sliced
½ tsp. salt
Dash of pepper
1 (3½ oz.) can French fried onion
rings

Cook asparagus according to package directions; drain. Place asparagus in greased 7x11 inch baking pan. Put on top asparagus, water chestnuts, mushrooms, and eggs. Combine soup, milk, salt, and pepper. Pour mixture over asparagus. Sprinkle onion rings on top. Bake, uncovered, in a 350° oven for 20 minutes. Serves 6.

Irene Heintz, Branch No. 3285, Bloomington, MN

EGGPLANT DELICIOUS

1 medium to large eggplant
4 Tbsp. butter or margarine
3 or 4 slices bread
1 Tbsp. butter or margarine

1 Tbsp. flour
1 c. milk
¼ lb. Cheddar or American
cheese, cubed

Pare eggplant; cut into cubes and cook in small amount of water for 10 to 15 minutes or until tender; drain. Melt 4 tablespoons butter in a skillet and brown the 3 or 4 slices of bread (cubed or crumbled in blender) until a golden brown.

Empty browned bread into a bowl, then put the 1 tablespoon butter and flour in the skillet. Stir in the milk and cook into sauce; season with salt and pepper. Add the drained eggplant, browned bread and cubed cheese. Mix together and serve.

P.S. Other vegetables can be used in place of the eggplant, such as carrots, cabbage, broccoli, etc.

Mrs. Victor Aufdenkamp, Branch No. 2078, Juniata, NE

CABBAGE-NOODLE CASSEROLE

1 green (firm) head cabbage
Several cloves of fresh garlic
1 stick butter
1 lb. cheese, grated or shredded
Salt and pepper
1 green pepper

1 can or 1 lb. fresh mushrooms
1 stick margarine
1 pkg. very fine egg noodles
Oregano
Chives

Shred or cut cabbage very thin. Save the outer dark leaves for color and flavor. Fry the cabbage (small batch at a time), garlic, and green pepper in margarine or butter. Saute the mushrooms and onions; add to cabbage mixture. Cook, drain and season the noodles. Combine the noodles and cabbage mixture. Grate the cheese into the cabbage and noodles.

Add cut up fried okra *(optional)*. Crumbled bacon or ham cubes could be added.

Geneva Maiden, Branch No. 3651, Chesterland, OH

RED CABBAGE

1 head red cabbage, thinly sliced	2 Tbsp. sugar
2 onions, sliced	½ tsp. salt
2 apples, cored and sliced	½ tsp. pepper
2 Tbsp. chicken fat (or margarine)	Cloves
1 c. water	Bay leaf
½ c. wine vinegar	

Heat fat in a large pan. Saute the onions and apples. Add water, vinegar and spices. Bring to a boil. Add cabbage and simmer for 2 to 3 hours.

Very good with pork or beef roulards.

Kay Wolfe, Branch No. 2716, Northglenn, CO

GREEN RICE

2 Tbsp. margarine	1 can cream of mushroom soup
1 small onion, chopped fine	(undiluted)
2 c. Minute rice	½ lb. Velveeta or Cheez Whiz
2 c. water	1 can French fried onions (for
½ tsp. salt (optional)	topping)
1 (20 oz.) pkg. frozen chopped	
broccoli	

In saucepan, melt margarine and saute onion just till soft. Mix with all remaining ingredients (except French fried onions) in a large bowl; pour into greased 9x13 inch pan. Bake in a 350° oven for 40 minutes. Place French fried onions on top the last 10 minutes of baking time.

Note: This recipe adapts very easily to number of servings needed. Just increase or decrease amount of rice and water in equal amounts to get the number of servings you need. Can increase rice and water to 4 cups each before altering other ingredients in recipe.

Donna Haselhorst, Branch No. 2793, Vandalia, IL

CARROTS AU GRATIN CASSEROLE

3 c. cooked, sliced carrots	½ c. fine bread crumbs
1 can cream of celery soup	2 Tbsp. melted butter
1 c. shredded process cheese	

Combine first 3 ingredients in 1 quart casserole. Combine crumbs and butter; sprinkle on. Bake for 35 minutes at 350°. Serves 4.

Adeline Ciriacks, St. Luke (ELCA), Branch No. 6304, Slinger, WI

COPPER PENNIES

2 lb. carrots
1 small green pepper
1 medium onion
1 c. tomato soup
½ c. salad oil

¾ c. sugar
¼ c. vinegar
1 tsp. prepared mustard
1 tsp. Worcestershire sauce
Salt and pepper to taste

Slice carrots and cover with water. Cook until tender, but firm. Cool in colander. Slice pepper and onion thinly. Layer with carrots in a casserole dish. Mix remaining ingredients thoroughly and pour over vegetables in casserole. Cover and refrigerate.

May be prepared several days ahead if desired. Serve cold as salad or heat at 350° for about ½ hour to serve as vegetable.

Mildred Gramzow, Branch No. 1700, Richmond, MI

COPPER PENNIES

5 c. sliced carrots
1 onion, sliced or diced
1 medium green pepper, sliced or
   diced
1 can tomato soup
⅓ c. salad oil

¾ c. vinegar
1 c. sugar
1 tsp. mustard
1 tsp. salt
1 tsp. pepper

Cook carrots for 5 minutes. Drain. Add onion and pepper. Set aside. Heat together remaining ingredients. Cover vegetables. Marinate for 24 hours.

Elinore Jones, Branch No. 1265, Creighton, MO

GREEN BEAN SCANDIA

1 (No. 2) can cut green beans
1 Tbsp. chicken broth base
2 Tbsp. oleo
1½ Tbsp. vinegar
1½ Tbsp. water
1 Tbsp. sugar

½ tsp. whole dill seed
Dash of pepper
1 Tbsp. cornstarch
1 Tbsp. cold water
2 c. packed, chopped cabbage

Drain liquid from beans. Add next 7 ingredients and heat to boiling, stirring. Stir cornstarch, mixed with water. Cook and stir until mixture thickens and is clear (about 5 minutes).

Add cabbage and heat to boiling! Simmer, covered, for 35 minutes (do not boil). Drain green beans. Add to mixture and serve at once.

Ms. Maxine Wilson, Branch No. 4734, West Lafayette, IN

MEXICAN BEANS

Have on hand 6 cans French style green beans.

Saute in butter:

1 c. celery, chopped
1 c. onions, chopped
1 c. green pepper, chopped
1 small can water chestnuts,
    chopped
1 small can mushrooms, chopped

1 clove garlic, minced
2 small cans tomato sauce
1 pt. or 2 c. whole tomatoes
1 Tbsp. sugar
1 Tbsp. flour and water
Salt and pepper to taste

Could add fried bacon and grease. Combine all ingredients and heat for ½ hour at 325°.

Mona Geidel, Branch No. 3107, Loveland, CO

BEAN CASSEROLE

2 cans red kidney beans, drained
8 slices bacon, cut up
1 medium onion, chopped
2 fresh tomatoes or 1 can whole
    tomatoes

1 c. brown sugar
1 small bottle catsup
1 green pepper, cut up

Mix well and bake in greased casserole at 350° for 1½ to 2 hours. Do not cover.

Great to serve with barbequed meat!

Julie Padilla, Branch No. 3107, Loveland, CO

GREEN BEAN CASSEROLE

3 cans green beans
2 Tbsp. melted butter
2 Tbsp. flour
12 oz. sour cream

1 lb. grated Swiss cheese
6 slices cooked and chopped
    bacon
Corn flakes

Layer beans in 9x13 inch pan. Top with Swiss cheese. Melt butter and add flour; mix well. Add sour cream and put on top of cheese. Top with bacon and crushed corn flakes. Bake for 30 minutes at 350°.

Sharon Bergemann, Branch No. 881, Good Thunder, MN

BAR BQ GREEN BEANS

3 cans green beans, drained
1 onion, chopped
6 slices uncooked bacon, cut in
    pieces

1 c. catsup
1 c. brown sugar

Mix all ingredients and bake in covered casserole at 275° for 4 hours.

Variation by Ella Mae Wagner: Substitute 3 quarts green beans for 3 cans green beans.

Lu Meyers, Branch No. 1098, Freemont, NE;
Ella Mae Wagner, Branch No. 6085, Bemidji, MN

170

CROCKERY COOKER BAKED BEANS

1 lb. dry pinto beans
6 c. water
1½ tsp. salt
1 tsp. dry mustard
½ tsp. pepper

½ c. chopped onion
½ c. molasses
½ c. brown sugar
½ lb. bacon, chopped

Place beans in boiling water (enough to cover) and simmer for 10 minutes. Combine beans, water and cooked bacon in crock. Cover and cook on LOW for about 12 hours. Drain beans, reserving liquid. Combine beans with remaining ingredients and add enough bean liquid to cover beans. Cover and cook on LOW for another 6 hours. Yield: 6 to 8 servings.

Sarah M. Anderson, Branch No. 6706, Brule, NE

SHARON'S BEACH BOILER BEANS

½ c. green pepper, chopped
½ c. onion, chopped
1 (1½ or 2 lb.) can pork and beans
⅓ c. light brown sugar

½ tsp. ground oregano
½ tsp. black pepper (coarse)
½ tsp. dry mustard

Mix all of the preceding ingredients together, then top with bacon (cut into small pieces). Bake, uncovered, at 300° for 2½ hours.

Can be made the day before. Cook for 2 hours and then bake for another ½ hour before serving.

Sharon Rohloff, Branch No. 5590, Casselberry, FL

GREEN BEAN-BACON ROLL-UPS

2 cans whole green beans, drained
Bacon slices, cut in thirds

½ c. brown sugar
¼ lb. margarine, melted

Combine brown sugar and melted margarine. Wrap 6 to 8 beans in 1 piece of bacon and secure with toothpick. Place in oblong baking dish. Pour sugar mixture over the roll-ups and bake in a 350° oven for 25 to 30 minutes, until bacon is cooked. Baste occasionally during cooking time to prevent beans from drying out. Makes 14 to 15 roll-ups.

Marty Tews, Branch 1221

THREE BEAN HOT DISH

1 lb. lean hamburger, browned
¼ c. brown sugar
¼ c. fine chopped celery
¼ c. chopped onion
1 large can pork and beans

1 can dark kidney beans
1 can navy beans or any kind of
    bean
½ c. Mesquite barbecue sauce

Mix all ingredients together, mixing well. Bake for ½ hour in a 350° oven.

May be put in a crock pot and heated well.

Rosemary Boxrucker, Branch 4693, Rhinelander, WI

BAKED BEANS

1 large can pork and beans
¼ c. catsup
⅓ c. sorghum

1 tsp. dry mustard
¼ c. minced onion
2 slices bacon, crumbled

Mix all ingredients and place in greased casserole. Bake till bubbly and lightly browned in conventional oven at 350° for approximately 30 to 45 minutes.

May be cooked in microwave. Be sure to cover and vent, stirring occasionally.

Alice Ahrens, Branch No. 5325, Stratford, IA

Notes

Notes

Meats, Poultry, Seafood

MEAT ROASTING GUIDE

Cut	Weight Pounds	Approx. Time (Hours) (325° oven)	Internal Temperature
BEEF			
Standing Rib Roast [1] (10 inch) ribs)	4	1¾	140° (rare)
[1] If using shorter cut (8-inch)		2	160° (medium)
ribs, allow 30 min. longer		2½	170° (well done)
	8	2½	140° (rare)
		3	160° (medium)
		4½	170° (well done)
Rolled Ribs	4	2	140° (rare)
		2½	160° (medium)
		3	170° (well done)
	6	3	140° (rare)
		3¼	160° (medium)
		4	170° (well done)
Rolled rump [2]	5	2¼	140° (rare)
		3	160° (medium)
		3¼	170° (well done)
Sirloin tip [2]	3	1½	140° (rare)
[2] Roast only if high quality.		2	160° (medium)
Otherwise, braise.		2¼	170° (well done)
LAMB			
Leg	6	3	175° (medium)
		3½	180° (well done)
	8	4	175° (medium)
		4½	180° (well done)
VEAL			
Leg (piece)	5	2½ to 3	170° (well done)
Shoulder	6	3½	170° (well done)
Rolled Shoulder	3 to 5	3 to 3½	170° (well done)

POULTRY ROASTING GUIDE

Type of Poultry	Ready-To-Cook Weight	Oven Temperature	Approx. Total Roasting Time
TURKEY	6 to 8 lbs.	325°	2½ to 3 hrs.
	8 to 12 lbs.	325°	3 to 3½ hrs.
	12 to 16 lbs.	325°	3½ to 4 hrs.
	16 to 20 lbs.	325°	4 to 4½ hrs.
	20 to 24 lbs.	300°	5 to 6 hrs.
CHICKEN (Unstuffed)	2 to 2½ lbs.	400°	1 to 1½ hrs.
	2½ to 4 lbs.	400°	1½ to 2½ hrs.
	4 to 8 lbs.	325°	3 to 5 hrs.
DUCK (Unstuffed)	3 to 5 lbs.	325°	2½ to 3 hrs.

NOTE: Small chickens are roasted at 400° so that they brown well in the short cooking time. They may also be done at 325° but will take longer and will not be as brown. Increase cooking time 15 to 20 minutes for stuffed chicken and duck.

MEATS, POULTRY, SEAFOOD

STEAK ROLLS

1 lb. round steak or 6 minute
   steaks
½ c. diced celery
½ c. mushroom stems and pieces
2 Tbsp. shortening

1 env. onion soup mix
½ c. catsup
¼ tsp. Worcestershire sauce
¼ tsp. garlic powder
1½ c. water

Pound meat thin. Combine celery and mushrooms. Place 2 tablespoons mixture in center of each piece of meat and roll, fastening with toothpicks. In medium size skillet, melt shortening and brown rolls.

Combine onion soup, catsup, Worcestershire sauce, garlic powder, and water. Pour into skillet. Simmer, covered, for 1½ hours.

Linda Meiburg, Branch No. 6715, Rock Rapids, IA

PEPPER STEAK

1 lb. lean boneless sirloin steak,
   trimmed
1 clove garlic, crushed
1 tsp. ground ginger
1 tsp. salt
½ tsp. pepper
2 Tbsp. oil
3 large green peppers, cut into
   strips

2 large onions, thinly sliced
½ tsp. sugar
¾ c. beef broth
¼ c. soy sauce
6 oz. water chestnuts, sliced
1 Tbsp. cornstarch, dissolved in ¼
   c. cold water

Place steak in freezer for 1 hour to firm for easier slicing. Cut across grain into ⅛ inch thick slices. Saute garlic, ginger, salt, and pepper in oil in skillet till garlic is golden. Add steak slices and brown lightly, about 2 minutes. Remove meat. Add green peppers and onions; cook for 3 minutes. Return meat to skillet along with sugar, broth, soy sauce, water chestnuts, and cornstarch, dissolved in water. Simmer for about 2 minutes or until sauce thickens. Serve plain or over hot cooked rice.

Ed and Barb Allen, Branch No. 837, Secor, IL

SMOTHERED STEAK ROLL-UPS

2 lb. thinly sliced round steak
2 c. herb seasoned stuffing,
   prepared as directed
2 Tbsp. butter or margarine

1 (10½ oz.) can condensed cream
   of mushroom soup
½ c. water
½ c. sour cream (if desired)

Pound steak with meat hammer or edge of heavy saucer. Cut into 6 pieces long enough to roll. Place ⅓ cup stuffing near center of each steak; roll pinwheel fashion. Fasten with toothpick or skewers. Brown roll-ups in butter. Add soup and water. Cover and cook over low heat for 1 hour or until tender. Spoon sauce over meat often during cooking. Stir in sour cream. Heat for a few minutes more. (Meat tenderizer sprinkled on steak before pounding speeds cooking time.) Makes 6 servings.

Margaret Flaaen, Branch No. 4909, Zumbrota, MN

FLANK STEAK ROLL-UPS

1½ lb. flank steak
2 to 3 long carrots
Cooking oil
1 small can tomato sauce

Nutmeg
Salt and pepper
Toothpicks

Pound steak till thin or cut in thin slices. (Partly freeze meat and cut in lengthwise slices.) Sprinkle each slice with nutmeg, salt and pepper. Place long cleaned carrot on each steak; roll like jelly roll. Secure with toothpicks, cut in 1½ inch pieces. Brown in heavy skillet. Drain fat. To meat, add 1 can tomato sauce and 1 can water. Bring to a boil; reduce heat and simmer until carrots are tender. Serve with noodles or mashed potatoes.

Lillian Umscheid, Branch No. 3436, Pico Rivera, CA

SWISS STEAK SPECIAL

4 lb. round steak (2 inch thick)
½ c. flour
1½ tsp. salt
¼ tsp. pepper
1 medium onion, chopped

4 Tbsp. oil
1 c. tomato sauce
½ c. diced celery
¼ c. water
12 carrots (whole - optional)

Pound steak. Pound the meat well. Mix flour, salt, and pepper; work it into the meat. Brown onion lightly. Remove from pan. Brown meat on both sides. Place in Dutch oven or roaster. Add onion, 1 cup or more of tomatoes, celery and water. Add carrots. Cover and bake at 350° till meat is done, 1½ or 2 hours. Place on platter. Garnish with carrots and parsley.

Elizabeth Gumz, Branch No. 341, Dorchester, WI

EASY COMPANY STEAK

Cut 5 minute steaks (or round steak) into pieces. Roll in flour. Brown in skillet in 2 tablespoons oleo or oil. Place in 3 quart casserole. Into skillet, pour 1½ cups water and 2 tablespoons dry onion soup mix. Stir, loosening all of the good fryings in the skillet. Pour this over steaks.

Place peeled and halved potatoes over top of steaks. Put lid or aluminum foil on casserole. Bake for 1 hour at 375°. Serves 5.

Shirley Lind, Branch 2248, Akron, CO

MARINATED STEAK

1½ c. salad oil
¾ c. soy sauce
⅓ c. fresh lemon juice
½ c. garlic flavored wine vinegar
½ c. Worcestershire sauce
2 Tbsp. dry mustard

1½ tsp. parsley flakes
2¼ tsp. salt
1 Tbsp. pepper
1 lb. sirloin steak, cut into 3 inch
   pieces

Mix all ingredients well. Drop pieces of sirloin steak into mixture and soak overnight.

Sauce can be kept in refrigerator for 1 week or frozen.

Kathy Burtchin, Branch No. 4119, Pemberville, OH

POOR MAN'S STEAK

3 lb. hamburg
1 c. cracker crumbs
1 c. water
1 Tbsp. salt

1 Tbsp. pepper
Flour
1 can mushroom soup

Combine meat, crumbs, water, and seasonings. Press onto 13x9x2 inch pan 1 inch thick. Refrigerate until cold. Cut into squares. Roll in flour and brown in skillet. Put squares in casserole dish. Pour soup over (do not dilute soup). Bake, covered, in a 350° oven for 1½ hours.

Kathy Burtchin, Branch No. 4119, Pemberville, OH

BAKED STEAK

2 lb. round steak
1 to 2 Tbsp. prepared mustard
1 pkg. dry onion soup mix

4 oz. drained mushrooms
6 slices bacon
1 can mushroom soup

Remove bone in steak, but don't tenderize. Lay steaks, side by side, on a large double layer of aluminum foil. Spread with mustard, dry soup mix, and mushrooms. Roll tightly in jelly roll. Top with bacon and mushroom soup. Lift edges of foil and add mushroom liquid. Seal foil around meat and place in jelly roll pan. Bake for 5 hours at 250°.

Alice Holscher, Branch No. 2616, Bertrand, NE

ITALIAN BEEF ROAST

4 to 6 lb. sirloin tip roast
1 (16 oz.) can Clamato juice
½ tsp. oregano

Salt and pepper to taste
1 medium chopped onion
1 pkg. dry onion soup mix

Place roast in Dutch oven. Mix all ingredients and pour over roast. Cover and bake for ½ hour per pound at 300°F. When done, remove from juice and let rest for a few minutes before carving.

For sandwiches, cut roast thinly, place back in juice and heat. Serve on a kaiser roll.

Terry Ohlendorf, Branch No. 2306, Remsen, IA

HOT BEEF

6 lb. chuck roast
4 stalks cut up celery
2 large onions, chopped
1 green pepper, chopped
1 large (32 oz.) bottle catsup
3 Tbsp. vinegar

3 Tbsp. barbeque sauce
1 tsp. Tabasco sauce
1 tsp. chili powder
1 tsp. salt
1 tsp. pepper
1½ c. water

Mix all ingredients, except roast, together. Place roast in large roasting pan; add ingredients. Cover and bake for 6 hours in a 300° oven. When done, take meat out and shred. (Be careful to get bone out of sauce.) Beat mixture in pan and thicken if desired. Add meat back to sauce mixture; stir and serve on buns.

Janet Tranberg, Branch No. 5285, Madison, WI

BEEF INTERNATIONAL

2 cans beef consomme
3 sprigs parsley
2 tsp. celery flakes
Dash of Tabasco
4 peppercorns
3 medium onions, halved
1 tsp. Accent
2 garlic cloves

1 bay leaf
1 tsp. oregano
2 tsp. salt
1 tsp. sugar
1 (12 oz.) can beer
6 or 7 lb. boned and rolled beef
    roast

Combine all ingredients in a Dutch oven and bring to a boil. Add meat. Cook at very low heat (325°), covered, in oven for at least 3 hours or until tender.

Horseradish Sauce (serve with roast-gravy):

3 c. broth in which meat was
    cooked
6 Tbsp. butter

6 Tbsp. flour
1 c. sour cream
¼ c. horseradish

Strain broth. Melt butter; blend in flour. Add to broth to make a gravy. Thicken over low heat. Stir in sour cream slowly, then add horseradish before serving.

Gertrude Kummer. Branch No. 3039, Dunlap, IL

176

ROULADEN MIT SPAETZLE

Hot spicy mustard
6 breakfast steaks
1 onion, chopped
4 Tbsp. parsley

6 slices bacon, partially precooked
6 dill pickle spears
2 cans beefy mushroom soup
2 cans mushrooms

Saute onion and parsley in a small amount of butter or margarine. Spread mustard on meat with onion and parsley. Place pickle and bacon slice on one end of meat and roll up. Secure with pick. Roll in flour and brown in skillet on all sides. Add a little water, mushrooms and both cans of soup. Simmer very slow for 2 to 3 hours in electric skillet or bake at 250°, covered. Uncover the last 30 minutes, turning meat once.

Can also be cooked in crock pot on LOW all day or for 5 hours on HIGH. Serve with Spaetzle (or egg noodles).

Nancy Lawfer, Branch No. 779, Savanna, IL

SPAETZLE

2¾ c. flour
1 tsp. salt
⅛ tsp. nutmeg

⅛ tsp. paprika
4 eggs
¾ c. water or part milk and water

Stir together flour, salt, nutmeg, and paprika. Add eggs and water. Beat until thick and smooth. Press into boiling water with spaetzle maker or spread dough very thin with spatula. Cut into small strips (dip spatula in water several times during cutting) and drop into large kettle of boiling, salted water. If noodles do not keep their shape, add a little flour to dough. Boil gently for about 5 minutes. Remove with slotted spoon. Drain well and add a little butter. Continue with remaining dough. Serve hot.

Nancy Lawfer, Branch No. 779, Savanna, IL

EASY MEAT PIES

½ lb. beef steak
1 small onion

Garlic salt to taste
Salt and pepper to taste

Trim and pound meat. Cut into strips ¼ inch wide. Cut strips into short pieces. Add onion and seasonings. Moisten with a few drops of water and mix well.

Dough:

1 c. flour
5 tsp. margarine

½ tsp. salt
4 Tbsp. cold water

Sift flour and salt. Work in margarine. Add water to form stiff dough. Divide dough into 2 parts. Roll each part in thin oval. Place half of the meat mixture on each. Fold over and crimp edges of each pie. Bake on cookie sheet in a 350° oven for ½ hour.

Olga Sobers, Branch No. 6928, St. Albans, NY

FLEMISH CARBONNADES

2 lb. round steak (1 inch thick)
1/4 c. flour
1 tsp. sugar
1/8 tsp. pepper

6 to 8 small potatoes, peeled
1 (1 1/2 oz.) env. dry onion soup mix
3/4 c. beer

Trim round steak and cut into serving portions. Combine flour, sugar, and pepper. Toss with steak to coat thoroughly. Place potatoes in crock-pot and cover with steak pieces. Thoroughly combine onion soup mix and beer. Pour over steak, moistening well. Cover and cook on LOW setting for 8 to 12 hours. Thicken gravy before serving if desired. Makes 4 to 6 servings (about 3 quarts).

Jean Landgraf, Branch No. 2568, Fredericktown, MO

MT. McKINLEY MOUNTAIN GOAT

5 to 7 lb. rump or loin roast
Fresh parsley
3 cloves garlic

6 bacon strips
Salt and pepper to taste

Wash and clean meat thoroughly. Wipe dry with a soft cloth. Make small, deep slits in meat. Into each, insert a piece of garlic and a sprig of parsley. Salt and pepper the whole roast. Lay bacon strips on top. Fix with toothpicks. Heat oven to 450°. Brown roast for 15 minutes in the hot oven, then reduce heat to 350° and bake for about 2 hours, or until done.

Lord of Life Lutheran, "Heavenly Dishes" Cookbook,
Branch 6677, North Pole, AK

ITALIAN BEEF

4 lb. roast beef
1 Tbsp. oregano
3 bay leaves
2 Tbsp. vinegar
2 tsp. caraway seed
2 medium onions, cut up

1/2 tsp. garlic powder
1/2 c. water
2 tsp. fennel seeds
4 green peppers, cut in strips
3 beef bouillon cubes

Salt and pepper roast. Place in Dutch oven. Add all other ingredients, except peppers and bouillon cubes. Cover and place on low heat. Simmer for 3 hours, adding more water, if necessary, to keep meat from sticking. Take out meat. Add to sauce, green peppers, 3 bouillon cubes, and 3 cups water; simmer for 1/2 hour. Slice or shred meat and return to Dutch oven with peppers. Cover and cook for 1/2 hour longer or until desired tenderness. Serve on French bread. (Take out bay leaves.)

Vera Fox, Branch No. 362, Michigan City, IN

BAKED CHUCK AND MUSHROOM SAUCE

2½ lb. boneless chuck
1 (10½ oz.) can cream of
   mushroom soup
1 can water (use soup can)
1 small bay leaf
½ tsp. Worcestershire sauce

1 garlic button, sliced
1 onion, sliced
1½ tsp. salt
¼ tsp. pepper
3 Tbsp. shortening

Cut chuck in serving pieces. Roll in flour and brown in skillet with shortening. Remove browned meat to baking dish. If desired, brown onion and garlic; add mushroom soup and water to shortening (drippings in skillet) and bring to a boil. Stir to blend. Add seasonings and pour over browned meat. Cover and bake in a 350° oven for about 2 hours. Uncover and bake for ½ hour longer. (Add more water if needed.) Serve over cooked noodles.

Lorina Rosenbrock, Branch No. 2579, Pinconning, MI

SAUERBRATEN - MARINATED BEEF

4 lb. pot roast (any beef pot roast)
2 c. vinegar
2 c. water
1 large onion
¼ c. sugar
2 tsp. salt

10 peppercorns
3 whole cloves
2 bay leaves
1 lemon, rinsed and cut into ¼
   inch slices

Wipe the roast clean and place it in a 3 to 4 quart bowl; set aside. Combine the rest of the ingredients (except the lemon) into a saucepan and heat it without boiling. Pour the hot mixture over the meat in the bowl and allow to cool. Add the sliced lemon. Cover and set in refrigerator. Marinate for 4 days, turning meat once each day.

When ready to cook the meat, remove it from the marinade; drain and heat the meat in a kettle over low heat, using 2 to 3 tablespoons of butter. Brown the meat slowly on all sides over medium heat. Add 2 cups of the marinade (keep the rest for making gravy).

Bring liquid to a boil; reduce heat and cover the kettle tightly. Simmer for 2 ½ to 3 hours, or until meat is tender when pierced with a fork. Add more marinade if necessary.

For gravy, melt ¼ cup butter and blend in ¼ cup flour; gradually add 3 cups of the reserved marinade, stirring constantly. Bring to a boil; cook until mixture thickens. One-half cup of thick sour cream may be added. Serve the meat and gravy with potato pancakes.

Monroe Teachenor, Branch No. 1540, Berkeley, CA

BEEF BRISKET IN BEER

3 to 4 lb. beef brisket
1 onion, sliced
¼ c. chili sauce

2 Tbsp. brown sugar
1 clove garlic, minced
1 (12 oz.) can beer

Season brisket with salt and pepper. Place meat in 9x13x2 inch baking dish. Cover with onion slices. In bowl, combine chili sauce, brown sugar, garlic, and beer; pour over meat. Cover with foil. Bake in a 350° oven for 3½ hours. Uncover and bake for 30 minutes more, basting occasionally with juices. To serve, cut meat diagonally across grain and return to juices.

Note: Delicious on rolls with mustard, mayonnaise and horseradish.
Sue Koerber, Branch No. 4115, League City, TX

BRISKET

Brisket (6 to 7 lb.)
Garlic salt
Onion salt
Celery salt

Liquid smoke
Salt
Pepper
Worcestershire sauce

Place heavy-duty foil in pan. Put roast in pan with fat side up. Sprinkle generously with garlic, onion and celery salts. Pour ½ bottle liquid smoke on it; seal tightly with foil and set in refrigerator overnight. Take out next morning and sprinkle with salt and pepper. Pour ½ small bottle Worcestershire sauce on it. Wrap up and seal again. Bake at 270° for 5 or 6 hours.
Kim Williams, Branch No. 5323, Lubbock, TX

BEEF BURGUNDY

3 lb. beef cubes (sirloin tip)
1 can cream of mushroom soup
1 can cream of celery soup
1 c. burgundy wine
1 Tbsp. Kitchen Bouquet

1 onion, sliced
1 lb. mushrooms (or as many as
   your pocketbook will handle)
Salt and pepper to taste

Put all in covered pot, except mushrooms, and put in preheated oven at 325° for 2 to 3¼ hours. Add mushrooms 2 hours after cooking time. Uncover the last ½ hour. Serve over rice or noodles. (Use a 2½ quart casserole with cover.)
Sandra Bunch, Branch No. 2785, Santa Maria, CA

BEEF BURGUNDY

½ stick oleo
6 onions, sliced
½ lb. mushrooms, sliced
2 lb. sirloin steak, cut in 2 inch
   cubes
Salt and pepper to taste
Accent to taste

½ tsp. thyme
½ tsp. marjoram
1½ Tbsp. flour
2 c. tomatoes (canned or fresh
   peeled)
½ c. burgundy wine

Brown onions and mushrooms in oleo till tender. Remove from skillet. Brown sirloin cubes in the same skillet a little bit at a time so it doesn't get too steamy. Add salt, pepper, Accent, marjoram, and thyme. Blend in flour and mix well to

180

thicken. Add tomatoes and wine. Cover and cook slowly for about 2 hours. Add onions and mushrooms. Heat. Serve over noodles.

You can substitute round steak for sirloin. This recipe freezes well.
Betty Meinke, Branch No. 3868, Highland Heights, OH

MOM'S SAUERKRAUT

1½ lb. country ribs
2 lb. sauerkraut
1 medium onion, sliced
1 large bay leaf

10 whole peppercorns
1 lb. smoked meat (such as picnic
    ham, pork chops, etc.)

Thoroughly brown country ribs on roasting pan. Drain juice from sauerkraut and add to country ribs. Add onion, bay leaf, peppercorns, and smoked meat at the same time. Continue baking for approximately 1 hour.
Martha H. Kahanak, Branch No. 3107, Loveland, CO

MARINADE FOR STEAKS

¾ c. olive oil
½ c. soy sauce
2 Tbsp. Worcestershire sauce
1 Tbsp. dry mustard
1 tsp. salt

1 tsp. coarse pepper
¼ c. wine vinegar
1 tsp. dried parsley flakes
2 cloves garlic, crushed (optional)
¼ c. lemon juice

Combine all ingredients and mix well. Store in refrigerator until ready to use. Yields 1¾ cups.

MEXICAN FLANK STEAK

2 flank steaks (1 lb. each)
Salt and pepper
Garlic salt
1 (15 oz.) can tamales
1 beef bouillon cube

¼ c. boiling water
1 (8 oz.) can tomato sauce
¼ tsp. ground cumin
½ tsp. chili powder

Trim steaks of fat and pound on both sides with meat tenderizer. Season with salt, pepper and garlic salt.

In small bowl, break tamales (with paper removed) into pieces and toss with sauce from can. Spread tamales over surface of steaks. Roll steaks lengthwise. Tie with string and place in 9x13 inch pan.

Dissolve bouillon cube in boiling water and stir into tomato sauce, ground cumin and chili powder. Spoon sauce over meat. Bake, uncovered, at 350° for 1 ¼ to 1½ hours, basting occasionally. Serves 8.

If you don't need both steak rolls for one meal, make them both and freeze one.

Vicki Bien, Loveland, CO

BEEF STROGANOFF AND RICE CASSEROLE

Beef Stroganoff:

3 lb. sirloin tip steak strips or
    cubes
2 cans cream of mushroom soup

1 env. Lipton onion soup
¾ c. sherry

Bake for 1½ hours at 350°, covered and 1½ hours, uncovered. Last hour of baking, add 4 ounce jar of mushrooms. Just before serving, add ½ pint sour cream. Serve over rice or noodles.

Rice Casserole:

1 (14 oz.) pkg. Minute rice
1 Tbsp. salt

½ c. butter
5½ c. boiling water

Put rice in casserole with butter, cut in pieces. Add salt. Pour boiling water over. Cover and bake at 450° for 20 minutes.

Arlene Bjorklund, Branch No. 5943, Roseville, MN

MY LAZY DAY STROGANOFF

1½ lb. round steak
1½ Tbsp. vegetable oil
2 onions, cut in slices and
    separated
1 can mushrooms (stems and
    pieces or sliced - reserve
    liquid)

1 can cream of mushroom soup
½ c. apple juice
Garlic salt
1 pkg. egg noodles
1 small container sour cream

Cut steak into strips. Brown in oil. Add onion when meat has browned. Cook until tender. Add mushrooms with liquid. Add soup, apple juice and garlic salt. Cook over medium to low heat for 1 hour. Stir occasionally. When meat is tender, add sour cream and serve over cooked noodles (or rice).

Branch No. 628, Farmington, MO

MARINATED CUBE STEAKS
(Low calorie)

4 (4 oz.) cube steaks
¼ c. low-cal Blue cheese or Italian
    dressing

1 tomato, cut into eighths

Place meat in coated pan. Pour dressing over. Let set for 20 minutes and turn once. Brown over medium high heat for about 4 minutes on each side. About 2 minutes before done, add tomato. Season with salt if desired. Serve topped with tomato and the juices. Makes 4 servings (250 calories each).

Sharon Verville, Branch No. 3107, Loveland, CO

CHINESE SPARERIBS

3 lb. spareribs, cut 2 inches long
3 tsp. cornstarch
1 Tbsp. sherry wine
2 thumb size ginger root, chopped
¾ c. vinegar

½ c. water
6 Tbsp. soy sauce
1 tsp. salt
2 cloves garlic, minced
¾ c. brown sugar

Soak spareribs in sauce of soy sauce, cornstarch, salt, and wine for about 10 minutes. Brown ginger root and garlic in oil. Brown spareribs. Drain oil. Add vinegar, sugar and water. Cook for about 45 minutes.

Alice Joerns, Branch No. 180, Denver, CO

CORNISH GAME HEN AND WILD RICE SUPREME

4 fresh or frozen Cornish game
    hens
2 Tbsp. butter or margarine,
    melted
1 (16 oz.) long grain and wild rice
    mix
1 (10¾ oz.) can chicken broth

2 Tbsp. butter or margarine
1 bunch green onions, sliced
6 large mushrooms, sliced, or 1
    (4.5 oz.) jar sliced mushrooms
½ c. dry white wine
2 bay leaves

Thaw hens if frozen. Remove giblets. Rinse hens and pat dry. Brush inside and out with melted butter. Remove seasoning packet from rice mix. Use 1 teaspoon seasoning per hen and rub inside and out. Pour chicken broth and ½ cup water into a shallow roasting pan. Bake, breast side up, for 15 minutes at 450°.

Meanwhile, melt 2 tablespoons butter in a skillet. Add green onions, mushrooms and rice packet from mix. Saute, stirring frequently. Slowly add 1¼ cups water, remaining seasonings from packet, wine, and bay leaves. Bring to a boil. Pour rice mixture into roasting pan. Make sure rice does not rest on top of hens. Brush hens with remaining butter. Cover loosely with foil. Reduce heat to 350° and bake for an additional 45 minutes or until all liquid is absorbed. Serve hens on a bed of rice. Makes 4 servings.

Mrs. Sheila Zasada, Branch No. 0356, Dubuque, IA

SOUTH DAKOTA PHEASANT

2 pheasants
Salt and pepper to taste
1 large onion, chopped
1 green pepper, chopped

1 c. celery, chopped
2 cans mushroom soup
2 soup cans water
½ c. cream

Cut pheasants into serving pieces. Roll in mixture of salt, pepper and flour. Brown in frying pan with butter or oil. Place browned pheasant in roaster or baking dish. Saute the onion, green pepper and celery in butter. Put on top of pheasants. Add mushroom soup and water which has been mixed well together. Add the ½ cup cream the last hour. Bake at 275° for 2 to 3 hours until tender. *Delicious!*

Leona Rieck, Branch No. 4029, Warner, SD

FRESH VENISON LIVER

2½ lb. venison liver, sliced ½ inch
    thick (best if cooked same day
    as kill)
½ c. flour
Salt and pepper

6 Tbsp. flour
2 Tbsp. lemon juice
3 red onions, sliced
3 Tbsp. butter

Saute onions in 3 tablespoons butter over fairly high heat. Remove to separate plate (keeping it warm). Dip liver in flour, salt and pepper. Saute over fairly high heat in the 6 tablespoons butter, turning once. (Cook for about 4 minutes on each side.) Stir lemon juice into dredging, adding more butter if necessary. Pour lemon sauce over liver. Arrange onions along side liver and serve with Cabernet Sauvignon wine.

Pastor Michael G. Warmbier, Branch No. 1393, Columbia Falls, MT

ELK PAPRIKA

2 lb. round elk or beef steak
1 tsp. paprika
1 beef bouillon, dissolved in 1 c.
    boiling water
1 Tbsp. Worcestershire sauce

2 Tbsp. flour
2 Tbsp. oil
1 tsp. salt
1 minced garlic clove
½ pt. sour cream

Heat oil and brown garlic while rubbing meat with salt and paprika. Brown the meat in the garlic oil. Add bouillon and Worcestershire sauce to meat. Cover and cook slowly for about 2 hours or until tender. Add water as needed. Beef will not take as long. Add sour cream and 1 teaspoon additional paprika. Simmer for a few minutes. Remove steak. Thicken the broth with the flour placed in ½ cup of water. Stir until smooth and serve over meat.

Sharon Verville, Branch No. 3107, Loveland, CO

VENISON STROGANOFF

2 lb. venison round steak, cut ¾
    inch thick
4 Tbsp. oleo
1 chopped onion
¼ tsp. basil
Pepper to taste

1¼ c. beef bouillon
1 c. sliced mushrooms
2 Tbsp. flour
1½ tsp. prepared mustard
1 c. sour cream

Remove fat from meat and cut meat into strips ¼ inch wide and 1½ inches long. Brown meat in 2 tablespoons oleo in a skillet. Transfer to an ovenproof casserole and add onion, basil and pepper. Heat bouillon in small skillet until it reaches the boiling point, scraping the bottom to loosen meat particles. Pour over the meat. Cover and bake in 350° oven for 1½ hours, turning twice during the baking time.

Saute mushrooms in 2 tablespoons oleo until lightly browned. Stir in flour and then liquid from the meat. Stir constantly until the mixture cooks and thickens. Add mustard and sour cream; bring to the boiling point. Pour over the meat and serve over cooked rice or broad noodles. Serves 4.

Gloria Lutz, Branch No. 5454, Pawnee, IL

LIVER DUMPLINGS

2 c. (2 to 3 day-old bread), ground
    up
1 onion
½ lb. ground liver
4 soda crackers, ground
3 eggs

1 tsp. sage
1½ tsp. salt
½ tsp. pepper
⅓ c. flour
½ c. milk

Mix the last 6 ingredients with the first 4. If needed, add ½ to 1 cup stuffing mix to make thicker batter. Form balls and drop in (slowly) boiling beef-vegetable broth. Cook for 10 to 12 minutes, covered.

Zona Schufletowski, Branch No. 1048, Muskego, WI

BARBECUED TROUT

8 fish (trout)
1 to 2 lemon wedges

¼ to ½ tsp. either parsley, basil or
    chives (herbs)

Marinade:

½ c. soy sauce
½ c. cooking sherry
¼ c. vegetable oil

1 Tbsp. lime or lemon juice
1 clove garlic, crushed

Put marinade ingredients into shaker and shake well. Brush trout cavity with juice from lemon wedge and sprinkle with herbs. Place in shallow pan and pour on marinade. Let stand for 1 hour, turning once. Cook over hot coals on well greased grill, turning once. Baste while cooking with strained marinade.

Total cooking time is 5 to 8 minutes per side.

Sheila Moureau, Branch No. 6439, Madison, WI

SEABURGERS

1 can tuna, drained
¼ c. onion
¼ c. sweet pickles
1 c. celery

¼ c. mayonnaise or salad dressing
¼ c. American cheese, cubed
½ c. catsup

Mix all ingredients together. Put on hamburger buns and wrap in foil. Place in a 350° oven until cheese melts (15 minutes).

Good for quick Friday night supper.

Carol Jean Eller, Branch No. 3304, Flushing, MI

SCALLOPED OYSTERS

1 (8 oz.) can oysters, drained (save
    liquid)
30 soda crackers (about)
1 large egg, slightly beaten

1¼ c. milk
4 pats butter or margarine
Salt and pepper to taste

Mix together slightly beaten egg, oyster liquid and milk; set aside. Crumble about 10 crackers in bottom of buttered casserole. Add ½ oysters. Add another layer of crackers, rest of oysters, and then rest of crackers. Add pats of butter. Do not add liquid until ready to put in oven. Bake at 350° for about 30 to 40 minutes (when crackers are raised in center). Can be doubled.

Arline Young, Branch No. 1265, Creighton, MO

BUTTER HERB BAKED FISH

½ c. butter
⅔ c. crushed saltine crackers
¼ c. grated Parmesan cheese
½ tsp. salt
½ tsp. basil leaves

½ tsp. oregano leaves
¼ tsp. garlic powder
1 lb. frozen fish fillets, thawed and
    drained

Heat oven to 350°. In 13x9 inch baking pan, melt butter in oven (5 to 7 minutes). Meanwhile, in 9 inch pie pan, combine cracker crumbs, Parmesan cheese, salt, basil, oregano, and garlic powder. Dip fish fillets in batter, then crumb mixture. Arrange fish fillets in baking pan. Bake for 25 to 30 minutes or until fish is tender and flakes with a fork.

Bernice Bergseth, Branch No. 1737, Finlayson, MN

POACHED SALMON ALA DISHWASHER

1 (3 lb.) whole salmon (head and
    tail removed)
Salt
Freshly ground pepper
2 Tbsp. butter, cut into pieces

1 small onion, sliced
1 small lemon, sliced
½ c. white wine
Watercress or parsley sprigs
Lemon wedges

Rinse salmon thoroughly. Pat dry. Sprinkle liberally with salt and pepper inside and out. Place on piece of foil large enough to wrap fish completely. Arrange butter, onion and lemon slices in cavity. Sprinkle with wine. Fold foil around fish, making a water tight package. Wrap several more layers of foil to seal completely. Place fish on top rack of dishwasher. *Do not* add detergent. Set washer for full cycle, including drying cycle.

When cycle is finished, remove fish package and unwrap. Discard onion and lemon slices. Carefully lift out backbone and smaller bones. (They should come out in one piece.) Scrape off any discolored spots. Remove fins. Serve warm or chilled on bed of watercress or parsley. Garnish with lemon wedges. Serve with favorite seafood sauce.

Mrs. Kenneth (Marion) Sheldon, Branch 2088, Shenandoah, IA

TUNA SOUFFLE

1 can tuna (I usually use 2)
3 egg yolks (or Egg Beaters)
4 Tbsp. butter, melted

1 Tbsp. flour
1 can mushroom soup
3 egg whites, beaten

Mix all together, except beaten whites. Fold whites into mixture. Pour into greased casserole. Bake at 350° for 20 to 25 minutes. Serves 5.

Esther Lou Wiedey, Branch No. 1387, Carrollton, MO

CRAB AND SHRIMP BAKE

1 medium size green pepper, chopped
1 medium size onion, chopped
1 c. celery, chopped
1 (6½ oz.) can crabmeat
1 (6½ oz.) can shrimp or equal amount of cooked shrimp

½ tsp. salt
⅛ tsp. pepper
1 tsp. Worcestershire sauce
1 c. mayonnaise
1 c. buttered crumbs

Combine ingredients, except crumbs. Place in casserole and sprinkle with buttered bread crumbs. Bake at 350° for 30 minutes. Serves 8.

Elaine Tiemann Johnson, Branch No. 2334, Pasadena, TX

MERMAID FISH FILLET

Mixture:

8 oz. *orange roughy,* patted dry (skin side up - 4 to 5 oz. fillets)
Lemon pepper

1 lb. imitation crabmeat
1 small bunch green onions
Mayonnaise (approx. 3 Tbsp.)

Pat fillets dry and sprinkle with lemon pepper. Chop 12 ounces to 1 pound imitation crabmeat (or use canned crab), small bunch of green onions (chopped also, use some tops), and 1 teaspoon lemon pepper. Mix enough mayonnaise to hold together (3 tablespoons). Spread mixture on fillets and roll up fillets from head to tail. Arrange on Pyrex baking plate.

Topping:

2 egg whites
1 tsp. lemon juice
4 Tbsp. mayonnaise

1 tsp. French's mustard
2 Tbsp. fresh dill or 2 tsp. dried dill

Garnish:

Radish roses
Parsley

Lemon wedges

Whip 2 egg whites and 1 teaspoon lemon juice stiff. Fold in mayonnaise, French's mustard, and fresh dill or dried dill. Mix and spoon over rolled fillets. Place dish on aluminum foil and shape up around edge of plate for sides. Bake at 425° for 20 to 25 minutes. Garnish with radish roses, parsley and lemon wedges.

Lloyd Williams, Branch No. 5844, Columbia City, IN

CRAB CASSEROLE

Dice 4 slices bread into a buttered dish.

Mix and add:

2 cans crab
½ c. mayonnaise
1 onion, chopped

1 green pepper, chopped
1 c. celery
Salt and pepper to taste

Place another 4 slices diced bread on top. Slightly beat 4 eggs and add 3 cups milk; pour over. Keep in refrigerator overnight. Bake at 350° for 15 minutes.

Remove and pour over 1 can mushroom soup. Top with grated cheese. Bake in 10x13 inch casserole at 325° for 60 minutes. Serves 10 to 12.

Bonnie Lutz, Branch No. 2630, Greeley, CO

BAKED OYSTERS AND NOODLES

1 pt. or 1 can drained oysters (save
   liquid)
4 Tbsp. butter
½ tsp. salt
Dash of pepper
½ tsp. paprika

1½ c. oyster liquid and rich milk
2 Tbsp. flour
2 c. uncooked, broken noodles
1 Tbsp. butter
½ c. bread crumbs

Saute oysters in 4 tablespoons butter very slowly until edges begin to curl. Add seasonings. Drain. Add rich milk to drained liquor to make 1½ cups. Add gradually to flour in saucepan, stirring well. Cook till thickened. Cook noodles in a large amount of boiling water till tender. Drain and add butter. Arrange half of the noodles in baking dish, then add oysters, then the other half of the noodles. Pour sauce over all. Top with crumbs. Bake at 450° for 15 minutes. Serve at once!! Serves 6.

Mrs. Margaret Greiner, Branch No. 2838, Wilmot, SD

SHRIMP-CLAM SAUCE WITH LINGUINI

¼ c. butter or margarine
¼ c. sliced green onion
1 small clove garlic, crushed
2 Tbsp. flour
1 Tbsp. Dijon mustard
2 (6½ oz.) cans chopped clams
   (*don't* drain - reserve liquid)
⅓ c. water

⅓ c. chopped parsley
¼ c. dry white wine
¼ tsp. basil leaves
¼ tsp. salt
½ lb. medium size shrimp,
   cooked, peeled and deveined
Hot cooked linguini

Melt butter in medium saucepan. Add onion and garlic. Cook over medium heat for 3 minutes. Stir in flour and mustard. Add the liquid from clams, water, wine, parsley, basil leaves, and salt. Simmer (covered) for 10 minutes, stirring occasionally. Stir in clams and shrimp. Heat to serving temperature. Serve over linguini. Yield: 4 servings.

Ellen Wagner, Branch No. 6245, Portage, WI

SHRIMP CREOLE

1½ c. chopped onion
1 c. finely chopped celery
2 medium green peppers, finely
    chopped
2 cloves garlic, minced
¼ c. butter or oleo
1 (15 oz.) can tomato sauce

1 c. water
2 tsp. minced parsley
1 tsp. salt
½ tsp. cayenne pepper
2 bay leaves, crushed
12 oz. raw shrimp
3 c. cooked rice

Cook and stir onion, celery, peppers, and garlic in butter for about 5 minutes. Remove from heat. Add tomato sauce, water, parsley, salt, pepper, bay leaves, and shrimp. Simmer for 10 minutes (add additional water if needed) and serve over hot cooked rice.

Mary Dietrich, Branch No. 2468, Friendswood, TX

LINGUINI WITH CLAM SAUCE

½ c. clarified butter
2 cloves garlic, finely chopped
4 c. good quality clams with sauce
6 Tbsp. white wine
White pepper to taste

6 sprigs parsley, chopped
3 tsp. roux (equal amounts butter
    and flour or thicken to taste)
1 lb. linguini, cooked al dente
Dried parsley (may be used)

In a 9 inch saucepan, lightly saute garlic in butter. Add clams and juice, wine, pepper, and half of the parsley. Simmer for 5 minutes. Just before serving, add the roux and thicken lightly. Pour over cooked linguini. Serve with remaining parsley. Makes 4 servings.

I've also added medium shrimp to the clams. *Delicious!*

Betty McCormick, Branch No. 4083, Brown Deer, WI

CODFISH CAKES

3 lb. codfish
1 qt. oil
½ lb. grated potatoes
4 eggs, beaten
1 Tbsp. baking powder

2 lb. scallions, chopped fine
6 cloves garlic
Crushed hot pepper to taste
Salt to taste
2 Tbsp. flour

Soak codfish in cold water for 12 hours. Place in boiling water and cook for 15 minutes. Remove from boiling water. Place in cool water, wash well, remove all bones, and chop in fine pieces. Put 1 quart of oil in a shallow saucepan. Put on a hot burner, but do not let smoke. Add the remaining ingredients, except the flour, to the chopped fish. Cream in the flour. Add water and mix with a wooden spoon until workable. Shape into cakes and drop into the hot oil, one by one. Remove when golden brown. Serve hot as an appetizer.

Elaine Thomas, Branch No. 6928, St. Albans, NY

SHRIMP JAMBALAYA

2 c. fully cooked ham
¾ c. chopped onion
½ tsp. garlic powder
2 Tbsp. margarine or butter
2 (15 oz.) cans tomato sauce with
    bits
1 (10½ oz.) can beef broth
1 c. uncooked long grain rice
1 bay leaf

1 tsp. sugar
½ tsp. ground thyme
¼ tsp. chili powder
Dash of freshly ground pepper
1 lb. cooked shrimp
¼ c. sliced pitted olives
1 medium green pepper, cut in ¾
    inch sq.

In large saucepan, cook ham and onion in butter till onion is tender. Add garlic powder, tomato sauce, beef broth, 1 cup water, rice, bay leaf, sugar, thyme, chili powder, and pepper. Cover and simmer until rice is tender, about 15 minutes.

Add shrimp, olives and green pepper squares. Simmer, uncovered, to desired consistency. Do not overcook shrimp! Five minutes should be sufficient. Cover and let set for another 5 minutes. Makes 4 to 6 servings.

Estelle Krist, Branch No. 1221

QUICK AND ELEGANT ORANGE ROUGHY
(Microwave)

1 to 1½ lb. orange roughy fillets
⅓ c. sliced mushrooms
¼ c. chopped onions
1 tsp. salt
½ tsp. pepper
1 tsp. marjoram

¼ c. dry white wine
2 tsp. lemon juice
¼ c. grated Monterey Jack cheese
¼ c. bread crumbs or dry stuffing
    mix
½ c. melted butter

Sprinkle onions and mushrooms over the bottom of an oblong glass dish. Arrange fillets over vegetables, overlapping only the thin part of the fillets. Season the fish with salt, pepper and marjoram. Sprinkle the wine and lemon juice over all. Top with cheese and bread crumbs; pour butter over all. Cover with wax paper and microwave for 5 to 7 minutes on HIGH or until flaky.

Note: This may be baked in a conventional oven at 400° for 7 minutes, covered, and for 5 minutes more, uncovered.

Cynthia Hunzeker, Branch No. 3107, Loveland, CO

CORNED OYSTERS

1 (8 oz.) can Cove oysters
1 (17 oz.) can whole kernel corn
3 c. milk

¾ lb. crackers (approx.)
¼ lb. butter or margarine

Grease well with butter or margarine a 2 quart glass covered casserole. Layer, using crackers, corn and oysters, and then dot generously with dabs of butter or margarine. (Makes about 3 layers.) Finish with layer of crackers and dots of butter or margarine. Save liquid off corn and oysters; pour them over finished casserole and then pour milk over to moisten. May find it necessary to add slightly more milk to moisten thoroughly. Bake, covered, in a 350° oven and then remove cover for 30 minutes more to brown top.

SWISS ALPINE PIE

1 (9 inch) pastry shell (unbaked)
1 pkg. frozen broccoli, cooked
2 c. (½ lb.) precooked ham, cubed
2 c. Swiss cheese, shredded
3 Tbsp. onion, chopped

½ c. milk
3 eggs, slightly beaten
⅛ tsp. salt
⅛ tsp. pepper

Drain and chop broccoli. Place broccoli, ham and cheese in alternate layers in pastry shell. Sprinkle onion over top. Set aside. Gradually stir milk into eggs; add seasonings. Pour into pastry shell. Bake for 10 minutes in preheated 450° oven. Reduce to 325° and continue to bake for an additional 30 to 35 minutes. Remove from oven. Allow to stand for a few minutes before serving in wedges.

Variation: Use 4 ounces of chiles instead of broccoli.

Glendis Parker, Branch No. 5604, Tucson, AZ

MOM'S HAM BALLS

1½ lb. ham, ground
1 lb. lean pork, ground
2 eggs, beaten

1 c. milk
2 c. bread crumbs (fine)

Mix ham, pork, eggs, milk, and bread crumbs together. Form into balls. Pour into 9x13 inch pan.

Sauce:

1½ c. brown sugar
3 Tbsp. cornstarch
1½ Tbsp. prepared mustard
½ tsp. cloves (optional)

1¾ c. pineapple juice
½ c. light Karo syrup
3 Tbsp. vinegar

Mix brown sugar, cornstarch, mustard, and cloves in saucepan. Add pineapple juice, syrup and vinegar. Bring to a boil, stirring constantly. Reduce heat and simmer for 3 minutes. Pour over ham balls and bake at 350° for 1 hour.

Jennifer Emery, Branch No. 6541, West Fargo, ND

HAM BALLS IN PINEAPPLE SAUCE

2 lb. ground ham
2 lb. ground pork
2 c. soft bread crumbs
4 eggs, slightly beaten

1 c. milk
½ c. finely chopped onion
Salt and pepper to taste

Combine ingredients and make into medium size balls. Place in a shallow baking pan and brown in oven (350°). Drain off grease. Bake for 1 hour.

Sauce:

2 (9 oz.) cans crushed pineapple
⅔ c. catsup
⅔ c. vinegar

¼ c. soy sauce
1 c. brown sugar
1 Tbsp. ginger

Combine all ingredients and spoon over balls. Bake, basting occasionally with sauce. Yield: 10 to 12 servings.

Joyce Mross, Branch No. 3383, Indianapolis, IN

HAM BALLS-HAM LOAF

2½ lb. ground smoked ham
2 lb. ground lean pork
1 lb. ground lean beef

3 eggs
3 c. crushed graham crackers
2 c. milk

Mix together all ingredients and place in greased loaf pan or make into balls and place in greased baking pan. Bake at 350° for 45 minutes for loaf pan and 25 minutes for ham balls. Drain any fats. Cover with sauce and bake for another 30 minutes. Baste with additional sauce every once in awhile.

Sauce:

2 c. tomato soup
¾ c. vinegar
1½ c. brown sugar

1 c. sorghum
2 tsp. dry mustard

Mix together all ingredients.

Alice Ahrens, Branch No. 5325, Stratford, IA

HAM LOAF

1 lg. ground smoked ham
1 lb. ground lean pork
3 c. *Wheaties*
2 eggs, beaten

1 c. milk
½ tsp. salt
⅛ tsp. pepper

Mix preceding ingredients thoroughly. Pack into greased 9x5x3 inch loaf pan.

For catsup topped loaf, spread 3 tablespoons catsup over top before baking. Bake at 350° (moderate oven) for 1½ hours. Unmold. Makes 8 servings.

Harriet B. Redman, Branch No. 5844, Columbia City, IN

ONE POUND PORK CHOPS

Have on hand six 1 pound pork chops.

Marinating Sauce:

2 c. soy sauce
1 c. water
½ c. brown sugar

1 Tbsp. dark molasses
1 tsp. salt

Mix soy sauce, water, brown sugar, molasses, and salt. Bring to a boil. Let cool. Put 6 chops on a pan with bone side up. Pour over chops and let stand overnight in refrigerator. Next day, take chops out of sauce, place in a baking dish and cover tightly with foil. Put in a 375° oven and bake until tender, about 2 hours. While chops are baking, combine all Red Sauce ingredients in heavy saucepan or double boiler.

Red Sauce:

1/3 c. water	1/2 c. brown sugar
1 (14 oz.) bottle ketchup	1 Tbsp. dry mustard
1 (12 oz.) bottle Heinz chili sauce	

Mix dry mustard, sugar and water together, leaving no lumps. Bring all ingredients to a slight boil and the Red Sauce is finished.

After chops are tender, remove them from the oven and dip in Red Sauce. After dipping, place chops in a baking dish and bake for 30 minutes or until slightly glazed. Keep chops at room temperature until you are ready to put them on the charcoal pit or grill. Have grill as high as possible over a small bed of coals. Grill chops slowly, no more than 15 minutes. A little blackening does not hurt. Both sauces can be reused if brought to a boil and refrigerated or frozen.

Lisa Rosendale, Augusta, IL

EASY COUNTRY STYLE RIBS

This recipe is very easy to double or even triple if the need arises.

2 to 3 lb. country style pork ribs	1 tsp. chile powder
1 c. catsup	1/2 tsp. (or more if you wish)
2 c. water	Tabasco sauce

Put the ribs in a small roaster or baking dish. Bake in a 375° oven for 1 1/2 hours. Drain off the accumulated fat. Mix together the catsup, water, chile powder, and Tabasco sauce. Pour over the ribs. Return to the oven for another 1 1/2 hours or until tender. The meat usually releases from the bone at the end of the baking time.

It is one of our family's favorite dishes.

Ann Kudrna, Branch No. 1149, Leigh, NE

MARINATED PORK STEAKS

4 to 6 pork steaks	1/4 c. salad oil
1 (8 oz.) can crushed pineapple	3 Tbsp. corn syrup
1 medium onion, chopped	1 tsp. ground ginger
1/2 c. soy sauce	

Drain pineapple, saving juice. Combine pineapple juice with onion, soy sauce, oil, corn syrup, and ginger in pint saucepan. Cook for 10 minutes, stirring to blend. Cool. Place pork steaks in flat utility dish. Pour cooled marinade over steaks. Cover and refrigerate for 4 to 6 hours (or overnight). Remove steaks. Cook on grill, 4 to 5 inches from coals. Turn and brush with remaining marinade. Takes approximately 30 minutes to cook.

Linda Ladage, Branch No. 640, Dwight, IL

BAKED PORK CHOPS AND APPLE DRESSING

1 small onion, chopped fine
1 rib celery, chopped fine
3 c. cubed rye bread
2 red or green apples, cored and
  chopped
1 c. shredded Swiss cheese (I use
  cheese substitute)
½ c. raisins
1 egg, beaten
1 chicken bouillon cube (optional)
¼ c. hot water
6 pork chops (each about 1 inch
  thick)

Preheat oven to 375°. In medium bowl, combine onion, celery, bread, apples, ¾ cup cheese, raisins, and egg. Dissolve bouillon cube in water and add to mixture into greased roasting pan. Place in pan atop mixture. Bake for 35 minutes. Sprinkle remaining ¼ cup cheese over chops and bake for 10 minutes until chops are cooked through.

Esther Lou Wiedey, Branch No. 1387, Carrollton, MO

ESPECIALLY GOOD PORK SHOULDER

6 lb. pork shoulder
½ c. drained crushed pineapple
⅓ c. finely chopped onion
2 Tbsp. brown sugar
2 Tbsp. soy sauce
1½ tsp. salt
1 tsp. vinegar
¼ c. pineapple juice
2 Tbsp. brown sugar
1 Tbsp. prepared mustard

Cut slits of ½ inch over top of pork shoulder with a sharp knife. In a bowl, mix crushed pineapple, onion, 2 tablespoons brown sugar, soy sauce, salt, and vinegar. Press the pineapple mixture into the slits. Cover and refrigerate overnight.

Place roast, fat side up, on rack in open roasting pan. Insert meat thermometer so bulb is in thickest part of roast, but not touching bone. Roast in a 325° oven for about 3½ hours or until thermometer registers 170°. The last 20 minutes of roasting, brush the pineapple juice, 2 tablespoons brown sugar, and mustard over the roast. Remove from oven and let stand for 10 minutes so roast firms up a bit.

Margaret Bicherb, Deerfield, WI, Branch No. 2017, Marshall, WI

KALUA PIG

1 (16 oz.) jar barbeque sauce   1 (6 to 8 lb.) boneless pork roast

Bake roast in crock pot for 8 hours. Drain. Cut off fat. Cut into bite-size pieces. Mix with barbeque sauce and heat through.

Sandi Seim, Branch No. 6255, Wahiawa, HI

PORK CHOPS 'N STUFFING

6 pork chops
3 to 4 c. soft bread crumbs
2 to 3 Tbsp. chopped onion
¼ c. celery with leaves
½ c. melted butter
½ c. water
¼ tsp. poultry seasoning
1 can cream of mushroom soup

Mix ½ cup water with ½ can soup. Combine with other stuffing ingredients. Brown chops. Place mound of stuffing on each. Use other ½ can of soup to pour over chops. Bake in a 350° oven for 1 hour, covered.

Stuffing is also good with chopped black olives or apple in it.

Sadie Johansen, Branch No. 3365, Rock Springs, WY

MAI TAI PORK LOIN

5 lb. pork loin
2 tsp. garlic salt
1 (20 oz.) can crushed pineapple

½ c. brown sugar, packed
1 tsp. grated orange peel
1 Tbsp. rum or ¼ tsp. rum extract

Place pork in roasting pan; sprinkle with garlic salt. Roast at 325° for 2½ hours. Drain pineapple. Combine with brown sugar, orange peel and rum. Spoon over pork and bake for ½ hour more, basting often.

Mary Schaffer, Loveland, CO

SPARERIBS WITH APPLES

4 lb. country style spareribs
2 Tbsp. margarine
½ c. minced onions
3 c. apple juice
½ c. vinegar

3 Tbsp. brown sugar
1½ tsp. cinnamon
2 tsp. salt
2 Tbsp. cornstarch
4 large apples

Brown ribs in Dutch oven. In saucepan, saute onions in margarine. Stir in 2¾ cups of the apple juice, the vinegar, brown sugar, cinnamon, and salt; heat to a boil. In a cup, combine cornstarch and ¼ cup apple juice; gradually add to hot liquid. Cook and stir until thickened. Drain fat off ribs. Pour on mixture. Cover and cook for 1½ to 2 hours. Cut each apple in quarters after coring. Add to ribs, spooning liquid over. Cook, covered, for 1 more hour.

Mary Schaffer, Loveland, CO

PORK CHOPS 'N STUFFING

6 pork chops
4 c. soft bread crumbs
2 Tbsp. chopped onion
½ c. melted butter
½ c. water

1 tsp. poultry seasoning
1 can cream of chicken or
mushroom or celery soup
½ c. water

Brown pork chops on both sides in ovenproof skillet; pour off drippings. Lightly mix bread crumbs, onion, butter, water, and poultry seasoning. Place a mound of stuffing on each pork chop. Blend soup and water; pour over stuffing. Bake at 350° for 1 hour. Yield: 6 servings.

Luanna Bauschlicher, Corning, AR

PORK CHOPS AND APPLES

8 pork chops
4 to 5 apples, cored and sliced
¼ c. brown sugar
½ c. raisins

½ tsp. salt and pepper
½ tsp. sage
1 c. hot water
1 Tbsp. vinegar

Flour and brown 8 pork chops on both sides. Place in single layer in Pyrex 9x13 inch pan. Top with 4 or 5 apples, cored and sliced. Mix together and sprinkle over top ¼ cup brown sugar, ½ cup raisins, ½ teaspoon salt and pepper, and ½ teaspoon sage. Mix 1 cup hot water and 1 tablespoon vinegar; pour over all. Bake, covered, in a 350° oven for 1½ hours.

Mrs. Henry Stern, Branch No. 1836, Maple Plain, MN

SUPREME PORK CHOPS

4 pork chops (about ¾ inch thick)
Salt to taste
4 thin onion slices

4 thin lemon slices
¼ c. brown sugar, packed
¼ c. ketchup

Sprinkle both sides of chops with salt. Place in ungreased shallow baking pan. Top each pork chop with onion slice, lemon slice, 1 tablespoon brown sugar, and 1 tablespoon ketchup. Cover and bake at 350° for 30 minutes. Uncover and bake for an additional 30 minutes more. Spoon sauce over chops occasionally while they are baking. Serves 4.

Jacky Garbade, St. Luke (ELCA), Branch No. 6304, Slinger, WI

SWEET AND SOUR PORK CHOPS

4 pork chops
4 Tbsp. ketchup
4 Tbsp. brown sugar

2 slices onion
2 lemon slices

Place pork chops in a covered pan and bake for 30 minutes at 350°. Remove from oven. Mix ketchup and brown sugar; cover pork chops. Place ½ slice onion and ½ slice lemon on each pork chop. Bake, uncovered, for 30 more minutes.

Renita Mohr, Branch No. 1587, Quincy, IL

CHINESE PORK ROAST

1 (3½ to 4 lb.) pork roast
¼ c. soy sauce
1 c. chicken stock
¼ c. honey
1 Tbsp. lemon juice

½ clove garlic
1 tsp. cinnamon
½ tsp. salt
¼ tsp. ginger

Combine last 8 ingredients; mix well. Pour over pork roast and marinate for 2 hours or overnight. Roast meat in sauce in glass or enamel pan, following standard time and temperature tables for the size of your roast. Skim fat from drippings and thicken to serve over rice.

Susan Tobin, Branch No. 6083, Lander, WY

MANDARIN PORK AND VEGETABLES

2 Tbsp. cornstarch
1¼ c. water
⅓ c. soy sauce
⅓ c. corn syrup
¼ to ½ tsp. crushed dried red
    peppers
1 lb. boneless pork, cut in thin
    strips (can also use chicken or
    beef)

2 garlic cloves, minced
2 c. broccoli, cut up
2 onions, sliced
1 carrot, cut in thin strips
½ lb. mushrooms
Vegetable oil

Make sauce. Mix cornstarch and water till smooth. Stir in soy sauce, corn syrup and red peppers; set aside.

In large skillet or wok, heat 2 tablespoons oil. Add meat and garlic. Stir-fry for 5 minutes or till tender. Remove from skillet. Heat 2 tablespoons oil. Add broccoli, onions and carrot. Stir-fry for 2 minutes; add mushrooms. Stir-fry for 1 minute more till vegetables are tender crisp. Return meat to pan. Stir in sauce and stir till hot. Serve over rice.

Barbara Alsum, Branch No. 3107, Loveland, CO

PORK DELIGHT

1½ lb. pork cubes
1½ c. apples, peeled and diced
1 qt. sauerkraut, drained

1 tsp. mustard
½ c. brown sugar (or to taste)

Dredge pork cubes in flour; season and brown. (Leftover pork roast may be used.) Place in casserole or crock pot. Pour remaining ingredients over pork. Stir and bake until pork is tender.

Letty Heumier, Branch No. 2935, Torrington, WY

HAM LOAF

2 lb. ground beef
2 lb. ground ham
3 eggs
1 c. oatmeal or bread crumbs

¾ c. brown sugar
1 tsp. mustard
¼ c. vinegar
¼ c. water

Combine beef, ham, eggs, and oatmeal (or bread crumbs). Form into 2 loaves and place in 9x13 inch pans. Bake at 350° until almost done (about 50 minutes).

While baking, prepare sauce by combining brown sugar, mustard, vinegar, and water; bring to a boil. Slice loaves thin and pour sauce over the loaves. Continue baking until done (another 15 minutes).

Mildred Bura, Branch No. 2049, Emporia, KS

TURKEY LOAF

2 c. chopped, cooked turkey
¼ c. margarine
1 c. hot milk
2 c. soft bread cubes
½ tsp. salt

¼ tsp. pepper
2 eggs, beaten
¼ c. chopped celery
¼ c. chopped onion

Melt margarine in milk. Combine all ingredients and pack lightly into greased loaf pan. Bake at 350° for 45 minutes. Let stand for about 5 minutes before slicing. Serves 6.

May also be baked as a casserole. Good too with chopped chicken or pork.
Marie Grossnicklaus, Branch No. 1412, Corvallis, OR

MARINATED TURKEY KABOBS

1 c. oil
2 tsp. Worcestershire sauce
1 Tbsp. lemon pepper

¼ c. soy sauce
⅔ c. water
Turkey breast

In a bowl, mix oil, Worcestershire sauce, lemon pepper, soy sauce, and water. Cut desired amount of turkey breast into kabobs. Put kabobs into the marinade and marinate for 4 hours or overnight. Put kabobs onto skewers and grill.
Mary Ann Wiedyk, Branch No. 2232, Auburn, MI

TURKEY ENCHILADAS

1½ c. shredded or chopped, cooked turkey
1½ c. picante sauce
1 (3 oz.) pkg. cream cheese
½ c. sliced green onion
¾ tsp. ground cumin

1½ c. shredded Monterey Jack or Colby cheese (I mix mine)
10 (6 to 7 inch) flour tortillas
Shredded lettuce
Radishes
Ripe olive slices

Combine turkey, ½ cup picante sauce, cream cheese, green onion, and cumin in skillet. Place over low heat until cheese is melted, stirring occasionally. Stir in ½ cup shredded cheese. Spoon scant ⅓ cup of the turkey mixture down center of each tortilla; roll up and place, seam down, in lightly greased 9x12 inch baking pan.

Spoon remaining picante sauce over enchiladas. Cover with remaining cheese. Bake at 350° for 20 minutes or until heated through. Garnish with lettuce, radishes, and olives. Serve with additional picante sauce.
Lorine Patschke, Branch No. 4899, Giddings, TX

EASY DOES IT TURKEY QUICHE

2½ to 3 c. stuffing (leftover) or 1 (6 oz.) box chicken flavor
1 c. chopped, cooked turkey

1 c. shredded Swiss cheese
4 beaten eggs
1 (5⅓ oz.) can evaporated milk

If using stuffing mix, prepare as directed on package. Press stuffing into a 9 inch pie plate or quiche pan, forming a crust. Bake in a 400° oven for 10 minutes. Combine meat and cheese.

In another bowl, beat eggs, milk and ⅛ teaspoon pepper. Sprinkle meat/cheese mixture into pie crust. Pour egg mixture on top. Lower oven temperature to 350°. Bake quiche for 30 to 35 minutes or till center is set. Let stand for 10 minutes before serving. Garnish with a tomato wedge. Makes 6 servings.

Microwave: Bake crust for 5 minutes on HIGH and for 15 minutes on HIGH after egg mixture is poured into crust over cheese-turkey mixture. Bake until done.

Delores Schuetze, Branch No. 4083, Brown Deer, WI

TURKEY LOAF

1 lb. ground turkey
1 c. herb seasoned stuffing
½ c. finely chopped parsley
2 ribs celery, grated
1 large pared carrot, grated

1 small onion, grated
½ tsp. salt
¼ tsp. pepper
1 egg, slightly beaten

Mix together turkey, stuffing, parsley, celery, carrot, onion, and seasonings in large bowl. Add egg and mix well. Turn into foil lined pan. Bake in preheated oven 350° for 40 to 45 minutes or until center is firm to the touch.

Doris Gueths, Branch No. 3227, Shawano, WI

HERB-SMOKED TURKEY

1 (8 to 14 lb.) turkey, thawed,
   cleaned and patted dry
½ c. butter or margarine, melted
2 garlic spears, minced
½ tsp. marjoram
½ tsp. dried thyme
½ tsp. rosemary
½ tsp. basil
¼ tsp. sage

2 Tbsp. parsley, chopped
½ tsp. salt
½ tsp. coarsely ground pepper
2 c. white wine (at room
   temperature)
Hickory chunks, soaked
Charcoal
Metal or foil drip pan (cake size)

Note: This recipe will not work on a gas grill, only a barbeque grill such as a kettle style. It is excellent served with cheese and crackers.

Build a charcoal fire around the drip pan. Pour wine into drip pan and add enough water to fill half full. When coals are glowing and ashy gray (30 to 40 minutes), add soaked wood chunks. Replace grill. Fold wings under back of turkey and place (breast side up) on grill over the drip pan. Do not allow to cook too fast.

Baste several times with a mixture of the butter and spices. Cook for 15 minutes per pound, adding more briquets and wood chips to the fire after 45 to 60 minutes to maintain a constant temperature. Let bird stand on platter or carving board for 10 to 20 minutes before slicing. The meat under the skin will be a pink color, due to the smoking.

Sheryl Zebell, Branch No. 3107, Loveland, CO

WILD AND CHEESY CHICKEN

1 (6 oz.) pkg. long grain rice with
    seasonings (I use Uncle Ben's)
2 Tbsp. butter
¼ c. green pepper, diced
½ c. celery, diced
½ c. green onion and tops,
    chopped

1 (4 oz.) can sliced mushrooms
1 can cream of mushroom soup
2 c. cooked chicken, cubed
1 c. grated Cheddar cheese

Prepare rice according to package directions. Grease a 7x11 inch pan and put rice in bottom. Melt butter in pan; add onion, celery, green pepper, and mushrooms. Saute till tender. Mix with remaining ingredients. Put on top of rice. Bake at 425° for 30 minutes, covered.

Barbara Alsum, Branch No. 3107, Loveland, CO

CHICKEN BREASTS PARMESAN
(Microwave)

1 (8 oz.) can tomato sauce
1 tsp. Italian seasoning
¼ tsp. garlic salt
⅓ c. corn flake crumbs
¼ c. grated Parmesan cheese
1 tsp. dried parsley flakes
2 large boneless chicken breasts
    (1½ to 2 lb.), split and skin
    removed

1 egg, beaten
½ c. shredded Mozzarella cheese
    (about 2 oz.)
Grated Parmesan cheese

1. Mix tomato sauce, Italian seasoning and garlic salt in 2 cup measure. Cover with waxed paper. Microwave on HIGH (100%) for 2 minutes. Stir. Reduce power to MEDIUM (50%). Microwave for 5 minutes, stirring once. Set sauce aside.

2. Mix corn flake crumbs, ¼ cup Parmesan cheese, and the parsley flakes. Dip chicken breasts in beaten egg, then in crumb mixture. Place in rectangular baking dish, 12x8 inches or 10 inch square casserole. Cover with waxed paper. Microwave at MEDIUM HIGH (70%) until chicken is tender, 9 to 14 minutes, rearranging after half the cooking time. (Do not turn over.)

3. Pour sauce over chicken. Sprinkle Mozzarella cheese over chicken breasts. Sprinkle with Parmesan cheese. Microwave on MEDIUM HIGH (70%) until Mozzarella cheese melts and sauce is hot, 2 to 5½ minutes.

Alison Ruesch, Branch No. 5844, Columbia City, IN

CHICKEN MANDARIN
(Low cholesterol)

2 whole chicken breasts, split,
    boned and skinned
2 Tbsp. oil
Green pepper, cut in strips

1 c. sliced celery
¼ c. honey
2 Tbsp. prepared yellow mustard
1 can mandarin oranges, drained

Cut chicken into narrow strips; brown in oil in large skillet. Add pepper and celery. Cook and stir for 2 or 3 minutes.

·Combine honey, mustard and oranges; add to chicken and mix slightly. Cook slowly for 2 or 3 minutes longer. Makes 4 or 5 servings.

May be served with rice.

Velma Swanson, Branch No. 3107, Loveland, CO

CHICKEN PRONTO

4 boneless chicken breast halves
¼ c. bottled Italian dressing
⅓ c. Italian seasoned dry bread crumbs

Dip chicken breasts in dressing, then in bread crumbs. Cover and bake at 450° for 20 minutes. Uncover and bake for 10 minutes more.

Julie Padilla, Branch No. 3107, Loveland, CO

MONTEREY CHICKEN

This recipe can be made in advance for dozens of guests and is easy to transport.

8 large (7 or 8 oz.) whole chicken breasts, skinned and boned
1 (7 oz.) can chopped mild green chilies
½ lb. Monterey Jack cheese, cut into 8 strips
½ c. fine dry bread crumbs
¼ c. freshly grated Parmesan cheese

1 to 3 tsp. chili powder
½ tsp. salt
¼ tsp. ground cumin
¼ tsp. freshly ground black pepper
6 Tbsp. butter, melted
Tomato Sauce (recipe follows)

Garnish:

Sour cream
Fresh limes

Pound the chicken breasts between 2 sheets of waxed paper until thin. Spread each breast with 1 tablespoon of the green chilies. Place 1 cheese strip on top of each portion of chilies. Roll up each chicken breast and tuck ends under.

Combine the bread crumbs, Parmesan cheese, chili powder, salt, cumin, and pepper in a shallow dish. Dip each stuffed breast into the melted butter and roll in the bread crumb mixture. Place the breasts in a baking dish, seam side down. Drizzle with remaining butter. Cover and chill for at least 4 hours or overnight. Preheat the oven to 400°F. Bake for 25 to 40 minutes, or until done. Serve with the Tomato Sauce and garnish with sour cream and fresh limes. Serves 8.

Tomato Sauce:

1 (15 oz.) can plain tomato sauce
½ tsp. ground cumin
⅓ c. sliced green onion
Salt and freshly ground black
    pepper to taste

Hot pepper sauce to taste
(optional)

In a small saucepan, combine the tomato sauce, cumin, green onion, salt, pepper, and hot pepper sauce if desired. Bring to a boil and cook, stirring constantly, until slightly thickened.

OVEN-FRIED CHICKEN

4 Tbsp. margarine
⅔ c. Bisquick baking mix
1½ tsp. paprika

1¼ tsp. salt
1 broiler or fryer chicken, cut up

Heat oven to 425°. Place margarine in several spots on bottom of oblong baking pan. Mix baking mix, paprika and salt in a plastic bag. Coat chicken with this mixture. Place chicken, skin sides down, on top of margarine in pan. Bake, uncovered, for 35 minutes. Turn. Bake until done, approximately 15 minutes.

Margie (Dias) Benes, Branch No. 3107, Loveland, CO

FRUITED CHICKEN

¾ c. flour
2 to 3 lb. cut up chicken
¼ tsp. garlic powder
¼ tsp. celery salt
¼ tsp. nutmeg

½ c. butter, melted
20 oz. pineapple tidbits
3 Tbsp. flour
⅓ c. soy sauce

Combine ¾ cup flour, the garlic powder, celery salt, and nutmeg. Coat chicken parts and brown in the melted butter. Remove the chicken to a baking dish. Reserve drippings. Drain the pineapple, reserving the juice. Arrange the fruit over the chicken. Stir the flour into the drippings. Add 1 cup juice and the soy sauce. Cook until thick. Spoon over meat. Bake for 1 hour.

Sharon Verville, Branch No. 3107, Loveland, CO

STUFFING FOR CORNISH HENS

4 Cornish game hens, thawed
1 box Uncle Ben's instant wild rice

1 (2 oz.) can mushrooms
¼ c. celery

Cook wild rice according to package directions. Dice mushrooms and celery; add to rice. Stuff each Cornish hen and bake for 1 hour and 15 minutes at 350°. Baste hens occasionally with butter.

Julie Padilla, Branch No. 3107, Loveland, CO

BAKED CHICKEN BREAST

4 oz. chipped or dried beef
8 deboned chicken breast halves
8 strips bacon

1 can cream of celery soup
1 c. sour cream

Wrap each chicken breast half with a piece of bacon. Place on top of beef that has been placed in the bottom of a glass pan or shallow casserole. Mix soup and sour cream; pour over chicken. Let marinate in refrigerator overnight. Bake in open casserole for 3 hours in a 275° oven.

Esther Prigge, Branch No. 127, Lake City, MN

CHICKEN CHEESE PIES

Chicken Base:

2 Tbsp. butter, melted
¼ c. flour
1 tsp. salt
1 tsp. sage
1 c. water
1 c. milk

1 chicken bouillon cube
2 c. chopped, cooked chicken
1 (10 oz.) pkg. frozen mixed
   vegetables, thawed
½ c. sliced celery
¼ c. chopped onion

Biscuit Topping:

¾ c. buttermilk baking mix
½ c. shredded Cheddar cheese

¼ c. milk

Melt butter over low heat. Stir in flour and seasonings. Cook until smooth, stirring constantly. Remove from heat. Gradually stir in water, milk and bouillon cube. Bring to a boil over medium heat, stirring constantly. Boil and stir until thickened. Add chicken and vegetables. Cover and simmer for 15 minutes or until vegetables are crisp tender. Spoon mixture into 4 buttered 2 cup individual casseroles or 1 large casserole.

Combine baking mix and cheese. Add milk, stirring only until moistened. Drop biscuit dough by tablespoonfuls over hot chicken mixture. Bake in preheated 375°F. oven for 14 to 16 minutes or until biscuits are lightly browned. Makes 4 servings.

Elfrieda Buettner, Branch No. 3227, Shawano, WI

CHICKEN WITH VEGETABLES

¼ c. cornstarch
¼ c. oil
1 c. zucchini strips
1 c. celery, sliced
1 clove garlic, minced or pressed
½ tsp. ginger

2 chicken breasts, cooked and cut
   in cubes
1 c. thinly sliced carrots
2 Tbsp. sliced green onion
¼ c. soy sauce

In shallow dish, stir together cornstarch and ginger. Coat chicken with cornstarch mixture. In large skillet, heat corn oil over medium high heat. Add chicken, stirring occasionally. Cook for 5 to 8 minutes or until browned. Add zucchini, carrots, celery, green onion, and garlic. Stir in soy sauce. Cover. Reduce heat and cook for 5 minutes or until vegetables are tender crisp. Serve over rice. Serves 4.

Anna Albert, Branch 545, Mosinee, WI

FORGOTTEN CHICKEN

1 chicken
1 pkg. dry onion soup
2 c. long grain rice

1 can cream of chicken
1 can water

Arrange chicken in casserole dish. Pour in rice. Sprinkle on soup mix, can of soup, and water. Bake for 1 hour at 375°.

Ruth Neeley, Branch No. 2254

ORANGE AVOCADO CHICKEN

4 whole chicken breasts, split
4 whole chicken leg quarters
1/4 c. butter
1 tsp. grated orange rind
1 c. orange juice, divided
1/2 c. chopped onion
1 tsp. salt

1 tsp. paprika
1/2 tsp. ground ginger
2 Tbsp. cornstarch
2 oranges, peeled and sliced
    crosswise
1 avocado, peeled and sliced
Fresh parsley

Rinse chicken and pat dry. Brown in butter over medium heat. Add orange rind, 1/2 cup orange juice, onion, and seasonings. Reduce heat to low; cover and cook for 30 minutes or until tender. Remove chicken to platter and keep warm. Combine remaining orange juice with cornstarch and add to pan drippings. Cook until thickened, scraping up brown bits from pan. Arrange oranges and avocado around chicken. Pour on sauce and garnish with parsley. Serves 8 to 12.

Donna Woerth, Branch No. 1810, Platte Center, NE

COUNTRY-STYLE CHICKEN POT PIE

3 Tbsp. butter
3 Tbsp. flour
2 c. chicken broth (instant, canned
    or reserved from cooking the
    chicken)
1 tsp. lemon juice
1/2 to 1 can chicken-mushroom
    soup

3 carrots, cooked and diced
1 (10 oz.) pkg. frozen green peas,
    cooked
1/8 tsp. curry and pepper, mixed
1 tsp. salt
2 large potatoes, cooked and diced
1 or 2 chicken fryers, cooked and
    cut in chunks

Melt butter. Add flour and allow to bubble 1 minute. Add broth and stir with wooden spoon. Bring to boil and simmer for a few minutes. Add lemon juice and soup. Drain vegetables and add to sauce; add seasonings and chicken. Pour into a deep 2 quart casserole. Preheat oven to 350°.

Topping:

1¼ c. Bisquick
⅓ c. shortening
2 Tbsp. butter

1 tsp. sugar
3 Tbsp. sour cream (very cold)

Topping: Use 2 knives or a pastry blender to cut the shortening, butter and sugar into the Bisquick. Mix in sour cream and knead gently. Roll between 2 sheets of waxed paper. Layer over the chicken mixture. Bake for 45 minutes. Serves 6 to 8.

This delicious pie can be made a day ahead. "Good enough for company."
Maxine Wolfmeyer, Branch No. 1587, Quincy, IL

ONION-CRUSTED CHICKEN

4 chicken breast halves, skinned
and boned
¼ tsp. pepper
½ c. butter or margarine, melted

1 Tbsp. Worcestershire sauce
1 tsp. dry mustard
1 (2.5 oz.) can French fried onion
rings

Place each piece of chicken between 2 sheets of plastic wrap and flatten to ¼ inch thickness, using a meat mallet or rolling pin. Combine butter, Worcestershire sauce, and mustard; stir well. Dredge chicken in butter mixture, then in crushed onion rings. Sprinkle with pepper. *Do not use salt in this recipe.*

Arrange chicken in a 9x13x2 inch pan. Top with remaining onion rings. Drizzle with part of remaining butter. Bake at 350° for 30 minutes. Serves 4.
Mary Lou Geldigan, Branch No. 3193, St. Louis, MO

HOT AND SPICY CHICKEN PIE

3 chicken breasts, skinned, boned
and cut in bite-size pieces
½ (10 oz.) frozen corn
½ c. chicken broth
½ c. sliced celery
1 medium onion, cut in wedges

½ c. salsa picante
4 tsp. cornstarch
1 (8½ oz.) corn bread mix
1½ c. Cheddar cheese, grated
2 (4 oz.) green diced chilies,
drained

Combine chicken, corn, broth, celery, and onion. Bring to a boil. Reduce heat and simmer for 10 to 15 minutes. Add salsa. Stir 2 tablespoons water into cornstarch. Add to chicken mixture. Cook and stir until bubbly. Cook for 2 minutes. Prepare corn bread mix. Pour chicken mixture into 10x6 inch dish. Sprinkle with cheese and chilies. Spoon corn bread mix on top. Bake at 425° for 20 minutes.
Judy Kugler, Branch No. 3679, Wheat Ridge, CO

SALSA CHICKEN BAKE

1 frying chicken
½ c. margarine
½ c. flour
½ c. Parmesan cheese

1 tsp. salt
Paprika
2 (10 oz.) pkg. frozen corn
1 can green chile salsa

Dip chicken pieces in margarine. Combine flour, cheese, and salt. Roll chicken in flour mixture. (It may be necessary to add more flour and cheese.) Sprinkle chicken on all sides with paprika. Arrange corn on bottom of greased pan, 9x12 inches. Spoon salsa over corn. Arrange chicken on top. Bake, covered, in a 375° oven for about 1 hour and 15 minutes or until tender.

Martha Broscheit, Branch No. 3679, Wheat Ridge, CO

OVEN CHICKEN WITH EASY BARBECUE SAUCE

2 to 2½ lb. frying chicken	Dash of pepper
½ c. pancake mix	¾ c. water
½ c. pancake mix	⅔ c. catsup
½ c. shortening	1 Tbsp. instant minced onion
2 tsp. garlic salt	1 Tbsp. parsley flakes (optional)

Shake the two 2½ pound chickens (quartered or cut in pieces) in ½ cup pancake mix. Combine other ½ cup pancake mix, ½ cup shortening, 2 teaspoons garlic salt, and dash of pepper to form a paste. Spread the mixture evenly over each piece of chicken with a spatula or knife. Bake, uncovered, on a lightly greased sheet for an hour in a 400° oven. Just before chicken is done, combine ¾ cup water, ⅔ cup catsup, 1 teaspoon onion, and 1 tablespoon parsley flakes in a saucepan. Bring to a boil and serve with the chicken. (I usually skip the barbecue sauce.)

Clarice Meyer, Branch No. 2148, Tobias, NE

MARINATED CHICKEN WINGS

Sauce:

1 c. water	¼ c. cooking oil
1 c. soy sauce	1 tsp. ginger
¼ c. pineapple juice	1 tsp. garlic powder

Pour sauce over wings. Let stand for 8 hours in refrigerator in 13x9 inch pan. Uncover and bake for 1½ hours till meat is tender.

Nancy Ericksen, Branch No. 4231, Necmeh, WI

CHICKEN DIVINE

2 c. broccoli, slightly cooked and chopped	1 can cream of mushroom soup
	½ c. mayonnaise
2 c. chicken breasts, cooked and chopped	3 c. grated Cheddar cheese
	½ c. bread crumbs

Mix soup and mayonnaise. Add broccoli that has been slightly cooked and chopped; add chicken (that has been cooked and chopped) and 2 cups of the cheese. Mix this thoroughly. Put in a 9x12 inch pan. Put 1 cup of cheese on top, then put the ½ cup bread crumbs on top of this. Bake at 350° for 30 minutes. Serve bubbling hot. *Enjoy!*

Mrs. Janet Schudde, Branch No. 02803, Buhl, ID

ORANGE-A-TANGY GOURMET CHICKEN

4 boneless chicken breasts, halved
½ tsp. pepper
⅓ c. oat bran
3 Tbsp. safflower oil
1½ c. orange juice
¼ c. finely diced onion
¼ c. finely diced green pepper

1 carrot, finely diced
Few broccoli flowerets
2 bay leaves
1 clove garlic, minced
⅛ tsp. paprika
2 Tbsp. slivered almonds

Remove skin from chicken. In paper bag, mix pepper and bran. Shake each chicken breast in a bag to coat with mixture. Brown chicken breast in safflower oil. Use large skillet.

Add 1½ cups orange juice, onion, green pepper, bay leaves, garlic, carrots, and broccoli flowerets. Bring to a boil on high heat. Turn heat down to low. Sprinkle chicken with paprika. Simmer, *uncovered,* for 45 minutes or until tender. (Note: If too much juice evaporates, add ½ cup more. You should end up with about 1 cup of orange sauce in the skillet from juice.)

To serve, spoon sauce over chicken. Sprinkle with almonds. Yield: 4 servings.

Good recipe from California (chicken, orange juice, vegetables, and almonds plentiful).

Henrietta Behrens, Branch No. 1927, Porterville, CA

HOT CHINESE CHICKEN

8 broiler fryer chicken thighs,
    skinned, boned and cut in 1
    inch pieces
¼ c. cornstarch
¼ c. oil
⅛ tsp. garlic powder or salt
1 large tomato, cut in chunks
1 (4 oz.) can mushrooms or 1 pkg.
    fresh mushrooms, sliced

1 c. chopped green onions
1 tsp. Accent
⅓ c. sliced water chestnuts
1 c. chopped celery
¼ c. soy sauce (or to taste
    preferred)
2 c. shredded iceberg lettuce

Recipe for the rice (Minute rice):

4½ c. rice
4½ c. water

5 beef bouillon cubes
½ c. onion

Roll chicken in cornstarch. Heat oil in *wok* over medium high heat. Add chicken and quickly brown. Sprinkle with garlic powder or garlic salt. Add tomato, water chestnuts, mushrooms, onion, and celery. Sprinkle with Accent and stir. Stir in the soy sauce. Now, cover and reduce heat to low; simmer for 5 minutes. Remove from heat.

When cooking the rice, add the onions and beef bouillon cubes right in with it.

After the Chinese chicken and rice are prepared, you can either put the lettuce under everything to eat it, or you can toss it in with the Chinese chicken after it is prepared. *Hope you enjoy this.*

Pam Young, Branch No. 2254, Flat River, MO

CHICKEN AND ALMONDS

3 Tbsp. oil
2 raw chicken breasts, diced
¼ tsp. pepper
2 Tbsp. soy sauce
2 c. diced celery
1 c. peas (fresh or frozen)
½ c. diced onions

1 (4 oz.) can button mushrooms, drained
½ c. hot chicken broth (water and bouillon)
1 Tbsp. cornstarch
2 Tbsp. water
½ c. blanched, toasted almonds

Heat the oil in a wok. Saute the chicken for 3 minutes. Add the salt, pepper, soy sauce, celery, peas, onions, and mushrooms (you may use fresh ones). Cook for 2 minutes. Stir in broth. Cover and cook over low heat for 5 minutes. Mix together cornstarch and water; stir into the mixture until thickened. Add almonds.

Carol Nielsen, Branch No. 4077, Racine, WI

MAKE AHEAD CHICKEN ROLLS

3 large chicken breasts, boned and split
1 Tbsp. oleo, divided

8 oz. cream cheese, whipped with chives and divided
6 slices bacon

Put chicken breasts between waxed paper and pound to ½ inch thickness. Spread each chicken breast with 3 tablespoons cream cheese mixture and ½ teaspoon oleo. Fold ends over filling. Wrap 1 slice bacon around each roll. Place, seam side down, in pan. Bake on top rack at 400° for 40 minutes. Broil 5 minutes or until bacon is crisp. Makes 6 servings.

This dish may be put together a day ahead of time and then refrigerated until time to bake.

Mary Ann Kindschi, Branch No. 6245, Portage, WI

ORIENTAL CHICKEN

¼ c. brown sugar
2 Tbsp. cornstarch
½ tsp. salt
¼ c. vinegar
1 Tbsp. soy sauce
1 (15¼ oz.) can pineapple chunks (undrained)
1 large green pepper, cut into strips

1 small onion, thinly sliced and separated into rings
2 whole chicken breasts, skinned and boned
¼ c. butter, melted
Hot cooked rice

208

Combine first 3 ingredients and stir until well blended. Gradually add vinegar and soy sauce, stirring until cornstarch mixture is dissolved. Stir in pineapple, green pepper and onion; set aside. Cut chicken into thin strips; cook in butter in a large skillet until lightly browned. Add pineapple mixture, stirring until smooth. Cover and simmer for 15 minutes. Serve over rice with Chinese noodles. Yield: 4 servings.

Doris Wohlschlegel, Branch No. 5425, Louisville, KY

ORIENTAL CHICKEN

1 lb. chicken breast	2 slightly beaten eggs
½ tsp. salt	1 can bean sprouts
½ tsp. cornstarch	1 can water chestnuts
1 tsp. soy sauce	Mushrooms
Dash of pepper	2 Tbsp. soy sauce
3 c. cooked rice	3 green onions (tops and all)

Skin and bone chicken; cut into ½ inch pieces. Toss with salt, cornstarch (mixed in the 1 teaspoon soy sauce), and pepper. Refrigerate for ½ hour. Drain and rinse bean sprouts and water chestnuts. Heat a large Teflon frying pan. Add 1 tablespoon oil and cook eggs just till done.

Remove from pan. Add 2 tablespoons oil to pan and cook chicken till white. Add bean sprouts, water chestnuts and mushrooms. Stir-fry for 2 minutes. Remove from pan. Add 2 tablespoons oil to pan. Stir-fry rice and 2 tablespoons soy sauce for 2 minutes. Add chicken, vegetables, eggs, and green onions. Heat through.

Debbie Link, Branch No. 3984, Washburn, ND

CHICKEN LICKEN

¼ c. butter or margarine	1½ tsp. ginger
4 large chicken breasts, cubed	¼ tsp. chili powder
1 large onion, chopped	1 (16 oz.) can tomatoes
1 clove garlic, minced	1 c. chicken broth
1½ tsp. salt	1 small can mushrooms
1½ tsp. paprika	1 c. half & half

Melt butter in skillet or Dutch oven and brown cubed chicken with onion and garlic. Add salt, paprika, ginger, tomatoes, broth, and mushrooms. Simmer, covered, for 40 minutes or until chicken is tender. Blend cornstarch (2 tablespoons) with half & half to form a smooth paste. Stir into chicken, stirring constantly. Serve immediately over noodles or rice. (I like grandma's frozen egg noodles.) Serves 4 to 6.

Lorna R. Brinser, Branch No. 2630, Greeley, CO

CHICKEN POT PIE

2 c. cooked, diced chicken	1 tsp. chicken bouillon
1 can chicken broth	

Bring this to a boil. Thicken with flour. To make gravy, pour into casserole. Top with the following Bisquick Batter.

Bisquick Batter:

1½ c. Bisquick	Milk
1 egg	

Mix to make a soft batter. Top chicken mixture with batter and bake at 350° for 30 minutes or until browned.

Edna Weber, Branch No. 2630, Greeley, CO

CHICKEN DINNER

4 large pieces chicken breast	1 pkg. chicken flavor Stove Top
1 pt. sour cream (or less)	stuffing mix
1 can cream of mushroom soup	

Cook the chicken until done. Remove bones and skin; cut into small pieces. Mix sour cream and soup together, then mix with chicken and put in buttered pan. Prepare stuffing mix according to instructions. Put on top of chicken mixture. Bake at 350° for 30 minutes. If you like it crisp, bake, uncovered; otherwise, cover while baking.

Phyllis Vogtmann, Branch No. 2232, Auburn, MI

PAPRIKA CHICKEN

1 Tbsp. low cholesterol margarine and corn oil (to cover bottom of skillet)	Warm water Green pepper slices (desired amount)
1 to 2 lb. skinless chicken breast (in strips)	Onion strips (desired amount) Chopped celery (desired amount)*
Lawry's chicken seasoning	
Paprika	Dash of minced garlic

Add chicken strips to oil/margarine in skillet. Sprinkle with chicken seasoning. Cook for about 2 minutes on each side. Should be slightly browned, then sprinkle paprika on each side. Add pepper, onion, celery, and garlic. Add warm water to cover bottom of skillet.

When water starts to boil, lower heat and cover with lid. Cook until tender, about 15 to 20 minutes. Add more water if necessary.

Use as a meat dish or chop into bite-size pieces and put on rice.

* Can use celery seed for chopped celery.

Jane Helton, Branch No. 5844, Columbia City, IN

MANDARIN CHICKEN

Frying chicken, cut in serving
    pieces
½ c. oil
1 Tbsp. Lawry's seasoned salt
2 tsp. paprika
1 tsp. black pepper
½ tsp. garlic salt
1½ c. water, combined with 2
    chicken bouillon cubes

Juice from 2 medium oranges
1 orange rind, grated
3 Tbsp. brown sugar
3 Tbsp. cornstarch, mixed with ½
    c. cold water
6 to 8 green onions, slivered
½ c. sliced almonds

Dry chicken pieces well. Combine oil, seasoned salt, pepper, garlic salt, and paprika. Rub pieces of chicken well with oil mixture. Place chicken pieces on a cookie sheet with an edge of 1 inch. Bake in a 375° oven for 15 minutes. Lower oven temperature to 350°. Continue to cook until tender (about 45 minutes).

Combine orange juice, sugar, bouillon water, and orange rind. Allow mixture to come to a boil. Thicken with cornstarch and water mixture. Sprinkle chicken with slivered green onions and almonds. Pour sauce over all. Serve with rice and a vegetable.

Hallie Stewart, Branch No. 4817, Youngstown, OH

SWEET AND SOUR CHICKEN WINGS

3 lb. chicken wings
1 c. cornstarch

3 eggs
Salt to taste

    Sauce:

1½ c. sugar
¾ c. vinegar
½ c. chicken broth

6 to 8 Tbsp. catsup
2 Tbsp. soy sauce
1 tsp. salt

Coat wings in cornstarch. Dip in beaten eggs. Fry until light brown. Heat sauce ingredients until sugar is dissolved. Place wings in shallow pan in single layer. Pour sauce over wings. Bake at 350° until tender and brown. Serve hot or cold. They freeze well.

Elsie Dittbenner, Branch No. 1293, Morgan, MN

BUSY DAY CHICKEN

1 cut up chicken
1 pkg. Lipton dry vegetable soup
1 can chicken broth

1 can cream of chicken soup
½ c. rice (not instant)

Place rice in bottom of casserole dish. Mix together soups and broth in a separate bowl. Place chicken pieces on top of rice in casserole dish. Pour soup mixture over top of chicken and rice. Bake at 350° for 1 to 1½ hours.

Mrs. Steve Bilyew, Branch No. 1878, Claflin, KS

BAKED CHICKEN-WINE SAUCE

8 boneless chicken breast
2 cans mushroom soup

1 c. sour cream
½ c. white wine

Mix soup, sour cream, and wine together till smooth. Pour ½ sauce on bottom of 9x13 inch pan. Put chicken on sauce. Pour remaining sauce on top of chicken. Bake at 350°, covered, for 1 hour. Bake, uncovered, for 15 minutes.

Carolyn Hurlbutt, Branch No. 2288, Hilton, NY

CHICKEN OREGANO

1 chicken, cut up
¼ c. vegetable oil
2 c. water
4 chicken bouillon cubes
4 to 5 medium potatoes, peeled
   and cut into quarters

2 Tbsp. oregano
1 tsp. parsley
2 tsp. garlic powder
Salt and pepper to liking

Preheat oven to 325°. Pour vegetable oil in bottom of baking dish. Lay pieces of chicken in pan. Add water, bouillon cubes and potatoes. Sprinkle remaining ingredients over the top. Cover pan and bake for 1 hour. Remove cover and bake for an additional ½ hour or until browned.

Debbie Goebig, New Lenox, IL

BAKED CHICKEN BREASTS SUPREME

2 c. sour cream
¼ c. lemon juice
4 tsp. Worcestershire sauce
   (optional)
1 tsp. celery salt

½ tsp. paprika
2 cloves garlic, chopped
6 chicken breasts
1¾ c. dry bread crumbs
½ c. butter

Combine the first 6 ingredients. Cut the chicken breasts in halves. Dip the chicken into the sour cream mixture. Lay in a shallow pan. Spread the remainder of the sour cream mixture over the chicken. Cover and refrigerate overnight.

The next day, remove the chicken from the sauce. Shake off excess and roll in bread crumbs. Arrange in baking pan in single layer. Melt butter and drizzle over chicken. Bake at 350° for 45 minutes to 1 hour until chicken is done and nicely browned.

Regina Stueber, Branch No. 1478, Clyman, WI

TEXAS RANCH CHICKEN

1 large chicken fryer, boiled and
  boned
1 large green pepper, chopped
1 large onion, chopped
1 can cream of mushroom soup
1 can cream of chicken soup
1 can cream of
  chicken/mushroom soup

1 can Ro-Tel tomatoes with chilies
1 lb. mild Cheddar cheese, grated
Season with garlic powder to taste
1 pkg. flour tortillas, torn in
  fourths

In oleo, cook pepper and onion until soft. Add soups, tomatoes, and garlic; blend well. In large casserole dish, layer ingredients in this order: Chicken, tortillas, soup mixtures, and grated cheese. Repeat this until dish is full; end with cheese. Bake at 325° for 50 minutes, uncovered.

Margit M. Buchman, Branch No. 1458, Houston, TX

COUNTRY CAPTAIN

1 (2½ to 3 lb.) broiler-fryer, cut up
½ c. flour, seasoned with 1¼ tsp.
  salt and ½ tsp. pepper
2 Tbsp. butter
2 Tbsp. oil
½ c. chopped onion
½ c. chopped green pepper
1 large clove garlic, crushed

2 tsp. curry powder
½ tsp. thyme leaves, crushed
1 small bay leaf, crumbled
¼ c. raisins or currants
1 lb. (1 can) tomatoes
Cooked rice (hot)
¼ c. sliced, salted, toasted
  almonds (optional)

Toss chicken pieces in seasoned flour to coat. Heat oil and butter in large skillet or Dutch oven. Brown chicken until golden. Remove. Add onion, green pepper and seasonings. Stir in currants and tomatoes (including liquid). Place chicken pieces in skillet. Heat to boiling, cover, reduce heat, and simmer for 20 to 30 minutes (until chicken is tender). Serve with hot rice and sprinkle almonds on top.

This is an English recipe of Colonial Indian origin.

Karen Holyer, Branch No. 6466, Batesville, AR

CHICKEN DIVAN

2 (10 oz.) pkg. frozen broccoli
  spears, cooked and drained
8 cooked chicken breasts,
  seasoned, then baked or
  simmered

⅛ tsp. curry powder
¾ c. grated sharp Cheddar cheese
1 c. bread crumbs, tossed with 1
  Tbsp. melted butter

Place broccoli in 9x13 inch pan. Place diced chicken over broccoli. Pour sauce over chicken. Sprinkle cheese over sauce. Top with bread crumbs. Bake for 1 hour at 325°.

213

Sauce:

2 cans cream of chicken soup   1 tsp. lemon juice
1 c. Hellmann's mayonnaise

Mix together for sauce.

Marion Schalow, Branch No. 48, Marshfield, WI

PAM'S PRETTY GOOD CHICKEN

¼ c. olive oil
1 medium onion, chopped
1 small green pepper, chopped
  (optional)
¼ to ½ tsp. minced garlic (to
  taste)
3 lb. chicken pieces (thighs,
  drumsticks, and wings),
  skinned and fat removed
2 cans ready cut tomatoes (3 large
  fresh)

½ tsp. oregano
½ tsp. thyme
½ tsp. parsley flakes or equal fresh
3 tsp. chicken bouillon crystals
2 qt. water
Salt (to taste)
1 small red bell pepper, chopped
  (optional)
Parmesan cheese (to taste)

This recipe works well in a slow cooker. In ¼ cup olive oil, soften chopped onion, green pepper, red bell pepper, and the minced garlic. Add chicken pieces. Add 2 cans tomatoes (or fresh). Stir in oregano, thyme, and parsley flakes. Add chicken bouillon, water, and salt (to taste). Cook on medium heat for 1 hour or until chicken is done and falls easily from bone. (Or, cook all day in slow cooker for 4 to 6 hours.) Serve on a bed of rice. Garnish with parsley and sprinkle lightly with grated Parmesan cheese.

Herb Rice (as much as needed):

1 tsp. minced onion
Rice
½ tsp. parsley flakes

1 Tbsp. oil
¼ tsp. chicken bouillon crystals

Cook rice (2 parts water to 1 part rice) to yield as much as you need. Add rice to boiling salted water. Stir in minced onion, parsley flakes and oil, also ¼ teaspoon bouillon. Boil rice, uncovered, for 10 minutes, stirring occasionally. Cover tightly and turn off heat. Let set for 10 minutes.

The next day, combine leftover rice with leftover chicken liquid for a fantastic soup.

Mrs. Fred (Pam) Bridgehouse, Branch No. 0916, Scotts Mills, OR

GARLIC ROASTED CHICKEN AND POTATOES

4 Tbsp. margarine (½ stick)
4 medium size chicken legs
4 chicken thighs
4 chicken breast halves
6 large potatoes (about 2 lb.)

12 to 24 garlic cloves *(unpeeled)*
1 tsp. salt
¼ c. maple or maple flavored
  syrup

About 1½ hours before serving:

214

1. In large roasting pan (about 17x11 inches) in a 400°F. oven, melt margarine. Remove pan from oven.

2. Meanwhile, cut potatoes into large chunks.

3. Place chicken pieces, potatoes and garlic in roasting pan; sprinkle with salt. Turn ingredients to coat with melted margarine; arrange chicken pieces, skin side up.

4. Bake for 40 minutes, basting the chicken and potatoes occasionally with drippings in pan.

5. Brush chicken with maple syrup; bake for 20 minutes longer or until chicken and potatoes are fork tender.

6. To serve, arrange chicken, potatoes, and garlic on large warm platter. Let each person cut through garlic skin and spread some soft, sweet tasting garlic onto chicken and potatoes.

Clara Mifflin, Branch No. 1358, Creal Springs, IL

MEXICAN CHICKEN

1 large fryer, boiled and boned
Tortilla chips (corn)

2 c. grated cheese (Colby or
    Cheddar)

Sauce:

1 tsp. cumin
1 tsp. oregano
1/8 tsp. garlic
1 Tbsp. plus 2 tsp. chili powder
1 can chopped green chilies

1 can cream of mushroom soup
1 can cream of chicken soup
1 c. chicken broth
1 large onion, diced

Mix sauce ingredients together in slow cooker. When blended, add cheese and chicken. Cook until cheese is melted and mixture is hot. Before serving, crumble and add enough tortilla chips to thicken mixture. Serve with tortilla chips.

May be made ahead, omitting crumbled chips, and frozen.

Mary Guerin, Branch No. 2311, Saginaw, MI

PARMESAN CHICKEN

1/2 c. fine bread crumbs (Italian
    style)
4 Tbsp. grated dry Parmesan
    cheese
1/4 tsp. oregano leaves, crushed
1/2 tsp. garlic powder

Dash of pepper
2 to 3 lb. chicken parts
1 can cream of chicken soup
1/2 c. milk
Paprika

Combine 2 tablespoons Parmesan cheese, oregano, garlic, and pepper. Roll chicken in mixture. Put in a greased 9x13 inch pan. Bake at 400° for 20 minutes. Turn chicken and bake for 20 minutes more. Blend soup and milk. Pour over chicken. Sprinkle with paprika. Bake for 20 minutes more or until done. Stir sauce left in pan with a little potato water and serve as a gravy.

Mrs. Barbara (Rev. David) Splett, St. John's Lutheran,
Branch No. 5488, Fayetteville, AR

MYSTERY CHICKEN

In 8x10 inch pan, place 8 to 10 chicken breast halves, boned and skinned. Cover with one 4 ounce package shredded Swiss cheese. Mix together 1 can cream of chicken (or mushroom) soup and ¼ cup sherry; spread over chicken and cheese. Top with 2 cups prepared stuffing mix. Melt ½ stick margarine and pour over all. Bake, uncovered, for 1 hour at 350°.

Estelle Krist, Branch 1221

SWEET-AND-SOUR CHICKEN

2 Tbsp. soy sauce
1 Tbsp. cornstarch
2 whole chicken breasts, halved, skinned, boned, and cut into bite-size cubes
1 Tbsp. vegetable oil
1 cucumber, scored lengthwise with tines of fork and cut into bite-size cubes

½ cantaloupe, seeded, rinded, and cut into bite-size pieces
1 sweet red pepper (or green pepper), cubed

Combine soy sauce and cornstarch. Coat chicken pieces thoroughly. Heat oil in large frypan (or wok). Stir-fry chicken for 3 to 4 minutes. Add cucumber, cantaloupe, and pepper.

Sweet-and-Sour Sauce:

2 Tbsp. brown sugar
2 Tbsp. vinegar
½ c. pineapple juice (unsweetened)

1 Tbsp. cornstarch in 2 Tbsp. cold water
3 oz. blanched whole almonds

Mix together sauce ingredients and add to chicken mixture. Heat, stirring often, until sauce boils and ingredients are heated through. Add almonds. Yield: 4 servings.

C. Wiitanen, Branch No. 3339, Esko, MN

CHICKEN-RICE BAKE

1½ c. regular rice
1 can condensed cream of mushroom soup
1 can condensed cream of chicken soup

1 can condensed cream of celery soup
1¾ c. milk
1 (3½ to 4 lb.) broiler-fryer, cut up
1 (1⅜ oz.) pkg. onion soup mix

Grease bottom of 13x9x2 inch pan. Add uncooked rice to make the bottom layer. Combine soups and milk; heat and pour over rice. Combine. Lay chicken pieces on top. Scatter the dry soup mix over chicken. Cover with aluminum foil. Bake in slow oven (325°) for 2 hours or until rice is tender. Makes 7 servings.

Mildred M. Deleo, Branch No. 1014, Cohocton, NY

GOURMET CHICKEN

1 c. raw rice
1 chicken, cut up
1 c. water

1 pkg. (env.) dry onion soup
1 can cream of chicken soup
2 Tbsp. milk

Put 1 cup raw rice on bottom of 9x13 inch pan. Arrange chicken over rice. Mix cream of chicken soup, water, milk, and onion mix. Stir well and pour over rice. Bake at 350° for 2 hours or until tender. Add extra water if necessary. (Add foil after cooked.)

Hazel Connelly, Branch No. 2089, Logan, IA

CHICKEN AND BROWN RICE BAKE

1 frying chicken, cut up
1½ c. brown rice
1 (10½ oz.) can mushroom soup

1 env. Lipton onion soup mix
1½ c. water

Butter generously a 9x13 inch baking dish. Put rice on bottom of dish, then chicken pieces (skinned and deboned if desired). Mix mushroom soup and water; pour over chicken. Sprinkle dry onion soup over top. Cover and bake at 350° for 1½ hours. (May add more water if desired.)

Lorraine Young, Branch No. 5325, Stratford, IA

CHICKEN AND RICE SURPRISE

1 c. raw rice
1 can cream of mushroom soup
Chicken pieces

1 can cream of chicken soup
2 c. water

Place raw rice in bottom of baking dish. Mix in the soups and water. Arrange chicken on rice mixture. Bake at 400° for 1½ hours. (Keep covered.)

Ruth Roper, Branch No. 2205, Granite, OK

CHICKEN CASSEROLE

1 can cream of celery soup
1 can cream of chicken soup
1 pkg. dry onion soup mix
½ c. water

1 (4 oz.) can mushrooms
1 c. uncooked rice
2 c. cut up chicken or turkey

Put ingredients in 1½ quart casserole. Bake for 1 hour and 15 minutes, covered. Remove cover and bake for 15 minutes. Bake at 350°.

Maxine Pulter, Branch No. 2295, Taylor, MI

CHICKEN AND RICE

1½ c. Minute rice
1 cut up chicken fryer
1 can cream of mushroom soup

1 can cream of chicken soup
½ c. milk
1 pkg. instant onion soup

Spread rice evenly on the bottom of a greased 9½ x 13 inch pan. Put cut up chicken on top of rice. Mix mushroom and chicken soups with milk; pour over chicken. Lastly, sprinkle ½ to 1 package of onion soup on top. Cover pan with foil and bake at 325° for 2 hours.

Pork chops may be used in place of chicken. Other soup combinations that may be used are: Tomato and Cheddar cheese and mushroom and tomato.

Mrs. Matt (Karen) Carter, Branch No. 3365, Rock Springs, WY

BAKED CHICKEN WITH RICE

1 chicken or pieces
1 (10¾ oz.) can cream of
   mushroom soup
1 (10¾ oz.) can cream of celery
   soup

1 (10¾ oz.) can cream of chicken
   soup
1 c. rice (uncooked)
Onion soup mix

Mix together soups and rice. Let set for ½ hour, stirring several times. Pour into 9x13 inch pan. Sprinkle onion soup mix over top of soup mixture. Arrange chicken on top of mixture and drizzle melted butter over chicken (or pat Miracle Whip on chicken pieces). Bake at 375° to 400° for 1 hour.

Can turn chicken over about half of baking time - not necessary.

Mrs. Dorothy Meinzen, Branch No. 5844, Albion, IN

SWEET-SOUR MEATBALLS

1½ lb. ground beef
⅔ c. cracker crumbs
⅓ c. minced onion
1 egg
1½ tsp. salt
¼ tsp. ginger
¼ c. milk
1 Tbsp. shortening

2 Tbsp. cornstarch
½ c. brown sugar
⅓ c. vinegar
1 Tbsp. (or more) soy sauce
1 (13½ oz.) can pineapple tidbits,
   drained (reserving juice)
Green pepper slices

Form beef, crumbs, onion, egg, salt, ginger, and milk into balls. Brown. Pour off excess grease. Cook shortening, cornstarch, sugar, vinegar, soy sauce, and pineapple juice until mixture thickens. Add pineapple and green pepper slices to meatballs. Pour sauce over and slowly simmer until ready to serve. Serve over cooked rice.

Velma Swanson, Branch No. 3107, Loveland, CO

SAUERBRATEN MEATBALLS

Meatballs:

1½ lb. ground beef
½ c. cracker crumbs
½ c. chopped onions
2 eggs, beaten

¾ tsp. salt
¼ tsp. pepper
2 Tbsp. water
2 Tbsp. lemon juice

Combine preceding ingredients and mix thoroughly. Shape into small balls. Brown in a small amount of hot oil (about 2 tablespoons) in a heavy skillet. Remove meatballs and to the drippings, add Meat Sauce (see following ingredients).

Meat Sauce:

2½ c. water	⅓ c. raisins
4 small bouillon cubes	¼ c. lemon juice
½ c. brown sugar	¾ c. gingersnap crumbs

Bring preceding ingredients to a boil and add meatballs. Reduce heat to simmer. Cover tightly and cook for 15 minutes. Turn meatballs and simmer for 5 to 10 minutes longer or until meatballs are done. Serve meatballs and sauce over noodles.

Martha H. Kahanak, Branch No. 3107, Loveland, CO

HAM BALLS

1 lb. ground ham	2 eggs
1½ lb. ground pork	1 c. milk
1 c. bread crumbs	

Mix first 5 ingredients and form into balls. Place on cookie sheet or cake pan.

Sauce:

1½ c. brown sugar	1 c. water
½ c. vinegar	1½ tsp. dry mustard

Mix sauce ingredients and pour over balls. Bake for 3 hours at 300°, turning every 45 minutes.

Esther Prigge, Branch No. 127, Lake City, MN

BARBECUES MEAT BALLS

1 (13 oz.) can evaporated milk	2 tsp. salt
3 lb. ground chuck	½ tsp. pepper
2 c. oatmeal	2 tsp. chile powder
1 c. chopped onion	2 eggs
½ tsp. garlic powder	

Mix together and shape into balls. Place on flat pans in a single layer. Bake in a 400° oven till browned. Remove and put in casserole or small roaster.

Sauce:

2 c. catsup	½ tsp. garlic powder
1½ c. brown sugar	½ c. chopped onion
2 Tbsp. liquid smoke	

Mix sauce and pour over meat balls. Bake at 350° for 1 hour.

Wanda Ogg, Branch 6940, Harrison, MI

SWEET AND SOUR MEATBALLS

2 eggs, slightly beaten
1 c. crushed saltine crackers
1 small onion
¼ tsp. pepper
2 lb. lean ground beef

1 Tbsp. cooking oil
1 (16 oz.) can whole cranberry
  sauce
1 (10¾ oz.) can tomato sauce
Hot rice

In large bowl, combine eggs, crackers, onion, and pepper. Add ground beef and mix well. Shape into 72 (1 inch) meatballs. Brown meatballs in hot oil until no pink color remains. Drain well on paper towels.

Combine cranberry sauce and tomato sauce; cook and stir until heated through. Put meatballs in a dish and pour sauce over. Serve with hot rice. Serves 8.

Edna Frerichs, Branch 2121, Chico, CA

STUFFED MEATBALLS

2 lb. hamburg
⅔ c. milk
2 cans cream of mushroom soup

2 Tbsp. Worcestershire sauce
2 Tbsp. ketchup
1 pkg. Stove Top stuffing, prepared

Prepare Stove Top stuffing according to instructions on the box. Set aside. Take 1 pound of hamburg. Add ⅓ cup of milk. Mix together. Divide and form into 5 patties on wax paper. Put ¼ cup of stuffing in the center of each patty. Close patty up over the stuffing. Repeat with second pound of hamburg. Put the 10 stuffed hamburgs into 13x9x2 inch pan.

Mix 2 cans of soup, Worcestershire sauce, and ketchup together. Pour over hamburgs. Put in oven and bake, uncovered, for 30 to 40 minutes at 350°. Leftovers freeze well.

Kathy Burtchin, Branch No. 4119, Pemberville, OH

PORCUPINE MEATBALLS

1 lb. ground beef or pork (or more)
½ c. uncooked rice
½ c. finely chopped onion
½ c. finely chopped celery
½ c. finely chopped green pepper
1 egg

1 Tbsp. Worcestershire sauce
2 tsp. prepared mustard
1 tsp. salt
¼ tsp. pepper
¼ tsp. garlic powder

Make in 1½ inch balls. Place in 2½ quart casserole.

Sauce:

1 can cream of mushroom soup
½ c. water

¼ c. ketchup

Boil and pour over balls. Cover and bake at 350° for 1 hour.

Optional: Put ⅓ cup cheese on last few minutes.

Pat Westrum, Branch No. 5325, Stratford, IA

PORCUPINE MEATBALLS
(Slow cooker)

1½ lb. ground beef
½ c. raw rice
½ c. onion, chopped fine

1 tsp. salt
¼ tsp. pepper
1 (10½ oz.) can tomato soup

Mix beef, rice, onion, salt, and pepper. Shape into 24 (1½ inch) meatballs. Place in pot. Pour tomato soup (undiluted) over meatballs. Cover and cook on MEDIUM heat or setting No. 3 on some cookers for 3 to 4 hours. Makes 4 to 6 servings.

Lorraine Young, Branch No. 5325, Stratford, IA

MEAT BALLS IN MUSHROOM GRAVY

1½ lb. ground beef
1 onion, minced
½ c. uncooked rice
1 egg, beaten
1½ tsp. salt
¼ tsp. pepper
1 c. bread crumbs

1 c. hot milk
1 can mushroom soup
1 c. water
1 Tbsp. bottled meat sauce
⅛ tsp. pepper
¼ tsp. salt

Combine first 8 ingredients and shape into golf ball size balls. Place in 2 quart casserole. Combine soup, water, meat sauce, salt, and pepper; pour over balls. Cover and bake at 350° for 1 hour and 45 minutes.

Janet Rissinger, Branch 5265, Herndon, PA

YUMMY MEATBALLS

2 lb. hamburger
1 c. milk
1 Tbsp. grated onion
1 c. crushed corn flakes

¼ c. vinegar
1 c. ketchup
½ c. brown sugar
2 Tbsp. grated onion

Mix hamburger, milk, onion, and flakes; form into small balls. Set aside. Mix remaining ingredients together; heat and pour over meatballs. Bake at 350° for 1 hour.

This can be prepared and put in the freezer until ready to use.

Irene Dankers, Branch No. 429, Goodhue, MN

FRIKADELLER - DANISH MEATBALLS

2 lb. hamburger
1 lb. sausage
3 eggs
Salt to taste

Pepper to taste
Onion pieces to taste
1 to 1½ c. oatmeal

Mix all ingredients together. Shape into round balls in palm of hand. Brown in oil or lard on both sides. Steam done in a moderate oven for 1 hour.

Deerburger or antelopeburger may be substituted for the hamburger.

Rosemary (Mrs. Donald) Matthiessen, Branch No. 1718, Gresham, NE

221

RICE MEAT BALLS

Meat Balls:

1 c. instant rice (right from the box)
1 lb. ground beef
1 egg, slightly beaten

2 tsp. dry minced onion
2 tsp. salt
Dash of pepper
½ c. tomato juice

Sauce:

1½ tsp. sugar

2 c. tomato juice

Mix the meat ball ingredients together lightly. Shape into 18 meat balls. Place in skillet and add sauce mixture. Bring to a boil, then cover and simmer for 15 minutes. Baste occasionally.

Jane M. Rottmann, Branch No. 4605, Highland, IL

MEATBALLS AND FRANKS

Have on hand 1 pound franks, cut in bite-size pieces.

Meatballs:

2 lb. ground beef
2 slightly beaten eggs
1 large grated onion

⅔ c. bread crumbs
Salt and pepper

Sauce:

1 bottle chili sauce
1 (10 oz.) jar grape jelly
Juice of 1 lemon

1 Tbsp. Worcestershire sauce
½ c. barbeque sauce

Mix ingredients for meatballs and shape into 50 to 60 small meatballs. Cook meatballs for about 10 minutes till browned. Mix ingredients for sauce in a crock pot. Add meatballs to crock pot and cook on LOW.

Gloria J. Boyer, Branch No. 5511, Dover, PA

MEAT BALLS STROGANOFF

1 lb. ground beef
1 small onion, grated
1 tsp. salt
¼ tsp. nutmeg
¼ tsp. ground cloves
Dash of pepper
2 Tbsp. flour

1½ tsp. dry mustard
1 env. instant beef broth or 1 beef flavor bouillon cube
1 c. water
1 c. dairy sour cream
2 Tbsp. chopped parsley

1. Mix ground beef lightly with onion, salt, nutmeg, cloves, and pepper. Shape into small balls.
2. Brown balls. Pour off drippings and remove balls from pan.
3. Mix flour and mustard; stir in instant beef broth or bouillon cube and water. Cook, stirring constantly, until sauce thickens.

4. Add sour cream and parsley to sauce. Heat slowly until hot.
5. Add meat balls and simmer for 5 minutes.
6. Serve with hot rice.

Doris Henschell, Branch No. 2086, Seattle, WA

BARBECUED VENISON MEAT BALLS

2 lb. ground venison	1 egg
1 pkg. onion soup mix	¼ c. bread crumbs

Combine venison, dry soup mix, egg, and bread crumbs. Shape into walnut size balls and brown, either in saute pan or arrange on cookie sheet and put under broiler till brown. Transfer to Dutch oven, casserole or crock pot. Add the sauce and simmer for about 30 to 40 minutes. Crock pot on LOW for 1½ hours.

Sauce:

1 (14 oz.) bottle or can pizza sauce	1 (10 oz.) currant or apple jelly
1 (14 oz.) bottle catsup	

Combine pizza sauce, catsup, and jelly in blender till smooth. (Must use blender.)

Can be made in advance and frozen.

Virginia Bellhorn, Branch No. 3819, Oviedo, FL

SWEDISH MEAT BALLS

1½ lb. hamburger	1 egg
1½ tsp. salt	½ c. minced onions
⅛ tsp. pepper	¾ c. fine dry bread crumbs
1 tsp. Worcestershire sauce	1 Tbsp. minced parsley
½ c. milk	

Mix all ingredients thoroughly. Shape mixture into balls the size of a walnut. Brown in ¼ cup oil. Remove meat balls from frying pan. Make gravy.

Gravy: Mix 1 can mushroom soup and 1 can water well. Return meat balls to gravy in pan. Cook for 15 to 20 minutes. Makes 6 to 8 servings.

Margret Stanke, Branch No. 5616, Tuttle, ND

KUMMEL KLOPS - GERMAN MEAT BALLS

1 lb. ground beef	¼ c. fine dry bread crumbs
1 tsp. salt	¼ c. milk
¼ tsp. pepper	1 Tbsp. chopped parsley
¼ tsp. poultry seasoning	1 slightly beaten egg

Sauce:

1 can beef broth	½ c. chopped onion
1 (3 oz.) can chopped mushrooms, drained	1 c. sour cream
	1 Tbsp. flour

Mix first 7 ingredients together and shape into 24 meat balls. Brown slowly in hot fat, turning frequently. Add beef broth, mushrooms and onion. Cover and simmer for 30 minutes. Take out meat balls.

Blend 1 cup sour cream and 1 tablespoon flour. Stir into the broth. Add meat balls and stir, bringing it to boiling, and cook for 5 minutes. Serves 6.

St. John's Lutheran Church, AAL Branch No. 1775, Columbus, NE

GRACE LUTHERAN'S SWEDISH MEATBALLS
(Serves 300)

10 doz. eggs
3 gal. milk
4 (24 oz.) loaves bread, made into
    crumbs
10 lb. onions, minced
3 lb. margarine

1 (4 oz.) poultry seasoning
100 lb. ground beef
1 (4 oz.) pepper
1 c. salt (season to taste)
1 (4 oz.) parsley flakes

Gravy:

2 large jars instant beef bouillon
10 large cans cream of mushroom
    soup

1 small jar dill weed

Saute onions in margarine until tender. Add eggs, milk, and crumbs into hamburger mixture. Add seasoning, salt, pepper, parsley, and onions. Mix all ingredients together and shape into meatballs. Brown in skillet until done.

Mix several cans of soup with bouillon mixed with water; sprinkle with dill weed. Pour over meatballs. This will keep them moist. Remainder of gravy can be used over mashed potatoes.

Grace Lutheran Church, Branch No. 4788, Denison, TX

MEATBALL YUMMIES

1 lb. ground beef
1 egg
2 Tbsp. oil
2 Tbsp. light brown sugar

1/3 c. dry bread crumbs
2 Tbsp. Prime Choice steak sauce
1/3 c. Prime Choice steak sauce
2 Tbsp. butter or margarine

Combine beef, bread crumbs, egg, and 2 tablespoons Prime Choice sauce. Mix and shape into 1 inch meatballs. Brown in oil in skillet. Drain fat from skillet. Combine 1/3 cup Prime Choice, brown sugar and butter with meatballs in skillet. Simmer, covered, for 15 minutes or until done. Makes about 2 dozen meatballs.

Judith Martino, Branch No. 545, Mosinee, WI

MINI BEEF BALLS

2 lb. lean ground beef
1 c. corn flakes
2 eggs, slightly beaten

1 (18 oz.) bottle barbecue sauce
1 (5 oz.) glass grape jelly
Juice of 1 lemon

Mix ground beef, corn flakes (crushed) and eggs. Form into small meatballs. Combine barbecue sauce, jelly and lemon juice; bring to a boil. Add meatballs (raw). Turn heat to low and simmer for about 30 minutes.

Edith Andersen, Yankton, SD

SAUSAGE BALLS

1 lb. seasoned sausage
1 egg, slightly beaten

⅓ c. finely chopped bread crumbs

Mix sausage, egg and crumbs. Shape into balls (any size). Brown and drain.

Sauce:

½ c. catsup
2 Tbsp. brown sugar

1 Tbsp. vinegar
1 Tbsp. soy sauce (optional)

Combine sauce ingredients and pour over meat balls. Simmer for 30 minutes for 1 ½ or 2 inch balls (less for cocktail size). Add water to sauce if it becomes too thick while simmering.

Shirley Aukamp, Lamplighter, Branch No. 483, Lincoln, IL

MEATBALLS IN SWEET SAUERKRAUT SAUCE

2 lb. ground beef
3 eggs

1 pkg. dry onion soup mix
1 c. bread crumbs

Mix hamburger, eggs, onion soup, and bread crumbs. Shape into meatballs and place in 9x13 inch pan.

Sauce:

1 c. brown sugar
1 (8 oz.) jar chili sauce
1 (8 oz.) jar water

1 (8 oz.) jar whole cranberry sauce
1 (16 oz.) can sauerkraut

Simmer brown sugar, chili sauce, water, cranberry sauce, and sauerkraut for 20 minutes. Pour over raw meatballs. Bake at 300°, covered, for 45 minutes, then uncover and bake for an additional 45 minutes.

Carolyn Olson, Branch No. 1094, Knapp, WI

APPLESAUCE MEATBALLS

2 c. corn flakes, crushed
3 Tbsp. chopped onions
1½ lb. ground beef
¼ tsp. sage

1½ tsp. salt
⅛ tsp. pepper
1 egg, slightly beaten
⅔ c. thick applesauce

Mix well. Shape into balls about 1¾ inches in diameter. Put in shallow pan.

Combine:

1¼ c. tomato soup	½ c. water

Mix and pour over meatballs. Bake in moderate oven at 350° for about 45 minutes. Serve immediately.

Ruth Voigt, Branch No. 2323, Caroline, WI

MEAT LOAF ROLL

1 (10 oz.) pkg. frozen chopped broccoli, spinach or French style green beans	½ tsp. salt
	¼ tsp. pepper
	¼ tsp. dried oregano
2 lb. hamburger	1 tsp. salt
2 eggs	1 (3 oz.) pkg. sliced ham
¾ c. soft bread crumbs	3 slices Mozzarella or Swiss
¼ c. catsup	cheese, cut diagonally into
¼ c. milk	halves

Rinse frozen vegetables under cold running water to separate; drain. Mix hamburger, eggs, bread crumbs, catsup, milk, ½ teaspoon salt, pepper, and oregano. Pat hamburger mixture into rectangle, 12x10 inches, on piece of aluminum foil, 18x15 inches.

Arrange vegetables on hamburger mixture to within ½ inch of edges; sprinkle with 1 teaspoon salt. Arrange ham on vegetables. Roll up rectangle carefully, beginning at 10 inch side and using foil to lift. Press edges at ends of roll to seal. Place on rack in shallow roasting pan. Bake, uncovered, in a 350° oven for 1¼ hours. Overlap cheese on top. Bake just until cheese begins to melt, about 1 minute longer. Garnish with celery leaves if desired. Serves 8.

Aurie Cosentine, Branch No. 6588, Port Washington, WI

SAVORY MEAT LOAF

2 lb. ground beef	1 tsp. salt
½ lb. ground salt pork	Dash of pepper
1 Tbsp. grated onion	½ c. tomato catsup
1 c. moist cracker crumbs	1 tsp. Worcestershire sauce
1 egg	

Mix ingredients in order given. Shape into a loaf. Place in baking pan and bake in a moderate oven (325° to 350°) for 1½ hours, basting frequently with a few tablespoons of cold water.

A delicious rich sauce may be made by thickening the juice in a pan with flour.

Esther Welker, Branch No. 2347, New Melle, MO

SAVORY MEAT LOAF

1½ lb. ground chuck
1¼ c. tomato juice
¾ c. uncooked oatmeal
1 beaten egg
½ c. finely chopped onion

1¼ tsp. salt
¼ tsp. pepper
½ tsp. chili powder
3 hard-boiled eggs (optional)*

Mix all ingredients together well. Press down into ungreased loaf pan. Bake for 1 hour and 10 minutes before slicing. Serve on platter and decorate around the meat loaf with parsley.

* For a special treat, press half of mixture into loaf pan. Place the 3 hard-boiled eggs in row on meat loaf mixture and cover with remaining mixture. Beautiful when sliced.

Coralee Haas, Branch No. 2578, Omer, MI

MEAT LOAF

1½ lb. ground beef
¾ c. rolled oats
1½ tsp. salt
¼ tsp. pepper

¼ c. chopped onion
1 egg, beaten
¾ c. milk

Combine all ingredients. Work together with hands. Spread topping on, then bake in skillet or loaf pan for 35 to 45 minutes at 350°.

Topping:

⅓ c. catsup
1 Tbsp. brown sugar

1 Tbsp. mustard

Mix together. Spread on meat loaf before baking.

Barb Sheets, Branch No. 5844, Columbia City, IN

GREEK MEAT LOAF

½ c. chopped onion
2 Tbsp. margarine
½ c. shredded carrot
½ c. shredded raw potato
2½ c. shredded eggplant
2 lb. meat loaf mix
2 eggs

1 c. diced tomatoes
1½ c. bread crumbs
3 tsp. salt
¼ tsp. pepper
½ tsp. cinnamon
2 Tbsp. lemon juice

Saute onion in margarine for 3 minutes. Remove from heat. Stir in carrot, potato, and eggplant, tossing to coat. Cover and cook for 5 minutes or until wilted, but crisp. Combine meat, eggs, tomatoes, bread crumbs, salt, cinnamon, pepper, lemon juice, and cooked vegetables in large bowl, mixing lightly. Press firmly into a loaf pan. Turn out into a lightly greased large shallow pan. Bake at 350° for 1 hour.

Bonnie Engelhardt, Branch No. 2232, Auburn, MI

TAMALE LOAF

1 chopped onion
Garlic
1 qt. tomatoes
2 c. corn meal
1 lb. hamburger
2 eggs

½ c. milk
1 pt. corn
1 tsp. salt
1 tsp. pepper
2 Tbsp. chili powder

Brown meat, onion, and garlic. Add corn meal and tomatoes. Cook for 15 minutes, stirring constantly. Combine eggs, milk, corn, salt, pepper, and chili powder. Add meat mixture. Put in greased casserole dish. Bake at 350°F. for 1 hour. Freezes well.

Linda Dodds, Branch No. 3107, Loveland, CO

CLASSIC MEAT LOAF
(Microwave)

1½ to 2 lb. ground beef
1 (8 oz.) can tomato sauce
1 egg, slightly beaten
1 c. quick cooking oatmeal

1 Tbsp. instant minced onion
⅛ tsp. salt
¼ tsp. pepper

Combine all of the ingredients. Put in a 9x9x2 inch loaf dish. Cook in the microwave on FULL power for 8 to 10 minutes.

Sauce (optional):

⅓ c. catsup
1 tsp. Worcestershire sauce

1 Tbsp. brown sugar
1 Tbsp. prepared mustard

Blend ingredients well. Pour over meat loaf halfway through cooking time. Cook till 160°F. is reached.

Hillard Peskey, Branch No. 6699, Iroquois, SD

SURPRISE MEAT LOAF

2 eggs
1 c. dry bread crumbs
½ c. powdered Pream
1 Tbsp. minced onion
2 tsp. salt
¼ tsp. pepper
3 Tbsp. catsup
1 c. water

2 lb. lean ground beef
2 strips bacon
5 slices American cheese, cut in
   halves diagonally
5 slices Swiss cheese, cut in halves
   diagonally
Paprika

In a large mixing bowl, beat eggs slightly. Add remaining ingredients, except bacon, eggs and paprika; mix well. Press meat mixture into a 9x5 inch loaf pan. Top with bacon. Bake for 60 minutes in a 350° oven. Remove from oven. Place cheese slices over top, alternating colors and overlapping points. Sprinkle with paprika. Continue baking until cheese is slightly melted, about 10 minutes. Serves 8 people.

Linda R. Keegan, Branch No. 6274, Lafayette, IN

GRAMMA'S SLOPPY JOES

1 c. catsup
4 Tbsp. vinegar
4 Tbsp. sugar
2 Tbsp. Worcestershire sauce

Minced onion
1 lb. extra lean hamburger
Hamburger buns

Combine the first 5 ingredients in saucepan. Bring to a boil. Add raw hamburger to preceding mixture. Cook until meat is brown. If too liquidy, you can add bread crumbs to absorb moisture. Spread on buns while hot. *Enjoy!*

Ron and Sue Going, Branch No. 3879, Billings, MT

SLOPPY JOES

25 lb. ground round
4 (10 oz.) cans tomato soup
22 oz. ketchup
3 (12 oz.) tomato paste
10 oz. sweet pickle relish
4 Tbsp. lemon juice

4 c. cooked, chopped onions
1 (32 oz.) can tomato juice
2 Tbsp. paprika
2 Tbsp. garlic salt
Salt to taste

1. Cook ground round and drain off grease.
2. Add cooked onions and all other ingredients.
3. Cook for 1½ hours at 350° the day before you need to use.
4. Heat up the next day. If necessary, add more tomato juice to moisten mixture.
5. Will serve 100 people.

This is a recipe used by Greenfield Peace Lutheran School for over 25 years.

Branch No. 2928, Detroit, MI

BEEFBURGERS

1 lb. ground beef
1 c. catsup
2 Tbsp. sugar
1 Tbsp. vinegar

½ tsp. salt
¼ tsp. ground cloves
2 Tbsp. prepared mustard
½ small onion, diced

Brown beef and drain off fat. Combine other ingredients and add to beef. Simmer for 20 to 30 minutes. Serve on buns. Serves 4 to 6.

Carol Jean Eller, Branch No. 3304, Flushing, MI

LONGBOY CHEESEBURGERS

1 lb. ground beef
1 tsp. salt
¼ tsp. pepper
¼ c. onion
1 loaf French bread, cut in half

½ c. corn flake crumbs
½ c. evaporated milk (1 small can)
1 Tbsp. Worcestershire sauce
¼ c. catsup
Cheese strips

Spread mixture on split loaves. Bake for 20 to 25 minutes at 325°. Add cheese strips last 5 minutes. Slice crossways to serve.

Phyllis Johnson, Branch No. 2089, Logan, IA

OVENBURGERS

1½ lb. hamburger
1 slice bread, crumbled
1 egg, slightly beaten

1 Tbsp. catsup
1 Tbsp. mustard
1 Tbsp. Worcestershire sauce

Mix together. Shape into meatballs (makes approximately 8). Place into ungreased glass pan. Bake for 20 to 25 minutes in a 325° oven.

Eugene Grant, Loveland, CO

B B Q

20 lb. hamburger
4 large onions
1 gal. catsup

⅔ c. mustard
1 lb. brown sugar
1 c. white vinegar

Brown hamburger and drain well. Add chopped onions and remainder of ingredients, plus salt and pepper to taste. Put into electric roaster and heat thoroughly for 1 hour. Will be enough for about 75 buns, depending on size of bun.

Dorothy Heiden, Branch No. 2670, Waco, NE

PORK BAR-B-QUE ON SKEWERS

4½ lb. pork
1 c. vinegar (or use ½ c. vinegar
    and ½ c. lemon juice)
3 cloves garlic, mashed

2 tsp. peppercorns, mashed
4 Tbsp. soy sauce
1 c. water

Cut pork into 1 inch cubes. Marinate for 2 hours or more in mixture of vinegar, garlic, peppercorns, soy sauce, and water. Place 5 or 6 cubes of meat on each skewer. Cook over charcoal, basting often. To baste, use marinating sauce with small amount of catsup added. Makes approximately 30 skewers, 2 or 3 per person.

Chicken cubes can be substituted for pork.

Mrs. Jean Gudenschwager, Reedsburg, WI, Branch No. 5935, Loganville, WI

BAR B Q

3 lb. ground beef, fried
2 small onions, cut fine
2 Tbsp. butter
2 tsp. prepared mustard
2 Tbsp. Worcestershire sauce
2 tsp. vinegar
Salt to taste

1 tsp. paprika
1 c. catsup
1 (10 oz.) can tomato soup
1 tsp. brown sugar
½ c. celery, cut fine
1 green pepper, cut fine

Mix all together and simmer for about 2 hours. Covers about 18 or 20 buns.

Jenny Bruss, Branch No. 840, Oak Creek, WI

230

BARBEQUE FOR 25

3½ to 3¾ lb. hamburger
2 Tbsp. fat (optional)
1 pt. celery, chopped
½ c. onion, chopped
5 Tbsp. cider vinegar

¼ c. brown sugar
1 Tbsp. dry mustard
2½ c. catsup (like Heinz)
1 Tbsp. salt
1½ c. water

In a Dutch oven, cook and stir hamburger until brown; drain. Cook celery and onion in fat until tender. Add cider vinegar, brown sugar, dry mustard, catsup, salt, and water to celery and onion. Cook for 5 minutes. Add browned hamburger. Simmer on top of stove for 1 hour.

Jacqulyn Hartfiel, Branch No. 3682, Beaver Dam, WI

BAR-B-Q
(One roaster - 100 servings)

20 lb. hamburger
4 large chopped onions
1 gal. ketchup

⅔ c. mustard
1 lb. brown sugar
1 c. white vinegar

Brown and drain hamburger. Salt and pepper to taste. Add all other ingredients. Put into electric roaster and heat for 1 to 1½ hours. Put a large spoonful on a hamburger bun. Makes one roaster. Serves 100.

Joan Gloystein (recipe of Kathy Schlechte), Branch No. 769, Utica, NE

BARBECUED BEEF LOAVES

6 Tbsp. dry bread (or 2 slices)
⅔ c. milk
1 lb. ground beef
1 egg, slightly beaten

¼ c. grated onion
1 tsp. salt
⅛ tsp. pepper
½ tsp. sage

Soak bread crumbs in milk. Add beef, egg, onion, salt, pepper, and sage. Mix well. Form into patties. Cover each meat loaf with Piquant Sauce. Bake in a 375° oven for 30 to 40 minutes.

Piquant Sauce:

3 Tbsp. brown sugar
4 Tbsp. catsup or chilli sauce

¼ tsp. nutmeg
1 tsp. dry mustard

Combine all ingredients and spread over patties.

Freada Reinhardt, Branch No. 2014, Stillwater, OK

CROCK POT BARBECUE RIBS

3 to 4 lb. spareribs
Salt and pepper

1 onion, sliced

Sauce:

1 tsp. dry mustard
1 tsp. red pepper
½ tsp. liquid smoke
2 c. catsup

1 tsp. celery seed
1 tsp. Worcestershire sauce
1 c. brown sugar
2 tsp. vinegar

Sprinkle ribs with salt and pepper. Place ribs in broiler pan under broiler for 30 minutes to brown and remove excess fat. Put sliced onion in crock pot. Slice ribs into serving pieces and put in crock pot. Pour in barbecue sauce. Cover and cook on LOW for 8 to 10 hours or HIGH for 4 to 5 hours.

AAL, Branch No. 3157, Ferncy, SD

BARBECUED RIBS

3 lb. country style spareribs
1 to 2 Tbsp. liquid smoke
1 c. catsup
¼ c. Worcestershire sauce
¼ c. lemon juice

1 tsp. salt
1 tsp. chili powder
1 c. water
1 tsp. celery seed

Put ribs in shallow baking pan, meaty side up. Brush with liquid smoke. Bake at 400° for 30 minutes. Heat rest of ingredients to boiling and pour over ribs. Reduce heat to 350° and bake for 1 hour, or until tender. Baste every 15 minutes.

Jan McLaughlin, Branch No. 3107, Loveland, CO

BARBECUE CHICKEN

1 lb. chicken (your family's
    favorite pieces)
1 (12 oz.) can Coke (sugar free can
    be used)

1 c. ketchup

Wash chicken and put in 10 inch skillet which you can cover. Add Coke and ketchup mixture, pouring over chicken. Cover and simmer for 1 hour. Stir occasionally. Sauce will thicken.

Annette Hartline, Loveland, CO

DIJON HAM 'N SWISS
(Meal in a loaf)

4 c. all-purpose flour
2 Tbsp. sugar
½ tsp. salt
2 pkg. RapidRise yeast
1 c. water
¼ c. Dijon mustard

2 Tbsp. oleo
1½ c. chopped, cooked ham
1 c. shredded Swiss cheese
½ c. chopped dill pickle
1 egg, beaten

Set aside 1 cup flour. Mix remaining flour, sugar, salt, and yeast. Heat water, mustard and oleo to 125°F. to 130°F. Stir into flour mixture. Mix in enough reserved flour to make a soft dough. Knead for 4 minutes.

On greased baking sheet, roll dough to 14x12 inches. Sprinkle ham, cheese and pickle down center third of dough length. Make cuts from filling to dough edges at 1 inch intervals along sides of filling. Bring strips from opposite sides of filling together; twist and place ends at an angle across filling. Cover. Place large shallow pan on counter; half fill with boiling water. Place baking sheet over pan. Let dough rise for 15 minutes.

Brush loaf with egg. Bake at 350°F. for 30 minutes or until done. Serve warm. Refrigerate leftovers. Reheat to serve.

Variation: For an even heartier loaf, ham may be increased up to 1 pound. Increase baking time to about 35 minutes.

Helen Hansen, Branch No. 1957, Creighton, NE

MOM'S PASTIES

2 c. Bisquick
½ c. cold water

5 raw potatoes
1½ lb. raw hamburger

Mix the Bisquick and cold water. Take small amount of dough and roll out, using a lot of flour on board. Cut up a few potatoes on the top of the rolled out dough, then add small amount of patted out burger on the top of potatoes. Season with salt and pepper. Fold together. Repeat steps until dough is gone. Put on margarined cookie sheet. Brush with milk. Bake at 350° till crust is golden brown.

Shelley Bourdeau, Branch No. 6245, Portage, WI

STUFFED CABBAGE - GOLABKI
(Polish)

Worldwide, this is one of the most popular and best-known Polish dishes.

1 (3 lb.) head green cabbage
¼ c. butter or margarine
1 small onion, chopped
1 lb. lean ground beef
1½ lb. lean ground pork
1½ c. cooked long grain white rice

1 tsp. salt
¼ tsp. freshly ground black pepper
3½ c. beef broth (bouillon broth)
1 (6 oz.) can tomato paste
2 Tbsp. all-purpose flour

With a sharp knife, remove core from cabbage. Carefully remove wilted or decayed outer cabbage leaves; discard. In a large saucepan, boil enough salted water to cover cabbage. Immerse cabbage in boiling water. Cook over medium high heat for 5 to 7 minutes. With fork or tongs, gently remove leaves as they become tender. Drain well. Let cool.

Preheat oven to 325°F. (165°C.). Trim main leaf stems. Melt 1 tablespoon butter or margarine in a small skillet. Add onion; saute over medium heat until golden brown.

In a large bowl, combine sauteed onion, beef, pork, rice, salt, and pepper. Spread a cabbage leaf flat. Depending on leaf size, place 2 tablespoons filling on cabbage leaf near base. Fold bottom of leaf over filling, then fold sides toward center. Roll tightly. Repeat with remaining filling and cabbage leaves.

Heat 1 tablespoon butter or margarine in a large skillet. Place filled cabbage leaves, seam down, in skillet. Cook over medium heat until browned, 8 to 10 minutes, turning once with a spatula. Arrange cabbage rolls, seam side down, in a medium roasting pan. Add 3 cups broth or bouillon.

In a small bowl, combine ½ cup broth or bouillon and tomato paste. Pour over stuffed cabbage. Cover and bake for 40 minutes or until fork tender. In a small skillet, melt remaining 2 tablespoons butter or margarine. Stir flour into butter or margarine until smooth. Cook over medium heat, stirring, until golden brown. Ladle 1 cup broth or bouillon from stuffed cabbage into flour mixture; blend. Pour mixture over stuffed cabbage. Cook, uncovered, until liquid bubbles and thickens slightly. Place stuffed cabbage on a large platter. Pour pan juices into a serving bowl. Serve hot with pan juices. Makes 10 to 12 servings.

LaVern Malinski, Branch No. 647, Carrington, ND

PEPPY CHILI STACK-UPS

1 lb. ground beef
1 (15 oz.) can kidney beans,
  drained
1 (24 oz.) can V-8 juice
1 pkg. Chili-O mix
⅓ c. chopped onion

Fritos corn chips
Shredded lettuce
Sour cream
Olives, sliced
Shredded cheese
Chopped onions

Brown ground beef; add onions, kidney beans, V-8, and Chili-O mix. Simmer for 45 minutes. Serve over corn chips. Garnish with shredded lettuce, sour cream, olives, shredded cheese, and chopped onions as desired.

Doreen Preuss, Branch No. 5016, Laguna Hills, CA

CHEATER BEANS

1 lb. hamburger
Onion, finely chopped
3 (1 lb.) can Bush's beans
1 c. brown sugar

1 c. catsup
¼ c. mustard
¼ c. dark molasses
Liquid hickory smoke

Brown hamburger with onion. Add remaining ingredients to hamburger-onion mixture. Pour in ovenproof bowl. Bake at 300° for 2 hours. *Enjoy!*

James E. and Elaine L. Lindquist, Branch No. 3339, Esko, MN

BIG-WHEEL BURGER SKILLET

1 Tbsp. instant minced onion
½ c. milk
1½ lb. ground beef
1 slightly beaten egg
½ c. quick cooking rolled oats
2 tsp. salt
¼ tsp. coarsely ground pepper

Kitchen Bouquet
1 (8 oz.) can (1 c.) spaghetti sauce
  with mushrooms
1 (8 oz.) can (1 c.) kidney beans
Buttered, toasted French bread
  slices

Soak onion in milk for 5 minutes; mix in ground beef, egg, rolled oats, salt, and pepper. Mound in 10 inch skillet. With wooden spoon handle, score in 5 or 6 wedges.

Brush top lightly with Kitchen Bouquet. Combine spaghetti sauce and kidney beans (with liquid). Pour over meat mixture. Simmer, uncovered, for 20 to 25 minutes or till done. Serve wedges on French bread slices. Spoon sauce over. Serves 5 or 6.

Florence Walter, Branch No. 2232, Auburn, MI

BAKED BEEF ROUNDS

2 lb. ground beef
1 c. soft bread crumbs
½ c. catsup
1 onion, chopped

1 tsp. Worcestershire sauce
1½ tsp. salt
¼ tsp. pepper
1 egg, slightly beaten

Mix all ingredients and shape into patties. Place in shallow baking dish. Spoon ½ cup tomato juice over top and cover with onion rings. Bake, uncovered, for 1 hour at 350°. Makes 4 to 6 servings.

Adeline McBride, Branch No. 6706, Brule, NE

EMPANADAS

Dough:

1½ c. flour
Pinch of salt

5½ Tbsp. whipped margarine
3 oz. dry vermouth

Combine flour and salt. Cut margarine into flour and work with finger tips until crumbly. Add vermouth and knead lightly into a pliable dough. This dough will be almost like velvet, yet easy to handle. Refrigerate for at least 1 hour.

Meat Filling:

½ lb. lean ground beef
1 Tbsp. minced onion
½ tsp. minced garlic
1 tsp. chili powder
1 tsp. cinnamon

1 tsp. sweet paprika
3 Tbsp. chili sauce or catsup
1½ tsp. salt and freshly ground
  pepper

Combine all ingredients in a skillet and saute the mixture, breaking up with a fork until meat is crumbly and no longer pink. Drain off excess fat and chill.

The Empanadas: Roll out on floured board about ½ of the chilled dough until very thin and almost transparent. Cut into 3 inch circles and fill each circle with 1 teaspoon Meat Filling. Moisten the edges with water. Fold in half and seal edges with tines of a fork. Repeat until dough and filling are used. Empanadas are ready for freezing or frying.

To fry, heat about 1 inch oil in a skillet until fairly hot (about 370°). Put filled dough into hot oil and reduce heat to low. Cook and brown for 2 or 3 minutes on each side. Drain on paper towels and serve very hot or slightly salted or bake straight from the freezer for 10 minutes at about 400°.

May be served with hot mustard, chili or sweet and sour sauces.
Al and Rosie Meinert, Lamplighters, Branch No. 5076, Topeka, KS

CABBAGE ROLLS

½ lb. ground beef
½ c. fine bread or cracker crumbs
½ onion, chopped
¼ small green pepper, chopped
½ tsp. salt
A little pepper
¼ tsp. celery salt

⅛ tsp. thyme
¼ tsp. (scant) sage
1 tsp. Worcestershire sauce
2 Tbsp. catsup, diluted to make ¼ c.
1 egg

Mix the preceding well and let stand for awhile. Select large loose head of cabbage. Core and carefully loosen large outer leaves under running water (about 10 leaves). Cook leaves for about 5 minutes in large saucepan until limp, but not mushy. Place a heaping tablespoonful meat mixture on the thin end of each leaf. Fold ends over and roll, then fasten with toothpick. Place in large skillet (with a lid). Pour over all a No. 2 can of tomatoes. Season with a little salt and pepper. Place 3 or 4 thin strips of green pepper and 1 strip of bacon on top. Cook, *uncovered,* in a 450° oven for ½ hour, then for 1 ½ hours, *covered,* in a 380° oven.
Mrs. Terry (Barbara) Sell, Branch No. 3365, Rock Springs, WY

JOHANNA MEZETTI

1 lb. 8 oz. ground beef
¼ c. onions, chopped
¼ lb. noodles (dry egg)
1 (10¼ oz.) can cream of mushroom soup

1¼ c. milk
¼ lb. American cheese, shredded
Salt and pepper to taste

1. Brown beef and onions.
2. Cook noodles in salted water until tender; drain.
3. Add cooked noodles, milk and mushroom soup to browned beef.
4. Blend in cheese.
5. Salt and pepper to taste.
6. Place in pan and bake for 30 minutes at 350°. Yield: 6 to 8 servings.

Note: If desired, you may just heat and not bake.
Maxine Wilson, Branch No. 4734, West Lafayette, IN

SUPPER ON A BREAD STICK

1 small can evaporated milk
1 lb. ground beef
½ c. bread crumbs
1 egg
½ c. chopped onion
1 tsp. salt

1 tsp. mustard
⅛ tsp. pepper
1 c. grated American or Cheddar
  cheese
1 loaf Italian bread

Mix all ingredients together. Cut bread in half lengthwise. Spread meat mixture on top of both halves. Wrap bread in foil. Bake at 350° for 1 hour.

Jean Germer (Mrs.), Branch No. 5776, Mount Joy, PA

MEAT FILLETS

2 lb. ground beef
1 c. applesauce
1 Tbsp. chopped onion
¼ c pimento (optional)

1 c. finely grated carrots
2 eggs
2 tsp. salt
1 tsp. pepper

Mix all ingredients well. Take a ½ cup measuring cup and measure out 12 balls. Slightly flatten and wrap 1 strip of bacon around and secure with a toothpick. Bake at 325°, covered, for ½ hour and uncovered for ½ hour.

Ronda Tucker, Branch No. 2512, Ord, NE

MOM SEDLAK'S GOULASH

3 Tbsp. cooking oil
5 medium onions, chopped
5 cloves garlic, chopped
⅛ tsp. red pepper
¼ tsp. paprika

5 lb. meat for stew (beef), cubed
1 whole green pepper
3 whole stalks celery
2 c. water
2 Tbsp. flour

In a large stew type pot, saute the onions and garlic in hot oil until golden. Stir in red pepper and paprika. Add the stew meat and cook over fairly high heat until all water has come out of the meat. Stir regularly so meat doesn't stick and burn. Add 1 whole green pepper and 3 stalks celery.

Cover, reduce heat to very low and simmer for 2 to 2½ hours. Add 2 cups water and 2 tablespoons flour for thickening. Simmer until flour is dissolved. Serve in a bowl by itself or over your favorite type noodles.

Allan Belko, Branch No. 822, St. Louis, MO

DELMOCETTI

1 large onion
1 green pepper
2 lb. ground beef
½ lb. Velveeta cheese

1 can tomato sauce
1 can stewed tomatoes
1 small can mushrooms
2 c. boiled shell noodles

Saute onion and green pepper. Add ground beef, cheese, tomatoes, tomato sauce, and mushrooms. Heat through until cheese has melted. Mix with cooked shells. Bake at 350° for 30 minutes.

Gayle Walther, Branch No. 2890, Wildomar, CA

MOSTACCIOLI

2 (10 oz.) pkg. mostaccioli
2 lb. hamburger
1 chili block
2 cans tomato soup
2 (8 oz.) cans tomato sauce

2 (1 lb.) cans tomatoes or 1 qt. home canned tomatoes
½ to 1 tsp. oregano
¼ tsp. garlic powder
Salt and pepper to taste

Break chili block into small pieces in a large saucepan. Add tomatoes, tomato soup, and tomato sauce, thinning the mixture with water. Simmer slowly. Brown the hamburger in a skillet; add oregano and garlic powder. Add to the tomato-chili mixture. Cook the mostaccioli in boiling salt water to which a few drops of oil have been added to prevent boiling over. Do not overcook. Drain and rinse. Combine the mostaccioli and the tomato-chili-meat mixture. Makes 16 to 20 servings.

Branch No. 1206, Crosstown, MO

CHILI LOAF

This looks complicated, but is not and my family loves it.

¾ lb. lean hamburger
1 small onion, chopped
⅓ c. tomato paste
⅓ c. water
2 Tbsp. chili powder

1 loaf French bread
½ c. butter or margarine, melted
2 tsp. garlic powder
1 can kidney beans, drained
½ c. sour cream

Brown hamburger with chopped onion. Add tomato paste, water and chili powder. Place bread on a cookie sheet and slice top off. Pull the inside of the loaf out (save for another dish). Using the melted butter with garlic added, butter inside of loaf. Put meat mixture in bottom of loaf. Top with kidney beans to which sour cream has been added. Place loaf top (which is also buttered) on top and bake at 400° for 10 minutes. Slice and serve.

Valerie Behnke, Branch No. 4292, Flagstaff, AZ

IRISH CORNED BEEF AND CABBAGE

5 lb. lean corned beef brisket
1 large onion, sliced
1 large carrot, peeled and sliced

½ tsp. rosemary leaves
1 (2 lb.) head cabbage, cut into quarters

In a 10 to 12 quart pan, cover beef with water. Boil for 5 minutes. Discard water. Add more water to cover meat, onion, carrot, and rosemary. Cover and simmer until meat is very tender when pierced (3½ to 4 hours). Lift out the meat. Keep warm on a platter. Bring stock to boiling. Add cabbage and cook, uncovered, until tender crisp when pierced. Reserve stock for Emerald Sauce. Slice meat across grain. Serve with sauce.

238

Emerald Sauce:

3 Tbsp. butter or margarine
3 Tbsp. all-purpose flour
1¾ c. corned beef stock

1½ to 2 Tbsp. horseradish
¼ c. sour cream
½ c. chopped parsley

In a 1 to 2 quart pan, melt butter. Add flour. Stir till bubbly. Add stock and stir to boiling. Add rest of ingredients. Stir till hot. Serves 6 to 8.

Dorinda Meyer, Branch No. 2714, Ogden, UT

CAJUN GUMBO FILÉ

2 Tbsp. vegetable oil
2 Tbsp. flour
1 large chicken, cut up
Water to cover chicken
Canned chicken broth (to add to
    broth from chicken to make 4
    c.)
½ lb. Brown and Serve sausage
1 lb. small frozen, peeled shrimp
½ c. finely chopped shallot (if
    available)

2 c. finely chopped onion
2 c. okra, cut into ½ inch pieces
    (or 2 c. canned, drained)
1 large can tomatoes (with juice)
2 pods pressed garlic
Salt and pepper to taste
¼ tsp. Tabasco
1 bay leaf
4 c. water
File powder to taste

Stew chicken; remove skin, fat and bones. Cut up into bite-size. Set aside. Measure broth. Add canned chicken broth to make 4 cups. In large, heavy pot, heat vegetable oil. Add flour, stirring constantly to make a dark brown roux.

In separate skillet, brown sausage. Drain and slice into ¼ inch rounds. Prepare shrimp if necessary. Saute shallot, onion, and okra, if raw. (If canned, add with other vegetables.) To pot containing roux, add broken up tomatoes and juice, garlic, salt, pepper, Tabasco, bay leaf, 4 cups chicken broth, 4 cups water, chicken, and sausage. Cover and simmer gently for at least an hour, stirring occasionally. Add shrimp. Heat until pink. Remove bay leaf. Sprinkle on file at very last. Serve over prepared rice (or with oyster crackers).

Olive M. Delezene, Branch No. 2568, Fredericktown, MO

BRATWURST

1 to 2 chopped onions
⅛ c. brown sugar
¼ c. vinegar
4 oz. ketchup
2 Tbsp. mustard

2 to 3 shakes of soy sauce
2 to 3 shakes of Worcestershire
    sauce
Cheap beer
Bratwursts

Add preceding mix to enough cheap beer to soak bratwurst in a kettle. Soak for 20 minutes. Bring mix to slow boil for 5 to 10 minutes. Finish them by browning them on a grill.

St. John's Lutheran Church, Branch AAL 1775, Columbus, NE

HOMEMADE SALAMI

2 lb. ground beef (hamburger)
½ tsp. garlic powder
½ tsp. mustard seed

2 Tbsp. liquid smoke
3 Tbsp. Morton's Tender-Quick
   salt

Blend all ingredients with hands. Form into two 12 to 18 inch rolls. Wrap in foil; refrigerate for 24 hours. Poke holes with fork into foil, piercing the meat deeply. (This will allow the fat to drain from the rolls as they bake.) Place rolls in foil on a broiler rack in a shallow pan of water. (The water keeps the grease from burning.)

Bake at 325° for 1½ to 2 hours. Unwrap and cool. Refrigerate or freeze. Slice thinly to serve. Recipe may be doubled or tripled.

This salami makes a tasty gift at Christmas time or anytime.
Mrs. David Pease, Branch No. 4896, Kalamazoo, MI

SUMMER SAUSAGE

2 lb. ground chuck
¾ tsp. mustard seed
¾ tsp. ground pepper
½ tsp. garlic powder

¼ tsp. liquid smoke (or smoke
   salt)
2½ Tbsp. Tender-Quick salt

Combine all of the ingredients and mix well. Place in tightly covered bowl and refrigerate for 24 hours. Divide in thirds; roll and form into sausages, or you can make 6 smaller sausages.

Wrap in foil and cook in water for 1 hour. Punch holes in foil and place on rack. When cooled a little, unwrap and rewrap in foil and refrigerate.
Joyce Duelm, Branch No. 514, Mt. Olive, IL

LAMB CURRY
(For Passover)

3 Tbsp. fat or pure vegetable oil
2 lb. lamb, cut in 1 inch cubes
1 c. chopped onion
2 cloves garlic, crushed
½ tsp. salt
½ tsp. ground ginger
¼ tsp. pepper
¼ tsp. ground cumin

1 to 2 Tbsp. curry powder (add
   least, you can always add
   more to taste)
1 tsp. flour
1 (10½ oz.) can condensed beef
   broth
1 c. water

Heat fat or oil in large skillet. Add meat and brown well. Remove and reserve. Saute onion and garlic until soft in fat or oil remaining in skillet. Add salt, ginger, pepper, cumin, curry powder, and flour. Cook for 2 minutes, stirring constantly. Return lamb to skillet. Add beef broth and water. Reduce heat, cover and cook, stirring occasionally, for about 45 minutes or until lamb is tender. Serve with Rice Pilaf and tomato chutney if desired.

This is a recipe that can be used if your church would like to observe/enact the Passover. This recipe does serve 6, but could serve more if each person only receives as taste.

Mona Geidel, Branch No. 3107, Loveland, CO

RICE PILAF
(For Passover)

⅔ c. chopped onion
3 Tbsp. butter or margarine
1 c. rice
1 tsp. leaf marjoram, crumbled

1 tsp. leaf rosemary, crumbled
½ tsp. leaf savory, crumbled
3 c. chicken broth

Saute onion in butter/margarine in skillet until soft. Add rice, marjoram, rosemary, and savory. Cook, stirring constantly, until rice starts to brown. Add chicken broth; simmer until rice is tender and liquid is absorbed.

Mona Geidel, Branch No. 3107, Loveland, CO

CARIBBEAN PICADILLO

5 lb. lean ground beef
2 to 3 Tbsp. vegetable oil
5 c. onions, chopped
4 large garlic cloves, minced
5 green bell peppers, chopped
4 c. canned or fresh tomatoes,
    peeled and chopped

1½ tsp. salt
½ tsp. freshly ground pepper
1 c. sliced pimento stuffed olives
½ c. capers with a few drops of
    juice
Hot cooked rice

Cook beef in oil in large skillet until meat loses red color. Crumble with long handled fork while cooking. Add onions and garlic; cook, stirring, until onions are translucent. Pour off fat. Stir in green peppers, tomatoes, salt, and pepper. Simmer, uncovered, for 10 minutes or until most of the liquid is evaporated. Stir now and then while cooking. Add olives and capers. Simmer for 2 minutes to blend flavors. Serve hot on rice.

Picadillo can be prepared ahead, refrigerated or frozen, and reheated in large skillet. Makes 18 to 20 servings, but is easy to divide or multiply. Two double recipes will serve 100 with salad, rice and bread.

Laura Johnson, Branch No. 2049, Emporia, KS

Notes

Casseroles
and
Breakfasts

RULES FOR USING HERBS

1. Use with a light hand—the aromatic oils are strong and objectional if too much is used.

2. Blend or heat with butter, margarine or oil to draw out and extend the flavor. Unsalted butter is best. When using herbs in French dressing, have the oil tepid.

3. Cut or chop leaves very fine. The more cut surface exposed, the more completely the aromatic oil is absorbed.

4. Dried herbs are two to four times as strong as fresh herbs, so that if you substitute dried for fresh herbs use ¼ to ½ the amount. Experimentation is the best guide.

5. The flavoring of herbs is lost by extended cooking.

6. To taste the true flavor of an herb you have not used before, mix ½ teaspoon crushed herb with 1 tablespoon cream cheese or sweet butter, let stand 10-15 minutes. Taste on a cracker.

7. The beginner should err on the side of too little rather than too much. It is easy to overseason and one flavor should never be allowed to overpower another. A person should not be able to recognize the presence of an herb or what accounts for the delicious flavor. More of an herb can be added, but it cannot be taken out.

8. Herbs are used in addition to salt and pepper.

9. For **herb butters**, 1 tablespoon of the minced fresh herb is mixed into ¼ pound softened butter or margarine. Let stand at room temperature for at least one hour, preferably more. After flavor has been absorbed into butter, it should be chilled in refrigerator. This will keep for several days if covered tightly so it does not absorb odors from refrigerator.

CASSEROLES AND BREAKFASTS

ORIENTAL HOT DISH

2½ c. chow mein noodles
1 can Chinese vegetables
1 can tomato soup
1 can cream of mushroom soup
1 can water
2 Tbsp. soy sauce

1 c. mushrooms
1 c. chopped celery
1 c. diced onion
1 can sliced water chestnuts
2 lb. lean ground beef
½ c. cashew pieces

Break up beef; brown well. Drain. Add onion and celery. Mix. Add rest of ingredients and pour into casserole. Bake for 1 hour at 350°.

Dorothy Ratzlaff, Branch No. 6714, Woodbury, MN

CHINESE BEEF AND POTATOES

1 Tbsp. salad oil
1 large onion, chopped
2 stalks celery, sliced in rings
1 lb. lean hamburger
2 garlic cloves, minced or pressed
¾ tsp. ground ginger

2 medium potatoes, peeled and cut
   in ½ inch cubes
2 c. water
1 beef bouillon cube
¼ c. soy sauce
1 (4 oz.) jar pimentos

Cooking Sauce:

2 Tbsp. cornstarch
2 Tbsp. water

¼ tsp. pepper
½ tsp. sesame oil (optional)

Quick fry onion and celery until tender and crisp; set aside. Crumble beef into pan. Add garlic and ginger. Fry meat until browned. Skim off oil. Add potatoes, water, bouillon cube, and soy sauce. Bring to a boil. Cover and simmer, stirring occasionally, until potatoes are tender when pierced (about 10 minutes). Add onion, celery, pimentos, and Cooking Sauce. Add salt to taste. Makes 3 to 4 servings.

Robin Fastert, Branch No. 6715, Rock Rapids, IA

HAM-CORN CHOP SUEY

2 lb. ham, cut up
1 can chicken rice soup
1 green pepper, cut up
1 onion, cut up

1 can pimentos
1 can whole kernel corn
1 (5 oz.) wide noodles

I use leftover ham. Cook noodles according to directions on package. Fry cut up green pepper and cut onion; saute in butter. Cut up pimentos and mix with whole kernel corn. Add prepared noodles and rest of ingredients in a 9x13 inch casserole. Top with buttered cracker crumbs. Bake in a moderate oven at 350° until done, about 1 hour.

Branch No. 2232, Auburn, MI

CHOW MEIN A LA ELTON

1 lb. hamburger
1 onion, cut up fine
1 c. celery, chopped
1 c. uncooked rice

1 can chicken rice soup
1 can cream of mushroom soup
1 can bean sprouts with liquid
1 can chow mein noodles

Brown hamburger; add onion and celery. Cook until vegetables are soft. Combine with rest of ingredients, except noodles, and put in casserole. Top with noodles and bake in moderate oven for 45 to 60 minutes, uncovered.

Elton Sprengeler, Branch No. 559, Fort Dodge, IA

CHOW MEIN HOT DISH

1½ lb. hamburger, browned
2 to 4 onions
1 can tomato soup
1 (4 oz.) can mushrooms
Chow mein noodles

3 c. celery
1 can mushroom soup
1 can celery liquid
4 Tbsp. soy sauce

Boil celery and onions for about 10 minutes with almost enough water to cover. Mix soups and add celery liquid, celery, onions, and meat. Put in flat baking dish, about 9x9 inches. Add chow mein noodles on top. Bake in a 325° oven for 1 ½ hours.

There is sufficient salt in soy sauce - *add no extra salt.*

Dorothy Sparby, Branch 545, Mosinee, WI

1950'S CHOW MEIN NOODLE CASSEROLE

1 lb. hamburger
6 stalks celery, diced
1 medium onion, diced
1 large can chow mein noodles
  (reserve a little to put on top of
  casserole)

1 can cream of mushroom soup
1 can tomato soup
3 Tbsp. soya sauce

Fry about 1 pound hamburger. Saute celery (diced) with onion (diced). Mix in large can of chow mein noodles, 1 can of mushroom soup, 1 can of tomato soup, and the soya sauce. Mix well. Add a little water to moisten. (Additional salt is not needed.) Top with noodles. Bake for ¾ hour at 350°.

Selma Nynas, Branch No. 3339, Esko, MN

SOUPER TUNA CRUNCH

1 can (about 3 oz.) Chinese
  noodles
1 can Campbell's cream of
  mushroom soup
¾ c. water
1 (6½ oz.) can tuna

1 c. cashews or peanuts
1 c. chopped celery
½ c. finely chopped onions
½ c. cooked peas
Soy sauce

Reserve ½ cup Chinese noodles. In 1½ quart casserole, combine remaining noodles, soup, water, tuna, nuts, celery, onions, and peas. Bake at 350° for 30 minutes or until hot; stir. Sprinkle remaining noodles around edge. Bake for 5 minutes longer. Serve with soy sauce to taste. Makes about 4½ cups.

Carol McFall, Branch No. 224, Grand Haven, MI

FIVE CAN CASSEROLE

1 can chicken and rice soup
1 can cream of mushroom soup
1 small can condensed milk
1 can chow mein noodles

1 small can Chicken of the Sea
   tuna or chicken
Crushed potato chips (over top)

Mix all together in large bowl. Put in 2 quart baking dish, greased. Bake at 325° until it bubbles. Let stand for a short time before serving.

Tuna may be used instead of chicken.

Lee Kehl, Branch No. 64, Elkhorn, WI

EASY SHRIMP CHOW MEIN

1½ c. sliced fresh mushrooms
1 c. sliced celery, diagonally cut
1 small green pepper, cut in strips
½ c. onion, sliced
2 Tbsp. salad oil
1 c. chicken broth

2 Tbsp. cornstarch
2 Tbsp. soy sauce
8 oz. frozen shrimp
½ c. water chestnuts, sliced
4 c. cooked rice or Chinese
   noodles

In skillet, brown mushrooms. Cook celery, onion and green pepper in salad oil until just tender. Add chicken broth, cornstarch and soy sauce. Cook until thick. Add shrimp and water chestnuts. Heat and serve over rice or noodles. Yield: 4 servings.

Gail Wollenzien, Branch No. 3715, Cottage Grove, WI

STIR-FRIED RICE

½ c. shrimp (small can)
1½ c. diced ham
4 eggs (1 per serving), beaten
2 c. frozen peas (8 to 16 oz. bag) or
   2 c. fresh peas
2 Tbsp. chopped green onion plus
   stem

½ c. mushrooms (small can)
4 c. cooked rice
12 Tbsp. peanut oil or 12 Tbsp.
   margarine
Soy sauce

Heat 2 tablespoons of oil each time and fry each of the first 6 ingredients separately, cooking each a few minutes. When cooked, add to a large casserole dish, mixing each gently. Heat oil and add cooked rice. Stir and add soy sauce till rice is brown in color. Add rice to rest of casserole. Mix well and heat before serving. Serves 4 to 6.

Mrs. Betty (Reinhard) Kufalk, Branch No. 4188, Beaver Dam, WI

HERBED CHICKEN CASSEROLE

3 large chicken breasts, cut in
    halves, or 1 cut up chicken
½ tsp. salt

⅛ tsp. pepper
¼ c. butter or margarine

    Browning Time:

1 can condensed cream of chicken
    soup
¾ c. sauterne wine (dry)
1 (5 oz.) can water chestnuts,
    drained and sliced
1 (No. 303) can broiled, sliced and
    drained mushrooms

2 Tbsp. minced onion or 3 thinly
    sliced scallions (including
    some green)
¼ tsp. thyme

Season chicken with salt and pepper. In large skillet, heat butter and chicken; brown well on all sides. Arrange browned chicken, skin side up, in a shallow roasting pan or casserole.

Combine soup with pan drippings; slowly add wine, stirring until smooth. Add remaining ingredients and heat to the boiling point. Pour sauce over chicken and cover with foil. Bake at 350° until chicken is almost cooked (about 40 minutes). Uncover and continue baking until fork tender. Serve with hot fluffy rice.

Ann Raquer, Branch No. 6958, Buffalo, MN

CHICKEN CHOW MEIN

About 3 lb. cooked chicken
1 pkg. chow mein noodles
1 can chop suey vegetables,
    drained
1 green pepper
1 medium onion
1 small jar pimento pieces

1 small water chestnuts
½ c. slivered almonds
1 can evaporated milk
1 can cream of chicken soup
1 can cream of mushroom soup
1 Tbsp. soy sauce

Cook chicken. Remove skin and bones; cut in small pieces. Layer ½ package chow mein noodles in a casserole, then cut up chicken, 1 can chop suey vegetables (drained), green pepper, onion, pimento, sliced water chestnuts (drained), and slivered almonds. Top with remaining chow mein noodles.

In a saucepan, mix and heat 1 can evaporated milk, cream of chicken soup, cream of mushroom soup, and 1 tablespoon soy sauce. Pour over the layers in the casserole. Poke with fork so liquid goes through. Bake at 350° for 1 hour.

Lillian Generotzke, Branch No. 840, Franklin, WI

CHICKEN WATER CHESTNUT CASSEROLE

5 or 6 slices white bread, crusts removed
2 c. cooked chicken or turkey, cubed
4 oz. water chestnuts, drained and sliced
4 oz. mushrooms, drained
1/4 c. mayonnaise
5 oz. undiluted mushroom soup
5 oz. undiluted celery soup
1/4 c. pimiento, chopped
5 slices Old English or American sliced cheese
1/2 c. eggs, beaten
1 c. milk
1/2 tsp. salt
1 c. herbed bread crumbs
1/8 c. margarine

Line a greased loaf pan with bread (on bottom only). Layer pan with 1 inch cubes of chicken or turkey. Add water chestnuts and mushrooms. Dot with mayonnaise. Combine soups and pour over ingredients in pan. Add pimiento and top with cheese. Mix eggs, milk and salt. Pour over layers in pan. Refrigerate for at least 4 hours (better overnight). Bake, covered, for approximately 1 1/2 hours at 350°F.

Combine bread crumbs and margarine. Sprinkle over the top. Bake, uncovered, for 30 minutes. Remove from oven 15 minutes before serving to allow setting time. Cut into serving portions. Serves 6 to 8.

Mrs. Juanita Mallett, Branch No. 5680, Cahokia, IL

BEEF AND BROCCOLI STIR-FRY

1 Tbsp. cornstarch
1/4 c. light or dark corn syrup
2 Tbsp. soy sauce
2 Tbsp. dry sherry
1 lb. boneless beef, cut into thin strips
5 Tbsp. Mazola corn oil
1/4 c. sliced onion
1 clove minced garlic
1/4 tsp. crushed, dried red pepper
1/2 c. sliced mushrooms
1/2 c. thin carrot strips
2 c. broccoli flowerets and sliced stems
1/2 c. chopped celery
1 (8 oz.) can water chestnuts, drained and sliced
1/2 c. beef broth

In bowl, stir together the first 4 ingredients until smooth. Add beef and toss to coat. Cover and refrigerate for 4 hours or overnight. Drain and reserve marinade. In large skillet or wok, heat 2 tablespoons oil over medium high heat. Add onion, garlic and red pepper. Stir-fry for 2 minutes. Remove with slotted spoon to large bowl. Add mushrooms to skillet. Stir-fry for 1 minute. Remove.

Add 2 tablespoons oil. Add carrots, broccoli, celery, and water chestnuts. Stir-fry for 2 minutes or until tender crisp. Remove. Add 1 tablespoon oil. Add beef and stir-fry for 3 minutes or until lightly browned. Add broth and reserved marinade, stirring constantly. Bring to a boil over medium heat and boil for 1 minute. Add the vegetables and the onion. Cook for 2 to 3 minutes or until heated. Serve over rice. Serves 4 to 6.

Bette Branda, Branch No. 6588, Port Washington, WI

EGG ROLLS

1 pack egg roll wrap
2 eggs
1 bunch bean thread
2 lb. pork chop
3 carrots, sliced
½ lb. cabbage, sliced
1 lb. onions, sliced

½ lb. bean sprouts
1 tsp. salt
1 tsp. sugar
2 tsp. fish sauce
½ tsp. black pepper
½ tsp. seasoning

Mix together the last 12 ingredients. Put a portion in each egg roll wrap and deep-fry in 3 or 4 inches of oil at 370° for 10 to 12 minutes.

Khamphong Hanlotxonphou, Branch No. 896, New Haven, IN

MOCK CHOP SUEY

1 lb. ground beef
4 Tbsp. margarine or butter
1 to 2 c. diced celery
2 onions
1 can condensed cream of
    mushroom soup (undiluted)
1 can condensed cream of chicken
    soup (undiluted)

1 can bean sprouts
¼ c. soy sauce
½ c. raw rice
1 soup can boiling water
1 c. Chinese noodles

Brown meat in 2 tablespoons butter. Saute celery and onions in 2 tablespoons butter. Mix all ingredients together, except noodles. Cover and bake at 350° for 30 minutes. Sprinkle top with noodles and bake for 15 minutes more. Serves 4 to 6.

Carol Jean Eller, Branch No. 3304, Flushing, MI

YAKI SOBA

1½ lb. hamburger
½ c. chopped onion
2 c. sliced or grated carrot and
    celery
3 to 4 c. shredded cabbage
¼ c. green pepper (optional)
2 Tbsp. soy sauce

2 c. water
1 (4 oz.) can mushrooms
    (undrained)
2 pkg. Ramen noodles
Salt to taste
1 can water chestnuts, sliced

Brown hamburger with celery and onion. Add rest of ingredients and cook until vegetables are tender and liquid is absorbed. Do not overcook.

Carol Sauder, Branch No. 837, Roanoke, IL

BEEF CHOW MEIN

1 lb. ground beef
2 cans Chinese vegetables
1 to 2 cans mushroom pieces

2 Tbsp. brown gravy sauce
3 Tbsp. soy sauce
3 Tbsp. cornstarch

Brown 1 pound beef. Drain if necessary. Pour off and reserve ½ cup juice from 2 cans Chinese vegetables. Drain mushrooms. Add vegetables and remaining juice as well as the mushrooms into hamburger. Add 2 tablespoons brown gravy sauce and 3 tablespoons soy sauce to mixture; bring to a boil.

Blend 3 tablespoons cornstarch with the ½ cup reserved juice and pour into the mixture, stirring constantly, until thickened. Reduce heat and simmer to desired consistency. Serve over rice or Chinese noodles.

Bob Meginnes, Branch No. 837, Secor, IL

PEPPERONI PIZZA CASSEROLE

1 lb. ground beef	1 (4 oz.) can mushrooms, drained
⅓ c. chopped green pepper	14 to 15 oz. pizza sauce
⅓ c. chopped onion	1 (3½ oz.) pkg. pepperoni
¼ tsp. garlic powder	1 c. water
2 c. uncooked egg noodles	1 c. Mozzarella cheese (added last)

Cover and cook ground beef, green pepper and onion until beef is no longer pink, about 5 minutes, on 100% power or HIGH. Drain ground beef. Add remaining ingredients to ground beef mixture and pour into a 2 quart casserole. Cook for 15 minutes on 100% power or HIGH, then for 7 minutes on 40% or 50% power until noodles are tender. Add Mozzarella cheese and let stand until cheese melts, about 5 minutes.

Duane D. Faas, Branch No. 2910, Ames, IA

PIZZA HOT DISH

1½ lb. ground beef	1 c. mushrooms
½ c. chopped onion	2 (10 oz.) cans pizza sauce
1 tsp. salt	1 (8 oz.) can tomato sauce
⅛ tsp. oregano	1 c. milk
¼ tsp. pepper	1 c. sliced pepperoni
1 (12 oz.) pkg. noodles	1 (8 oz.) pkg. Mozzarella cheese
¼ c. green olives, chopped	

Brown together beef, onion, salt, oregano, and pepper. Cook noodles. Mix noodles and beef with olives, mushrooms, pizza sauce, tomato sauce, and milk. Put in 9x13 inch pan. Top with pepperoni and Mozzarella cheese. Bake at 350°, covered, for 45 minutes. Uncover and bake for 15 minutes more.

Mrs. Arline Schroeder, Branch No. 1131, Worthington, MN

PIZZA CASSEROLE

1 lb. ground beef	½ c. diced onion
1 can Cheddar cheese soup	½ tsp. oregano
½ c. milk	¼ tsp. pepper
4 c. thinly sliced potatoes	½ tsp. salt
1 (15 oz.) can tomato sauce	

Brown hamburger; add remaining ingredients. Put in 9x13 inch pan. Cover with foil and bake for 45 to 60 minutes at 375°. Remove from oven. Cover with ½ cup Parmesan cheese and 8 ounces Mozzarella cheese. Bake for 15 minutes, uncovered.

Carol Wiedebush, Branch No. 2560, Mansfield, SD

POURED PIZZA

1 c. flour
1 tsp. salt
⅛ tsp. pepper
1 lb. ground beef
1 onion, chopped
Salt and pepper to taste

2 eggs, beaten
⅔ c. milk
⅛ tsp. oregano
1 (15 oz.) can tomato or pizza
sauce
1½ c. shredded cheese

Saute meat and onion until meat is lightly browned. Drain. Season with salt and pepper. Combine ingredients for batter and pour into a greased 9x13 inch pan. Top with meat mixture and bake at 400° for 15 to 20 minutes. Remove from oven and pour tomato sauce over top. Sprinkle with cheese. Return to oven and bake for another 15 minutes. Serves 6.

This is a family favorite for potlucks.

Donna Giermann, Branch No. 6470, Kiron, IA

UPSIDE-DOWN PIZZA

1 lb. hamburger
1 env. spaghetti mix
1 env. taco mix
1 large onion

1 can tomato sauce
½ c. water
1 (8 oz.) pkg. Mozzarella cheese
½ c. Parmesan cheese

Brown hamburger and onion; pour off excess fat. Add sauces, tomato sauce, and water. Simmer for 10 minutes.

Mix together:

2 eggs
1 c. milk
1 Tbsp. oil

1 c. flour
¼ tsp. salt

Beat eggs, milk and flour. Add flour and salt. Blend until smooth. Pour hamburger mixture in 9x13 inch dish. Top with Mozzarella cheese. Pour batter over hot filling. Cover all. Sprinkle with Parmesan cheese. Bake at 400° for 30 minutes.

Lenore Ruppert, Branch No. 3837, Nokomis, IL

PIZZA HOT DISH

10 to 12 potatoes (depends on size)
1 can Cheddar cheese soup
¾ c. milk
1½ lb. hamburger
1 medium size onion

1 green pepper (if desired)
1 tsp. salt
1 jar Pizza Quick sauce
1 lb. Mozzarella cheese (more or
less as desired)

Line a 9x13 inch cake pan about 1 inch thick with peeled, sliced potatoes. Cover potatoes with can of Cheddar cheese soup mixed with ¾ cup milk. Brown in pan on stove the hamburger with onion and, if desired, green pepper. Sprinkle with salt. Add this to potato mixture. Top with Pizza Quick sauce. Cover cake pan with tin foil.

Bake for about 1 hour and 15 minutes at 350°F. to 375°F. Remove from oven and take tin foil off. Cover hot dish with Mozzarella cheese. Put back in oven and brown for about 20 minutes.

Arlas Johnson, Branch No. 186, Minnesota City, MN

PAUPER'S PIZZA

1 c. buttermilk
1 Tbsp. sugar
2 Tbsp. butter
1 pkg. active dry yeast

2 c. sifted flour
1 tsp. salt
¼ tsp. baking soda
4 oz. shredded Cheddar cheese

Combine buttermilk, sugar and butter in large saucepan. Heat to lukewarm. Remove from heat and add yeast. Stir to dissolve. Stir in flour, salt and soda till well blended. Knead on floured surface until smooth (about 1 minute). Let rest for 10 minutes. Pat out dough onto greased 12 inch pizza pan or cookie sheet. Spread with topping. Sprinkle with cheese. Bake at 400° for 20 to 30 minutes. Serves 8.

Topping:

1 (11½ oz.) can bean and bacon
    soup
1 Tbsp. instant minced onion

¼ c. catsup
2 Tbsp. prepared mustard
1 lb. wieners, cut in ½ inch slices

Combine and mix well.

JoAnne Einspahr, Branch No. 2630, Greeley, CO

PIZZA PINWHEEL CRESCENTS

1 (16 oz.) pkg. hot roll mix
1 lb. hamburger
½ c. finely chopped green pepper
¼ c. chopped onion

1 c. shredded Mozzarella cheese
2 Tbsp. snipped parsley
½ c. spaghetti sauce

Mix roll mix according to directions through kneading. Cover and let rest while preparing meat mixture. In skillet, brown hamburger, pepper, and onion; drain well. Add remaining ingredients.

Divide dough in half. On lightly floured surface, roll one half into 8x10 inch rectangle. Spoon half of meat mixture over dough to within an inch of edges. Roll up dough from one long edge. Pinch edges to seal. Place seam side down. Cut 3 places on side of loaf. Repeat with other half of dough. Let rise for ½ hour. Bake at 375° for 25 minutes. Cut each loaf into 8 slices.

Cheryl Schultz, Branch No. 3107, Loveland, CO

SPAGHETTI OR PIZZA SAUCE

Saute in heavy saucepan until tender:

2 Tbsp. oil
2 cloves garlic, minced

½ green pepper, chopped
1 onion, chopped

Add and saute until brown ½ pound ground beef (optional).

Add:

2 c. tomato sauce
¾ c. tomato paste
1 tsp. Worcestershire sauce
1 c. stock, beef broth or bouillon
¼ tsp. oregano

¼ tsp. basil
¼ tsp. thyme
¼ tsp. cumin
Salt and pepper to taste

Simmer over low heat for 1 hour. Use for spaghetti, lasagne or pizza sauce.

Mary Vander Top, Loveland, CO

GOOD AND EASY PIZZA DOUGH

1 pkg. yeast
1 c. warm water
1 tsp. sugar

1 tsp. salt
2 Tbsp. oil
2½ c. flour

Dissolve yeast in warm water. Stir in remaining ingredients. (Dough handles better if it is kneaded a few times.) Divide in half and pat out on 2 greased 10 to 12 inch pizza pans or use 1 large baking sheet. Let dough set for about ½ an hour, then spread with sauce and toppings of your choice. Bake at 425° until browned (15 to 20 minutes).

Barbara Alsum, Branch No. 3107, Loveland, CO

PIZZA SPAGHETTI

2 lb. hamburger
1 medium onion
1 green pepper
1 (4 oz.) can mushrooms
1 (32 oz.) jar spaghetti sauce

1 (10½ oz.) can pizza sauce
1 tsp. salt
4 c. uncooked macaroni twists
1 lb. Mozzarella cheese

Boil twists and drain. Chop onion into frying pan. Add hamburger and brown. Add chopped green peppers. Stir in pizza and spaghetti sauce. Add twists, mushrooms and salt. Pour into 13x9 inch baking pan. Cover with grated cheese. Bake at 350° for 45 minutes.

Muriel Nickel, Branch No. 2579, Pinconning, MI

SPAGHETTI

1 lb. ground beef
2 onions, chopped
3 garlic cloves, minced
1½ Tbsp. oil
2 (29 oz.) cans tomatoes
2 (6 oz.) cans tomato paste

1 can mushrooms
⅓ c. parsley (dried)
1½ Tbsp. sugar
1 Tbsp. salt
2 tsp. oregano
1 bay leaf (optional)

Brown ground beef and onion. Add rest of the ingredients. Simmer for 2 hours. Serve over noodles. Makes 2 quarts.

GRAMS SPAGHETTI

1½ lb. ground beef
28 oz. tomatoes
6 oz. tomato paste
1 chopped onion
1 clove garlic

1 Tbsp. sugar
½ tsp. cloves
1 c. mushrooms
½ c. Parmesan cheese
1 bell pepper, chopped

Combine in a Dutch oven and simmer for 2 to 3 hours. *It's thick and yummy.*
Sharon Verville, Branch No. 3107, Loveland, CO

SPAGHETTI SAUCE

¼ c. olive oil
2 large onions, chopped
2 minced garlic cloves
1 lb. ground beef
2 large cans tomatoes
2 (6 oz.) cans tomato paste
½ c. water

½ c. chopped celery
2 Tbsp. parsley flakes
1 Tbsp. salt
1 tsp. sugar
1 bay leaf
¼ tsp. pepper

Brown ground beef and drain. Add onions, garlic and olive oil. Add rest of ingredients and simmer for 2½ to 3 hours. Stir occasionally until sauce thickens. Makes 3½ pints.

Can freeze extra. Serve on cooked spaghetti noodles and sprinkle with Parmesan cheese if desired.

Jan McLaughlin, Branch No. 3107, Loveland, CO

SPAGHETTI CASSEROLE

2 lb. ground beef
1 c. chopped onion
½ tsp. garlic salt
1 (28 oz.) can tomatoes
1 (15 oz.) can tomato sauce
1 (4 oz.) jar sliced mushrooms,
   drained

2 tsp. sugar
1½ tsp. oregano
1 tsp. basil
8 oz. spaghetti, broken, cooked
   and drained
2 c. Mozzarella cheese
⅓ c. Parmesan cheese

Brown the ground beef and onion; drain. Stir in all of the seasonings, tomatoes and mushrooms. Simmer for 20 minutes. Stir in the spaghetti. Place half of mixture in a 9x13 inch pan. Sprinkle with Mozzarella cheese. Add remaining meat mixture. Top with the Parmesan cheese. Bake at 375° for 30 minutes.

Mrs. Robert (Marilynn) Claus, Branch No. 1971, Pilger, NE

DJ'S CAVENTINI

1⅛ c. pasta twists
1⅛ c. pasta shells
8 oz. hamburger
5 oz. sausage
¾ c. onion
½ c. green pepper

4 oz. mushrooms
15½ oz. spaghetti sauce
8 oz. Mozzarella cheese, divided
2½ Tbsp. Parmesan cheese
2 oz. pepperoni

Cook twists in boiling water for 9 minutes. Cook shells in boiling water for 7 minutes. Brown hamburger and sausage; drain. Chop and saute onion, green pepper and mushrooms. Mix. Bake in 8x8 inch dish with 5 ounces of Mozzarella cheese and spaghetti sauce. Top with slices of pepperoni, Parmesan cheese and remaining 3 ounces of Mozzarella cheese. Bake at 350° for 15 minutes and at 250° for 15 minutes.

Marilyn Berglund, Branch No. 5325, Stanhope, IA

MANICOTTI

2 c. homemade spaghetti sauce
1 lb. (2 c.) Ricotta cheese or
  cottage cheese
1 c. shredded Mozzarella cheese
10 oz. frozen spinach, cooked
½ tsp. garlic salt
½ tsp. basil

⅛ tsp. pepper
12 manicotti shells, cooked
  according to pkg. directions
  and drained
2 Tbsp. grated Parmesan cheese
2 eggs

Prepare homemade spaghetti sauce. While simmering, stir together Ricotta, Mozzarella, egg, garlic salt, spinach, basil, and pepper. Stuff manicotti with mixture. Pour 2 cups homemade spaghetti sauce in 9x13x2 inch baking dish. Place manicotti on sauce. Pour remaining sauce over manicotti. Sprinkle with Parmesan. Cover tightly with foil and bake at 350° for 30 minutes.

Lorraine Tucker, Branch No. 4845, Youngstown, OH

MOSTACCIOLI

¼ lb. bacon
½ lb. fresh mushrooms
¼ c. chopped onion
1 minced garlic clove
16 oz. tomatoes with liquid, cut up

1 small can peas
1 Tbsp. basil
½ tsp. salt
3 c. mostaccioli noodles

Fry bacon and crumble. Reserve liquids to saute mushrooms for 2 to 4 minutes until tender, but not brown. Add tomatoes, peas, basil, and salt. Bring to a boil over medium heat. Reduce to simmer. Stir occasionally. Cook pasta as directed on box. Toss with sauce and top with bacon. Makes 4 to 6 servings.

Sharon Verville, Branch No. 3107, Loveland, CO

COMPANY CASSEROLE

1 lb. ground beef	1 can cream of mushroom soup
1 tsp. salt	1 soup can water
½ medium onion, chopped	1 (4 oz.) can mushrooms
½ green pepper, chopped	1 c. shredded sharp cheese
8 oz. cooked spaghetti	Garlic powder to taste (optional)
1 can tomato soup	

Brown the beef in skillet, then add the onion, green pepper and salt. After these have cooked a little, add the cooked spaghetti, soups, water, and mushrooms, and garlic (if desired). Pour into a 3 quart casserole and top with the shredded sharp cheese. Bake, uncovered, in a 350° oven for about 35 minutes. Serves 8.

Sadie Jackson, Branch No. 4817, Youngstown, OH

SPAGHETTI PIZZA LASAGNA

1 lb. spaghetti, cooked and drained	Salt and pepper to taste
1 c. milk	Oregano to taste
2 eggs, beaten	Garlic to taste
32 oz. spaghetti sauce	1 pkg. pepperoni
1 lb. hamburger	3 c. (or more) shredded cheese of choice

Combine cooked spaghetti, milk and eggs. Place in 9x13 inch pan. Spread spaghetti sauce over spaghetti. Brown hamburger. Season with salt, pepper, oregano, and garlic. Place hamburger over spaghetti sauce. Add a layer of pepperoni next. Top with shredded cheese. Bake, uncovered, for ½ hour at 350°.

Deb Jorgensen, Branch No. 2306, Marcus, IA

CRAFTY CRESCENT LASAGNE

Meat Filling:

½ lb. ground sausage	½ tsp. leaf basil (optional)
½ lb. ground beef	½ tsp. leaf oregano
¾ c. chopped onion	½ tsp. salt
½ clove garlic, minced (optional)	Dash of pepper
1 Tbsp. parsley flakes	1 (6⅓ oz.) can tomato paste

Brown meats and drain. Add remaining ingredients. Simmer for 5 minutes. May be made ahead and refrigerated.

Cheese Filling:

½ to 1 c. cottage cheese
1 egg

¼ c. Parmesan cheese

Combine all ingredients.

Crust:

2 cans crescent rolls
2 (7x4 inch) slices Mozzarella
cheese

1 Tbsp. milk (optional)
1 Tbsp. sesame seeds (optional)

Unroll crescents into 8 rectangles. Place on ungreased cooky sheet, overlapping edges (15x13 inches). Press edges together. Spread half of meat down center of dough to within 1 inch of 13 inch end. Top meat with Cheese Filling. Put on remaining meat. Place cheese slices on top. Fold 1 inch edges over filling. Pull sides over filling. Pinch edges to seal. Brush with milk and sprinkle on seeds. Bake at 375° for 20 to 25 minutes until golden brown.

Tip: May be prepared ahead of time, covered with plastic wrap, and refrigerated for 2 to 3 hours before baking. Bake for 25 to 30 minutes.

Rose Borck, Branch No. 1098, Fremont, NE

RAVIOLI

1 medium onion, chopped
3 or 4 garlic cloves
1 lb. pork
1 lb. veal or beef
1 stalk celery, chopped
Sage to taste
Salt and pepper to taste

½ c. water
2 Tbsp. grated cheese
½ tsp. cinnamon
½ tsp. nutmeg
1 egg
Broth (add from meat until moist)

Dough:

6 c. flour
6 eggs

1½ tsp. salt
7 Tbsp. water

Brown your meats, onion, garlic, and celery. Add sage, salt, pepper, and water. Stew all this together until tender. Trim off fat and bones. Grind in meat grinder. Add grated cheese, cinnamon, nutmeg, egg, and enough broth until moist. Make dough roll very thin. Cut into 2x2 inch squares. Put small ball of meat in the middle of dough squares. Fold over and crimp edges with a fork. Let them dry out (like you would noodles). Cook in boiling water until tender. Add to tomato sauce or chicken broth.

John and Karla Enrietto, Branch No. 5454, Pawnee, IL

POTLUCK LASAGNA

2 qt. tomatoes
4 (8 oz.) cans tomato paste
2 tsp. salt
3 tsp. oregano
1/4 tsp. pepper
2 tsp. onion salt
2 c. onions

2 minced garlic
1/3 c. oil
2 lb. ground beef
1 lb. medium wide noodles
2 tsp. salt
1 lb. Mozzarella cheese
1 c. Parmesan cheese

Simmer first 6 ingredients in saucepan. Saute onions and garlic in oil. Fry ground beef and add with onions to tomato mixture. Simmer for 1/2 hour. Arrange in casserole 1 layer noodles, 1 layer of tomato mixture, slices of Mozzarella cheese, and Parmesan cheese. Repeat. Bake for 50 minutes at 350°. Serves 16.

Note: Makes one 12x18 inch or two 9x13 inch pans.

Clara Schultz, Branch No. 736, Essexville, MI

MEXICAN LASAGNA

2 lb. ground beef
1 c. chopped onion
Garlic
1 can cream of chicken soup
1 can cream of mushroom soup
1 (10 oz.) can enchilada sauce

1 c. milk
1 c. sliced pitted black olives
1 (4 oz.) can chopped green chilies
12 flour tortillas, cut in 4 strips
2 c. Monterey Jack cheese
2 c. Colby cheese

In a large skillet, brown beef, onion and garlic. Drain fat. In another large pan, mix the milk, olives, chilies, and soups; bring to boil. Add the meat and mix together. Remove from heat.

In a large cake pan, spread sauce, 1/3 tortillas, sauce, and 1/3 cheese. Add 2 more layers like the last, ending with cheese. Bake at 350°, covered with foil, for 30 minutes. Uncover and bake for another 20 minutes or until hot and bubbling and the cheese is browned. Let stand for a few minutes before serving.

Deb Austin, Branch No. 3887, Greeley, CO

BAKED LASAGNE

1 lb. ground beef
1 clove garlic, minced
1/2 tsp. salt
1/2 c. dry red wine (optional)
1 qt. spaghetti sauce
1 (6 oz.) can tomato paste
1 (16 oz.) pkg. lasagna noodles

2 eggs, slightly beaten
1 1/2 c. cottage cheese
1/2 c. grated Parmesan cheese
2 Tbsp. parsley flakes
Dash of pepper
1 lb. Mozzarella cheese, shredded
    or sliced thin

Cook noodles in 4 quarts of boiling water for 5 minutes. Drain and rinse with cold water. Set aside.

Brown ground beef in skillet. Drain off fat. Add minced garlic, salt and wine. Simmer for 3 to 5 minutes. Stir in spaghetti sauce and tomato paste. Cook for 10 to 15 minutes.

Combine beaten eggs, cottage cheese, Parmesan cheese, parsley, and pepper. Blend well. Layer meat sauce, noodles, egg, cottage cheese mix, and Mozzarella cheese. Repeat layers. Bake at 350° for 1 hour. Makes two 9x13 inch pans or you can use one 9x13 inch pan for a deep dish lasagna.

Mabel Biel, Branch No. 4534, Litchfield, MN

QUICK LASAGNE

2 lb. hamburger
1 env. onion soup mix
3 cans (8 oz.) tomato sauce
1 c. water
8 oz. broad cooked noodles
8 oz. Mozzarella cheese, sliced

Brown meat. Stir in soup mix, tomato sauce, and water. Simmer for 15 minutes. Alternate sauce, cooked noodles and cheese. End up with cheese. Bake at 400° for about 20 minutes or until cheese is melted.

Elaine Maison, Branch No. 6940, Harrison, MI

LASAGNA

1 lb. Italian sausage
1 lb. ground beef
1 large can tomato sauce or 1 (16 oz.) can tomatoes, pureed
2 (6 oz.) cans tomato paste
10 oz. lasagne or wide noodles
3 c. fresh Ricotta or creamy cottage cheese
½ c. grated Parmesan or Romano cheese
2 Tbsp. parsley flakes
2 beaten eggs
1 lb. Mozzarella cheese, sliced very thin

Brown meat slowly and spoon off excess fat. Add tomato sauce and tomato paste. Simmer, uncovered, for 20 minutes, stirring occasionally. Cook noodles in large amount of boiling, salted water till tender; drain and rinse. Combine remaining ingredients, except Mozzarella cheese.

Place half of the noodles in 13x9x2 inch baking dish. Spread with half of the cottage cheese filling. Add half of the Mozzarella cheese and half the meat sauce. Repeat layers. Bake at 375° for 30 minutes. Let stand for 10 minutes before cutting into squares. Filling will set slightly. Makes 12 servings.

Or, assemble early and refrigerate. Be sure to allow 15 minutes longer in the oven.

Bernice Ave, Branch No. 3107, Loveland, CO

QUICK LASAGNE

1½ lb. hamburger
1 Tbsp. basil
1 tsp. garlic salt
1½ tsp. salt
½ tsp. cumin
1 (1 lb.) can stewed tomatoes
1 (6 oz.) can tomato paste
4 oz. lasagne noodles
1 egg
1 small ctn. cottage cheese
2 Tbsp. parsley
½ c. Parmesan cheese
1 tsp. salt
½ tsp. pepper
¾ lb. shredded Mozzarella cheese

Brown meat with garlic salt, salt, basil, and cumin. Add tomato paste and stewed tomatoes after draining grease. Simmer, uncovered, for 30 minutes. Stir occasionally.

Cook noodles in large amount of water until tender. Drain and rinse. Beat egg. Add cottage cheese, Parmesan cheese, parsley, salt, and pepper. Layer ½ of noodles in baking dish; spread ½ of cheese mixture, ½ of Mozzarella cheese, and ½ of meat mixture. Repeat. Bake at 375° for 30 minutes. Let stand for 10 minutes before serving.

Julie Padilla, Branch No. 3107, Loveland, CO

CLASSIC LASAGNA

½ pkg. (16 oz.) lasagna noodles
1 lb. lean ground beef
1 lb. Italian sausage (mild or hot)
1 medium onion, chopped
1 rib celery, chopped
½ green pepper, chopped
¼ tsp. garlic powder
Salt and pepper to taste
1 tsp. oregano

1 can tomato soup
1 (6 oz.) can tomato paste
1 (8 oz.) can tomato sauce
1½ c. water
¾ lb. Mozzarella cheese
Parmesan cheese
1 (12 oz.) container Ricotta cheese
(optional)

Cook lasagna noodles according to package directions. Brown meat and sausage. Drain off liquid. Add tomato soup, sauce and paste. Add spices and water, celery, green pepper, and onion. Mix well and cook for 1 hour.

To assemble, pour ½ cup sauce on bottom of a 9x13 inch pan. Layer lasagna noodles, slices of Mozzarella cheese and sauce. Sprinkle with Parmesan cheese. Repeat layers, ending with Mozzarella cheese and sauce. Sprinkle with Parmesan cheese. (You can fill one layer with Ricotta cheese if you like.) Bake in a 375° oven for 40 minutes. Let stand for 10 minutes before cutting.

Martha Krentz, Branch No. 3107, Loveland, CO

LASAGNE

Spaghetti Sauce:

1 lb. hamburger
1 small clove garlic, chopped fine
½ bay leaf
1 full tsp. oregano

1 full tsp. sugar
½ tsp. salt
1 (12 oz.) can tomato paste
2 (12 oz.) cans tomato sauce

Brown hamburger. When lightly browned, add chopped garlic, then put all other ingredients in pan plus four 6 ounce cans of water. Simmer over low heat for about 2 hours. More water can be added if sauce becomes too thick.

Lasagne:

Spaghetti sauce
1 (1 lb.) ctn. cottage cheese
1 (12 oz.) Mozzarella cheese
Parmesan cheese

1 (8 oz.) pkg. lasagne noodles,
cooked according to pkg.
directions

Layer ingredients in this order in 9x13 inch pan: Noodles, cottage cheese, Mozzarella cheese, sprinkling of Parmesan cheese, and then spaghetti sauce. Repeat until all ingredients are used. Bake at 350° for about 45 minutes to 1 hour.

Helen Frey, Branch No. 1061, Saline, MI

LASAGNA

1 to 1½ lb. ground beef
3 Tbsp. flour
1 large can whole tomatoes
1 small onion
¼ tsp. pepper
2 tsp. oregano
1 tsp. basil
½ tsp. garlic salt (optional)

½ lb. or 8 large lasagna noodles, cooked and drained
½ lb. Mozzarella cheese
½ c. grated Parmesan cheese
¼ c. catsup
¼ c. brown sugar
2 c. cottage cheese

Brown meat, adding ¾ teaspoon salt; drain and rinse. Mix flour with ½ cup tomato juice until smooth. Stir into meat with remaining tomatoes and juice, onion, and seasonings. Cook slow for 15 minutes. Grease 9x12 inch dish and place alternate layers of noodles, meat and cheese. Sprinkle with Parmesan cheese and bake at 375° for 25 to 30 minutes.

Carol Lydy, Branch No. 896, New Haven, IN

EASY LASAGNA

½ lb. lasagna noodles, boiled
1 garlic clove, minced
1 onion, chopped
1 Tbsp. oregano
2 tsp. basil (optional)
½ tsp. salt
2 cans (8 oz.) tomato sauce

1 (6 oz.) can tomato paste
1½ lb. hamburger
1 egg
1 (24 oz.) ctn. cottage cheese
12 oz. Mozzarella cheese
½ c. Parmesan cheese

Brown hamburger with garlic and onion. Salt and pepper to taste. Add tomato sauce, paste, oregano, and basil. Let simmer for 20 to 30 minutes. Mix 1 egg and cottage cheese.

After hamburger mixture simmers, layer in 9x13 inch pan the noodles, cottage cheese mix, Mozzarella cheese, and meat sauce (usually 3 layers). Sprinkle top with Parmesan cheese. Bake at 350° for 35 to 45 minutes.

Robin Fastert, Branch No. 6715, Rock Rapids, IA

LAZY LASAGNA
(Microwave)

¾ lb. lean hamburger
2 eggs
2 c. cottage cheese
¼ c. grated Parmesan cheese
1 (32 oz.) jar spaghetti sauce

¼ c. water
1½ tsp. dried Italian seasoning, crushed
10 uncooked lasagna noodles
12 oz. sliced Mozzarella cheese

In a large bowl, break up hamburger. Cover and microwave on HIGH for 3½ to 4 minutes, stirring and breaking up meat after 2 minutes. Drain well. In separate bowl, beat eggs with a fork. Stir in cottage cheese until blended; set aside.

To meat, add spaghetti sauce, water and seasoning; stir until blended. In 12x8x2 inch baking dish, layer 1½ cups of sauce, 5 noodles, half of the cottage cheese mixture, 6 Mozzarella slices, 1½ cups of sauce, remaining noodles, remaining cottage cheese mixture, and remaining sauce. Cover tightly with plastic wrap, turning one corner back. Heat on HIGH for 8 minutes. Rotate ¼ turn. Microwave on 50% power for 30 minutes or until noodles are tender, rotating ¼ turn after 15 minutes.

Top lasagna with remaining 6 slices Mozzarella cheese. Sprinkle with additional Parmesan cheese if desired. Microwave, uncovered, on HIGH for 1 minute. Remove from oven. Cover tightly with foil. Let stand for 15 minutes or until set.

Cheryl Schultz, Branch No. 3107, Loveland, CO

GREEN CHILI CASSEROLE

1 cooked, boned chicken or 3
   cooked chicken breasts
   (bite-size pieces)
1 c. chicken broth
1 can cream of mushroom soup

1 can cream of chicken soup
2 small cans diced green chilies
½ lb. grated Longhorn cheese
1 pkg. corn tortillas

Combine all, except cheese and tortillas. Beginning with tortillas, layer into a large 10x14 inch pan, alternating with the meat, chilies and soup mixture. Top with grated cheese. Bake at 400° until heated through (30 to 40 minutes).

Darlene Rowe, Branch No. 1122, Brighton, CO

CHICKEN ENCHILADAS

2 c. diced chicken
1½ lb. Colby or Cheddar cheese
1 can cream of mushroom soup
1 can cream of chicken soup

1 (4 oz.) can diced chiles
1 (4 oz.) can chopped black olives
1 pt. sour cream
18 to 24 corn tortillas

Stir together soups, chiles, olives, sour cream, and diced chicken. Shred cheese. Stir half into preceding mixture. Warm tortillas either in microwave or by dipping in hot oil to make them pliable. Spoon some mixture into the center of the tortilla, then roll each of 2 sides over the mixture.

Place, face down, in a large pan. Continue filling tortillas until you have used about ⅔ of the mixture. Spread the remaining mixture over the top, covering completely. Sprinkle with remaining cheese. Bake in a 350° oven or microwave until cheese melts and enchiladas are warmed through.

Linda Sedlacek, Branch No. 3107, Loveland, CO

DAD'S CHILI RELLENOS

1 (26 oz.) can whole green chilies
3 lb. Monterey Jack cheese

2 (16 oz.) pkg. egg roll skins

Rinse seeds out of chilies and pat dry. Cut cheese into blocks about 4 inches long and an inch or so square. You'll want about 30 blocks. Using 2 chilies for 3 rellenos, put chilies and cheese block on egg roll skin. Roll up and seal with a little water on the edges. Deep fat fry in ¾ inch of oil at 375° till golden brown. Serve topped with green chili.

Rellenos can be frozen, individually wrapped. No need to defrost before cooking, but take out of the freezer about an hour beforehand. Makes 30.

Lynn Schmidt, Loveland, CO

CHICKEN ENCHILADAS

9 to 12 corn tortillas
Chicken bouillon or broth
1 (4 oz.) can chopped green chilies
2 cans cream soup (chicken or
    mushroom)

2 cans (5 oz.) canned chicken or
    leftover chicken or turkey
Grated Cheddar cheese

Make sauce from 2 cups chicken bouillon and 2 cans (undiluted) cream style soup. Set aside. Prepare large casserole or 9x12 inch cake pan with cooking spray. Place torn taco shells in thin layer on bottom of pan. Continue layers, alternating chicken, chilies, tortillas, and cheese and adding sauce between layers. Bake at 300° until casserole holds together.

May be topped with cheese and broiled for 5 minutes before serving.

Judy Castner, Branch No. 6902, El Paso, TX

CHILI RELLENOS

1 pkg. egg roll wrappers
2 cans green chilies
12 slices Cheddar cheese

Cooking oil
Flour and water paste
Salsa

Heat oil to fry rellenos. Clean chilies and cut so you have 12 pieces of chilies. Lay chili and cheese slice in center of one egg roll wrapper; fold and seal with paste. Fry for a few minutes in heated oil and serve with salsa on top. Serves 6.

A great side dish with this is Spanish rice.

Jane Tonjes, Branch No. 2616, Bertrand, NE

GREEN CHILLI AND FLOUR TORTILLAS

2 c. pork (cooked or raw)
1 c. green chilli peppers
1 large can tomatoes (or fresh)

1 medium onion, minced
1 clove garlic
Jalapeno pepper to taste

If pork is raw, cube and brown lightly in oiled pan. (If cooked, just cube in little pieces.) Add remaining ingredients and simmer till the onion is tender. Serve plain or use over burritos.

Tortillas:

4 c. flour
2 tsp. salt

½ c. shortening
1 c. lukewarm water

Sift flour and salt in mixing bowl. Add shortening and mix well. Add luke-warm water. Blend well. Turn out on a lightly floured board; knead 50 strokes. Divide into 12 balls. Cover and knead for 15 minutes. Roll balls flat to form 8 inch tortillas.

Cook on an ungreased skillet (iron) until golden brown in spots. Turn over once, being careful not to break the air bubbles. Use medium heat.

Peggy Wasem, Branch No. 2716, Northglenn, CO

ENCHILADAS

2 lb. ground beef
1 can cream of mushroom soup
1 can cream of chicken soup
3 small cans green chili peppers
  (mild), diced

1 small can evaporated milk
20 oz. shredded mild Cheddar
  cheese
18 corn tortillas

Brown chili peppers in vegetable oil (just enough to cover bottom of pan). Remove peppers and set aside. Brown beef and drain grease. Return peppers to pan; add soups, milk and ½ cup of the cheese. Cook over low heat, stirring, until blended.

Meanwhile, fry tortillas as directed on package. Drain and place 6 tortillas in oblong pan. Add ⅓ of meat, then ⅓ of cheese. Repeat twice, ending with cheese. Bake in preheated 350° oven until cheese is melted.

Gabi Stroud, Branch No. 1221

GREEN ENCHILADAS

1 tall can evaporated milk
2 cans cream of chicken soup
1 lb. Velveeta cheese
1 flat can chopped green chilies
1 can chopped pimentos
1 lb. ground beef

1 large onion, chopped
Dash of salt
Dash of pepper
20 corn tortillas
½ lb. grated Longhorn cheese

Melt first 5 ingredients together on low fire for Cheese Sauce. Avoid scorching.

Brown ground beef; salt and pepper to taste. Add onion and continue cooking until onion is done. Pour Cheese Sauce to cover bottom of long, shallow baking dish.

Soften corn tortillas. Put 1 or 2 tablespoons meat mixture, grated Longhorn cheese and raw chopped onion in tortillas; roll up. (Adjust beef and cheese to equal amounts.) Place rolled tortillas in baking dish and cover completely with remaining Cheese Sauce. Bake at 350° for about 30 minutes or until cheese is melted and bubbling. This will make approximately 20 enchiladas.

Shirley Springer, Branch No. 4570, Andrews, TX

ENCHILADA CASSEROLE

1 lb. ground meat (2 for a crowd)
1 can cream of mushroom soup
1 can cream of chicken soup
1 (10 oz.) can enchilada sauce
1 can Ranch Style beans (2 if you like beans)

1 pkg. corn tortillas (buy 2 - use one for bread)
Cheese, grated
Sauteed onion and/or green pepper (may be added)

Brown and drain the ground meat. Add soups, sauce and beans; stir well. Layer into casserole dish or pan (it fills a 9x13 inch cake pan). Starting with sauce mixture, then the torn or broken tortillas, make about 3 layers. Cover with lots of cheese. Bake at 350° till bubbly.

Mrs. Mary D. Lange, Branch No. 3365, Rock Springs, WY

ENCHILADA PIE

12 corn tortillas
1 lb. ground beef
1 medium clove garlic, minced
½ medium onion
1 (4 oz.) can green chiles, drained and diced (2 cans if you want it hotter)

1 can mushroom soup
1 can stewed tomatoes
¼ tsp. chili powder
Salt and pepper to taste
1 lb. Longhorn cheese, shredded

Cut tortillas in quarters. Dip quarters in a small amount of hot oil for just a few seconds on both sides until slightly crisp. Drain on paper towels. Crumble beef into heated skillet. Add garlic and onion. Cook over moderate heat, stirring occasionally, until meat loses red color. Drain off grease.

Combine chiles, soup and tomatoes in a bowl. Add to meat mixture with chili powder, salt and pepper. Mix well. Arrange half of the quartered tortillas in rows, slightly overlapping in a greased 9x13 inch baking pan. Spoon half of meat mixture on top of tortillas. Sprinkle half of the cheese on top. Repeat layers, ending with cheese. Cover loosely with foil. Bake at 350° for ¾ to 1 hour.

Jan McLaughlin, Branch No. 3107, Loveland, CO

SPANISH RICE

1 lb. ground beef (lean)
1½ c. long grain white rice
4 strips bacon
1 qt. tomatoes
½ c. catsup
1 large onion, chopped

1 green pepper, chopped
½ tsp. pepper
2 tsp. salt
1 tsp. chili powder (or more to taste)

Brown bacon. Remove bacon from pan and crumble. Add rice to bacon grease in pan and brown lightly. Add ground beef and cook until its color is gone. Add the chopped onion and green pepper to the meat and rice mixture. Saute a short time. Next, add the tomatoes, catsup, salt, pepper, chili powder, and crumbled bacon. Bring to a boil, then lower heat. Cover and cook until rice is done. If mixture seems dry, add water. Stir occasionally.

Marilyn Rehley, Branch No. 1412, Corvallis, OR

MEXICAN CASSEROLE

2 lb. ground beef
½ c. onions
1 large can chili beans
1 can mushroom gravy or soup
½ c. milk

2 Tbsp. chili pepper
Salt
Black pepper
3 c. shredded Cheddar cheese
6 tortillas

Brown ground beef and onion. Add remaining ingredients, except for cheese and tortillas; mix well. Lay ½ of the tortillas at the bottom of large casserole dish. Pour ½ of ingredients over tortillas in the casserole dish. Top with 1½ cups Cheddar cheese. Repeat process, ending with the last of the Cheddar cheese on top. Cover and bake at 325° for 1½ hours.

Sharon Walters, Branch No. 3107, Loveland, CO

BEEF-TACO CASSEROLE

2 lb. hamburger
1 onion
1 Tbsp. margarine
1 tsp. salt
1½ tsp. garlic salt

2 (8 oz.) cans tomato sauce
2 Tbsp. chili powder
1 (1 lb.) can chili or kidney beans
½ lb. grated cheese
1 pkg. tortilla chips

Brown meat and onion. Drain. Add remaining ingredients, except margarine, cheese and tortilla chips. Cover and simmer for 15 minutes. Melt margarine in 9x13 inch pan. Cover bottom of pan with crushed chips. Spread meat mixture over chips. Sprinkle with cheese. Bake in a 375° oven for 20 minutes.

Cathy Glaser, Branch No. 6083, Lander, WY

TACO CASSEROLE

1 Tbsp. vegetable oil
1 onion, chopped
1 tsp. minced garlic
1½ lb. chopped beef
1 (15 oz.) tomato sauce

1 pkg. taco mix
1 can kidney beans
2 c. Cheddar cheese
1 (12 oz.) pkg. taco chips
½ c. taco sauce

Brown meat and onion; add tomato sauce and taco mix. Remove from heat. Rinse beans and mix with 1 cup cheese. Layer taco chips in bottom of pan. Layer bean and cheese mixture. Layer with another layer of chips. Spoon meat mixture over chips. Top with a layer of chips. Drizzle taco sauce over chips and top with remaining cheese. Bake for 25 minutes at 350° in a 9x13 inch pan.

Lois Hall, St. Matthew Ev. Lutheran Church,
Branch No. 6588, Port Washington, WI

MEXICALLI MEAT PIE

Filling:

1 lb. ground beef
1 c. whole kernel corn
1/4 c. green pepper, chopped
1/4 c. onion, chopped
1/4 c. corn meal

1/2 tsp. oregano
1 Tbsp. chili powder
1/2 tsp. salt
1/8 tsp. pepper
1 (8 oz.) can tomato sauce

Crust:

1 c. flour
2 Tbsp. corn meal

1/3 c. bacon drippings
3 to 4 Tbsp. water

Mix like a pie crust. Roll out and place in a 9x9 inch square pan. Place filling in pastry lined pan and bake at 425° for 25 minutes.

Topping:

1 egg, beaten
1/4 c. milk
1/2 tsp. salt
1/2 tsp. dry mustard

1/2 tsp. Worcestershire sauce
4 stuffed olives, sliced
Reserved bacon pieces

Fry 6 slices bacon until crisp and then break into large pieces; set aside. Mix topping ingredients, except olives and bacon slices; spread on pie. Top with olives and bacon. Bake for 5 minutes or until cheese melts. Let stand for 10 minutes before serving.

Barbara Rasmussen, Branch No. 4077, Sturtevant, WI

EASY MEXICAN CASSEROLE

2 lb. hamburger
1 onion
1 small can chopped green chilies
1 can enchilada sauce

1 can mushroom soup
1 can pinto or chile beans
Corn or flour tortillas
1 lb. grated Longhorn cheese

Brown hamburger and diced onion. Add the chilies, enchilada sauce, soup, and beans. Layer in pan in this order: Corn or flour tortillas, hamburger mixture, and grated Longhorn cheese. Bake at 350° for 25 to 30 minutes or until cheese is melted.

Nyla Jane M. Koopman, Branch No. 421, Battle Creek, NE

RIO GRANDE SUPPER

1 lb. ground beef
1/2 c. chopped onion
1/2 c. chopped green pepper
1 (12 oz.) can corn, drained

1 (8 oz.) jar Cheez Whiz
3/4 c. barbecue sauce
1 Tbsp. chili powder
1 bag corn chips

266

Brown meat and drain. Add onion and green pepper; cook until tender with beef. Add corn, Cheez Whiz, barbecue sauce, and chili powder. Simmer for 20 minutes. Stir occasionally. Serve with corn chips on each serving.

Marge Spencer, Trinity Lutheran, Branch No. 796, Jackson, MI

MEXICAN CASSEROLE

1 (12 count) pkg. tortillas
2 lb. ground beef
Salt
Chili powder
Garlic powder
1 chopped onion

2 cans Ranch Style beans
1 lb. Velveeta cheese, sliced
1 can cream of chicken soup
1 can Ro-Tel or Kuner's tomatoes
    and green chiles

Line bottom of greased 9x11 inch dish with half of the tortillas. Brown ground beef; season with salt, chili powder and garlic powder to taste. Spread in layers on tortillas the beef, onion, beans, sliced cheese, and rest of tortillas. Repeat layers of beef, onion, beans, and cheese. Mix soup with tomatoes and green chiles. Pour over top layer. Cover with foil and bake for 1 hour at 350°.

If you don't want it too "beany," you can use only 1 can instead of the 2 called for in the recipe.

Frances Wehmeier, Branch No. 2049, Emporia, KS

REUBEN CASSEROLE

1 (16 oz.) can kraut, drained
1 (12 oz.) can corned beef
2 c. shredded or cubed Swiss
    cheese

½ c. mayonnaise or salad dressing
¼ c. Thousand Island dressing
2 tsp. melted margarine
1 c. toasted bread crumbs

Layer (or can be mixed together) the kraut, corned beef, cheese, mayonnaise, and Thousand Island dressing. (Slice 2 medium tomatoes across top of casserole - optional). Add margarine to bread crumbs. Put on top and bake for ½ hour in a 350° oven. Use 1½ quart casserole dish.

Helen Foreman, Branch No. 224, Grand Haven, MI

CORNED BEEF CASSEROLE

1 can corned beef, flaked
1 can cream of chicken soup
1 c. milk

¼ c. chopped green onions
½ c. chopped American cheese
8 oz. macaroni, cooked

Mix first 5 ingredients together and combine with cooked macaroni. Put in baking dish and top with buttered cracker crumbs. Bake for 30 to 40 minutes at 350°.

Ferne Hansen, Branch No. 2986, Torrance, CA

DRIED BEEF CASSEROLE

1 c. milk
1 can cream of mushroom soup
2 Tbsp. chopped onion
½ green pepper, chopped

1 c. uncooked elbow macaroni
1 can water chestnuts, sliced thin
1 small jar pimento
1¼ c. shredded Cheddar cheese

Mix all together. Marinate for 8 hours. Bake for 1 hour, uncovered. Sprinkle ¼ cup cheese on top for last 15 minutes.

Verna Tessean, Branch No. 4845, Youngstown, OH

BEEF STEW CASSEROLE

3 lb. beef stew meat
2 (10½ oz.) cans cream of
    mushroom soup

1 (6 oz.) can mushrooms
¾ c. sherry wine
½ pkg. onion soup mix

Mix and pour all ingredients into a greased casserole. Cover tightly with foil. Bake at 325° for 3 hours. Don't peek! Serve with rice or noodles. Serves 8 to 10.

Elaine Behnke, Branch No. 952, Dolton, IL

GOOD-BYE TURKEY CASSEROLE

1 *can cream* of mushroom or
    cream of chicken soup
½ can water
2 c. turkey or chicken gravy

2½ c. diced leftover turkey
2½ c. leftover stuffing
1 c. leftover mashed potatoes or
    leftover rice

Combine the soup, water and gravy. Heat to simmer. Set aside. In 1½ quart casserole dish, layer soup, stuffing, turkey, and potatoes, starting and ending with the soup mixture. Cover and bake at 350° for 35 minutes. Remove cover and bake for an additional 10 minutes.

Darla Springer, Peshtigo, WI, Branch No. 5515, Marinette, WI

CROCK POT DRESSING

1 c. oleo
1 c. chopped onion
1 c. chopped celery
1½ tsp. salt
1½ tsp. sage

½ tsp. pepper
12 to 13 c. dry bread cubes
3½ to 4½ c. broth and/or milk
2 well beaten eggs

Pack lightly in crock pot. Cover and set on HIGH for 45 minutes, then on LOW for 4 to 8 hours.

Kathy Busch

CHICKEN ZUCCHINI CASSEROLE

6 c. zucchini, sliced
3 c. chicken, cooked and cubed
1 c. dairy sour cream
1 can cream of chicken soup
¼ c. chopped onions

½ c. melted margarine
1 pkg. chicken flavored stuffing
mix
1 c. shredded carrots

Cook zucchini and onion together until tender and drain. Blend sour cream and chicken soup. Add zucchini, cooked chicken and carrots to cream mixture. Mix well. Add melted margarine to stuffing mix. Put ½ in a 9x12 inch pan. Spread other ingredients on top. Bake for 30 minutes at 350° in a conventional oven or for 7 minutes in a microwave oven at FULL power. Serves 8.

Lillian Knop, Branch No. 507, Ellisville, MO

CHICKEN CASSEROLE

1 (6 oz.) box stuffing (if desired,
use your own stuffing)
1 (16 oz.) can green beans (French
style), partially drained
1 c. (or more) chicken or turkey

Water chestnuts or almonds
(optional)
1 can cream of mushroom or
celery soup and milk (as can
directs)

Prepare stuffing according to directions on the box. Set aside 1⅓ cups of stuffing (about half of mixture). Place the rest of the stuffing in the bottom of a small roaster or casserole. Spread green beans over the stuffing. Place the chicken over the green beans. Add chestnuts or almonds if desired. Top with set aside stuffing. Over this, add the soup and milk which has been mixed together. Bake at 400° for 30 to 40 minutes. Serves 8 to 12.

Jeannette Wubbena, Branch No. 2578, Standish, MI

CHICKEN AND DRESSING CASSEROLE

¼ c. oleo
1 medium onion
5 c. cubed bread
1 tsp. poultry seasoning

1 can chicken rice soup
3 to 4 c. cubed chicken, cooked
1 pkg. mixed vegetables or carrots
or peas

Melt oleo. Add chopped onion. Cook until clear. Add bread cubes and seasoning, then add chicken rice soup. Alternately layer chicken dressing mix and vegetables. Bake in covered casserole for 1 hour at 350°. Makes a good all around casserole.

Note: I sometimes mix all items together and bake.

Anita R. Schmidt, Branch No. 2232, Auburn, MI

TURKEY CASSEROLE

1 c. liquid
¼ c. turkey fat plus oleo
2 eggs, beaten
1 c. fresh bread crumbs
¼ c. sharp cheese, grated
¼ c. American cheese, grated
2 c. diced turkey
1½ c. cooked macaroni

1 Tbsp. green pepper
1 Tbsp. minced parsley
1 Tbsp. minced onion
1 can golden mushroom soup
Salt and pepper to taste
2 c. cooked, diced carrots or 1 c.
    carrots and 1 c. peas
Crushed Ritz crackers

Heat liquid and fat together; add all remaining ingredients, except cracker crumbs. Place in roasting pan; top with cracker crumbs. Bake at 350° for 1 hour. Cut in squares to serve. Yield: About 8 servings.

Lorraine Schultz, Branch No. 192, Hilbert, WI

TURKEY DRESSING

4 c. bread cubes
3 Tbsp. chopped onion
1 c. celery, chopped and cooked
1 tsp. salt (omit for preseasoned
    sausage)
¼ tsp. pepper

⅓ c. butter, melted
¼ tsp. poultry seasoning
Sage to taste
¼ lb. pork sausage
Water (as instructed on pkg. of
    cubes)

Use method of mixing as directed on package of bread cubes. Salt, pepper, poultry seasoning, and sage can be omitted if using preseasoned bread cubes.

Mrs. Loren (Beulah) Wessel, Branch No. 0743, Truman, MN

DRESSING FOR TURKEY

1 loaf toasted bread
5 c. broth
⅔ c. milk
3 eggs
4 Tbsp. margarine
⅔ tsp. poultry seasoning

½ tsp. pepper
¼ to ½ c. chopped celery
¼ c. sugar
2 Tbsp. chopped onion
1 tsp. salt

Mix together all ingredients and line pan with turkey. Top the turkey with the dressing. Bake at 350° for 1 hour.

Mrs. Robert (Marilyn) Nussbaum, Branch No. 1374, Jackson, MO

FRANKENMUTH DRESSING

15 slices stale bread
2 c. cooked chicken (including
    liver and giblets), ground
3 c. chicken broth
½ c. chopped onion
½ c. chopped celery
½ tsp. marjoram

¼ c. margarine
2 eggs
1 Tbsp. salt
¼ Tbsp. pepper
¼ Tbsp. chopped parsley
¼ Tbsp. sage

Mix all together, adding eggs last. Put in a baking dish, but do not pack. Bake for 1¼ hours at 350°.

Wanda Ogg, Branch No. 6940, Harrison, MI

MUSHROOM-GARDEN STUFFING

4 to 6 Tbsp. butter
1 c. chopped onion
3 c. sliced celery
Turkey liver, cut up and seasoned
1 lb. fresh mushrooms, sliced

4 c. bread cubes
2 c. peeled and chopped apple
½ tsp. sage
Salt and pepper to taste

Heat 4 tablespoons butter in a skillet and add the onion and celery. Cook, stirring, until lightly browned. Transfer to a bowl. Brown the liver and mushrooms in the same skillet, adding more butter as needed. Add to the bowl. Toast bread cubes in the same skillet; add to the bowl. Add the apple. Add seasonings and mix gently just until combined. Use to stuff turkey or bake in a covered casserole at 325° for 1 hour. Uncover last 30 minutes to brown top and baste with pan drippings.

Janet Maeder, Branch No. 640, Dwight, IL

TURKEY DRESSING

2 loaves dry bread, cubed
¼ lb. butter, melted
¼ c. carrots, ground
½ c. onions, ground
¼ lb. hamburger, ground
½ c. celery, ground

Giblets, cooked and ground
1 tsp. poultry seasoning
Salt and pepper to taste
Liquid from giblets that were
    cooked plus enough extra
    warm water to moisten

Cut bread into cubes and let dry overnight. Grind giblets, carrots, onions, and celery. Add hamburger, salt, pepper, and poultry seasoning. Mix with bread cubes and add melted butter. Mix with hands until well mixed. Place in a greased pan or inside the turkey. Serves 20 people.

St. Peter's Lutheran Church Mission Circle, Branch No. 2379, Easton, MN

TUNA NOODLE CASSEROLE

6 oz. (3 c.) noodles
2 (6½ oz.) cans tuna, drained
½ c. mayonnaise
1 c. celery, sliced
⅓ c. onion, chopped
¼ c. green pepper, chopped
¼ c. pimento, diced

½ tsp. salt
1 pkg. frozen peas, thawed
1 can cream of celery soup
½ c. milk
4 oz. Cheddar cheese, shredded
½ c. toasted slivered almonds
Butter

Cook noodles. Combine with tuna, mayonnaise, celery, onion, pepper, pimento, salt, and peas. Blend and heat soup, milk and cheese. Add to noodle mixture. Turn into 2 quart casserole. Top with almonds. Dot with butter. Bake, uncovered, at 425° for 20 minutes.

Doris Fabian, Branch No. 449, Lockport, NY

TUNA-NOODLE CASSEROLE

Cook 6 ounces (3 cups) medium noodles, using package directions; drain. Combine noodles, one 6½ or 7 ounce can tuna (drained), ½ cup mayonnaise, 1 cup sliced celery, ⅓ cup chopped onion, ¼ cup chopped green pepper, ¼ cup chopped canned pimiento (optional), and ½ teaspoon salt. Blend one 10½ ounce can condensed cream of celery soup and ½ cup milk; heat through. Add 4 ounces sharp process American cheese, shredded (1 cup). Heat and stir till cheese melts. Add to noodle mixture. Turn into 2 quart casserole. Bake, uncovered, at 425° for 20 minutes.

If desired, top with ½ cup toasted slivered almonds 5 minutes before removing casserole from oven. Makes 6 servings.

Audrey Loka, Branch 4693, Gleason, WI

NOODLE HOT DISH
(Large crowd - 18 to 25)

¾ c. green pepper, chopped
3 c. diced celery
2 medium onions
¼ c. margarine
3 cans mushroom soup
1½ c. milk

3 c. shredded cheese
1 (24 oz.) pkg. noodles (medium
   wide to wide)
4 c. tuna
¾ c. pimento (optional)
1½ c. mayonnaise

Cook pepper, celery, onions, and margarine until tender. Heat in saucepan the soup, milk and cheese. Cook noodles. Combine all ingredients. Bake in a 350° oven for 45 to 50 minutes.

Can be sprinkled with chow mein noodles or crushed potato chips before baking.

Margaret Lubben, Branch No. 1018, Fergus Falls, MN

272

TUNA NOODLE BAKE

1 (10½ oz.) can condensed cream of celery or cream of mushroom soup
½ c. milk
2 c. cooked noodles (about 4 oz. uncooked)
1 (7 oz.) can tuna, drained and flaked
2 Tbsp. diced pimiento or diced olives
1 Tbsp. dried parsley flakes
½ c. buttered crumbs or crushed potato chips

1. Preheat oven to 375°F.
2. Blend soup and milk.
3. Add cooked noodles, tuna, parsley, pimiento, and olives.
4. Mix ingredients and spoon into a quart casserole.
5. Sprinkle crumbs on top.
6. Bake in a moderate oven (375°F.) for about 25 minutes or until hot and bubbling. Makes 4 servings.

Budget stretcher: Substitute white sauce or cheese sauce for soup. Use chopped celery and onion in place of olives and pimiento. Add leftover peas for more color.

Miss Adelheid Kirmis, Branch No. 2042, Lisbon, ND

PARTY CRAB BAKE

6 oz. large shell macaroni
1 (8 oz.) pkg. cream cheese
½ c. dairy sour cream
½ c. cottage cheese
¼ c. sliced green onions and tops
1 (7½ oz.) can crabmeat, flaked (imitation crab works well also)
2 medium tomatoes, peeled and sliced
¼ tsp. salt
1½ c. shredded sharp Cheddar cheese

Cook macaroni as directed on package. Drain and set aside. Combine cream cheese, sour cream, cottage cheese, and green onions; mix well. Arrange ½ of macaroni in bottom of greased 2½ quart casserole. Spread ½ of cheese mixture over macaroni. Top with ½ of the crab. Repeat these layers. Top the top layer with tomatoes and sprinkle with the salt. Spread Cheddar cheese over all. Bake in moderate oven (350°) for 30 minutes. Serves 6 to 8.

SHELLS AND SHRIMP

1 (8 oz.) pkg. medium shell macaroni
2 (6 oz.) pkg. frozen cooked bay shrimp
1 can condensed cream of shrimp soup
½ c. mayonnaise
1 tsp. dried dill weed (or seed)
½ tsp. garlic salt
⅛ tsp. pepper

Preheat oven to 375°. Grease 1½ quart casserole. Cook macaroni according to package directions. Drain. Meanwhile, place shrimp in colander. Run hot water over shrimp for 1 minute or until thawed. Drain well.

In medium bowl, mix pasta, shrimp, soup, mayonnaise, dill, garlic salt, and pepper. Pour into casserole. Cover and bake for 35 minutes.

Cheryl Schultz, Branch No. 3107, Loveland, CO

GAMAZETTA

1 lb. hamburger
⅛ c. onions, chopped (optional)
1 to 2 c. cooked noodles
1 small can corn, drained

1 can tomato soup
1 can cream of mushroom soup
Cheese slices

Brown hamburger and onions together. Combine in casserole dish the hamburger/onion mixture, cooked noodles, corn, and the 2 soups. Bake for 1 hour at 350°. Just before done, top with cheese slices. Serve when cheese is melted.

Reba Bergt, Branch No. 2346, Schuyler, NE

CHICKEN CASSEROLE

1 chicken
1 (5 oz.) pkg. egg noodles
1 large green pepper, chopped
1 large onion, chopped
3 large celery stalks, chopped

1 can mushroom or celery soup
1 (2 oz.) can mushroom pieces
1 (4 oz.) can pimentos
1 c. grated Cheddar cheese
Salt and pepper to taste

Boil chicken tender; bone. Cook egg noodles in broth. Cook green pepper, onion and celery in small amount of water just until tender. Add to noodles, along with the soup, mushroom and pimentos. Add salt and pepper to taste. Pour into baking dish. Sprinkle with cheese. Bake at 350° for 20 to 30 minutes. Serves 8 to 10.

Margaret Sutton, Branch No. 4477, Claremore, OK

CHICKEN CASSEROLE

8 oz. uncooked elbow macaroni
2 c. milk
1 can cream of celery soup
1 can cream of mushroom soup

½ c. grated cheese
¼ c. diced onion
1 c. frozen peas
2 c. cut up, cooked chicken

Put in 2 quart casserole dish. Refrigerate overnight. One hour before baking, remove from refrigerator to bring to room temperature. Bake for 1½ hours at 350°, uncovering last 15 minutes and topping with bread crumbs. Stir once during baking.

Mrs. June Werth, Branch No. 965, North Tonawanda, NY

MACARONI AND CHEESE CASSEROLE

1 pkg. macaroni and cheese
10 oz. frozen or fresh broccoli

1 lb. ground beef or sausage
1 can celery soup

274

Cook macaroni as directed. Cook broccoli till tender crisp. Brown ground beef or sausage. Mix all 3 and pour into greased baking dish. Top with soup and bake at 350° for 30 minutes. Top with package of dry cheese mixture the last 15 minutes.

Nancy Neese, Branch No. 5325, Stratford, IA

HAMBURGER CASSEROLE

Boil one 15 ounce package wide noodles according to directions.

1 lb. ground beef, browned	⅛ tsp. pepper
1 (8 oz.) can tomato sauce	1 c. cottage cheese
1 tsp. salt	1 c. sour cream
¼ tsp. garlic salt	⅛ c. chopped onions

Combine in layers in a 2 quart casserole. Top with grated cheese. Bake at 350° for 30 minutes or till cheese is melted.

Leona Becher, Columbus, NE

HOMEMADE BEEF AND NOODLES

3 eggs	2 c. flour
¼ c. water	Beef roast or boiling beef
2 tsp. salt	

Mix with fork. Divide into 4 pieces. Roll and let dry. Cut. Bake roast with water to cover or boil boiling beef. Boil broth and add noodles. Add pieces of beef to boiling noodles. Turn down to medium until noodles are tender.

Melonie Buelow, St. John's AAL, Branch No. 3806, Center Point, IA

HAM AND NOODLE CASSEROLE

2 c. ground ham (raw or cooked)	2 (6 oz.) pkg. fine noodles
½ lb. American cheese	¼ lb. (1 c.) sliced mushrooms
½ green pepper	1 can condensed tomato soup
1 c. chopped celery	

Cut cheese into small pieces and mince green pepper. Mix all ingredients, including soup (diluted with an equal amount of water), with noodles which have been cooked in boiling salted water until tender and drained. Bake in casserole in a moderate oven (350°) for 1 hour. Serves 8.

Earl A. Holl, Branch No. 3383, Indianapolis, IN

FOR THE CROWD CASSEROLE

1½ lb. ground beef, fowl or other
    meat
1 c. chopped onions
1½ c. (12 oz. can) whole kernel
    corn or other vegetable
1 can condensed cream of chicken
    soup
1 can condensed cream of
    mushroom soup

1 c. dairy sour cream
¼ tsp pimento
¾ tsp. salt
½ tsp Accent (optional)
3 c. cooked noodles (medium size)
1 c. bread crumbs

Brown ground beef; add onions and cook till tender. Add next 8 ingredients; mix well. Stir in noodles. Pour into 2 quart casserole (or 9x13 inch pan). Sprinkle crumbs over top. Bake at 350° for about 30 minutes till heated through.

Curtis Bremer, Zion Ev. Lutheran Church, Branch 2543, McHenry, IL

DAIRY-BURGER CASSEROLE

1 (8 oz.) pkg. noodles, cooked in
    salted water

Add:

2 (8 oz.) cans tomato sauce
1 tsp. salt

Combine:

1 c. cottage cheese
¼ c. sour cream
1 (8 oz.) pkg. cream cheese

1 lb. ground beef, browned
2 Tbsp. butter

1 Tbsp. Worcestershire sauce

¼ c. green onion *or* onion flakes
2 Tbsp. green pepper, chopped

Use 2½ quart casserole, greased with butter. Spread ½ of noodles in casserole. Cover with cheese mixture, then remaining noodles. Pour 2 tablespoons melted butter over noodles. Cover with meat sauce. Garnish with parsley flakes. Bake at 350° for 35 to 40 minutes. Serve hot with salad and rolls for a complete meal. Serves 6 to 8.

Winnifred Laabs, Hortonville, WI, Branch No. 1162, Dale, WI

COMPANY CASSEROLE

1 small pkg. thin noodles
1 (8 oz.) pkg. cream cheese
1 c. sour cream
6 green onions, diced
1½ lb. ground round

1 tsp. salt
1 tsp. sugar
1 tsp. pepper
2 small cans tomato sauce

Cook noodles and place in casserole (8x10 inches or larger). Cream the cream cheese, sour cream and onions; spread over noodles. Brown meat. Add the salt, pepper, sugar, and tomato sauce. Spread meat mixture on top of cream cheese mixture. Cover top with grated cheese and bake at 350°F. until cheese melts and mixture bubbles.

Burdean Werschky, Branch No. 180, Denver, CO

CHICKEN AND RICE SUPREME

1 (6 oz.) box long grain wild rice
¼ c. melted margarine
⅓ c. chopped onion
2 to 3 c. diced chicken
⅓ c. flour
1 c. milk
1 c. chicken broth

1 tsp. salt
¼ tsp. pepper
⅓ c. chopped pimento
¼ c. chopped parsley
¼ c. slivered almonds
1 c. frozen peas (need not be cooked)

Cook rice as directed on package. Saute onion in melted margarine. Blend in flour, salt, and pepper; gradually add liquids to make a white sauce. Cook till thickened as a creamed gravy. Add chicken, rice, pimento, parsley, almonds, and peas. Transfer to a 2 quart casserole dish. Bake at 425° for 30 minutes.

This is an excellent dish to take to someone just home from the hospital, etc., as it is very tasty, but not too spicy.

Barbara Cochran (Mrs. Robert), Branch No. 2678, Laramie, WY

WILD RICE

1 c. wild rice
¼ lb. butter
½ c. slivered almonds
2 Tbsp. chopped green pepper

2 Tbsp. chopped onion
½ lb. (8 oz. can) sliced mushrooms
3 c. chicken broth

Mix all ingredients, except broth, and cook on top of stove until rice turns from gray to yellow color. Add broth Place in casserole. Cover and bake at 325° for 1 hour.

May be cooked slowly on top of stove instead of in oven.

Joyce Miller, Branch No. 932, Minneapolis, MN

SPANISH RICE

1 lb. ground beef
¼ c. green peppers, chopped
1 medium onion, chopped
1 to 1½ stalks celery, chopped
1 c. uncooked white or brown rice
1 tsp. salt
⅛ tsp. pepper

2 c. water
¼ c. catsup
1 Tbsp. Worcestershire sauce
16 oz. (2 c.) tomatoes (undrained), cut up
Cheddar cheese

Brown beef, onion, green peppers, and celery. Drain off fat. Add remaining ingredients, except for cheese. Simmer, covered, for 30 to 4 minutes or until rice is tender and liquid is absorbed. Top with cheese. Return lid and let stand till cheese is melted. Serves 5 to 6 people.

A Dutch oven works really well with this recipe.

Jewell Bork, Branch No. 5985, Midland, SD

CHICKEN AND RICE CASSEROLE

1 (10¾ oz.) can cream of
   mushroom soup
1 (10¾ oz.) can cream of celery
   soup

1 c. milk
1 small pkg. dry onion soup mix
1 chicken, cut up
1 c. instant rice

Into large well greased bowl, mix rice, both cans of soup and milk together. Skin pieces of chicken and press into mixture. Sprinkle top with dry onion soup mix. Bake at 350° for approximately 1½ to 2 hours.

Eugene Grant, Loveland, CO

CHICKEN AND RICE CASSEROLE

1⅓ c. Minute rice
1 can cream of chicken soup
1 can cream of mushroom soup

1¼ c. milk
½ to 1 pkg. dry onion soup mix
Chicken pieces

Mix soups and milk together. Add rice. Pour into baking dish. Lay desired number of chicken pieces on top (skinned or skin side up). Sprinkle dry onion soup mix over top of chicken. Cover with foil. Bake at 300° for at least 3 to 4 hours.

Julie Padilla, Branch No. 3107, Loveland, CO

CARYN'S CASSEROLE

3 (15 oz.) cans Hormel "no bean"
   chili
3 c. prepared Minute rice

1 (15 oz.) can stewed tomatoes
3 c. shredded Cheddar cheese
Sliced tomatoes (optional)

Preheat oven to 350°. Prepare rice as directed. In large casserole (3 quart), combine chili, rice, and stewed tomatoes. Reserve ½ cup Cheddar cheese; add remainder to casserole. Mix well. Sprinkle top with reserved cheese and sliced tomatoes (optional). Bake until cheese is melted; approximately ½ hour.

Cheryl O'Brien, Branch No. 4718, New Lenox, IL

HAMBURGER CASSEROLE
(Microwave)

2 lb. hamburger, browned
2 c. Minute rice, cooked
1½ c. diced green peppers
1 (10 oz.) can cream of celery soup

1 (10 oz.) can onion soup
1½ tsp. salt
½ tsp. black pepper

Brown hamburger; mix in the other ingredients and place in a glass baking dish that has been sprayed with a vegetable spray. Place tater tots or quick taters on top and bake for 30 to 45 minutes at 400° in conventional oven or on HIGH for 20 minutes in microwave.

Erna C. Boggs, Winnetoon, NE, Branch No. 1957, Creighton, NE

SWISS CHICKEN AND HAM CASSEROLE

2 c. cooked, chopped chicken
1 can cream of chicken soup
1 green onion, thinly sliced
2 c. diced ham

3 c. cooked rice
½ c. sour cream
½ c. milk
½ c. Swiss cheese

In a mixing bowl, combine chicken, soup, onion, ham, sour cream, and milk. Place rice in a 9x13 inch pan. Spread meat mixture over rice. Put in a 350° oven for 30 minutes. Add cheese. Let melt and serve.

Linda Connor, Branch No. 1976, Cornelius, OR

CAJUN SAUSAGE AND RICE

1 c. rice
8 oz. sliced, smoked link sausage
½ c. chopped onion
½ c. chopped green pepper
2 c. sliced okra
1 (16 oz.) can whole tomatoes

1 (10¾ oz.) can chicken broth
2 c. water
1 tsp. sage
1 tsp. hot sauce
Salt and pepper to taste

In a large pan, combine all ingredients. Bring mixture to a boil. Cover, reduce heat and simmer for 20 minutes. Remove lid and simmer for an additional 5 to 10 minutes. Yield: 8 to 10 servings.

Luanna Bauschlicher, Corning, AR

SAUSAGE-RICE CASSEROLE

1 lb. pork sausage, browned
1 small onion, chopped
½ c. celery, diced
½ c. green pepper, diced

1 c. uncooked rice
2 cans cream of chicken soup
½ c. water

Mix all ingredients together. Place in a greased 1½ quart casserole and bake at 350° for 30 minutes.

Phyllis Carlson, Branch No. 5617, Schuyler, NE

SAUSAGE AND RICE CASSEROLE

1 lb. bulk pork sausage
1 onion, chopped
1 c. rice (uncooked)
1 c. celery

2 cans cream of chicken soup
1 can water
1 can sliced mushrooms

Fry pork and drain. Add all other ingredients and bake in oven at 350° for 50 minutes.

Marjorie Tjepkema, Branch No. 767, Norwood, MN

CHICKEN AND RICE BAKE

1 (10¾ oz.) can condensed cream
   of mushroom soup
1 c. milk
1 env. onion soup mix
1 (3 oz.) can chopped mushrooms
1 c. regular rice

1 (10 oz.) pkg. frozen peas (or
   mixed vegetables), thawed
Paprika
1 (2½ or 3 lb.) ready to cook
   broiler-fryer chicken, cut up
   and thawed

I roll the chicken lightly in flour and brown lightly in oil.

In bowl, stir together mushroom soup, milk, dry onion soup mix, and un-drained mushrooms. Remove ½ cup of the soup mixture and set aside. Stir un-cooked rice and thawed vegetables into remaining soup mixture.

Turn rice mixture into a 12 x 7½ x 2 inch baking dish; arrange chicken pieces on top. Pour soup mixture over chicken. Sprinkle chicken pieces with paprika. *Cover tightly* with foil. Bake at 375° till rice is tender, 1¼ to 1½ hours. Makes 4 to 6 servings.

Thelma L. Meinert, Branch No. 5425, Louisville, KY

WILD RICE CASSEROLE

1 (6 oz.) Uncle Ben's wild rice
Dash of salt
½ c. margarine
8 slices American cheese
1 large green bell pepper, chopped

2 medium onions, chopped
1 c. half & half coffee cream
1 (4 oz.) can mushroom pieces
2 chicken breasts, cooked

Prepare rice. Saute pepper, onions, and mushrooms in margarine. Layer rice, sauteed mixture, chicken, and half of the cheese broken up in oblong casserole dish. Layer rest of cheese on top. Pour half & half cream over entire mixture. Bake in a 400° oven for 30 minutes.

Norma McKinnis, Branch No. 2568, Fredericktown, MO

CHICKEN AND RICE

1 frying chicken, cut up
1 can cream of celery soup
2 cans cream of mushroom soup

1 c. milk
2 c. rice
1 env. dry onion soup mix

Combine soups and milk; add rice and mix well. Place ½ mixture in a greased 9x12 inch baking dish. Lay chicken on mixture. Cover with remaining mix-ture. Sprinkle dry onion soup mix on top. Seal with foil and bake at 325° for 2 hours and 15 minutes. Yield: 6 servings.

Phyllis Koehn, Niobrara, NE

CHICKEN CASSEROLE

2 c. cooked rice
2 cans cream of chicken soup
½ c. *mayonnaise*
1 tsp. salt
½ c. chopped onion
1 (8 oz.) can water chestnuts,
    diced

5 tsp. lemon juice
1 c. chopped celery
2 (4 oz.) cans mushrooms
5 c. chicken chunks

Mix all ingredients in large bowl. Put in 9x13 inch greased pan. Top with ¼ cup butter and 1 cup crushed soda crackers. Bake at 350° for 1 hour. Makes 10 to 12 generous servings.

Mary L. Spangler, Branch No. 5383, Sumner, IA

CHICKEN CASSEROLE

Cook a chicken with ¼ medium onion, ½ stalk celery, 1 teaspoon salt, and ½ teaspoon pepper. Have 4 cups of cooked rice on hand. Remove chicken from bones and cut up. Cut up 4 slices of bread in cubes. Beat 2 eggs. Add 1 can of cream of mushroom soup and ½ can of broth. Lay 4 slices of Velveeta cheese on top. Mix all. Put in 9x13 inch pan. Bake at 325° for 1½ hours.

Leona Becher, Columbus, NE

FALL ROUNDUP CASSEROLE

3 eggs, beaten
1½ tsp. salt
1 tsp. paprika
2 Tbsp. chopped onion
2 c. cooked, cubed chicken

2 Tbsp. parsley
1 c. cooked rice
1 c. bread crumbs
3 c. chicken broth

Blend first 4 ingredients. Add remaining ingredients. Supplement broth with milk, if necessary, to have 3 cups. Pour all into a greased 1½ quart casserole. Set in a pan of water. Bake at 350° for 45 minutes or until set. Serve with undiluted cream of mushroom or cream of chicken soup heated, as a sauce.

Mrs. Delbert Radtke, Branch No. 6896, Mahnomen, MN

TURKEY-WILD RICE CASSEROLE

Cook 1 cup wild rice.

Saute until tender:

½ c. onion

½ c. butter

Remove from heat.

Combine:

⅔ to ¾ c. flour
Juice from 1 (6 oz.) can
    mushrooms and chicken
    broth to make 1½ c.

1½ c. milk

Cook until thick. Add rice, mushrooms, 3 cups turkey or chicken (cubed), ¼ cup pimento, 2 teaspoons parsley (preferably fresh), and salt and pepper to taste. Put into 2 quart dish. Cover with ½ cup blanched, slivered almonds. Place in 350° oven for 30 to 45 minutes until almonds are toasted. Serves 10.

Mona Geidel, Branch No. 3107, Loveland, CO

TURKEY CASSEROLE

2 to 4 c. cooked or leftover turkey
1 pkg. Uncle Ben's wild rice
2 cans mushroom soup

2 cans milk
1 tsp. salt and pepper

Cook rice as directed on box. Cut up turkey into bite-size chunks. Combine and bake in cake or casserole dish at 350° for 25 minutes or until bubbly and brown. Preheat oven to 350° and bake for 25 minutes. Serves 6 to 8.

Lori Thatcher, Loveland, CO

WILD RICE CASSEROLE

3 Tbsp. chopped onion
½ c. butter
3 (4 oz.) cans mushrooms

1 c. wild rice
1 can beef broth
¾ c. water

Saute onion and butter. Wash and parboil the wild rice for 20 minutes. Mix all ingredients together. Bake for 1 to 1½ hours at 350°.

Lonn and Deb Kiel, Branch No. 1073, Crookston, MN

WILD RICE DISH

1 c. wild rice, soaked in cold water
    for 2 hours
½ c. white rice
2 c. chopped celery
1 large chopped onion

2 cans mushrooms and juice
½ c. butter
6 to 8 chicken bouillon cubes
4 c. hot water

Soak wild rice. Dissolve bouillon cubes in hot water. Mix all together and bake at 300° for 2 hours.

Millie Darge, Branch No. 881, Good Thunder, MN

WILD RICE

¼ c. butter
1 c. wild rice
½ c. blanched, slivered almonds

2 Tbsp. chopped onions (or chives)
2 (2 oz.) cans mushrooms, drained
3 c. chicken broth

Put all ingredients, except broth, in heavy fry pan and cook over medium high heat for about 20 minutes until almonds are brown. Stir often. Heat oven to 325°. Add broth to rest of ingredients. Pour mixture in 1½ quart baking dish. Bake for 1½ hours.

Nada Foede, Branch No. 881, Good Thunder, MN

NO. 6 RAVISHING RICE

1 lb. bulk hot sausage
1 large onion, chopped
1 large green pepper, chopped
1 c. celery, chopped
4½ c. boiling water

2 env. chicken noodle soup mix
½ c. raw rice
Slivered almonds or grated
    Cheddar cheese

Cook the sausage in a large skillet, pouring off grease now and then. Stir meat until crumbled and brown. Add chopped onion, green pepper, and celery; continue cooking until wilted. Bring water to a boil. Add soup mix and rice; cook for 15 minutes. Do not drain.

Combine soup mixture, vegetables and sausage; mix well. Pour into 2 quart casserole. Sprinkle top with almonds or cheese. Cover. Place in medium warm oven for just a few minutes.

Betty Ahrent, Branch No. 1936, Corning, AR

LUTHERAN CASSEROLE

1 can water chestnuts, sliced
3 c. celery
1 tsp. salt
2 cans cream of mushroom soup
1 onion, minced
5 c. cooked rice

4 to 6 c. diced ham or chicken
3 c. mayonnaise
3 Tbsp. lemon juice
½ c. Cheddar cheese
Bread crumbs

Set aside cheese and bread crumbs or potato chips. Mix together all other ingredients. Put in large casserole. Cover with crumbs. Bake in a 400° oven. Add grated cheese toward end of baking. Chicken or ham or both may be used and mushroom or chicken soup or both may be used. Bake for 30 to 35 minutes. Use large casserole.

Flavors blend in if made the night before.

Sherry Bathke, Branch No. 286, Bloomer, WI

CRUNCHY ONION HAMBURGER CASSEROLE

1 can French fried onions
1 lb. hamburger
1 pkg. onion gravy mix
¼ tsp. garlic salt

1½ c. water
⅓ c. rice (uncooked)
1 pkg. frozen peas, thawed
1 can water chestnuts (optional)

Brown hamburger. Blend in gravy mix, salt, water, and rice. Boil. Reduce heat to low; cover and simmer for 15 minutes. Stir in thawed peas and chestnuts (continue to simmer until rice is tender). Stir in onions. Serves 4 to 6.

May serve with soy sauce if desired.

Mary Vander Top, Loveland, CO

MINNESOTA WILD RICE CASSEROLE

Gourmet Version:

2 c. raw wild rice
4 c. water
2 tsp. salt
2 lb. ground round
1 lb. fresh mushrooms
½ c. chopped celery
1 can sliced water chestnuts

1 c. chopped onion
½ c. butter
¼ c. soy sauce (Kikkoman)
2 c. sour cream
2 tsp. salt
¼ tsp. pepper
½ c. slivered almonds

More economical version: Use part long grain or brown rice instead of all wild rice. Use hamburger instead of ground round. Use cans of canned mushrooms instead of fresh, button or even stems and pieces. I used two 4 ounce cans, undrained.

Cook rice until tender in salt water; drain if necessary. Should have 6 to 7 cups. Brown beef and set aside. If hamburger is used, then drain it. Saute either fresh or canned mushrooms, celery and onion in butter for 5 to 10 minutes. Combine soy sauce, sour cream, salt, and pepper. Add rice, hamburger, vegetables, and almonds. Toss lightly.

Place mixture in a 3 quart buttered casserole. Bake at 350° for 1 hour, uncovered. Stir several times. Add water and more seasoning if needed. Garnish with slivered almonds and sprigs of parsley. Serve piping hot.

The dish can be made in advance and refrigerated. Bake just before serving. If cold, may need 15 minutes more in the oven. Freezes well.

Florence Springstroh, Salem Lutheran Church,
Branch No. 6714, Woodbury, MN

NO. 5 BEEF CASSEROLE OLE

3 c. cooked rice
1 lb. ground beef
½ c. chopped onion
½ c. chopped green pepper
1 garlic clove, minced
2 (8 oz.) cans tomato sauce

2 tsp. chili powder
1 tsp. salt
1 (15 oz.) can pinto beans
1 c. crushed corn chips
1 c. Cheddar cheese, shredded

Brown ground beef; drain excess fat. Stir in onion, green pepper and garlic. Continue to cook until vegetables are barely tender. Blend in tomato sauce, chili powder and salt.

In lightly greased 2 quart casserole, layer the meat sauce, rice and beans, beginning and ending with the meat sauce. Sprinkle with corn chips and bake at 350°F. for 15 minutes. Sprinkle with cheese and bake for an additional 5 minutes. Serves 6.

Martha Ahrent, Branch No. 1936, Corning, AR

RICE-HAMBURGER HOT DISH

1 lb. hamburger
2 small onions
Salt and pepper
1 can cream of mushroom soup
1 can cream of chicken soup

2 Tbsp. soy sauce
½ c. long grain uncooked rice
1 c. finely chopped celery
2 c. water

Brown hamburger with onions; season with salt and pepper. Mix in other ingredients and put in a 3 quart casserole. Bake at 350° for 1½ hours.

Arlene Twardokus, AAL Branch No. 1400, Hartford, WI

WILD RICE-HAMBURGER CASSEROLE

2 c. boiling water
⅔ c. uncooked, washed wild rice
1 (10 to 12 oz.) can chicken rice
   soup
1 small can sliced mushrooms,
   drained

½ c. water
1 tsp. salt
¼ tsp. celery salt, garlic salt and
   paprika
1 small onion, chopped
1 lb. hamburger

Pour boiling water over rice. Cover and let stand for 15 minutes. Drain. Place rice in 2 quart casserole. Add soup, mushrooms with liquid, water, and seasonings. Mix gently and let stand for a few minutes. Brown the hamburger and the onion together; add to the casserole. The casserole can be refrigerated at this point. When ready to bake, cover and bake at 325° for 2 hours. Serves 4.

Marion Bittorf, Branch No. 4095, New Hope, MN

CHEESY CHICKEN CASSEROLE

1 (4 lb.) stewing chicken or 6
   chicken breasts
2 c. milk
1 tsp. salt
2 (10 oz.) pkg. frozen broccoli
   spears

2 (8 oz.) cream cheese
¾ tsp. garlic salt
1½ c. Parmesan cheese

Simmer chicken until done. Remove skin and bone. Cook broccoli until done. Cut into bite-size pieces. Arrange in bottom of greased casserole dish.

In heavy saucepan, blend milk and cream cheese until smooth; stir in ¾ cup Parmesan cheese until smooth. Pour 1 cup of sauce over broccoli. Top with all of the chicken and cover with rest of sauce. Sprinkle ¼ cup Parmesan cheese over the top. Bake for 30 minutes at 350°. Sprinkle with rest of the cheese before serving. Serves 6. (Use casserole approximately 8x10 inches.)

Marty Williams, Branch No. 5844, Columbia City, IN

CHICKEN BROCCOLI

2 pkg. broccoli spears (fresh or if
    frozen, thawed and drained)
3½ to 4 lb. chicken, cooked and
    boned
¼ lb. Velveeta cheese slices

1 can cream of mushroom soup
    (rinse can with ½ c. milk)
½ c. mayonnaise
1 can water chestnuts, drained
1 can French fried onion rings

Place broccoli in a greased 9x13x2 inch pan. Cut chicken in large pieces and spread over broccoli. Cover chicken with cheese slices. Mix soup, mayonnaise and milk together. Spread over cheese. Sprinkle sliced water chestnuts over top. Bake for 40 minutes at 350°. Take out and sprinkle onion rings over top. Return to oven and bake, uncovered, for 20 minutes more.

Bernice Luebke, Branch No. 2408, Port Huron, MI

CHICKEN BROCCOLI CASSEROLE

2 bunches broccoli, cooked
2 cans cream of chicken soup (or 1
    can cream of chicken and 1
    can cream of mushroom)
1 c. mayonnaise

¼ tsp. curry powder
1 tsp. lemon juice
2 to 3 c. cooked chicken or turkey,
    diced
½ c. seasoned bread crumbs

Put layer of broccoli in buttered 9x13 inch pan. Next put a layer of chicken, then layer of rice. Repeat. Mix together soup, mayonnaise, lemon juice, and curry powder. Pour over casserole mixture. Top with bread crumbs. Bake at 350° for 35 minutes.

Henrietta Hinrichs, Branch No. 7063, Albany, OR

BROCCOLI-RICE CASSEROLE

1¾ c. raw rice
¾ c. chopped onion
¾ c. chopped green pepper
1 c. chopped celery
4 Tbsp. butter

2 (10 oz.) pkg. frozen broccoli
1 (8 oz.) jar Cheez Whiz
1 can cream of mushroom soup
1 (3 oz.) can mushrooms, drained

Cook rice. Saute onion, green pepper and celery in butter. Cook broccoli and drain. Combine with Cheez Whiz, vegetables, undiluted soup, and mushrooms. Fold in cooked rice and put into a 3 quart buttered casserole. Bake at 350° until hot and bubbly (about 20 to 30 minutes).

Can be made a day ahead and bake just before serving.

Veloren Osladil, Branch No. 1737, Finlayson, MN

GREEN RICE

2 c. cooked rice
1 c. chopped onion
½ c. butter
1 (10 oz.) pkg. broccoli, cooked
    and chopped in little pieces

6 c. grated aged cheese
1 (10¾ oz.) can celery soup
1 (10¾ oz.) can mushroom soup

Cook chopped onion and butter in microwave for 6 minutes on HIGH. Combine all ingredients and bake at 325° for 1 hour.

Vivian Engel, Branch 2525, Larsen, WI

COUNTRY HAM CASSEROLE

1 lb. Velveeta pasteurized cheese
    spread, cubed
1 c. milk
½ c. Miracle Whip salad dressing
2 c. chopped, cooked ham

1 (10 oz.) pkg. frozen chopped
    broccoli, cooked and well
    drained
1 tsp. chopped chives
5 oz. cooked spaghetti

Heat process cheese spread, milk and salad dressing over low heat. Stir until sauce is smooth. Add remaining ingredients and mix well. Pour into 2 quart casserole dish and bake at 350° for 35 to 40 minutes or until hot. Makes 6 to 8 servings.

Mrs. Lucille Riechmann, Branch No. 0356, Dubuque, IA

HAM AND BROCCOLI DINNER CASSEROLE

3 c. rice
2 (10 oz.) pkg. broccoli
4 c. cubed ham
2 c. milk
½ stick butter

3 Tbsp. flour
1 large onion, chopped
4 oz. Cheddar cheese
1 c. dry bread crumbs

Put cooked rice in the bottom of a buttered 2½ quart casserole dish. Next layer is broccoli. Next layer is cubed ham. Make a sauce by cooking milk, butter, flour, and onion until thick. Pour this over top of 3 layers. Next, sprinkle on shredded Cheddar cheese and finally decorate with bread crumbs. Bake at 350° for 40 minutes.

Irene Wilke, Branch No. 817, Sturgeon Bay, WI

BROCCOLI PIE

1 lb. ground beef

½ c. onion

Brown and drain.

1 (3 oz.) pkg. cream cheese
4 oz. Monterey cheese
2 eggs

2 Tbsp. flour
¾ tsp. garlic salt

Mix broccoli, hamburger, cheese, etc. Put into crust. Put top crust on as for pie and bake until golden brown at 350°

Crust:

1¼ c. lard
3 c. flour

1 tsp. salt
½ c. water, mixed with ½ c. flour

Mix lard, flour and salt. Make hole in mixture; add flour and water. Mix together and roll as for pie crust. Put in 9 inch pan.

Velma Hornicke, Branch No. 2512, Ord, NE

BLUE RIBBON HAM CASSEROLE
(Microwave)

¼ c. chopped onion
1 Tbsp. butter
½ lb. Velveeta, cubed
¼ tsp. salt

¼ c. milk
3 c. diced, cooked potatoes
1 c. chopped ham

Heat onion and butter in 2 quart casserole on HIGH for 3 minutes. Add cheese and milk. Heat on HIGH for 3 to 4 minutes till cheese is melted. Add remaining ingredients and stir. Cover and heat on MEDIUM for 8 minutes or till heated through.

Cheryl Schultz, Branch No. 3107, Loveland, CO

ONE DISH SUPPER

1 lb. chopped meat
1 can whole kernel corn or peas
    and carrots

Mashed potatoes
1 small onion
Butter or grated cheese

Brown 1 pound chopped meat and 1 chopped onion. Drain. In casserole, place meat mixture. Top with drained corn or peas and carrots. Top with freshly made or leftover mashed potatoes. Top with butter and/or grated cheese. Bake in a 375° oven until heated, usually 30 to 40 minutes.

Lillian Umscheid, Branch No. 3436, Pico Rivera, CA

SHEPHERD'S PIE

1½ lb. ground beef
½ c. cream of mushroom soup (or
    tomato sauce)
½ c. dry bread crumbs
¼ c. chopped onions
2 Tbsp. chopped parsley (optional)
1 egg, beaten

½ tsp. salt
⅛ tsp. pepper
2 (10 oz.) cans beef gravy
4 medium to large potatoes,
    cooked and mashed with
    butter, salt and milk

Combine first 8 ingredients. Shape into loaf. Place loaf in greased flat baking dish (9x13 inches). Pat meat gently to edges of pan, about 1 to 1½ inches thick. Don't press hard. Bake for 45 minutes at 350°.

Meanwhile, cook and mash potatoes. When meatloaf is done, cut into squares with knife (about 1½ inches). Pour gravy over meat in pan. Spoon hot mashed potatoes over gravy. Return to oven for 20 minutes or until potatoes are brown at tips. Serves 8. Serve with hot vegetable, salad and rolls.

Eloise Brodbeck, Branch No. 5124, Alma, MI

HAMBURGER PIE

1 lb. lean ground beef
1 small onion, diced
1 pkg. instant onion soup mix
1 small can mushroom pieces

1 can green beans
3 medium potatoes, cooked and
   mashed

Brown meat with diced onion until nicely browned. Drain fat. Add onion soup mix, green beans with juice, and mushrooms in juice. Bring to a boil and thicken as for gravy. Add salt and pepper to taste. Pour into casserole and top with mashed potatoes. Dot with margarine and bake until lightly browned in a 350° oven.

May also sprinkle with grated cheese.

Edna Weber, Branch No. 2630, Greeley, CO

DELICIOUS CROCK POT CASSEROLE

2 large potatoes
1 (16 oz.) can pork and beans

Hot dogs, browned hamburger or
   diced ham

Peel and thinly slice the potatoes into the crock pot. Add the can of pork and beans and meat that you have available. Four hot dogs, sliced, is a good proportion. Cover and cook on LOW heat for 3 hours.

Phyllis Carlson, Branch No. 5617, Schuyler, NE

ESCALLOPED POTATOES AND HAM

6 medium potatoes, sliced
1 can cream of celery soup
½ can milk
½ can mushroom soup

1 medium onion, diced
½ c. celery, cut up
1½ lb. ham, diced
Salt and pepper to taste

Mix all together. Bake at 375° for 1 hour and 45 minutes, stirring twice.

DeEtta Peltier, Branch No. 4095, New Hope, MN

TATER TOTS CASSEROLE

1½ lb. hamburger
1 pkg. dry onion soup mix
1 large bag frozen mixed
   vegetables

2 cans cream of chicken soup
1 large bag frozen tater tots
   potatoes

Pat hamburger into bottom of 11x13 inch pan; sprinkle with dry onion mix. Add mixed vegetables and then the 2 cans of soup (undiluted). Cover with tater tots close together. Bake at 350° for 35 to 45 minutes or until bubbly. This recipe freezes well.

Gladys Meier, Branch No. 2986, Torrance, CA

TATER TOTS CASSEROLE

1 lb. ground beef
1 medium onion
1 pkg. frozen tater tots

1 can corn
1 can cream of mushroom soup
Grated cheese

Brown beef with onion; drain. Drain corn, reserving juice. Add soup, corn, and 1 soup can liquid (½ milk and ½ corn juice). Mix well. Pour mixture into 9x13 inch dish. Spread cheese over mixture and top with tater tots. Bake at 425°F. for 30 minutes or until tater tots are brown and crispy.

Elaine Gynther, Branch No. 1349, Sandy, OR

TATER TOTS HOT DISH (FOR A CROWD)

4 lb. ground beef
1 c. chopped onion
2 (10 oz.) pkg. frozen mixed
   vegetables
3 cans cream of mushroom soup

1½ c. chopped celery
3 c. milk
3 c. shredded Cheddar cheese
2 (32 oz.) pkg. tater tots

Brown ground beef and onion. Stir together soup, celery and milk. Add to beef. Add frozen vegetables. Divide into two 9x13 inch pans. On top of each, add 1 ½ cups cheese and 1 package tater tots. Bake for 1 hour at 350°, uncovered. Serves 20 people (or freeze one pan for later use).

Vivian Merkel, Lamplighter, Branch No. 3984, Washburn, ND

TATER TOTS CASSEROLE

1 lb. ground beef
1 can cream of celery or
   mushroom soup
1 small onion, chopped
⅔ can water in the soup can

Salt and pepper to taste
1 bag mixed frozen vegetables
American cheese
1 small bag tater tots

Brown ground beef and onion; drain off grease. Steam frozen vegetables until almost done. Drain off water. Add salt and pepper to taste. Mix ground beef, vegetables with 1 can of soup, and ⅔ can of water; pour this mixture into baking dish. Cover with grated American cheese and top with tater tots. Bake at 350° for 1 hour.

Judy Schmidter, Branch No. 72, Burlington, WI

TATER TOTS CASSEROLE

1½ lb. hamburger
½ chopped onion
2 cans mushroom soup
1 qt. green beans

Grated American cheese
Tater tots
Salt

For 160 servings, use:

30 lb. hamburger
3 chopped onions
4 (52 oz.) cans mushroom soup

8 lb. grated American cheese
7 (5 lb.) bags tater tots
Salt

Brown meat and onion. Add mushroom soup and green beans. Put in greased 9x13 inch pan. Top with grated cheese, tater tots and salt. Bake for 30 to 45 minutes at 350°F.

School Cooks, Cedar Rapids, NE; Linda Dodds, Loveland, CO

GROUND BEEF-VEGETABLE CASSEROLE

2 lb. ground chuck
3 or 4 large potatoes, sliced
5 carrots, sliced
2 large onions, sliced

1 can peas (reserve juice)
1 can tomato soup
Salt and pepper

Brown meat just so all red color is gone. Drain. Spray 2 quart baking dish with Pam. Layer vegetables in baking dish with potatoes, then carrots, onions, and salt and pepper to taste. Add peas, then ground beef. Mix reserved juice from peas with soup and pour over meat. Cover with foil and bake at 350° for 1½ hours or until potatoes and carrots are done.

Variation by E. Krist: May use one 10 ounce package frozen peas. Add ½ cup water to tomato soup.

Hattie Erdman, Branch 1221; E. Krist

CASSEROLE DINNER

5 medium potatoes (raw), sliced or
    diced
1 can tomato sauce, tomato soup
    or vegetable soup

1 lb. hamburger
1 can water
1 medium onion

Slice potatoes. Add ground beef, onion, and soup. Salt and pepper to taste. Mix in 1 can water. (Optional: Add 4 to 5 medium carrots, 1 stalk celery, ½ cup uncooked rice, 1 green pepper, ½ cup grated cheese, and pimento.) Bake for 1 ½ hours at 350°.

Tyyne Kivi, Branch No. 5691, Hurley, WI

POTATO HOT DISH

¾ gal. diced potatoes
2 cans tomato soup
2 to 5 onions, chopped
2 stalks celery, diced

2 c. sour cream
2 lb. ground beef, formed into
   small balls
Salt and pepper to taste

Combine all ingredients. Put into casserole. Bake at 325° for 4 hours.

Mrs. Franis Thompson, Mrs. Emma Klebe, Branch No. 1248, Willow City, ND

MEAL-IN-ONE CASSEROLE

3 to 6 medium potatoes
1 lb. ground beef
½ tsp. salt
½ tsp. pepper

1 medium onion
1 can pork and beans
1 can tomato soup

Slice raw, peeled potatoes and place in greased casserole. Crumble ground beef over potatoes. Add salt and pepper. Slice onion and spread over ground beef. Spread pork and beans over the onion. Cover all with undiluted tomato soup. Bake for 1 hour and 40 minutes in a 350° oven.

Mary Margarette Clark, Branch No. 1927, Porterville, CA

ONE-POT DINNER

½ to 1 lb. ground beef
¾ lb. bacon, cut in small pieces
1 c. chopped onion
2 (1 lb. 15 oz.) cans pork and
   beans
1 (1 lb.) can kidney beans, drained
1 (1 lb.) can butter limas, drained

1 c. catsup
¼ c. brown sugar
1 Tbsp. liquid smoke
3 Tbsp. white vinegar
1 tsp. salt
Dash of pepper

Brown ground beef in skillet; drain off fat and put beef in crock-pot. Brown bacon and onion; drain off fat. Add bacon, onion and remaining ingredients to crock-pot. Stir together well. Cover and cook on LOW for 4 to 6 hours.

Linda Bura, Branch No. 2049, Emporia, KS

THREE-BEAN BAKE
(Microwave)

1 (31 oz.) can pork and beans in
   tomato sauce
1 (16 oz.) can cut green beans,
   drained
1 (15 oz.) can garbanzo beans or
   chickpeas, drained

1 small onion, chopped
3 Tbsp. brown sugar
1 Tbsp. prepared mustard
¼ c. catsup
3 slices bacon, cut into pieces

Combine all ingredients, except bacon, in 2 quart glass casserole. Top with bacon. Microwave, covered, for 14 to 16 minutes or until heated through.

Mrs. Lawrence Greiner, Branch No. 2838, Wilmot, SD

CALICO BEANS

¼ lb. bacon
½ c. chopped onion
1 lb. hamburger
½ c. brown sugar
½ c. catsup
2 Tbsp. vinegar
1 Tbsp. mustard

1 tsp. salt
1 can kidney beans
1 can green or white lima beans,
    drained
1 can pork and beans
1 pkg. hot dogs, sliced

Brown ¼ pound bacon, ½ cup onion, and 1 pound hamburger. Add remaining ingredients and bake at 350° for 1½ hours, or simmer in crock pot for 3 hours or more.

Sharon Walters, Branch No. 3107, Loveland, CO

SAVORY BEANS

1 (32 oz.) pkg. beans (pinto)
6 qt. water
1 tsp. salt
1 (12 oz.) jar picante sauce (mild)

1 lb. bacon, chopped
1 lb. ham, cubed
1 tsp. seasoned salt

Soak beans overnight in 3 quarts of water with 1 teaspoon salt. Pour off water after soaking. Add 3 quarts clean water. Add picante sauce and meat to beans. Cook on low for 5 to 6 hours, stirring occasionally. Add seasoned salt. Cook for ½ to 1 hour longer.

These beans gain flavor after a day or two of refrigeration. They may also be frozen and microwaved.

Anna Schultz, Branch No. 6196, Marion, TX

FOUR BEAN CASSEROLE

½ lb. bacon
1 lb. hamburger
1 medium onion
1 can kidney beans
1 can green limas

1 can butter beans
1 can pork and beans
½ c. catsup
¾ c. brown sugar

Brown bacon and drain fat; crumble. Brown hamburger with onion. Add the 4 cans of beans (don't drain liquid), catsup, brown sugar, and crumbled bacon. Mix and put in baking dish. Bake at 350° for 1½ hours. Serves 8.

Corry McDowell, Loveland, CO

HAMBURGER CASSEROLE

Fry 1 pound hamburger with onion; drain liquid.

Add:

¼ c. barbeque sauce	1 (8 oz.) can Van Camp's baked
¼ c. syrup molasses	beans
1 chopped up apple	

Fry 4 slices bacon and cut up. Add ½ teaspoon salt. Bake for 1 hour at 350° in casserole.

Emma Berghoefer, Branch No. 554, Hampton, IA

SEVEN-BEAN CASSEROLE

½ lb. bulk sausage (mild), mixed with ½ lb. bulk sausage (hot)	1 can chili beans (with juice)
2 medium onions, chopped	1 can pork and beans
1 can green beans	1 can tomato soup
1 can yellow beans	3 Tbsp. catsup
1 can lima beans	1 c. brown sugar
1 can kidney beans	2 Tbsp. mustard
1 can butter beans	Strips of bacon

Saute onions. Roll sausage into small meatballs and brown. Mix chili, kidney and pork and beans in a large bowl. Drain remaining beans. Add and toss gently.

Combine tomato soup, catsup, sugar, mustard, and onions. Carefully mix with beans. Fold in sausage. Place strips of bacon on top. Bake at 350° for 1 hour, uncovered, in deep 9x13 inch pan or a large casserole dish.

Noreen Chernock, Branch No. 1848, Lorain, OH

WIENER AND BEAN POT CASSEROLE
(Microwave)

1 clove garlic, crushed	1 can kidney beans
½ c. chopped onions	½ c. brown sugar
2 Tbsp. margarine	1 c. catsup
1 pkg. wieners, cut in quarters	1 Tbsp. prepared mustard
1 can baked beans	½ tsp. salt
1 can lima beans	¼ tsp. pepper

Combine onions, garlic and margarine in 3 quart casserole. Microwave on HIGH for 1 to 2 minutes till onions are translucent. Add remaining ingredients. Push wieners to bottom. Cover and microwave for 13 to 15 minutes. Stir after ½ of the time.

June Maynus, Branch No. 6902, El Paso, TX

ONE POT DINNER

½ to 1 lb. ground beef
¾ lb. bacon, cut in small pieces
1 c. chopped onion
2 (1 lb. 15 oz.) cans pork and
    beans
1 (1 lb.) can kidney beans, drained
1 (1 lb.) can lima beans, drained

1 c. ketchup
¼ c. brown sugar
3 Tbsp. white vinegar
1 Tbsp. liquid smoke
Salt
Pepper

Brown ground beef in skillet; drain off fat and put beef in crock pot. Brown bacon and onion; drain off fat. Add bacon, onion, and remaining ingredients to crock pot. Stir together well. Cover and cook on LOW for 4 to 9 hours.

If using the 2 quart crock pot, reduce this recipe by half.

Connie Davis, Branch No. 3107, Loveland, CO

RANCH BEANS

1 lb. ground beef, browned
1 pkg. onion soup mix
½ c. water
1 c. catsup

2 tsp. vinegar
2 Tbsp. mustard
2 (1 lb.) cans baked beans
1 can kidney beans

Mix all ingredients together and bake at 400° for 30 minutes.

Wonderfully quick and easy and usually a crowd pleaser.

Mrs. Paul (Barbara) Dickman, Branch No. 0916, Mt. Angel, OR

SKILLET DINNER

1 lb. hamburger
1 pt. frozen corn or 1 can corn
1 medium can pork and beans

1 small can tomato sauce
Salt and pepper to taste
Tabasco sauce to taste

Brown hamburger in skillet. Onions can also be added if you like. Add corn, pork and beans and tomato sauce with salt and pepper to taste. Heat thoroughly and serve. Tabasco sauce can be added at the table to each person's taste.

This is one of my favorite meals and is quick and easy.

Dale Brehe, Branch No. 3707, Agar-Onida, SD

CALICO BEAN BAG

½ lb. bacon, chopped
1 lb. ground beef, browned
1 c. onion, chopped
¾ c. brown sugar
½ c. ketchup

1 tsp. mustard
2 tsp. vinegar
1 can kidney beans, drained
1 can lima beans, drained
1 can pork and beans

Mix all ingredients together in a casserole dish. Bake at 350° for 40 minutes.

Ruth Peppler, Branch No. 6719, Moses Lake, WA

LIMA BEAN CASSEROLE

¼ to 3 c. diced celery
1 (1 lb.) bag frozen lima beans
3 slices bacon
1 can cream of celery soup

⅓ c. milk
1 Tbsp. flour
¼ lb. cheese

Cook celery and lima beans with a very small amount of water for 30 minutes. Brown bacon and crumble. Combine milk and flour until smooth. Add the soup, bacon, beans, and celery. Dice cheese and stir into mixture. Bake at 350° for 25 minutes.

Casserole may be prepared a day ahead, but increase baking time to 40 to 45 minutes.

June Reiners, Branch No. 2078, Juniata, NE

TACO CREPES

Crepes:

1 c. flour
½ c. corn meal
1½ c. milk

3 eggs
¼ tsp. salt

Filling:

1½ lb. ground beef
1 onion, chopped, sauteed with
    finely chopped celery
1 can refried beans

1 can creamed corn (optional)
2 (8 oz.) tomato sauce
1 env. taco seasoning mix

Garnish:

4 oz. shredded Cheddar cheese

⅓ c. ripe olives

Use ¼ cup crepe mixture and fry in *small* amount of hot oil in small skillet. (Tilt the skillet to make thin crepe.) Fry only till very lightly browned; turn. Simmer filling while making crepes. Put 2 tablespoons meat mixture on each crepe. Roll up and place in 9x13 inch pan. Pour any remaining filling over top of all. Top with cheese and olives. Bake at 375° for 20 minutes (longer if cold). Serve with sour cream and/or guacamole.

Marilyn Vogel, Loveland, CO

REUBEN PIE

1 lb. ground beef
¼ lb. ground pork
⅓ c. quick oats
¼ c. Worcestershire
1 egg
¼ tsp. pepper

¼ tsp. garlic powder
1½ tsp. caraway seed
1 lb. sauerkraut
2 c. shredded Swiss cheese
1 (3 oz.) can French fried onions

Combine ground meats, oats, Worcestershire, egg, pepper, and garlic powder. Press into deep 9 inch pie plate. Spread evenly over bottom and up sides. Bake, uncovered, at 350° for 15 minutes. Remove from oven and drain liquid.

While meat is baking, combine sauerkraut, cheese, caraway seed, and ¼ of onions. Fill partially baked meat crust with mixture. Return to oven for 20 minutes. Sprinkle onions over top and bake for 3 to 5 minutes longer. Cut into wedges.

Can be served with chili sauce.

Marilyn Vogel, Loveland, CO

TUNA CASSEROLE WITH ALMOND SAUCE

2 (10 oz.) pkg. frozen asparagus	¼ c. flour
(or fresh when in season)	½ tsp. salt
2 (7 oz.) cans tuna	Dash of pepper
½ c. sliced almonds	2 c. skim milk
¼ c. unsaturated oil	Paprika

Cook asparagus according to directions on package; drain and arrange in an oiled baking dish. Drain tuna, then arrange over the asparagus. Saute the almonds in the unsaturated oil until lightly browned. Blend in the flour, salt, and pepper. Add the skim milk gradually and stirring, cook until smooth and thick. Pour sauce over tuna. Dust with paprika. Bake in a moderate oven at 350° for 30 minutes or until hot and bubbling. Serves 6 (348 calories per serving).

Phyllis Pundt, Branch No. 239, Brainerd, MN

STUFFED PEPPERS

1 lb. ground beef	1 tsp. Worcestershire sauce
6 medium bell peppers	1 c. shredded Cheddar cheese
1 small onion, chopped	½ tsp. salt
1 (8 oz.) can tomato sauce	⅓ c. catsup
½ c. packed precooked rice	¼ tsp. pepper
¼ c. water	

Cut stem and top off of each pepper. Discard stems. Chop tops and reserve. In bowl, combine peppers and remaining ingredients, except catsup. Stuff peppers with meat mixture. Top each with 1 tablespoon catsup. Place peppers in circle in 10 inch round baking dish, leaving center empty. Cover with wax paper or lid. Cook for 18 to 20 minutes. Let stand, covered, for 5 minutes before serving. Makes 6 servings.

Edna Leister, Branch No. 1131, Worthington, MN

REUBEN CASSEROLE
(Microwave)

1 box noodles romanoff, prepared as directed
1 (16 oz.) can sauerkraut, drained

Corned beef (fresh baked or canned)
6 slices Swiss cheese

Layer ingredients as listed in 8x8 inch casserole. Bake at 80% for 15 minutes, turning once. Be sure casserole is covered.

Cheryl Schultz, Branch No. 3107, Loveland, CO

GREEN BEAN CASSEROLE

2 cans green beans
1½ lb. hamburger

1 can tomato soup
1 can mushrooms

Bake for 30 minutes, then top with onion rings and bake for 10 to 15 minutes longer

Hilma Guffy, Branch No. 2630. Greeley, CO

ZUCCHINI CASSEROLE

1 lb. ground beef
1 clove garlic

Onion to taste
Green pepper to taste

Brown. Spread in bottom of casserole. Put 1 layer sliced zucchini, 1 layer Velveeta cheese, and 1 layer zucchini. Pour 1 can cream of mushroom soup plus ½ cup milk over top. Top with cracker crumbs. Bake for 40 minutes at 350°.

Debbie Meisel, Zion Lutheran, Branch 2232, Auburn, MI

ZUCCHINI HOT DISH

1 lb. lean ground beef
1 large onion, chopped fine
1 c. raw rice
1 (16 oz.) stewed tomatoes with
   green peppers and celery

1 qt. chopped zucchini
1 tsp. salt
½ tsp. pepper (black)
2 to 3 c. hot water

Brown ground beef and onion in frying pan. Add rice, stewed tomatoes, zucchini, salt, pepper, and water. Simmer for about 1 hour or until rice is soft.

You may need to add a bit more water. Use your own judgement.

Ethel Bauer, Branch No. 5616, Regan, ND

BEEF-CABBAGE BAKE

½ c. uncooked long grain rice
1⅓ c. boiling water
½ tsp. salt
1 medium onion, chopped
1 Tbsp. butter or margarine
¾ lb. ground beef
1 tsp. Worcestershire sauce

½ tsp. seasoned salt
⅛ tsp. black pepper
4 c. finely shredded cabbage
1 (16 oz.) jar mild herb style Italian
   cooking sauce or spaghetti
   sauce

Cook rice in boiling water seasoned with salt for 25 minutes or until rice is tender. Drain if necessary. In medium skillet, saute onion in butter until tender. Add beef and cook, breaking up with fork, until meat is browned. Stir in Worcestershire sauce, seasoned salt, and black pepper. Add rice and mix well. Layer half of the cabbage in a 2 quart casserole. Add beef mixture and press down. Add remaining cabbage. Sprinkle lightly with salt and pepper. Press down. Pour sauce over top. Cover and bake at 350°F. for 1 hour. Makes 4 servings.

Les and Carol Gillmore, Branch No. 4930, Kenosha, WI

STUFFED CABBAGE

¾ lb. ground beef	1 large onion
¾ lb. ground pork (lean)	1 small can sauerkraut
1 Tbsp. salt (or salt to taste)	1 large head cabbage
1 tsp. pepper	1 link sausage (Eckrich or
¾ c. uncooked rice, washed	kielbasa)

Wilt cabbage in boiling water (salted). As cabbage wilts, cut off leaves. Drain and trim off thick center vein on cabbage leaf. Line bottom of roaster with sauerkraut. Save some for on top. Add cabbage rolls. Cut up sausage and add in between cabbage rolls. (Sausage can be omitted.) Cover with tomatoes. Use about ¾ tomatoes and rest water. Put remaining sauerkraut on top. Add 2 teaspoons of brown sugar to tomatoes and water.

Bake in a 350° oven till it starts to boil, then turn down to 275°. Cook for about 1½ hours till rice is done.

Better the next day warmed up.

Olga Domine, Branch No. 2295, Allen Park, MI

CABBAGE AND BEEF CASSEROLE

1 lb. ground beef	1 can water
1 c. chopped onion	2 Tbsp. sugar
1 medium head cabbage	1 Tbsp. vinegar
½ c. uncooked rice	Salt to taste
1 large can tomato soup	

Brown beef with onion until beef loses its red color and onion is transparent. When beef is brown, stir in raw rice. While beef is cooking, shred cabbage more coarsely than for slaw. Place in a greased baking dish or shallow casserole. Place beef mixture in a layer over the cabbage. Mix soup, water, sugar, and vinegar together. Pour over beef and cabbage layers. Cover with lid or foil. Bake at 350° for 1 hour.

Laura Kyle, Branch No. 812, Medina, NY

SAUERKRAUT BALLS

1 (16 oz.) pork sausage, seasoned
   to taste
½ c. finely chopped onion
1 lb. sauerkraut, all juice squeezed
   out
¼ c. dry bread crumbs or soda
   crackers

8 oz. cream cheese
¼ c. parsley flakes
2 tsp. yellow mustard
½ tsp. garlic salt
¼ tsp. pepper

Brown in skillet the pork sausage and onion. Drain. Mix with drained sausage the cream cheese, parsley flakes, mustard, garlic salt, and pepper till soft. Refrigerate until cold. Shape into balls. First, roll balls in flour, then 2 beaten eggs, then in sauerkraut-bread crumb mixture. (May freeze.) Bake at 400° for 15 to 20 minutes. Makes about 40 to 50 balls.

Paula Tellock, Branch No. 2525, Larsen, WI

SAUSAGE CASSEROLE

1 lb. sausage

1 (16 oz.) can creamed corn

Brown sausage in skillet. Drain. Stir in creamed corn and heat to bubbling.

Lisa Rosendale, Augusta, IL

SQUASH CASSEROLE

3 long yellow summer squash
2 onions
2 grated carrots (for color)

1 pt. sour cream
1 can cream of chicken soup
Buttered bread crumbs

Boil for 5 minutes the sliced squash, onions, and carrots. Stir in sour cream and cream of chicken. Bake for ½ hour at 350°. Add bread crumbs the last 15 minutes. Serves 12.

Mary Windelbauer, Branch No. 6303, Lodi, OH

CHICKEN CASSEROLE

1 chicken or 6 to 8 chicken breasts
2 cans cream of chicken soup
   (undiluted)
1 (8 oz.) ctn. sour cream

2 c. crushed Ritz crackers
2 tsp. poppy seeds
1½ c. butter or margarine, melted

Cook chicken and cut into bite-size pieces. Combine soup and sour cream. Add chicken, making sure all pieces are coated. Put into a 9x13 inch casserole pan. Add crackers to melted butter and mix well. Spread over chicken and sprinkle with poppy seeds. Bake at 350° for 30 to 40 minutes.

Sherrie Proft, Branch No. 4115, Houston, TX

CHICKEN AND PEA CASSEROLE

1 (6½ oz.) can boned chicken
1 can peas, drained
1 can cream of chicken soup
2 c. milk
2 c. crushed potato chips

Grease a 3 quart casserole dish. Combine ingredients and blend until thoroughly mixed, reserving the chips. Layer into casserole, ending with chips covering top. Bake at 350° for 30 to 35 minutes.

May be served over toast or muffins or plain.

Luellan Hammerand, Branch No. 1720, Sherrill, IA

MIXED VEGETABLE CASSEROLE
(Freezes well)

1 (No. 2) can green beans, drained
2 c. sliced raw carrots
2 c. celery, cut up
1½ c. raw onion, cut in long strips
1 Tbsp. sugar
¾ c. green pepper, cut in long
    strips
2½ tsp. salt
¼ tsp. pepper
3 Tbsp. Minute tapioca
6 Tbsp. melted butter
1 (No. 2½) can stewed tomatoes

Place preceding ingredients in order listed in greased large 3 quart casserole. Cover and bake at 350°.

Edna W. Tegtmeier, Branch 2910, Ames, IA

CASSEROLE MIX

2 c. powdered milk
¾ c. cornstarch
¼ c. chicken bouillon
4 tsp. dry onion mix (onion flakes)
1 tsp. thyme
1 tsp. basil
½ tsp. pepper

Mix all ingredients in bowl. Place in large container and store in refrigerator. Mix 4 teaspoons to 1¼ cups water when using for casseroles.

Erma Nauman, Branch No. 1720, Sherrill, IA

SWEET POTATO CASSEROLE

3 c. cooked, mashed sweet
    potatoes
¼ lb. melted butter or margarine
2 eggs
½ c. granulated sugar
1 tsp. pumpkin pie spice
1 c. drained crushed pineapple
1 tsp. vanilla

Combine all ingredients, except topping ingredients. Mix well and pour in baking dish.

Topping:

1/3 c. margarine

1/3 c. flour

1 c. brown sugar

1 c. chopped pecans

Combine all topping ingredients and sprinkle over casserole. Bake for 30 minutes in a preheated oven. Serves 6.

Mary Brown, Branch No. 6928, St. Albans, NY

HOT CROSSED TUNA CASSEROLE

2 (6½ or 7 oz.) cans tuna, drained

1 (10 oz.) pkg. frozen peas, thawed

1 c. shredded cheese

1 c. celery slices

½ c. bread crumbs

¼ c. chopped onion

¼ tsp. salt

⅛ tsp. pepper

1 c. Miracle Whip salad dressing

1 (8 oz.) can refrigerated crescent
   rolls

Combine all of the ingredients, except the crescent rolls, and mix well. Spoon into an 8x8 inch baking dish. Cut crescent rolls into strips and place strips over casserole into a lattice design. Brush lightly with salad dressing and sprinkle with sesame seeds. Bake at 350° for 35 minutes or until lattice is golden brown.

Corry McDowell, Loveland, CO

COUNTRY COTTAGE CASSEROLE

1 lb. ground beef (lean)

1 (16 oz.) can Veg-All (mixed
   vegetables)

1 pkg. frozen crescent rolls

1 Tbsp. dried minced onions

½ tsp. salt

¼ tsp. seasoned pepper

¼ tsp. ground nutmeg

2 Tbsp. cornstarch

Reserved liquid from the canned
   vegetables

4 slices Velveeta cheese, cut into 8
   triangles

Brown ground meat in a frying pan. Season with the salt, minced onion, seasoned pepper, and nutmeg. Drain liquid from the Veg-All. Stir Veg-All into the meat. Stir the cornstarch in the reserved liquid. Add to meat mixture and stir until thickened.

Preheat oven to 375°F. Line a lightly greased 7x11 inch baking pan with the crescent rolls. Overlap edges to form a crust up the sides of the pan. Pour meat mixture into the crust. Spread evenly. Bake for 10 minutes. Cut Velveeta into thin triangles. Lay over top to form a nice pattern. Bake for an additional 5 minutes or till crust is browned.

Harriet Wilkens, Branch No. 2716, Northglenn, CO

CHEESEBURGER CASSEROLE

1 lb. hamburger

¼ c. chopped green peppers

¼ c. chopped onion

⅛ tsp. pepper

¼ c. catsup

1 (10 oz.) can tomato soup

1 (8 oz.) American cheese, sliced

1 pkg. ready to bake biscuits

302

Brown hamburger, green pepper and onion. Drain if needed. Stir in pepper, tomato soup, and catsup. Heat. After thoroughly heated, put in 2 quart casserole, alternating meat and cheese. Arrange the unbaked biscuits around the edge of pan. Bake at 400° for 20 to 25 minutes or till biscuits are done.

Gladys Graumenz, Branch No. 1409, St. Peter, IL

CHEESEBURGER PIE

2 Tbsp. fat
1 lb. hamburger
¼ c. onions, chopped
¾ tsp. salt
⅛ tsp. pepper

1 (8 oz.) can tomato paste
¼ c. catsup
Grated cheese
1 tube biscuits

Brown fat, hamburger and onion. Drain off juice; add salt and pepper to drained meat. Add tomato paste and catsup; heat thoroughly. Put in 9 inch pie pan. Sprinkle with grated cheese and top with biscuits. Bake at 425° until biscuits are done. Serve hot.

Jo Manke, Branch No. 5985, Midland, SD

CRESCENT ROLL CASSEROLE

2 pkg. crescent rolls
1 lb. hamburger
1 (8 oz.) can tomato sauce
1 pkg. Sloppy Joes mix
Mushrooms

Onions
Season with oregano (if desired)
1 pkg. Mozzarella cheese,
   shredded
1 pkg. Cheddar cheese, shredded

Lay one package of crescent rolls in a 9x13 inch greased cake pan. Brown hamburger. Add tomato sauce, Sloppy Joes mix, mushrooms, onions, and oregano. Spread over rolls in pan. Cover with cheeses. Top with second package of rolls and bake at 350°F. for 25 minutes.

Lucy Hadler, Branch No. 3285, Bloomington, MN

HAM AND EGG QUICHE

1 small container whipping cream
4 eggs
½ to 1 tsp. nutmeg
Salt and pepper to taste

¼ to ½ c. chopped up ham
½ c. shredded Cheddar cheese
1 pie crust, baked for 6 minutes

Mix cream and eggs; beat well. Add nutmeg. Put ham, cheese and onion (if desired) in bottom of prebaked pie shell. Add egg mixture. Bake at 350° for 30 to 50 minutes.

Marilyn Vogel, Loveland, CO

QUICK BREAKFAST ROLLS

2 pkg. refrigerator biscuits
⅔ c. brown sugar
½ c. nuts
Handful of butterscotch chips

1 tsp. cinnamon
⅓ c. butter
2 Tbsp. water

Cut biscuits into fourths and place in an 8x8 inch pan. Mix remainder of ingredients in saucepan and heat till all is melted and blended. Stir frequently. Pour over biscuit pieces. Bake at 350° for 10 to 15 minutes.

Marilyn Vogel, Loveland, CO

SCRAMBLED EGGS

75 eggs
1½ qt. milk

2 Tbsp. salt

Break eggs into bowl. Beat slightly. Heat milk and salt, then combine with eggs. Melt 4 ounces butter in electric roaster. Add egg mixture and bake for about an hour at 325°. Stir often. You may add ham or cheese as you wish. Serves about 45 people.

We use this recipe for our Sunrise service breakfast on Easter morning. Have used it for over 10 years and have always had good luck.

Dorothy Heiden, Branch No. 2670, Waco, NE

BREAKFAST PIZZA

1 lb. pork sausage
1 c. cooked rice
1 (8 count) pkg. refrigerated
    crescent rolls
4 eggs, slightly beaten

¼ c. milk
½ tsp. salt
⅛ tsp. pepper
½ c. shredded Cheddar cheese
½ c. shredded Mozzarella cheese

Brown and drain sausage; mix with rice. Separate crescent rolls and place, side by side, in pizza pan. Press together to form a crust. Combine eggs, milk and seasonings. Set aside. Spoon rice and sausage mixture over crust. Top with cheeses and pour egg mixture over all. Bake in a 350° oven for 30 minutes. Serves 6 to 8.

Luanna Bauschlicher, Corning, AR

BREAKFAST PIZZA

1 lb. pork sausage
1 (8 count) pkg. crescent rolls
1 c. frozen loose pack hash brown
    potatoes, thawed
1 c. shredded sharp Cheddar
    cheese (4 oz.)

5 eggs
¼ c. milk
½ tsp. salt
⅛ tsp. pepper
2 Tbsp. grated Parmesan cheese

In a skillet, cook sausage till browned; drain off excess fat. Separate crescent dough into 8 triangles. Place in an ungreased 12 inch pizza pan with points toward the center. Press over bottom and up sides to form a crust; seal perforations. Spoon sausage over crust. Sprinkle with potatoes. Top with Cheddar cheese.

In a bowl, beat together eggs, milk, salt, and pepper. Pour into crust. Sprinkle Parmesan cheese over all. Bake in a 375° oven for 25 to 30 minutes. Makes 6 to 8 servings.

Pam Lonnquist, Branch No. 2151, Hamburg, WI

BREAKFAST PIZZA

1 lb. sausage	1 c. (4 oz.) shredded Swiss cheese
1 (8 oz.) pkg. refrigerated crescent rolls	5 eggs
	¼ c. milk
1½ c. frozen loose packed hash brown potatoes, thawed	½ tsp. salt
	¼ tsp. pepper
1 c. (4 oz.) shredded sharp Cheddar cheese	2 Tbsp. grated Parmesan cheese

In a skillet, brown sausage and drain. Separate crescent rolls into 8 triangles. Place in an ungreased 12 inch pizza pan with points toward the center. Press over bottom and up sides to form a crust; seal perforations. Spoon sausage over crust. Sprinkle with potatoes. Top with Cheddar and Swiss cheeses.

In a bowl, beat together eggs, milk, salt, and pepper. Pour onto crust. Sprinkle Parmesan cheese over all. Bake in a 375° oven for 25 to 30 minutes.

Variation: Add ½ cup chopped onion and bell pepper after cheese.

This recipe has Swiss cheese in it also.

Jean Spencer, Branch No. 1618, Hickory, NC

BREAKFAST PIZZA

1 lb. bulk pork sausage	5 eggs
1 (8 count) pkg. refrigerator crescent rolls	¼ c. milk
	½ tsp. salt
1 c. frozen loose pack hash brown potatoes, thawed	⅛ tsp. pepper
	2 Tbsp. grated Parmesan cheese
1 c. shredded sharp Cheddar cheese	

In skillet, cook sausage until browned. Drain. Separate crescent dough into 8 triangles. Place in ungreased 12 inch pizza pan with points toward center. Pat dough to fit bottom and sides of pan, sealing perforations. Spoon sausage over dough. Sprinkle with the potatoes. Top with Cheddar cheese.

In a bowl, beat together eggs, milk, salt, and pepper. Pour over preceding ingredients and top with Parmesan cheese. Bake in a 375° oven for 25 minutes. Makes 6 to 8 servings.

Marlene Griffith, Branch No. 1221

APPLE-SAUSAGE BRUNCH PIE

1 lb. link sausage	1 c. American cheese, shredded
1 (20 oz.) can apple pie filling	½ c. light brown sugar
11 oz. (2 crusts) pie crust mix	

Make ½ of pie crust. Put in pie pan. Prick and bake for 10 minutes at 375°. Cook sausage. Spoon pie filling on cooled crust. Arrange sausage on top in spoke fashion. Sprinkle American cheese on next. Mix rest of pie crust with brown sugar. Sprinkle on top of pie. Bake for 25 minutes at 350°. Serves 4 to 8.

LesLee Heusinkveld, Branch No. 3107, Loveland, CO

BRUNCHY EGG ALA JACQUE CASSEROLE

Egg Dish:

½ c. Velveeta cheese (1 c.),
  shredded
4 to 6 slices bacon
¼ c. chopped onion
1 doz. eggs, slightly beaten

½ tsp. salt
1 (4 oz.) can mushroom slices
3 slices bread, cubed, and 2 Tbsp.
  oleo

Dice and fry bacon. Drain grease. Saute onion with bacon. Scramble eggs to soft stage. Fold in bacon, onion, mushrooms, and eggs into White Sauce. Pour into 12 x 7 x 2½ inch baking dish. Cover with buttered bread cubes. Sprinkle with paprika. Cover and refrigerate overnight. Bake, uncovered, at 350° for 30 minutes.

White Sauce:

2 Tbsp. butter or oleo
2 Tbsp. flour

2 c. milk

Combine and heat until it starts to thicken. Add cheese.

This is our breakfast dish we serve at our church for Easter breakfast. Everybody loves it.

Ethel Krause, Branch No. 4374, Chesaning, MI

ZUCCHINI PANCAKES

⅓ c. Bisquick
¼ tsp. salt
¼ c. grated Parmesan cheese

2 beaten eggs
2 c. shredded zucchini

Mix first 4 ingredients. Add zucchini. Fry in small amount of vegetable shortening or oil.

Vi White, Branch No. 2568, Fredericktown, MO

WHOLE WHEAT FRUIT PANCAKES

1 egg
1 c. whole wheat flour
1 c. milk
2 Tbsp. vegetable oil

3 tsp. baking powder
½ tsp. salt
¼ tsp. cinnamon
⅔ c. fruit*

Beat egg with hand beater until fluffy. Beat in rest of ingredients, except fruit, just until smooth. Stir in fruit last. Pour ¼ cup batter onto hot griddle that has been greased if necessary. Cook pancakes until puffed and dry around edges. Turn and cook other sides until golden brown.

* Use fresh or frozen *blueberries* (thawed and well drained), fresh *raspberries* or fresh (peeled), frozen (thawed and drained) or canned (drained) *peaches* that have been cut up (about 1 medium peach).

Linda Biebert, Branch No. 3682, Beaver Dam, WI

POTATO PANCAKES

¼ c. milk
2 eggs
3 c. diced raw potatoes
1 small onion, quartered

3 Tbsp. flour
1 tsp. salt
¼ tsp. baking powder

Put all ingredients in blender in order listed. Cover and blend just until all potatoes go through blades. Do not overblend or potatoes will be liquefied. Pour small amounts onto a hot, greased griddle or frying pan. Fry until brown on both sides, turning once.

Esther Fitzner, Branch No. 559, Fort Dodge, IA

FARMER'S BREAKFAST

2 Tbsp. margarine
4 medium potatoes, cooked and
  chopped
1 to 2 c. cooked meat, cut into
  small pieces

6 eggs, beaten
1 c. cheese, grated (Colby,
  American or other)
¼ c. chopped onion (optional)

Saute onion in large skillet. Fry potatoes and meat until heated through. Add beaten eggs to meat and potatoes. Add cheese. Cook slowly until eggs are set. Stir occasionally. Serve hot. Serves 6.

Ron Bork, Branch No. 625, Perry, OH

KROPSU OVEN PANCAKE

4 eggs
1 Tbsp. salt
1 qt. milk

2 c. flour
½ c. butter

Beat eggs and salt; add milk and flour gradually. Mix well. Put butter in a 9x13 inch baking pan. Keep pan hot, but not enough to brown the butter. Add egg mixture and bake at 400° for 30 to 35 minutes. Serve immediately with crushed fruit, jam or syrup.

Tyyne Kivi, Branch No. 5691, Harley, WI

EGG CASSEROLE

3 Tbsp. butter
2 medium onions, chopped
1 lb. fresh mushrooms
2 green peppers
12 slices white bread, crusts
    trimmed off
2 c. Cheddar cheese, shredded

1 lb. boiled ham, chopped
8 eggs
2 c. milk
1 Tbsp. Worcestershire sauce
1 tsp. salt
¼ tsp. pepper

Brown onions, green peppers and mushrooms in butter. Place 6 slices bread in bottom of 9x13 inch greased pan as a lining. Place half of the ham and a third of the cheese on the bread. Place half of the browned vegetable mixture on the cheese. Repeat layers, starting with the bread; end with a cheese layer on top.

Mix together the eggs, milk, Worcestershire sauce, salt, and pepper. Pour over the layers, making sure that all bread and the corners are covered with the egg mixture. Cover and refrigerate overnight. Remove cover and check corners to make sure bread is covered with egg mixture. If not, add more milk mixed with an egg. Bake, uncovered, at 350° for 50 to 60 minutes or until egg is set. Let stand for 10 minutes before cutting to serve.

Larry and Doris Taubmann, Branch No. 1359, Milwaukee, WI

CRUSTY POTATO PANCAKES

6 medium potatoes, peeled
1 small onion, grated
3 eggs

¾ c. flour
2 tsp. salt
Oil (for frying)

Grate potatoes coarsely into a bowl filled with cold water. This keeps the potatoes from turning dark and removes some of the excess starch, making the pancakes crispier. In another bowl, combine the onion, eggs, flour, and salt. Drain potatoes, pressing out all liquid. Beat potatoes into batter. Heat oil. Spoon heaping tablespoons of batter into oil, spreading with the back of a spoon into 4 inch rounds. Brown on one side. Turn and brown on the other side. Brown the pancakes slowly so potatoes will have a chance to cook through properly. Drain on absorbent paper. Serve hot with applesauce.

Joel H. Timian, Branch No. 1412, Corvallis, OR

HEAT AND HOLD SCRAMBLED EGGS

¼ c. butter
12 eggs
1⅓ c. milk

1 tsp. salt
⅛ tsp. pepper
2 Tbsp. flour

Melt butter in large skillet. Mix rest of ingredients together and pour in skillet. Cook, stirring from outside in, until eggs have cooked to a creamy texture. May be held on low up to 2 hours before serving.

This recipe is used for our AAL Easter breakfasts.

Ardith Mueller, Columbus, NE

LEFSE

3½ c. boiled and mashed potatoes
¼ c. melted butter
½ tsp. salt

1 c. flour
¼ c. half & half
½ tsp. sugar

Combine potatoes, butter and salt; set aside to cool. Add flour, half & half, and sugar when you are ready to roll. Roll as thin as possible. Bake on pancake or lefse grill. Turn once. When baked, stack rounds and cover with cloth so they won't dry out.

Ardis Zimney, Branch No. 6541, West Fargo, ND

HAM AND POTATO BREAKFAST

1 pkg. Betty Crocker hash browns
1½ c. shredded Cheddar cheese
1 c. finely chopped ham
½ c. sliced green onions
1½ c. water
1 c. milk

1 tsp. salt
1 tsp. dry mustard
Dash of ground red pepper
5 eggs, beaten
Paprika

Heat oven to 350°. Mix all ingredients, except paprika, in large bowl. Pour into ungreased rectangular baking dish, 12x17x2 inches. Sprinkle with paprika. Bake, uncovered, until knife inserted in center comes out clean. Bake for 40 to 45 minutes.

Marsha Ruesch, Branch No. 5844, Columbia City, IN

FRENCH TOAST SUPREME

½ c. butter
2 Tbsp. white corn syrup
1 c. brown sugar
French bread *or* Texas toast

5 eggs
1 c. Carnation milk
1 tsp. vanilla
¼ tsp. salt

Boil together butter, corn syrup and brown sugar for 1 minute. Grease a 9x13 inch pan and put the caramel mixture in bottom. Slice French bread about 1 inch thick *or* use Texas toast. Put slices close together on top of the caramel sauce. Beat together eggs, milk, vanilla, and salt. Pour over the top of the bread. Cover and refrigerate overnight. Bake at 350° for 45 minutes. When ready to serve, turn the pieces over and the caramel will be on top. *A good brunch recipe.*

Marcella Reinking, Branch No. 5383, Sumner, IA

DUTCH BABY

For 2 to 3 quart pan size (2 servings), use:

¼ c. butter
3 eggs

¾ c. milk
¾ c. flour

For 3 to 4 quart pan size (2 to 3 servings), use:

⅓ c. butter
4 eggs

1 c. milk
1 c. flour

For 4 to 4½ quart pan size (3 to 4 servings), use:

½ c. butter   1¼ c. milk
5 eggs   1¼ c. flour

For 4½ to 5 quart pan size (4 to 6 servings), use:

½ c. butter   1½ c. milk
6 eggs   1½ c. flour

Preheat oven to 425°. Put butter in baking dish (I use large wok). Set in oven to melt, being careful not to scorch butter. In blender, mix eggs at high speed for 1 minute. With blender running, pour in milk, then slowly add flour. Remove pan from oven and pour batter into hot melted butter. Bake at 425° for 20 to 25 minutes, until puffy and well browned. Remove. Serve immediately with butter and syrup, jam, fruit, or other fruit topping.

Cheryl Schwab-Ambrose, Branch No. 02803, Buhl, ID

BREAKFAST BLINTZ

6 eggs   1½ c. milk
1 c. flour   2½ Tbsp. oil
¾ tsp. salt

Shake, mix or blend until smooth. Cook ½ cup at a time in an 8 inch skillet. Remove to plate and fill with applesauce, strawberries or favorite filling. Fold in half and sprinkle with powdered sugar or cinnamon. Serve warm.

Lois Heiden, Branch No. 3651, Chesterland, OH

BREAKFAST CASSEROLE

10 slices bread   2 c. milk
2 lb. ham or sausage links   1 tsp. salt
½ lb. cheese   1 tsp. dry mustard
5 eggs   ¼ to ½ tsp. garlic powder

Butter a 9x14 inch pan well. Whisk eggs till foamy. Add milk, salt, mustard, and garlic powder. Mix well; set aside. Cube or grind coarsely the ham or fry sausage. Grate cheese and cube bread. Start with a layer of bread cubes on bottom of pan. Add meat, then cheese. Put the rest of the bread cubes on top. Pour egg mixture over all. Pack down with potato masher. Cover tightly with foil and refrigerate. This is best when prepared and refrigerated for a day or two before baking. Can be frozen. Also, you may add diced green pepper, onion, black olives, and mushrooms. Bake for 1 hour at 350°

Branch No. 3207, Mt. Vernon, WA

BREAKFAST CASSEROLE

6 to 12 slices bread   1 tsp. salt
1 c. shredded Cheddar cheese   2 c. milk
½ to 1 lb. bacon, fried crisp   ¾ c. melted butter
10 eggs

Butter bottom of 9x13 inch pan. Cut bread into quarters. Cover bottom of pan so that pieces touch. Cover with cheese. Add crumbled bacon, then another layer of bread. Beat eggs, salt, butter, and milk together. Pour over bread. Cover and refrigerate overnight. Bake at 370° for about 45 minutes, uncovered.

You may add mushrooms, peppers, frozen chopped spinach, ham, etc.

Mrs. Dorothy H. Meyer, Branch No. 5935, Loganville, WI

HOMEMADE PANCAKES

2 eggs
2 c. buttermilk
2 c. flour
2 Tbsp. sugar

1 tsp. salt
1 tsp. baking soda
2 Tbsp. melted butter

Beat together eggs and buttermilk. Add flour, sugar, salt, and soda. *Fold* this flour mixture into egg mixture with melted butter. Stir - don't beat.

Connie Davis, Branch No. 3107, Loveland, CO

EGGS O'BRIEN
(Microwave)

4 slices bacon, cut in halves
3 c. frozen hash browns with
    onions and peppers (12 oz.)
1 Tbsp. butter

½ tsp. salt
⅛ tsp. pepper
4 eggs
Paprika

Place bacon in 9 inch microwavable pie plate. Cover with a paper towel. Microwave on HIGH for 3 minutes or till crisp. Set bacon aside. Drain off all but 1 tablespoon drippings.

Into drippings in pie plate, stir potatoes, butter, salt, and pepper. Microwave on HIGH for 7 minutes or till potatoes are almost tender, stirring twice. Crumble bacon and stir into potatoes. With the back of a spoon, make 4 shallow depressions in potato mixture. Place an egg in each hollow. Cover tightly with plastic wrap, turning one edge back. Microwave at 50% for 6 to 8 minutes or till eggs are almost done. Remove from oven. Sprinkle with paprika if desired.

Cheryl Schultz, Branch No. 3107, Loveland, CO

BREAKFAST CASSEROLE

4 c. frozen hash brown potatoes
5 eggs, beaten
½ c. cottage cheese
1 c. Jack cheese, shredded
1 whole green onion, sliced
1 tsp. salt

Pepper (as desired)
4 drops of Tabasco (optional)
6 slices bacon, cut into pieces and
    browned
Paprika

Stir together all ingredients, *except* bacon and paprika. Spoon into a well buttered 10 inch pie plate or quiche pan. Sprinkle with bacon pieces and paprika. Bake at 350° for 30 to 40 minutes until lightly browned and set in the center. Serves 6 to 8.

We serve this at our branch Member Awareness Breakfasts along with English muffins, cantaloupe wedges, jelly, orange juice, and coffee.

Branch No. 5189, San Diego, CA

HAMBURGER-CHEESE QUICHE

1 lb. ground meat, cooked and drained
2 c. grated sharp cheese (or 1 c. each sharp and Mozzarella)
½ c. mayonnaise
¼ c. milk

2 eggs
1 Tbsp. cornstarch
¼ c. chopped green onions
1 (10 oz.) cream of mushroom soup
2 unbaked 9 inch pie crust shells

Mix all ingredients. Pour into pie shells. Bake at 350° for 40 to 45 minutes until puffed across top and golden brown.

Eileen Kay Smith, Branch No. 3405, Affton, MO

SAUSAGE AND PASTA QUICK AND EASY MAIN DISH MEAL

Great for potluck dinners. Keeps well in slow cooker. Makes a large main dish. Preparation time: 15 to 20 minutes.

1 lb. Polish kielbasa or smoked sausage
1 small cooking onion, chopped
1 Tbsp. margarine

1 lb. macaroni (shells or spirals)
1 (1 lb.) pkg. frozen corn or peas (can use both together)
½ c. Parmesan cheese

In large skillet, melt margarine and cook chopped onion until tender. Cut meat into bite-size pieces and add to skillet. Cook until heated thoroughly. Cook pasta in separate pan while skillet mixture is cooking. As meat begins to get hot, add corn or peas or both to make dish larger and cover skillet.

Drain pasta. Turn into large serving bowl. Pour ¼ cup cheese into skillet. Mix. Add to pasta in bowl. Pour in remaining grated cheese. Stir until mixed. Serve immediately.

Linda Lampman, Branch No. 449, Lockport, NY

EGG CASSEROLE

½ stick margarine
1 c. evaporated milk
1 (4 oz.) jar mushrooms
2 c. Cheddar cheese, shredded

2 Tbsp. prepared mustard
¼ tsp. pepper
12 eggs
½ lb. bacon, fried and crumbled

Melt margarine in bottom of 9x13 inch baking dish. Layer mushrooms, bacon and cheese in dish. Mix eggs, milk, mustard, and pepper; pour over other ingredients. Bake at 325° for 40 to 50 minutes. Serves 10 to 12.

Ingredients may be halved and baked in an 8 inch round cake pan. Will serve 5 or 6.

Chopped pieces of ham, diced sausage links or bulk sausage (browned and drained) may be substituted for the bacon.

Carol Hoffman, Branch No. 5844, Columbia City, IN

EGG COVER-UP

2 Tbsp. oil	1 small pkg. breakfast sausage
2 medium potatoes, sliced round	3 eggs, beaten
1 small onion, sliced	Salt and pepper

Brown onion and potatoes in oil. Drain and set aside. Cook sausage until done; drain. Combine with potatoes in fry pan. Pour beaten eggs over potatoes and sausage. Cook until done. Serves 4.

Carolyn Roney, Branch No. 4817, Youngstown, OH

BREAKFAST CASSEROLE

1 lb. sausage	2 c. milk
6 slices bread	1 tsp. mustard
1 c. shredded Cheddar cheese	1 tsp. salt
6 eggs	

Fry sausage; drain and set aside. Beat eggs and add other ingredients. Mix with sausage. Put in casserole dish. Let casserole set in refrigerator overnight. Bake at 375° for about 45 to 60 minutes and center is firm. Serves 6.
Variations: May add to basic recipe such as mushrooms, green peppers.

Marty Williams, Branch No. 5844, Columbia City, IN

EGG-SAUSAGE CASSEROLE

6 eggs	½ tsp. salt
2 tsp. Worcestershire sauce	1 lb. sausage (Jimmy Dean)
Dash of Tabasco	2 c. grated Cheddar or Colby
6 to 8 slices bread	cheese
Instant onions	1 (4 oz.) can chopped green chilies
3 c. milk	(optional)

Trim crusts from bread and place in a buttered 9x13 inch pan. Sprinkle onion flakes and cheese over bread. Brown sausage and green chilies; drain and sprinkle over bread. Mix remaining ingredients well and pour on top. Cover and let stand overnight in refrigerator. Bake at 350° for 30 to 40 minutes.

Great for Christmas morning brunch and we have used for our church's Easter breakfast. Can be spicy or toned down according to your taste.

Hallie A. Hurd, Branch No. 6961, Albany, OR

Notes

Breads
and
Rolls

EQUIVALENT CHART

3 tsp...	.1 tbsp.
2 tbsp..	.⅛ c.
4 tbsp..	.¼ c.
8 tbsp...	.½ c.
16 tbsp	.1 c.
5 tbsp. + 1 tsp.	.⅓ c.
12 tbsp...	.¾ c.
4 oz....	.½c.
8 oz....	.1 c.
16 oz....	.1 lb.
1 oz.	.2 tbsp. fat or liquid
2 c.	.1 pt.
2 pt.	.1 qt.
1 qt.	.4 c.
⅝ c.	.½ c. + 2 tbsp.
⅞ c.	.¾ c. + 2 tbsp.
1 jigger.	.1½ fl. oz. (3 tbsp.)
8 to 10 egg whites.	.1 c.
12 to 14 egg yolks.	.1 c.
1 c. unwhipped cream	.2 c. whipped
1 lb. shredded American cheese	.4 c.

¼ lb. crumbled Bleu cheese	.1 c.
1 lemon.	.3 tbsp. juice
1 orange	.⅓ c. juice
1 lb. unshelled walnuts	.1½ to1¾ c. shelled
2 c. fat	.1 lb.
1 lb. butter	.2 c. or 4 sticks
2 c. granulated sugar.	.1 lb.
3½ - 4 c. unsifted powdered sugar	.1 lb.
2¼ c. packed brown sugar	.1 lb.
4 c. sifted flour.	.1 lb.
4½ c. cake flour.	.1 lb.
3½ c. unsifted whole wheat flour.	.1 lb.
4 oz. (1 to 1¼ c.) uncooked macaroni.	.2¼ c. cooked
7 oz. spaghetti	.4 c. cooked
4 oz. (1½ to 2 c.) uncooked noodles	.2 c. cooked
28 saltine crackers	.1 c. crumbs
4 slices bread	.1 c. crumbs
14 square graham crackers.	.1 c. crumbs
22 vanilla wafers	.1 c. crumbs

SUBSTITUTIONS FOR A MISSING INGREDIENT

1 square **chocolate** (1 ounce) = 3 or 4 tablespoons cocoa plus ½ tablespoon fat.

1 tablespoon **cornstarch** (for thickening) = 2 tablespoons flour.

1 cup sifted **all-purpose flour** = 1 cup plus 2 tablespoons sifted cake flour.

1 cup sifted **cake flour** = 1 cup minus 2 tablespoons sifted all-purpose flour.

1 teaspoon **baking powder** = ¼ teaspoon baking soda plus ½ teaspoon cream of tartar.

1 cup **sour milk** = 1 cup sweet milk into which 1 tablespoon vinegar or lemon juice has been stirred; or 1 cup buttermilk (let stand for 5 minutes).

1 cup **sweet milk** = 1 cup sour milk or buttermilk plus ½ teaspoon baking soda.

¾ cup **cracker crumbs** = 1 cup bread crumbs.

1 cup **cream, sour, heavy** = ⅓ cup butter and ⅔ cup milk in any sour milk recipe.

1 teaspoon **dried herbs** = 1 tablespoon fresh herbs.

1 cup **whole milk** = ½ cup evaporated milk and ½ cup water or 1 cup reconstituted nonfat dry milk and 1 tablespoon butter.

1 package **active dry yeast** = 1 cake compressed yeast.

1 tablespoon **instant minced onion, rehydrated** = 1 small fresh onion.

1 tablespoon **prepared mustard** = 1 teaspoon dry mustard.

⅛ teaspoon **garlic powder** = 1 small pressed clove of garlic.

1 lb. **whole dates** = 1½ c. pitted and cut.

3 medium **bananas** = 1 c. mashed.

3 c. **dry corn flakes** = 1 c. crushed.

10 **miniature marshmallows** = 1 large marshmallow.

GENERAL OVEN CHART

Very slow oven	.250° to 300° F.
Slow oven.	.300° to 325° F.
Moderate oven	.325° to 375° F.
Medium hot oven	.375° to 400° F.
Hot oven.	.400° to 450° F.
Very hot oven	.450° to 500° F.

CONTENTS OF CANS

Of the different sizes of cans used by commercial canners, the most common are:

Size:	Average Contents
8-oz.	.1 cup
picnic	.1¼ cups
No. 300	.1¾ cups
No. 1 tall	.2 cups
No. 303	.2 cups
No. 2	.2½ cups
No. 2½	.3½ cups
No. 3	.4 cups
No. 10	.12 to 13 cups

BREADS AND ROLLS

RAISED GREBBLE

3 eggs
1 c. half & half cream
½ c. milk
2 Tbsp. sugar

1 tsp. salt
1 tsp. vanilla
1 cake yeast

Dissolve yeast in a little warm water. Add 4 to 4½ cups flour (no more). Make a medium stiff dough. Let rise twice. Roll out and cut oblong strip. Make a slit and pull through. *Fry* in hot oil. Sprinkle a little sugar on Grebble.

Roberta Kallsen, Branch No. 3107, Loveland, CO

STRAWBERRY BREAD

½ c. butter
¾ c. sugar
½ tsp. vanilla
2 eggs
1½ c. flour
½ tsp. salt

½ tsp. cream of tartar
¼ tsp. baking soda
⅔ c. strawberry preserves
⅓ c. strawberry yogurt
½ c. chopped nuts (optional)

Cream together butter, sugar and vanilla until light and fluffy. Add eggs, one a time, beating well. Mix together flour, salt, cream of tartar, and soda. Combine preserves and yogurt. Add yogurt mixture to creamed mixture alternately with dry ingredients. Stir in nuts. Pour into a greased 9x5 inch loaf pan. Bake at 350° for 1 hour. Cool for 20 minutes. Remove from pan.

It is best if it is refrigerated overnight before slicing.

Sherry Pike, Branch No. 3679, Wheat Ridge, CO

STRAWBERRY BREAD

3 c. flour
1 tsp. salt
1 c. oil
2 c. sugar
1 Tbsp. cinnamon

1 tsp. soda
3 eggs
2 boxes frozen strawberries,
    thawed

Combine preceding ingredients. Grease small loaf pans with butter. Coat with sugar. Fill pans ½ to ¾ full. Bake at 350° for 1 hour.

Raspberries may be substituted for strawberries, but omit the cinnamon.

Jan Rulison, Loveland, CO

BANANA BREAD

1 c. ripe bananas (2 or 3 medium)
1 egg
¾ c. milk
3 Tbsp. salad oil
3½ tsp. baking powder

1 tsp. salt
1 c. sugar
2½ c. flour
1 c. chopped nuts (optional)

Heat oven to 350°. Grease and flour loaf pans. Place peeled bananas in large mixing bowl. Beat until almost a puree. Add ingredients as listed, mixing well after each addition. Pour into pan. Bake loaves for 55 to 65 minutes. Test with wooden pick. Bread is done when tester comes out clean. Bake muffins for 45 to 50 minutes. Remove from pans to cool on wire racks. Makes one 9 x 5 x 3 inch loaf, two 8½ x 4½ x 2½ inch loaves, or 24 muffins.

Linda Lampman, Branch No. 449, Lockport, NY

BANANA BREAD

½ c. shortening
1 c. sugar
1½ c. flour
1 tsp. salt

1 tsp. baking soda
2 eggs
3 ripe bananas, mashed

Cream shortening and sugar. Add remaining ingredients in order given. Bake in a well greased loaf pan at 350° for 45 minutes.

Eugene Grant, Loveland, CO

HONEY WHEAT CROCK POT BREAD

A crock pot Bread 'N Bake pan is required.

¼ c. dry milk
2 Tbsp. vegetable oil
¼ c. honey
¾ tsp. salt
1¾ c. warm water

1 pkg. or 2½ tsp. active dry yeast
1 c. whole wheat flour
¾ c. white flour
1¾ c. warm water
2 c. whole wheat flour

Preheat crock pot on HIGH setting for 30 minutes. Mix together dry milk, vegetable oil, honey, yeast, salt, 1 cup whole wheat flour, salt, and ¾ cup white flour. Add 1¾ cups warm water; mix well. Beat with electric mixer for approximately 2 minutes. Add the other 2 cups whole wheat flour and mix well with a spoon.

Place in a greased Bread 'N Bake pan. Cover. Let stand for 5 minutes. Place pan in crock pot. Cover and bake on HIGH setting for 2 to 3 hours. Remove pan and uncover. Let stand for 5 minutes. Unmold and serve warm. Store in refrigerator.

Is great toasted with butter!

Margie (Dias) Benes, Branch No. 3107, Loveland, CO

SPECIAL DATE BREAD

1 pkg. dry yeast
1½ c. warm water
3 Tbsp. sugar
3 egg yolks
½ c. milk
4 c. flour

1 tsp. salt
1 c. shortening
3 egg whites, stiffly beaten
¾ c. sugar
1½ tsp. cinnamon
Chopped dates and nuts

Dissolve yeast in the warm water. Add the 3 tablespoons sugar. Next, stir the egg yolks in the milk. Take the flour, salt and shortening; mix until crumbly. Stir the yeast and egg yolk mixture into the flour mixture. Mix well. Form into a ball. Place in greased bowl and chill overnight. Divide dough into 3 parts.

On a lightly floured board, roll into a rectangle. Take 3 egg whites and stiffly beat; add ¾ cup sugar and 1½ teaspoons cinnamon. Spread ⅓ of egg white mixture over each dough rectangle, leaving ½ inch around the edge. Sprinkle with chopped dates and nuts. Roll as for jelly roll. Let rise until double. Bake for 25 minutes at 350°. Frost with powdered sugar glaze and decorate as desired. *Nice for Christmas.*

Velda Zeeck, Branch No. 6699, Cavour, SD

WHODUNITS

1 cake yeast or 1 pkg. yeast
½ tsp. sugar
½ c. shortening
1 c. milk
1 c. hot water
7 to 7½ c. flour

½ c. lukewarm water
½ c. sugar
1 egg
2 tsp. salt
Cinnamon and sugar mixture
Tiny marshmallows

Dissolve 1 cake of yeast or 1 package of yeast in ½ cup lukewarm water; add ½ teaspoon sugar. Let stand for 30 to 45 minutes. Cream together ½ cup sugar and ½ cup shortening; add yeast and 1 egg. Beat. To this, add 1 cup milk poured into 1 cup hot water and 2 teaspoons salt. Cool to lukewarm and add yeast mixture. Stir well and add enough flour to make a soft dough; knead until smooth. It takes about 7 to 7½ cups of flour. Cover and let rise in a warm place until doubled.

Prepare tiny marshmallows by coating the marshmallows with melted oleo and then a mix of cinnamon-sugar. Roll in the mixture. Take a small amount of bread dough and wrap around the 2 marshmallows; seal thoroughly, then roll each prepared ball in oleo and cinnamon-sugar mix. Place in prepared pans (use the tiny tart pans or make into a Bundt cake, layering approximately 3 full layers). Singles should bake for about 12 minutes and Bundt cake for approximately 1 hour. After 45 minutes of baking at 325°, covered with foil, remove and bake for 15 minutes. Cool upside-down to let all of the cinnamon-sugar mixture run down the sides. Cool for approximately 30 minutes and remove from the pan. Cool thoroughly before freezing, or cut while still warm.

Eileen Graumann, Branch No. 2205, Granite, OK

POPPY SEED STOLLEN OR ALMOND TEA RING

4¾ c. flour
1 c. scalded milk
¼ c. butter
½ c. sugar
1 tsp. salt

2 yeast cakes or 2 pkg. dried yeast
2 eggs
1 can Solo almond filling or 1 can
    Solo poppy seed

Pour hot milk over butter, sugar, and salt; stir well. Crumble yeast into luke-warm water (115°) and dissolve. Cool milk to lukewarm; add yeast and well beaten eggs. Gradually pour this into the flour to make a soft dough. Put on floured board and knead. Form into ball and place in greased bowl. Cover and let rise until double in bulk.

When yeast dough is light, roll into rectangular square about ½ inch thick. Brush lightly with melted butter; spread around and then spread the filling. Roll into jelly roll style and place on greased cookie sheet. Form into a ring and cut almost through with scissors at 1 inch intervals, then twist slices. Cover and let rise until double in bulk. Bake at 350° for 30 minutes.

Butter Frosting:

1 c. confectioners sugar, sifted
2 Tbsp. milk

2 Tbsp. melted butter
¼ tsp. vanilla

Blend sugar and butter. Add milk and vanilla. Blend until smooth. Spread over stollen. Sprinkle with ground nuts and halved maraschino cherries or halved walnuts and the cherries.

Idelle Clemons, Branch No. 5844, Columbia City, IN

PUMPKIN BREAD

1 c. oil
3 c. sugar
2 eggs
2 c. pumpkin
3 c. flour

1 tsp. baking soda
½ tsp. baking powder
1 tsp. cloves
1 tsp. cinnamon
1 tsp. nutmeg

Preheat oven to 350°. Combine oil, sugar, eggs, and pumpkin. Add dry ingredients, which have been sifted together. Pour into well greased and floured loaf pans (3 small pans). Bake for about 45 minutes, till toothpick is clean.

Mary Manz Simon, Branch No. 1717, Belleville, IL

PUMPKIN BREAD

3 c. sugar
1 c. salad oil
4 eggs
1¼ tsp. salt
1 tsp. cinnamon
⅔ c. water

3½ c. flour
2 c. cooked pumpkin
3 tsp. soda
1 c. chopped pecans
1 tsp. nutmeg

Combine all ingredients and mix. Divide batter into 3 greased bread pans. I use coffee cans. Bake at 350° for 1 hour or until done. Freezes well.

Marcia K. Sieker, Branch No. 1351, Ellinwood, KS

PUMPKIN BREAD

4 eggs
3 c. sugar
1 c. salad oil
⅔ c. water
1½ c. pumpkin

3½ c. flour
2 tsp. soda
1 tsp. nutmeg
1 tsp. cinnamon
1½ tsp. salt

Blend all ingredients in order. Blend lightly. Bake in well greased loaf tins at 350° for about 1 hour. Makes 3 pans.

JoAnne Scott, Branch No. 545, Mosinee, WI

PUMPKIN BREAD
(3 loaves at once!)

Dry Ingredients:

3½ c. flour
3 c. sugar
2 tsp. soda

1½ tsp. salt
1 tsp. cinnamon
1 tsp. nutmeg

Wet Ingredients:

1 c. salad oil
⅔ c. water

4 eggs
2 c. canned pumpkin

Mix together all dry ingredients in large bowl; set aside. Mix together all other wet ingredients in smaller bowl. Make a well in the center of the dry ingredients and pour the liquid ingredients in. Mix well, scraping bottom. Pour evenly into 3 greased and floured bread pans. Bake at 350° for 1 hour. Makes 7 baby sized bread loaves.

Julie Padilla, Branch No. 3107, Loveland, CO

CRANBERRY BREAD

1 c. sugar
1 egg
½ c. orange juice
2 Tbsp. hot water
2 Tbsp. melted shortening
2 c. flour

½ tsp. baking powder
½ tsp. salt
½ tsp. baking soda
½ c. chopped cranberries
½ c. chopped nuts

Beat sugar and egg. Add orange juice, water and shortening to egg mixture. Combine flour, soda, salt, and baking powder; add to batter. Mix well. Add cranberries and nuts. Bake at 375° for 30 to 35 minutes. After baking, brush loaves with melted butter. Wrap loaves well and refrigerate for 3 hours. Freezes well. Makes 4 small loaves.

Branch No. 5903, Dunlap, IL

CRANBERRY BREAD

Juice and rind of 1 orange (grind
  the rind)
1/4 c. butter or margarine
2 eggs
1 1/2 c. raw cranberries, halved
3/4 c. nutmeats, chopped

1 c. sugar
2 c. flour
1/2 tsp. baking powder
1 tsp. salt
1 tsp. soda

Pour juice in cup and fill to top with *hot* water. Pour in bowl. Add butter and cool. Beat eggs until thick and lemon colored. Add sugar, 1/4 cup at a time. Beat well. Sift dry ingredients and add to egg mixture alternately with orange juice. Fold in orange rind and nuts. Bake 2 medium loaves for 45 minutes and 3 small loaves for 40 minutes at 350°.

Joan Schleif, Branch No. 6958, Buffalo, MN

DILLY BREAD

1 pkg. dry yeast, dissolved in 1/4 c.
  warm water
1 c. cottage cheese, heated to
  lukewarm
2 Tbsp. sugar
1 Tbsp. instant onion

1 egg
1 Tbsp. butter
2 tsp. dill seed
2 1/2 c. flour
1 tsp. salt
1/4 tsp. baking powder

Combine all ingredients. May have to add additional flour to make stiff dough. Cover and let rise until double in bulk, about 50 to 60 minutes. Stir down and turn into greased 1 1/2 quart casserole or bread pan. Let rise for 30 to 40 minutes. Bake at 350° for 40 to 50 minutes or until golden brown. Brush with butter. Serve warm.

Leona Zander, Branch No. 3619, Waverly, IA

DILLY BREAD

2 pkg. dry yeast
1/2 tsp. soda
1 Tbsp. salt
4 Tbsp. dill seed
1/2 c. warm water
2 eggs (unbeaten)

4 Tbsp. butter or margarine
4 Tbsp. sugar
2 Tbsp. minced onion
2 c. creamed cottage cheese,
  warmed
4 1/2 to 5 c. flour

Soften yeast in warm water; set aside. Combine soda, salt, dill seed, eggs, onion, cottage cheese, sugar, and yeast mixture. Add flour to make a soft dough. Cover and let rise till double (about 1 hour). Stir down. Turn into well greased round or square pans. Brush with soft butter or margarine. Sprinkle with a little salt. Let rise until double. Bake for 40 to 50 minutes at 350° till golden brown.

Very good with turkey or ham, fish, any meat, or just plain buttered bread.

Variations: May be kneaded on floured surface with flour to keep from sticking. Place in regular bread pans, butter tops and sprinkle with salt. Bake as before.

For a darker bread, 2 cups rye flour and 1 cup whole wheat flour may be used to replace white flour. Finish with white flour.

Ruth Schnoor, Branch No. 1712, Baudette, MN

APPLE BREAD

1/2 c. butter or oleo
1 c. sugar (white)
2 eggs
1 tsp. vanilla
1/2 tsp. salt

1 tsp. soda, dissolved in 2 Tbsp. sour milk
2 c. diced apples
2 c. flour

Topping:

2 Tbsp. butter
2 Tbsp. flour

2 Tbsp. sugar
1 tsp. cinnamon

Cream butter and sugar. Add eggs, vanilla, salt, and soda. Add apples and flour. Turn into 2 small or 1 large greased and floured tins. Mix together and sprinkle on top loaf the topping. Bake for 1 hour at 325°.

Kathaleen Reese, Branch No. 5844, South Whitley, IN

APPLE BREAD

3 eggs, beaten
1 c. oil
1 1/2 c. sugar
2 c. cubed apples

3 c. flour
1 tsp. baking soda
1/2 tsp. salt
1 tsp. vanilla

Mix all together, except cubed apples. Fold them in last. Put in 2 loaf pans, each 5 x 8 1/2 or five (3 x 6 inch) pans. Bake at 350° for 50 minutes.

Violet M. Ulrich, Branch No. 640, Dwight, IL

BOSTON BROWN BREAD

2 c. water
2 c. raisins
2 tsp. baking soda
4 c. sifted all-purpose flour
1/2 tsp. salt

1/2 c. shortening
2 c. sugar
2 eggs
2 tsp. vanilla
1 c. chopped nuts

Combine water and raisins in a saucepan. Bring to a boil. Boil for 5 minutes. Remove from heat; add baking soda and stir to mix. Set aside to cool. Sift together flour and salt into a bowl. Combine shortening and sugar until light; add eggs and vanilla. Beat until light and fluffy. Add dry ingredients alternately with raisin mixture. Mix well. Stir in walnuts.

Preheat oven to 350°. Spoon mixture into 3 well greased and floured 1 pound coffee cans, filling each half full. Bake for 1 hour or until toothpick inserted in center comes clean. Remove from pan.

Mathilda Dibbert, Branch No. 2331, Wausa, NE

BEST BROWN BREAD

1 (1 lb.) box raisins	2 c. sugar
2 c. boiling water	4 c. flour
2 tsp. baking soda	1 tsp. salt
2 heaping Tbsp. shortening	2 tsp. cinnamon
2 eggs	1 c. chopped nuts

Combine raisins, shortening, baking soda, and boiling water. Mix well and let stand overnight (at least several hours). Beat the eggs and sugar. Add to raisin mixture. Sift the flour, salt and cinnamon; add to mixture. Mix well. Add the nuts. Half fill 9 or 10 soup cans that are well greased. Bake in 350° oven for 50 to 60 minutes. Cool. Open closed end of can and gently push out bread. Wrap individually in foil or Saran Wrap. These freeze well.

Mrs. Leona Lintner, Branch No. 1182, Perryville, MO

OVERNITE ROLLS

1 c. warm water	1 Tbsp. salt
1 pkg. dry yeast	½ c. melted shortening
1 Tbsp. sugar	2 eggs
2 c. warm water	8 to 10 c. flour
1 c. sugar	

Filling:

Butter	Cinnamon
Sugar	Raisins or nuts (if desired)

At 5:00 p.m., dissolve 1 package yeast in 1 cup warm water and 1 tablespoon sugar. In large bowl, mix 2 cups warm water, 1 cup sugar, 1 tablespoon salt, and ½ cup melted shortening. Add 2 eggs and yeast mixture. Work in 8 to 10 cups flour to make soft dough. Cover and let rise. Stir down every hour.

At 10:00 p.m., roll out. Cover with cinnamon-sugar and butter. Shape into rolls. Cover with towel and let rise overnight. Next morning, bake at 350° for 15 to 25 minutes. Frost if desired.

Joy Roggow, Branch No. 1552, Breckinridge, Enid, OK

OVERNIGHT BUNS

3 c. lukewarm water	½ pkg. dry yeast (1½ tsp.)
½ c. melted butter	1 c. sugar
2 eggs, well beaten	1 Tbsp. milk
10 to 12 c. flour	

Start about 5:00 p.m. Dissolve yeast in warm water. Add melted butter, sugar, and salt; add beaten eggs. Add flour. Mix and knead. Set in warm place to rise. Knead down every hour until 9:30 p.m. or 10:00 p.m. Make into buns. Cover with towel. Let rise until morning. Bake in a 350° oven until brown.

Marge Gebert, Branch No. 840, Franklin, WI

OVERNIGHT BUNS

1 pkg. dry yeast	1 c. sugar
3 c. lukewarm water	2 eggs
½ c. shortening (Crisco)	12 c. flour
1 Tbsp. salt	

Soak yeast in ½ cup water. Mix other ingredients and knead until smooth, starting them at about 5:00 p.m. Knead down every hour. Put in well greased pans at about 10:00 p.m. Let rise all night and bake at about 7:00 a.m. the next morning. Cover with plastic and light weight blanket while they are rising so they don't dry out. Makes about 7 dozen buns.

Twyla Zaske, Branch No. 1784, Renville, MN

GRAHAM GEMS

1 egg, well beaten	1 c. sour milk
¼ c. sugar	½ tsp. soda
1 c. flour	1 c. graham flour

Mix all together. Put into muffin tins. Bake in moderate oven for 15 to 20 minutes.

Rosemary (Mrs. Donald) Matthiessen, Branch No. 1718, Gresham, NE

SEMMEL - HARD ROLL

12 c. flour	2 pkg. yeast (2 scant tsp.)
5 c. lukewarm water (5½ to 6 in winter)	2 Tbsp. salt

Dissolve the yeast with water in a large bowl (6 quart or larger). Add salt and flour; beat with a large wooden spoon until dough begins to form blisters on surface and dough is shiny and smooth. Cover and allow to rise till double, or place in the refrigerator overnight. Lightly stir down and drop by large spoonfuls onto a well greased cookie sheet (12x15 inches), 6 Semmel per sheet.

Bake in a 425° to 450° oven for about 15 minutes or until nicely browned. Serve hot with butter and honey or jam or make sandwiches with cheese or meat. Slice rolls horizontally with a table knife. This recipe is fine for a family of 5 or 6. Extra batter can be kept in the refrigerator for several days, baking as needed.

Mrs. Don (Phyllis) Brandt, Branch No. 1998, Beatrice, NE

SWEDISH PANCAKES

1½ c. sifted flour
3 Tbsp. sugar
½ tsp. salt

3 eggs
2 c. milk
2 Tbsp. melted butter

Sift together into a large bowl and set aside the flour, sugar and salt. Beat the eggs in a bowl until thick and piled softly. Beat in until blended the milk and melted butter. Add to dry ingredients.

Heat skillet over low heat. Lightly grease skillet with butter. Pour about ¼ cup (or a little more if you like) into skillet and rotate skillet until the batter covers the bottom of the skillet. Cook over medium heat until lightly browned on the bottom. Loosen edges; turn and lightly brown second side.

Margaret M. Golick, Branch No. 5196, Trafford, PA

PLÄTTAR · SWEDISH PANCAKES

3 eggs
3 c. milk
1 Tbsp. sugar

½ tsp. salt
1½ c. flour
3 Tbsp. melted butter

Beat eggs. Add milk and flour alternately. Add sugar and salt. Mix well. Let stand for an hour. Add melted butter. Heat griddle or "Platt" pan; butter it. For each pancake, spoon about 1 tablespoon batter onto griddle. (Pancakes should be about 3 inches in diameter.) Brown on both sides. Serve with butter and syrup or spread with jam and roll up.

Myrtle Anderson, Branch No. 5325, Stratford, IA

DOUGHNUTS

1 c. sugar
2 Tbsp. melted shortening
1 egg
1 c. sour milk or buttermilk
1 tsp. soda
1 tsp. baking powder

1 tsp. salt
½ tsp. vanilla
⅛ tsp. nutmeg
3½ c. flour (a little more may be
        added)

Mix all ingredients. Roll out and cut into doughnuts. Cook in hot grease.

Hilda Johnson, Branch No. 2121, Chico, CA

HONEY WHEAT BREAD

2 pkg. yeast
½ c. warm water
2 c. warm milk
⅓ c. honey
2 tsp. salt

2 eggs, slightly beaten
½ c. oil
2½ c. whole wheat flour
3 c. white flour

Mix in order given; stir well. Knead in more white or wheat flour if dough needs to be stiffer. Knead well. Put in greased bowl and let rise till double in bulk. Knead down. Put in pans and let rise till double. Bake for 25 minutes at 325°. Makes 2 loaves.

Ester Mohr, Branch No. 670, May City, IA

PUMPKIN SWIRL BREAD

Filling:

1 (8 oz.) pkg. cream cheese,
   softened

¼ c. sugar
1 egg, beaten

Batter:

1¾ c. flour
1½ c. sugar
1 tsp. baking soda
1 tsp. cinnamon
½ tsp. salt

¼ tsp. ground nutmeg
1 c. canned pumpkin
½ c. margarine, melted
1 egg, beaten
⅓ c. water

1. Combine cream cheese, sugar and egg, mixing until well blended; set aside.

2. Combine dry ingredients. Add combined pumpkin, margarine, egg, and water, mixing just until moistened. Reserve 2 cups pumpkin batter; pour remaining batter into a greased and floured 9x5 inch loaf pan.

3. Pour cream cheese mixture over pumpkin batter; top with reserved pumpkin batter. Cut through batters with knife several times for swirl effect.

4. Bake at 350° for an hour and 10 minutes or until wooden pick inserted in center comes out clean. Cool for 5 minutes; remove from pan.

YELLOW CROOKNECK SQUASH BREAD

3 eggs
1 c. vegetable oil
2½ c. sugar
3 tsp. vanilla
2 c. shredded squash (yellow
   crookneck)

3 c. flour
1 tsp. salt
1 tsp. soda
½ tsp. baking powder
3 tsp. cinnamon
1 c. chopped nuts

Sift flour, salt, soda, baking powder, and cinnamon in bowl. Beat eggs. Add oil, sugar and vanilla. Mix until well blended. Slowly add flour mixture and alternate squash into it. Put in greased and floured loaf pans. Bake for 40 to 50 minutes at 350°.

Hilde Johnson, Chico, CA

STICKY OVERNIGHT ROLLS

1 pkg. frozen dough balls
1 c. brown sugar
½ c. oleo

1 tsp. cinnamon
½ c. chopped nuts
4 Tbsp. white syrup

Grease a Bundt pan and sprinkle bottom with chopped nuts. Arrange frozen balls in pan. Melt oleo. Stir in brown sugar, 1 teaspoon cinnamon and 4 tablespoons white syrup. Pour over frozen dough balls. Cover with wax paper and set on counter until morning. Bake at 350° for 30 to 40 minutes. Invert on plate while still warm.

Ramona Wienck, Branch No. 4516, Wymore, NE

OATMEAL-BLUEBERRY MUFFINS

1 c. plus 2 Tbsp. flour
6 oz. uncooked quick oats
⅓ c. plus 1 Tbsp. sugar
1 Tbsp. baking powder
½ tsp. salt

1 c. skim milk
1 egg
¼ c. vegetable oil
1 c. blueberries, thawed
1 tsp. ground cinnamon

Preheat oven to 425°. Combine flour, oats, ⅓ cup sugar, baking powder, and salt. In small bowl, using fork, combine milk, egg and oil. Add to flour mixture. Fold in blueberries. Pour into muffin cups. Combine 1 tablespoon sugar with cinnamon and sprinkle evenly over muffins. Bake for 20 to 25 minutes (until lightly browned and toothpick comes out dry). Makes 12 muffins.

Susan Gubsch, Branch No. 6719, Moses Lake, WA

OATMEAL MUFFINS

1 c. quick oats
1 c. sour milk
1 beaten egg
½ c. brown sugar
1 c. flour
⅓ c. melted shortening (oleo)

½ tsp. salt
1 tsp. baking powder
½ tsp. baking soda
½ tsp. cinnamon
½ to 1 c. raisins

In a bowl, soak the oats in the sour milk for a few minutes. In the meantime, mix flour with brown sugar, salt, baking powder, soda, cinnamon, and raisins. Add egg and shortening to oat mixture. Add flour mixture and mix well with spoon. Put into muffin tin which has been lined with cupcake liners. Bake at 350° for 20 minutes until done. Makes 12 large muffins.

Phyllis Vogtmann, Branch No. 2232, Auburn, MI

OATMEAL MUFFINS

1 c. oats
1 c. all-purpose flour
1 Tbsp. baking powder
½ tsp. cinnamon
1 c. skim milk
½ c. mashed ripe banana

½ c. dates
¼ c. vegetable oil
¼ c. firmly packed brown sugar
1 egg white
1 c. nuts (optional)

Heat oven to 400°F. Line muffin cups with paper baking cups. Combine oats, flour, baking powder, and cinnamon. Add combined remaining ingredients and mix just until dry ingredients are moistened. Fill prepared muffin cups ¾ full. Bake for 20 to 25 minutes. Yield: 1 dozen muffins.

Sandee Scanlan, Branch No. 2714, Ogden, UT

RONOAKE ROLLS

1 c. milk
½ c. sugar
1 tsp. salt
6 Tbsp. margarine

1 c. warm water
2 pkg. yeast
3 eggs
9 c. flour (about)

Scald milk. Add sugar, salt and margarine. Cool till lukewarm. Measure water in large bowl. Add yeast. Stir, then add mixture of milk, eggs and ½ of the flour. Stir till smooth. Add flour till dough leaves side of bowl. Knead for 10 minutes. Grease and set in warm place till double (about 1¼ hours). Roll ¾ inch thick. Cut and let rise. Bake at 350° for 20 minutes.

Irene Braun, Branch No. 812, Medina, NY

DINNER ROLLS

2 c. warm water
1 tsp. salt
⅓ c. oil
½ c. sugar

2 eggs
2 pkg. yeast
6½ c. flour

Beat water, salt, oil, sugar, and eggs till mixed; add yeast. Stir until it is dissolved. Add flour and knead until smooth and elastic. Let rise until double, about 1 hour. Punch down and make into rolls. Let rise in a greased baking pan until double in size. Bake at 350° for 25 minutes. Use dough for bread, dinner rolls and cinnamon rolls.

Barbara Alsum, Branch No. 3107, Loveland, CO

POPOVERS
(Quick and easy)

½ c. milk
⅓ c. sugar
½ tsp. salt
½ tsp. vanilla
1 tsp. shortening

1 egg
1¼ tsp. baking powder
1⅓ c. flour (unsifted)
2 dashes of nutmeg (optional)

Mix all ingredients together; stir until smooth. Drop from teaspoon into deep hot fat or oil (about 375°). They will pop over by themselves. Fry until they are a golden brown; drain and roll in granulated sugar. Makes 36 to 40 (1 inch) round ball cake type donuts.

I sometimes add a little cinnamon to the sugar that I roll them in.

June Oehl, Branch No. 1255, Friedheim, MO

SOUTH PACIFIC MUFFINS

1 (20 oz.) can crushed pineapple
½ c. sliced almonds
2 c. all-purpose flour
1 tsp. baking soda
1 tsp. salt
1 (3 oz.) pkg. cream cheese

1 c. sugar
2 tsp. vanilla
1 egg, beaten
½ c. dairy sour cream
¼ c. coconut

Drain pineapple. Reserve juice. Heavily grease muffin pans and line with almonds. Mix flour with soda and salt. Blend cream cheese, sugar, and vanilla until smooth. Stir in the egg. Add flour mixture alternately with sour cream. Fold in drained pineapple and coconut. Spoon into prepared pans.

Bake at 350°F. for 35 minutes, or until golden brown. Let stand in pan for 5 to 10 minutes. Turn out onto wire rack.

Glaze:

1 Tbsp. butter or margarine
1 c. powdered sugar

1 Tbsp. reserved pineapple juice

Blend butter, powdered sugar and pineapple juice for glaze. Drizzle over warm muffins. Makes about 2 dozen muffins.

Helen Hansen, Branch No. 1957, Creighton, NE

JEAN'S HEAVENLY CLOUD BISCUITS

2 c. flour
1 Tbsp. sugar
4 tsp. baking powder
½ tsp. salt

½ c. shortening
1 egg, slightly beaten
⅔ c. milk

Sift dry ingredients. Cut in shortening. Combine egg and milk; add to dry ingredients and shortening. Stir dough until it follows fork around bowl. Turn on lightly floured board. Knead gently. Roll and cut out biscuits. Place on ungreased cookie sheet. Bake until golden brown (10 to 14 minutes) at 450°.

Mrs. June Werth, Branch No. 965, North Tonawanda, NY

KAVRING

1 c. whole wheat flour
1 c. white flour
½ c. sugar
2 tsp. baking powder
½ tsp. soda

½ tsp. cream of tartar
½ tsp. salt
½ c. butter or oleo
¾ c. buttermilk

Cut butter into dry ingredients (like pie crust) until the consistency of fine meal. Add buttermilk. Mix well. Roll out ¼ inch thick on floured cloth. Cut with small cookie cutter. Bake at 400° for 10 to 12 minutes. While warm, cut in half. Toast with cut side up in slow oven until dry and browned.

Myrtle Anderson, Branch No. 5325, Stratford, IA

BUNS

1 c. milk
½ c. margarine
1 tsp. salt
Scant ½ c. sugar
1 c. cold water

2 pkg. yeast
¼ c. warm water
¼ tsp. sugar
1 egg
6 to 8 c. flour

Heat milk, margarine, salt, and sugar to melt margarine. Add cold water. Dissolve yeast in warm water and sugar. Add to first mixture. Beat in egg and flour to make stiff dough. Turn out onto lightly floured board; knead until smooth and elastic, about 8 to 10 minutes. Place in greased bowl, turning to grease top. Cover and let rise in warm place until doubled in bulk.

Punch dough down. Let rise again until almost double. Divide into equal size pieces. Form into smooth ball. Place on greased baking sheets about 2 inches apart. Press to flatten. Cover and let rise until double. Bake at 350° for 15 to 20 minutes.

Edna Lundquist, Branch No. 5325, Stratford, IA

OAT AND HONEY BRAN MUFFINS

1 c. rolled oats
¾ c. wheat germ
½ c. natural bran
½ tsp. salt
½ tsp. cinnamon
1 c. buttermilk
½ c. honey

2 eggs, beaten
½ c. oil
1 c. whole wheat flour
2 tsp. baking powder
1 tsp. baking soda
½ c. raisins

Combine oats, wheat germ, bran, salt, cinnamon, and buttermilk. Mix well and let stand for 15 minutes. Add honey, eggs, and oil. Mix well. Combine flour, baking powder and baking soda. Add to first mixture. Stir in raisins. Fill well greased muffin cups ¾ full. Bake at 375° for 20 to 25 minutes. Loosen edges and turn out on wire racks to cool. Makes 1½ dozen muffins.

Walda Mann, Branch No. 0916, Mt. Angel, OR

JUMBO CEREAL MUFFINS

1 c. flour
½ c. whole wheat flour
1 Tbsp. baking powder
½ tsp. salt
½ c. brown sugar, packed
½ tsp. cinnamon
¼ tsp. nutmeg

1 c. milk
1 egg, slightly beaten
⅓ c. oil
2 c. Post Toasties Corn Flakes (or
    similar cereal)
¼ c. chopped nuts

Mix flours with baking powder and salt in bowl. Combine sugar, cinnamon, nutmeg, milk, egg, and oil. Add to flour. Mix till just moistened. Stir in cereal and nuts. Bake in 6 paper lined 6 ounce custard cups at 400° for 30 to 35 minutes or until cake tester inserted in center comes out clean. (To make regular size, bake in 12 regular muffin cups for 20 to 25 minutes.) *Delicious and nutritious!*

Vivian Merkel, Branch No. 3984, Washburn, ND

BELLIN'S BRAN MUFFINS

1 c. 100% bran
1 c. boiling water
½ c. margarine
½ tsp. salt
1½ c. sugar
2 eggs
2 c. buttermilk

¼ lb. chopped dates
¼ lb. raisins (about 1 c.)
1 c. chopped walnuts
2½ c. flour
2½ tsp. baking soda
2 c. 100% bran

Mix 1 cup bran and water; let stand for about ½ hour. Cream together margarine, salt, sugar, and eggs. Add 2 cups of buttermilk and mix. Add dates, raisins and nuts. Add flour, baking soda and 2 cups bran; stir just until blended. Add bran and water mixture. Stir only to blend. Bake at 350° for 20 to 25 minutes. Batter keeps in refrigerator up to 6 weeks. Makes 24 to 30 muffins.

Ruth Borchardt, Branch No. 2412, Green Bay, WI

BANANA NUT MUFFINS

2 c. sifted flour
3 tsp. baking powder
½ tsp. salt
½ c. shortening
1 c. sugar

2 eggs
1⅓ c. mashed bananas (approx. 3 medium)
1 c. chopped walnuts

Sift together flour, baking powder and salt. Cream together shortening and sugar in a bowl until light and fluffy. Beat in eggs, one at a time, blending well after each addition. Stir in mashed bananas. Add dry ingredients, stirring just enough to moisten. Do not overbeat. Batter will be lumpy. Gently mix in chopped nuts. Fill greased 3 inch muffin pan ⅔ cup full. Bake in a 350° oven for 20 minutes or until muffins are golden brown. Makes 18.

Kerry Niederbaumer, Branch No. 2620, Yale, SD

HUCKLEBERRY MUFFINS

½ c. margarine (soft)
1 c. honey
2 eggs
2 c. whole wheat flour
2 tsp. baking powder
½ tsp. salt

½ c. milk
1 tsp. vanilla
2½ c. huckleberries
Sugar (for sprinkling tops of muffins)

Grease muffin pans or use paper baking cups. Preheat oven to 350°. In bowl, cream margarine and honey until fluffy. Add eggs, one at a time, beating well. Combine flour, baking powder, and salt. Add alternately to creamed mixture with milk and vanilla. Crush ½ cup berries and add to batter. Fold remaining berries and spoon into pan. Sprinkle with sugar. Bake for 30 minutes. Makes 18 muffins.

JoAnne Sherman, Branch No. 1393, Kalispell, MT

NEVER-FAIL BUNS

To 3 cups of lukewarm water, add:

½ c. white sugar   1½ tsp. salt
2 pkg. yeast

When yeast rises to top, add:

4 eggs, well beaten   10 c. flour
½ c. vegetable oil

Mix and knead well. Let rise to double in size, about 2 hours. Punch down and let rise again. Make into buns. Place on greased pan and let rise for 1 hour or until light. Bake at 375° for 20 minutes (I bake mine longer). When removed from oven, brush tops with melted butter. When thoroughly cool, store in plastic bags. Freeze well.

Mrs. Margaret Greiner, Branch No. 2838, Wilmot, SD

DINNER ROLLS

1 c. milk, scalded   2 Tbsp. melted butter
¼ c. warm water   ¼ c. sugar
1 oz. yeast, dissolved in water and 1 egg, beaten
    ¼ tsp. sugar   About 4 c. flour
1 tsp. salt

When milk is cool, add beaten egg, butter, yeast, sugar, and salt to flour. Beat well. Let rise once until double. Put in pans. Let rise again. Shape as desired. Bake at 350° for 15 minutes. Makes about 18 rolls.

Helen Krueger, Branch No. 817, Sturgeon Bay, WI

QUICK AND EASY ROLLS

2 c. whole wheat flour   1 c. plain yogurt
2 to 2½ c. unbleached white flour   ¾ c. water
2 pkg. yeast   ½ c. butter or margarine
1 tsp. salt   ¼ c. honey
½ tsp. soda

Combine whole wheat flour, yeast, salt, and soda in mixing bowl. Stir together yogurt, water, butter or margarine, and honey. Warm over low heat or in microwave until very warm. Add to yeast mixture and mix until blended, then beat on medium speed for 2 minutes. Add remaining flour (enough to make a soft dough). Knead for several minutes or use dough hooks on mixer for 2 minutes.

Cover with plastic wrap and a towel; let rise for 20 minutes in a warm place. Uncover and punch dough down. Divide in half. Shape rolls to fit 2 greased 8 inch pans. Cover and let rise for 20 minutes. Bake at 400° for 15 to 20 minutes.

Note: This recipe makes very good communion bread if baked in 2 round loaves instead of rolls.

Linda Olson, Branch No. 5285, Madison, WI

APPLE MUFFINS

2 c. flour
½ tsp. salt
4 tsp. baking powder
¼ c. sugar
¾ tsp. cinnamon

¼ tsp. nutmeg
1 egg, beaten
1 c. milk
⅓ c. salad oil
¾ c. peeled, chopped apple

Combine dry ingredients. Combine egg, milk and salad oil; add dry ingredients and mix just to moisten. Add chopped apple and mix well. Fill greased muffin pans ⅔ full. Bake at 375° for 25 minutes. Yield: 1 dozen.

Margaret Smeyak, Branch No. 3819, Oviedo, FL

ZUCCHINI-NUT MUFFINS

2 c. Bisquick baking mix
¾ c. packed brown sugar
¼ c. vegetable oil
3 eggs
2 tsp. ground cinnamon

1 tsp. ground nutmeg
1 tsp. vanilla
¼ tsp. ground cloves
1½ c. shredded zucchini
½ c. chopped nuts

Heat oven to 400°. Grease bottoms only of 16 muffin cups, 2½ x 1¼ inches, or line with paper baking cups. Mix baking mix, brown sugar, oil, eggs, cinnamon, nutmeg, vanilla, and cloves. Beat vigorously for 30 seconds. Stir in zucchini and nuts. Fill muffin cups about ⅔ full. Bake until golden brown, about 15 minutes. Makes 16 to 20 muffins.

High altitude directions (3500 to 6500 feet): Heat oven to 425°.

Gloria Byrd, Santa Maria, CA

CORN-OATS GRIDDLE CAKES

1 egg
2 Tbsp. oil
1¼ c. buttermilk
½ c. corn meal
½ c. quick cooking rolled oats

¼ c. flour
½ tsp. soda
1½ tsp. baking powder
Salt

Beat egg. Add oil, buttermilk, corn meal, and oats. Stir together well. Let stand for 10 to 15 minutes. Mix flour, soda, baking powder, and salt. Add to first mixture and stir until just blended. Bake on hot griddle. Flour amount may be adjusted according to how thick you want them to be.

Eileen Larson, Branch No. 5325, Stratford, IA

PINEAPPLE ZUCCHINI BREAD

3 eggs
1 c. oil
2 c. sugar
1 tsp. vanilla
2 tsp. soda
1 tsp. salt
1 (8½ oz.) crushed pineapple, well
    drained

3 c. flour
1½ tsp. cinnamon
½ tsp. baking powder
1 c. nuts
¾ tsp. nutmeg
2 c. shredded zucchini

Beat eggs. Add oil, sugar and vanilla. Mix well. Add remaining ingredients and mix well. Pour into greased and floured bread pans. Bake at 350° for 45 to 60 minutes depending on pan size.

Cream Cheese Frosting:

3 oz. cream cheese
½ c. butter
1 tsp. vanilla

1½ tsp. milk
¾ tsp. cinnamon
4 c. powdered sugar

Mix together all ingredients. Frost cooled bread.

Lois McDermed, Branch No. 3412, Commerce City, CO

WHOLE WHEAT FREEZE BREAD

8 c. flour
3 c. whole wheat flour
1 c. wheat germ
½ c. brown sugar
2 tsp. salt

4 c. milk
1 c. water
½ c. butter
2 Tbsp. yeast

Mix as usual bread. Divide dough as you wish and freeze. Can be kept for 4 weeks or can bake right away at 375°.

Alvena Eckert, Branch No. 5985, Midland, SD

BANANA-WHEAT QUICK BREAD

1¼ c. all-purpose flour
½ c. whole wheat flour
1 c. sugar
1 tsp. soda
1 tsp. salt
1½ c. (3 medium) mashed
    bananas

¼ c. margarine or butter, softened
2 Tbsp. orange juice
¼ tsp. lemon juice
1 egg
¼ or ½ c. raisins

Heat oven to 325°. Grease and flour bottom of a loaf pan. In large bowl, blend all ingredients and beat for an additional 3 minutes at medium speed. Pour batter into prepared pan. Bake for 60 to 70 minutes or until toothpick inserted in center comes out clean. Remove from pan immediately. Cool.

Jewell Bork, Branch No. 5985, Midland, SD

SWEDISH OATMEAL BREAD

2 c. quick oatmeal
2 c. boiling water
⅓ c. shortening
½ c. molasses

1 Tbsp. salt
1 pkg. yeast
1½ c. warm water
6 to 7 c. flour (or more)

Combine in large bowl the oats, molasses, shortening, salt, and boiling water. Blend well and cool to lukewarm. Add the yeast which is softened in warm water. Gradually add flour to form a stiff dough. Knead for 10 minutes. Place in greased bowl and let rise until doubled, about 2 hours. Punch down and let rise again for 30 minutes. Place dough on floured board. Divide in 3 parts. Let rise for 15 minutes. Shape into 3 loaves. Let rise until doubled. Bake at 350° for 40 minutes. Makes 3 loaves.

Mrs. Lawrence Greiner, Branch No. 2838, Wilmot, SD

ZUCCHINI BREAD

3 eggs, beaten
1 c. oil
2 c. sugar
2 c. pureed zucchini
2 tsp. vanilla
3 c. flour

1 tsp. soda
½ tsp. baking powder
1 tsp. salt
1 tsp. cinnamon
½ c. nuts

Mix together all dry ingredients. Add all liquids. Mix together thoroughly. Place in 2 greased pans. Bake for 1 hour at 325°.

Barb Sheets, Branch No. 5844, Columbia City, IN

NOTTINGHAM BREAD

½ c. oleo
¾ c. sugar
1 egg
1 tsp. vanilla
½ tsp. salt
1 tsp. soda

2 c. dates
1 c. water
1 c. raisins
1 c. nutmeats
2 c. flour

Heat oven to 350°. Cut dates into pieces and add water. Bring to a boil. Cool. Cream oleo and sugar. Add egg, raisins, nutmeats, and vanilla. Sift flour, salt, and soda. Add alternately with date mixture. Mix thoroughly. Bake for 1 hour. Makes 4 small loaves.

Luella Ittner, Branch No. 2232, Auburn, MI

WHOLE WHEAT CHEESE BREAD

1¼ c. whole wheat flour
1¼ c. all-purpose flour
⅓ c. firmly packed brown sugar
1 tsp. baking powder
1 tsp. baking soda
½ tsp. salt
2 c. shredded Cheddar cheese
1 c. chopped pecans
2 tsp. grated orange peel
1¼ c. milk
¼ c. butter or margarine, melted
¼ c. light molasses
1 egg, slightly beaten

Preheat oven to 350°F. Combine dry ingredients in large mixing bowl. Stir in cheese, nuts and orange peel. Combine milk, butter, molasses, and egg. Stir liquid ingredients into dry ingredients, stirring just until they are blended. Spread batter evenly in buttered 9½ x 5½ inch loaf pan. Bake for 55 to 60 minutes or until a knife inserted in center comes out clean. Let rest in pan for 10 minutes. Remove and cool for at least 1½ hours on a wire rack. Serve warm with butter.

Sally J. Smith, Branch No. 2232, Midland, MI

CHOCOLATE ZUCCHINI BREAD

1 c. brown sugar
1 c. sugar
½ c. margarine
½ c. oil
3 eggs
1 tsp. vanilla
¾ c. buttermilk
3 c. flour
1 tsp. cinnamon
½ tsp. salt
2¼ tsp. baking soda
5 Tbsp. cocoa
2½ c. grated zucchini
½ c. milk chocolate chips
½ c. raisins
½ c. chopped nuts (optional)

Beat sugar, oil and margarine until dissolved. Add eggs, one at a time. Add buttermilk and vanilla. Sift all dry ingredients. Add to batter alternately with zucchini. Fold in chips, raisins and nuts. Pour into greased 9x13 inch pan. Bake at 350° for 1 hour. *Improves with freezing.*

Sadie Jackson, Branch No. 4817, Youngstown, OH

HEARTY OATS AND WHEAT BREAD

1¾ c. lukewarm water
½ c. honey
½ c. butter
2 eggs
3 pkg. dry yeast
2 to 2½ c. bread flour
1 c. rolled oats
2 c. whole wheat flour
⅓ c. sesame seeds

Combine water, honey, butter, eggs, and yeast. Butter does not need to melt. Let set to dissolve yeast. Add remaining ingredients. Mix in mixer with dough hook or knead by hand, about 5 to 10 minutes until elastic. Dough will be soft. Place in greased bowl. Cover and let rise until double, 45 minutes to 1 hour. Punch down and divide. Pat into 2 loaves. Place in greased 9x5x3 inch bread pan. Let rise for 45 minutes to 1 hour. Bake at 350° for 30 to 40 minutes. Makes 2 loaves.

Mrs. Carol (Richard) Wehland, Branch No. 4188, Beaver Dam, WI

NUTS AND SEEDS BREAD

1½ c. flour
½ c. whole wheat flour
1 tsp. baking powder
1 tsp. baking soda
½ tsp. salt
1 c. lightly packed brown sugar
½ c. chopped nuts

2 Tbsp. wheat germ
2 Tbsp. sesame seeds
2 Tbsp. poppy seeds
1 egg, beaten
1 c. buttermilk
¼ c. oil

Combine all dry ingredients and mix thoroughly. Combine egg, buttermilk and oil. Add to dry ingredients and stir together just until blended. Turn into greased 9x5 inch loaf pan. Bake at 350° for 1 hour.

Mrs. Robert Eldridge, Branch No. 2320, Fowler, MI

POPPY SEED BREAD

3 eggs
2¼ c. sugar
1½ c. milk
1¼ c. cooking oil
3 c. flour
1½ tsp. salt

1½ tsp. baking powder
1½ tsp. almond flavoring
1½ tsp. vanilla
1½ tsp. butter flavoring
1½ tsp. poppy seeds

Mix all ingredients for 2 minutes with electric mixer. Pour into 2 greased loaf pans. Bake for 1 hour at 350° or until toothpick comes out clean. Top of bread will crack. When bread is done, remove from pans.

Frost while warm with:

¼ c. orange juice
½ c. sugar
½ tsp. butter flavoring

½ tsp. almond flavoring
½ tsp. vanilla

Betty Evans, Branch No. 06439, Madison, WI

APPLE SWIRL BREAD

3¾ to 4¼ c. all-purpose flour
1 (1 layer size) pkg. white cake mix
1 pkg. active dry yeast
1¼ c. warm water (120° to 130°)
½ tsp. salt
1 egg
2½ c. finely chopped, peeled apple

⅓ c. sugar
⅓ c. finely chopped pecans
   (optional)
1 or 2 tsp. cinnamon
2 or 3 Tbsp. melted butter or
   margarine

In a large mixer bowl, combine 1½ cups flour, cake mix and yeast. Combine water and salt; add to flour mixture. Add egg. Beat with electric mixer on low speed for 30 seconds. Beat at high speed for 3 minutes. Using a spoon, stir in as much remaining flour as you can. Turn dough out onto a lightly floured surface. Knead in enough flour to make a moderately stiff dough that is smooth and elastic (6 to 8 minutes).

Place in lightly greased bowl; turn once to grease surface. Cover and let rise until double (about 1½ hours). Punch dough down; divide in half. Cover and let rise for 10 minutes.

Meanwhile, stir together apple, sugar, pecans, and cinnamon. On a lightly floured surface, roll half of the dough into a 12x8 inch rectangle. Brush surface with some margarine. Sprinkle with half of the apple mixture. Roll up jelly roll style, beginning at narrow end. Seal edge and ends. Place in greased 8x4x3 inch loaf pan. Brush top with margarine. Repeat with remaining dough. Cover and let rise until nearly double (about 1½ hours). Bake in a 375° oven for about 35 minutes or until top is golden. Remove from pans immediately. Cool on wire rack.

Mrs. Howard Mueller, Branch No. 1137, Pocahontas, MO

COMMUNION BREAD

2 c. whole wheat flour
½ c. white flour
¾ tsp. soda
¾ tsp. salt

3 Tbsp. shortening
1 scant c. water
3 Tbsp. honey

Mix the dry ingredients well. (Be sure to sift them.) Add shortening and blend well. Add the water and the honey. Knead until you have a good texture. You can spread the dough into a pan or you can roll it flat with a rolling pin, then place it into a pan. Divide the dough into about 5 balls and roll each one less than ½ inch thick and 5 or 6 inches in diameter. Make a cross design on dough with a fork. Place on greased cookie sheet and bake at 350° for 10 to 12 minutes.

Doris Holste, Branch No. 4453, Hays, KS

WHOLE WHEAT BREAD

2 pkg. dry yeast
½ c. warm water
2 c. buttermilk
½ c. oleo
½ c. honey

¼ tsp. soda
1 tsp. salt
3 eggs
3 c. whole wheat flour
5 c. white flour

Dissolve yeast in warm water. Heat oleo and buttermilk until oleo melts. In large bowl, combine honey, soda, salt, and eggs. Add buttermilk mixture and yeast; stir well. Slowly add whole wheat flour, mixing with fork, then add white flour, a little at a time, until you must use your hands.

When dough becomes soft and satiny, knead 10 minutes. Place in greased bowl. Cover with plastic wrap and towel. Let rise until double (1 hour). Punch down. Let rise again. Turn on floured board. Knead lightly. Make into loaves. Let rise until double, about 45 minutes. Bake in 350° oven for 35 to 45 minutes.

Lucille Hejtmanek, Branch No. 1149, Leigh, NE

POPPY SEED BREAD

3 c. flour, sifted
1½ tsp. salt
1½ tsp. baking powder
2½ c. sugar
3 eggs
1½ c. milk

1 c. + 2 Tbsp. salad oil
3 Tbsp. poppy seed
1½ tsp. vanilla
1½ tsp. almond flavoring
1½ tsp. butter flavoring

Glaze:

3 c. powdered sugar
¼ c. fresh orange juice
½ tsp. vanilla

½ tsp. almond flavoring
½ tsp. butter flavoring

Add ingredients into mixer bowl in the order given. Beat for 2 minutes. Bake in 2 large loaf pans or 4 smaller ones. Use a 350° oven and watch carefully for 55 minutes; may take less time for small pans. Do not overbake.

Mix glaze while bread bakes. Remove bread from pans and immediately glaze. As they cool, reapply glaze.

Caroline Geisert, Branch No. 1412, Corvallis, OR

QUICK CINNAMON BREAD

½ c. shortening
2 eggs
1 c. sugar
1 tsp. vanilla

1 c. buttermilk
2 c. flour
1 tsp. soda
1 tsp. baking powder

Topping:

¼ c. sugar
1 Tbsp. cinnamon

¼ c. walnuts or pecans

Mix shortening, eggs, sugar, vanilla, and buttermilk. Sift flour, soda, and baking powder together; add to first mixture. Pour ½ of the batter in greased loaf pan and sprinkle with most of the cinnamon mixture. Pour remaining batter over topping mix and then the remaining cinnamon mix. Swirl through batter with knife. Bake at 350° for 60 minutes.

Edna Lundquist, Branch No. 5325, Stratford, IA

MEXICAN CORN BREAD
(Mississippi style)

1 c. corn meal
½ tsp. baking soda
½ tsp. salt
2 eggs
1 can green chillies

¼ c. cooking oil
1 c. chopped onion
3 cloves garlic
1 can creamed corn
1 c. grated Cheddar cheese

338

Place last 7 ingredients in blender. Blend. Add dry corn meal, soda and salt; mix. Pour into 10x15 inch pan. Bake at 425° for 30 to 35 minutes.

Note: Moist and also good cold.

Jean Fadler, Branch No. 2568, Fredericktown, MO

FESTIVE HOLIDAY BREAD

1½ c. flour	2 lb. whole pitted dates
1 tsp. baking powder	1 (8 oz.) maraschino cherries,
5 eggs	drained
1½ c. sugar	1 lb. Brazil nuts
1 tsp. salt	1 lb. English walnuts

Mix dry ingredients and eggs. Add uncut dates, cherries, and nuts. Pour into 3 greased bread pans. Bake at 325° for 1 hour.

Betty Eilers, Branch No. 1128, Webster City, IA

TOASTED BUTTER PECAN LOAF

1 c. sugar	2 eggs
½ c. milk	1 tsp. vanilla
1½ tsp. baking powder	1½ c. flour
½ tsp. salt	3 Tbsp. butter
½ c. pecans	1 c. 10X sugar
½ c. butter, cut into 10 pieces	2 to 3 tsp. milk

Grease and flour one 9x5 inch loaf pan. Brown 3 tablespoons butter and pecans in small saucepan. Drain nuts and save butter. In food processor, process 1 cup sugar, ½ cup milk, 1½ teaspoons baking powder, ½ teaspoon salt, ½ cup butter, 2 eggs, 1 teaspoon vanilla, and toasted pecans for 30 seconds. Add flour and process for 5 seconds.

Pour into pan and bake at 350° for 50 to 60 minutes. Cool completely. Mix saved butter, 1 cup 10X sugar, and 2 to 3 teaspoons milk. Spread on cake.

Dee Fritz, Branch No. 5776, Mount Joy, PA

YELLOW BREAD

1 pkg. yellow cake mix (dry - Duncan Hines)	1 pkg. instant vanilla pudding mix (dry)

Stir together and add:

4 eggs	1 tsp. vanilla extract
¾ c. warm tap water	1 tsp. butter extract

Mix for 5 minutes on high with electric mixer. Layer in 2 greased and floured bread pans with 3 tablespoons sugar and 1 teaspoon cinnamon. (Begin and end with batter.) Bake for 40 minutes at 350°.

This bread is very easy to make - not real sweet. Very good with a cup of coffee! By far the best recipe I've had in 35 years of cooking!!

Janis Erlandson (Mrs. Merle), Branch No. 4730, Fergus Falls, MN

SHEPHERD'S BREAD

7 c. flour
¼ c. honey
1 c. milk
¼ c. butter

1 Tbsp. salt
2 pkg. dry yeast
1½ c. warm water

Mix flour, salt, honey, and yeast. Combine the milk, water and butter. Heat over low heat until warm. Gradually add liquid mixture to dry ingredients and beat with electric mixer on medium speed for 2 minutes. If still sticky, add additional flour to make soft dough. Knead on lightly floured board for 8 to 10 minutes or until smooth and rubbery to the touch.

Shape into large ball and place into greased bowl. Cover and let rise until double in bulk. Punch down and let rise again, 15 minutes. Divide dough. Shape into 2 round balls. Place on baking sheet. Let rise again until double in bulk and bake at 400° for 30 minutes.

Betty Urbanek, Branch No. 4570, Andrews, TX

DAKOTA BREAD

1 pkg. active dry yeast
½ c. warm water (105° to 115°)
2 Tbsp. sunflower oil
1 egg
½ c. cottage cheese
¼ c. honey
1 tsp. salt

2 to 2½ c. bread flour
½ c. whole wheat flour
¼ c. wheat germ
¼ c. rye flour
¼ c. rolled oats
Corn meal

Sprinkle yeast in warm water; stir to dissolve. In a large bowl, mix sunflower oil, egg, cottage cheese, honey, and salt. Add dissolved yeast and 2 cups bread flour, beating until flour is moistened. Gradually stir in whole wheat flour, wheat germ, rye flour, and oats, plus enough bread flour to make a soft dough. On a floured surface, knead dough for 10 minutes or until dough is smooth and elastic.

Place dough in greased bowl, covered loosely with oiled plastic wrap. Let rise in warm place until doubled in size, about 30 minutes. Punch down dough. Shape into 1 round loaf. Place in a greased pan and sprinkle with corn meal. Cover with oiled plastic wrap and let rise until double in size, about 1 hour.

Brush with egg white and sprinkle with wheat germ, sunflower seeds, and/ or oatmeal. Bake at 350° for 35 to 40 minutes. If too dark, cover loosely with foil the last 10 to 15 minutes of baking.

Marlys Russett, Branch No. 5980, Arlington, SD

DATE BREAD

1 c. dates, cut up
½ c. chopped nutmeats

3 Tbsp. melted butter
1 tsp. soda

Put these ingredients into bowl. Pour 1 cup boiling water over all.

With electric mixer, mix together, adding one at a time (the following):

1 c. sugar   1 tsp. vanilla
2 beaten eggs   1½ c. flour

Add the date mixture. Pour into well greased and lined loaf pan or two small pans. Bake in a 350° oven for approximately 1 hour.

Dorothy Tiedeman, Branch No. 6330, Beresford, SD

BROWN BREAD (OR DATE BREAD)

1 (6½ oz.) dates (or 8 oz.)   2 beaten eggs
3 tsp. soda   4 c. sifted flour
2 c. boiling water   1 tsp. salt
2 Tbsp. butter   2 tsp. vanilla
2 c. sugar   ½ c. nuts, chopped

Chop dates and cover with cold water. Cook until mushy, about 10 minutes. Do not drain. Add soda, boiling water and butter. Let cool. Add remaining ingredients. Grease six No. 2 cans and fill a little less than half full or use 8 soup cans. Bake at 325° for 1¼ hours. Baking time depends on size of cans used. (When top of bread is golden brown and pops up after tapping, it is done or use toothpick method.) Bread baked in soup cans gets done in about 30 minutes.

Make a mixture of cream cheese and salad dressing (just enough dressing to add zip to the cream cheese) and spread on rounds of bread (optional), but oh, so scrumptious!

Priscilla Scholl, Branch No. 2150, Tomball, TX

FINNISH CHRISTMAS RYE BREAD OR JOULULIMPPU

2 c. rye flour   ½ c. oil
1 qt. mashed potatoes   ½ c. sugar
2 c. potato water   3 Tbsp. salt
1 large cake fresh yeast or 1 oz.   1 Tbsp. anise seed
   dry yeast, dissolved in ¼ c.   1 c. golden raisins
   water (warm)   2 c. rye flour
1½ c. dark molasses   18 to 20 c. all-purpose flour
5 c. warm water

In large bowl, combine 2 cups rye flour with the mashed potatoes, potato water and yeast. Stir and cover. Let stand at room temperature for 2 days. Stir in molasses, warm water, oil, sugar, salt, anise, raisins, and rye flour. Add all-purpose flour to make a stiff dough. Turn out onto floured surface and knead until dough loses its stickiness. Place into greased bowl and let rise in a warm place until doubled. Shape into loaf or round pans. Let rise until doubled. Bake at 375°F. for about 40 to 50 minutes or until loaf sounds hollow when tapped. Makes 9 to 10 loaves.

Donna Saari, Branch No. 6035, Maple, WI

STOLLEN

1 pkg. dry yeast
¼ c. warm water
1 c. milk
½ c. butter (or margarine)
¼ c. sugar
1 tsp. salt

¼ tsp. cardamon
1½ c. white raisins
¼ c. candied fruit (optional)
¼ c. slivered almonds
1 Tbsp. orange rind
Flour

Mix the yeast and warm water; scald the milk. Remove from heat and add the butter, sugar and salt. *Cool.* Add the yeast and remaining ingredients. Knead in enough flour to make a stiff dough. Let rise, punch down and put in 3 small bread tins. Let rise until doubled in bulk. Bake at 350° for 30 minutes. Frost with powdered sugar frosting.

St. Peter's Ev. Lutheran Church, Moltke Township, Gibbon, MN

FINNISH COFFEE BREAD - NISUA

2 pkg. yeast
2 c. milk
1 c. sugar
1 cube butter

1 tsp. salt
3 eggs, beaten
7½ c. flour
2 tsp. cardamom

Heat milk to scalding point (do not boil). Add sugar, butter, and salt; cool to lukewarm. Add yeast, dissolved in a little warm water (about ½ cup). Don't mix yeast until milk is lukewarm. Put yeast into milk mixture. Add eggs, about 1½ cups flour and cardamom; beat with a mixer real well. Add a little more flour until it is spongy, but doesn't come up the beater. Take beaters out and knead in enough flour to handle easily, but not too stiff. Be sure to get flour on bottom mixed in.

When still a little tacky, put butter on your hands and knead a little more. It will stop it from getting too stiff and handle easily. Grease bowl and put back in bowl. Cover and let rise in warm place until a little more than double; knead a little. Make into small loaves and let set for about 5 minutes. Make into loaves or braids and let rise until double or light. Bake in a 375° oven for about 40 minutes. Take about ½ cup hot water; add 1 teaspoon oleo and about 1 tablespoon sugar. Brush on top while still hot and lightly sprinkle with sugar.

If making in jelly roll form, spread with melted butter and sprinkle with a mixture of cinnamon, about ½ cup sugar and 1½ teaspoons cinnamon. Roll up.

For braids, put sugar and cinnamon on board; roll in sugar and cinnamon. Braid. Pinch and tuck under both ends. Braid loosely. Makes 3 loaves.

Mrs. John (Maxine) Johansen, Branch No. 3365, Rock Springs, WY

YULEKAKE - NORWEGIAN CHRISTMAS BREAD

4 pkg. yeast
4 c. scalded milk
1⅓ c. margarine, melted
2 c. granulated sugar
4 eggs, beaten

4 tsp. salt
3 Tbsp. cardamom, freshly ground
14 c. sifted flour
4 c. seedless raisins
1⅓ c. finely cut citron

In bowl, combine milk, margarine and sugar; stir well. Cool until lukewarm. Add eggs, salt and cardamom. Stir in 8 cups flour to which the yeast has been added. Beat until smooth. Add raisins and citron; stir in remaining 6 cups flour. Mix well. Cover and let rise in warm place until double in bulk, about 2 ½ to 3 hours. Punch down and let rise until double again.

Turn out onto lightly floured board; knead lightly. Form into 4 loaves and place in greased pan. Let rise for 15 minutes. Grease top of loaves and bake in a 325° oven for 20 minutes and then for 40 minutes in a 300° oven. Grease loaves with margarine when they come out of the oven.

Mrs. John (Maxine) Johansen, Branch No. 3365, Rock Springs, WY

PEANUT BUTTER TEA RING

1 Tbsp. dry yeast
½ c. warm water
1 Tbsp. sugar
1 c. milk, scalded and cooled some
2 eggs, beaten

½ c. sugar (scant)
⅓ c. oil or shortening
1 tsp. salt
3½ to 4 c. flour

Filling:

1 c. cream style peanut butter
¼ c. sugar

Raisins (optional)

Topping:

Powdered sugar frosting

Chopped peanuts

Soak yeast in the warm water and sugar in mixing bowl for 5 minutes. Stir in a little of the flour to make a paste. Add warm milk, beaten eggs and remaining ingredients. Mix by hand until blended. Knead on floured board until elastic. Put in buttered bowl and let rise for 1 hour in a warm place.

Roll dough into rectangle ¼ inch thick. Spread with peanut butter. Sprinkle with sugar and raisins. Roll up lengthwise and place on buttered cookie sheet, joining ends to form a circle. With scissors, cut through the roll within an inch of the bottom. Let rise for about 45 minutes. Bake at 350° for 30 to 35 minutes.

While warm, spread the top only with powdered sugar frosting, allowing it to trickle down sides. Sprinkle with chopped peanuts. Serve warm. *Enjoy!*

Emma Gaub Haevischer, Branch No. 3017, Portland, OR

CINNAMON ROLLS

3½ to 4 c. flour
1 pkg. yeast
1¼ c. milk
¼ c. sugar

¼ c. shortening (Crisco)
1 tsp. salt
1 egg

In a mixing bowl, combine 1½ cups flour and yeast. Heat milk, sugar, shortening, and salt in a pan until warm (115° to 120°), stirring constantly. Add to dry mixture and add egg. Beat at low speed of electric mixer for ½ minute, scraping the bowl. Beat for 3 minutes at high speed.

With dough hooks or by hand, stir in remaining flour to make a soft dough. Add enough flour so you can pinch the dough and it won't stick to your fingers. Shape into a ball, place in lightly greased bowl, and flip once in bowl. Cover with a towel and place in a warm place until doubled in size. Punch down and let rise for 10 more minutes. Flour table and shape into desired rolls. Bake for 20 to 25 minutes in a 350° oven. Makes 2 to 3 dozen rolls.

Caramel Sauce (optional):

½ c. maple syrup
½ c. brown sugar

¼ c. margarine
¼ tsp. maple flavoring

Heat together in microwave on HIGH for 1 minute. Mix well and pour into 9x13 inch pan for caramel rolls. Pour sauce in first and rolls on top.

Carol Kirchner, Branch No. 615, Grand Island, NE

QUICK CARAMEL ROLLS
(Easy for children)

1 tube buttermilk biscuits
½ stick margarine
½ c. brown sugar

Walnuts or pecans
Maple syrup

Melt margarine in ring pan in microwave (30 seconds to 1 minute on HIGH). May use glass pie pan with drinking glass in center. Sprinkle nuts and brown sugar over margarine. Arrange biscuits evenly around the ring. Pour a little maple syrup over the biscuits. Microwave on HIGH for 2 minutes. Turn ring ½ turn; microwave for 2 minutes more till biscuits feel dry on top. (If not done, add 30 seconds more.)

Invert pan over a plate. Let rest for 1 minute before removing.

Vivian Merkel, Branch No. 3984, Washburn, ND

SCANDINAVIAN CINNAMON COFFEE ROLLS

4 c. flour
¼ c. sugar
1 tsp. salt
1 c. margarine, softened

1 pkg. dry yeast, dissolved in ¼ c.
very warm water
3 egg yolks, beaten
1 c. milk, scalded and cooled

Mix all ingredients and store overnight in refrigerator. Divide dough in half and roll each half into 12x10 inch rectangle. Brush each with melted butter and sprinkle with ¼ cup sugar and ¾ teaspoon cinnamon. Roll up and cut in 1 inch slices. Let rise for 1 hour. Bake in a 375° oven for about 20 to 25 minutes.

Frosting:

1½ c. powdered sugar
3 Tbsp. margarine, softened

½ tsp. vanilla
2 Tbsp. hot water

Combine all ingredients and frost rolls.

Leona Zander, Branch No. 3619, Waverly, IA

344

STOLLEN OR CHRISTMAS LOAF

2 pkg. dry yeast or 1½ cakes
   compressed yeast
1½ c. water or milk, scalded and
   cooled
6 c. all-purpose flour, sifted before
   measuring
½ lb. raisins
½ lb. blanched, chopped almonds
½ c. chopped candied citron (red
   and green, or other candied
   fruit)

¾ c. sugar, sifted
1½ c. butter, softened
3 eggs
¾ tsp. salt
¾ tsp. grated lemon rind
2 Tbsp. brandy or rum (or several
   drops of rum extract)
Melted butter

Have all ingredients at about 75°. Dissolve yeast in lukewarm (85°F.) water or milk, about 10 minutes. Add 1 cup of the flour. Permit this sponge to rise in a warm place until doubled in bulk. Sprinkle a little of the sifted flour over the nuts and fruits. Set aside. Beat the butter in a large bowl until very soft. Add the sugar gradually, blending until light and creamy. Beat the eggs in one at a time. Add the salt, lemon rind and brandy or extract.

Add the sponge and remaining flour. Knead the dough until smooth and elastic. Permit it to rise until almost doubled in bulk. Toss it onto a floured board and knead in the fruits and nuts.

Divide into 2 loaves and place them in greased pans. Brush tops with melted butter. Let the loaves rise, covered, until they again almost double in bulk. Preheat oven to 350°. Bake the loaves for about 45 minutes. When cool, they may be dusted with confectioners sugar or iced with confectioners sugar icing.

These should be aged one day before cutting and eating. Store, tightly covered. May be frozen for up to 2 months.

Rev. Fred Mildenburger, Branch No. 2413, Dudleytown, IN

MAMMOTH PECAN BRAID

1 pkg. dry yeast
¼ c. warm water
½ c. sugar
½ c. margarine
½ tsp. salt
1 c. milk, scalded
5 c. flour
1 egg, well beaten

¾ c. margarine, softened
1½ c. powdered sugar
1 tsp. vanilla
1 c. chopped pecans
2 Tbsp. orange juice
½ tsp. vanilla
2 c. powdered sugar
Pecan halves

Dissolve yeast in the water in a measuring cup. Set aside for 5 to 10 minutes. Put the sugar, margarine and salt in large bowl. Pour in hot milk. Cool to lukewarm, stirring until margarine is melted. Beat in 1 cup flour until smooth. Add yeast. Beat in 2 cups flour until very smooth. Beat in the egg. Beat in the remaining 2 cups flour to make a soft dough.

Turn dough onto floured board. Let rest for 10 minutes. Knead smooth. Place in greased bowl; turn dough over. Cover and let rise for 2 hours. Punch down. Turn onto floured board. Let rest for 10 minutes. Divide in half. Roll each half into a 9x18 inch rectangle. Cut each into 3 long strips.

Mix the ¾ cup margarine, 1½ cups powdered sugar and 1 teaspoon vanilla. Mix in the chopped pecans. Spread 1/6 of this filling over each of the strips, leaving a little margin on one long edge. Roll each strip lengthwise, sealing edges *well*. Braid in thirds. Leave in 2 braids or shape into 1 large or 2 small wreaths. Place on greased baking sheet. Let rise for 30 minutes. Bake at 350° for 25 minutes. Frost with next 3 ingredients. Decorate with pecan halves.

Mrs. Robert Bishop (or Joyce Bishop), Branch No. 441, Bloomington, IL

SWEET BUNS

2 qt. milk (whole)	2 c. sugar
4 pkg. yeast	8 tsp. salt
2 tsp. sugar	2 c. oil (Mazola)
1 c. water	22 c. flour (approx.)
6 eggs	

Scald 2 quarts milk. Add sugar (2 cups), salt and oil. While this mixture cools down, set the yeast, sugar (2 teaspoons) and 1 cup water to dissolve. Add eggs to milk mixture; stir in some flour. Add risen yeast mixture. Add flour until the dough still has some stickiness to it, being careful not to get too much flour in (which makes for not so light buns or bread). Cover and let rise until double (1 hour). Punch down. Let rise again. Form into buns. Let rise for 1½ to 2 hours. Bake at 350° until buns are golden brown. Makes about 144 buns.

Arlene E. Knutson, Branch No. 5616, Tuttle, ND

SWEDISH COFFEE ROLL

½ c. scalded milk	½ cake or 1 pkg. dry yeast,
Salt	dissolved in warm water (½
½ c. sugar	c.) with 1 tsp. sugar
½ c. oleo	3 to 4 c. flour
2 eggs	

Pour scalded milk over softened oleo, salt and sugar. Cool to lukewarm. Add dissolved yeast and beaten eggs. Work in flour (enough to make a *soft* dough). Knead. Dough should be soft! Let rise till double in bulk. Roll out in a rectangular shape, thin as possible. Spread with oleo, brown sugar, cinnamon, and nuts. Roll from length side. Form in ring on baking sheet. Cut nearly through with scissors and let rise again. Bake in a 350° oven for 25 to 30 minutes (no more). Ice and sprinkle with nuts if desired.

Grace Ahlberg, Branch No. 5915, Lanse, PA

BOHEMIAN KOLACHES

¾ c. lard or butter
¾ c. sugar
3 eggs
1 oz. yeast

1 tsp. salt
2 c. water or scalded milk (milk takes longer to rise)
5½ to 6 c. flour

Pour hot milk (or water) over lard, sugar, and salt. Crumble yeast in little water. Cool milk to lukewarm, then add eggs and yeast. Beat with electric beater with 3 cups flour, about 3 minutes. Add remainder of flour; stir with a spoon. This will be a very soft dough. Let rise in warm place until double. With buttered hands, form small balls (size of a walnut or golf ball). Place on greased baking sheet. When double in size, make a depression in center and fill with either of the following fillings. Makes 5 dozen.

Filling Recipes for Kolaches -

Poppy Seed Filling:

1 can Solo poppy seed filling
1 egg, beaten
2 Tbsp. milk
1 graham cracker, crushed

1 Tbsp. vanilla
2 Tbsp. butter
3 Tbsp. brown sugar

Let come to boil in Teflon pan. Stir all the time. Makes enough filling for ½ recipe.

Prune Filling:

1 lb. pitted prunes, cooked and mashed or ground
1 tsp. cinnamon

1 c. sugar
½ tsp. salt

Cottage Cheese (to be used with Prune Filling):

1 ctn. cottage cheese
½ c. sugar
1 egg, beaten

Pinch of salt
1 Tbsp. corn starch

Cook until thick, stirring constantly. Put 1 teaspoon in center of Prune Filling. Bake at 375° for 15 to 18 minutes.

Olive Hoffmann, Branch No. 2323, Caroline, WI

CINNAMON ROLL TOPPING
(Microwave)

2 c. brown sugar
¼ c. milk
1 Tbsp. white vinegar
½ tsp. vanilla

½ tsp. rum extract
¼ c. white syrup
1 stick oleo
⅛ tsp. salt

Cook for 1 minute. *Cool.* Pour over sweet rolls and bake.
Betty Bierwagen, Branch No. 2672, Milesville, SD

WHOLE WHEAT MUFFINS
(No eggs used)

1 c. white flour
1 c. wheat flour
½ c. sugar
1 c. sour milk (add 1 Tbsp. vinegar
　　to 1 c. milk)

1 tsp. soda
½ tsp. salt
2 Tbsp. oil

Preheat oven to 350°. Grease 12 serving muffin pan. Mix dry ingredients (flour, sugar, salt, and soda). Add milk and oil. Stir until moistened. (Batter will be quite thick.) Spoon into greased muffin pan. Bake for 15 minutes until lightly browned. Serve warm.

These store well and can be reheated in microwave nicely, about 15 seconds for an individual muffin.

Paula Scheirer, Loveland, CO

GLAMOUR BREAD PUDDING

6 slices bread, cubed
2 c. milk
2 eggs
⅓ c. sugar
¼ tsp. salt

1 tsp. vanilla
⅓ c. brown sugar
1 Tbsp. milk
⅓ c. nuts

Place cubed bread in a 2 quart casserole. Scald milk. Beat 2 eggs. Add sugar, salt and vanilla. Stir milk into egg mixture, then pour over bread. Place casserole into a pan with 1 inch of water in the bottom. Bake at 350° for 1 hour or until set. Mix brown sugar, milk, and nuts; sprinkle over top and broil until lightly browned.

Leona Becher, Columbus, NE

BRUNCH APPLE KUCHEN

2 c. apples
1 c. sugar
½ c. brown sugar
1 c. shortening
2 eggs

1 c. sour milk
1 tsp. soda
½ tsp. baking powder
2 tsp. cinnamon
2½ c. flour

Topping:

½ c. sugar
¼ tsp. cinnamon

½ c. chopped nuts

Chop or shred apples; set aside. Stir soda into the sour milk and mix with all of the other ingredients. Add apples and pour into a 9x13 inch pan that has been greased. Sprinkle with topping and bake for 1 hour at 300°.

Doris Ruhs, Branch No. 3107, Loveland, CO

HOBO BREAD

2 c. seedless raisins
2 c. hot water

4 tsp. soda

Let set overnight.

2 c. sugar
4 Tbsp. oil or butter
1 c. nuts

4 c. flour
1 tsp. salt

Mix in well. Place in 3 greased 1 pound cans. Bake at 350° for 1 hour and at 325° for 10 to 15 minutes. Test with pick.

Rosella Hemmen, Loveland, CO

BEER BREAD

2 pkg. yeast
½ c. lukewarm water
¼ c. sugar
1½ tsp. salt

3 Tbsp. oil
1 (12 oz.) can warm beer
5 to 5½ c. flour
Corn meal

In large bowl, dissolve yeast in water. Stir in sugar, salt, oil, and warm beer. Stir in flour until dough is sticky. Beat until dough pulls away from spoon. Turn onto floured surface; knead until smooth and elastic. Put in greased bowl, turning to grease top. Cover and let rise till double (about 1 hour).

Knead dough briefly; make into 2 loaves. Sprinkle cookie sheet with corn meal. Place loaves on it. Cut 3 or 4 diagonal slashes across each loaf. Let rise till double. Bake at 375° for 30 to 35 minutes. Cool on rack.

Cheryl Schultz, Branch No. 3107, Loveland, CO

YELLOW SQUASH PUFFS

¾ lb. yellow squash, sliced
1 egg, beaten
⅓ c. all-purpose flour
⅓ c. corn meal

1 tsp. baking powder
½ tsp. salt
1 medium onion, grated
Oil

Cook squash, covered, in boiling water until tender. Drain and mash enough to measure 1 cup. Combine squash and egg; stir well. Combine flour, corn meal, baking powder, and salt; stir well. Add squash mixture and onion; stir until blended. Drop squash mixture by level tablespoons into hot oil. Cook until golden brown, turning once. *Drain well* on paper towel.

Doris Wohlschlegel, Branch No. 5425, Louisville, KY

SWEDISH BUTTER HORNS

1 cake yeast
1 Tbsp. sugar
¼ c. lukewarm water
1 c. margarine or butter
2½ c. flour

¼ tsp. salt
1 egg and 2 yolks
½ c. sugar
1 tsp. cinnamon
2 egg whites

Mix first 3 ingredients and let rise for 10 minutes. Mix next 3 ingredients like pie dough. Beat well 1 egg and 2 yolks; add to flour mixture. Stir well until smooth. Divide dough into 3 parts. Roll each as thin as possible. Mix sugar and cinnamon. Take 2 egg whites (beaten stiff) and spread over dough, then sprinkle with sugar and cinnamon. Cut into pie fashion. Roll each wedge as jelly roll. Put loosely into greased cookie sheet. Let stand in warm place for 20 minutes or so. Bake at 400° until light brown. Spread with frosting.

Jean Brockmann, Branch No. 64, Elkhorn, WI

FRENCH BREAD STICKS

3½ to 4 c. all-purpose flour,
    divided
2 tsp. salt
2 tsp. sugar
1 pkg. dry yeast
1¼ c. warm water (105° to 115°)

Corn meal
2 egg whites
2 Tbsp. water
Poppy seeds
Sesame seeds

Combine 1¼ cups flour, salt, sugar, and yeast in large bowl. Add 1¼ cups water and beat on low speed to combine. Beat for 3 minutes at high speed. Add remaining flour and mix or knead until dough is smooth and elastic. Place dough in lightly greased bowl and turn to coat all sides. Cover and let rise (85°), free from drafts, until double in bulk. Punch down. Cover and let rise again until double. Punch down; knead until smooth. Divide into 36 equal pieces. Roll each into 8 x ½ inch sticks. Place sticks 1 inch apart on well greased baking sheet. Sprinkle with corn meal.

Combine egg whites and 2 tablespoons water; beat lightly. Brush sticks with mixture. Let rise for about 50 minutes until double. Brush again; sprinkle with poppy or sesame seeds. Bake in oven at 400° and put pan of water on bottom shelf for 15 minutes. Brush again and bake for 10 to 12 minutes more, or until golden brown. Makes 3 dozen.

Mona Geidel, Branch No. 3107, Loveland, CO

ERNA'S CINNAMON BRAIDS

1 c. scalded milk
⅓ c. sugar
⅓ c. margarine
1 tsp. salt
2 eggs
2 c. wheat flour

2 pkg. dry yeast
½ c. warm water
1 Tbsp. sugar
White flour
1 Tbsp. cinnamon
½ c. sugar

Combine milk, ⅓ cup sugar, margarine, and salt. When cooled slightly, add eggs and wheat flour. Dissolve yeast in warm water and sugar. Add yeast mixture to dough and keep adding white flour until mixture is no longer sticky while you knead it. Let rise until double in bulk.

Punch down. Divide into 2 parts. Divide each part into thirds. Roll each third in the mixture of cinnamon and sugar. Make ropelike lengths of each third and braid. Place each braid on cooky sheet and let rise. Recipe makes 2 braids. Bake at 350° for 20 minutes.

Glaze braids with a mixture of margarine, powdered sugar and hot coffee. (Braids may be placed in loaf pans if preferred.)

Velma Swanson, Branch No. 3107, Loveland, CO

SAUSAGE BREAD

2 loaves frozen bread dough
1 (1 lb.) pkg. Bob Evans mild
  sausage
1 (8 oz.) pkg. shredded Mozzarella
  cheese
1 medium onion, chopped
1 small green pepper, chopped

Let dough rise. Roll out to ½ inch thickness on floured surface. Fry sausage. Crumble. Add green pepper and onion. Drain off grease. Sprinkle sausage mixture and shredded cheese on bread; roll. Bake at 350° for 25 to 35 minutes on greased cookie sheet.

Denise Blystone, Helen Kolb, Branch No. 4806, Sheffield, OH

ZUCCHINI NUT BREAD
(Low sugar - diabetic)

1 c. oil
½ c. honey
2 Tbsp. Sweet 'N Low liquid
  (equivalent of ½ c. sugar)
3 eggs
2 tsp. vanilla
3 c. flour*
1½ tsp. baking powder
1 tsp. soda
½ tsp. allspice
3 tsp. cinnamon
1 tsp. salt
3 c. finely grated, unpeeled
  zucchini
1½ c. finely grated carrots
1 c. raisins
¾ c. chopped nuts
¼ c. chopped sunflower seeds

Beat eggs until foamy. Add oil, honey, Sweet 'N Low, and vanilla. Mix well. Sift together in separate bowl the flour, baking powder, soda, allspice, cinnamon, and salt. Set aside. Measure together in another bowl the zucchini, carrots, raisins, nuts, and seeds. Add dry ingredients, approximately 1 cup at a time, alternately with zucchini mixture to the egg mixture. Stir well after each addition. Pour batter evenly divided into 2 greased and floured loaf pans. Bake for 1 hour at 350°. Remove from pan immediately. Cool and slice or cool slightly and wrap in foil to freeze for later.

* May use ½ cup soy flour and ½ cup whole wheat flour for the third cup.

Adell Brott, Branch No. 3086, Citrus Heights, CA

Notes

Puddings, Pies, Pastries, Desserts

APPROXIMATE 100 CALORIE PORTIONS

Almonds (shelled)—12 to 15 nuts
Angel cake—1¾ inch cube
Apple—1 large
Apple pie—⅓ normal piece
Apricots—5 large
Asparagus—20 large stalks
Bananas—1 medium
Beans—⅓ cup canned baked
Beans—green string—2½ cups
Beets—1⅓ cups sliced
Bread—all kinds—slice ½ inch thick
Butter—1 tablespoon
Buttermilk—1⅛ cups
Cabbage—4 to 5 cups shredded
Cake—1¾ inch cube
Candy—1 inch cube
Cantaloupe—1 medium
Carrots—1⅔ cups
Cauliflower—1 small head
Celery—4 cups
Cereal—uncooked—¾ cup
Cheese—1⅛ inch cube
Cottage cheese—5 tablespoons
Cherries—sweet fresh—20 cherries
Cookies—1 to 3 inches in diameter
Corn—⅓ cup
Crackers—4 soda crackers
Crackers—graham—2½ crackers
Cream—thick—1 tablespoon
Cream—thin—4 tablespoons
Cream sauce—4 tablespoons
Dates—3 to 4
Doughnuts—½ doughnut
Eggs—1⅓ eggs
Fish—fat—size of 1 chop
Fish—lean—size of 2 chops
Flour—4 tablespoons
Frankfurter—1 small
French dressing—1½ tablespoons
Grapefruit—½ large
Grape juice—½ cup
Grapes—20 grapes
Gravy—2 tablespoons
Ice cream—½ cup
Lard—1 tablespoon
Lemons—3 large
Lettuce—2 large heads

Macaroni—¾ cup cooked
Malted milk—3 tablespoons
Marmalade and jelly—1 tablespoon
Marshmallows—5 marshmallows
Mayonnaise—1 tablespoon
Meat—cold sliced—⅛ inch slice
Meat—fat—size ½ chop
Meat—lean—size 1 chop
Milk—⅝ cup (regular)
Molasses—1½ tablespoons
Onions—3 to 4 Medium
Oranges—1 large
Orange juice—1 cup
Peaches—3 medium fresh
Peanut butter—1 tablespoon
Pears—2 medium fresh
Peas—¾ cup canned
Pecans—12 meats
Pie—¼ ordinary serving
Pineapple—2 slices 1 inch thick
Plums—3 to 4 large
Popcorn—1½ cups
Potatoes—sweet—½ medium
Potatoes—white—1 medium
Potato salad—1 cup
Prunes—dried 4 medium
Radishes—3 dozen red button
Raisins—¼ cup seeded or
  2 tablespoons seeded
Rhubarb—stewed and sweetened
  —½ cup
Rice—cooked ¾ cup
Rolls—1 medium
Rutabagas—1⅔ cups
Sauerkraut—2½ cups
Sherbet—4 tablespoons
Spinach—2½ cups
Squash—1 cup
Strawberries—1⅓ cups
Sugar—brown—3 tablespoons
Sugar—white—2 tablespoons
Tomatoes—canned—2 cups
Tomatoes—fresh—2 to 3 medium
Turnips—2 cups
Walnuts—8 to 16 meats
Watermelon—¾ slice 6 inches
  diameter

PUDDINGS, PIES, PASTRIES, DESSERTS

DELICIOUS VANILLA PUDDING
(Microwave)

2 eggs
1¾ c. milk
1¼ tsp. vanilla
½ c. whipping cream

6 Tbsp. flour
⅔ c. sugar
¼ tsp. salt

Mix dry ingredients in microwave dish. Add eggs and milk. Stir to combine. Microwave on SIMMER for 16 to 18 minutes, stirring every 4 minutes. When thickened, add 1¼ teaspoons vanilla. Chill. When chilled, whip ½ cup cream and fold into mixture.

May add coconut and bananas if desired.

Emma J. Wegner, Branch No. 2366, Shawmut, MT
(Branch address - Harlowton MT)

BANANA TORTE

1½ c. flour
½ c. butter or margarine
½ c. chopped nuts
8 oz. cream cheese
3 c. + 2 Tbsp. milk

1 c. powdered sugar
8 oz. Cool Whip
4 bananas
2 (3 oz.) pkg. instant vanilla
   pudding

Combine flour, butter and nuts. Press in a 9x13 inch pan. Bake for 10 minutes at 375°. Cool. Mix together cream cheese, 2 tablespoons milk, powdered sugar, and ½ of 8 ounce container of Cool Whip. Pour over cooled crust. Slice 4 bananas over top. Mix 3 cups of milk with 2 packages of pudding. Pour over bananas. Top with the rest of the Cool Whip. Sprinkle with chopped nuts. Chill.

Ruth Brisbine, Branch No. 1976, Cornelius, OR

CHERRY FLUFF

1 can cherry pie filling
1 can crushed pineapple
1 pkg. chopped pecans

1 can Eagle Brand milk
1 large ctn. Cool Whip

Open all of the cans; drain the pineapple and mix all the ingredients in a large bowl. Cool and serve.

Linda R. Keegan, Branch No. 6274, Lafayette, IN

SWEDISH RICE PUDDING

8 c. milk
1 c. rice

1 cinnamon stick
Salt to taste

Stir all ingredients together and pour into a 3 quart baking dish. Bake at 350° for 3 hours. Do not stir or cover. The following is to be used as a topping for the pudding.

Kräm:

3 c. grape juice
1 c. sugar

2 Tbsp. lemon juice
4 Tbsp. cornstarch

Mix cornstarch with sugar. Add to juice and boil until thick. Cool. Serve over Swedish Rice Pudding.

Eleonora Martin, Branch No. 5076, Topeka, KS

SWEDISH RICE PUDDING

¾ c. rice (uncooked - not Minute rice)
4 c. milk
2 c. more milk
2 eggs

1¼ c. sugar
1 tsp. salt
1 Tbsp. cornstarch
1 tsp. vanilla

Put rice and 4 cups milk in double boiler over boiling water; cook slowly for about 1 hour and 15 minutes till soft and rice has absorbed milk. Stir occasionally. Beat together 2 cups milk and 2 eggs. Mix together sugar, salt and cornstarch. Put egg and milk mixture together with dry ingredients, then add rice mixture and vanilla. Bring to a boil and thicken in regular saucepan. Put in bowl and sprinkle cinnamon on top.

Grace Lardy, Branch No. 3879, Billings, MT

RICE PUDDING

½ c. rice
1 c. water
3 eggs

3 c. milk
1 c. sugar

Boil water with a little salt. Add rice and cook. Add 3 cups milk and continue cooking. Beat 3 eggs with 1 cup sugar. Mix with rice and milk mixture. Bake at 350° until thick.

Virginia Heczko, Branch No. 5691, Ironwood, MI

RICE PUDDING

1 c. rice (uncooked)
4 c. water
½ tsp. salt
2 c. milk
¼ c. margarine or butter
1 egg

½ to 1 c. milk (depending on thickness of rice)
1 tsp. vanilla
¾ c. sugar
½ c. raisins

Bring first 3 ingredients to a boil. Stir, cover and turn to simmer for 15 minutes. Add next 2 ingredients and simmer for 15 minutes, stirring occasionally. Beat together last 5 ingredients and add to rice mixture. Simmer, uncovered, stirring often, for 10 to 20 minutes until pudding is thick and coats the spoon. Top with cinnamon. *Delicious warm or cold!*

Branch No. 1206, Crosstown, MO

RICE PUDDING

1 c. rice
1 tsp. salt
1 qt. plus 2 c. milk
¾ c. sugar

1 egg
1 tsp. vanilla
Cinnamon

Rinse 1 cup rice and drain. Put in heavy bottom kettle. Cover with water and 1 teaspoon salt. Boil till water disappears. Add 1 quart plus 1 cup milk and ¾ cup sugar. Slowly boil this till rice is done. Stir often. Add 1 egg (beaten with fork) in 1 cup milk to rice. Return to stove and let it come only to a slow boil, stirring constantly. Do not *overboil* after egg is added. Add 1 teaspoon vanilla. Pour into serving dish and sprinkle with cinnamon.

Irma Jaekel, Branch No. 1836, Maple Plain, MN

MOM'S RICE PUDDING

1 c. rice
¾ c. sugar
5 c. milk (whole)

1 tsp. vanilla
Cinnamon

Boil rice with 2 cups water, a little butter and salt for 20 minutes (like the package says). Add sugar and milk; bring to a boil. Turn stove on low, cover and cook for approximately 45 minutes. Add vanilla. Pour in bowl and sprinkle with cinnamon. Cool. (This will thicken as it cools.) Keep refrigerated.

Connie Davis, Branch No. 3107, Loveland, CO

RICE PUDDING

½ c. rice
3 c. scalded milk
½ c. sugar
3 Tbsp. cornstarch

¾ c. cold milk
3 eggs, separated
8 Tbsp. sugar

Cook the rice until tender; add the scalded milk to rice. Mix the sugar with the cornstarch and mix with the cold milk. Add to the hot mixture and cook until thick. Add beaten egg yolks and cook for 2 minutes more. Put into a buttered dish. Cover with meringue and brown.

Meringue:

3 egg whites
¼ tsp. cream of tartar

3 Tbsp. sugar

Beat egg whites and cream of tartar until stiff. Add sugar gradually and put on top of pudding.

St. Peter's Ev. Lutheran Church, Moltke Township, Gibbon, MN

OSTAKAKA - SWEDISH CUSTARD

6 qt. milk
½ rennet tablet
1 Tbsp. warm water
1 c. flour
1 c. milk (cold)

6 eggs
1½ c. sugar
1 tsp. salt
2 c. cream
1 qt. milk

Heat milk to 85°. Mix flour and cold milk; add to warmed milk, stirring constantly for 3 minutes. Immediately stir in crushed rennet dissolved in warm water. Stir for 1 minute; cover and let set until like gelatin. Whey will appear on top. Cut wih knife approximately ½ inch apart in each direction to release whey. Let stand, then cut again and again, carefully pouring off the whey until you can dump curds into colander to drain. When well drained, break curds with pastry blender to look like cottage cheese.

Beat eggs. Add sugar, salt, cream, and milk. Add cheese curds and pour into 4 quart baking dish. Bake at 325° to 350° for approximately 1 hour or until a knife comes out clean when checking center of the pudding.

Lucille Larson-Quick, Branch No. 5325, Stratford, IA

PEANUT PUDDING TORTE

⅔ c. dry roasted peanuts, chopped
1 c. flour
½ c. butter
⅓ c. peanut butter
1 (8 oz.) cream cheese
1 c. powdered sugar

1 c. Cool Whip
1 small pkg. instant vanilla
   pudding
1 small pkg. instant chocolate
   pudding
2⅔ c. milk

First layer: Blend flour and butter. Add peanuts. Put in a 9x13 inch pan and bake for 20 minutes at 350°. Cool.

Second layer: Cream together peanut butter and cream cheese. Add powdered sugar and mix well. Blend in Cool Whip. Spread on first layer.

Third layer: Mix pudding and milk well. Spread over cream cheese layer (second layer). Layer top with additional Cool Whip. Shred 1 Hershey's bar over the top and sprinkle with ⅓ cup chopped peanuts. Refrigerate.

Bonnie Sielaff, Branch No. 3729, Appleton, WI

GLORIFIED TAPIOCA

1 large can fruit cocktail
1 can mandarin oranges
1 pkg. orange tapioca pudding
1 pkg. vanilla tapioca pudding or 2
   pkg. vanilla tapioca pudding

3 c. colored marshmallows
1 c. whipping cream or Cool Whip

Drain juice from fruits. Add water to make 3 cups liquid. Mix with tapioca puddings in saucepan. Cook and stir over medium heat until mixture comes to a full boil. Cool for 20 minutes, stirring a few times. Add fruit and marshmallows. Whip cream and fold into mixture. Makes a large bowl.

This recipe works well to make the day before using it.
Blanche Holmes, Branch No. 5943, New Brighton, MN

CARROT PUDDING

1 sq. butter	1 tsp. baking soda
1 c. sugar	½ tsp. cinnamon
2 eggs	½ tsp. nutmeg
1 c. grated carrots	¼ tsp. salt
1 c. grated potatoes	1 c. raisins
1½ c. flour	

Cream butter and sugar; add eggs (beaten). Add carrots and potatoes; mix well. Add flour that has been sifted together with the other dry ingredients. Last, add raisins and steam for 2½ hours. Do not uncover during the steaming.

Carrot Pudding Sauce:

1 c. brown sugar	1½ c. hot water
2 Tbsp. flour	2 Tbsp. butter
Pinch of salt	1 tsp. vanilla

Mix brown sugar and flour. Add salt and hot water. Mix in butter and cook until thickened. Add vanilla. Serve hot or cold on pudding.
Mrs. John (Maxine) Johansen, Branch No. 3365, Rock Springs, WY

BUTTERSCOTCH PUDDING

1 c. brown sugar	1½ c. milk
2 eggs	¼ c. butter
2 Tbsp. flour (slightly rounded)	

Mix together brown sugar, eggs and flour. Add milk and butter. Cook over medium heat, stirring constantly. Cook until thick.
Barb Sheets, Branch No. 5844, Columbia City, IN

PINEAPPLE PUDDING

½ c. butter	5 pieces bread
1 c. sugar	1 (16 or 20 oz.) can crushed
4 eggs	pineapple

Drain pineapple slightly. Break bread into small pieces. Cream butter and sugar. Add eggs and beat well. Add pineapple and bread. Stir. Bake in 1½ quart casserole (uncovered) at 350° for 1 hour or until brown.

This is a delicious side dish for baked ham.
June Gise, Branch No. 5511, Dover, PA

OREO COOKIE-WALNUT PUDDING

2 (4 oz.) instant vanilla pudding
4 c. cold milk
1 (12 oz.) Cool Whip, thawed

2 c. broken Oreo cookies
½ c. chopped walnuts
2 Oreos, crumbled (to garnish)

Prepare puddings according to package directions. Fold in Cool Whip until well blended. Fold in cookies and walnuts. Sprinkle crushed Oreos over top. Makes approximately 12 servings.

Best if chilled overnight so cookies can soften. Great for picnics and potlucks.

Hollee Milz, Branch No. 2295, Allen Park, MI

PERSIMMON PUDDING

1 c. sugar
1 egg
½ c. margarine
2 c. persimmon pulp

1 c. milk
1 c. flour
1 tsp. baking powder

Cream together sugar, egg and margarine. Mix baking powder with flour. Mix persimmon pulp, milk, flour, and baking powder with sugar mixture. Pour into greased 9x13 inch pan and bake at 350°F. for 35 minutes or until done. Cut into 12 squares and serve topped with whipped cream.

Patricia Darlage, Branch No. 2413, Dudleytown, IN

BREAD PUDDING

3 eggs
1 qt. milk
½ c. sugar
2 tsp. vanilla

4 to 6 slices stale bread, broken
   into pieces
Nutmeg
½ c. raisins

Beat eggs. Add milk, sugar and vanilla; mix thoroughly. Add bread, submerging into mixture. Add raisins. Sprinkle top with nutmeg. Bake, uncovered, for 55 to 60 minutes in a 400° oven. Serve hot or cold.

Elizabeth Eaton, Branch No. 4012, East Jordan, MI

BREAD PUDDING

4 c. dried bread crumbs
4 c. milk
3 eggs
1 c. sugar
1 Tbsp. butter

1 tsp. cinnamon
¼ tsp. salt
1 tsp. vanilla
½ c. raisins

Butter 2½ quart dish. Soak bread in milk for 5 minutes. Add sugar, butter, salt, and cinnamon. Add eggs, vanilla and raisins (optional). Mix well. Bake at 375° for about 70 minutes.

Carol Loewe, Branch No. 1589, Pilger, NE

358

CHERRY TORTE

Crust:

2 doz. crushed graham crackers   ½ c. sugar
½ c. soft butter

In a 9x13 inch pan, combine the crackers, butter and sugar with a fork. Spread evenly in pan.

Torte:

1 (8 oz.) pkg. cream cheese   1 c. sour cream
¾ c. sugar   1 tsp. vanilla
2 eggs

Beat cream cheese with sugar. Add eggs, sour cream and vanilla. Beat until smooth. Pour into graham cracker crust. Bake for 25 minutes at 350°. Cool. Top with one 21 ounce can thickened cherries. Top with whipped cream before serving.

Marie Mach, Branch No. 17, Kewaunee, WI

APRICOT KOLACKIES

1 loaf frozen white or sweet bread   1 tsp. grated orange or lemon peel
    dough   ¼ c. finely chopped nuts (if
¾ c. cooked apricots, cut up   desired)
2 Tbsp. sugar

Thaw 1 loaf frozen white or sweet bread dough. (I put it in the fridge overnight or all day.) Let it rise until doubled in size. Divide into 18 pieces. Flatten each piece of dough, shaping into 3 inch round or square. Place on greased cookie sheets. Cover and let rise in a warm place for 30 minutes.

With floured fingers, make an impression in centers. Top each with a teaspoonful of filling. With squares, bring opposite corners together and seal tightly. Bake filled rolls at 375° for 15 to 18 minutes. Frost with powdered sugar icing.

Filling:

¾ c. cooked apricots, cut up   ¼ c. finely chopped nuts (if
2 Tbsp. sugar   desired)
1 tsp. grated orange or lemon peel

Combine the preceding ingredients.

Jeanie Coleman, Loveland, CO

NUT SQUARES

1 lb. oleo   4½ c. flour
1 (8 oz.) cream cheese   1 tsp. vanilla
4 egg yolks   4 Tbsp. sugar

Cream together oleo and cream cheese. Add egg yolks, flour, vanilla, and sugar. Knead on lightly floured board. Refrigerate for 1 hour. Separate into 3 portions. Use powdered sugar on board. Roll out. Cut into 3 inch squares. Fill with Nut

Filling. Fold over. Bake at 350° until lightly browned. Sprinkle with powdered sugar.

Nut Filling:

1 lb. ground nuts   1 c. brown sugar
4 egg whites

Beat egg whites. Mix together with nuts and sugar.

Mrs. Fred Neuman, Branch No. 625, Jefferson, OH

HUCKLEBERRY BUCKLE

¼ c. butter   ½ c. milk
½ c. sugar   2 c. huckleberries
1 c. sifted flour   ¾ c. sugar
1 tsp. baking powder   ½ c. boiling water
¼ tsp. salt   1 Tbsp. butter

Cream ¼ cup butter and ½ cup sugar. Sift flour, baking powder and salt. Add dry ingredients to creamed mixture along with the milk. Stir briefly to blend. Spread butter in deep 8 or 9 inch pan. Toss berries with ¾ cup of sugar. Pour this over dough in pan. Melt 1 tablespoon of butter in the ½ cup boiling water. Pour this over the berries and dough in pan. Bake at 350°. If using glass pan, bake at 325°. Serve with whipped cream or ice cream.

Carol Ondor, Branch No. 1393, Kalispell, MT

RASPBERRY AND PRETZEL DESSERT

2½ c. pretzels, crushed   3 Tbsp. sugar
¾ c. melted butter

Mix and press in a 9x13 inch pan. Bake at 350° for 10 minutes and cool.

1 (8 oz.) cream cheese   2 small pkg. raspberry jello
1 c. sugar   2 c. boiling water
1 (8 oz.) Cool Whip   2 pkg. frozen raspberries

Mix cream cheese and sugar. Add Cool Whip and put on top of crust. Mix jello and boiling water. Add raspberries. Stir until partially set. Put on top of filling. Chill. Serve with topping. Can substitute strawberries.

Stella Scheffler, Branch No. 4909, Pine Island, MN

CHERRY DREAM SQUARES

1 pkg. Pillsbury Plus white cake   1 egg
  mix   1 (21 oz.) can cherry fruit pie filling
1¼ c. rolled oats   ½ c. chopped nuts
½ c. margarine or butter, softened   ¼ c. firmly packed brown sugar

Heat oven to 350°. Grease a 9x13 inch pan. In large bowl, combine cake mix, *6 tablespoons* margarine, and *1 cup* rolled oats. Mix until crumbly. Reserve 1 cup crumbs for topping. To remaining crumbs, add 1 egg; mix until well blended. Press into pan. Pour cherry pie filling over crust. Spread to cover.

To reserved crumbs in large bowl, add remaining ¼ cup rolled oats, 2 table-spoons margarine, nuts, and brown sugar. Beat until thoroughly mixed. Sprinkle over cherry mixture. Bake at 350° for 30 to 40 minutes or until golden brown. Cool completely. If desired, serve with Cool Whip or whipped cream. Serves 12.

Doris Seevers, Branch No. 382, St. Louis, MO

CRANBERRY DESSERT

Mix together:

1 c. oatmeal	½ c. coconut
¾ c. brown sugar	½ c. flour

Cut in ⅓ cup butter.

1 (No. 1) can whole cranberry sauce	1 Tbsp. lemon juice

Pack half of recipe on bottom of 8x8 inch pan. Put on No. 1 can whole cranberry sauce and 1 tablespoon lemon juice. Put remainder of recipe on top. Bake for 40 minutes at 350°.

Audrey Hakkila, Branch No. 6034, Poplar, WI

GREBBLE

½ c. sugar	1 tsp. soda
¾ c. sour cream	1 tsp. baking powder
1½ c. buttermilk	1½ tsp. salt
5 egg yolks	¼ tsp. allspice
2 egg whites	5 c. flour

Mix sour cream, butter, sugar, and salt in a bowl. Beat yolks and whites till thick and silky. Add flour to other dry ingredients. Add enough flour to make a soft dough. Let rise for about 2 hours. Roll out on cutting board and cut into strips about 2½ x 2½ inches. Cut 2 slits, stretch, and pull one of the ends through the slit. Deep-fry. May sprinkle with cinnamon-sugar or powdered sugar.

Lydia Bernhardt, Branch No. 2630, Greeley, CO

DANISH AEBLESKIVER

8 eggs	2 tsp. baking soda
1 qt. buttermilk	1 tsp. salt
4 c. flour	2 Tbsp. sugar
2 tsp. baking powder	

Beat eggs separately. Add buttermilk slowly to beaten egg yolks. Add sifted dry ingredients. Beat egg whites stiff and fold in last. Bake in special monk pans. Fill pans ¼ full with oil. When hot, fill each hole full of batter and bake slowly until golden brown, turning with knitting needle. Serve sprinkled with powdered sugar together with jam, jelly and applesauce. Yield: Approximately 58 portions.

This Danish delicacy is served every fall in early November at the annual Aebleskiver Day at Redeemer Lutheran Church.

Redeemer Lutheran Church, Branch No. 1568, Waukegan, IL

STRAWBERRY VANILLA PUDDING

½ small angel food cake
1 pkg. instant vanilla pudding
1 c. cold milk
1 pt. vanilla ice cream

1 pkg. strawberry jello
1½ c. water
10 oz. frozen strawberries

Tear cake in pieces and place in bottom of 9x9 inch pan. In mixing bowl, combine pudding and milk. Add ice cream and beat at low speed until well mixed. Pour over cake pieces and let set until firm. Dissolve jello in water and add frozen berries. Stir until thickened and pour over pudding. Chill.

ANGEL-APRICOT DESSERT

1 small angel food cake
1 (3 oz.) pkg. instant vanilla
   pudding

1½ c. milk
1 c. commercial sour cream
1 can apricot pie filling

Break or cut angel food cake into small pieces. Spread in 7x11 inch pan. Mix vanilla pudding mix and milk. Blend in the sour cream. Pour over cake, working it in. Spread pie filling over top. Refrigerate for 6 to 8 hours before serving. Serves 8.

Allison Reinking, Branch No. 5383, Sumner, IA

EASY PEACH COBBLER

½ c. butter
¾ c. self-rising flour
¾ c. milk

1 c. sugar
1 (20 oz.) can sliced peaches with
   juice

Melt butter in a 9x13 inch pan. Mix flour, milk and sugar together. Spread mixture on top of butter. Pour peaches and juice on top. Bake at 350° for 1 hour.

Sandee Scanlan, Branch No. 2714, Ogden, UT

APPLE-CRANBERRY CRISP

3 c. chopped apples
2 c. raw cranberries

¾ to 1 c. sugar

Topping:

1½ c. oatmeal
½ c. brown sugar
⅓ c. flour

⅓ c. chopped pecans
½ c. melted butter

Combine apples, cranberries and sugar in an 8 inch square baking dish. Mix thoroughly to blend. Set aside. Combine the topping and mix until crumbly. Spread evenly over the fruit layer. Bake in a 350° oven for 1 hour or until the fruit is fork tender. Serve warm with ice cream or whipped cream. Makes 8 servings.

Mrs. William (Hilda) Scheve, Branch No. 1998, Beatrice, NE

ROSE-BLUSH APPLE TORTE

Crust:

¾ c. butter or margarine	⅛ tsp. salt
1½ c. flour	1 egg yolk
1½ Tbsp. sugar	

Mix ingredients for crust together until smooth like rich cooky dough. Press evenly into ungreased 9x13 inch pan, bringing dough up the sides a little. Bake at 350° for about 8 minutes until crust is set and very lightly browned on edges.

Filling:

1 c. sugar	2 drops of red food coloring
¼ tsp. salt	1 tsp. vanilla
3 Tbsp. cornstarch	5 c. thinly sliced, peeled apples
1 c. water	

Combine sugar, cornstarch, salt, and water in saucepan for filling. Cook over medium heat until thickened (about 5 minutes), stirring constantly. Remove from heat; add food coloring, vanilla and apples. Spread over partially baked crust.

Streusel Topping:

⅔ c. flour	¼ c. butter
⅔ c. sugar	⅛ tsp. cinnamon

Cover with topping of flour, sugar, butter, and cinnamon, mixed together with finger tips until small crumbs are formed. Sprinkle evenly over filling and bake at 350° for ½ hour. Serve plain or with ice cream.

Elsie Schultz, Branch No. 341, Curtiss, WI

PASTEL MINT DESSERT

Crush 32 chocolate sandwich cookies (Hydrox) and put half in bottom of a buttered 9x13 inch pan. Whip 1 pint heavy cream. Add 1 cup pastel after dinner pillow mints and 2 cups miniature pastel marshmallows. Fold in well, but carefully. Spread over crumbs. Top with remaining crumbs, patting lightly to press into cream filling. Refrigerate for at least 2 or 3 days, then it may be frozen. Thaw before serving.

Hilma Hoerneman, Branch No. 3650, Lester Prairie, MN

DELICIOUS APPLE TORTE

2 c. flour	¾ c. quick oatmeal
1 c. brown sugar	¾ c. margarine or butter

Mix the preceding ingredients together like pie crust. Save 1 cup and press remainder into a pan, 13x9x2 inches. Set aside.

Peel and slice 6 to 8 large apples into a large mixing bowl. Set aside.

Bring to a boil and cook until thick:

¾ c. sugar   1 c. water
1 Tbsp. corn starch

Remove from heat. Add ¼ teaspoon salt, 1 teaspoon cinnamon and 1 teaspoon vanilla. Pour over apple slices; mix well and pour into crust. Top with 1 cup reserved topping. Bake for 15 minutes at 450°. Reduce heat to 350° for 30 minutes. Serve warm with Cool Whip or ice cream.

Note: You may also add some crushed pecans to the topping before baking.
Dorothy Priddy, Branch No. 6466, Batesville, AR

GRAHAM CRACKER FLUFF

11 double graham crackers,   4 egg yolks
   crushed   2 env. Knox gelatine
1 stick oleo or butter, melted   1 tsp. vanilla
6 Tbsp. brown sugar   4 egg whites
1½ c. rich milk (evaporated)   8 oz. Cool Whip
¾ c. sugar

Mix the brown sugar with the melted oleo. Mix in the graham cracker crumbs. Pat in 9x13 inch pan. Bake for 10 minutes at 300°. Save 1 cup for the top.

Cook rich milk, sugar and eggs for 1 minute; add the vanilla. Dissolve gelatine in ⅓ cup cold water. Add to hot milk mixture and cool until partially set. Fold into the following and add Cool Whip. Fold into 4 beaten egg whites. Pour on cooled crust and sprinkle on remaining crumbs. Chill overnight.
Velma Rickertsen, Branch No. 997, Charlotte, IA

CHERRY BERRIES ON A CLOUD

Meringue:

6 egg whites   ¼ tsp. salt
½ tsp. cream of tartar   1¾ c. sugar

Beat egg whites until frothy. Add cream of tartar and salt; continue to beat until soft peaks form. Gradually add sugar, 2 tablespoons at a time, beating constantly until stiff and glossy. Draw a circle 10 inches in diameter on a piece of brown paper. Pile meringue lightly in circle, spreading it to fill completely. Place paper backed meringue on cookie sheet and bake at 275° for 1 hour. Turn off oven heat and allow meringue to cool completely, about 8 hours in oven.

Filling:

6 oz. cream cheese, softened   2 c. whipping cream, whipped
1 c. sugar   2 c. miniature marshmallows
1 tsp. vanilla

Topping:

1 can cherry pie filling
½ tsp. lemon juice
2 c. fresh strawberries, sliced and
sweetened, or 16 oz. frozen
strawberries

Filling: Mix cream cheese, sugar and vanilla. Fold in marshmallows, then whipped cream. Pull meringue off of paper and place on torte plate. Pile filling on lightly. Refrigerate for 12 hours.

Note: Meringue may be baked in a buttered 9x13 inch pan if desired.
Kathleen Kloehn, Branch No. 48, Marshfield, WI

PUMPKIN ROLL

⅔ c. pumpkin
3 eggs
1 c. white sugar
1 tsp. vanilla
¾ c. flour

1 tsp. ginger
2 tsp. cinnamon
1 tsp. baking powder
½ tsp. nutmeg
½ tsp. salt

Fold mixture together and spread onto greased medium size cookie sheet. Spread 1 cup chopped nuts over raw mixture and bake at 350° for 15 minutes. Turn upside-down while still warm onto a towel sprinkled with powdered sugar. Roll up like a jelly roll. Roll towel with this. Let cool.

Filling:

½ tsp. vanilla
1 c. powdered sugar

3 (4 oz.) pkg. cream cheese
4 Tbsp. oleo

Beat until smooth.

When roll is cooled (usually in refrigerator overnight), then fill the following day. Spread filling on and reroll. Keep refrigerated so filling stays firm. (Don't forget to take towel out.) Slice like jelly roll. Can be frozen.
Elaine Maison, Branch No. 6940, Harrison, MI

VENETIAN TORTE

1 (3 oz.) pkg. lime jello
1 (3 oz.) pkg. raspberry jello
3 c. Kraft miniature
marshmallows

1 (13½ oz.) can crushed
pineapple, well drained
1 c. heavy cream, whipped
12 to 15 ladyfinger cookies

Dissolve jello in separate containers, using only 1½ cups of water per package. Pour each flavor into separate layer cake tins and chill until firm. Cut jello into cubes. Mix jello cubes with marshmallows, pineapple and whipped cream. Line a serving dish with ladyfingers and pour jello mixture over top. Jello mixture served by itself is good also. Chill until ready to serve.
Edla Johnson, Branch No. 2408, Port Huron, MI

365

RHUBARB CRUNCH

4 c. fresh rhubarb pieces
1 c. sugar
2 Tbsp. flour
2 Tbsp. butter
1 c. sugar

1 c. sifted flour
1 tsp. baking powder
¼ tsp. salt
1 large egg, beaten

Cut rhubarb into ½ inch lengths. Sift 1 cup sugar and 2 tablespoons flour together; mix with rhubarb. Pour into an 8 or 9 inch baking pan and dot with butter. Sift together the remaining sugar and flour with salt and baking powder; stir in beaten egg. The mixture will be crumbly.

Sprinkle it over the rhubarb and shake the pan a little so the crumbs will settle down in the rhubarb. Bake for about 40 minutes at 350° or until the crust is a delicate brown. Serve warm or cold with cream or vanilla ice cream.

If your family likes a bit of spice with its rhubarb, mix about ½ teaspoon of cinnamon or nutmeg with the rhubarb. This dessert freezes beautifully. Reheat in oven before serving.

Mrs. Dorothy H. Meyer, Branch No. 5935, Loganville, WI

PUMPKIN SQUARES

1¾ c. graham cracker crumbs
   (about 24)
⅓ c. sugar
½ c. margarine, melted
2 eggs
¾ c. sugar
1 (8 oz.) pkg. cream cheese,
   softened
1 (16 oz.) can pumpkin (about 2 c.)
3 egg yolks

½ c. sugar
½ c. milk
½ tsp. salt
2 tsp. ground cinnamon
1 env. unflavored gelatin (1 Tbsp.)
¼ c. cold water
3 egg whites
¼ c. sugar
Whipped topping

Mix graham cracker crumbs, ⅓ cup sugar and the margarine in a 9x13x2 inch baking dish. Pat down evenly. Beat eggs, ¾ cup sugar and cream cheese until light and fluffy. Pour over graham cracker crust. Bake at 350° for 20 minutes. Set aside.

Beat pumpkin, yolks, ½ cup sugar, milk, salt, and cinnamon in the top of double boiler. Cook over boiling water, stirring frequently, until thick, about 5 minutes. Sprinkle gelatin on water in small saucepan. Stir over low heat just until dissolved; stir into pumpkin mixture. Cool. Beat egg whites until foamy. Gradually beat in ¼ cup sugar; beat until stiff and glossy. Gently fold beaten egg whites into pumpkin mixture. Pour over baked mixture. Chill to set. Cut into 15 squares. Serve with a dollop of whipped topping on each.

Mrs. Robert Bishop (or Joyce Bishop), Branch No. 441, Bloomington, IL

PUMPKIN SQUARES

Crust:

1¾ c. graham cracker crumbs	2 eggs
⅓ c. sugar	¾ c. sugar
½ c. melted butter	1 (8 oz.) cream cheese

Pumpkin Mix:

1 (16 oz.) canned pumpkin	2 tsp. ground cinnamon
3 egg yolks (save whites)	1 env. unflavored gelatin
½ c. sugar	¼ c. cold water
½ c. milk	3 egg whites
½ tsp. salt	¼ c. sugar

1. Mix cracker crumbs and ½ cup sugar; stir in melted butter. Pat in a 13x9 inch baking dish.
2. Beat 2 eggs, ¾ cup sugar and cream cheese until light and fluffy. Pour over graham cracker crumbs and bake at 350° for 20 minutes.
3. Beat pumpkin, egg yolks, ½ cup sugar, milk, salt, and cinnamon in top of double boiler. Cook, stirring frequently, until thick (5 minutes).
4. In saucepan with ¼ cup cold water, sprinkle unflavored gelatin until dissolved.
5. Beat egg whites until foamy. Gradually beat ¼ cup sugar until stiff, gently fold in pumpkin. Pour over crust. *Refrigerate.* Garnish with whipped cream.

Beth Strablow, Branch No. 449, Lockport, NY

LEMON LUSH

1 stick margarine	½ c. crushed nuts
1 c. flour	

Press top mixture into 13x9x3 inch glass pan. Bake at 350° for 25 to 30 minutes.

1 (8 oz.) pkg. cream cheese	1 c. Cool Whip
1 c. powdered sugar	

When crust is cool, spread this mixture carefully over. Mix 2 small packages of instant chocolate or lemon pudding with 2½ cups milk. Spread over cheese filling and top with more crushed nuts and remainder of Cool Whip.

Sharon Stoll, Branch No. 5677, LaMesa, CA

CHOCOLATE DELIGHT

First layer:

1 c. flour	1 c. oatmeal and/or nuts
1½ sticks butter or margarine, melted	

Combine and pat into 13x9 inch pan. Bake at 350° for 15 minutes. Cool.

Second layer:

1 c. Cool Whip   8 oz. softened cream cheese
1 c. confectioners sugar

   Blend in mixer.

   Third layer:

1 large pkg. instant chocolate   4 c. milk
   pudding
1 large pkg. instant vanilla
   pudding

   Mix with whip.

   Topping:

Rest of 8 oz. container Cool Whip   1 Hershey's bar

   Spread Cool Whip over layers. Grate Hershey's bar on top. Refrigerate for 3
to 4 hours.

Janine Ritter, Branch No. 4477, Claremore, OK

CHOCOLATE OR LEMON DELIGHT

1 c. flour   1 c. Cool Whip
¼ c. softened butter   3 to 3½ oz. pkg. *instant* chocolate
½ c. chopped walnuts   (or lemon) pudding
8 oz. cream cheese   3 c. milk
1 c. powdered sugar

   Preheat oven to 350°F.

   Crust: Mix flour, butter and walnuts together; press evenly into a sheet cake
pan. Bake for 15 minutes, then cool.

   Next, mix together cream cheese, powdered sugar and Cool Whip. Spread
this cream cheese mixture on cooled crust. Be careful not to break up crust.

   Filling: Mix chocolate (or lemon) pudding with milk. This mixture will be
thick and smooth. Spread pudding mixture over cream cheese layer. Top with remaining Cool Whip and sprinkle with chocolate sprinkles or nuts. Refrigerate for a
couple of hours. Serve.

   Note: Purchase 12 ounce tub of Cool Whip.

Ethel Pullmann, Branch No. 1345, Rio Linda, CA

CREAM CHEESE TART

Vanilla wafers   1 Tbsp. lemon juice
2 (8 oz.) cream cheese   1 tsp. vanilla
2 eggs   Fruit pie filling
¾ c. sugar

368

Place one wafer in the bottom of a muffin cup (paper or foil). Beat remaining ingredients until fluffy. Fill muffin cups ½ to ⅔ full. Bake in a 375° oven for 15 to 20 minutes. Top with choice of fruit pie filling. Chill and serve. Makes 20 to 24 servings.

Paul Beckman, Branch No. 5285, Madison, WI

CHEESECAKF CUPCAKES

2 (8 oz.) pkg. cream cheese
2 eggs
2 tsp. vanilla
½ c. sugar
Salt to taste
Vanilla wafers
Prepared pie filling

Do not let cream cheese soften to room temperature. Beat first 5 ingredients together for 5 minutes. Place one vanilla wafer in the bottom of a cupcake paper in muffin tin. Fill half full with cream cheese mixture. Bake for 15 minutes at 375°. Cool. Top with choice of prepared pie filling. Refrigerate. Makes about 2 dozen.

Diane Zeh, Branch No. 1014, Cohocton, NY

NILLA CHEESECAKE TARTS

Vanilla wafers
3 (8 oz.) pkg. softened cream
   cheese
1 c. sugar
4 eggs
1 tsp. vanilla
Fruit pie filling

Mix together well till creamy the cream cheese, sugar, eggs, and vanilla. Place small tart muffin papers in tin and put 1 vanilla wafer in the bottom of each. Spoon cheese mixture in each, ½ to ¾ full. Bake at 325° for 25 minutes. Cool completely, then refrigerate overnight. Peel off tart papers carefully (much easier if cakes are chilled). Top with desired flavor of fruit pie filling. Makes 24 tart sized cheesecakes.

Julie Padilla, Branch No. 3107, Loveland, CO

CHERRY DESSERT

⅔ stick oleo (margarine)
1½ c. graham crackers, crushed
¼ c. sugar
1 c. whipping cream
1 (8 oz.) pkg. cream cheese
2 cans cherry pie filling

Mix margarine, crackers and sugar. Press into 9x13 inch pan. Mix cream and cream cheese, then spread over crust. Top with cherry pie filling.

Marti Conrad, Loveland, CO

BLUEBERRY DESSERT

11 graham crackers
½ c. melted butter
¼ c. brown sugar
½ tsp. cinnamon
3 eggs
8 oz. soft cream cheese
½ c. sugar
1 tsp. vanilla
1 can blueberry pie mix

1. Melt butter. Add brown sugar and cinnamon.
2. Crush graham crackers and add to butter mixture.
3. Pack in a 9 inch pie pan.
4. Beat eggs. Add cream cheese, sugar and vanilla.
5. Spread egg mixture on top of crust.
6. Bake for 25 minutes at 350°.
7. Cool. Spread can of blueberry pie mix on top.
8. Serve with a spoon of Cool Whip on top.

Doris Henschell, Branch No. 2086, Seattle, WA

PUMPKIN TORTE

24 graham crackers, crushed
½ c. butter, melted
2 eggs, beaten
¾ c. sugar
8 oz. cream cheese
2 c. pumpkin
3 egg yolks
½ c. sugar
½ c. milk
½ tsp. salt
1 Tbsp. pumpkin spice
1 env. plain gelatin
¼ c. cold water
3 egg whites
¼ c. sugar
½ pt. Cool Whip

Mix graham crackers and butter; press into 9x13 inch pan. Mix eggs, ¾ cup sugar and cream cheese; pour over crust. Bake for 20 minutes at 350°. Cook pumpkin, egg yolks, ½ cup sugar, milk, salt, and pumpkin spices until mixture thickens. Remove from heat and add gelatin, dissolved in cold water. Cool. Beat egg whites and ¼ cup sugar. Fold into pumpkin mixture. Pour over cooled baked crust. Top with Cool Whip.

When cooled, put in the refrigerator until they need to be served.

Miss Gladys Noeske, Branch No. 2578, Standish, MI

PUMPKIN TORTE

2 c. graham cracker crumbs
⅓ c. sugar
½ c. melted butter
2 eggs
¾ c. sugar
1 (8 oz.) cream cheese
1 can pumpkin (1 pie size)
3 egg yolks
½ c. milk
½ c. sugar
½ tsp. salt
1 tsp. cinnamon
1 env. Knox gelatine
¼ c. cold water
3 egg whites
¼ c. sugar
Cool Whip

Mix crumbs, sugar and melted butter together; press into 13x9 inch pan. (Pat on bottom, not up the sides.) Beat eggs, ¾ cup sugar and cream cheese, then pour over crust. Bake at 350° for 15 to 20 minutes. Cool!

Mix and cook pumpkin, 3 egg yolks, ½ cup sugar, ½ cup milk, ½ teaspoon salt, and 1 teaspoon cinnamon in a saucepan till thick. Remove from heat. Mix 1 envelope Knox gelatine and ¼ cup cold water. Add to preceding mixture and cool. Beat 3 egg whites until stiff, then add ¼ cup sugar. Fold in pumpkin mixture. Mix and pour over crust. Chill until firm. Serve with Cool Whip.

Patricia Schaefer, Branch No. 192, Hilbert, WI

KRINGLE

4 c. flour
3 Tbsp. sugar
1 c. shortening
2 pkg. dry yeast, dissolved in ½ c.
    warm water
1 c. scalded milk

1 tsp. salt
2 egg yolks
2 egg whites, beaten
1 Tbsp. sugar
Filling (apple, cherry or blueberry)

Add milk to sugar, salt and beaten egg yolks. Add yeast and half of the flour. Beat till smooth. Add remaining flour. Knead until smooth and dough leaves sides of bowl. Refrigerate overnight or for at least 2 hours. Roll into 2 rectangular shapes. Place on cookie sheet. Brush with egg whites which have been beaten and the sugar added.

Place on cookie sheet (center). Spread filling down center of dough. With scissors, clip in sides 1 inch apart and crisscross over. Brush top with egg whites. Let rise for 1 hour. Bake at 375° until done. Decorate with icing, cherries, nuts, etc.

Myrtle Prestebak, Branch No. 341, Dorchester, WI

KRINGLE

Crust:

1 c. butter or margarine
2 c. sifted flour

1 c. sour cream or buttermilk

Cut butter into flour as for pie crust. Add sour cream and mix well. Chill for 1 hour or more. Divide into 4 parts and roll each into a 6x12 inch rectangle on a floured pastry cloth. Spoon in filling (one 21 ounce can cherry pie filling) and overlap. Bake at 375° for 25 minutes or until delicately browned on an ungreased pan.

Frosting:

1 c. powdered sugar

2 Tbsp. warm milk

Blend frosting and drip over warm pastry.

Werna Johnson, Branch No. 4077, Racine, WI

DANISH PUFF

½ c. butter or margarine, softened
1 c. Gold Medal flour
2 Tbsp. water
½ c. butter or margarine

1 c. water
1 tsp. almond extract
1 c. Gold Medal flour
3 eggs

Heat oven to 350°. Cut ½ cup butter into 1 cup flour. Sprinkle 2 table-spoons water over mixture; mix. Round into ball and divide in half. On ungreased baking sheet, pat each half into strip, 12x3 inches. Strips should be about 3 inches apart.

Heat ½ cup butter and 1 cup water to rolling boil in medium saucepan. Remove from heat and quickly stir in almond extract and 1 cup flour. Stir vigorously over low heat until mixture forms a ball, about 1 minute. Remove from heat. Beat in eggs (all at once) until smooth and glossy.

Divide in half. Spread each half evenly over strips. Bake for about 60 minutes or until topping is crisp and brown. Cool. (Topping will shrink and fall, forming the custardy top of this puff.) Frost with sugar glaze and sprinkle generously with nuts.

Confectioners Sugar Glaze:

1½ c. confectioners sugar	1½ tsp. vanilla
2 Tbsp. butter or margarine,	1 to 2 Tbsp. warm water
softened	Chopped nuts

Mix confectioners sugar, butter, vanilla, and warm water until smooth and of spreading consistency.
Jean Bohr, Branch No. 2189, Oregon City, OR; Helen Kopischke, Branch No. 1293, Morgan, MN; Yvonne Mettler, Branch No. 849, Vancouver, WA

CARAMEL DUMPLINGS

2 Tbsp. shortening	1½ c. boiling water
1½ c. brown sugar	Pinch of salt

Cook gently in a 2 quart saucepan for 5 minutes.

Make a batter of:

1¼ c. flour	⅓ c. sugar
1½ tsp. baking powder	⅛ tsp. salt

Sift ingredients and cut in 2 tablespoons shortening. Add ⅓ cup milk and ½ teaspoon vanilla. Drop by spoonfuls into hot syrup. Cover tightly and boil slowly for 20 minutes. Do not uncover while boiling. Serve warm or cold. Top with whipped cream.

APPLE DUMPLINGS

Basic Pie Dough:

2 c. flour	1 tsp. salt
1 c. Crisco	¼ c. cold water

Make Basic Pie Dough. Use about 1½ inch ball for each dumpling. Roll out to about 6 inches in diameter.

4 apples (cooking preferred)	1 c. sugar
½ stick butter	

Syrup

1¼ c. water   1 c. sugar

Place handful peeled and diced apples on rolled out pie dough. Melt butter in sugar. Spoon 1 tablespoon on top of apples. Fold crust over apples and sugar mixture, making a small dumpling and place in baking pan. After all dumplings (8) are made, bake in 450° oven until slightly browned, approximately 15 minutes. Reduce heat to 250°.

Boil water and sugar; pour half over apple dumplings. Bake for 20 minutes. Add the remainder syrup (reheat to boiling). Bake for another 25 minutes. Serve warm with ice cream.

Doris V. Tormoehlen, Branch No. 3437, Seymour, IN

APPLE DUMPLINGS

Apple Dumplings (per dumpling):

½ cored sliced apple   ⅛ tsp. nutmeg
1 tsp. sugar   1 pat butter
¼ tsp. cinnamon

Prepare your favorite pie crust for a double crust pie. Divide into 8 balls. Roll out each ball into a 6 to 8 inch circle. Place the preceding Apple Dumpling in the center of each circle. Bring edges of circle up over apples and seal on top. Place on baking sheets and bake at 400° for 20 to 25 minutes.

Apple Dumpling Sauce:

½ c. flour   ½ tsp. nutmeg
1 c. sugar   4 c. milk
1 tsp. cinnamon   2 pats butter

Mix flour, sugar, cinnamon, and nutmeg. Add milk and butter. Cook over medium heat, stirring constantly, until bubbly and thick. Serve warm over dumplings.

Irene Clements, Branch No. 6196, Marion, TX

CHERRY SQUARES

1½ c. graham cracker crumbs   2 Tbsp. milk
⅓ c. melted margarine   1 c. nuts, chopped
1 (8 oz.) pkg. light cream cheese   1½ c. Cool Whip
1 c. powdered sugar   1 can cherry pie filling

Combine graham cracker crumbs and margarine. Press in bottom of buttered 8x8 inch pan. Bake for 10 minutes at 350°.

Mix cream cheese, sugar and milk. Spread over cooled crust. Sprinkle on the nuts. Spread Cool Whip over nuts. Spread pie filling over Cool Whip. Refrigerate for at least 2 hours.

Marilyn Goeglein, Branch No. 1868, Yuma, CO

APPLE CRISP

10 to 12 c. pared, sliced apples
½ c. water
2 tsp. cinnamon
1 tsp. salt

2 c. brown sugar
1½ c. flour
⅔ c. butter or margarine

Mix water, cinnamon and salt. Sprinkle over apples in greased 9x13 inch pan. Combine brown sugar, flour and butter until crumbly. Spread over apples. Bake at 350° for 40 minutes.

Millie Hetzner, Branch No. 2311, Saginaw, MI

RHUBARB COBBLER
(Microwave)

4 c. sliced rhubarb
¾ c. sugar
2 Tbsp. cornstarch
¾ c. water

1 tsp. vanilla
½ tsp. cinnamon
1 (6 oz.) can refrigerated
  cinnamon rolls with icing

In 9 inch round microwavable baking dish, microwave rhubarb on HIGH for 5 to 6 minutes, stirring after 3 minutes. Drain well. Set aside.

In 2 cup measuring cup, stir sugar and cornstarch. Stir in water. Microwave, uncovered, on HIGH for 2 to 3 minutes or until thick and bubbly, stirring every minute. Stir in vanilla and cinnamon. Stir into rhubarb. Microwave, uncovered, on HIGH for 2 minutes or until hot and bubbly, stirring after 1 minute. Stir again.

Cut each cinnamon roll in half. Arrange rolls, cinnamon side up, on top of hot rhubarb around edge of dish. Microwave, uncovered, on HIGH for 7 minutes or until rolls are firm to the touch and no longer sticky, rotating dish ¼ turn every 1½ minutes. Let stand for 5 minutes. Microwave container of icing on HIGH for 20 seconds. Drizzle over rolls.

Cheryl Schultz, Branch No. 3107, Loveland, CO

PANNUKAKKUA - FINNISH CUSTARD

3 c. warm milk (not scalded)
3 eggs
¾ c. flour

¼ c. sugar
½ tsp. salt
½ stick butter or oleo

Place butter in a 9x13 inch pan, then place pan into oven while the oven warms to 400° temperature. Beat eggs. Add sugar and salt. Add warm milk alternately with flour. Batter will be thin. Pour into hot pan with the melted oleo and bake for 30 minutes. Serve with syrup or berries.

Siiri Mellstrom, Branch No. 4843, Hancock, MI

COLORADO PEACH CREAM PIE

Crust:

½ c. butter
1½ c. flour

½ tsp. salt

Mix the crust ingredients together. Press into pie plate. Bake for 15 minutes at 400°.

Filling:

4 c. fresh sliced peaches	¼ tsp. salt
¼ c. sugar	¼ tsp. vanilla
2 Tbsp. flour	¾ c. sugar
1 egg	1 c. sour cream

Mix together the peaches and ¼ cup sugar. Let stand while preparing the rest of the filling. Mix the flour, egg, salt, vanilla, and ¾ cup sugar, then fold in sour cream. Put into crust and bake for 20 minutes at 350°.

Topping:

⅓ c. sugar	¼ c. butter
⅓ c. flour	1 tsp. cinnamon

Mix topping ingredients and sprinkle on pie. Bake for 10 minutes at 400°.

Kathy Leininger, Branch No. 3107, Loveland, CO

EASY PECAN PIE

3 eggs, slightly beaten	1 tsp. vanilla
1 c. light or dark corn syrup	1½ c. pecan halves
1 c. sugar	1 unbaked 9 inch pie shell
2 Tbsp. margarine, melted	

In large bowl, stir first 5 ingredients until well blended. Add pecan halves. Pour into pie shell. Bake in a 350°F. oven for 50 to 55 minutes until knife comes out clean. Cool. Serves 8.

Adele Hogue, Branch No. 952, Dolton, IL

FABULOUS PECAN PIE

1 unbaked pie shell	1 c. sugar
3 eggs	2 Tbsp. melted butter
1 c. dark corn syrup	1 tsp. vanilla
Dash of salt	1 c. chopped or whole pecans

Beat eggs slightly. Mix in the sugar, butter, vanilla, salt, and nuts. Pour into the pie shell and bake at 400° for 15 minutes. Reduce heat to 350° and bake for 30 to 35 minutes. Filling should be softer in center. *Very good and rich!*

Myrtle Askelson, Branch No. 3866, Audubon, MN

PECAN (CORN MEAL) PIE

2 eggs, slightly beaten
½ c. milk
1 c. white sugar
1 c. brown sugar
½ stick butter or oleo (soft or melted)

2 Tbsp. flour
2 Tbsp. corn meal
1 c. coconut
1 tsp. vanilla
Chopped pecans (for topping)

Mix in order given. Put in unbaked 9 inch pie shell. Sprinkle finely chopped pecans over the top before baking. Bake for 40 to 45 minutes at 350°. Serves 6 to 8.

Jeanette Peterson, Branch No. 2295, Allen Park, MI

ABBY'S PECAN (OR WALNUT) PIE

1 c. white corn syrup
1 c. dark brown sugar
⅓ tsp. salt
⅓ c. melted butter

1 tsp. vanilla
3 whole eggs
1 heaping c. shelled pecans (or walnuts)

Mix syrup, sugar, butter, and vanilla. Add slightly beaten eggs. Pour into a 9 inch unbaked pie shell. Bake in a 350° oven for approximately 45 minutes.

May be topped with Cool Whip or ice cream.

Esther V. Ruesch, Branch No. 3107, Loveland, CO

SWEET POTATO PECAN PIE

Have on hand pie dough for one 8 inch pie shell (deep).

Potato Filling:

1 c. baked sweet potatoes
½ c. light brown sugar
2 Tbsp. granulated sugar
1 Tbsp. heavy cream
1 Tbsp. unsalted butter

1 Tbsp. vanilla
1 tsp. salt
⅛ tsp. allspice
¼ tsp. ground cinnamon
⅛ tsp. nutmeg

Syrup Mixture:

¾ c. sugar
¾ c. dark corn syrup
2 small eggs
1½ Tbsp. unsalted butter

¾ c. pecan halves
2 tsp. vanilla
Pinch of salt
Pinch of cinnamon

1. Combine the ingredients for Potato Filling and beat at medium speed until smooth (2 to 3 minutes).

2. Combine the ingredients for Syrup Mixture in a mixing bowl. Beat in mixing bowl for 1 to 2 minutes on low speed. Add pecans and set aside.

3. Line an 8 inch deep pie pan with your pie dough. Spoon Potato Filling in the lined pan. Pour the Syrup Mixture over the Potato Filling. Bake at 325° until a knife inserted in the center comes out clean, about 1¾ hours.

Patricia Garbe, Branch No. 1646, Wheeler, IL

SWEET POTATO PIE

3 c. sweet potatoes (fresh or
   canned)
⅔ c. sugar
2 eggs

½ c. butter
¼ c. Carnation milk
1 c. coconut
1 tsp. vanilla

Beat the preceding ingredients together.

Topping:

1 c. chopped pecans
½ c. butter

1 c. brown sugar
½ c. flour

Mix topping ingredients together and spread over potato mixture. Bake at 350° for 20 minutes.

Esther Dumler, Branch No. 3107, Loveland, CO

PUMPKIN PECAN PIE

3 eggs, slightly beaten
1 c. canned pumpkin
1 c. sugar
½ c. dark corn syrup
1 tsp. vanilla

½ tsp. cinnamon
¼ tsp. salt
1 c. chopped pecans
1 unbaked 9 inch pie shell

Combine eggs, pumpkin, sugar, syrup, vanilla, cinnamon, and salt. Mix well. Spoon into pie shell. Sprinkle pecans on top. Bake in a 350° oven for 40 minutes or until knife inserted comes out clean. Top with whipped cream.

Deb Austin, Branch No. 3887, Greeley, CO

RHUBARB CUSTARD PIE

3 c. rhubarb, cut in 1 inch pieces
1¼ c. sugar
¼ c. flour

2 eggs
1 unbaked pie shell

Combine rhubarb, sugar, flour, and eggs. Mix lightly. Pour into pie shell. Bake at 400° for 55 minutes.

Gladys Graumenz, Branch No. 1409, St. Peter, IL

RHUBARB PIE

1 unbaked pie crust, filled with
   chopped rhubarb
2 eggs, beaten

1 c. sugar
Pinch of salt

Topping:

½ c. brown sugar
½ c. flour

¼ c. butter

Beat eggs. Add sugar and pinch of salt. Pour mixture over rhubarb in pie shell. Mix topping ingredients like pie crust and sprinkle on top. Bake at 425° for 10 minutes. Reduce heat to 350° and bake for an additional 35 minutes or until bubbling and brown.

Irene Nelson, Branch No. 1737, Finlayson, MN

RHUBARB CUSTARD PIE

1 (11 oz.) pkg. pie crust mix*
2½ c. unpeeled rhubarb, cut in 1
   inch lengths
1½ c. sugar
¼ c. flour

2 eggs, slightly beaten
2 tsp. lemon juice
Dash of salt
2 Tbsp. butter
1 Tbsp. sugar

Place bottom crust in deep 9 inch pie pan. Heat oven to 450°. In large bowl, combine rhubarb, sugar, flour, eggs, lemon juice, and salt. Turn into lined pie plate. Dot with butter. Roll out pastry for top crust. Either cut in strips to make lattice top or roll out and cut slits in for top crust. Moisten edges of bottom crust. Place top crust on pie. With fingers, press edges together to seal, so juices cannot run out. Sprinkle with 1 tablespoon sugar. Bake at 450° for 10 minutes. Reduce heat to 350° and bake for 30 minutes or till lightly browned.

* I make my own crust and make a lattice top crust.

Thelma Meinert, Branch No. 5425, Louisville, KY

APPLE PIE FILLING

5 c. sugar
1 c. cornstarch
2 tsp. cinnamon
½ tsp. nutmeg

½ tsp. cloves
10 c. cold water
3 Tbsp. lemon juice
24 c. sliced apples

Blend all ingredients together well. Cook over medium heat until bubbly, stirring frequently. Pack into sterilized hot jars. Seal. Process in a pressure cooker for 10 minutes at 10 pounds pressure. Makes about 7 quarts. Use as for commercial pie filling.

Mrs. Delbert Radtke, Branch No. 6896, Mahnomen, MN

FAVORITE SUGARLESS APPLE PIE

6 medium size apples
1 (6 oz.) can apple juice
   concentrate, thawed
1½ Tbsp. cornstarch

1½ Tbsp. water
1 tsp. cinnamon
Whole wheat pastry crust

Peel and slice apples. Place apples and undiluted juice in a large pan. Bring to a boil; reduce heat and simmer, covered, for about 5 minutes. Dissolve cornstarch in water. Gently stir cornstarch into apple mixture. Bring to a boil; reduce heat and simmer, covered, for 10 to 15 minutes or until apples begin to soften and mixture thickens. Gently stir in cinnamon. Fill 9 inch pastry shell with apples. Dot with margarine. Cover with top crust and cut several slits in top crust. Bake for 45 minutes or until crust is brown in a 350° oven.

Sandra teVelde, Loveland, CO

HOLIDAY APPLE PIE

1 Ritz pie shell
2 c. apple slices
1/2 c. white sugar
1/2 c. brown sugar
2 Tbsp. butter or margarine
1/4 tsp. cinnamon

1/4 tsp. allspice
1 egg
1/2 c. milk
1 Tbsp. lemon juice
1/4 c. raisins
1/4 c. chopped pecans

Place sliced apples in unbaked pie shell. Sprinkle white and brown sugars over apples. Mix other ingredients together. Pour over apples. Bake at 425° for 30 to 50 minutes. *Enjoy your pie!*

Mrs. Beulah Graeber, Branch No. 5968, Greensboro, NC

PEAR AND APPLE PIE

3 c. pears, pared and thinly sliced
3 c. apples, pared and thinly sliced
3/4 c. sugar
3 Tbsp. flour

1/2 tsp. cinnamon
1/4 tsp. salt
1 (9 inch) unbaked pie shell

Combine pears, apples, sugar, flour, cinnamon, and salt. Place in unbaked pie shell.

Topping:

1/3 c. margarine
1/2 c. brown sugar

1 c. flour

Cream margarine and brown sugar. Mix in flour. Sprinkle over top of pie.

Fold a 14 inch circle of foil loosely over top and around sides of pie. Bake at 400° for 40 to 45 minutes. Remove foil and continue baking for 20 minutes longer.

Thane Malison, Branch No. 5903, Dunlap, IL

FRESH STRAWBERRY PIE

2 c. water
1 1/4 c. sugar
1/4 c. cornstarch
2 or 3 drops of red food coloring

2 baked pie shells
6 c. sliced strawberries
1 small pkg. strawberry jello

Combine water, sugar, cornstarch, and food coloring in a saucepan; cook till thickened. Add strawberry jello and remove from heat; cool slightly. Fold in sliced strawberries and put in baked pie shells. Chill in refrigerator for 2 to 3 hours. Top with Cool Whip at serving time.

Mrs. Robert (Shirley) Aufdenberg, Branch No. 1374, Jackson, MO

FRESH STRAWBERRY PIE

4 Tbsp. cornstarch
3 Tbsp. cold water
1 c. sugar
1 c. water
¼ tsp. salt

Several drops of red food coloring
1 qt. fresh strawberries, washed
and hulled
1½ to 2 c. whipping topping

Mix cornstarch and cold water. Boil 1 cup water and the sugar plus the cornstarch mixture. Add the salt and the red food coloring. Cool, then add the strawberries. Put in the Baked Pie Shell. Top with the whipped topping and a few fresh strawberries. Refrigerate the leftover pie.

Baked Pie Shell:

1 c. Gold Medal flour
½ tsp. salt

⅓ c. plus 1 Tbsp. Crisco

Mix in bowl with pastry blender. Sprinkle with 2 tablespoons cold water. Make a ball of dough. Roll out and put in pie plate. Prick with a fork. Bake at 475° for 8 to 10 minutes.

Pearl Johannes, Branch No. 1149, Leigh, NE

STRAWBERRY-FRESH PIE

1 (4 serving size) pkg. Jell-O brand
vanilla flavor pudding and pie
filling
1 (3 oz.) pkg. Jell-O brand
strawberry flavor gelatin
2 c. water

1 tsp. lemon juice
1½ c. prepared Dream Whip
whipped topping
1 c. sliced strawberries
1 baked 9 inch pie shell, cooled

Combine pudding mix, gelatin, water, and lemon juice in a saucepan. Cook and stir over medium heat until mixture comes to a boil. Pour into a bowl and chill until thickened. To hasten chilling, place bowl of pudding mixture in larger bowl of ice and water, then stir until thickened. Fold in whipped topping, blending well. Stir in strawberries. Pour into pie shell and chill until set, 1 to 2 hours. Garnish with additional whipped topping and strawberries.

Eunice Brakhane, Branch No. 507, Ellisville, MO

PUMPKIN PIE

1 (16 oz.) can pumpkin
⅔ c. brown sugar
¼ tsp. salt
1 tsp. ground cinnamon
½ tsp. ground ginger

¼ tsp. ground nutmeg
¼ tsp. ground cloves
2 eggs, beaten
1 (13 oz.) can evaporated milk

Beat all ingredients together until mixed well. Pour into 9 inch unbaked pastry shell. Bake for 45 to 60 minutes.

Ethel Bauer, Branch No. 5616, Regan, ND

PUMPKIN PIE

Mix:

2 eggs
1 lb. canned pumpkin
⅔ c. brown or white sugar

½ tsp. salt
2 tsp. pumpkin pie spice

Mix first 5 ingredients. Stir in 1⅔ cups evaporated milk. Pour into 9 inch crust. Bake at 425° for 15 minutes, then at 350° for 45 minutes. Let cool and eat.

Shelia Schroeder, Branch No. 2347, New Melle, MO

PUMPKIN PIE

3 c. cooked pumpkin
1 c. white sugar
½ c. brown sugar
¼ c. honey
1½ tsp. cinnamon
¾ tsp. nutmeg
½ tsp. salt

¼ tsp. ginger
¼ tsp. cloves
4 Tbsp. melted butter
4 eggs
1 qt. milk (canned milk diluted half
    and half)

Combine pumpkin, sugars, honey, spices, and salt. Mix thoroughly. Add milk and butter. Store overnight in refrigerator. This greatly improves the flavor. Add slightly beaten eggs and bake in 2 pastry lined 9 inch pie pans at 400° for 30 to 35 minutes.

Katherine Nielson, Branch No. 5604, Tucson, AZ

FROZEN PEACH PIE

2 qt. peeled, sliced peaches
1 c. sugar
Scant ½ c. tapioca

Dash of salt
¼ c. lemon juice

Combine all ingredients and mix well. Line a 9 inch pie tin with foil, extending beyond edge. Put in filling with foil loosely up around tin and freeze until firm. When frozen, remove from tin and wrap with more foil; store in freezer. When ready to use, line pie tin with pastry, drop in frozen filling, dot with margarine, and add top crust. Brush with milk. Sprinkle with sugar and slit top.

Set pan on foil crumpled up around pan and loosely cover top with cooking bag held up with toothpicks. Bake at 450° for 30 minutes and turn down to 350°. Bake for 30 minutes or till brown.

Pastry for one 9 inch pie:

1¾ c. flour
¾ tsp. salt
About ½ c. ice water

2 tsp. baking powder
⅔ c. Crisco

Mix dry ingredients. Cut in Crisco. With fork, lightly mix in water so sticks together when put together with fingers. Mix for about 5 minutes. May be chilled before rolling out.

Anna Parsley, Branch No. 2121, Chico, CA

FRESH PEACH SINGLE CRUST PIE

¾ c. sugar
2 Tbsp. butter, softened
5 large fresh peaches, peeled and
   sliced

1 unbaked 9 inch pie shell
Vanilla ice cream
⅓ c. flour
¼ tsp. nutmeg

Cream together sugar and butter. Add flour and nutmeg. Mix until mixture is mealy. Spread ½ of this on bottom of unbaked pie shell. Arrange peaches on top. Sprinkle the remaining sugar mixture over peaches. Bake in oven preheated to 450° for 10 minutes. Reduce heat to 350°. Continue to bake for 40 minutes or until crust edges and top are light brown. Serve warm or cold with ice cream.

This pie is not overly sweet - just right with ice cream.

Lorna Miller, Branch No. 3107, Loveland, CO

PEACH PIE
(Fresh)

Crust:

1½ c. flour
2 Tbsp. sugar
2 Tbsp. milk

½ c. oil
½ tsp. salt

Mix and press into 9 inch pie pan. Bake for 30 minutes at 325°. Cool well.

Filling:

1 c. sugar
2 Tbsp. white syrup
3½ Tbsp. corn starch

1 c. boiling water
3 Tbsp. peach jello

Combine sugar, syrup, corn starch, and water; cook till clear and thick. Add 3 tablespoons peach jello. Set aside and cool. Add 6 to 8 sliced fresh peaches. Pour into crust and refrigerate. Serve with Cool Whip or whipped cream.

Arlene Kropp, Branch No. 634, Omaha, NE

COLORADO PEACH CREAM PIE

Crust - Mix:

½ c. butter
1½ c. flour

½ tsp. salt

Press into 1 very large or 2 small pie plates.

Filling: Slice 4 cups fresh sliced peaches into a bowl and sprinkle with ¼ cup sugar. Let stand while preparing ¾ cup sugar, 2 tablespoons flour, 1 egg, ¼ teaspoon salt, and ½ teaspoon vanilla. Fold in 1 cup sour cream and stir this mixture into the sugared peaches. Pour into the crust. Bake at 400° for 15 minutes, then at 350° for 20 minutes.

Now, sprinkle on the top of pie the topping mixture, consisting of ½ cup sugar, ⅓ cup flour, ¼ cup butter, and 1 teaspoon cinnamon. Bake at 400° for 10 minutes.

Get ready to enjoy one of the best peach pies ever!!!

Leona Sletmoen, Branch No. 3866, Audubon, MN

COOL PEACH PIE

½ lb. vanilla wafers
1 c. powdered sugar
¼ c. butter
2 well beaten egg yolks

1 large can peach halves
1 c. whipping cream
1 Tbsp. powdered sugar

Crush vanilla wafers and form into a 9 inch pie crust. (Save a portion of crumbs to sprinkle on top.) Cream 1 cup powdered sugar with ¼ cup butter. Add the egg yolks. Spread this on the crust. Place 6 peach halves, round side up, on the creamed mixture close to edge of pie pan (so each pie slice will have a peach). Whip the 1 cup cream and sweeten with the 1 tablespoon powdered sugar. Spread over peaches. Top with remaining crumbs. Refrigerate for 24 hours before serving.

Very nice for it can be made ahead of time!

Jan McLaughlin, Branch No. 3107, Loveland, CO

PEACH MERINGUE

3 egg whites
½ tsp. baking powder
1 c. white sugar
½ c. crushed corn flakes
¼ c. finely chopped nuts
½ c. coconut, toasted

½ pt. whipping cream
2 Tbsp. sugar
½ tsp. vanilla
⅛ tsp. almond extract
4 fresh peaches

Beat egg whites and baking powder till stiff. Add the 1 cup sugar slowly. Keep beating, then add ½ cup crushed corn flakes and ¼ cup nuts. Bake in a buttered pie plate at 300° for 35 to 40 minutes. Cool.

Meanwhile, toast ½ cup coconut. Beat ½ pint whipping cream. Add 2 tablespoons sugar, 2 teaspoons vanilla and ½ teaspoon almond extract. Put half of mixture in cooled crust, then add 4 fresh peaches sliced on, then the other half of mixture. Top with toasted coconut. *Chill.*

Easy and delicious - never fails!

Sue Heckendorf, Branch No. 4083, Brown Deer, WI

GOLDEN COCONUT PEACH PIE

4 to 4½ c. sliced fresh peaches
½ c. sugar
3 Tbsp. flour
¼ tsp. nutmeg
⅛ tsp. salt
¼ c. orange juice
1 (9 inch) unbaked pie shell

2 Tbsp. butter
2 c. flaked coconut
½ c. evaporated milk
1 egg, beaten
¼ to ½ c. sugar
¼ tsp. almond extrac.

Mix together peaches, sugar, flour, nutmeg, salt, and orange juice in medium bowl. Pour mixture into pie shell. Dot with butter. Bake at 450° for 15 minutes. Meanwhile, combine coconut, milk, egg, sugar, and almonds. Pour over hot peach mixture. Reduce heat to 350° and bake until coconut is toasted, about 30 minutes. Chill pie unless eaten at once.

Paul Schutte, Branch No. 1589, Wisner, NE

FRESH COCONUT PIE

1¼ c. coconut juice and water
3 c. grated coconut, packed
1 tsp. vanilla

1¾ c. sugar
Pastry for 2 crust pie

Boil sugar and liquid until it nearly threads. Add grated coconut and cook for about 10 minutes longer, so that coconut absorbs syrup. When cool, pour into pastry lined 9 inch pie pan. Place top crust and seal well all around. Make several slits near center of pie. Bake at 425° for 15 minutes, then reduce heat to 375° for 30 to 45 minutes.

Note: If using fresh coconut, drain off juice by punching out "eyes." Break nuts by hitting with a hammer between the eyes. Grate with food grinder. Or, may use packaged unsweetened grated coconut.

Esther Williams, Branch No. 6255, Wahiawa, HI

MILLIONAIRE PIE

1 can Eagle Brand milk
½ c. lemon juice
1 can crushed pineapple, drained,
    or 1 pkg. unsweetened
    strawberries

1 c. chopped pecans
1 (12 oz.) Cool Whip

Mix together and pour into two 8 inch graham cracker pie crusts. Cool for 1 hour in refrigerator.

Waymer Martin, Branch No. 4817, Youngstown, OH

MILLION DOLLAR PIES

1 (16 oz.) can crushed pineapple
1 (16 oz.) can sliced peaches
1 (14 oz.) can Eagle Brand milk
1 (12 oz.) ctn. Cool Whip

½ c. ReaLemon lemon juice
2 (9 inch) graham cracker pie
    crusts

Drain pineapple and peaches. Cut peaches in thirds. In large bowl, mix together pineapple and peaches, *adding* Eagle Brand milk. Mix well. Add lemon juice slowly while stirring and mix well. Fold in the thawed Cool Whip. Pour into 2 pie shells and chill in the refrigerator. Makes 2 pies.

Note: Pies made a day ahead have a better flavor.

Bonnie Spoerke, Branch No. 5844, Columbia City, IN

RHUBARB ORANGE CREAM PIE

Pastry for 9 inch pie shell
3 eggs, separated
1¼ c. sugar
¼ c. soft butter or margarine
3 Tbsp. frozen orange juice
    concentrate
¼ c. flour
¼ tsp. salt
2½ c. rhubarb, cut in ½ inch
    pieces

Make crust and line pan. Beat egg whites until stiff. Add ¼ cup of the sugar gradually, beating well after each addition. Add butter and juice concentrate to egg yolks; beat thoroughly. Add remaining 1 cup sugar, flour and salt. Beat well. Add rhubarb to yolk mixture and stir well. Gently fold in meringue. Pour into pastry lined pan. Bake on bottom rack in moderate oven (375°) for 15 minutes. Reduce heat to 325° and bake for 45 to 50 minutes more.

Linda Iverson, Branch No. 4909, Zumbrota, MN

RHUBARB CREAM PIE

1 Tbsp. butter
1¼ c. sugar
2 Tbsp. cornstarch
Pinch of salt
4 c. rhubarb
3 egg yolks
¼ c. milk
Baked 9 inch pie shell

Melt butter in pan. Add rhubarb and 1 cup sugar. Cook till rhubarb is tender, about 10 minutes. Combine remaining ingredients (except pie shell), stirring constantly, till thick. Turn into pie shell.

Meringue:

½ c. water
¼ c. sugar
Pinch of salt
1 Tbsp. cornstarch
3 egg whites

For meringue, stir first 4 ingredients over low heat till thick and clear. Beat egg whites till stiff; add cooled mixture and stir just till mixed. Spread over pie filling. Bake in 350° oven for 15 to 20 minutes. Refrigerate.

Cheryl Schultz, Branch No. 3107, Loveland, CO

PEAR RHUBARB PIE

1 (29 oz.) can Bartlett pears
2½ c. rhubarb, cut in ½ inch
   pieces
Pastry for 2 crust 9 inch pie
1 c. sugar

⅓ c. flour
½ tsp. salt
¼ tsp. mace
2 Tbsp. butter or margarine
Sugar (for sprinkling on top)

Drain juice from pears. Cut into bite-size chunks and toss with fresh rhubarb. Place half of the fruit in the pastry lined 9 inch pie plate. Combine sugar, flour, salt, and mace; sprinkle ½ over fruit. Add remaining fruit; top with remaining flour-sugar mixture. Dot with butter. Place woven lattice crust over the pie. Flute the edges. Sprinkle lightly with white granulated sugar. Bake at 450°F. for 10 minutes. Reduce heat to 350°F. and continue baking for 40 minutes. Serve warm as is, or with ice cream. Makes 6 servings.

Phyllis Shaffer, Branch No. 5844, Columbia City, IN

AMAZING COCONUT PIE

2 c. milk
¾ c. sugar
½ c. Bisquick mix
4 eggs

¼ c. melted margarine
1½ tsp. vanilla
1 c. coconut

Heat oven to 350°. Combine milk, sugar, Bisquick, eggs, margarine, and vanilla in blender. Cover blender and blend on low for 3 minutes. Pour into greased 9 inch pie pan. Let stand for about 5 minutes. Sprinkle coconut on top. Bake at 350° for 40 minutes. Serve warm or cool.

Nita Schmidt, Branch No. 2630, Greeley, CO

IMPOSSIBLE PIE
(Supposed to form its own crust)

2 c. milk
4 eggs
1 c. sugar
1 stick softened oleo

½ c. flour
2 tsp. vanilla
1 c. cocoanut

Mix all ingredients in blender; pour into greased and floured pie pan. Bake at 350° for 50 to 60 minutes.

Edna W. Tegtmeier, Branch No. 2910, Ames, IA

CHOCOLATE BAVARIAN CREAM

1½ sq. chocolate (unsweetened)
⅔ c. sugar
½ c. milk
1 Tbsp. Knox gelatine

¼ c. cold water
1 pt. whipping cream
1 tsp. vanilla
Vanilla wafers (or ladyfingers)

Combine chocolate, sugar, and milk. Cook over medium heat, stirring until chocolate is melted, then add gelatine soaked in cold water. Cook until dissolved. Cool until it begins to thicken. Beat mixture until very light. Fold in cream whipped until thick and the vanilla. Line a mold with wafers. Pour in part of mixture, then a layer of wafers, ending with mixture. Chill.

Mrs. John (Maxine) Johansen, Branch No. 3365, Rock Springs, WY

BLUEBERRY BANANA PIE

2 baked pie shells	1 c. milk (for Dream Whip)
1 (8 oz.) cream cheese	1 tsp. vanilla
1 c. powdered sugar	1 can blueberry pie filling
2 env. Dream Whip	4 bananas

Cream powdered sugar and cream cheese. Fold into prepared Dream Whip. Slice bananas and line pastry shells. Add vanilla to cheese mixture. Pour half cheese mixture over bananas in each shell. Sprinkle half can blueberry pie filling over each pie. Refrigerate for 2 or 3 hours or overnight.

Betty Kiesling, Branch No. 1250, Vernon, TX

BUTTERSCOTCH PIE

2 c. sweet milk	1/4 tsp. salt
1 1/3 c. brown sugar	2 eggs
5 Tbsp. white flour	2 Tbsp. butter

Scald 1 1/2 cups milk with brown sugar, but do not come to boil. Mix white flour with salt and 1/2 cup cold milk; mix well. Add to the hot milk, stirring constantly, over hot fire until it has boiled for a few minutes. Remove from fire and add beaten egg yolks. Return to fire and stir constantly until it boils. Add butter and remove from fire. Let cool slightly, then pour into a baked pie shell. Cover with the beaten egg whites in which a little sugar is used, then place in oven to brown.

Bernice Sheets, Branch No. 5844, Columbia City, IN

SOUR CREAM PIE

1 c. raisins	1 c. water

Boil together for 10 minutes.

3 egg yolks	3 Tbsp. corn starch
1 c. sour cream	Pinch of salt
1 c. sugar	

Add to top mixture and cook until thick. Add 1/4 teaspoon cinnamon. Boil together the raisins and water for 10 minutes. Add rest of the ingredients and cook until thick. Pour into a baked pie crust. Cover with meringue and brown.

Meringue:

3 egg whites	½ tsp. cream of tartar
⅛ tsp. salt	

Beat until thick and slowly add ⅓ cup sugar. Bake for 10 to 15 minutes to brown at 350°.

Mrs. Lawrence Greiner, Branch No. 2838, Wilmot, SD

MOM'S EGGNOG PIE

1 env. Knox gelatine	6 egg yolks
2 c. milk	2 Tbsp. butter
¼ c. cornstarch	2 tsp. vanilla
1 c. sugar	2 c. whipping cream
⅛ tsp. salt	

Soak gelatine in ¼ cup cold water. Cook the milk, cornstarch, sugar, and salt in double boiler until slightly thickened. Beat egg yolks. Add 1 cup hot mixture to yolks, stirring constantly. Add yolk mixture to cooked mixture and cook for a few minutes. Remove from heat. Add gelatine, 2 tablespoons butter and 2 teaspoons vanilla. Cool.

Beat cream to soft peaks. Slowly add cooled mixture. Pour into baked 10 inch pie shell. Sprinkle generously with nutmeg. Chill overnight. Serves 8 to 10.

Ruth Glaystein, Branch No. 769, Utica, NE; Janet Peterson, Branch No. 4390, Appleton, Wi; Jeanie Wittkopf, Branch No. 2714, Ogden, UT

AMBROSIA PIE (COCONUT CRUST)

2 c. wide coconut or 2¼ c. shredded coconut	6 oz. orange juice concentrate
	2 (17 oz.) cans apricot halves, drained (reserve the juice)
¼ c. sugar	
⅔ c. soft margarine	5 Tbsp. cornstarch or tapioca
1 c. slivered or crushed almonds	Water (add to orange juice and apricot juice to make 3 c. liquid)
1 large orange	
1 tsp. zest of orange	
½ c. sugar	1 tsp. vanilla

Make zest. Peel orange and cut up into juices. Add thickening and sugar. Cook till clear. Cool. If tapioca is used, soak in the juices before cooking. Add vanilla.

Mix coconut, sugar, margarine, and nuts. Press into two 9 inch pie plates. Bake at 325°F. for 20 minutes or until light brown. Cool.

Arrange the apricots on the bottom or alternate the juice filling with the apricot halves in the shells. Cool for several hours or overnight. Mix a few nuts and coconut; sprinkle around the edge of the pie. Fill the middle with Cool Whip before serving.

Loraine Jorgensen, Loveland, CO

LEMON VELVET PIE

1⅓ c. sugar
6 Tbsp. cornstarch
¼ tsp. salt
1½ c. boiling water
3 eggs, separated
2 Tbsp. butter or margarine
1 Tbsp. grated lemon peel
⅓ c. strained fresh lemon juice

1 tsp. vanilla
1 env. unflavored gelatin
¼ c. cold water
1 c. light cream
1 baked 10 inch pie shell
1 c. heavy cream, whipped
6 to 8 walnut halves (optional)

In saucepan, thoroughly mix together sugar, cornstarch and salt; add boiling water, stirring constantly. Bring to boil over medium heat. Continue stirring; boil for 3 to 4 minutes. Beat egg yolks slightly; add some of hot mixture to yolks and blend well. Return mixture to saucepan. Add butter and cook for 2 minutes longer, stirring constantly. Do not boil.

Remove from heat; stir in lemon peel, juice and vanilla. Remove a generous ½ cup of filling; reserve for topping. Soften gelatin in water; add to hot mixture, stirring until thoroughly dissolved. Blend in light cream. Chill until slightly thickened, but not set.

Beat egg whites until stiff, but not dry. Carefully fold into chilled mixture. Pour into baked pie shell; chill until partially set. Spread reserved filling completely over top of pie; chill until firm. Top with whipped cream. Garnish with walnut halves if desired.

Dorothea Albright, Branch No. 2793, Vandalia, IL

LEMON PIE

1 baked pie shell
1 c. sugar
4 Tbsp. corn starch

Juice of 1 lemon
1½ c. water
4 eggs, separated

Meringue:

3 egg whites

6 Tbsp. sugar

Mix cornstarch and sugar. Add lemon juice, water and egg yolks. Cook until clear and thick. Make meringue by beating 3 egg whites until thick, but not dry. Add 6 tablespoons sugar gradually until glossy. Put meringue over pie while hot. Bake at 425° for 5 to 6 minutes.

Mrs. Arthur Wegener, Branch No. 2232, Midland, MI

FROSTY LEMONADE PIE

1¼ c. crushed pretzels
¼ c. sugar
½ c. butter or margarine, melted
1 qt. (4 c.) vanilla ice cream,
    softened

1 (6 oz.) can frozen lemonade,
    thawed
Few drops of yellow food coloring

Butter an 8 to 9 inch pie pan. In small bowl, combine pretzel crumbs, sugar and margarine. Press in bottom and up sides of pan. Refrigerate for 15 minutes. In large bowl, combine ice cream, lemonade and food coloring. Blend well. Spoon into prepared crust. Freeze until firm. Let stand at room temperature for a few minutes before serving.

Cheryl O'Brien, Branch No. 4718, New Lenox, IL

STRAWBERRY ANGEL PIE

1 (1 lb.) bag marshmallows   1 c. milk

Melt together in large bowl in microwave for 2 minutes. Stir and cook for another 2 minutes until marshmallows are melted. Do not overheat. Cool.

Add:

10 oz. (or more) frozen   1½ c. whipped cream
   strawberries

Pour over graham cracker crust in 10x13 inch pan. Refrigerate or freeze.

Use any fruit desired. Fresh peaches are very good.

Ardith Mueller, Branch No. 1775, Columbus, NE

ANGEL PIE
(Dessert)

1 pkg. Nabisco cookies, crushed   Juice of 2 to 3 lemons
1 large pkg. lemon jello   1 can Milnot
1 pinch of salt   Cherries
1 c. sugar   2 c. boiling water

Juice 2 to 3 lemons. Mix 2 cups boiling water with 1 large lemon jello, salt, sugar, and juice of 2 to 3 lemons. Put in the refrigerator. When it begins to thicken, stir it into a can of cooled whipped Milnot. Have the Nabisco crumbs in a large 13x9 inch dish. Pour whipped mixture and sprinkle with a few crumbs on top. Top each square with a cherry.

May also be put in pie pans.

Ruth Ann Broers, Branch No. 3837, Nokomis, IL

MONTGOMERY PIES

Bottom Part:

1 lemon juice and rind   1 egg
1 c. sugar   2 Tbsp. flour
1 c. molasses   1 pt. water

Top (Cake Part):

2 c. sugar
½ c. shortening
2 eggs

1 c. milk
3 c. flour
3 tsp. baking powder

Bring first 6 ingredients to a boil. Cool. Put in 2 unbaked pie shells. Mix top as given as you would a cake. Bake at 350° for 30 minutes.

Meda Miller, Branch No. 5265, Herndon, PA

GREEN TOMATO PIE

Pastry for 2 crust pie
3½ c. sliced green tomatoes
¾ c. raisins
1½ tsp. grated lemon rind
2 Tbsp. lemon juice
1 Tbsp. vinegar

½ tsp. salt (scant)
1½ c. sugar
3 Tbsp. flour
½ tsp. cinnamon
½ tsp. ginger
2 Tbsp. butter or margarine

Combine first 5 ingredients. Combine sugar, flour and spices; add to the tomato combination. Place the tomato mixture into the pastry lined pie pan and dot with butter. Lay on the top crust and seal. Bake for 15 minutes in a 425° oven, then reduce heat to 350° and bake for 40 minutes longer or until done.

Mrs. Hildegarde Gordon, Branch No. 2090, Dowagiac, MI

FEBRUARY'S FAVORITE PIE

Fit pastry for single crust pie into a 9 inch pie pan and form a high crimped edge. Spoon one No. 2 can of sour pitted cherries (drained), mixed with 2 tablespoons corn starch and ½ cup sugar into the unbaked crust. Bake in a 375° oven for 30 minutes.

Combine:

2 eggs, well beaten
½ c. sugar
¼ c. melted butter

2 tsp. lemon juice
¼ tsp. vanilla
½ c. flaked coconut

Pour mixture carefully over the cherries. Return pie to oven and bake for 20 to 25 minutes longer.

Betty Hay, Branch No. 5677

PLUM DEEP-DISH PIE

1¼ c. sugar
3 Tbsp. flour
⅛ tsp. salt
¼ tsp. almond extract

2 Tbsp. butter or margarine
4 c. halved, pitted plums (about 2½ lb.)

Combine sugar, flour, salt, extract, and butter. Arrange plums in 10x6x2 inch baking dish; sprinkle with sugar mixture. Place a single pie crust over top of plums. Sprinkle crust with sugar. Bake at 450° for 45 to 50 minutes. Makes 6 servings.

Margaret M. Golick, Branch No. 5196, Trafford, PA

CONFETTI PIE

1 (4 oz.) pkg. chocolate pudding
   and pie filling mix
1 (2 oz.) pkg. dessert topping mix

1 c. multicolored mini
   marshmallows
¼ c. chopped nuts (if desired)

Crust:

1 c. graham cracker crumbs
2 Tbsp. sugar

⅓ c. butter

Prepare crust. Mix graham cracker crumbs and sugar in 9 inch pie pan. Melt butter. Add to crumbs. Mix and press against bottom and sides of pan. Set aside.

Prepare the pudding as directed on the package. Cool. Prepare the dessert topping as directed. Carefully fold ½ of the topping, the marshmallows and nuts into the pudding. Spoon into crust. Garnish with remaining topping and sprinkle with more mini marshmallows.

This is a great recipe for children to help with.

Sharon Verville, Branch No. 3107, Loveland, CO

LIME PINEAPPLE PIE

1 can sweetened condensed milk
½ c. *fresh* lime juice
1 (10 oz.) can crushed pineapple,
   drained

Green food coloring (if desired)
1 baked pie shell
Whipped topping

Mix first 3 ingredients together. Pour into baked pie shell. Chill for 3 hours. Pour on whipped topping or whipped cream.

Mary Schaffer, Loveland, CO

PUDDING PIE

Pudding pie mixes (2 flavors)   1 pie crust

Mix one flavor of the pudding pie mix. Pour into already cooked pie crust. Make the second flavor. Pour on top of the pudding already in the pie crust. Chill for 2 hours. Serve.

Jajay Lothe, Branch No. 5285, Deforest, WI

CRANBERRY-RAISIN PIE

1½ c. cranberries
1 c. raisins
½ c. water
1 Tbsp. butter
1 tsp. vanilla

1 c. sugar
4 Tbsp. cornstarch
1 Tbsp. grated orange peel
1 c. chopped nuts
Baked pie crust

Cook the cranberries and raisins in the ½ cup of water until the cranberries crack. Add 1 tablespoon butter and 1 teaspoon vanilla. Mix together 1 cup sugar, 4 tablespoons cornstarch, and 1 tablespoon grated orange peel. Add to cranberry mixture. Cook until thick. Add 1 cup chopped nuts. Cool and pour into baked pie shell. This may be topped with whipped cream or Cool Whip.

Phyllis Carlson, Branch No. 5617, Schuyler, NE

PUMPKIN FLUFF PIE
(Diabetics may use)

1 (16 oz.) can pumpkin
1 (12 oz.) evaporated skim milk
2 egg yolks, beaten
½ tsp. ground cinnamon
¼ tsp. ground ginger
⅛ tsp. ground nutmeg
8 packets Equal

1 env. unflavored gelatin
¼ c. cold water
3 egg whites
1 tsp. vanilla
¼ tsp. cream of tartar
1 baked 8 inch pie shell

Beat well in large saucepan the pumpkin, milk, and egg yolks. Stir in spices. Thoroughly heat over medium heat, stirring occasionally. Remove from heat and stir in Equal. Combine gelatin and cold water. Let stand for 1 minute. Cook over low heat for 5 minutes or till gelatin completely dissolves. Stir into pumpkin mix. Cool.

Combine egg whites and cream of tartar at room temperature in medium bowl; beat until soft peaks form. Add vanilla. Beat till stiff peaks form. Fold into pumpkin mix. Spoon into baked pie shell. Chill.

One-eighth pie equals 163 calories, 18 g carbohydrate, 8 g protein, and 7 g fat.

Ruth Flowers, Branch No. 3436, Pico Rivera, CA

LOW CHOLESTEROL PUMPKIN PIE FILLING

1 c. cooked pumpkin
⅔ c. (may use 1 c.) dry milk
  (skim), dissolved in 1 c. warm
  water
¼ c. flour
⅔ c. sugar
⅓ c. molasses
1 whole egg

4 egg whites
¼ tsp. salt
1 tsp. cinnamon
½ tsp. cloves
¼ tsp. nutmeg
¼ tsp. ginger
1 unbaked pie shell

Mix together pumpkin, flour, sugar, molasses, 1 egg and whites, salt, and spices. Beat with mixer until smooth. Add milk on low speed. Fill shell. Bake at 400° for 10 minutes; reduce heat to 350°. Bake for 30 minutes more or until done.

Mrs. Lorna Klein, Branch No. 239, Brainerd, MN

FRENCH CHERRY PIE

Crust:

3 egg whites
12 soda crackers
½ c. chopped pecans or walnuts
1 tsp. baking powder

1 c. sugar
1 tsp. vinegar
Vanilla

Filling:

1 pkg. cream cheese
½ c. powdered sugar

1 tsp. vanilla
1 (12 oz.) ctn. whipped cream

Beat egg whites until frothy. Gradually beat in sugar. Fold in crackers, vinegar, nuts, baking powder, and vanilla. Spread in buttered pie plate (sides and bottom). Bake at 325° for 20 minutes.

Beat cream cheese with powdered sugar. Stir in whipped cream and vanilla. Pour over cooled crust. Cover with 1 can cherry pie filling. Chill.

PEANUT BUTTER CREAM PIE

½ c. sugar
1 c. powdered milk
2 Tbsp. corn starch
½ c. water

2 egg yolks
1½ c. hot water
1 tsp. vanilla
½ c. peanut butter

Mix together sugar, powdered milk, corn starch, ½ cup water, and egg yolks. Add to hot water, stirring constantly and cooking on moderate heat until thickened. Remove from heat; add vanilla and peanut butter. Put into 9 inch cooked pie crust and top with meringue.

Pat Woolington, Branch No. 2935, Torrington, WY

TOFFEE ICE CREAM PIE

17 to 18 vanilla wafers (or as needed)

½ gal. vanilla ice cream
1 c. chopped Heath bars*

Sauce:

1½ c. sugar
1 c. evaporated milk
¼ c. butter

¼ c. light corn syrup
Dash of salt

394

Soften ice cream. Stir in ½ cup Heath bars. Pour into pie pan lined with vanilla wafers. Mix together sauce ingredients in saucepan and boil for 1 minute. Stir remaining candy into sauce. To serve, pour cooled sauce over frozen slice of pie.

* Use ½ cup bars in pie itself and other ½ cup in sauce.

Kathy Wessel, Branch No. 0743, Truman, MN

HERSHEY'S BAR PIE

½ c. milk
16 large marshmallows
1 large Hershey's bar with
    almonds (½ lb.)

1 c. whipped cream

Heat milk and marshmallows in top of a double boiler. Add the Hershey's bar and mix until melted and blended. Cool. Fold into the chocolate mixture the whipped cream. Pour into a graham cracker crust and chill.

Grace Reich, Branch No. 1349, Sandy, OR

GRAPE PIE WITH CRUMB TOPPING

3½ c. Concord grapes
¾ c. sugar
¼ c. flour
¼ tsp. salt

1 Tbsp. lemon juice
1½ Tbsp. melted butter
1 (8 inch) unbaked pie shell

Crumb Topping:

½ c. sugar
¾ c. flour

⅓ c. butter

Wash grapes and slip off skins. Set skins aside to add later. Cook the pulp until soft. Press through a sieve to remove seeds. Combine sugar, flour, salt, lemon juice, skins, butter, and grape pulp. Pour into pie shell. Sprinkle with Crumb Topping. Bake at 450° for 10 minutes, then reduce heat to 350° and bake for 25 additional minutes.

Helen Baysinger, Branch No. 771, Elizabeth, IL

GRASSHOPPER PIE

1½ c. chocolate wafer cookie
    crumbs
¼ c. butter or margarine, melted
32 large or 3 c. miniature
    marshmallows

½ c. milk
1½ c. chilled whipping cream
¼ c. creme de menthe
3 Tbsp. white creme de cacao
Few drops of green food coloring

Heat oven to 350°. Mix crumbs and butter in 9 inch pie pan; press firmly and evenly against bottom and side of pan. Bake for 10 minutes. Cool.

Melt marshmallows with milk over low heat, stirring constantly. Chill until thickened. In chilled bowl, beat cream until stiff. Stir marshmallow mixture to blend. Gradually stir in creme de menthe and creme de cacao. Fold into whipped cream. Fold in food coloring. Pour into baked crust. Chill for at least 4 hours.

Dorothy Sahlhoff, Branch No. 0823, Bremen, IN

MINCEMEAT
(Filling for pie)

2 qt. beef or venison, cooked and chopped fine or ground	1 pt. rich stock
	1 Tbsp. salt
8 qt. peeled apples	1 small tsp. black pepper
2 lb. raisins	1 small Tbsp. cinnamon
2 lb. currants	1 tsp. cloves
1 lb. suet, ground	1 small tsp. allspice
3 c. brown sugar	½ tsp. nutmeg
1 pt. dark syrup or sorghum	Some apple, pickle juice or ½ c.
1 pt. apple cider	vinegar

Boil all together for ½ hour or until done. Stir often. Cook slow. Recipe equals about 8 quarts or filling for 8 pies.

I can extra mincemeat, but it can be put in containers and frozen for future use.

Phyllis Schenck, Branch No. 422, Reedsburg, WI

BUTTER CRUNCH CRUST

½ c. butter or oleo	1 c. sifted flour (Gold Medal)
¼ c. brown sugar, packed	
½ c. chopped pecans, walnuts or cocoanut	

Heat oven to 400°. Mix all ingredients with hands. Spread in oblong pan, 13 x 9 ½ x 2 inches. Bake for 15 minutes. Take from oven. Stir with spoon. Save ¾ cup for topping. Immediately press rest of mixture against bottom and sides of 9 inch pie pan. Cool. Pour in your favorite lemon chiffon or creamy pie filling. Sprinkle reserved crumbs over top. Chill for 1 hour. Makes 8 servings.

Ida Ouillette, Branch No. 2579, Pinconning, MI

EASY PIE CRUST

1½ c. flour	½ c. oil
1 tsp. salt	2 Tbsp. milk
1½ tsp. sugar	

Put all ingredients into pie plate and mix until they form a ball. Pat out to form pie crust. Prick with fork and bake at 425° for 10 to 15 minutes. Cool and fill or fill unbaked pie shell with your favorite filling and bake per instructions of pie filling.

Nancy M. Luft, Branch No. 6303, Lodi, OH

STIR-N-ROLL PASTRY

2 c. sifted flour
1 tsp. salt

½ c. Wesson, Mazola or Kraft oil
¼ c. cold milk

Mix together the flour and salt. Pour into measuring cup, but don't stir the oil and milk. Pour all at once into flour. Stir lightly until mixed. Round out dough and divide in half. Flatten each half slightly. Place half between 2 sheets of waxed paper. Roll out gently until circle reaches edge of paper. Peel off top paper. Bake at 450° for 10 to 12 minutes. Makes two 9 inch pie shells. Use half for shell.

Marge Milz, Branch No. 2295, Detroit, MI

NEVER FAIL PIE CRUST

1 c. lard
½ c. boiling water

1 tsp. salt
3 c. flour

Blend lard and water with mixer until smooth. Add salt and flour; beat with mixer until moistened. Roll crust between 2 sheets of wax paper.

Jamy Manke, Branch No. 5985, Midland, SD

PIE CRUST - FAILPROOF

3 c. flour

1 tsp. salt

Cut in 1 cup shortening. Measure 1 egg yolk and milk to equal ⅔ cup. Reserve egg white. Beat with 1 teaspoon water and use as glaze on top crust of pie. Add egg yolk-milk mixture to flour mixture and combine thoroughly. Roll crust on flour or cloth in usual manner. Any crust is usually easier to work with if left to set for a few minutes before rolling, or put into refrigerator for a few minutes.

Mona Geidel, Branch No. 3107, Loveland, CO

NORWEGIAN NEVER FAIL PIE CRUST

1¼ c. shortening
3 c. flour
1 egg

5 Tbsp. water
1 tsp. salt
1 tsp. vinegar

Combine dry ingredients and cut in the shortening. Mix rest of ingredients and toss with fork to make soft dough. Roll out as usual.

Erna Koelsch, Branch No. 6940, Harrison, MI

PIE CRUST - "BOB'S MOMS"

1½ c. shortening
3 c. flour
1 egg

5 Tbsp. water
1 tsp. vinegar
¼ tsp. salt

Cut shortening into flour. Beat together the egg, water, vinegar, and salt. Mix the egg liquid with flour and shortening, using a fork. Gather dough together and roll out as for other pie dough. Use plenty of flour to roll. Makes 3 "two crust" 8 inch pies.

Evalyn Storm, Branch No. 4665, Knoxville, TN

FLAKY PASTRY

4 c. flour
1¾ c. solid shortening
1 Tbsp. sugar
2 tsp. salt

1 Tbsp. vinegar
1 egg
½ c. water

With fork, mix first 4 ingredients. In small bowl, combine and beat water, vinegar, and egg. Add to first mixture and blend with fork until dry ingredients are moistened. Must be chilled for at least 15 minutes before being used. Will stay for 3 days in refrigerator. Makes 5 single crusts.

Marguerite Boerger, Branch No. 4734, Delphi, IN

MOM'S PIE CRUST

5 c. flour
2 tsp. salt
3 tsp. sugar
2 tsp. baking powder
2 c. shortening

1 egg yolk
3 tsp. vinegar
1 egg white (for top crust)
Ice water (enough to fill cup)

Combine flour, salt, sugar, and baking powder. Cut shortening into dry ingredients. Put egg yolk in a cup and beat it with a fork. Add vinegar to blended egg yolk. Fill cup with ice water. Sprinkle a small amount of liquid over the flour and shortening mixture; blend it together with a fork to make a soft dough. Continue adding water as needed. The dough will be easier to roll out if the dough rests for an hour. Roll out. Will make 2 or 3 two crust pies.

Blend egg white with 1 teaspoon water and brush it on the top crust. Sprinkle a little sugar on top. Bake at 425° until bubbly and lightly browned. *Yum-yum-good!*

Sharon Willweber, Granada Hills, CA, Branch No. 4859, Mission Hills, CA

NEVER-FAIL-PIE-CRUST-OR-TURNOVERS

5 c. flour
1 c. oleo
1 c. shortening

1 tsp. salt
2 egg yolks
1 c. milk

Mix first 4 ingredients, then put 2 egg yolks in 1 cup measuring cup. Fill to top with milk. Mix with other ingredients. Dough will be a little moist. Can be rolled out and rerolled - will not get tough.

Janette McCann, Branch No. 2232, Midland, MI

SIX CRUST-PIE CRUST

6 c. flour
2½ c. shortening (only 2 c. if lard
   is used)

1 egg, beaten slightly in a 1 c.
   measure*

Blend with fork or pastry blender. Work dough with your hands until all flour is mixed in well and dough is consistency of play dough. You can't overmix, so mix thoroughly. This makes at least 6 pie crusts. Roll out flat pie pan size rounds. Wrap in wax paper and store in freezer until needed.

* Fill cup with milk and add to the crumb mixture (flour, shortening and 1 tablespoon salt.

Lydia Busick, Branch No. 5844, Columbia City, IN

CHOCOLATE MINT PIE

3 Tbsp. butter
36 vanilla wafers, crushed
1/4 lb. butter
1 c. powdered sugar, *sifted*

2 eggs
1/2 tsp. mint extract
2 sq. baking chocolate, melted
1 medium tub Cool Whip

Combine crushed vanilla wafers and butter. Pat into pie plate. Bake at 350° for 10 minutes and cool.

Mix *sifted* powdered sugar and butter. Add eggs, mint extract and melted chocolate squares. Fold in Cool Whip. Pour in cooled crust and chill.

NO BAKE PEANUT BUTTER CHIFFON PIE

1 env. unflavored gelatin
1/2 c. cool water
4 oz. cream cheese (soft)
1 c. confectioners sugar

1/3 c. smooth peanut butter
1 (9 oz.) container Cool Whip
1 (9 inch) graham cracker crust
1/4 c. finely chopped peanuts

Whip cheese till soft and fluffy. Beat in sugar and peanut butter. Dissolve gelatin in water. Slowly add to mixture, blending thoroughly. Fold Cool Whip into mixture. Pour into pie shell. Sprinkle with peanuts. Chill until firm, 1 to 2 hours.

Marilyn Vogel, Loveland, CO

BANANA BOATS
(Microwave)

2 ripe bananas, peeled
3 Tbsp. brown sugar
1 Tbsp. butter or margarine, cut in
    pieces

1 Tbsp. chopped walnuts

Split bananas lengthwise and place in 8x8 inch baking dish. Cut sides up. Sprinkle brown sugar over bananas. Dot with butter. Scatter nuts on top. Microwave for 1 minute on HIGH. Garnish with whipped cream or chocolate syrup if desired.

Cheryl Schultz, Branch No. 3107, Loveland, CO

BANANAS FOSTER
(Microwave)

2 Tbsp. butter	½ tsp. cinnamon
2 large bananas, quartered	2 Tbsp. orange liqueur
2 Tbsp. brown sugar	2 Tbsp. rum

Place butter in 1 quart casserole. Microwave on HIGH till butter melts. Roll bananas in butter. Mix brown sugar and cinnamon. Sprinkle over bananas. Microwave for 2½ to 3 minutes on HIGH, or till sugar begins to melt. Remove from oven. Pour liqueur and rum over bananas. Ignite. When flame dies down, serve bananas and sauce on ice cream or a thin slice of pound cake.

Cheryl Schultz, Branch No. 3107, Loveland, CO

ECLAIR DESSERT

Bottom layer:

1 c. water	1 c. flour
1 stick margarine	4 eggs

Boil water and margarine. Add flour and stir until it leaves side of pan. Add eggs, one at a time, beating by hand until mixed. Spread in 9x13 inch pan. Bake at 400° for 25 minutes. Cool.

Filling:

8 oz. cream cheese	2 small pkg. vanilla instant
3 c. cold milk	pudding

Beat cream cheese and cold milk until smooth. Add pudding and mix well. Pour on crust.

Topping:

1 (9 oz.) container Cool Whip	Chocolate syrup

Spread with Cool Whip. Drizzle with chocolate syrup. Refrigerate till serving.

Delores Schrimpf, Branch No. 127, Lake City, MN

PINK CLOUD DESSERT

1 (3 oz.) pkg. strawberry jello	2 c. sliced bananas
1 c. crushed vanilla wafers	Whipped topping
1 (3½ oz.) pkg. vanilla pudding	
(the kind you cook)	

Prepare jello. Chill until partially set. Spread half of wafer crumbs in an 8x8 inch pan. Prepare pudding and spoon hot pudding over crumbs. Arrange half of the banana slices over pudding, top with remaining crumbs and cool. Pour partially set jello over crumbs and arrange rest of banana slices on top. When jello is set, spread whipped topping over top. Cut into squares to serve.

Doris Maier, Branch No. 6569, Seward, NE

FROZEN RASPBERRY DESSERT

Crust:

3¼ c. vanilla wafer crumbs
1 stick margarine, melted

6 Tbsp. sugar

Combine crust ingredients and press into a 9x13 and 8x8 inch cake pan. Bake at 375° for 8 minutes. Cool.

Filling:

6 egg yolks
2 tsp. vanilla
½ tsp. raspberry flavor
2 (8 oz.) pkg. cream cheese,
  softened

¼ tsp. salt
2 c. sugar
2 (9 oz.) ctn. Cool Whip
6 egg whites
2 (10 oz.) pkg. frozen raspberries

Beat vanilla, raspberry flavor and egg yolks until creamy. Add and beat in the cream cheese. Add salt and sugar; beat until smooth. Fold in sugar and Cool Whip. Beat egg whites until they form peaks and then blend into mix. Mash and swirl the raspberries into the mix. Pour mix over the 2 crusts. Put remaining raspberries on top. Freeze.

This is rich so cut into small squares to serve.

Mrs. John (Mardelle) Goeller, Branch No. 1971, Pilger, NE

GRANDMA ED'S CREAM PIE

This is a favorite recipe that my grandmother used to make. It came from her grandmother.

1 qt. sour cream*
½ c. brown sugar

½ c. white sugar

Mix brown and white sugars. Simmer sour cream for about 7 to 10 minutes. Add sugar to sour cream and simmer until syrupy (5 to 10 minutes). Stir constantly. Cool down until warm.

Have prepared a 9x12 inch pan of *baked* sweet yeast dough. Fork sour cream mixture into sweet dough and cover top. *Good while warm.*

* Farm cream is preferred or substitute 1 pint cultured sour cream and 1 pint sweet cream. Allow to stand overnight to finish souring. Add 1 teaspoon vinegar if necessary.

Pennie Tomac, Branch No. 4374, Chesaning, MI

BUTTERSCOTCH FONDUE

½ c. butter or margarine
2 c. brown sugar
1 c. light corn syrup

1 (15 oz.) can sweetened
  condensed milk (1⅓ c.)
1 tsp. vanilla

In saucepan, melt butter; stir in sugar, corn syrup, and 2 tablespoons water. Bring to boiling. Stir in milk. Simmer, stirring constantly, till mixture reaches thread stage (230°). Add vanilla. Pour into fondue pot. Place over fondue burner. Spear "dippers" with fondue forks. Dip in fondue. (If mixture becomes too thick, stir in a little milk or water.)

Suggested "dippers": Pound cake, vanilla wafers, apples, and popcorn. (To keep apple slices from browning, put in diluted orange juice.

Lanette Ude, Branch No. 1868, Yuma, CO

NORWEGIAN RICE

½ gal. milk
1 c. white rice
¾ c. sugar
½ c. half & half

1 egg
1 tsp. salt
1 tsp. flour
1 tsp. vanilla

Pour boiling water over the 1 cup of rice to cover the rice. Let stand just 5 minutes and drain well. Scald the milk. Add rice to milk; let cook for 20 to 30 minutes until tender, but not mushy. Beat the egg. Add sugar, salt, and flour. Beat mixture together and add the half & half. Add to rice mixture and cook for 5 minutes more. Add vanilla after removing from heat. Serve either warm or cold with a sprinkling of cinnamon.

Betty Leland, Branch No. 6872, Bricelyn, MN

QUICK PEAR DESSERT

Fresh or thawed frozen raspberries
Pear halves

Sour cream
Ginger snap cookies

In dessert dishes, spoon raspberries over pear halves. Top with dollop of sour cream. Accompany with ginger snap cookies.

Julie Padilla, Branch No. 3107, Loveland, CO

LIME DESSERT

2 pkg. lime jello
1 pkg. cream cheese
2 c. hot water
1 large can crushed pineapple

1 small jar maraschino cherries
Nuts
2 c. whipped cream

Dissolve jello and cream cheese in water. Mix well and chill until partially set. Add rest of ingredients and chill.

Ilene Ring, Branch No. 3330, McIntire, IA

FORGOTTEN DESSERT

6 egg whites
¼ tsp. salt
½ tsp. cream of tartar
1½ c. sugar (added slowly)
1 tsp. vanilla

⅛ tsp. almond flavoring
1 pkg. lemon pudding
1 pt. whipping cream
Crushed nuts

Beat egg whites, salt, cream of tartar, sugar (add the sugar a little at a time), vanilla, and almond flavoring into a stiff meringue. Have oven heated to 400°F. Put meringue into a 9x13 inch pan; place pan into oven. Turn off heat and leave in oven overnight.

Cook lemon pudding as directed on package. Cool. Whip 1 pint whipping cream. Spread half of the whipped cream over the meringue. Spread the cooled pudding over that, then spread the remainder of the whipped cream over the pudding layer. Sprinkle with crushed nuts. Refrigerate.

Selma Nynas, Branch No. 3339, Esko, MN

LEMON DELIGHT

1 c. flour
½ c. margarine
½ c. chopped pecans
1 (8 oz.) pkg. cream cheese
1 (9 oz.) ctn. Cool Whip

1 c. powdered sugar
2 (3½ oz.) pkg. lemon instant
   pudding
3 c. milk

Mix flour, margarine and pecans together. Press into the bottom of a 9x13 inch pan. Bake to light brown at 375°. Cool. Mix cream cheese, sugar and 1 cup Cool Whip together. Spread over cooled first layer. Beat pudding and milk until thick; spread over the 2 layers in the pan. Spread the remaining Cool Whip over the top. Sprinkle with toasted pecans. Chill thoroughly.

Vera Krueger, Branch No. 2716, Northglenn, CO

LEMON TORTE

50 Waverly crackers
½ c. plus 2 Tbsp. butter
5 egg whites
1 c. sugar

1 large box cook type lemon
   pudding or 1 (21 oz.) can
   lemon pie filling
Whipping cream

Roll crackers into crumbs. Melt butter. Put into 10x15 inch pan.

Filling: Beat egg whites till frothy. Add sugar gradually, beating till stiff. Spread over crust and bake at 350° for about 20 minutes. Prepare lemon pudding or filling. Spread over cooled shell and top with whipped cream. Serve.

Lorraine Roecker, AAL Branch No. 1400, Allenton, WI

RHUBARB DELIGHT

Crust:

2 c. flour
2 Tbsp. sugar

1 c. softened butter

Mix together and press into a 9x13 inch greased pan. Bake at 350° until golden brown.

Filling:

4 c. diced rhubarb	1½ c. sugar
3 egg yolks	2 Tbsp. flour
½ c. milk	

Beat egg yolks and add milk until smooth. Add remaining ingredients and cook over medium heat for 30 minutes. Pour over crust and bake at 350° for 40 minutes.

Topping:

3 stiffly beaten egg whites	1 tsp. vanilla
⅓ c. sugar	

Spread on top and bake for 10 minutes until golden brown. Cut while warm.
Maria Bremer (Curtis Bremer), Branch No. 2543, McHenry, IL

SUMMER PEACH DESSERT

1 white cake mix	1 c. toasted coconut
½ c. butter	Fresh peaches, sliced and drained
4 Tbsp. sugar	2 tsp. cinnamon
1 egg, slightly beaten	1 c. sour cream

To toast coconut, place in a 9x13 inch pan and place under broiler for 5 minutes or until golden. Mix coconut with dry cake mix and butter. Press in a 9x13 inch pan, ½ inch up on sides. Bake at 350° for 10 to 15 minutes. Cool.

Layer with peaches. Sprinkle peaches with 2 tablespoons sugar and 1 teaspoon cinnamon. Combine egg and sour cream. Pour over peaches. Sprinkle sour cream mixture with 2 tablespoons sugar and 1 teaspoon cinnamon. Bake at 350° until sour cream is set and peaches are tender, about 20 to 30 minutes.
Karen K. Riesberg, Branch No. 1957, Creighton, NE

APRICOT DESSERT

2 c. crushed Ritz crackers	4 egg whites
1 stick margarine, melted	1 c. granulated sugar

Topping:

1 can Wilderness apricot pie filling	Toasted flaked coconut (about ¼
1 large container Cool Whip	c.)

Combine crackers and margarine. Press into a 9x13 inch pan. Beat egg whites until frothy and add sugar, 1 tablespoon at a time, and beat until thick and glossy. Pour over crust and bake at 300° for 60 minutes. Cool. Spread filling over all. Add Cool Whip over filling. Sprinkle coconut on top. Refrigerate overnight. Cut into squares.

To make toasted coconut: Melt 1 teaspoon margarine and add coconut. Stir until lightly browned. Dry on paper towel.
Doris Heuer, Branch No. 4095, New Hope, MN

MANDARIN ORANGE DESSERT

60 Hi-Ho or Ritz crackers, crushed   ½ c. sugar
½ c. margarine, melted

Mix well and pat into 9x13 inch pan. Save ⅔ cup to sprinkle on top. Chill. Beat 1 cup sweetened condensed milk on high for 7 minutes. Add 1 can concentrated thawed orange juice.

Fold in one 9 ounce carton of Cool Whip. Add 1 can of drained mandarin oranges (cut in halves). Pour over crust. Sprinkle remaining ⅔ cup crumbs on top. Chill for at least 4 hours.

Eileen Voss, Branch No. 6714, Woodbury, MN

BANANA SPLIT DESSERT

2 c. graham cracker crumbs
½ c. melted margarine (not butter)
3 Tbsp. sugar
2 eggs
1 c. margarine (not butter)
2 c. sugar (powdered)

3 or 4 sliced bananas
1 medium size can drained
    crushed pineapple
1 (9 oz.) ctn. Cool Whip
½ c. maraschino cherries
¾ c. chopped nuts

First layer: Mix together cracker crumbs, ½ cup margarine and 3 tablespoons sugar. Pour into pan.

Second layer: Cream together eggs, 1 cup margarine, and 2 cups powdered sugar for 10 minutes; spread over the crumbs.

Third layer: Cover with 3 or 4 ripe banana slices, then 1 medium size can of crushed drained pineapple.

Fourth layer: Top all with one 9 ounce carton Cool Whip. Garnish nuts and cherries.

Note: Keeps well for several days, so it may be made up to 2 days ahead of time.

Linda Sedlacek, Branch No. 3107, Loveland, CO

BANANA SPLIT

⅔ c. oleo, melted
2 c. graham cracker crumbs
2 eggs
2 c. sifted powdered sugar
¾ c. butter or oleo, softened
1 tsp. vanilla
1 (20 oz.) can crushed pineapple,
    well drained

3 large or 4 medium bananas
1 (9 oz.) ctn. frozen whipped
    topping, thawed
½ c. coarsely chopped pecans
1 (4 oz.) jar maraschino cherries,
    drained

Combine melted margarine and cracker crumbs. Pat in bottom of 13x9x2 inch pan. Beat eggs on high speed of electric mixer until light, about 4 minutes. Add powdered sugar, softened butter, and vanilla. Beat for 5 minutes. Spread over crumbs. Chill for 30 minutes. Spread pineapple over creamed mixture. Arrange

405

bananas over pineapple. Cover with whipped topping. Sprinkle with pecans. Cover and refrigerate for 6 hours or overnight. Garnish with maraschino cherries (chopped).

Mrs. Jim (Kay) Pfluger, Branch No. 1648, Eden, TX

BLUEBERRY DESSERT

¼ lb. saltine crackers
¼ lb. soft margarine
⅓ c. sugar
1 (8 oz.) pkg. cream cheese

2 c. powdered sugar
1 (8 oz.) container Cool Whip
18 oz. blueberry pie filling

Crust and Topping: Crush saltine crackers. Mix with margarine and sugar. Press mixture in a 9x13 inch pan, saving ¾ cup for topping. Bake at 350° for 10 to 12 minutes. Cool.

Filling: Mix powdered sugar and softened cream cheese together. Fold in Cool Whip. Pour mixture on crust. Put pie filling on cream cheese mixture and top with crushed cracker mixture. Cool in refrigerator.

Susan A. Vrondran, Branch No. 4012, Boyne City, MI

SODA CRACKER CHERRY DESSERT

3 egg whites
1 tsp. cream of tartar
1 c. sugar
23 crushed soda crackers

½ c. nuts
1 tsp. vanilla
Cherry pie filling
Whipped topping

Beat egg whites till frothy. Add cream of tartar and slowly add sugar, beating till stiff. Add crushed crackers, nuts and vanilla. Bake at 350° for 25 minutes. Cool. Cover with cherry pie filling and whipped topping. Chill for several hours.

Leona Becher, Columbus, NE

CHERRY BERRIES ON A CLOUD

Meringue:

6 egg whites (room temperature)
½ tsp. cream of tartar
¼ tsp. salt

1¾ c. sugar
1 tsp. vanilla

Filling:

6 oz. cream cheese, softened
1 c. sugar
1 tsp. vanilla

2 c. whipping cream, whipped
2 c. miniature marshmallows

Topping:

1 c. cherry pie filling
½ tsp. almond extract or lemon
 juice

2 c. sliced raspberries or
 strawberries

406

1. Day before serving, turn oven to 450°. Beat egg whites until foamy; add cream of tartar, salt, sugar, and vanilla. Beat for 15 minutes longer. Turn off oven. Butter a 9x13 inch pan (or larger) well. Pour in meringue and keep in oven overnight or for 8 hours.

2. Cream the cream cheese with the sugar and vanilla. Fold in the whipped cream and marshmallows. Before serving, pour cream cheese mixture over meringue. Refrigerate.

3. Combine pie filling with extract. Add berries carefully (try not to break up berries). Spread some over top of cheese mixture. Save the remainder to spoon over individual servings. Cut into squares. Makes 16 servings.

Mildred Bertram, Branch No. 840, Franklin, WI

CHERRY DESSERT

6 egg whites
2 c. sugar
¾ tsp. cream of tartar
2 c. soda crackers

¾ c. chopped pecans
8 oz. Cool Whip
1 can cherry pie filling

Beat egg whites until frothy. Gradually add sugar and cream of tartar while beating. Beat until peaks form and sugar is dissolved. Fold in broken soda crackers and pecans. Bake in greased 9x13 inch cake pan at 350° for 20 to 25 minutes. Allow meringue to cool completely. Spread on top 8 ounces of Cool Whip. Carefully spread cherry pie filling on top of Cool Whip. Refrigerate for several hours or overnight.

Joanne Ross, Branch No. 779, Savanna, IL

GRACE LUTHERAN'S FRUIT MAGIC

2 cans pie filling*
1 (18 oz.) yellow cake mix

½ c. margarine
1 c. chopped nuts

Spread pie filling in bottom of 13x9 inch pan. Combine cake mix and margarine; mix until crumbly. Add nuts. Sprinkle over top of pie filling. Bake at 350° for 45 to 50 minutes. It will be golden brown when done. Serve with vanilla ice cream or a dab of whipped cream.

This is a quick and easy dessert for unexpected company.

* Any flavor may be used (cherry, peach, strawberry, blueberry, etc.).

Grace Lutheran Church, Branch No. 4788, Denison, TX

FRUIT PIZZA

1 pkg. Pillsbury slice and bake
   sugar cookies
1 (8 oz.) pkg. cream cheese
⅓ c. granulated sugar
½ tsp. vanilla

Fresh strawberries
Bananas
Fresh blueberries
Green grapes

Glaze:

½ c. preserves (apricot, apple or peach) 2 Tbsp. water

Slice cookie dough in ⅛ inch pieces. Overlap in 14 inch pizza pan. Bake for 8 minutes at 350°. Blend softened cream cheese, sugar, and vanilla. Spread over cooled crust. Arrange assorted fruits in circles over filling (strawberries in outer ring, then 2 rings of banana slices, then 1 ring blueberries, 1 ring green grapes, and bananas in the center). Brush with glaze (preserves thinned with water).

Doris E. Wendt, Branch No. 1293, Morgan, MN

WHITE DESSERT

1 angel food cake
1 pkg. Knox gelatine
½ c. milk
3 egg yolks
1 c. sugar
1½ c. milk
½ pt. whipping cream
½ tsp. vanilla
Cherry pie filling or thickened
strawberries

Break angel food cake into 9x13 inch pan. Mix the Knox gelatine with ½ cup milk. Cook 3 egg yolks, 1 cup sugar and 1½ cups milk to thin custard. Do not overcook. Add gelatine to custard. Cool. Beat the 3 egg whites. Whip the ½ pint cream and add to the egg whites. Add to the cooled custard and add the vanilla. Pour over the angel food cake. Let stand overnight. Top with prepared pie filling or thickened strawberries.

Delores Bierstedt, Branch No. 1846, Cylinder, IA

STRAWBERRY PRETZEL DESSERT

2 c. crushed pretzels (small sticks)
½ c. sugar
¾ c. margarine, softened
⅓ c. coarsely chopped pecans
1 (8 oz.) pkg. cream cheese,
softened
1 scant c. sugar
1 (9 oz.) tub whipped topping
1 (6 oz.) box strawberry jello
2 c. boiling water
2 boxes (10 oz.) frozen
strawberries

Mix crushed pretzels (not too fine), ½ cup sugar, margarine, and pecans together. Press mixture very lightly into a greased 9x13x2 inch pan. Bake for 10 minutes in a 350° oven. Cool.

Combine cream cheese, 1 cup sugar and whipped topping. Spread on top of first layer. Dissolve jello in boiling water. Add frozen strawberries. When 75% congealed, put on top of first layer. Refrigerate for several hours or overnight before serving.

Different fruits and jello flavors may be used.

Hilda Roggow, Branch No. 1552, Breckinridge, OK;
Laura H. Meyer, Branch No. 1149, Leigh, NE

STRAWBERRY DESSERT

Vanilla wafers
½ c. butter
½ c. butter (additional)
1½ c. powdered sugar

3 eggs
Drained strawberries
Whipped topping
8 oz. tiny marshmallows

Blend 2 cups crushed vanilla wafers with ½ cup melted butter. Press into an 8x10 inch pan. Cream ½ cup butter, powdered sugar and 3 eggs (added singly), beating after each addition. Pour over crumbs. Cover with a layer of strawberries. Stir marshmallows into whipped topping and top dessert with it.

Leona Becher, Columbus, NE

BERRIES AND BITS

1 (14 oz.) can sweetened
  condensed milk
1½ c. cold water
1 (3½ oz.) pkg. instant vanilla
  pudding

2 c. heavy cream
36 vanilla wafers
1 qt. strawberries, halved
¾ c. semi-sweet chocolate bits

In large mixing bowl, combine sweetened condensed milk and water. Add instant pudding mix. Beat until well blended. Chill for 5 minutes. Fold in whipped cream. Spoon 2 cups pudding mix into 3 quart glass serving bowl. Top with half of each of the vanilla wafers, strawberries, and ¼ cup bits. Repeat layering, ending with pudding. Garnish with additional berries and the last ¼ cup bits. Chill thoroughly. Serves 8 to 10.

May substitute 2 cups blueberries, sliced peaches, grapes, or raspberries.

Martha Ogg, Branch No. 6940, Harrison, MI

LAST MINUTE DESSERT

1 (3 oz.) box instant vanilla
  pudding
1 c. sour cream

1 c. milk
Fresh strawberries
Bananas

Mix pudding, sour cream and milk. Refrigerate. When ready to serve, add fruit.

Karen K. Riesberg, Branch No. 1957, Creighton, NE

ANGEL JELLO

¾ baked angel food cake, torn into
  pieces
2 small pkg. strawberry jello
2 c. hot water

1 c. cold water
1 (16 oz.) container frozen
  strawberries
1 (8 oz.) container Cool Whip

Tear angel food cake into pieces and place in the bottom of a 9x13 inch pan. Mix jello and water; add frozen strawberries. Using a mixer on low speed, blend into jello ¾ container of Cool Whip. Pour mixture over cake pieces and refrigerate until set. Frost with the rest of the Cool Whip and garnish with chopped nuts.

Betty J. Boggs, Branch No. 1957, Creighton, NE

PINEAPPLE DESSERT

1 regular yellow cake mix
1 (20 oz.) can crushed pineapple
   (do not drain)
9 oz. Cool Whip

1 (3 oz.) pkg. instant vanilla
   pudding mix
¾ c. milk
Coconut

Mix cake as per directions and bake in a 9x13 inch pan. Cool. Punch holes in top of cake with a toothpick. Spread the pineapple with juice evenly over top of cake. Mix the ¾ cup milk with the pudding mix. Fold in Cool Whip. Spread on cake and sprinkle with coconut.

Winnifred Bitterman, Branch No. 1868, Yuma, CO

PINEAPPLE-COCOANUT CREAM DESSERT

1 small yellow cake mix
¼ tsp. lemon flavoring
1 (15 oz.) can crushed pineapple
1 small box instant cocoanut
   cream pudding mix

1½ c. milk
4 oz. cream cheese
Whipped topping or Cool Whip
¾ c. cocoanut

Mix cake mix (Jiffy size) according to box directions. Add lemon flavoring. Pour into a 9x13 inch pan and bake the allotted time. Drain part of the juice off the pineapple. When cake is baked and cool, prick cake with a long tined fork and spoon the pineapple with some juice over the cake. Cream the cheese. Add the pudding mix and milk; beat until blended and spread over the pineapple layer. Top with topping. Sprinkle flaked cocoanut on top. Refrigerate.

Doris Ruhs, Branch No. 3107, Loveland, CO

SCALLOPED PINEAPPLE

7 slices toasted bread
¾ c. melted butter
2 c. sugar

3 beaten eggs
½ c. milk
1 (16 oz.) can crushed pineapple

Mix all ingredients together in order given. Pour into glass casserole baking dish. Bake at 350° for 40 minutes or longer until knife inserted comes out clean.

Dorothy Redeker, Branch No. 3837, Nokomis, IL

FRUIT COCKTAIL PUDDING

1 c. sugar
1 c. flour
1 tsp. soda
¼ tsp. salt
1 egg

1 can fruit cocktail
½ c. brown sugar
½ c. nuts
Whipped topping

Mix together sugar, flour, soda, salt, egg, and fruit cocktail. Pour into a greased 9 inch square pan. Sprinkle brown sugar and nuts on top. Bake at 300° for 1 hour. Serve with whipped topping or ice cream.

Leona Becher, Columbus, NE

APPLE SQUARES

2 c. flour
2 tsp. baking soda
½ tsp. salt
1 Tbsp. cinnamon
3 eggs

1½ c. sugar
1 c. oil
4 c. apples, pared and diced
1 c. chopped nuts

Sift together dry ingredients. Combine eggs and sugar; beat well. Stir in oil and dry ingredients. Fold in apples and nuts. Batter will be thick. Spread in greased 11x17 inch cookie sheet. Bake at 350° for 25 to 30 minutes. Cool in pan. Cut into squares.

May sprinkle with powdered sugar. Do not cover.

Elsie Kirchenbauer, Branch No. 6303, Lodi, OH

APPLE TORTE

2 eggs
1½ c. sugar
3 tsp. vanilla
2 c. chopped apples
¾ c. nuts

⅔ c. flour
3 tsp. baking powder
½ tsp. salt
Whipped topping

Beat eggs. Add remaining ingredients (except for whipped topping). Bake in a 9x12 inch pan at 350° for 40 minutes. Serve with whipped topping.

Leona Becher, Columbus, NE

APPLE DESSERT

1 c. granulated sugar
½ c. shortening
1 beaten egg
2 c. grated raw apples
½ tsp. nutmeg

½ tsp. cinnamon
½ tsp. salt
1 c. flour
1 tsp. soda
½ c. nutmeats

Cream sugar and shortening; add egg and mix well. Mix all dry ingredients together and add to creamed mixture. Add apples and nuts last. Bake for 45 minutes at 350°. Serve warm with the following sauce.

Sauce:

½ c. margarine
½ c. canned milk

½ c. brown sugar
½ c. granulated sugar

Cook preceding in double boiler until fully mixed. Add 1½ teaspoons vanilla.

Mrs. Mabel Musolf, Loveland, CO

PUMPKIN DESSERT

6 eggs
1½ c. white sugar
1 tsp. salt (sparingly)
1 large (29 oz.) can pumpkin

2 tsp. cinnamon
1 tsp. ginger
2 c. Carnation milk

Beat eggs well; add sugar and beat again. Add all of the rest of the ingredients and mix. Pour into a 9x13 inch pan.

Topping:

1 pkg. yellow cake mix
1 stick oleo

Few nutmeats

Mix together cake mix and oleo until crumbly. Sprinkle over the top of first layer, adding a few nutmeats. Bake for 1 hour at 350°. Serve with Cool Whip.

"I make this a lot as it serves quite a few poeple."
Irene Miller, Branch No. 3558, Schleswig, IA

PUMPKIN FREEZER DESSERT

Crust:

24 graham cracker sq., crushed
1 c. chopped English walnuts

½ c. butter or margarine
½ c. sugar

Mix together first 4 items until crumbly in 9x13 inch pan. Bake for 4 minutes at 400°. Remove half of mixture and reserve. Pat remainder in pan.

Filling: Spoon ½ gallon vanilla ice cream (softened) over mixture in pan. Put in freezer while you prepare next layer.

Topping:

8 oz. Cool Whip
1 c. solid pack pumpkin
¾ c. sugar
½ tsp. salt

½ tsp. ginger
2 tsp. cinnamon
½ c. chopped nuts

To 8 ounces of Cool Whip, fold in 1 cup solid pack pumpkin, sugar, salt, ginger, cinnamon, and chopped nuts. Pour over ice cream. Add remaining crumbs on top and freeze. Thaw slightly before cutting into squares. Serves 12 to 15.
Linda L. Aper, Branch No. 483, Lincoln, IL

PUMPKIN DESSERT

1 box yellow cake mix
¾ c. margarine
4 eggs
1 large (2 pie size) can pumpkin
½ c. packed brown sugar

⅔ c. milk
2 tsp. cinnamon
½ c. granulated sugar
Chopped nuts

Mix by hand 1 box yellow cake mix (reserve 1 cup for topping), ½ cup margarine and 1 egg, then pat in greased 9x13 inch pan.

In a large bowl, mix 1 large can pumpkin, ½ cup packed brown sugar, 3 eggs, ⅔ cup milk, and 2 teaspoons cinnamon. Mix thoroughly with electric mixer; pour over first layer.

Blend the 1 cup reserved cake mix, ½ cup granulated sugar, and ¼ cup cold margarine; spread evenly over the pumpkin. Sprinkle with chopped nuts. Bake at 350° for 55 minutes, or until top is light brown. Serve with whipped topping. Keeps well in refrigerator for several days.

Doris Wohlschlegel, Branch No. 5425, Louisville, KY

PUMPKIN PIE DESSERT

1 c. flour	1½ c. sugar
¼ c. brown sugar	1 tsp. salt
½ c. butter or margarine	1 tsp. nutmeg
4 eggs, beaten	1 tsp. cinnamon
2 cans pumpkin	½ tsp. vanilla
½ c. milk	

Mix flour, brown sugar and butter or margarine for crust. Pat in 9x13 inch cake pan. Bake at 350° for 10 minutes. Mix balance of ingredients for filling and pour over crust. Bake at 350° for 30 to 40 minutes or till done.

Note: Great for pumpkin pie lovers who hate to make and roll out a crust. *Enjoy!*

James E. and Elaine L. Lindquist, Branch No. 3339, Esko, MN

PUMPKIN TORTE

24 sq. crushed graham crackers	½ c. sugar
⅓ c. sugar	½ tsp. salt
½ c. oleo or butter	½ tsp. cinnamon
2 eggs	⅛ tsp. nutmeg
¾ c. sugar	⅛ tsp. ginger
8 oz. cream cheese	1 env. unflavored gelatin
2 c. pumpkin	¼ c. water
3 egg yolks (mix with milk following)	3 egg whites
	¼ c. sugar
½ c. milk	

Mix together the graham crackers, ⅓ cup sugar and ½ cup melted oleo or butter. Press preceding mixture in 9x13 inch pan. (It really takes 1½ times the recipe to make the pan full enough. I double the recipe and put it in a little larger pan.)

Beat the following ingredients well and pour over the crust: Two beaten eggs, ¾ cup sugar and 8 ounces cream cheese. Bake for 20 minutes in a 350° oven. (I bake my doubled recipe in a large glass pan at 325° for 35 minutes.) Cool.

Cook egg yolks, pumpkin, ½ cup sugar, milk, salt, and spices until mixture thickens in a heavy pan, stirring often (approximately 30 minutes total time on the stove). Remove from heat. Add gelatin that has been dissolved in cold water, then cool. Beat egg whites to soft peaks and then gradually beat in ¼ cup sugar. Fold in pumpkin mixture. Pour over cooled, baked crust. Refrigerate at least overnight. Serve topped with whipped cream or other whipped topping.

Gwen Grantz, Branch No. 997, Charlotte, IA

MINI CHEESE CAKES

1 (8 oz.) pkg. softened cream
   cheese
2 eggs
¾ c. sugar

1 Tbsp. lemon juice
Vanilla wafers
Cherry pie mix
Whipped topping

Beat together cream cheese, eggs, sugar, and lemon juice. Place a little dough into a cupcake paper to hold wafer in place. Place in a muffin pan. Place a vanilla wafer in the bottom, then fill ⅔ full with batter. When cool, top with cherry pie mix and whipped topping. Makes 15 servings.

Leona Becher, Columbus, NE

LINDY'S CHEESECAKE

Pastry Crust:

1 c. sifted all-purpose flour
¼ c. sugar
1 Tbsp. grated lemon peel
1 egg yolk

½ c. (1 stick) butter (room
   temperature)
½ tsp. vanilla

Filling:

5 (8 oz.) pkg. cream cheese (room
   temperature - 2½ lb.)
1¾ c. sugar
3 Tbsp. flour
1½ tsp. grated orange peel
1½ tsp. grated lemon peel

¼ tsp. vanilla
5 eggs
2 egg yolks
¼ c. heavy cream (whipping
   cream)

Preheat oven to 400°F. Combine flour, sugar and lemon peel. Make a well in center and drop in egg yolk, butter and vanilla. Quickly work together until well blended. Wrap in wax paper and chill for 1 hour. Roll out about ⅓ of the dough ⅛ inch thick. Fit over bottom of buttered 9 inch springform pan. Trim and save extra dough. Bake circle of dough for about 8 to 10 minutes or until golden. Cool! Butter sides of pan and place sides over bottom. Turn oven to 500°F. Roll out remaining dough and line pan ¾ of the way up the sides.

Blend together cheese, sugar, flour, grated peels, and vanilla until smooth. Add eggs and yolks, one at a time, mixing well after each addition. Blend in cream thoroughly. Turn cheese mixture into springform pan and bake for 10 to 12 minutes. Reduce heat to 200°F. and bake for 60 to 70 minutes. Cool in draft free place. Top with fresh or canned cherries, blueberries or strawberries. Makes 12 to 14 servings.

Pam Kaumeyer, Branch No. 5845, Joliet, IL

MACAROON DESSERT

3 apples (or 2 c.), peeled, cored
   and sliced thin
½ c. sugar

2 Tbsp. flour or corn starch
¼ tsp. cinnamon (optional)

Combine apple mixture in a well greased pan, 8x8 or 6x10 inches. Cover with dough. This dough does not need to cover every bit - it will cover while baking.

Dough:

½ c. sugar
2 Tbsp. soft butter
1 Tbsp. water

1 egg
1 tsp. vanilla
⅓ tsp. salt

Beat all well with electric mixer. Add ¾ cup flour and ½ teaspoon baking powder.

This can be used for most any kind of fruit desired. The crust is crisp and can be served with ice cream or other topping.

Mrs. Gertrude Bergt, Branch No. 2346, Schuyler, NE

BUTTERFINGER DESSERT

6 Tbsp. oleo
1½ tsp. vanilla
1½ c. powdered sugar
3 beaten egg yolks

2 pkg. Dream Whip
1 bar angel food cake
2 to 4 small Butterfinger candy
   bars

Melt oleo in double boiler; add rest. Mix and cool. Add 2 packages Dream Whip (beaten). Slice a bar of angel food cake thinly (approximately 8 slices). Put one layer of each in 9x13 inch pan and alternate the layers. Crush 2 to 4 small Butterfinger candy bars and sprinkle on the top. Refrigerate and serve.

Mary Vander Top, Branch No. 3107, Loveland, CO

SUPER BUTTERFINGER DESSERT

2 c. crushed graham crackers
1 c. crushed soda crackers
½ c. melted margarine
2 (3¾ oz.) pkg. instant vanilla
   pudding

2 c. milk
1 qt. soft vanilla ice cream
1 (8 oz.) ctn. whipped topping
2 frozen crushed Butterfinger
   candy bars

Combine crackers with margarine. Spread ⅔ of the mixture in a 9x13 inch pan. Reserve ⅓ for topping. Mix pudding, milk and ice cream. Spread on top of crust. Spread topping over pudding. Combine crushed candy bars and reserved crumbs. Sprinkle on top of whipped topping. Refrigerate.

Dee Frantz, Branch No. 2049, Emporia, KS

BUTTERSCOTCH DESSERT

1 c. flour
1 stick butter, softened
½ c. chopped nuts
1 (8 oz.) pkg. cream cheese
1 container Cool Whip

1 c. powdered sugar
2 pkg. instant butterscotch
  pudding
3 c. milk

Mix together flour, butter and chopped nuts; press into 9x13 inch pan. Bake at 375° for 10 to 15 minutes. Mix the following together: Cream cheese, 1 cup Cool Whip and 1 cup powdered sugar. Pour over crust. Cool and chill for 15 minutes. Mix instant butterscotch pudding with 3 cups milk. Pour over crust and cover with Cool Whip and nuts if desired.

Bernice Sheets, Branch No. 5844, Columbia City, IN

RITZ-PISTACHIO DESSERT

2 c. Ritz crackers, crushed

½ c. or 1 stick margarine

Pat into a 9x13 inch pan.

2 c. softened vanilla ice cream
2½ c. milk
2 (3½ oz.) pkg. pistachio instant
  pudding

1 small container Cool Whip
Chocolate shavings

Pat Ritz cracker mixture into 9x13 inch pan. Beat ice cream, milk and pudding mixture until thick; spread on crust. Cover with Cool Whip and chocolate shavings.

Mona Geidel, Branch No. 3107, Loveland, CO

PISTACHIO TORTE

First layer:

1½ c. flour
2 Tbsp. sugar

1 stick oleo
½ c. fine pecans

Mix together ingredients for first layer. Pat into bottom of 13x9 inch pan. Bake at 350° for 15 to 20 minutes. Cool!

Second layer:

8 oz. cream cheese
½ large Cool Whip

¾ c. powdered sugar

Whip together ingredients for second layer. Pour over cool first layer and refrigerate.

Third layer:

2 pkg. instant pistachio pudding

2½ c. milk

Blend together ingredients for third layer. Pour over second layer. Cool.

Fourth layer:

½ large Cool Whip   ½ c. chopped pecans

Spread Cool Whip over third layer. Sprinkle pecans on top. Refrigerate.
Lois Martin, Branch No. 840, Franklin, WI

BROKEN GLASS DESSERT

Graham Cracker Crust:

1½ individual pkg. graham   ⅔ c. sugar
   crackers   ⅔ c. butter or margarine, melted

Crush crackers in 9x13 inch cake pan. Mix in butter and sugar; pack. Reserve about ¾ cup for topping.

1 pkg. orange jello and 1½ c. hot   1½ pkg. Knox gelatine
   water   1 c. cold pineapple juice
1 pkg. raspberry jello and 1½ c.   ¾ c. pineapple juice
   hot water   ½ c. sugar
1 pkg. lime jello and 1½ c. hot   2 c. whipped cream
   water

Mix together the Knox gelatine and 1 cup of *cold* pineapple juice. Heat together ¾ cup pineapple juice and ½ cup sugar; add to gelatine mixture and let stand until syrupy. Add 2 cups of whipped cream to the gelatine mixture.

Make 1 package each of orange, raspberry and lime jello with 1½ cups hot water; put in small pans (bread pans). Refrigerate until hard. Cube and add to preceding mixture. Pour over crust and add topping. Refrigerate.
Sue Folken, Branch No. 1149, Leigh, NE

FOUR-LAYER DESSERT

First layer:

2 c. flour   1 c. chopped walnuts
1 c. butter or margarine

Mix like pie crust. Press in pan, 9x13 inches. Bake at 350° for 15 to 20 minutes.

Second layer:

2 c. Cool Whip   2 (8 oz.) cream cheese
2 c. powdered sugar

Beat until fluffy and spread over cooled crust.

Third layer:

2 large pkg. instant chocolate pudding   **5 c. cold milk**

Mix as directed on package. Pour over second layer.

Fourth layer: Top with Cool Whip and sliced walnuts. Keeps for 3 days.

Ethel M. Voigt, Branch No. 72, East Troy, WI

FOUR-LAYER DESSERT

You can make this a couple days ahead if you want.

First layer:

1 c. flour   **½ c. pecans, chopped**
½ c. margarine, melted

Combine all ingredients and mix thoroughly. Pat into a 9x13 inch pan. Bake for 15 minutes in a 350° oven. Cool.

Second layer:

1 (8 oz.) pkg. cream cheese,   **1 c. powdered sugar**
softened to room temperature   **1 c. Cool Whip**

Mix ingredients together and spread on top of first layer. Chill thoroughly.

Third layer:

2 pkg. instant pudding mix (any   **1 tsp. vanilla**
flavor)   **1 tsp. burnt sugar (optional)**
3 c. milk

Mix together and beat until thick. Pour over top of second layer. Chill again.

Fourth layer: Top with additional Cool Whip and sprinkle chopped pecans over top. Chill.

TEXAS DESSERT

1 c. flour   **2 c. Cool Whip**
½ c. oleo   **2 (3 oz.) Jell-O instant pudding**
½ c. chopped pecans   **(lemon or chocolate)**
8 oz. cream cheese   **2½ c. milk**
1 c. powdered sugar   **2 c. Cool Whip**

First layer: Combine and pack into 9x13 inch pan the flour, oleo and chopped pecans. Bake for 15 minutes at 350°. Cool before adding second layer.

Second layer: Beat softened cream cheese, powdered sugar and Cool Whip. Put over cooled crust.

Third layer: Beat until thick 2 packages instant pudding and 2½ cups milk. Put over second layer.

Topping: Spread 2 cups Cool Whip over pudding mixture and garnish with chopped pecans. Chill overnight.

Justine Beaver, St. John's, Branch No. 3806, Center Point, IA

CHOCOLATE ECLAIR DESSERT

1 c. water
½ c. butter
1 c. flour
4 eggs
1 large pkg. instant vanilla
    pudding

2½ c. milk
8 oz. cream cheese, softened
1 large container Cool Whip
Chocolate syrup

Bring water and butter to a boil; remove from heat. Stir in flour. Add eggs, beating after each one. Spread in greased jelly roll pan. Bake at 400° for 25 minutes. Cool. Mix 1 large instant vanilla pudding with 2½ cups milk and 8 ounces cream cheese. Spread over crust. Top with large container of Cool Whip. Drizzle with chocolate syrup.

Ruth Hines, Branch No. 48, Marshfield, WI

CHOCOLATE ECLAIR DESSERT

1 box graham crackers
2 (3 oz.) boxes French vanilla
    pudding

3 c. milk
1 (8 or 9 oz.) Cool Whip

Butter sides and bottom of 9x13 inch pan. Line bottom with whole crackers. Beat pudding with milk until thick. Fold in Cool Whip. Mix well. Pour ½ of the pudding mixture over crackers. Place second layer of crackers over top of pudding, then second layer of pudding and third layer of crackers. Pour frosting over third layer of crackers. Spread gently. Refrigerate for 24 hours.

Frosting:

3 Tbsp. margarine
2 oz. unsweetened chocolate
2 Tbsp. white Karo syrup

3 Tbsp. milk
1 Tbsp. vanilla
1½ c. powdered sugar

Melt margarine and unsweetened chocolate. Add all ingredients to melted margarine and chocolate. Mix well.

Jeanie Coleman, Loveland, CO

CHOCOLATE CHIP TREATS

1 c. + 2 Tbsp. flour
½ tsp. soda

⅛ tsp. salt

Sift and set aside.

½ c. margarine	1 egg
6 Tbsp. sugar	½ tsp. vanilla
6 Tbsp. brown sugar	

Sift together first 3 ingredients and set aside. Cream together the next 3 ingredients. Blend in beaten egg and vanilla. Add flour mixture. Mix thoroughly. Put a rounded tablespoonful of dough in greased muffin tin (12). Bake at 325° for 12 minutes or until they show a depression in the center. Take out of oven and put a tablespoon of topping in depression. Return to oven and bake for 12 minutes at 350°.

Topping:

½ c. brown sugar	1 tsp. vanilla
1 egg	

Beat until thick. Stir in chocolate chips and nuts.

Charmaine Santema, Branch No. 2611, Sac City, IA

MERINGUE KISSES

2 egg whites	Salt
⅔ c. sugar	1 (6 oz.) pkg. chocolate chips
1 tsp. vanilla	

Preheat oven to 350°. Grease and flour cooky sheet. Stiffly beat egg whites, adding ⅔ cup sugar and pinch of salt. Add vanilla and stir in chocolate chips. Drop by teaspoonfuls. Bake for 1 minute. Turn off oven. Leave in oven for 3 hours or overnight.

For holidays, add red coloring and ½ teaspoon peppermint.

Kathy Burtchin, Branch No. 4119, Pemberville, OH

BUSTER BAR DESSERT

1 large pkg. Oreo cookies	1 can chocolate topping
½ c. margarine	1 pkg. salted peanuts
½ gal. ice cream (vanilla, English toffee or butter brickle)	1 (8 oz.) ctn. Cool Whip

Crush cookies. Mix with margarine. Save ¼ crumbs for top. Pat remaining crumbs into 9x13 inch pan. Soften ice cream. Spread on top of crumbs. Freeze. Top with chocolate topping and peanuts. Freeze. Top with Cool Whip. Sprinkle remaining crumbs on top. Freeze. Serves 12.

Ann Lubeck, Branch No. 2611, Sac City, IA;
Patricia Christian, Branch No. 2256, Plymouth, NE

OREO CREME DE MENTHE DESSERT

20 Oreos
1 stick oleo
3 sq. unsweetened chocolate
3 beaten eggs

2 c. powdered sugar
½ gal. vanilla ice cream
¼ c. creme de menthe

Crush Oreos in blender. Reserve ¼ cup of crumbs. Pat remaining crumbs in bottom of ungreased 9x13 inch pan. Melt oleo and chocolate squares. Add eggs and sugar. Cook and stir until fudgy. Spread over Oreos. Place in freezer for at least 30 minutes. Soften ice cream and mix with creme de menthe. Spread over fudge layer. Top with reserved Oreo crumbs. Cover and freeze until serving.

Sally Mueller, Branch No. 3107, Loveland, CO

COCONUT ICE CREAM DESSERT

60 Ritz crackers, crumbled
½ gal. vanilla ice cream, softened
2 pkg. instant coconut cream pie
    filling

1½ c. milk
½ c. oleo
1 large container Cool Whip

Mix ice cream, pudding and milk together. Melt ½ cup oleo or butter in large pan (9x13 inches). Sprinkle ½ of the cracker crumbs over oleo. Add mix to top of crumbs; spread 1 large container of Cool Whip over ice cream mixture. Spread with remaining crumbs and refrigerate.

Can even be frozen, but will have to be taken out of freezer about 15 minutes before eaten.

Irene Wattjes, Branch No. 3837, Nokomis, IL

ORANGE SHERBET DESSERT

2 pkg. orange jello
2 c. hot water
1 pt. orange sherbet
1 (No. 2) can crushed pineapple,
    drained

2 c. mandarin oranges, drained
2 c. bananas, cut up
½ pt. heavy cream, whipped, or 1
    pt. Cool Whip

Dissolve gelatin in hot water. Add sherbet immediately. When slightly thickened, add fruit. Fold in whipped cream. Place in a 9x13 inch pan and chill.

Marie Wasson, Branch No. 2630, Greeley, CO

FROZEN YUM YUM

Graham Cracker Crust:

1½ individual pkg. graham
    crackers

⅔ c. sugar
⅔ c. butter or margarine, melted

Crush crackers in 9x13 inch cake pan and mix in butter and sugar. Pack. Reserve about 1½ cups for later.

Filling:

⅔ c. butter	Pinch of salt
2 c. powdered sugar	1 tsp. vanilla
3 egg yolks (save whites)	½ gal. vanilla ice cream
2 sq. unsweetened chocolate	

Cream butter and sugar. Add the egg yolks, melted chocolate, salt, and vanilla. Beat egg whites until stiff and fold into the chocolate mixture. Spread over the crust and freeze. Next, cover chocolate layer with ½ of the crumbs. Spread ice cream over chocolate layer. Sprinkle remaining crumbs and chocolate curls.

Sue Folken, Branch No. 1149, Leigh, NE

CHOCO-MINT FREEZE

2 c. finely crushed vanilla wafers   1 stick melted oleo
   or graham crackers

Toss and press into a 9x13 inch pan. Save a few crumbs for topping. Spread ½ gallon of mint ice cream over crust and freeze.

Topping: Melt ½ cup butter and 2 squares of unsweetened chocolate over low heat; gradually stir into mixture 3 well beaten egg yolks, 1½ cups confectioners sugar, ½ cup chopped pecans, and 1 teaspoon vanilla. Cool thoroughly. Beat egg whites until stiff peaks form. Beat chocolate mixture until smooth; fold in egg whites. Spread chocolate mixture over ice cream. Top with reserved crumb mixture and freeze.

Mary Vander Top, Branch No. 3107, Loveland, CO

ICE CREAM TORTE

1 c. crushed graham crackers   ½ c. melted butter
1 c. crushed soda crackers

Mix and put in 9x13 inch pan. Bake at 350° for 10 minutes. Cool.

Take:

1 qt. butter pecan ice cream   2 pkg. instant vanilla pudding
1 c. milk

Mix and put over crust. Top completely with 12 ounces Cool Whip. Crush 4 or 5 Heath bars. Sprinkle over top. Refrigerate or place in freezer to chill completely before serving.

Myrtle Callies, Branch No. 53, Hartford, WI

ICE CREAM DESSERT

2 pkg. vanilla instant pudding	½ angel food cake
1¾ c. milk	1 Butterfinger candy bar
1 qt. ice cream (vanilla)	

TUTTI FRUITTI HOMEMADE ICE CREAM

1 (3 oz.) raspberry jello
3 lemons
3 oranges
3 bananas

2 c. sugar
2 c. cream
1 can evaporated milk
3 c. milk

In blender, put juice of lemons, orange sections (take seeds out if any), and peeled bananas. Mix until well blended. Add dry jello and sugar; mix thoroughly. Put evaporated milk, cream and fruit mixture in ice cream container. Add milk. Freeze.

Carolyn Manke, Branch No. 5985, Midland, SD

STRAWBERRY-BANANA-WALNUT ICE CREAM

1 c. milk
2 eggs
⅔ c. honey
2 tsp. vanilla
1 c. sliced strawberries

2 ripe bananas
3 Tbsp. orange juice *or* apple juice
1 Tbsp. lemon juice
1 c. heavy cream
½ c. chopped walnuts

1. Blend all ingredients, except heavy cream and walnuts, until smooth.
2. Whip cream lightly and combine with fruit mixture.
3. Churn. Freeze.
4. After taking dasher out of the freezer can, pour walnuts on top of mixture and slowly mix them throughout.

For gallon size, use 4 times these amounts.

Mrs. Walter Schroeder, Branch No. 7101, Tucson, AZ

HOMEMADE ICE CREAM

3 c. sugar
3 Tbsp. (rounded) cornstarch
½ tsp. salt
4 eggs

4 c. milk
1 to 1½ Tbsp. flavoring
Cream or half & half

Beat 4 eggs in bowl, then add sugar, cornstarch and salt. Warm 4 cups of milk and add a little warm milk to egg mixture. Add mixture to the rest of the milk. Cook, stirring constantly, until coats spoon or begins to boil. Cool down. Pour into freezer. Add cream or half & half to the fill line in freezer and freeze. Makes 5 quarts.

Susan Stich, Branch No. 2820, Chanute, KS

CRANBERRY ICE

1 lb. cranberries
3 c. water
1 to 1½ c. sugar

⅓ c. lemon juice
2 c. cold water

Cook cranberries in 3 cups water for about 10 minutes or until they "pop." Rub berries through sieve to make pulp. Stir in sugar, juice and cold water. Pour into a 9x13 inch dish. Freeze. Let stand at room temperature for 10 minutes. Cut into cubes and serve in glasses or cups. Additional sugar may be sprinkled on to your taste.

This recipe is a holiday tradition with my family.

Cindy Hein, Branch No. 3879, Billings, MT

Notes

Notes

Cakes,
Fillings,
Frostings

HANDY CHART OF KITCHEN MATH
(Size of Pans and Baking Dishes)

Cooking need never become a crisis, when you use our handy charts. Need a 4 or 6-cup baking dish? Will your fancy mold be the right size for the recipe? See below for the answers.

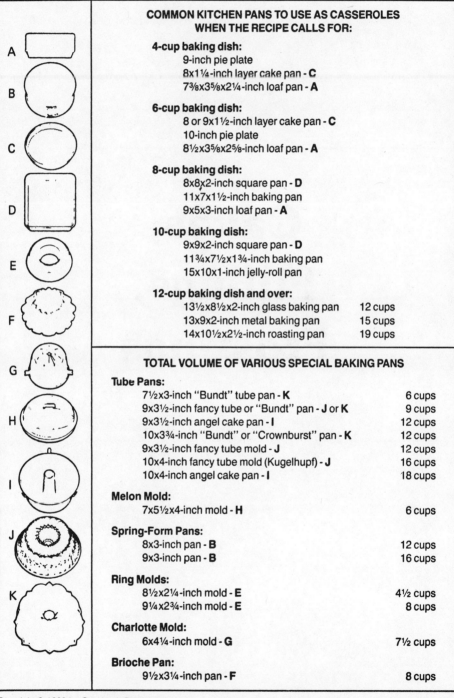

COMMON KITCHEN PANS TO USE AS CASSEROLES WHEN THE RECIPE CALLS FOR:

4-cup baking dish:
   9-inch pie plate
   8x1¼-inch layer cake pan - **C**
   7⅜x3⅝x2¼-inch loaf pan - **A**

6-cup baking dish:
   8 or 9x1½-inch layer cake pan - **C**
   10-inch pie plate
   8½x3⅝x2⅝-inch loaf pan - **A**

8-cup baking dish:
   8x8x2-inch square pan - **D**
   11x7x1½-inch baking pan
   9x5x3-inch loaf pan - **A**

10-cup baking dish:
   9x9x2-inch square pan - **D**
   11¾x7½x1¾-inch baking pan
   15x10x1-inch jelly-roll pan

12-cup baking dish and over:
   13½x8½x2-inch glass baking pan   12 cups
   13x9x2-inch metal baking pan   15 cups
   14x10½x2½-inch roasting pan   19 cups

TOTAL VOLUME OF VARIOUS SPECIAL BAKING PANS

Tube Pans:
   7½x3-inch "Bundt" tube pan - **K**   6 cups
   9x3½-inch fancy tube or "Bundt" pan - **J** or **K**   9 cups
   9x3½-inch angel cake pan - **I**   12 cups
   10x3¾-inch "Bundt" or "Crownburst" pan - **K**   12 cups
   9x3½-inch fancy tube mold - **J**   12 cups
   10x4-inch fancy tube mold (Kugelhupf) - **J**   16 cups
   10x4-inch angel cake pan - **I**   18 cups

Melon Mold:
   7x5½x4-inch mold - **H**   6 cups

Spring-Form Pans:
   8x3-inch pan - **B**   12 cups
   9x3-inch pan - **B**   16 cups

Ring Molds:
   8½x2¼-inch mold - **E**   4½ cups
   9¼x2¾-inch mold - **E**   8 cups

Charlotte Mold:
   6x4¼-inch mold - **G**   7½ cups

Brioche Pan:
   9½x3¼-inch pan - **F**   8 cups

CAKES, FILLINGS, FROSTINGS

BLUEBERRY CHEESECAKE

Crust:

⅓ (1 lb.) box graham crackers, crushed

¼ c. melted butter or margarine
¼ c. sugar

Filling:

1 (8 oz.) pkg. softened cream cheese
3 c. cold milk

2 small boxes lemon instant pudding

Have on hand 1 can blueberry pie filling for topping. (Can also use cherry or other desired flavor.)

Mix together graham cracker crumbs, sugar and melted butter. Press into a 9x13 inch pan or two 9 inch pie pans. Gradually beat milk into cream cheese until smooth. Add pudding mix and beat until well blended. Pour immediately onto crust and refrigerate for 30 minutes until set. Spread pie filling over top.

Judy Maseman, Branch No. 3999, Centralia, MO

CHEESECAKE

Graham cracker crumbs
1 lb. small curd cottage cheese
2 (8 oz.) pkg. cream cheese, softened
1½ c. sugar
4 eggs, slightly beaten

⅓ c. corn starch
2 Tbsp. lemon juice
1 tsp. vanilla
½ c. margarine, melted
1 pt. sour cream

Grease one 9 inch spring form pan; dust with graham cracker crumbs. Sieve cottage cheese into large mixing bowl. Add cream cheese. Beat with high speed of electric mixer until well blended and creamy. Beating at high speed, blend in sugar, then eggs. Reduce speed to low. Add corn starch, lemon juice and vanilla. Beat until blended. Add melted margarine and sour cream. Blend at low speed. Pour into prepared pan. Bake in a 325° oven for about 1 hour and 10 minutes or until firm around edges. Turn off oven. Let cake stand in oven for 2 hours. Remove and cool completely on wire rack. Chill. Remove sides of pan. Makes about 12 servings.

Note: Cheesecake may be frozen and later topped with fruit.

Norma McKinnis, Branch No. 2568, Fredericktown, MO

CHEESE CAKE

Crust:

15 graham crackers, crushed
½ c. sugar

½ tsp. cinnamon
¼ c. butter, melted

Combine crust ingredients. Press into a 9 inch pie pan. Bake at 400° for 6 minutes. Cool.

Filling:

2 eggs
½ c. sugar
2 tsp. vanilla

1½ c. sour cream
2 (8 oz.) pkg. cream cheese (soft)
2 Tbsp. butter, melted

Blend eggs, sugar, vanilla, and sour cream for 15 seconds in blender. Continue blending and gradually add the cream cheese. Add the butter; blend well and pour filling into cooled crust. Bake at 325° for 35 minutes. Center will be soft, but will firm up as cake cools. Top with cherry pie filling or other topping as desired.

Kris Metzler, Branch No. 932, Minneapolis, MN

CHEESE CAKE

2 c. finely crushed graham
   crackers

½ c. margarine, melted
3 Tbsp. sugar

Mix together and line bottom of 9x13 inch pan with crumb mixture. Reserve ½ cup for topping. Bake at 375°F. for 6 to 8 minutes. Chill.

Dissolve one 3 ounce package lemon jello in 1 cup hot water. Stir until dissolved. *Cool* until like syrup, *but not set*. Whip one 12 ounce can evaporated milk. (Will whip best if cold.)

Cream together one 8 ounce package cream cheese (have at room temperature) with 1 cup sugar. Add to whipped milk. Add chilled jello mixture. Mix together and pour into chilled crumb crust. Top with reserved crumbs.

For variation, can be topped with cherry pie filling, blueberry pie filling, or a strawberry glaze. Serves 15.

Mabel Prahl, Branch No. 1068, Murdo, SD

CREAM CHEESE CAKE

1 lb. cream cheese, softened
3 eggs
⅔ c. sugar
½ tsp. almond extract

1 c. commercial sour cream
3 Tbsp. sugar
1 tsp. vanilla

Beat cream cheese, eggs, ⅔ cup sugar, and almond extract together until smooth, thick and lemon colored. Bake in a greased 9 inch pie plate for 25 minutes. While cheese cake is cooling (cool for 20 minutes), beat sour cream, 3 tablespoons sugar and vanilla together thoroughly. Pour over top of cream cheese cake and bake at 350° for 10 minutes more. Cool before serving. Sprinkle slivered Brazil nuts on top before serving if desired.

Note: Make the cake the day before being served as it needs to be chilled thoroughly.

Florence Brown, Branch No. 3819, Oviedo, FL

CHEESE CAKE

2 (8 oz.) cream cheese
1 (16 oz.) Cool Whip
½ c. powdered sugar

6 c. crushed Rice Krispies
1 c. margarine
½ c. sugar

Melt margarine; add sugar and crushed Rice Krispies. Press in 9x13 inch cake pan. Bake at 350° for approximately 5 minutes. Cool.

Beat cream cheese, Cool Whip and powdered sugar together. Spread over cooled crust. Top with favorite pie filling or crushed pineapple, drained well.

Judy Czarnecki, Branch No. 2232, Coleman, MI

CHERRY CHEESE CAKES

2 (8 oz.) pkg. cream cheese,
   softened
¾ c. sugar
2 eggs

1 Tbsp. lemon juice
1 tsp. vanilla
24 vanilla wafers
1 (21 oz.) cherry pie filling

Beat cream cheese, sugar, eggs, lemon juice, and vanilla until light and fluffy. Line small muffin pans with paper baking cups and place a vanilla wafer in bottom of each cup. Fill the cup ⅔ full with cream cheese mixture. Bake in a 325° to 350° oven for 15 minutes. Cool. Top each with about 1 tablespoon pie filling. Chill. Makes 2 dozen.

Susan Stich, Branch No. 2820, Chanute, KS

CRESCENT CHEESE CAKE

2 pkg. crescent rolls
1 egg, separated
2 (8 oz.) cream cheese

1 c. sugar
1 tsp. vanilla

Topping:

Chopped nuts
¼ c. sugar

Cinnamon to taste

Grease a 9x13 inch pan. Lay 1 package of crescent rolls on bottom of pan. In bowl, mix cream cheese, egg yolk, sugar, and vanilla. Spread on bottom layer of crescent rolls. Cover with second package of crescent rolls. Beat egg whites until foamy. Spread on top of roll mix. Sprinkle with topping mix. Bake at 350° for 30 to 35 minutes. Store in refrigerator.

Marge Gebert, Branch No. 840, Franklin, WI

CHOCOLATE MACADAMIA NUT CHEESECAKE

Crust:

¾ c. butter
1¼ c. flour
¼ c. sugar

1 egg yolk
⅛ tsp. vanilla
1 c. chopped macadamia nuts

429

Preheat oven to 400°F. Beat first 4 ingredients until well mixed, then add macadamia nuts and vanilla. Cover and refrigerate for 15 minutes. Spread ⅓ of dough into bottom of 10 inch springform pan. Bake bottom crust for 8 minutes or until lightly browned. Cool. Turn oven to 475°.

5 (8 oz.) pkg. cream cheese	⅛ tsp. salt
2 egg yolks	6 oz. semi-sweet chocolate,
5 eggs	melted
1¾ c. sugar	⅓ c. chopped macadamia nuts
2 Tbsp. flour	

Meanwhile in a large bowl, beat cream cheese just until smooth. Do not over-beat. Gradually beat in sugar, eggs, flour, salt, and melted chocolate until blended. Beat at high speed for 5 minutes. Press reserved dough around sides of pan; do not bake. Pour cheese mixture into pan and sprinkle top with ⅓ cup chopped macadamia nuts. Bake for 12 minutes. Decrease oven temperature to 300°F. and continue baking for 45 minutes. Turn oven off. Leave in for additional 30 minutes. Cool in pan on rack for 1 hour, then refrigerate for 12 hours.

Glaze:

8 oz. Baker's sweet chocolate	¼ tsp. vanilla
1 Tbsp. shortening	

Melt sweet chocolate and shortening with vanilla over low heat. Drizzle over top of cheesecake in a lace pattern 1 hour before serving.

Paul Gregor, Branch No. 6255, Wahiawa, HI

FLAVORED CHEESECAKE

Crust:

2 c. graham cracker crumbs	⅔ c. sugar
½ c. oleo	

Mix crust ingredients together and put in 9x13 inch pan.

1 (3 oz.) pkg. apricot jello	1 c. sugar
1 c. hot water	1 (8 oz.) ctn. Cool Whip
1 (8 oz.) pkg. cream cheese	1 can blueberry pie filling
1 tsp. vanilla	

Mix jello and hot water together. Set aside until it starts to jell. Mix together cream cheese, sugar and vanilla. Add jello mixture and last of all the Cool Whip. Put on top of crust. After it sets, cover with pie filling.

Mrs. Gale (Vonita) Marx, Branch No. 2227, Pilger, NE

GINGER'S CHOCOLATE CHEESECAKE

1 c. vanilla sandwich cookies, crushed	½ c. brown sugar
	1 tsp. vanilla
2 Tbsp. Parkay, melted	4 eggs
3 (8 oz.) pkg. cream cheese	1 (8 oz.) chocolate bar

Mix cookies and oleo. Press in 9 inch springform pan. Bake at 350° for 10 minutes. Cream brown sugar and cream cheese. Add vanilla and eggs, one at a time. Grate chocolate bar and add to mixture. Pour over crust and bake at 350° for 35 minutes.

Ruth Schultz, Branch No. 2232, Auburn, MI

JACKIE'S CHEESECAKE

1¼ c. graham cracker crumbs	1 c. sugar
2 Tbsp. sugar	1 Tbsp. lemon juice
4 Tbsp. margarine or butter, melted	1 tsp. vanilla
	4 large eggs
3 (8 oz.) pkg. cream cheese, softened	1 c. sour cream, mixed with 2 Tbsp. sugar and 1 tsp. vanilla

Heat oven to 350°. Mix cracker crumbs, 2 tablespoons sugar and the butter. Press in bottom of a springform pan. Bake for 10 minutes. Cool.

Heat oven to 300°. Beat cream cheese in large mixer bowl. Add 1 cup sugar gradually, beating until fluffy. Add the lemon juice and vanilla. Beat in 1 egg at a time, mixing well. Pour over crumb mixture in pan. Bake until center is firm (about 1 hour). Spread sour cream mixture carefully over the top. Cool to room temperature. Refrigerate for at least 3 hours before cutting.

This cake freezes very well and it is very yummy.

Jackie Popke, Branch No. 5677, La Mesa, CA

NO-BAKE CHEESECAKE

1 env. unflavored gelatin	1 tsp. grated lemon rind
½ c. sugar	1 pt. small curd cottage cheese
¼ tsp. salt	1 Tbsp. lemon juice
2 egg yolks	1 tsp. vanilla
½ c. milk	½ c. heavy cream, whipped

Mix together the gelatin, sugar and salt in the top of a double boiler. Beat together the egg yolks and milk; add to gelatin mixture. Cook over boiling water, stirring constantly, until gelatin is dissolved and mixture thickens, about 10 minutes. Remove from heat; add grated lemon rind and cool. Stir in cottage cheese, lemon juice and vanilla. Chill, stirring occasionally, until mixture mounds slightly when dropped from spoon.

While mixture is chilling, make Crumb Topping as follows. Mix 2 tablespoons melted butter, 1 tablespoon sugar, ½ cup graham cracker crumbs, ¼ teaspoon cinnamon, and ¼ teaspoon nutmeg; set aside.

Fold in stiffly beaten egg whites and whipped cream into chilled mixture. Turn into 8 inch layer pan or 9 inch pie plate and sprinkle top with Crumb Mixture. Chill until firm. If desired, use 8 or 9 inch square or 9x5 inch loaf pan. Line with waxed paper and press Crumb Mixture in bottom of pan and turn in gelatin mixture. Chill.

Mrs. John (Maxine) Johansen, Branch No. 3365, Rock Springs, WY

SPEEDY CHEESE CAKE

1¼ c. graham cracker crumbs
¼ c. butter, melted
8 oz. cream cheese
½ c. sugar
1 Tbsp. lemon juice
½ tsp. vanilla

Dash of salt
2 eggs
1 c. sour cream
2 Tbsp. sugar
½ tsp. vanilla

Combine cracker crumbs and melted butter. Press into bottom and sides of buttered 8 inch pie pan. Beat cream cheese until fluffy. Gradually blend in ½ cup sugar, lemon juice, ½ teaspoon vanilla, and salt. Add eggs, one at a time, beating well after each. Pour into crust. Bake at 325°F. for 25 to 30 minutes or until set.

Combine sour cream, sugar and vanilla. Spoon over top of pie. Bake for 10 minutes more. Cool. Chill for several hours.

Ruth Olson, Branch No. 1643, Eden, ID

PINEAPPLE CHEESECAKE
(Low calorie)

Crust:

1 c. graham cracker crumbs   3 Tbsp. margarine, melted

Mix crumbs and margarine. Press into bottom of an 8 inch square pan and chill.

Filling:

1 (4 serving size) pkg. diet lemon
   gelatin
1 c. boiling water
1½ lb. 2% lowfat cottage cheese

2 Tbsp. sugar
1 Tbsp. water
1 (8½ oz.) can crushed pineapple
2 tsp. cornstarch

Dissolve gelatin in boiling water and cool until lukewarm. Blend cottage cheese and sugar in blender until smooth. Slowly add dissolved gelatin and mix well. Pour onto crust and chill until firm. Stir cornstarch and 1 tablespoon water in saucepan until smooth. Blend pineapple and its juice into cornstarch mixture; bring to a boil, stirring constantly. Cool for 15 minutes. Spread cooling pineapple mixture over cheesecake and chill for 1 hour or more (or overnight).

Can use 10 ounce box frozen strawberries in place of pineapple. Cut to yield 12 servings (each serving contains 1 teaspoon fat).

Olga Franzen, Branch No. 445, Beatrice, NE

CHERRY COFFEE CAKE

½ c. butter
1 c. sugar
1 egg
1 tsp. vanilla

2 c. flour
2 tsp. baking powder
1 c. milk
1 can cherry pie filling

Cream together butter and sugar. Add egg and vanilla. Alternately add the flour and baking powder with the milk. Pour batter into greased 9x13 inch pan. Pour the cherry pie filling over the batter.

Topping:

½ c. butter   1 c. sugar
1 c. flour

Mix butter, flour and sugar together; sprinkle over pie filling. Bake at 350° for 30 minutes, or longer if needed.

Walene Heerman, Branch No. 2227, Pilger, NE

COFFEE CAKE DELIGHT

¼ c. butter   2 tsp. baking powder
1¼ c. sugar   1 egg (unbeaten) plus milk to
2¼ c. flour   make 1¼ c.

Mix the butter, flour, sugar, and baking powder like pie crust. Add the egg mixture. Stir smooth. Spread in a greased 12x18 inch cooky sheet pan.

Topping:

1 c. flour   ½ c. butter
1 c. sugar   Pinch of baking powder

Mix the preceding ingredients like pie crust for topping. Sprinkle ½ of topping over dough. Pour over 1 can of cherry pie filling (or other kind). Add the rest of the topping and nuts if desired.

In preheated oven, bake at 350° for 40 minutes. When cool, drizzle over with powdered sugar frosting. Freezes well.

Irma Prill, Branch No. 1036, Manawa, WI

COFFEE CAKE PULL APART

1 pkg. active dry yeast   1 tsp. salt
¼ c. water   1 egg
¼ c. shortening   ¾ c. milk, scalded and cooled
¼ c. sugar   3 c. flour

Soften yeast in ¼ cup water. Cream shortening, sugar and salt. Add softened yeast and milk. Blend in flour, 1 cup at a time, until last cup. Add the last cup at ⅓ cup at a time. Turn on floured board, using ½ cup flour. Knead until dough is soft and elastic. Place in greased bowl and cover tightly. Let rise in warm place until double in size. Press down and let rise again. Roll dough in small size rolls (walnut size).

Glaze:

⅔ c. granulated sugar   1 Tbsp. cinnamon
½ c. chopped pecans   ½ c. oleo or butter

In small saucepan, melt ½ cup butter. In small bowl, mix sugar, nuts and cinnamon. Line an angel food cake pan (greased) with cherries and pecan halves. Roll each roll first in butter, then in sugar mixture. Place in pan. Let rise until double in size. Bake at 375° for 30 or 35 minutes.

Thelma L. Meinert, Branch No. 5425, Louisville, KY

DATE NUT COFFEE CAKE

1½ c. flour
⅔ c. sugar
2½ tsp. baking powder
½ tsp. salt

4 Tbsp. soft shortening
1 egg
1 c. milk

Sift flour, sugar, baking powder, and salt. Add shortening, egg and milk; mix. Spread half of the batter in an 8 inch square pan. Cover evenly with Date Filling, then add remaining batter and sprinkle rest of filling on top. Bake at 375° for 30 minutes.

Date Filling:

½ c. brown sugar
2 Tbsp. flour
2 tsp. cinnamon

2 Tbsp. soft butter or margarine
½ c. chopped walnuts
½ c. chopped dates

Combine ingredients (except dates) and divide in half. Add dates to one half and use for middle layer. Use remaining half for topping.

Mrs. Grace Polley, Branch No. 283, Leavenworth, KS

FRUIT-FILLED COFFEE CAKE

¾ c. margarine
1 c. sugar
2 beaten eggs
1 c. sour cream
2½ c. flour
1 tsp. salt

1 tsp. baking soda
1 (1 lb. 5 oz.) can blueberry pie
    filling
½ c. sugar
½ tsp. cinnamon
Nuts

Cream margarine and sugar. Combine eggs with sour cream. Add to creamed mixture. Stir in flour, salt and soda; mix well. Spread half of batter in greased 13x9 inch pan. Spread pie filling over batter. Combine sugar and cinnamon; sprinkle half over pie filling. Top with remaining batter, then sprinkle with remaining sugar-cinnamon mixture. Garnish with nuts. Bake at 350° for 45 minutes

Other pie fillings such as cherry, peach or raisin may be used.

Connie Davis, Branch No. 3107, Loveland, CO

FRUIT SWIRL COFFEE CAKE

4 c. Bisquick baking mix
½ c. sugar
¼ c. margarine, melted
½ c. milk
1 tsp. vanilla

1 tsp. almond extract
3 eggs
1 (21 oz.) can cherry, apricot or
    blueberry pie filling

Grease jelly roll pan, 15½ x 10½ x 1 inches, or 2 square pans, 9 x 9 x 2 inches. Mix all ingredients, except pie filling. Beat vigorously for 30 seconds. Spread ⅔ of the batter (about 2½ cups) in jelly roll pan or ⅓ of batter (about 1¾ cups) in each pan. Spread pie filling over batter. Drop remaining batter by teaspoonfuls onto pie filling. Bake at 350° until light brown, 20 to 25 minutes. Drizzle with glaze while warm. Serve warm or cool. Makes 18 servings.

Glaze: Beat 1 cup powdered sugar and 1 to 2 tablespoons milk until smooth and of desired consistency.

Nita Schmidt, Branch No. 2630, Greeley, CO

FRUIT SWIRL COFFEE CAKE

1½ c. sugar
½ c. shortening
1 tsp. vanilla
4 eggs
½ c. softened oleo

1½ tsp. baking powder
1 tsp. almond flavoring
3 c. flour
1 (21 oz.) can cherry pie filling

Blend in large mixing bowl the sugar, shortening, vanilla, eggs, oleo, baking powder, and almond flavoring. Stir in the flour. Grease lightly a jelly roll pan. Spread ⅔ of batter in jelly roll pan. Spread cherry pie filling over the batter. Drop remaining batter by tablespoonfuls onto pie filling. Bake for 30 minutes or until golden brown in a 350° oven. While warm, drizzle with the glaze.

Glaze:

1 c. powdered sugar

1 to 2 Tbsp. milk

Mix thoroughly.

Viola E. Gnadt, Branch No. 2801, McFarland, KS

MARY'S FAVORITE COFFEE CAKE

Dough:

2 c. flour
½ c. sugar
3 Tbsp. baking powder
½ c. margarine

½ tsp. salt
2 eggs
1 c. milk

Filling can be:

Canned fruit (any kind), drained
Jams
Cream Cheese Filling (recipe
    following)

Chocolate chips (1 (12 oz.) pkg.)

Streusel Topping:

1 c. sugar
½ c. flour
⅛ lb. margarine

Pinch of salt
Spice

Mix first 5 ingredients in large bowl till like small peas. Mix eggs and milk together. Add milk mixture to flour mixture. Pour into a greased pan. Put fruit, jam or Cream Cheese Filling on top of dough. Top that with Streusel Topping. Bake at 350° for about ½ hour.

Cream Cheese Filling:

1 (8 oz.) pkg. cream cheese	¼ c. sugar
1 egg	½ tsp. lemon peel or vanilla
2 to 3 Tbsp. milk	1 Tbsp. flour

Soften cream cheese. Add egg and blend. Add milk, sugar and flour. Flavor to taste with lemon peel or vanilla.

Theresa Wilke, Kasson, MN

LEMON SUGAR COFFEE CAKE

Sift 2 cups sifted flour, 3 teaspoons baking powder and 1 teaspoon salt together. Mix ½ cup shortening and ½ cup sugar well. Add 2 eggs and beat well. Add flour mixture alternately with 1 cup milk and ¼ teaspoon lemon extract. Pour into greased 8 inch pan. Sprinkle with lemon-sugar topping made by blending ½ cup sugar, 1 tablespoon lemon rind, ⅛ teaspoon nutmeg, and 1 tablespoon melted butter. Bake in a 400° oven for about 30 minutes.

More lemon (which seems to be a universally appealing flavor): Mrs. James Leckband of rural Worthington sends this lemon coffee cake which she has enjoyed making in her kitchen. Maureen Leckband advises, "I use fresh lemon rind in this and see to it that we have lemonade or something, so the lemon isn't wasted."

Mrs. Maureen Leckband, Branch No. 1131, Worthington, MN

OLD-FASHIONED COFFEE CAKE

Mix in bowl:

1½ c. flour	½ tsp. salt
½ c. brown sugar	1 tsp. baking powder
½ c. white sugar	¼ c. instant Pet dry milk
½ tsp. soda	½ c. shortening

Blend until crumbly. Save ½ cup for topping.

In another bowl, mix:

½ c. water	1 well beaten egg
1½ tsp. vinegar	½ tsp. lemon flavoring

Add dry ingredients to liquid and mix thoroughly. Sprinkle the ½ cup topping over batter before baking. Bake for about 30 minutes at 350° in greased and floured 9 inch square pan.

Marjorie Bley, Branch No. 2630, Greeley, CO

RHUBARB COFFEE CAKE

½ c. margarine
1½ c. sugar
1 egg
1 c. sour milk or buttermilk
1 tsp. vanilla
1 tsp. soda

½ tsp. salt
2½ c. flour
3 c. rhubarb, cut up
½ c. brown sugar and nuts (if desired)

Mix together sugar, margarine, egg, sour milk or buttermilk, vanilla, soda, and salt. Add flour and mix well. Add rhubarb. Put in a 9x13 inch pan, greased and floured. Sprinkle ½ cup brown sugar and nuts. Bake at 350° for 45 minutes or less. After cake is baked and still warm, pour over this topping.

Topping:

¼ c. margarine
½ c. sugar

1 tsp. vanilla
9 Tbsp. evaporated milk

Boil for 3½ minutes. Beat until thickened a little and pour over warm cake.

This is also good for a dessert with whipped cream.

Berniece Rodemeyer, Branch No. 554, Hampton, IA

SOUR CREAM COFFEE CAKE

1 pkg. yellow cake mix
4 eggs
1 c. sour cream

1 pkg. vanilla or lemon instant pudding
½ c. salad oil

Topping:

¼ c. sugar
1½ tsp. cinnamon

½ c. chopped nuts

Combine all ingredients. Mix for 8 minutes. Pour half of batter in greased and floured Bundt cake pan. Sprinkle half of the topping over; add rest of batter and sprinkle other half of topping over. Cut through batter and topping with knife. Bake in a 350° oven for approximately 45 minutes.

Connie Davis, Branch No. 3107, Loveland, CO

SOUR CREAM PUMPKIN COFFEECAKE

½ c. butter
¾ c. sugar
1 tsp. vanilla
3 eggs
2 c. flour
1 tsp. baking powder

1 tsp. baking soda
1 c. sour cream
1 (16 oz.) can pumpkin
1 slightly beaten egg
⅓ c. sugar
1 tsp. pumpkin pie spice

Cream first 3 ingredients in mixer bowl. Add eggs, beating well. Combine flour, baking powder and baking soda. Add to butter mixture alternately with sour cream. Combine pumpkin, beaten egg, sugar, and pie spice. Spoon half of the batter into a 13x9x2 inch baking pan; spread to corners. Sprinkle with half of the streusel. Spread pumpkin mixture over streusel. Carefully spread remaining batter over pumpkin mixture. Sprinkle with remaining streusel. Bake at 325° for 50 to 60 minutes or until toothpick inserted in center comes out clean. Makes 12 servings.

Streusel:

1 c. firmly packed brown sugar	2 tsp. cinnamon
⅓ c. butter	1 c. chopped nuts

Cut first three ingredients until blended. Stir in nuts.

June Nelson, Branch No. 4930, Kenosha, WI

GOOEY BUTTER CAKE

1 pkg. yellow cake mix	1 c. powdered sugar
4 eggs	1 (8 oz.) pkg. cream cheese
1 stick butter (soft)	

Mix cake mix, 2 eggs, and softened butter until smooth. Mixture will be thick and hard to spread. Press into greased and floured 9x13 inch pan. Mix remaining 2 eggs, powdered sugar and cream cheese. Pour over cake mixture. Bake at 350° for 35 minutes.

Vi White, Branch No. 2568, Fredericktown, MO

GOOEY BUTTER CAKE

1 box yellow cake mix	1 (8 oz.) pkg. cream cheese
4 eggs (large)	1 lb. powdered sugar
¼ c. butter or margarine, softened	

Mix cake mix, 2 eggs and butter by hand until smooth. Spread into a 13x9x2 inch cake pan that has been buttered and floured.

Beat softened cream cheese, 2 eggs and powdered sugar with a mixer until smooth. Pour over the cake batter in the pan. Bake in preheated 350° oven for 45 minutes. Sprinkle powdered sugar over the top when cool (optional).

Marcella Bartz, Branch No. 822, St. Louis, MO

COCONUT CAKE

1 (18½ oz.) pkg. butter flavored cake mix	1 (12 oz.) pkg. coconut
2 c. sugar	1½ c. frozen whipped topping, thawed
16 oz. sour cream	

Prepare cake mix according to directions, making two 8 inch layers. When completely cool, split both layers, making 4. Combine sugar, cream and coconut. Blend well and chill. Reserve 1 cup mixture for frosting and spread remainder between cake layers.

Combine reserved mixture and whipped topping. Blend until smooth. Spread on top and sides of cake. Seal cake in airtight container and refrigerate for 3 days before serving.

Charlene

THREE LAYER COCONUT-WALNUT CAKE

1 pkg. yellow cake mix
1 (4 serving) pkg. instant pudding
   and pie filling (vanilla)
1½ c. water

4 eggs
¼ c. oil
2½ c. flaked coconut
1 c. chopped walnuts

Blend cake mix, pudding mix, water, eggs, and oil in large mixer bowl. Beat at medium speed of mixer for 4 minutes. Stir in coconut and walnuts. Pour into 3 greased and floured 9 inch layer cake pans. Bake at 350° for 35 minutes. Cool in pans for 15 minutes. Remove and cool on rack. Fill and frost with Coconut-Cream Cheese Frosting (recipe for frosting found under frosting section).

Meg Bray, Branch No. 4122, Spearfish, SD

ITALIAN CREAM CAKE

½ c. Crisco
1 stick oleo
2 c. sugar
1 tsp. vanilla
1 tsp. soda
1 c. buttermilk

2 c. flour
1 tsp. salt
2 c. coconut
1 c. chopped nuts
5 eggs, separated

Icing:

1 stick softened oleo
1 (8 oz.) cream cheese
1 tsp. vanilla

1 box powdered sugar (3 c.)
1 c. chopped nuts

Cream oleo and Crisco well. Cream in sugar. Add egg yolks, one at a time, beating after each. Mix all dry ingredients and add alternately with buttermilk. Stir in coconut and pecans, then fold in stiffly beaten egg whites. Bake in 3 layer pans at 350° for 40 minutes.

Amarylis E. Kottman, Branch No. 6862, Unionville, MO

MOCHA CAKE

4 eggs
3 Tbsp. cold water
1 c. sugar

1 tsp. vanilla
1 c. sifted cake flour
1 tsp. baking powder

Beat the 4 eggs until thick. Add cold water and vanilla, then the sugar. Slowly add the flour mixture. Put in a 9x13 inch greased and floured pan. Bake in a 350° oven. Cool. Cut into squares and frost with thin powdered sugar frosting and turn in ground peanuts (I use about 1 pound of salted peanuts).

Mathilda Dibbert, Branch No. 2331, Wausa, NE

MOON CAKE

½ c. margarine
1 c. flour

4 eggs

Topping:

2 small boxes instant vanilla
   pudding
8 oz. cream cheese

8 oz. Cool Whip
Chocolate sauce
Chopped nuts

Bring to a boil 1 cup water and margarine. Add at once the flour and stir rapidly. Mixture will form a ball. Remove and cool slightly. Beat in eggs, one at a time. Beat well after each egg. Spread on cookie sheet that has been sprayed with Pam. Bake at 400° for 30 minutes. Cool. Mix pudding according to package directions. Mix in softened cream cheese. Spread on crust. Refrigerate for at least 20 minutes. Top with Cool Whip. Drizzle with chocolate sauce and nuts.

Fran Kelley, Branch No. 779, Savanna, IL

OATMEAL CAKE

1¼ c. boiling water
1 c. quick oatmeal (uncooked)
1 stick margarine
1 c. white sugar
1 c. brown sugar
2 eggs

1⅓ c. sifted flour
1 tsp. baking soda
½ tsp. salt
1 tsp. cinnamon
2 tsp. vanilla

Put oatmeal and margarine in mixing bowl. Pour boiling water over them and let stand for 20 minutes. Add 2 eggs and vanilla; beat well. Add remaining ingredients and beat together. (Sift together flour, salt, soda, and cinnamon.) Pour batter into greased and floured 9½ x 13 inch pan. Bake at 350° for 35 minutes or until done. Cool slightly and spread with topping.

Topping - Mix together and heat:

6 Tbsp. margarine
½ c. brown sugar
¼ c. milk

1 c. cocoanut
1 c. chopped nuts

Spread on top of cake. Put cake under broiler for just a few minutes to brown frosting. Watch carefully or frosting will burn.

Laverne Altschuh, AAL Branch No. 452, St. Louis, MO

OATMEAL CAKE

1¼ c. boiling water
1 c. quick oatmeal
½ c. margarine
2 eggs
1 c. brown sugar

1 c. white sugar
1⅓ c. flour
1 tsp. soda
1 tsp. cinnamon
½ tsp. salt

Pour boiling water over oatmeal. Let stand until cool. Beat margarine well. Add sugar, eggs, cinnamon, salt, soda, and flour. Add oatmeal mixture. Bake in a 9x13 inch pan at 375° for 30 to 35 minutes.

440

Frosting:

6 Tbsp. margarine	1 c. coconut
⅔ c. brown sugar	½ c. chopped nutmeats
¼ c. evaporated milk	1 tsp. vanilla

Mix all ingredients. Spread over baked cake and put under broiler for 10 minutes.

Alvena Eckert, Branch No. 5985, Midland, SD

OKLAHOMA CAKE

White cake mix	Flaked coconut
1 can cream of coconut	Cool Whip
1 can Eagle Brand condensed milk	

Bake the white cake as directed on package in a 9x13 inch pan. While cake is baking, mix together 1 can cream of coconut and 1 can condensed milk. When cake is done, punch holes in it with a straw. While the cake is still warm, pour the sweetened condensed milk and cream of coconut mixture over the cake. This forms a glaze and soaks down into the holes. Serve it with Cool Whip and flaked coconut over the top.

Marjorie Tjepkema, Branch No. 767, Norwood, MN

BETTY'S POUND CAKE

2 sticks butter	1 tsp. vanilla extract
½ c. Crisco	½ tsp. lemon extract
5 eggs	½ tsp. almond extract
Dash of salt	3 c. sugar
1 c. evaporated milk	3 c. flour

Cream butter, Crisco and sugar well. Add eggs, one at a time. Add salt and flavorings. Add flour and evaporated milk alternately. Bake in greased and floured tube pan (angel food cake pan) in a 300° oven for 1 hour and 30 minutes.

Baking the day before serving makes the cake settle and taste even better!

Mrs. Barbara (Rev. David) Splett, St. John's Lutheran,
Branch No. 5488, Fayetteville, AR

RICH RUM CAKE

1 c. pecans	4 eggs
1 white cake mix	½ c. cold water
1 (3⅝ oz.) pkg. vanilla pudding	½ c. oil
mix	½ c. dark rum

1. Preheat oven to 325°F.
2. Butter and flour a large Bundt or angel food pan. Sprinkle pecans into the bottom of the pan.
3. In a large bowl, combine the cake mix, pudding mix, eggs, water, oil, and rum; pour over pecans. Bake for 1 hour.
4. Remove cake from oven. Allow to cool and invert on a platter.

5. Using a toothpick, poke holes about 1 inch apart in the top and sides of the cake. Spoon hot glaze over cake.

Glaze:

1 stick butter	1 c. sugar
¼ c. water	¼ to ½ c. dark rum

1. In a saucepan over medium heat, bring butter, water and sugar to a boil; lower heat slightly and continue to cook for 5 minutes, stirring constantly.
2. Remove saucepan from heat and stir in rum. Serves 12 to 15.

LeAnn Duchow, Branch No. 0985, Moses Lake, WA

SEVEN-UP CAKE

1½ c. butter (use real butter)	3 c. flour
3 c. sugar	2 Tbsp. lemon extract
5 eggs	¾ c. 7-Up

In a large bowl, use electric mixer to cream butter and sugar until fluffy (2 minutes). Add eggs, one at a time, beating well after each addition. Add flour and extract, beating until just combined. Add 7-Up and mix thoroughly.

Turn batter into a well greased and floured 12 cup Bundt pan. Bake at 325° for 60 minutes. Remove from oven and cool on rack for 15 minutes before removing from pan. After cool, sprinkle with confectioners sugar or slice and dribble homemade jelly over slice.

JoAnn Wilson, Branch No. 1646, Wheeler, IL

GRANDMA'S SPONGE CAKE
(Easy)

Put in bowl:

2 c. sugar	Pinch of salt
4 eggs, mixed singly into the sugar	1 tsp. vanilla

Mix well.

Sift together and add to first mixture:

2 level tsp. baking powder	2 c. sifted flour

Add 1 cup boiled milk and mix thoroughly. Bake in a 9x13 inch pan at 350° for 40 minutes. Do not overbake.

Frosting:

1½ c. brown sugar	½ c. cream
½ c. melted butter	2 c. coconut

Mix together and spread on cake. Broil for a few minutes until browned.

Or, use any frosting desired. Cake is a nice moist cake. Can also be used topped with fruit for dessert.

Ardith Mueller, Branch No. 1775, Columbus, NE

442

TOFFEE BAR CAKE

2 c. brown sugar
2 c. flour
¾ tsp. soda
½ tsp. salt
½ c. butter or margarine

1 egg
1 c. milk
1 tsp. vanilla
½ c. chopped nuts
8 (5 cent) Heath bars, crushed

Mix sugar, flour, soda, and salt. Cut in butter as for pie crust. Reserve 1 cup crumb mixture. To remaining mixture, add egg, milk, and vanilla. Beat only until blended. Mixture will be thin and lumpy. Pour into greased 9x13 inch pan. Sprinkle with reserved crumb mixture, nuts and candy. Bake at 350° for 30 minutes or until toothpick comes out clean when inserted. Serve with ice cream or whipped cream while still warm.

Ruth Leitch, Branch No. 5844, Avilla, IN

NEVER FAIL WHITE CAKE

1½ c. sugar
½ c. shortening (part butter, part
    lard)
1 c. liquid (either milk or water)
2½ c. cake flour, sifted

3 tsp. baking powder
1 tsp. vanilla
4 egg whites, stiffly beaten
Pinch of salt

Work sugar, shortening, flour, salt, and baking powder as for pie crust until all dry ingredients and shortening are finely crumbled. Add vanilla and liquid; beat until a smooth batter. Add stiffly beaten egg whites. Fold together. Bake in a 350° oven until cake tests done. Pan size needed is a 9x13 inch pan.

Linda Matter, Branch No. 6699, Cavour, SD

FRENCH CREAM CAKE

Cake:

1 c. cake flour
1 c. sugar
6 eggs, separated

1 tsp. cream of tartar
1 tsp. vanilla
Pinch of salt

Sift cake flour and measure. Beat egg whites and cream of tartar until stiff. Slowly add sugar, beating at a lower speed. Fold in cake flour, using wire whip. Beat egg yolks until lemon colored. Fold egg yolks into egg white mixture. Add flavoring and salt. Bake in 2 layers, using 8 inch round pans. Bake at 350° until a toothpick inserted comes out clean. Cut layers in two and put filling between each layer. Sprinkle powdered sugar on top.

Filling:

1½ c. milk
¾ c. sugar
3 egg yolks
2 Tbsp. cornstarch

¼ tsp. salt
1 tsp. vanilla
1 Tbsp. butter

443

Heat milk; do not boil. Add sugar, egg yolks, cornstarch, and salt. Cook. When thickened, add vanilla and 1 tablespoon butter. Cool and spread between layers.

Lorena Groener, Branch No. 422, Reedsburg, WI

TWINKIE CAKE

1 box yellow cake mix	½ c. vegetable shortening
1 c. milk	1 c. sugar
¼ tsp. salt	5 Tbsp. flour
½ c. margarine	1 tsp. vanilla

Prepare cake mix as directed and bake in a 9x13 inch pan. Let stand to cool. Remove from pan and cut in half lengthwise. (Dental floss can be used sawing back and forth.) Boil flour and milk in saver pan until thick, stirring constantly. Set aside.

Cream together sugar, shortening and margarine. Add salt and vanilla. Add cream mixture and flour mixture; beat until fluffy. Put filling on bottom half of cake (using 9x13 inch pan cake was baked in). Put other half of cake on top. Cover cake with remaining filling and refrigerate one day before serving.

Mrs. Dorothy Meinzen, Branch No. 5844, Albion, IN

BUTTERMILK CAKE

2 c. sugar	2 c. raisins
1½ c. butter	1 c. nuts
2 c. buttermilk	¼ tsp. allspice
3 c. flour	1 tsp. cinnamon
2 tsp. soda	½ tsp. nutmeg

Cream sugar and butter. Add buttermilk into which soda has been added. Mix raisins, nuts, and spices into flour. Add to the preceding and mix well. Grease and flour 9x13 inch pan. Pour into pan and bake in slow oven at 350° until tested with a toothpick which comes out clean.

Mrs. Lawrence Greiner, Branch No. 2838, Wilmot, SD

CLOVE CAKE

1 c. brown sugar	1 c. sour cream
1 egg	1½ c. flour
1 tsp. cloves	1 tsp. soda
Pinch of salt	

Mix in order given. Put the soda in the sour cream and spices in the flour. Bake at 350° until done or tester comes out clean.

Gladys Austin, Branch No. 545, Mosinee, WI

SPICE CAKE

Cake:

1 c. sour cream
1 c. white sugar
2 eggs
Pinch of salt
¼ tsp. cinnamon
¼ tsp. cloves
1 tsp. baking soda

2 c. flour
1 tsp. vanilla
1 c. raisins, cooked in a small
    amount of water and drained
    before adding to mixture
½ c. walnuts

Cream together the sour cream, sugar and eggs. Sift together the dry ingredients and add to creamed mixture. Mix well. Add vanilla, raisins and nuts. Stir to mix. Bake at 350° until it tests done. Frosting with Caramel Frosting.

Caramel Frosting:

½ c. butter
1 c. brown sugar, packed

¼ c. milk
1¾ c. powdered sugar

Melt butter in saucepan. Stir in brown sugar. Boil and stir over low heat for 2 minutes. Stir in milk. Bring to a boil, stirring constantly. Cool to lukewarm (120°). Gradually stir in powdered sugar. Place in pan of ice water and stir until thick enough to spread.

Ida Robertson, Branch No. 6479, Minnewaukan, ND

GINGER SPICE CAKE

1 box Betty Crocker gingerbread
    mix
1 c. applesauce

½ c. raisins
½ c. nuts
¾ c. warm water

Mix all ingredients well. Turn out in a greased 9x9 inch pan. Bake for 35 to 40 minutes in a 350° oven.

Martha Kreutz, Branch No. 3107, Loveland, CO

CHOCOLATE CHIP OATMEAL CAKE

1¾ c. boiling water
1 c. quick oatmeal
1 c. brown sugar
1 c. white sugar
1 Tbsp. cocoa
½ c. margarine

2 eggs
1¾ c. flour
1 tsp. soda
½ tsp. salt
2 c. chocolate chips
½ c. chopped nuts

Pour boiling water over oatmeal and let stand for 10 minutes. Add sugars, cocoa and margarine. Stir until margarine is melted. Add eggs, flour, soda, salt, and 1 cup chocolate chips. Pour into greased 9x13 inch pan. Sprinkle with nuts and 1 cup chocolate chips. Bake at 350° for 40 minutes.

Bobbie Bierman, Branch No. 2560, Mansfield, SD

DATE CHOCOLATE CHIP CAKE

1 c. diced dates
1 tsp. soda
¾ c. shortening
1 c. sugar

2 eggs
1½ c. flour
¾ tsp. soda

Topping:

½ c. chocolate chips
½ c. chopped walnuts

⅓ c. sugar

Place dates and 1 teaspoon soda in a bowl. Pour 1¼ cups boiling water over the date mixture. Cool. Cream shortening, sugar and eggs in a mixing bowl. Add the cooled date mixture, flour, and ¾ teaspoon soda; stir. Pour the batter in a greased 9x13 inch cake pan. Sprinkle each ingredient of the topping on in the order given. Bake at 350° for 30 minutes.

Delicious served with ice cream or whipped cream. Cake freezes well.

Jean Parkhurst, Branch No. 1098, Fremont, NE

CHOCOLATE CHIP TORTE

1¾ c. sifted all-purpose flour
2 Tbsp. cocoa
½ tsp. salt
1 c. finely cut dates
1 c. boiling water
1 tsp. baking soda
¼ lb. margarine (must be 1 stick)

½ c. Crisco
1 c. sugar
2 eggs, beaten
1 tsp. vanilla
1 c. chopped pecans
1 (6 oz.) pkg. chocolate chips

Pour the 1 cup boiling water over the cut up dates and the soda. Cool. Sift flour, salt and cocoa together. Cream shortening and sugar together. Beat well. Add eggs and vanilla. Beat until fluffy. Add flour mixture alternately with the cooled date mixture to this batter until all has been used. Spread in a greased 9x13 inch pan. Sprinkle nuts and chips evenly over the top. With the back of a spoon, lightly press down into batter. Bake at 350° for 40 minutes. Serve as is or with a dollop of Cool Whip.

Elsie Grotheer, Branch No. 4582, New Port Richey, FL

CHOCOLATE CREAM FILLED CUPCAKES

2½ c. flour
1 c. sugar
5 Tbsp. cocoa
1 tsp. vanilla
½ c. oil

½ c. buttermilk
½ c. hot water
½ tsp. salt
2 eggs

Mix all ingredients, beating until well blended. Fill paper cups ⅔ full. Bake at 375° for 15 to 20 minutes.

Filling:

2/3 c. sugar   1/3 c. milk
1/2 tsp. salt   2/3 c. shortening

Mix all ingredients until fluffy. After cupcakes are cool, put filling in cookie press and press some of the filling into center of cupcake.

Make frosting with your favorite chocolate frosting.

Alvena Eckert, Branch No. 5985, Midland, SD

FUDGY CUPCAKES

1 c. margarine	1 c. flour
4 sq. semi-sweet chocolate	4 eggs
1½ c. pecans	1 tsp. vanilla
1¾ c. sugar	

Melt together margarine and chocolate. Add the pecans. In separate bowl, stir by hand the sugar, flour and eggs. Add chocolate mixture to this and add 1 teaspoon vanilla. Fill metal cupcake shells 2/3 full. Bake at 325° for 35 minutes.

Fanelda Westphalen, Branch No. 3558, Kiron, IA

NEVER FAIL CUPCAKES

1 egg	1 tsp. soda
½ c. cocoa	1 c. sugar
½ c. shortening	1 tsp. vanilla
1½ c. flour	½ c. hot water
½ c. sour milk	

Put in bowl in order given. Do not mix until last item has been added, then beat well. Bake in cupcake pans in moderate oven (350°) for 17 minutes.

Evelyn L. Decker, Branch No. 5433, New Comerstown, OH

ALL-AMERICAN CHOCOLATE CAKE

2 c. sugar, sifted	2 eggs, slightly beaten
2 c. flour, sifted	½ c. buttermilk or ½ c. milk plus
1 stick margarine (or ½ c.)	1½ tsp. vinegar
½ c. shortening	1 tsp. soda
4 Tbsp. cocoa	1 tsp. cinnamon (optional)
1 c. water	1 tsp. vanilla

In a bowl, place sugar and flour; set aside. In a saucepan, put margarine, shortening, cocoa, and water. Bring to a boil, then add to flour and sugar. Mix well. Add beaten eggs, buttermilk, soda, cinnamon, and vanilla; mix well, then pour into a 9x13 inch greased pan. Bake at 350° for 25 minutes.

Frosting (make while cake is baking and frost while still *hot):*

1 stick margarine (or ½ c.)	3½ c. powdered sugar
4 Tbsp. cocoa	1 tsp. vanilla
1/3 c. milk	Nuts (if desired)

Melt in a saucepan the margarine, cocoa and milk. Remove from heat and add powdered sugar, vanilla and nuts. Beat well and spread on hot cake still in pan. Serves 12 to 15.

"This fast and easy cake is wonderful for any holiday dessert. Frosting sets up like fudge candy."

Shirley Christian, Branch No. 2121, Chico, CA

ALWAYS MOIST CHOCOLATE CAKE

3 c. flour	2 c. cold water
1/3 c. cocoa	1 tsp. vanilla
1 tsp. salt	3/4 c. oil
2 c. sugar	2 Tbsp. lemon juice
2 tsp. soda	

Sift dry ingredients in large bowl. Mix well. In another bowl, mix liquid ingredients. Gradually add liquids to dry mixture. Mix well and pour into a greased 9x13 inch pan. Bake at 350° for 30 minutes. Frost when cool.

Barbara Alsum, Branch No. 3107, Loveland, CO

CHOCOLATE CAKE

3/4 c. shortening	Salt
1 1/2 c. granulated sugar	1/2 c. boiling water
2 eggs	1/2 c. buttermilk or sour milk
2 c. sifted flour	1 tsp. soda and vanilla
1/2 c. cocoa	

Cream 3/4 cup shortening. Mix in 1 1/2 cups granulated sugar and add 2 eggs. Mix well. Place 2 cups sifted flour in sieve; add 1/2 cup cocoa and salt. Add flour mixture to creamed mixture alternately with 1/2 cup boiling water and 1/2 cup buttermilk or sour milk to which 1 teaspoon soda has been added. Add vanilla. Bake in a 350° oven.

Easy Fudge Icing:

2 to 3 sq. unsweetened chocolate	2 c. sifted confectioners sugar
3 Tbsp. butter or margarine	1/4 tsp. salt
5 Tbsp. milk	1 tsp. vanilla

Heat together 2 to 3 squares unsweetened chocolate, 3 tablespoons butter or margarine, and 5 tablespoons milk just until melted over very low heat. Blend in 2 cups sifted confectioners sugar, 1/4 teaspoon salt, and 1 teaspoon vanilla. Stir until spreadable. To thicken, stir over ice water. To thin, stir over hot water. Ices two 8 inch layers or 8x8x2 inch square pan.

Loretta Fick, Branch No. 2232. Auburn, MI

CHOCOLATE CAKE

2 eggs, beaten
1½ c. sugar
Dash of salt
1 c. sour cream (add 1 tsp. soda to cream)

½ c. cocoa (add water to make paste)
2 c. flour, sifted
1 tsp. vanilla
1 c. boiling water

Beat eggs; gradually add sugar and beat until thick. Add sour cream and soda; beat until thick. Add cocoa paste. Add sifted dry ingredients. Bake in waxed paper lined 9x13 inch pan in moderate oven (350°) for 45 to 50 minutes.

Mrs. Marlys Dick, Branch No. 2042, Englevale, ND

CHOCOLATE BUTTERMILK CAKE

Boil together to a quick boil:

1 stick oleo
½ c. oil

1 c. water
4 Tbsp. cocoa

Mix with·

2 c. sugar

2 c. flour

Beat till creamy.

Add:

½ c. buttermilk with 1 tsp. soda added
2 beaten eggs

1 tsp. vanilla
¼ tsp. salt

Bake at 400° for 20 minutes.

Frosting - Bring to a boil:

1 stick oleo
¼ c. cocoa

⅓ c. buttermilk

Remove from heat.

Add:

1 lb. powdered sugar
1 tsp. vanilla

Nuts (if desired)

Ardith Mueller, Branch No. 1775, Columbus, NE

CHERRY CROWN CHOCOLATE CAKE
(Microwave)

1 (21 oz.) can cherry pie filling
1 box devil's food chocolate cake mix
3 eggs

½ c. water
¼ c. vegetable oil
2 tsp. almond extract

Generously grease 12 cup microwavable fluted tube pan. Sprinkle with about 2 tablespoons sugar to thoroughly coat. Evenly spoon half of the pie filling into bottom of tube pan; set aside pan.

In large mixer bowl, place remaining pie filling and other ingredients. Beat at low speed until moistened. Increase speed to medium; beat for 3 minutes. Pour into tube pan. Microwave, uncovered, at 50% for 12 minutes, rotating ¼ turn every 3 minutes. Microwave on HIGH for 7 to 8 minutes or until top springs back when touched and begins to pull away from side of pan. Remove from oven. Cover tightly with foil. Let stand for 10 minutes. Invert onto serving plate. Let stand for 1 minute before lifting off pan. Cool completely.

Cheryl Schultz, Branch No. 3107, Loveland, CO

CHOCOLATE CAKE PUDDING

Cake:

¾ c. granulated sugar
1 c. sifted flour
¼ tsp. salt
2 tsp. baking powder

2 Tbsp. cocoa
½ c. milk
3 Tbsp. melted butter, cooled
1 tsp. vanilla

Topping:

½ c. granulated sugar
½ c. brown sugar

¼ c. cocoa
1½ c. water

Sift sugar, flour, salt, baking powder, and cocoa together in a 9 inch square baking pan. Stir in milk, butter and vanilla. Spread batter in pan. Mix topping sugars and cocoa; sprinkle over batter. Pour water over all and bake in a 350°F. oven for 45 minutes or until top springs back when lightly touched. Serve warm or cool with cream or sour cream. Serves 6 to 8.

Agnes R. Sauers, Branch No. 5196, Monroeville, PA

CHOCOLATE PEPSI CAKE

2 c. sugar
2 c. flour
2 sticks margarine
1 c. Pepsi
3 Tbsp. cocoa
½ c. buttermilk

2 eggs
1 tsp. vanilla
1 tsp. soda
½ c. chopped nuts
1½ c. miniature marshmallows

In saucepan, melt the margarine. Add the Pepsi and cocoa. Bring to a rolling boil. Pour into mixture of sugar and flour. Beat. Add the buttermilk, eggs, vanilla, and soda. Beat together until well mixed; add the chopped nuts and marshmallows. Bake in a 9x13 inch pan, greased. Bake at 350° for 45 minutes.

Frosting:

6 Tbsp. Pepsi   1 stick margarine
3 Tbsp. cocoa

Boil, then add 1 pound powdered sugar. Mix in 1 teaspoon vanilla and 1 cup chopped nuts. Pour over cake while cake and frosting are warm.

Dorothy Heiden, Branch No. 2670, Waco, NE

CHOCOLATE SAUERKRAUT CAKE

4 Tbsp. cocoa   2½ c. flour
2 c. sugar   2 tsp. baking soda
½ c. shortening   1 c. drained sauerkraut
¾ c. milk   ½ tsp. vanilla
2 eggs   ¾ c. hot water

Mix together cocoa, sugar, shortening, and milk; set aside. Mix together remaining ingredients. Add to the chocolate mixture. Mix well. Pour into 9x13 inch pan. Bake at 350° for 40 minutes.

Mrs. Estrella Hamburg, Branch No. 5935, Loganville, WI

CHOCOLATE ZUCCHINI CAKE

½ c. margarine, softened   4 Tbsp. cocoa
½ c. oil   1 tsp. soda
1¾ c. sugar (granulated)   ½ tsp. salt
2 eggs   ½ tsp. cinnamon (optional)
1 tsp. vanilla   ½ tsp. cloves (optional)
½ c. sour milk or buttermilk   2 c. finely grated zucchini
2½ c. flour

Mix the first 6 ingredients. Add and mix the next 6 ingredients, then add and mix the grated zucchini. Pour batter into 9x13 inch greased and floured pan. Sprinkle ½ cup chocolate chips and ½ cup nuts on top. Bake in a 325°F. oven for 45 minutes, or until center is done.

Lenette Schuldheisz, Branch No. 1349, Sandy, OR

EASY NO-FROST CHOCOLATE CAKE

1 (3¾ oz.) pkg. chocolate pudding   1 small pkg. chocolate chips
2 c. milk   Nuts
1 pkg. chocolate cake mix

Combine pudding and milk in pan and place over heat; just bring to a boil. Remove from heat and stir in regular size cake mix. Pour into a greased 9x13 inch cake pan. Sprinkle chips over top. Add nuts if desired. Bake at 350° for 30 minutes. The chips do not melt while baking.

Lou Ann Vogtman, Branch No. 2232, Auburn, MI

FUDGE PUDDING CAKE

1 c. brown sugar
½ c. cocoa
2 c. water

12 marshmallows
Chocolate cake mix

In 13x9 inch pan, mix 1 cup brown sugar and ½ cup cocoa. Stir in 2 cups water. Add 12 marshmallows cut into quarters. Spoon over this chocolate cake batter. Top with 1 cup of broken nuts. Bake at 350° for 45 to 50 minutes. Top with whipped cream.

Donna Phillips, Branch No. 2512, Ord, NE

HERSHEY'S FUDGEY CHOCOLATE TORTE

¾ c. butter or regular stick
   margarine
6 Tbsp. Hershey's cocoa
1 c. sugar, divided
⅔ c. ground blanched almonds

2 Tbsp. flour
3 eggs, separated
2 Tbsp. water
Chocolate Glaze (recipe follows)

Melt butter in medium saucepan over low heat. Stir in Hershey's cocoa and ¾ cup sugar; blend until smooth. Remove from heat; cool for 5 minutes. Blend in almonds and flour. Beat in egg yolks, one at a time. Stir in water.

In medium bowl, beat egg whites until foamy. Gradually add remaining sugar, beating just until soft peaks form. Gently fold chocolate mixture into egg whites, blending thoroughly. Pour into greased and floured 9 inch layer pan. Bake at 350° for 30 minutes or until tester comes out clean. Cool for 10 minutes (cake will settle slightly). Remove from pan onto wire rack. Cool completely. Invert cake onto serving plate. Spread top and sides with Chocolate Glaze. Garnish as desired. Makes 8 to 10 servings.

Chocolate Glaze: Melt 2 tablespoons butter or regular stick margarine in small saucepan over low heat. Add 2 tablespoons Hershey's cocoa and 2 tablespoons water; stir constantly until mixture thickens. Do not boil. Remove from heat; add ½ teaspoon vanilla. Gradually add 1 cup confectioners sugar, beating with whisk until smooth.

Grace Claussen, Branch No. 3420, Sioux City, IA

HUNNGIAN CHOCOLATE CAKE

½ c. butter or oleo
1 c. brown sugar
¼ c. shortening
½ c. white sugar
2 eggs
1 tsp. vanilla

2½ sq. semi-sweet chocolate,
   melted
2¼ c. cake flour
1½ c. buttermilk
1½ tsp. baking soda, dissolved in
   1½ Tbsp. boiling water

Cream well first 4 ingredients (oleo, brown sugar, shortening, and white sugar). Add 2 eggs (well beaten), 1 teaspoon vanilla, 2½ squares semi-sweet chocolate (melted). Add 2¼ cups cake flour and 1½ cups buttermilk; last add 1½ teaspoons baking soda in 1½ tablespoons boiling water. Add this to cake mixture. Grease and flour three 9 inch cake pans. Bake at 350° for 30 minutes or until done.

Icing:

1 c. milk
½ c. shortening
1 c. sugar

4 Tbsp. flour
1 stick oleo

Cook flour and milk together. When cool, add shortening, oleo and sugar; beat well. Put between cake layers. This can also be used to frost sides or frost sides with favorite chocolate frosting.

Pauline A. Richter, Branch No. 1137, Pocahontas, MO

LOW CHOLESTEROL CHOCOLATE CAKE

½ c. shortening
1 c. sugar
¼ tsp. salt
1 tsp. vanilla
½ c. cocoa
⅓ c. water

2½ c. sifted cake flour
1 c. more water
3 egg whites
¾ c. more sugar
1⅓ tsp. soda
2 Tbsp. boiling water

Cream together shortening, 1 cup sugar, salt, and vanilla; add the cocoa and ⅓ cup water mixed together to make a paste. Add alternately the flour and the 1 cup water. Beat egg whites until foamy. Add the ¾ cup sugar and beat until stiff. Blend into preceding mixture. Combine soda and boiling water; add to batter. Mix well. Bake at 350° for 35 to 40 minutes or until tests done. I always get everything ready and beat the egg whites first and proceed from there - no changing or washing of beaters!!

This is a low cholesterol cake, depending on the shortening used and is a fine textured cake.

Eileen Larson, Branch No. 5325, Stratford, IA

MISSISSIPPI MUD CAKE

Cake:

2 c. white sugar
4 eggs
2 sticks oleo, melted
1½ c. flour
⅓ c. cocoa

1 tsp. vanilla
½ c. chopped nuts
1 c. coconut
1 (7 oz.) jar marshmallow creme

Mix first 3 ingredients together. Add next 3 ingredients and mix. Add nuts and coconut. (This recipe does *not* have baking soda or baking powder.) Pour into greased 9x13 inch pan. Bake in a 350° oven for 30 to 35 minutes. As soon as you remove from oven, cover with marshmallow creme. Let cool.

Frosting:

1 stick oleo
1/3 c. cocoa
6 Tbsp. milk

1 tsp. vanilla
1 lb. powdered sugar

Beat frosting ingredients together and spread on cooled cake.

Mrs. James (Sharon) Bickel, Branch No. 5844, Frankenmuth, MI

CHOCOLATE CAKE

2½ c. flour
1/3 c. cocoa
3½ tsp. baking powder
2/3 c. corn oil
3/4 c. water

½ c. milk (skim)
1 tsp. vanilla
4 egg whites
1/4 tsp. cream of tartar
1¾ c. sugar

Oil and flour cake pans. Sift flour, cocoa and baking powder together. Add oil, water, milk and vanilla together. Batter will resemble a thick paste. Beat eggs till foamy. Add cream of tartar and gradually add sugar, beating until egg whites form soft peaks. Fold egg whites into batter. Bake at 350° for 30 minutes.

Contains 235 calories without frosting, trace of saturated fat, and 0 mg *cholesterol.*

Annabell Meyer, Branch No. 0714, Fairmont, OK

MISSISSIPPI MUD CAKE

2 sticks soft margarine
2 c. sugar
3 Tbsp. cocoa
4 eggs
3 tsp. vanilla

1¼ c. plain flour
1⅓ c. coconut
1 c. chopped nuts
½ tsp. salt

Combine sugar and cocoa, then margarine. Beat well with mixer. Add eggs, one at a time, beating until light and fluffy. Add vanilla. Sift flour and salt; add and mix well. Beat for 1 to 2 minutes. Add coconut and nuts. Bake in greased 9x13 inch pan in a preheated 350° oven for 35 minutes. Spread one 7 ounce jar marshmallow cream on cake while hot

Frosting:

1 box powdered sugar
1/3 c. cocoa
1 stick margarine

1 tsp. vanilla
½ c. chopped nuts
Hot water

Mix margarine and cocoa. Add vanilla. Mix. Add powdered sugar and hot water to make icing. Spread on cooled cake. Sprinkle with nuts.

Variation for cake from Branch No. 6557 (San Antonio, Texas): Use 1 teaspoon vanilla, 1½ cups flour, 1½ cups coconut, and no salt.

Variation for frosting from Branch No. 6557 (San Antonio, Texas): Use ½ cup cocoa, no nuts, no water, and ½ cup evaporated milk.

Annaliese Griffin, Branch No. 2276, Louisville, KY;
Branch No. 6557, San Antonio, TX

NO EGG-ORANGE COCOA CAKE

1 c. all-purpose flour
⅔ c. sugar
¼ c. unsweetened cocoa powder
¾ tsp. baking soda

½ c. skim milk
½ c. orange juice
⅓ c. corn oil

Sift flour, sugar, cocoa, and soda together. Add milk, orange juice and oil. Beat well. Set oven at 350°. Spray an 8x8x2 inch pan with nonstick spray. Bake for 30 to 35 minutes. Cool. Top with sifted powdered sugar. *This is low cholesterol.*

Arvilla Passow, Branch No. 433, Alma, WI

SEVEN-UP CHOCOLATE CAKE BARS

Cake:

2 c. sugar
2 c. flour
1 c. margarine
1 c. 7-Up
4 Tbsp. cocoa
½ c. buttermilk

2 eggs, beaten
1 tsp. soda
1 tsp. vanilla
½ tsp. salt
1 c. nuts

Sift flour and sugar in a large bowl. Bring margarine, 7-Up and cocoa to a boil. Pour hot liquid onto the flour and sugar mixture. Add buttermilk, eggs, soda, salt, and vanilla. Beat well and stir in nuts. Bake at 350° for 20 to 25 minutes in a greased 10x15 inch pan.

Icing:

½ c. margarine
4 Tbsp. cocoa
1 tsp. vanilla

4 Tbsp. milk
1 lb. powdered sugar
1 c. chopped nuts

Five minutes before the cake is done, prepare the frosting. Bring margarine, cocoa and milk to a boil. Add powdered sugar, vanilla and nuts. Stir until mixed. Spread on warm cake. Add a little milk if frosting is too thick. Cut into 1x2 inch bars when cool.

Alda Muhly, Branch No. 1976, Cornelius, OR

SOUR CREAM CHOCOLATE CAKE

1½ c. sugar

2 Tbsp. butter

Beat well. Add 2 eggs.

Sift together and add:

1¾ c. flour   **Salt**
⅓ c. cocoa

Add 1 cup sour cream and beat well.

Stir in:

⅔ c. hot water   **1 tsp. soda**

Bake at 325° for 40 minutes. *Very moist cake!*

RED CAKE

½ c. shortening	**1 tsp. vanilla**
1½ c. sugar	**1 tsp. salt**
2 oz. red food coloring	**1 tsp. soda**
2 heaping Tbsp. cocoa	**1 Tbsp. vinegar**
1 c. buttermilk	**2 eggs**
2¼ c. cake flour	

Cream shortening, sugar and eggs. Make a paste of food coloring and cocoa; add to creamed mixture. Add buttermilk alternately with sifted flour and salt. Add vanilla. Add soda to vinegar, but hold over bowl as it foams. Add this to the mixture, blending it in instead of beating. Bake for 24 to 30 minutes at 350° in two 8 inch greased and floured pans. Cool on rack. Split each layer in half and add frosting between layers and outside.

Butter Cream Frosting:

3 Tbsp. flour	**1 tsp. vanilla**
1 c. milk	**1 c. butter**
1 c. sugar	

Cook flour and milk until very thick, stirring constantly. Cool. Cream sugar, butter and vanilla until fluffy. Add to the first cooled mixture. Mix together until well blended. (Should be consistency of whipped cream). Frost all 4 layers.

Francis V. Sedlacek, Branch No. 3107, Loveland, CO

HO HO'S

Base:

½ c. oil	**2 eggs**
½ c. oleo	**1 tsp. soda**
1 c. water	**3 Tbsp. cocoa**
½ c. buttermilk	**2 c. sugar**
2 c. flour	

Combine all base ingredients and pour into a greased and floured 13x9 inch pan or two 9x9 inch pans so one can be frozen when recipe is completed. Bake at 350° for 20 to 30 minutes. Let cool.

Filling:

1 c. sugar
1 c. Crisco
½ c. milk
1 Tbsp. water

¼ tsp. salt
1 tsp. vanilla
1 c. powdered sugar

Combine all filling ingredients, except powdered sugar, and beat for 5 minutes. Add powdered sugar and mix well. Spread on cool base.

Frosting:

½ c. sugar
½ c. milk

6 Tbsp. oleo
1½ c. chocolate chips

Boil sugar, milk and oleo for 1 minute. Remove from heat and add chocolate chips. Beat until thick. Frost while still warm. Cut into squares.

Cheryl Manke, Branch No. 5985, Midland, SD

SOUR CREAM FUDGE TORTE

Torte:

1 pkg. Pillsbury Plus devil's food
    cake mix
3 eggs

⅓ c. oil
1 c. water

Heat oven to 350°. Grease and flour two 8 inch pans. In large bowl, blend cake mix, eggs, water, and oil at low speed until moistened, then beat at high speed for 2 minutes. Pour into pans. Bake for 30 to 40 minutes or until toothpick comes out clean. Cool cake in pans for 15 minutes. Remove from pans. Cool completely. Split each layer in half to make 4 layers.

Filling:

2 c. dairy sour cream
1 c. sugar
3 c. coconut

3 c. non-dairy whipped topping or
    3 c. Cool Whip

Make filling by combining sour cream, sugar and coconut. Fold in whipped topping. Fill and frost layers with filling. Store in refrigerator, covered.

May also use lemon or strawberry cake mix. Can be made several days ahead as cake improves with age, as the flavors blend.

Viola Albrecht, Branch No. 1781, Elizabeth, IL

THE BLACK FOREST CAKE

1 box chocolate cake mix
1 c. water
3 eggs

¼ c. oil
Cherry pie filling
Cool Whip

Mix together cake mix, water, eggs, and oil. Let stand. Line bottom of two 9 inch quiche pans with wax paper. Divide batter evenly. Place in microwave, covered with another quiche pan, and bake for 6 minutes on 100% power. Let stand to finish cooking. Put part of the cherry pie filling between layers. Frost around cake with Cool Whip. Put rest of cherry filling on top of cake.

Mr. and Mrs. Terry L. Albrecht, Coffeyville, KS

BLACK FOREST CHERRY TORTE

Cake:

1 pkg. German chocolate cake mix
¼ c. oil
2 Tbsp. rum

Have on hand one large can cherry pie filling for filling.

Prepare cake following package directions, but substitute oil for ¼ cup water in basic recipe. Bake in 9 or 10 inch springform pan for 35 to 40 minutes. Cool completely. Slice cake in half. Sprinkle both halves with rum. Let stand.

Filling: Set 10 to 12 cherries aside. Spread rest of filling on center of one cake layer. Leave about 1 inch free on edges.

Frosting and decorating:

2 c. whipping cream
½ c. powdered sugar
1 tsp. vanilla
Chocolate strussels

Whip cream until almost stiff. Add powdered sugar and beat lightly. Stir in vanilla. Fill edges of cherry filled cake layer with whipped cream about ¾ inch high. Put second layer on top. Press down lightly. Spread whipped cream on top and sides; save some for decorating. Decorate top with cookie press. Garnish with extra cherries. Put chocolate strussels all around cake.

Christa Zentgraf, Branch No. 2714, Ogden, UT

MOCHA CHOCOLATE CREAM TORTE

Crust:

1½ c. chopped nuts
½ c. powdered sugar
¼ c. butter, melted

Heat oven to 375°. In small bowl, combine crust ingredients. Mix well. Press firmly into bottom of 9 inch springform pan. Bake at 375° for 8 to 10 minutes; cool.

Fudge Layer:

1 c. chocolate chips
1 Tbsp. instant coffee
1 c. whipping cream
¼ c. butter

In small saucepan over low heat, melt chocolate chips, instant coffee, and whipping cream, stirring constantly until smooth. Remove from heat; stir in ¼ cup butter. Refrigerate until slightly thickened. Spread over crust. Freeze until firm.

Chocolate Cream Layer:

1 c. sugar
1 c. butter, softened
3 eggs

3 oz. (3 sq.) semi-sweet chocolate,
melted and cooled

In medium bowl, cream sugar and 1 cup butter until light and fluffy. Add eggs, one at a time, beating at medium speed for 2 minutes after each addition. (Batter may look curdled; beat until smooth.) Blend in melted chocolate. Spread over fudge layer.

Topping:

1 Tbsp. powdered sugar
1 tsp. unsweetened cocoa

½ c. whipping cream, whipped

In small bowl, fold powdered sugar and cocoa into whipped cream. Spoon topping into pastry bag with desired tip. Pipe rosettes evenly spaced around top edge of torte. May spread topping over all evenly.

Garnish with candied coffee beans or chocolate chips. Store in refrigerator. Makes 16 servings.

Julia Riedel, Branch No. 3107, Loveland, CO

DIRT CAKE

1½ large pkg. Oreo cookies
8 oz. cream cheese
⅓ c. powdered sugar
½ stick margarine

2 small pkg. French vanilla instant
pudding
4 c. milk
1 (12 oz.) container Cool Whip

Crush Oreo cookies. Mix the next 3 ingredients until blended. Mix and allow to set the pudding with the milk. Blend the Cool Whip into the pudding. Combine the cream cheese mixture with the pudding mixture.

Using a container that is see-through and looks like a flower pot, place and layer the cookies and pudding, beginning and ending with "cookie dirt." Place some silk flowers in the center and use as a centerpiece. Remove flowers when ready to serve. What a surprise to your guests!!

Mary E. Asplund, Branch No. 4883, Odenton, MD

DIRT CAKE

1 large pkg. Oreo cookies
8 oz. cream cheese
2 (3½ oz.) pkg. instant vanilla
pudding

½ stick butter
1 c. powdered sugar
3½ c. milk
12 oz. Cool Whip

Cream butter and cream cheese with sugar. Set aside. Mix pudding and milk according to package instructions. Add Cool Whip. Crush cookies in blender. Mix ½ of the crumbs with cream cheese mixture and pudding mixture. Pour into 8 inch planter. Cover with rest of cookie crumbs. Serve with a trowel. *Very rich!*

Sharon Schober, Branch No. 4077, Racine, WI

TURTLE CAKE

1 box German chocolate cake mix
1 (14 oz.) bag caramels
¾ c. butter

½ can evaporated milk
1 c. chocolate chips
1 c. chopped pecans

Prepare cake batter per cake package instructions. Pour half of the batter into 9x13 inch pan. Bake for 15 minutes at 350°. Meanwhile, melt caramels, butter and milk in saucepan over low heat, stirring constantly. Pour over hot half baked cake. Top with chocolate chips and pecans. Pour the rest of the cake batter on top. Bake at 350° for 20 minutes.

Variation by Nancy Welker: Use ½ cup Pet milk (instead of ½ can evaporated milk). Frost with favorite chocolate frosting.

Rhonda Hill, Branch No. 0823, Bremen, IN;
Nancy Welker, Branch No. 401, Washington, MO

NEXT BEST THING TO TOM SELLECK

1 pkg. German chocolate cake
  mix
1 can Borden's sweetened
  condensed milk
1 jar Mrs. Richardson's
  butterscotch caramel ice
  cream topping

1 (8 oz.) Cool Whip
2 or 3 Heath candy bars

Bake cake at 350° for 30 to 35 minutes as directed on a package in a 9x13 inch pan. Take out of oven and poke holes in the cake with a wooden spoon. Pour sweetened condensed milk in holes, then pour ice cream topping over the milk. Frost with Cool Whip. Crush candy bars and sprinkle over the top. Refrigerate.

Carol Schultz, Branch No. 1612, Rothsay, MN

APPLE PUTTING CAKE

1 c. flour
1 c. nutmeats
4 c. chopped apples
1 c. brown sugar
1 c. white sugar
2 eggs
½ c. shortening

1 tsp. vanilla
1 c. flour
½ tsp. salt
1 tsp. soda
1 tsp. cinnamon
½ tsp. nutmeg
1 tsp. allspice

Mix together flour, nuts and apples. Add both sugars, eggs, shortening, and vanilla. Sift rest of ingredients and add to mixture. Bake in greased jelly roll pan at 350° for 40 minutes.

Hilde Johnson, Branch No. 2121, Chico, CA

APPLE CAKE
(Microwave oven)

1 (9 oz.) pkg. lemon cake mix
¼ c. butter, softened
2 eggs

2 c. sliced apples
1 c. sour milk or cream

Combine cake mix, butter and 1 egg; blend well. Spread batter in glass baking dish. Cook on HIGH (9) for 3 to 4 minutes. Arrange apple slices over cake base. Blend sour milk and remaining egg; spread evenly over apples.

Topping:

1 c. graham cracker crumbs
⅓ c. butter, softened
⅓ c. brown sugar

1 tsp. cinnamon
½ tsp. ground nutmeg

Combine topping ingredients in small glass bowl. Sprinkle topping mixture over sour milk layer. Bake on HIGH (9) for 1 minute. Turn dish. Bake on ROAST (6) for 7 to 9 minutes. Serve warm or cold.

Dorothy Albert, Branch No. 1646, Wheeler, IL

CAROLINA APPLE CAKE

3 c. unsifted flour
1 tsp. baking soda
1 tsp. cinnamon
1 tsp. salt
¼ tsp. mace
2 c. sugar
1 c. salad oil

3 eggs
2 tsp. vanilla
3 c. diced, pared tart apples
1 c. chopped walnuts
½ c. raisins
Confectioners sugar

Combine flour, baking soda, cinnamon, salt, and mace; set aside. In large bowl of mixer, beat together sugar, oil, eggs, and vanilla at a medium speed until well combined. Gradually beat in flour mixture until smooth. Fold in apples, walnuts and raisins. Turn into greased and floured Bundt pan. Bake at 325°F. for 1 hour and 15 minutes or until cake tester comes out clean. Cool cake for 10 minutes, then remove from pan. Cool completely.

To serve, sprinkle with confectioners sugar. If you bake in smaller pans, allow less baking time.

Dorothy Buege, Branch No. 1781, Elizabeth, IL

DUTCH APPLE CAKE

2 tsp. cinnamon
5 Tbsp. sugar
3 or 4 baking apples, sliced thin
3 c. flour
2 c. sugar

3 tsp. baking powder
4 eggs
1 c. salad oil
2 tsp. vanilla
⅓ c. orange juice

461

Mix together first 3 ingredients; set aside. Mix together remaining ingredients in large bowl. Put in greased 10 inch tube pan. Place both mixtures in pan alternately, beginning and ending with batter. Batter will be thick. Bake at 350° for 1 hour and 10 minutes. Cake can be stored for days; will become more moist.

Ruth M. Peitsch, Branch No. 552, Dundalk, MD

DUTCH APPLE CAKE

Crust:

1¼ c. flour	½ c. butter
¾ tsp. baking powder	1 egg yolk, beaten
½ tsp. salt	2 Tbsp. milk
1 tsp. sugar	

Topping:

3 to 4 c. peeled, chopped or sliced apples	1½ Tbsp. flour
¾ c. sugar	½ tsp. cinnamon
	3 Tbsp. butter

To make crust, sift flour with baking powder, salt and sugar. Cut the butter into the flour mixture; moisten with the egg and milk mixture. Press into bottom of 11x7 inch pan.

Press prepared apples over the dough of the crust. Sprinkle with topping ingredients which have been mixed like coarse crumbs. Bake at 375° for 50 minutes or until apples are done.

Doris Kiehnau, Branch No. 817, Sturgeon Bay, WI

DUTCH APPLE CAKE

1 c. sugar	1½ c. flour
⅓ c. shortening (margarine)	1½ tsp. baking powder
1 egg	½ tsp. salt
1 c. milk	1 tsp. vanilla

Cream sugar and shortening. Add egg, milk and sifted dry ingredients. Stir by hand.

Top with following:

4 peeled apples	2 Tbsp. melted butter
1 c. sugar	1 tsp. cinnamon
2 Tbsp. flour	

Put apples on top of cake batter. Mix sugar, flour and butter like corn meal. Sprinkle over apples. Sprinkle cinnamon over this. Bake at 350° for 35 minutes or more. Test with toothpick. Serve with ice cream or whipped cream.

Recipe can be doubled to a 9x13 inch pan, but needs to bake for about 50 minutes.

Ann Raquer, Branch No. 6958, Buffalo, MN

462

GERMAN APPLE CAKE

2 eggs
1 c. sugar
1 tsp. vanilla
1 c. salad oil
2 c. sifted flour

2 tsp. cinnamon
1 tsp. baking soda
½ tsp. salt
½ to 1 c. chopped English walnuts
4 c. apples, *thinly sliced*

Beat eggs lightly. Add sugar, vanilla, and oil; blend thoroughly. Add dry ingredients and stir, then add chopped and thinly sliced apples. Batter will be stiff. *Do not use a mixer.* Spread into a greased and floured 13x9x2 inch pan. Bake at 350° for 45 to 60 minutes. Serve cake with whipped cream or frost with icing.

Icing:

2 (3 oz.) pkg. cream cheese
3 Tbsp. melted butter

1 tsp. vanilla
1½ c. powdered sugar

Blend ingredients together and frost.

Becky Steinbrueck, Branch No. 507, Ellisville, MO

APPLE TIME CAKE

1 c. sugar
¼ c. margarine
1 egg
1 c. flour
1 tsp. baking soda
¼ tsp. salt

¼ tsp. cinnamon
2 Tbsp. hot water
2½ c. raw apples, chopped
1 tsp. vanilla
Nuts

Beat sugar, margarine and egg together. Sift in flour, soda, salt, cinnamon, hot water, apples, vanilla, and nuts. Bake in a greased 9x9 inch pan at 350°.

St. Peter's Lutheran Church Mission Circle, Branch No. 2379, Easton, MN

RAW APPLE CAKE

4 c. raw apple
2 c. sugar
2 eggs
½ c. oil
1 tsp. vanilla

2 c. flour
¾ tsp. salt
2 tsp. cinnamon
2 tsp. soda
½ c. walnuts (or more)

Dice apples into a large bowl. Break eggs over apple and mix with a fork. Add sugar, nuts, oil, cinnamon, and vanilla. Sift flour, salt and soda. Add to mixture. Grease and flour 9x12 inch pan. Bake at 325° for about 1 hour.

Mrs. Agnes Carpenter, Branch No. 1540, Berkeley, CA

RAW APPLE CAKE

4 c. chopped apples (with peelings on)
2 whole eggs
2 c. sugar
1 c. nuts, chopped
½ tsp. salt
½ c. Wesson oil
2 tsp. cinnamon
2 c. flour
2 tsp. soda

Mix all together with heavy spoon. Grease and flour a 9x13 inch pan. Spread batter evenly in pan. Bake at 350° for 55 minutes or until done.

Optional: Glaze with powdered sugar when partly cooled.

Lois Schember, Branch No. 2232, Auburn, MI

RAW APPLE CAKE

2 c. flour
2 tsp. soda
2 tsp. cinnamon
1 tsp. salt
1 tsp. vanilla
2 c. white sugar
½ c. oil
4 c. diced apples
2 eggs, well beaten
½ to 1 c. chopped nuts

Pour sugar over apples. Add oil and stir well. Blend in eggs and vanilla. Sift all dry ingredients (flour, soda, cinnamon, and salt) together. Add to apples and mix. Add nuts. Bake at *350°* for *35 to 40* minutes.

Frosting:

1 c. brown sugar
2 eggs, well beaten
¼ c. butter

Make frosting. Melt butter. Add sugar and eggs. Bring just to a boil. Remove from heat and cool. Whip ½ pint whipping cream. Add together.

Hilder Smerda, Branch No. 545, Mosinee, WI

APPLESAUCE CAKE

Cake:

1 box yellow layer cake mix
2 eggs, beaten
1 can applesauce
1 small box vanilla instant pudding mix
¼ c. water
½ c. oil
¾ c. walnuts or pecans
½ tsp. cinnamon

Topping:

3 Tbsp. sugar
1 tsp. cinnamon

Preheat oven to 350°. Lightly grease (Crisco) a 9x13 inch pan. Place all ingredients in cake pan. Mix thoroughly with a fork. Bake for 30 to 40 minutes or until a toothpick inserted in the center of cake comes out clean. Sprinkle with cinnamon and sugar mixture while hot. Serve when cooled.

Jane M. Rottmann, Branch No. 4605, Highland, IL

DIABETIC APPLESAUCE CAKE

1¾ c. flour
1 tsp. salt
1 tsp. cinnamon
2 tsp. baking powder
½ tsp. soda
1 tsp. vanilla

1 egg, beaten
½ c. milk
1 c. unsweetened applesauce
½ c. salad oil
1 Tbsp. Sweet-10

Mix all ingredients together. Beat until mixed well. Pour into 9x13 inch pan. Bake at 350° for 55 to 60 minutes.

Ella Riebe, Branch No. 5616, Wilton, ND

BANANA TUBE CAKE

1½ c. sugar
1 c. butter or oleo
10 Tbsp. sour cream
4 eggs

3 c. flour
2 tsp. soda
6 medium bananas, mashed

Cream together sugar and butter; add the sour cream and eggs. Mix in the flour and soda. Add the mashed bananas last. Bake in greased Bundt or angel food pan at 350° for 1 to 1½ hours.

Can serve plain or drizzle plain white icing over cake.

Zona Schufletowski, Branch No. 1048, Muskego, WI

BANANA SPLIT CAKE

1 yellow cake mix
1 (5⅝ oz.) *instant* vanilla pudding
2 c. milk
2 (8 oz.) pkg. cream cheese (room temperature)
6 to 8 bananas, chilled
2 (20 oz.) cans crushed pineapple, drained and chilled

2 (8 oz.) containers Cool Whip, thawed
2 (10 oz.) pkg. frozen strawberries (fresh are better), thawed and drained

Prepare cake mix as directed and bake in a 12x18 inch pan or two 9x13 inch pans for *only* 15 to 17 minutes. Cool cake. Mix pudding with *only* 2 cups milk. Blend cream cheese into pudding. Spread this mixture onto cake. Cut up bananas in small pieces on top of pudding/cheese spread. Spread crushed pineapple over top of bananas. Spread Cool Whip over top of pineapple and place strawberries on top of Cool Whip. Serves 30 to 35.

"This may be used for Fourth of July by covering the upper left corner with well drained blueberries topped with "stars" of Cool Whip and placing the strawberries as "stripes" across the cake which has been spread with Cool Whip to resemble a flag."

Shirley Christian, Branch No. 2121, Chico, CA

BANANA SPLIT CAKE

1 Jiffy cake (white or yellow)
Bananas
2 c. milk
1 (8 oz.) cream cheese
1 pkg. instant vanilla pudding

1 pkg. frozen strawberries, thawed
and drained
1 large Cool Whip
Hershey's syrup
Nuts

Bake cake in a 9x13 inch pan. Cool. Slice bananas over cake. Mix milk and cream cheese. Add pudding mix and mix together for 2 minutes. Pour over bananas. Add strawberries over bananas. Spread Cool Whip over strawberries. Drizzle chocolate syrup over Cool Whip. Sprinkle nuts over the top.

Krista Scharrer, Branch No. 2280, Hemlock, MI

BANANA SPLIT CAKE

Combine:

2 c. graham cracker crumbs
1 stick butter

⅓ c. sugar

Combine graham cracker crumbs, butter and sugar; press into 9x13 inch pan. Bake for 10 minutes at 375°.

Combine:

2 (8 oz.) pkg. cream cheese

1 c. sugar

Beat well and spread on baked crust.

Slice 3 or 4 bananas over cheese. Spread one 20 ounce can crushed pineapple (drained) over bananas. Spread 1 large package frozen strawberries (drained) over pineapple. Cover with slightly sweetened whipped cream (1 pint) or large Cool Whip. Refrigerate for several hours or overnight. Serves 12 to 16.

Marylyn Muzer, Branch No. 2785, Santa Maria, CA

BETTER THAN SEX CAKE

1 yellow cake mix
20 oz. crushed pineapple (in heavy
syrup)
1 c. sugar
4 sliced bananas

1 instant vanilla pudding
12 oz. Cool Whip
Nuts
Cocoanut
Maraschino cherries

Prepare and bake cake mix as directed in a 9x13 inch pan. Boil together the pineapple and sugar for 5 minutes; pour over hot cake. Cool. Add sliced bananas, vanilla pudding (which has been prepared) and then Cool Whip. Top with nuts, cocoanut and cherries. Refrigerate for 2 days! *Enjoy!!*

Phyllis Vogtmann, Branch No. 2232, Auburn, MI

HUMMINGBIRD CAKE

3 c. all-purpose flour
2 c. sugar
1 tsp. salt
1 tsp. baking soda
½ tsp. cinnamon
3 eggs, beaten
1½ c. oil

1 tsp. almond flavoring
1 tsp. vanilla
1 (8 oz.) can crushed pineapple
   with juice
1 c. chopped nuts
2 c. chopped bananas

Combine flour, sugar, salt, baking soda, and cinnamon. Add eggs and oil. Stir until moistened, but do not beat. Stir in vanilla, almond flavoring, pineapple, bananas, and nuts. Pour into 10 inch tube pan. Bake at 325° for 1 hour and 20 minutes.

Icing:

1 c. butter
4 (3 oz.) pkg. cream cheese
1 Tbsp. cocoa

1½ (16 oz.) boxes powdered sugar
2 tsp. vanilla
1 c. chopped nuts

Combine all ingredients. Whip until smooth.

Jeanie Coleman, Branch No. 3107, Loveland, CO

HUMMINGBIRD CAKE

3 c. flour
2 c. sugar
1 tsp. soda
1 tsp. salt
2 c. diced bananas
1 c. pecans

1½ c. Wesson oil
3 beaten eggs
1 tsp. cinnamon
1 (8 oz.) can crushed pineapple
   (undrained)

In large mixing bowl, combine flour, sugar, soda, salt, cinnamon, oil, and eggs. Add pineapple, bananas and pecans. Pour into tube pan and bake at 300° for 1 hour and 15 minutes.

Frosting:

1 (3 oz.) pkg. cream cheese
1 stick oleo

2 c. powdered sugar
1 tsp. vanilla

Mix all together and frost cake.

Donna Long, Branch No. 1351, Ellinwood, KS

HUMMINGBIRD CAKE

Cake:

3 c. flour
2 c. sugar
1 tsp. baking soda
1 tsp. salt
1 tsp. cinnamon
3 eggs, beaten

1 c. vegetable oil
½ tsp. vanilla
1 (8 oz.) can undrained crushed
   pineapple
1 c. chopped pecans
2 c. chopped bananas

Combine first 5 ingredients in a large bowl. Add eggs and oil, stirring until dry ingredients are moistened. *Do not beat.* Stir in vanilla, pineapple, pecans, and bananas. Spoon batter into 3 greased and floured 9 inch cake pans. Bake at 350° for 25 to 30 minutes. Cool in pans for 10 minutes and remove. Frost when cool.

Frosting:

1 (8 oz.) pkg. cream cheese
½ c. butter

1 (16 oz.) pkg. powdered sugar
1 tsp. vanilla

Combine cream cheese and butter. Add powdered sugar and vanilla. Beat until light and fluffy. A small amount of crushed pineapple and pineapple juice may be added to the frosting.

Rosalind A. Burger, Branch No. 1468, Fort Smith, AR

BAKELESS CAKE

Graham crackers
1 c. sugar
½ c. butter
2 eggs
1 c. nutmeats

1 c. crushed pineapple
3 Tbsp. cream
2 boxes red jello
Whipped cream

Line 9x13 inch pan with graham crackers. Cream together sugar and butter. Beat egg yolks slightly. Beat egg whites stiffly. Fold sugar, butter and egg yolks into the egg whites. Add nutmeats, pineapple and cream. Pour half of mixture over graham crackers. Place another layer of graham crackers on top. Pour remaining half of mixture over crackers. Top with 2 boxes of prepared red jello slightly thickened. Cover with whipped cream. Freeze or refrigerate.

Ardith Gronwoldt, Branch No. 3330, LeRoy, MN

DUMP CAKE

1 (20 oz.) can crushed pineapple
1 (20 oz.) can cherry pie filling
1 pkg. dry yellow cake mix

1 c. chopped nuts
1 stick sliced butter

Layer in 9x13 inch ungreased cake pan the crushed pineapple with juice, cherry pie filling, dry yellow cake mix, chopped nuts, and butter. Bake at 325° for 40 minutes.

Paula Kocken, Branch No. 7029, DePere, WI

CHOP SUEY CAKE

2 c. flour
1¾ c. sugar
¼ c. brown sugar
2 eggs
Nuts

2 tsp. baking soda
½ tsp. salt
1 (20 oz.) can crushed pineapple
  (juice and all)

Mix ingredients together and put in 11x13 inch greased and floured pan. Bake at 350° for 25 to 35 minutes.

Frost with:

½ cube butter or margarine
1 c. powdered sugar
Nuts on top

1 tsp. vanilla
3 oz. cream cheese

Eleanor E. Kreidt, Branch No. 3436, Pico Rivera, CA

PINEAPPLE SHEET CAKE

2 c. flour
2 c. sugar
1 tsp. soda

½ tsp. salt
¾ c. salad oil
2 eggs

Mix dry ingredients. Add oil and eggs; mix well. Pour into cookie sheet or jelly roll pan. Bake for about 25 minutes or until light brown at 350°.

Frosting:

⅔ c. (small can) evaporated milk
1 (15½ oz.) can crushed pineapple
1 c. sugar

½ c. butter or margarine
Few grains of salt

Bring to a boil and simmer for 8 minutes, stirring constantly. Add 1 cup coconut and ½ cup chopped nuts. Spread on warm cake.

Mrs. May Thede, Branch No. 2004, Palmer, NE

PINEAPPLE SHEET CAKE

2 c. flour
2 eggs
1 tsp. soda

2 c. sugar
20 oz. crushed pineapple (juice
  too)

Combine all ingredients. Pour into 10x15 inch greased and floured pan. Bake for 25 minutes in a 350° oven.

Frosting: Five minutes before cake is done, combine 1½ cups sugar, 1 small can Pet milk (⅔ cup), and 1 stick oleo. Bring to a boil and boil for 3 minutes. Remove from heat. Add 1 small package coconut (about 1 cup), one 10 ounce package nutmeats, and 1 teaspoon vanilla. Pour over warm cake.

Mrs. Lloyd Atton (Shirley), Branch No. 2232, Midland, MI

PINEAPPLE TORTE

1 pkg. Jiffy yellow cake mix
2 c. milk
1 large pkg. cream cheese (at
   room temperature)
Nuts, chopped fine

1 large can crushed pineapple,
   drained
1 large ctn. Cool Whip
1 small pkg. instant vanilla
   pudding mix

Make cake as directed on package. Let cool. Mix milk and cream cheese until smooth. Add pudding mix and beat until thick. Pour over cake. Top with drained pineapple, then cover with Cool Whip. Sprinkle with nuts and refrigerate. (Use 9x13 inch pan.)

Marguerite Boerger, Branch No. 4734, Delphi, IN

PINEAPPLE-YELLOW CAKE DESSERT

1 (1 lb. 2¼ oz.) yellow cake mix
1 (20 oz.) can crushed pineapple
½ c. sugar
1 (3 oz.) pkg. instant vanilla
   pudding

1 (8 oz.) tub whipped topping,
   completely thawed
Coconut and/or nuts

Prepare 9x13 inch pan. Bake cake mix as directed on package. *Cool thoroughly.* Boil for 1 minute crushed pineapple and sugar. Place on cooled cake. Mix pudding as directed and pour over warm pineapple mixture. Top with whipped topping. Sprinkle with coconut, nuts or both. Keep refrigerated.

Ruth Westmeyer, Branch No. 1810, Platte Center, NE

SWEDISH PINEAPPLE CAKE

Cake:

2 c. sugar
2 c. flour
1 (20 oz.) can crushed pineapple
   (undrained)

1 tsp. vanilla
2 eggs
2 tsp. soda
½ c. nutmeats

Combine sugar, flour, eggs, pineapple, vanilla, and nutmeats in bowl. Do not use a mixer. Pour batter in 9x13 inch greased and floured pan. Bake in a 350° oven for 35 to 40 minutes.

Frosting:

1 (8 oz.) pkg. cream cheese
1 stick margarine
1¾ c. powdered sugar

1 tsp. vanilla
½ c. nutmeats

Combine cream cheese, margarine, powdered sugar, vanilla, and nuts. Beat well and frost cooled cake.

Marge Yurges, Branch No. 2616, Bertrand, NE

470

Cook in double boiler until boiling point. Thicken with 2 tablespoons corn starch and 2 tablespoons water. Cook enough to thicken. Serve sauce hot. This will freeze well.

Mrs. Iris Kluever, Branch No. 1131, Worthington, MN

WISCONSIN CRANBERRY CAKE

1½ Tbsp. melted Wisconsin butter	½ c. sugar
1 egg	½ c. Wisconsin milk
1 c. sifted flour	1½ tsp. baking powder
½ tsp. salt	1 c. fresh *Wisconsin* cranberries

Cake: Mix 1½ tablespoons melted Wisconsin butter with the sugar. Add 1 Wisconsin egg (beaten) and the Wisconsin milk. Add alternately with the following: Sifted flour, baking powder, salt, and 1 large cup fresh or frozen Wisconsin cranberries. Bake in flat 9 inch pan for 30 minutes at 350°.

Sauce: Cook ½ cup Wisconsin butter, 1 cup sugar, and ½ cup Wisconsin cream for 10 minutes. Add 1 teaspoon vanilla. Cook at slow boil, stirring frequently. Sauce should be served hot. (Suggestion: Use double boiler to keep sauce hot.) Makes 9 servings.

Note: This recipe is from Melvin Laird, a former Congressman. I won a prize for this at Fox Valley Technical School.

Melda Mortensen, Branch No. 432, Manawa, WI

RHUBARB OR CRANBERRY CAKE

Cake:

1½ c. sugar	1 tsp. soda
½ c. shortening	½ tsp. salt
1 egg	1 tsp. vanilla
1 c. sour milk	1½ to 2 c. rhubarb or cranberries
2½ c. flour	½ c. nuts

Cream sugar and shortening; add egg (well beaten). Gradually add sour milk, flour, soda, salt, vanilla, rhubarb or cranberries, and nuts.

For rhubarb, sprinkle brown sugar and cinnamon on top. For cranberry, sprinkle white sugar on top; serve with sauce. Bake at 350° for 25 minutes.

Sauce:

½ c. melted butter	1 c. sugar

Add ¾ cup cream and serve.

Mrs. Don Estabrooks, Branch No. 6085, Bemidji, MN

RHUBARB CAKE

½ c. butter
1½ c. sugar
1 egg
1 tsp. vanilla
2 c. flour

1 tsp. baking soda
½ tsp. salt
1 c. milk
2 c. chopped rhubarb

Cream butter and sugar. Add egg and vanilla. Stir to mix. Add dry ingredients and alternate with milk. Fold in rhubarb. Put in a 9x13 inch buttered pan. Sprinkle topping over. Bake at 350° for 40 minutes. Be sure it's done.

Topping:

½ c. sugar
½ tsp. cinnamon

¾ c. coconut
½ c. nuts

Mix and put on top of cake before you bake.

Ethel M. Voigt, Branch No. 72, East Troy, WI

RHUBARB CAKE

¾ c. margarine
1 egg
1½ c. sugar
1¼ tsp. soda

2 c. + 2 Tbsp. flour
1 c. sour cream or yogurt
1 tsp. vanilla
3 c. diced rhubarb

Topping:

½ c. brown sugar
1 tsp. cinnamon

1 Tbsp. margarine

Cream the first 3 ingredients. Gradually add the next 5 items. Mix the topping ingredients and crumble on top of batter in greased 9x13 inch pan. Bake for 45 minutes at 350°.

Mary Schaffer, Branch No. 3107, Loveland, CO

RHUBARB DELIGHT

5 c. rhubarb, cut fine
1 (3 oz.) pkg. red jello
1 c. sugar
3 c. miniature marshmallows

Yellow or white cake mix,
    prepared according to
    directions on pkg.

Place chopped rhubarb in buttered 9x13 inch pan. Sprinkle jello over this and sugar over jello, then marshmallows and cake batter last. Bake for 1 hour at 350°. Serve with whipped cream.

Mrs. Corrine K. Schlomer, Branch No. 1292, Mobridge, SD

BEST FRUIT CAKE EVER

1 c. butter	1 tsp. salt
1 c. sugar	Lemon juice
4 large eggs	1 c. brown sugar
1 c. dried fruit	Nuts
1 tsp. baking powder	1 or 2 qt. whiskey
1 tsp. baking soda	

Before you start, sample the whiskey to check for quality. Good, isn't it? Now go ahead. Select a large mixing bowl, measuring cup, etc. Check the whiskey again as it must be just right. To be sure the whiskey is of the highest quality, pour 1 level cup into a glass and drink it as fast as you can. Repeat.

With an electric mixer, beat 1 cup of butter in large fluffy bowl. Add 1 teaspoon of thugar and beat again. Meanwhile, make sure that the whiskey is of the finest quality. Cry another tup. Open second quart if necessary. Add 2 arge leggs, 2 cups of fried druit and beat till high. If druit gets stuck in beaters, just pry it loose with a drewscriver. Sample the whiskey again, thecking for tonsicisity, then sift 2 cups of salt or anything, it really doesn't matter. Sample the whiskey. Sift ½ pint lemon juice. Fold in chopped butter and strained nuts. Add 1 babblespoon of brown thugar, or whatever color you can find and wix mell. Grease oven and turn cake pan to 350°. Now pour the whole mess into the coven and ake. Check the whiskey again, and bo to ged.

NO-BAKE FRUIT CAKE

¾ c. butter	2 tsp. vanilla
1 (16 oz.) pkg. miniature marshmallows	4 c. pecans
	2 (8 oz.) pkg. pitted dates
1 (13½ oz.) pkg. graham cracker crumbs	1 lb. candied cherries
	1 lb. candied pineapple
4 Tbsp. brown sugar	¼ lb. citron (optional)

Melt butter and marshmallows in double boiler. Mix all other ingredients together. Add the hot marshmallow mixture and mix together. Press into a greased tube pan or loaf pan. Refrigerate. Makes a 7 pound fruit cake.

Gladys Bole, Branch No. 806, Cincinnati, OH

FRUIT CAKE

1 lb. dates, cut up	1 c. boiling water
1 tsp. soda	

Mix and set aside.

2 Tbsp. butter	1 tsp. baking powder
1 c. brown sugar	1 c. nuts, chopped
2 eggs	1 lb. orange slices, cut up
2 c. flour	¼ tsp. salt

Mix butter and sugar. Add eggs. Add dry ingredients. Add to batter the nuts and orange slices. Last, add dates, water and soda mixture. Bake for 1 hour at 350°. Makes 2 loaves or use angel food cake pan.

Viola Lueck, Branch No. 422, Reedsburg, WI

FRUIT CAKE

Boil 2 cups seedless raisins (or 1 cup raisins and 1 cup chopped dates) in 2 cups water. Cook until tender (until ⅔ cup juice remains). Pour hot juice over 1 cup sugar, 1½ teaspoons butter, 1 teaspoon cinnamon, ½ teaspoon cloves, 1 teaspoon nutmeg, and ½ teaspoon salt. Add 1 beaten egg, 1 teaspoon soda, ¼ teaspoon baking powder, 1¾ cups sifted flour, 1 cup nuts, and 1 cup chopped gumdrops (no black ones). You may use 2 loaf pans or an angel food pan. Line pans with wax paper. Bake in a slow oven (325°) for 35 to 45 minutes.

Edna Leister, Branch No. 1131, Worthington, MN

SOUTHERN FRUIT CAKE

3 eggs	1 c. buttermilk
2 c. sugar	1 tsp. soda
1 c. butter	1 Tbsp. allspice
1 c. nuts (pecans)	1 Tbsp. cinnamon
1½ c. coconut (flaked kind)	1 c. raisins
1 c. blackberry seedless jam	3 c. flour

Cream butter and sugar; add eggs, flour, soda, and spices. Add buttermilk, jam, coconut, pecans, and raisins. Pour batter into lightly greased pans*. Bake at 350°F. for 1 hour.

Filling:

1½ c. sugar	½ c. butter

Cook until thick (approximately 20 minutes).

* I like to put the batter into a spring mold type pan and when done, drizzle the filling over the top of warm cake. Chill, then slice and serve.

Arla J. Petrie, Branch No. 3086, Rocklin, CA
(Branch address - Citrus Heights, CA)

WHITE FRUIT CAKE

1½ lb. dates (leave whole)	4 large eggs, beaten separately, then put them together
1 lb. walnuts in shells (or 8 oz. shelled - leave whole)	1½ c. sugar
1 lb. Brazil nuts in shells (or 7 oz. shelled - leave whole)	1½ c. flour
¼ to ½ lb. candied cherries (leave whole - I use both red and green)	1 tsp. baking powder
	Pinch of salt

Put fruit and nuts in dish. Sprinkle with flour and other ingredients. Pour beaten eggs over all and mix well with hands. Bake in slow oven at 300° for about 1¼ hours. Makes 2 loaves.

Bea Laruwe, Branch No. 7101, Tuscon, AZ

FRUIT COCKTAIL CAKE

Cake:

1 (No. 303) can fruit cocktail (16 to 17 oz.)	**2 tsp. baking soda**
2 c. sifted flour	**½ tsp. salt**
2 c. granulated sugar	**1 tsp. cinnamon**
2 eggs	**1 Tbsp. vanilla**

Blend all ingredients in a mixing bowl and beat for 3 minutes. Pour into a lightly greased and floured 13x9x2 inch cake pan. Bake in a preheated 350° oven for 35 minutes. Remove from oven and top with following icing.

Icing:

¾ c. evaporated milk	**1½ c. granulated sugar**
6 Tbsp. butter or margarine	**1½ c. flaked coconut**

Combine milk, butter and sugar in a saucepan; bring to a boil over medium heat. Remove from heat. Stir in coconut and pour over hot cake.

Marcella Bartz, Branch No. 822, St. Louis, MO

FRUIT COCKTAIL CAKE

2 c. flour	**2 eggs**
1 c. sugar (1½)	**1 large (17 oz.) can fruit cocktail**
½ tsp. salt	**½ c. brown sugar**
2 tsp. soda	**½ c. nuts**

Mix dry ingredients. Add beaten eggs and 2 tablespoons juice from fruit cocktail; mix in rest of ingredients. Pour into greased and floured pan. Sprinkle ½ cup brown sugar and ½ cup nuts over the top. Bake at 350° for 40 minutes.

Icing:

1 cube oleo	**¾ c. canned milk**
¾ c. white sugar	

Boil for 3 minutes. Add 1 cup coconut and spread on cake.

Pat Spaeth, Branch No. 180, Denver, CO

A CAKE FROM THE BIBLE (SCRIPTURE CAKE)

1 c. Judges 5:25 (last clause -
   butter or margarine)
1¾ c. Jeremiah 6:20 (sugar)
¼ c. Proverbs 24:13 (honey)
6 Job 39:14 (eggs)
1 Kings 10:2 (spices - 1½ tsp.
   cinnamon, ½ tsp. cloves, 1
   tsp. allspice, and 1 tsp.
   nutmeg)
3 tsp. Amos 4:5 (baking powder)
   plus 1 tsp. baking soda

1 tsp. Leviticus 2:13 (salt)
3¾ c. 1 Kings 4:22 (unsifted
   all-purpose flour)
1 c. Genesis 24:11 (water)*
2 c. 1 Samuel 30:12 (second
   clause - raisins)
2 c. Revelations 6:13 (cut up dried
   figs - I used dates or raisins)
1 c. Numbers 17:8 (chopped
   almonds or nuts)

1. Preheat oven to 300°F. Heavily grease and flour a 10 inch tube or Bundt pan or two 9x5x3 inch loaf pans.

2. In large bowl, with electric mixer at medium speed, beat butter until smooth. At low speed, add sugar gradually; beat in well. Clean beaters. Blend in honey at low speed.

3. Add eggs, one at a time, beating at medium high speed after each addition.

4. On large sheet of wax paper, combine cinnamon, cloves, allspice, nutmeg, baking powder, baking soda, salt, and 3¼ cups flour.

5. Add blended dry ingredients to butter alternately with buttermilk. Toss reserved ½ cup flour with raisins, figs and nuts. Gently fold fruit and nuts into batter.

6. Pour batter into pan. Cut through batter with knife to distribute evenly. Bake for about 1½ hours or until cake tester pushed into center comes out clean. Let cool in pan for 30 minutes, then turn out on rack to cool completely. (Doesn't need a frosting.) Makes 1 large tube cake or 2 loaf cakes (very large cake).

* We substituted 1 cup cold buttermilk (I used sour milk).

Linda Cornell, Branch No. 2232, Auburn, MI

ANGEL FOOD CAKE SUPREME

1 angel food cake, baked in tube
   pan
1 c. diced pineapple
1 c. cocoanut, cherries or
   strawberries

2 c. whipped topping
½ lb. miniature marshmallows
1 c. salted pecan nuts

With 2 forks, carefully remove the inside of cake, leaving a firm shell. Tear the center of the cake in small pieces and blend with whipped topping, cocoanut, pineapple, and marshmallows. Fill the ring and let stand in refrigerator for several hours. To serve, add more topping and sprinkle berries and salted nuts on top.

Erna C. Boggs, Winnetoon, NE, Branch No. 1957, Creighton, NE

ANGEL FOOD TORTE

1 day-old angel food cake
3 eggs, separated
½ c. orange juice
Juice of 1 lemon

Pinch of salt
¾ c. sugar
1 env. unflavored gelatin
Whipped cream or topping

Beat egg yolks. Add juices, salt and sugar. Cook in double boiler until slightly thickened to coat a silver spoon. Dissolve 1 tablespoon (1 envelope) of unflavored gelatin in ¼ cup cold water. Add dissolved gelatin to hot mixture, stirring to dissolve. Cool to set like a syrup consistency. Beat egg whites to stiff peaks. Slowly beat in ¾ cup sugar. Fold into cool custard.

Pour a layer of custard in bottom of springform pan. Break cake into bite-size pieces. Place half of cake in pan. Pour over *half* of the remaining custard. Layer remaining cake pieces and cover with remaining custard. Refrigerate for at least 12 hours.

To serve: Remove outer ring and cut. Serve plain or cover with whipped cream or topping.

Note: Sunshine cake may be used in place of angel food.
Mabel M. Neumann, Branch No. 1359, Milwaukee, WI

CHOCOLATE PUDDING CAKE

1 angel food cake
2 (3 oz.) pkg. chocolate pudding
   (regular)

1 (12 oz.) container Cool Whip

Break the angel food cake into pieces. Put in a 9x12 inch baking dish. Prepare the chocolate pudding. Pour over cake while hot. Cover and refrigerate overnight. Next day, frost with Cool Whip.
Marilyn Lengyel, Branch No. 1848, Lorain, OH

BETTER THAN SEX CAKE

1 c. flour
1 c. walnuts
¼ lb. butter
8 oz. cream cheese

1 c. powdered sugar
2 (8 oz.) tubs Cool Whip
3 c. milk
2 pkg. *instant chocolate pudding*

Mix flour, walnuts and softened butter. Press into 9x13 inch greased pan. Bake at 350° for 20 minutes, then cool. Combine cream cheese, powdered sugar, and one 8 ounce Cool Whip. Beat until mixed. Spread over pastry and refrigerate. Mix milk and pudding mixture with beater on low setting for 3 minutes. Spread over cream cheese layer. Top with second tub of Cool Whip. Refrigerate until ready to serve.

Liz Clark, Branch No. 6439, Madison, WI

BLACK FOREST CHERRY TORTE

Cake:

⅔ c. butter, softened	2¾ c. flour
1¾ c. sugar	2½ tsp. baking powder
2 eggs	1 tsp. salt
1½ tsp. vanilla	1¼ c. milk

Combine first 4 ingredients until fluffy. Beat for 5 minutes. Blend in remaining ingredients alternately with milk, mixing on low speed. Pour into 2 greased and floured 9 inch round pans. Bake at 350° for 30 minutes. Cool for 10 minutes and remove from pans.

Filling:

2 Tbsp. cornstarch	1 c. reserved cherry juice
2 Tbsp. sugar	1 Tbsp. brandy flavoring
1 (16 oz.) can pitted dark sweet cherries, drained	

Mix cornstarch and sugar in pan; stir in cherry liquid. Cook, stirring constantly, until mixture thickens and boils; boil and stir for 1 minute. Cool to lukewarm. Add brandy flavoring. Dip 36 cherries into filling, saving them for top of cake. Cut up remaining cherries and stir into filling. Chill.

Topping:

1½ c. whipping cream, chilled	4 oz. sweet chocolate, grated
¼ c. confectioners sugar	

Beat whipping cream and sugar until very stiff. Place 1 layer of cake on serving plate. Make rim of whipped cream around edge of cake. Fill center with filling. Place second layer on top and spread whipped cream on side and top of cake. Press chocolate onto side. Place reserved cherries on top and decorate, as desired, with piping border of whipped cream around edge and spoke design on top. Store in refrigerator.

St. John's Lutheran Church, AAL Branch No. 1775, Columbus, NE

PRONTO CHERRY CRUNCH

2 cans cherry pie mix	1 c. dry quick cooking oatmeal
1 pkg. white cake mix	1 c. chopped nuts
2 cubes butter or margarine	

Spread cherry pie mix on the bottom of a 9x13 inch pan. Sprinkle with the cake mix. Melt butter or margarine and pour over cake mix. Mix oatmeal and chopped nuts together; sprinkle evenly over mixture. Bake for 45 to 50 minutes in a 350° oven. Serve with whipped cream or a dip of vanilla ice cream on top.

You can also substitute apricot pie mix for the cherry for a delicious change.
Darlene Scheideler, Branch No. 445, Beatrice, NE

CHOCOLATE RASPBERRY TORTE

3 eggs, separated
1/8 tsp. cream of tartar
1/8 tsp. salt
1 1/2 c. sugar
1 c. sweet cream butter, melted
1 1/2 tsp. vanilla
1/2 c. all-purpose flour

1/2 c. unsweetened cocoa
3 Tbsp. water
3/4 c. finely chopped almonds
1/3 c. raspberry preserves
1 c. whipping cream, whipped
Sweetened raspberries (fresh)

Heat oven to 350°. Grease 9 inch round cake pan. Line with aluminum foil, leaving excess foil over edges. Grease foil. Set aside. In small mixer bowl, combine egg whites, cream of tartar and salt. Beat at high speed, scraping bowl often, until soft peaks form (1 to 2 minutes); set aside.

In large mixer bowl, combine egg yolks, sugar, butter, and vanilla. Beat at medium speed, scraping bowl often, until well mixed (1 to 2 minutes). Add flour, cocoa and water. Continue beating until well mixed. Stir in almonds. Fold egg whites into chocolate mixture. Put in pan. Bake for 45 to 55 minutes or until wooden pick comes out clean. Cool for 1 hour. Remove from pan by lifting out aluminum foil. Cool for 2 to 3 hours.

Remove foil and place on serving plate. Spread raspberry preserves on top. Pipe sweetened cream to form a lattice top. Garnish with raspberries. Serves 12 pieces.

Mrs. Madelyn (Roland) Beske, Branch No. 4188, Beaver Dam, WI

COTTAGE CHEESE CAKE

1 1/2 c. graham crackers
1/2 c. sugar

1 tsp. cinnamon
1 stick butter or margarine, melted

Mix and press in bottom of a greased 9x13 inch pan.

Mix and pour over graham crackers:

4 eggs, beaten
4 Tbsp. flour
1 c. sugar
1/4 tsp. salt
3/4 tsp. vanilla

2 Tbsp. lemon juice
1 c. canned milk
2 c. cottage cheese, put through
sieve or put in blender

Sprinkle cracker crumbs on top. Bake at 325° for 1 1/4 hours.

Can be topped with cherry pie filling.

Mrs. Elma Doberstein, Branch No. 2090, Dowagiac, MI

CREME DE MENTHE CAKE

1 pkg. *Pillsbury Plus white cake
    mix*
4 Tbsp. green creme de menthe

1 can Hershey's fudge topping (no
    substitutes - for First Frosting
    Layer)

Second Frosting Layer:

1 (8 oz.) ctn. Cool Whip (see Note 1)   2 Tbsp. green creme de menthe

Follow instructions on box, adding creme de menthe at same time other ingredients are added. Follow baking instructions also, baking cake in 9x13 inch pan or a 10 inch springform pan. *Do not* try to make a layer cake out of this. When cake has cooled, spread top *only* with whole can of *Hershey's Fudge Topping.* Cover fudge with Cool Whip to which has been added 2 tablespoons creme de menthe. Chocolate shot is pretty on top. Refrigerate.

Note 1: If you take cake from baking pan to display it, you need to frost the sides. Get 12 ounce size Cool Whip, adding *3* tablespoons creme de menthe. It's too much, so freeze the remainder in dollops, using to top other desserts.

Note 2: Try substituting Amaretto or cherry brandy or Kahlua or apricot brandy for the creme de menthe.

Mary Lou Geldigan, Branch No. 3193, St. Louis, MO

DATE CAKE

1½ c. dates, cut up	2 eggs
1½ tsp. soda	2¼ c. flour
1½ c. water	½ tsp. salt
¼ c. butter	1 tsp. vanilla
1½ c. sugar	1 c. chopped nuts

Dissolve soda in water and add to cut up dates. Let set while creaming together the butter, sugar and eggs. Add flour, salt and vanilla. Beat well and add to date mixture. Add chopped nuts. Bake in a 9x13 inch greased pan for 40 minutes at 350°.

Lyman Bich, Branch No. 2620, Yale, SD

DUTCH PLUM CAKE

1 c. sifted flour	5 (or more) plums, cut into eighths
1½ tsp. baking powder	1 tsp. cinnamon
½ tsp. salt	¼ tsp. nutmeg
6 Tbsp. sugar	3 Tbsp. melted butter
¼ c. shortening	⅓ c. currant or pomegranate jelly
1 egg	1 Tbsp. hot water
¼ c. milk	

Sift flour, baking powder, salt, and 3 tablespoons sugar. With 2 knives, cut in shortening until mixture is like coarse corn meal. With fork, stir in combined egg and milk. Spread dough in greased 12x8x2 inch baking pan. On top, arrange plums, slightly overlapping, in parallel rows. Sprinkle with combined cinnamon, nutmeg, 3 tablespoons sugar, and butter. Bake for 35 minutes at 400° or until plums are tender. Beat jelly with hot water and brush over fruit. Serve warm and cut into squares.

Phyllis Kesti, Branch No. 5604, Tucson, AZ

ECLAIR CAKE

1 box graham crackers
2 pkg. French vanilla instant
   pudding

2¾ c. milk
1 (12 oz.) Cool Whip

Mix instant pudding with milk as directed on box only use 2¾ cups milk. Add Cool Whip to pudding and mix well. Place a single layer of graham crackers on bottom of 9x13x2 inch pan. Do not crumble crackers. You will have to break some to fit pan. Spread ½ of pudding over crackers. Cover with another layer of graham crackers and remainder of pudding mixture. Top with another layer of graham crackers and cover with frosting.

Frosting:

2 pkg. premelted unsweetened
   chocolate
2 Tbsp. margarine, softened
2 Tbsp. white Karo syrup

1½ c. powdered sugar
3 Tbsp. milk
1 tsp. vanilla

Beat all ingredients until smooth. Spread over top of crackers. Refrigerate overnight. Must be kept in the refrigerator.

Sue Koerber, Branch No. 4115, League City, TX

FOUR LAYER DELIGHT

First layer:

1 cube butter or margarine
1 c. flour

½ c. finely chopped pecans

Cream together and press into a 9x13 inch pan. Bake for about 20 minutes at 350°. Let cool.

Second layer:

1 (8 oz.) pkg. Philly cream cheese
1 c. powdered sugar
1 c. Cool Whip (buy 9 oz. size)

1 tsp. vanilla
1 c. Angel Flake coconut

Mix together and spread over first layer. Cover generously with coconut.

Third layer:

2 pkg. instant lemon pudding

3 c. milk

Mix together and spread on second layer.

Fourth layer: Spread remainder of Cool Whip on the pudding. Sprinkle with 1 cup coconut and ½ cup chopped pecans. Refrigerate for about 3 hours before serving. When cutting to serve, be sure to include the crust.

Ruth Maas, Branch No. 3436, Pico Rivera, CA

LEMON-ORANGE CAKE

1 pkg. yellow cake mix
1 (3 oz.) pkg. orange gelatin
¾ c. water

¾ c. vegetable oil
4 eggs

Mix all ingredients together until smooth. Bake at 350° for 30 to 35 minutes. While still hot, poke holes in the cake with a fork. Saturate the cake with Lemon Sauce.

Lemon Sauce:

2 c. powdered sugar

¼ c. lemon juice

Blend for cake topping.

Myra Vrudny, Branch No. 239, Brainerd, MN

LEMON POPPY SEED CAKE

1 box lemon cake mix
4 whole eggs
¾ c. vegetable oil
1 (5¼ oz.) box instant vanilla
   pudding

1¼ c. cold water
½ c. poppy seeds
1 (21 oz.) can lemon pie filling
1 pt. Rich Whip or Cool Whip

Combine dry cake mix, eggs, oil, dry pudding, water, and poppy seeds. Mix well with electric mixer for about 4 minutes. Bake at 350° in a 9x13 inch pan. Cool. Spread lemon pie filling on top of cake. Frost with whipped cream. Refrigerate for at least 4 hours before serving.

Marion Behm, Waterloo, WI, Branch No. 2017, Marshall, WI

MANDARIN ORANGE CAKE

2 c. flour
2 c. sugar
2 eggs
1 tsp. soda

1 tsp. vanilla
2 c. mandarin oranges, drained
1 tsp. salt

Mix all ingredients together. Bake for 35 minutes at 375°. When done, use fork and pull cake back from side of pan, then pour on the following topping.

Topping:

1½ c. brown sugar
6 Tbsp. butter

5 Tbsp. milk
½ tsp. salt

Bring to a boil. Spoon over cake while cake is real hot.

Kathryn Price, Branch No. 0823, Nappanee, IN

NUTTY PEACH CRUNCH

1 (29 oz.) can sliced peaches
1 pkg. butter brickle cake mix
½ c. margarine, melted

1 c. coconut
1 c. chopped pecans

Place peaches in a 10x13 inch cake pan. Sprinkle cake mix over peaches Drizzle melted margarine over. Top with coconut and pecans. Bake at 325° for 55 to 60 minutes.

This is very quick and easy.

Eloise Winkelman, Branch No. 1351, Ellinwood, KS

CARROT CAKE

2½ c. flour	¼ c. buttermilk
1½ tsp. baking soda	1 c. margarine
1½ tsp. cinnamon	2 c. white sugar
½ tsp. salt	4 eggs
¼ tsp. nutmeg	1 tsp. vanilla
1½ c. grated carrot	¾ c. chopped pecans

Sift flour with soda, cinnamon, salt, and nutmeg. Combine carrot and buttermilk. Beat margarine and sugar until light. Add eggs and vanilla. At low speed, beat in flour mixture alternately with carrot mixture. Stir in nuts. Bake at 350° for 40 to 50 minutes in a 9x13 inch pan.

Virginia Hakes, Branch No. 6817, Cornell, WI

SWEET POTATO SURPRISE CAKE

1½ c. oil	¼ tsp. salt
2 c. sugar	1 tsp. cinnamon
4 eggs, separated	1 tsp. nutmeg
4 Tbsp. hot water	1½ c. grated raw sweet potato
2½ c. sifted flour	½ c. chopped nuts
3 tsp. baking powder	1 tsp. vanilla

Combine oil and sugar; beat until smooth. Add egg yolks and beat well. Add hot water, then dry ingredients which have been sifted together. Stir in grated sweet potato, nuts and vanilla; beat well. Beat egg whites until stiff and fold into mixture. Bake in three 8 inch layer pans that have been greased and floured at 350° for 25 to 30 minutes. Cool and frost.

Frosting for Sweet Potato Surprise Cake:

1 large can evaporated milk	1 stick oleomargarine
1 c. sugar	3 egg yolks

Cook all for 12 minutes. Stir constantly. Remove from heat and add 1 teaspoon vanilla, 1⅓ cups coconut, and ½ cup chopped nuts. Frost all layers, between sides and top.

Evalyn Storm, Branch No. 4665, Knoxville, TN

GREEN TOMATO CAKE

1½ c. oil
2 c. sugar
1 tsp. salt
1 tsp. soda
1 tsp. baking powder
1½ tsp. cinnamon

1 tsp. nutmeg
1 tsp. vanilla
4 eggs, beaten
2½ c. flour
3 c. green tomatoes
1 c. nuts, chopped

Grind tomatoes and drain, then measure. Mix the ingredients in the order given. Bake in a 350° oven for 1 hour.

Mrs. Joyce Gross, Branch No. 1998, Beatrice, NE

TOMATO SOUP CAKE

2 c. flour
4 Tbsp. shortening
1 c. sugar
1 egg, well beaten
1 can tomato soup
½ tsp. cloves

½ tsp. nutmeg
½ tsp. soda
3 tsp. baking powder
1 c. raisins
½ c. nutmeats

Mix all together and bake in a 9x12 inch pan at 350° for 1 hour.

Edna Weber, Branch No. 2630, Greeley, CO

ZUCCHINI CAKE

Cake:

3 c. grated zucchini
3 c. all-purpose flour
3 c. sugar
4 eggs
1½ c. oil

1 c. chopped nuts
2 tsp. cinnamon
2 tsp. baking powder
1 tsp. baking soda

Beat all ingredients together for cake. Pour into greased 9x13 inch pan. Bake for 1 hour at 350°.

Frosting:

½ c. softened butter
3 oz. cream cheese

2 c. confectioners sugar
1 tsp. vanilla

Beat all ingredients together for frosting.

Meda Miller, Branch No. 5265, Herndon, PA

PAUL'S PUMPKIN BARS

4 eggs
1⅔ c. sugar
1 c. cooking oil
1 (16 oz.) can pumpkin
2 c. flour

2 tsp. baking powder
1 tsp. baking soda
1 tsp. salt
2 tsp. cinnamon

Topping:

1 (3 oz.) pkg. soft cream cheese
½ c. soft margarine

1 tsp. vanilla
2 c. sifted powdered sugar

1. Beat eggs.
2. To beaten eggs, add sugar, cooking oil, pumpkin, baking powder, baking soda, salt, cinnamon, and flour in that order.
3. Bake for 20 minutes at 350° in a 15x10x1 inch greased pan.
4. Let cool.
5. Mix ingredients for topping and spread on top of cooled, baked bars.

Doris Henschell, Branch No. 2086, Seattle, WA

PUMPKIN CAKE WITH CREAM CHEESE ICING

Cake:

2 c. sugar
4 eggs
1 c. vegetable oil
2 c. canned pumpkin

2 c. flour
2 tsp. cinnamon
2 tsp. baking soda
½ tsp. salt

Combine all ingredients in order given in large bowl. Pour into a 13x9 inch greased and floured baking pan. Bake at 350° for 35 minutes or until toothpick comes out clean.

Cream Cheese Icing:

½ c. (1 stick) butter or margarine
1 (1 lb.) box powdered sugar
1 (8 oz.) pkg. cream cheese

2 tsp. vanilla
1 c. chopped nuts

Combine all ingredients, except nuts; beat with mixer. Spread on cooled cake. Sprinkle nuts on top. Refrigerate. Serves 16.

Barbara Hackbart, Branch No. 3802, Fort Worth, TX

PUMPKIN CAKE ROLL

3 eggs
1 c. sugar
⅔ c. pumpkin
1 tsp. lemon juice
¾ c. flour
1 tsp. baking powder

2 tsp. cinnamon
1 tsp. ginger
½ tsp. nutmeg
½ tsp. salt
1 c. nuts

Filling:

1 c. powdered sugar
2 (3 oz.) pkg. cream cheese

4 Tbsp. butter or margarine
½ tsp. vanilla

Beat eggs on high for 5 minutes. Gradually beat 1 cup sugar. Stir in ⅔ cup pumpkin and 1 teaspoon lemon juice. Stir together ¾ cup flour, baking powder, cinnamon, ginger, nutmeg, and salt. Fold into pumpkin. Spread in greased and floured 15x10x1 inch pan. Top with finely chopped nuts. Bake at 375° for 15 minutes.

Turn out on towel sprinkled with powdered sugar. Starting at narrow end, roll towel and cake together. Cool. Unroll. Combine and beat until smooth the powdered sugar, cream cheese, butter, and vanilla. Spread over cake. Roll up again. Chill. Makes 8 servings.

Jane Bach, Branch No. 3107, Loveland, CO

PUMPKIN CAKE

1 large can pumpkin
4 eggs
1½ c. sugar
Pinch of salt
2 tsp. cinnamon
1 tsp. ginger

½ tsp. nutmeg
1 can evaporated milk
1 box yellow cake mix
1 stick margarine
1 large container Cool Whip

Mix in a large bowl 4 eggs, 1½ cups sugar, pinch of salt, 2 teaspoons cinnamon, 1 teaspoon ginger, ½ teaspoon nutmeg, and 1 can evaporated milk. Place these preceding ingredients in an *ungreased* cake pan. Over these ingredients, sprinkle a box of yellow cake mix, then melt 1 stick of margarine and pour over cake mix. Bake at 350° for 1 hour. When cake is cool, cover with Cool Whip.

Bertha M. Davidson, Branch No. 5124, Alma, MI

PUMPKIN DESSERT CAKE

1 yellow cake mix (white works
   too!)

½ c. butter or margarine
1 egg

Reserve 1 cup mix and pat rest into bottom of 9x13 inch pan.

2 eggs
⅔ c. evaporated milk
1 lb. or 1½ c. pumpkin
¾ c. sugar
½ tsp. vanilla

½ tsp. salt
1 tsp. cinnamon*
½ tsp. ginger*
⅛ tsp. cloves*

Pour pumpkin mixture over cake crust in pan.

Add to 1 cup of reserved cake mix:

¼ c. sugar
1 tsp. cinnamon

¼ c. margarine

Bake at 350° for 55 minutes.

* An equal amount of pumpkin pie spice in place of these 3 spices is fine.

Mona Geidel, Branch No. 3107, Loveland, CO

PUMPKIN PIE CAKE

1 (16 oz.) can pumpkin
5 eggs
1½ c. sugar
1 tsp. salt
1 tsp. cinnamon

1 box yellow or white cake mix
  (with pudding)
2 sticks oleo
⅔ c. pecans

Beat together first 5 ingredients. Pour into greased 9x13 inch pan. Sprinkle cake mix on top. Melt the 2 sticks of oleo and pour over top of cake mix. Sprinkle ⅔ cup pecan pieces on top. Bake at 350° for 1 hour or until knife comes out clean.

Best when served warm and topped with Cool Whip or ice cream.

Leona Grandt, Branch No. 1409, St. Peter, IL

PUMPKIN PIE CAKE

4 eggs
1½ c. sugar
1 large can evaporated milk
1 tsp. cinnamon

1 (No. 303) can pumpkin
1 pkg. yellow cake mix
1 c. melted butter or margarine
1 c. chopped nuts

Mix first 5 ingredients in order given. Pour into a 9x13 inch pan. Sprinkle the cake mix on top. Dribble the melted butter or margarine over the cake mix. Sprinkle with 1 cup nuts. Bake for 1 hour at 350° or until knife comes clean when inserted in center. Serve as is or with whipped topping.

Variation by Bernice Ave: Omit cinnamon.

Variation from Branch No. 628 (Farmington, Missouri): Use 1 cup sugar, ¼ teaspoon salt, ½ teaspoon allspice, and ½ teaspoon cinnamon.

Esther Schwede, Branch No. 2347, New Melle, MO; Bernice Ave, Branch No. 3107, Loveland, CO; Branch No. 628, Farmington, MO

PUMPKIN SQUARES

4 eggs
1⅔ c. sugar
1 c. vegetable oil
1 (16 oz.) can pumpkin
2 c. flour

1 tsp. salt
2 tsp. baking powder
1 tsp. soda
2 tsp. cinnamon

Beat together eggs, sugar, oil, and pumpkin. Combine flour, salt, baking powder, soda, and cinnamon. Stir pumpkin mix into flour mixture. Spread into ungreased 15x10 inch pan. Bake at 350° for 25 to 30 minutes. Cool on rack.

Frosting:

3 oz. cream cheese
½ c. butter, softened

2 c. powdered sugar
1 tsp. vanilla

Cream the cream cheese and butter; add vanilla and add sugar in small amounts, stirring after each addition. Spread over cooled pumpkin cake and cut into squares.

Mrs. Edna Johnson, Branch No. 5968, Greensboro, NC

PUMPKIN TORTE

Crust: Combine 1⅔ cups crushed graham crackers with ⅓ cup sugar and ½ cup melted butter. Press into a 9x13 inch pan.

Second layer - Beat well:

2 eggs	¾ c. sugar
8 oz. cream cheese	

Pour over crust. Bake for 20 minutes at 350°F.

Third layer - Mix and cook until thick:

3 egg yolks	2 c. pumpkin
½ c. sugar	1 Tbsp. cinnamon
½ c. milk	

Remove from heat and add 1 envelope Knox gelatine which has been dissolved in ¼ cup cold water. Cool well. Beat 3 egg whites, adding ¼ cup sugar and beating until soft peaks form. Fold into pumpkin mixture. Pour over baked mixture. Chill overnight. Add whipped cream for topping as desired. Cut into squares.

Eunice Cahoon, Branch No. 51, Marquette, WI

PUMPKIN TORTE

Crust:

24 crushed graham crackers	½ c. sugar
½ c. margarine or butter	

Mix and pat lightly in a 9x13 inch pan.

Beat the following:

2 eggs	2 (8 oz.) pkg. cream cheese,
¾ c. sugar	softened

Put on top of crust. Bake for 20 minutes at 350°. *Cool.*

Mix and cook:

1 can pumpkin (2 c.)	½ c. sugar
3 egg yolks	½ tsp. salt
½ c. milk	½ tsp. cinnamon

Cook until thick, about 3 to 4 minutes. Remove from heat. Add 1 envelope Knox gelatine, dissolved in ¼ cup cold water. *Cool well.* Beat 3 egg whites until stiff. Add ¼ cup sugar. Fold into pumpkin mixture. Pour on baked crust. Let set. Top with whipped cream. Sprinkle with nuts.

Verna Beatty, Branch No. 2417, Moores Hill, IN

PINEAPPLE UPSIDE-DOWN CAKE
(Microwave)

2 Tbsp. butter or margarine
1 (8 oz.) can crushed pineapple
½ c. firmly packed brown sugar

6 maraschino cherries
1 (9 oz.) pkg. yellow cake mix

Heat butter or margarine in an 8 inch round glass baking dish. Drain pineapple, reserving juice. Blend together butter (margarine), brown sugar and drained pineapple; spread evenly in bottom of pan. Arrange maraschino cherries in bottom of pan. Prepare cake mix as directed on package, substituting the reserved pineapple juice for water. Pour batter evenly over pineapple mixture. Cook for 5 to 7 minutes, rotating dish one-quarter turn halfway through cooking time. Let cool for 5 minutes until cake pulls away from sides of pan. Invert onto serving dish.

Note: If desired, pineapple slices may be used. Blend the melted butter and the brown sugar in baking dish and arrange slices on top of mixture. Place cherries in holes of pineapple. Other fruits, such as apricots or peaches, may be used also.

Linda Bura, Branch No. 2049, Emporia, KS

FRUIT COCKTAIL CAKE

Cake:

2 c. flour
1½ c. sugar
2 tsp. baking soda

2 eggs
1 (15 oz.) can fruit cocktail
¼ c. brown sugar

Mix all ingredients, except the brown sugar, in a cake pan. Use a fork or large spoon so you don't crush the fruits. Sprinkle brown sugar over cake. Bake at 325° for 45 minutes. Frost while warm.

Note: This mixture may be mixed in a bowl and put in the cake pan after well mixed.

Frosting:

1 stick oleo
1½ c. sugar
½ c. condensed milk

1 tsp. vanilla extract
1 c. coconut
1 c. pecans

Mix all ingredients in saucepan. Bring to a boil and boil for 3 minutes. Pour over warm cake.

Linda Bura, Branch No. 2049, Emporia, KS

FAST FIXIN' CHOCOLATE CHIP CAKE

1 pkg. Duncan Hines devil's food
    cake mix
¼ c. oil
2 eggs

1¼ c. water
1 (3 oz.) pkg. chocolate instant
    pudding
1 c. chocolate chips

Preheat oven to 350°. Pour oil into 9x13 inch pan. Tilt pan till bottom is covered. Put remaining ingredients into pan; stir with a fork or spoon until blended (2 minutes). Scrape sides and spread evenly. Bake for 35 to 45 minutes.

Alternate: Prepare pan as directed before, using ¼ cup oil. Add cake mix, 2 eggs, ½ cup water, and 1 can cherry pie filling. Mix, bake and serve.

Renae Tegtmeier, Branch No. 2049, Emporia, KS

PUMPKIN TWINKIE DESSERT

Have on hand 1 package Hostess Twinkies, Zingers or other cream filled cakes or ladyfingers.

Combine in double boiler (or microwave dish):

¾ c. brown sugar	¼ tsp. salt
1 (16 oz.) can pumpkin	1 tsp. cinnamon
3 egg yolks, beaten	½ tsp. nutmeg
½ c. milk	

Cook until thick. Add 1 envelope unflavored gelatin dissolved in ¼ cup cold water. Chill until cool. Beat 3 egg whites and ¼ cup sugar until stiff, but not dry. Fold into chilled mixture. Split Twinkies in halves and line the bottom of a 15x20 (or 9x13) inch pan with them. Add the cooled pumpkin mixture. Top with Cool Whip and chopped pecans.

Margaret Bernstein, Branch No. 2334, Pasadena, TX

FRIENDSHIP CAKE

1 c. greetings	⅔ c. love
½ c. smiles	1 tsp. sympathy
2 large handshakes	2 c. hospitality

Cream greetings together with smiles. Add handshakes separately. Add love slowly. Sift sympathy and hospitality; fold in carefully. Bake in a warm heart. Serve often.

Ruby Rohlfs, Branch No. 483, Lincoln, IL

FILLING FOR ANGEL FOOD

1 env. Knox gelatine	1½ c. milk
¼ c. cold water	1 (10 oz.) whipped topping
5 egg yolks	1 c. nuts
1 c. sugar	1 tsp. vanilla
1 Tbsp. flour	

Dissolve gelatine in cold water. Beat egg yolks well. Add sugar, flour and milk. Boil till slightly thickened. Remove from heat and *cool*. Add whipped topping, nuts and flavoring. Spoon over slices of angel food. Top with a maraschino cherry.

Leona Becher, Columbus, NE

ALWAYS MOIST CHOCOLATE CAKE FROSTING

1 c. brown sugar
3 tbsp. milk

5 Tbsp. oleo
½ c. cocoa or chocolate chips

Combine brown sugar, milk and oleo in saucepan. Bring to a boil. Remove from heat and add cocoa or chocolate chips. Stir until mixed well. Let stand for about 5 minutes to cool, then spread on cake.

Barbara Alsum, Branch No. 3107, Loveland, CO

CARAMEL ICING

2 c. brown sugar
½ c. hot water
Vanilla

½ c. cream
Lump of butter

Dissolve brown sugar in hot water. Boil and slowly add cream. Boil until it forms a soft ball in cold water. Flavor with vanilla. Add butter and beat until thick enough to spread on cake. If this becomes too hard while spreading, add a little cream and stir together.

Bernice Sheets, Branch No. 5844, Columbia City, IN

COCONUT-CREAM CHEESE FROSTING

4 Tbsp. butter or margarine
2 c. flaked coconut
1 (8 oz.) pkg. cream cheese

2 tsp. milk
3½ c. sifted confectioners sugar
1 tsp. vanilla

Melt 2 tablespoons butter in skillet. Add coconut; stir constantly over low heat until golden brown. Spread coconut on absorbent paper to cool. Cream 2 tablespoons butter with cream cheese. Add milk and sugar alternately, beating well. Add vanilla. Stir in 1¾ cups of the coconut. Spread on tops and sides of cake layers. Sprinkle with remaining coconut.

Meg Bray, Branch No. 4122, Spearfish, SD

UNCOOKED FROSTING

1 c. sugar
Pinch of salt
1 tsp. vanilla

1 egg white
¼ tsp. cream of tartar

Put all ingredients in bowl and mix slowly. Add ½ cup boiling water. Beat for 10 to 15 minutes with electric mixer. Makes sufficient frosting for a large cake.

Mrs. Lawrence Greiner, Branch No. 2838, Wilmot, SD

Notes

Bars,
Cookies,
Candies

TEMPERATURE TESTS
FOR CANDY MAKING

There are two different methods of determining when candy has been cooked to the proper consistency. One is by using a candy thermometer in order to record degrees, the other is by using the cold water test. The chart below will prove useful in helping to follow candy recipes:

TYPE OF CANDY	DEGREES	COLD WATER
Fondant, Fudge	234 - 238°	Soft Ball
Divinity, Caramels	245 - 248°	Firm Ball
Taffy	265 - 270°	Hard Ball
Butterscotch	275 - 280°	Light Crack
Peanut Brittle	285 - 290°	Hard Crack
Caramelized Sugar	310 - 321°	Caramelized

In using the cold water test, use a fresh cupful of cold water for each test. When testing, remove the candy from the fire and pour about ½ teaspoon of candy into the cold water. Pick the candy up in the fingers and roll into a ball if possible.

In the SOFT BALL TEST the candy will roll into a soft ball which quickly loses its shape when removed from the water.

In the FIRM BALL TEST the candy will roll into a firm but not hard ball. It will flatten out a few minutes after being removed from water.

In the HARD BALL TEST the candy will roll into a hard ball which has lost almost all plasticity and will roll around on a plate on removal from the water.

In the LIGHT CRACK TEST the candy will form brittle threads which will soften on removal from the water.

In the HARD CRACK TEST the candy will form brittle threads in the water which will remain brittle after being removed from the water.

In CARAMELIZING, the sugar first melts then becomes a golden brown. It will form a hard brittle ball in cold water.

BARS, COOKIES, CANDIES

CHOCOLATE RASPBERRY TRUFFLE BROWNIES

Brownie:

1¼ c. semi-sweet real chocolate
   morsels
½ c. margarine
¾ c. brown sugar
2 large eggs

1 tsp. instant coffee crystals
   (optional)
2 Tbsp. water
½ tsp. baking powder
¾ c. all-purpose flour

In heavy saucepan over low heat, melt chocolate morsels with margarine. Cool slightly. In a large mixing bowl, beat sugar and eggs together. Add chocolate mixture and coffee crystals dissolved in water, mixing well. Stir in baking powder and flour; blend well. Spread evenly into greased 9x9 inch baking pan. Bake for 30 to 35 minutes at 350° or until toothpick inserted in center comes out clean. Cool on wire rack.

Truffle Filling:

1 c. semi-sweet real chocolate
   morsels
¼ tsp. instant coffee crystals
   (optional)

8 oz. cream cheese, softened
¼ c. powdered sugar
⅓ c. seedless red raspberry
   preserves

Melt chocolate morsels with coffee crystals in heavy saucepan over low heat. Set aside. In small mixing bowl, beat cream cheese until fluffy. Add powdered sugar and raspberry preserves; beat until fluffy. Beat in melted chocolate, mixing until well blended. Spread over top of brownies.

Glaze:

¼ c. semi-sweet real chocolate
   morsels

1 tsp. vegetable shortening

In small heavy saucepan over low heat, melt chocolate morsels with shortening. Drizzle over top of truffle mixture. Chill for at least 1 or 2 hours. Cut into bars. *Enjoy!*

Shirley Scholz, Branch No. 2234, Milwaukee, WI

TWIX BARS

Line a 9x13 inch pan with club crackers (not crushed).

½ c. brown sugar
½ c. white sugar
½ c. margarine

¼ c. milk
1 c. graham crackers, crushed

Simmer all for 5 minutes. Pour over the cracker layer and top with another of club crackers.

Melt over low heat:

½ c. peanut butter
½ c. chocolate chips

½ c. butterscotch chips

Pour over top and spread. Cool and cut into squares. Keep refrigerated.
Elsie R. Napp, Branch No. 2476, Deerwood, MN

YUMMY BARS

Club crackers
1 c. crushed graham crackers
1 stick oleo
⅓ c. milk

¾ c. brown sugar
½ c. white sugar
⅔ c. chunky peanut butter
1 c. chocolate chips

Place layer of club crackers on bottom of buttered 9 x 13 inch pan or 11¾ x 7½ x 1¾ inch Pyrex dish. Boil for 5 minutes the crushed graham crackers, oleo, milk, brown sugar, and white sugar. Pour over crackers while hot. Add another layer of club crackers. Melt peanut butter and chocolate chips; pour on top and spread. Put in refrigerator to make firm. Cut into squares. (Must be club crackers.)
Imogene Seabaugh, Branch No. 1255, Friedheim, MO

CINNAMON CHEESE SQUARES

2 pkg. refrigerated crescent rolls
2 (8 oz.) pkg. cream cheese, softened
1 c. granulated sugar
1 egg, separated

1 tsp. vanilla
½ tsp. ground cinnamon
½ c. granulated sugar
½ c. sliced almonds

Spread 1 package of rolls in bottom of 9x13 inch pan. Mix softened cream cheese, 1 cup sugar, egg yolk, and vanilla until smooth. Spread over crust. Place second package of rolls over cheese mix to form top crust. Beat egg white until frothy. Spread over top crust. Mix cinnamon, ½ cup sugar and nuts. Spread over top crust. Bake at 350° for 30 to 35 minutes.
Norma McKinnis, Branch No. 2568, Fredericktown, MO

CHEESE BARS

1 egg yolk
1 c. sugar
2 pkg. (8 oz.) cream cheese, softened

1 tsp. vanilla
1 pkg. crescent rolls (unrolled)

Mix the preceding together. Line the bottom of 9x13 inch Pyrex pan with 1 package of crescent rolls (unrolled). Spread cream cheese mixture over the top of the dough and cover with another package of crescent rolls (unrolled) over the top. Beat egg white and spread on top. Sprinkle with ¼ cup sugar and ½ teaspoon cinnamon mixture. Also, sprinkle ½ cup of slivered almonds on top. Bake at 350° for 30 minutes.

Penny Graham, Branch No. 6719, Moses Lake, WA

FROSTED CHEWS

1 c. sugar
1 c. light corn syrup
1 c. peanut butter
6 c. Special K cereal, slightly
   crushed

1 c. (6 oz.) semi-sweet chocolate
   morsels
1 c. (6 oz.) butterscotch morsels

In medium size saucepan, stir to combine the sugar and corn syrup. Cook over medium heat. Stir frequently until mixture boils. Remove from heat. Add peanut butter and mix well. Add cereal. Stir till evenly coated. Press mix evenly and firmly in buttered 13x9 inch pan. Cool.

Melt chocolate and butterscotch morsels over low heat, stirring constantly. Spread evenly over mixture in pan. Let stand in cool place till firm. Cut into bars. Yield: 4 dozen Frosted Chews, 2x1 inch.

Lu Krugler, Branch No. 3436, Pico Rivera, CA

PEANUT BUTTER BARS

1 c. white Karo syrup
1 c. white sugar
1 (6 oz.) pkg. chocolate chips

1 (12 oz.) jar peanut butter
6 c. Special K cereal
1 (6 oz.) pkg. butterscotch chips

Melt sugar and syrup. Add peanut butter. Mix thoroughly. Add cereal and mix well. Put into greased 9x9 inch pan. Let cool. Melt chocolate and butterscotch chips; spread over top. Cool and cut into squares.

Elizabeth Rice, Branch No. 2996, Hale, MI

YUMMY CHOCOLATE BARS

2 c. sifted flour
2 c. white sugar
½ c. oleo
4 Tbsp. cocoa
¼ c. Crisco oil
1 c. water

½ c. buttermilk
1 tsp. vanilla
1 tsp. soda
1 tsp. cinnamon
2 eggs, beaten

In large bowl, combine 2 cups sifted flour and 2 cups sugar. In small saucepan, melt oleo. Add cocoa, oil, and water. Bring to a boil, then add to flour-sugar mixture. Mix thoroughly by hand or beater, then add buttermilk, vanilla, soda, cinnamon, and eggs. Beat all together for 2 minutes until mixed well. Bake in a 13x18 inch pan for 20 minutes at 400°.

Frosting:

½ stick oleo
1½ Tbsp. cocoa
3 Tbsp. evaporated milk

1 tsp. vanilla
¼ tsp. cinnamon
2 c. powdered sugar

Cream all ingredients together and frost bars while warm.

Margret Stanke, Branch No. 5616, Tuttle, ND

CHOCOLATE BARS

2 c. flour
2 c. sugar
½ tsp. salt
1 stick oleo
½ c. shortening
1 c. water

3 Tbsp. cocoa
2 eggs, beaten
1 tsp. soda
½ c. buttermilk
1 tsp. vanilla

Sift flour, sugar and salt together; pour in bowl. Melt oleo, shortening, water, and cocoa; bring to a boil. Pour cocoa mixture over flour mixture and mix well. In another bowl, mix eggs, soda, buttermilk, and vanilla. Add all together and bake at 350° for 20 minutes.

Icing:

1 stick oleo
3 Tbsp. cocoa
6 Tbsp. milk

1 box powdered sugar
½ c. nuts
1 tsp. vanilla

Beat oleo, cocoa, and milk. Add powdered sugar, nuts and vanilla. Mix well. Put on bars as soon as bars come from the oven.

Marilyn Robbins, Branch No. 3966, Craig, MO

CHOCOLATE REVEL BARS

1 c. butter
2 c. brown sugar
2 eggs
2 tsp. vanilla

2½ c. flour
1 tsp. soda
1 tsp. salt
3 c. oatmeal

Chocolate Filling:

1 (12 oz.) pkg. chocolate chips
1 can Eagle Brand milk
2 Tbsp. butter

½ tsp. salt
2 tsp. vanilla
Nuts (optional)

Cream together butter, sugar, eggs, and vanilla. Add dry ingredients. Melt very slow in microwave, stirring occasionally, or over low heat on burner the Chocolate Filling. Spread ⅔ of the oatmeal mixture in large cake pan (jelly roll pan). Cover with chocolate mixture. Dot with patches of remaining oatmeal mixture. Bake at 350° for 25 to 30 minutes.

Sue Folken, Branch No. 1149, Leigh, NE

CHEWY CHOCOLATE BAR

½ c. butter or margarine
1¾ c. brown sugar
1¼ c. flour
1½ oz. bar chocolate
2 eggs

1 tsp. vanilla
¼ tsp. salt
½ tsp. baking powder
½ c. nuts
1 c. coconut

Mix the ½ cup of the butter, ¼ cup of the brown sugar and 1 cup of flour. Press in 9x13 inch pan. Bake for about 15 minutes in a 325° to 350° oven. Mix the balance of the ingredients and pour on the prebaked crust. Put back in oven and bake for about 30 minutes longer. Watch closely as edges will tend to brown and get hard if left in too long. Cool and cut into bars.

Mrs. Darlene Meyer, Branch No. 2004, Palmer, NE

SCRUMPTIOUS CHOCOLATE LAYER BARS

2 c. (12 oz. pkg.) semi-sweet
   chocolate chips
1 (8 oz.) pkg. cream cheese
⅔ c. evaporated milk
1 c. chopped walnuts
½ tsp. almond extract*

3 c. unsifted all-purpose flour
1½ c. sugar
1 tsp. baking powder
½ tsp. salt
1 c. butter or margarine, softened
½ tsp. almond extract*

Combine chocolate chips, cream cheese and evaporated milk in medium saucepan. Cook over low heat, stirring constantly, until chips are melted and mixture is smooth. Remove from heat; stir in walnuts and ½ teaspoon almond extract. Blend well; set aside.

Combine remaining ingredients in large mixer bowl; blend well with mixer until mixture resembles coarse crumbs. Press half of mixture in greased 13x9 inch pan. Spread with chocolate mixture. Sprinkle rest of crumbs over filling. Bake at 375° for 35 to 40 minutes or until golden brown. Cool and cut into bars. Makes about 3 dozen bars, depending on size of bars cut.

* Both ½ teaspoons are needed at 2 different times.

Lynne Schultz, Branch No. 1700, Richmond, MI

SPICY CHOCOLATE BARS

1½ c. shortening
1½ c. sugar
1½ c. brown sugar, packed
4 eggs
2 tsp. vanilla

4 c. unsifted flour
2 tsp. baking soda
2 tsp. salt
4 tsp. cinnamon
2 c. chocolate chips

Cream shortening and sugars. Add eggs, one at a time. Add vanilla. Blend dry ingredients into creamed mixture. Add chocolate chips. Spread in 2 ungreased 15 ½ x 10½ x 1 inch cookie sheets and bake at 375° for 20 minutes. Yield: 80 bars.

Donnajean Kangas, Branch No. 192, Hilbert, WI

CHOCOLATE DESSERT BARS

1 box brownie mix
1 (10½ oz.) miniature
   marshmallows
1 (12 oz.) semi-sweet chocolate
   chips

1 c. broken walnut meats or other
   nutmeats

Heavily grease 9x13 inch glass pan (or use Pam). Mix brownie mix according to box directions and spread in pan (will be thin in pan). Bake as directed on box, being careful not to overbake.

When brownie mixture is baked, do not turn oven off. Slide out oven rack with brownie pan on it. Spread miniature marshmallows over brownies and slide back into oven for about 5 minutes until marshmallows are melted. Slide rack out and smooth marshmallows with back of buttered spoon. Add walnuts sprinkled evenly over marshmallows. Sprinkle chocolate chips evenly over the marshmallows. Slide pan back into oven until chocolate is melted. Take from oven and turn oven off. Use back of buttered spoon to spread chocolate chips. Cool and cut into bars.

Doris A. Anderson, Branch No. 1412, Corvallis, OR

CHOCOLATE BARS

2 c. sugar	2 c. flour
1 tsp. cinnamon	1/8 tsp. salt

Sift preceding into a bowl.

1 stick oleo	1/2 c. cooking oil
1/4 c. cocoa	1 c. water

Bring to boil and pour over flour mix.

Add:

1 tsp. soda in 1/2 c. buttermilk	1 tsp. vanilla
2 eggs	

Beat well. Put in 1 inch deep 12x18 inch cookie sheet. Preheat oven to 400°. Bake for 20 minutes. Frost when cool.

Barb Koch, Branch No. 6470, Kiron, IA

CHOCOLATE CRUMBLE BARS

1/2 c. butter	1/4 tsp. salt
3/4 c. sugar	1/4 tsp. baking powder
2 eggs	2 c. mini marshmallows
1 tsp. vanilla	1 c. chocolate chips
3/4 c. flour	1 c. peanut butter
1/2 c. chopped nuts	1 1/2 c. rice cereal
2 Tbsp. cocoa	

Cream butter and sugar. Beat in eggs and vanilla. Stir in flour, nuts, cocoa, baking powder, and salt. Spread in 13x9 inch pan. Bake at 350° for 15 to 20 minutes. Sprinkle marshmallows evenly on top and return to oven for 3 minutes.

In small saucepan, combine chocolate pieces and peanut butter. Stir over low heat until chocolate is melted. Stir in the rice cereal. Spread on cooled bars. Chill.

Arvella Passow, Branch No. 433, Alma, WI

DOUBLE CHOCOLATE CRUMBLE BARS

½ c. margarine
¾ c. sugar
2 eggs
1 tsp. vanilla
¾ c. flour
2 Tbsp. cocoa
½ tsp. baking powder

½ c. nuts (optional)
Miniature marshmallows (enough
    to cover 9x13 inch pan)
1 (6 oz.) pkg. chocolate chips
¾ c. peanut butter
1½ c. crispy Rice Krispies

Cream together margarine and sugar. Add eggs, cocoa, baking powder, and nuts. Spread on greased 9x13 inch pan and bake in a 350°F. oven for 15 minutes. Remove from oven and sprinkle marshmallows over top. Return to oven for 3 minutes.

In large saucepan, melt chocolate chips with peanut butter. Add crisp Rice Krispies and spread over top of baked mixture. Refrigerate or put in very cool place. Cut into bars.

Mary Barks, Branch No. 1255, Friedheim, MO

BROWNIES

Bars:

½ c. oleo
1 c. sugar
1 c. flour

4 eggs
1 (1 lb.) can chocolate syrup

Combine ingredients well. Pour into 9x13 inch pan and bake at 350° for 30 minutes.

Frosting:

½ c. oleo
¼ c. milk
1 c. sugar

½ c. chocolate chips
1 tsp. vanilla

Cook oleo, milk and sugar until bubbly. Count to 60 and remove from heat. Add chips and vanilla. Cool a bit and frost brownies.

Karla West, Branch No. 6399, Orange City, IA

HERSHEY'S CHOCOLATE BROWNIES

½ c. butter
4 eggs
⅔ c. nuts (optional)
1 c. sugar

1 tsp. vanilla
1 (16 oz.) can Hershey's syrup
1 c. + 3 Tbsp. flour

Mix butter, eggs, and sugar well. Add 1 teaspoon vanilla, then full 16 ounce can syrup. Slowly add 1 cup plus 3 tablespoons flour. Add nuts if desired. Use 15x10 inch pan for brownies, 9x13 inch is higher brownie. Bake at 350° for 25 to 30 minutes.

Frosting:

6 Tbsp. butter
6 Tbsp. cream

1½ c. sugar
6 oz. chocolate chips

Mix butter, cream, and sugar. Boil for ½ minute when bubbles begin. Take from heat. Blend in 6 ounces chips. Spread on slightly cooled brownies.

Florence Colrud, Branch No. 545, Mosinee, WI

BROWNIES

½ c. butter
1 c. sugar
4 eggs
1 tsp. vanilla
1 (1 lb.) can chocolate syrup (1½ c.)
1 c. plus 1 Tbsp. flour
½ tsp. baking powder

¼ tsp. salt
½ c. walnuts (optional)
6 Tbsp. butter
6 Tbsp. milk
1 c. sugar
½ c. chocolate chips
1 tsp. vanilla

Beat ½ cup butter with 1 cup sugar until light and fluffy. Beat in eggs, two at a time, and 1 teaspoon vanilla. Mix well. Stir in chocolate syrup. Sift together flour, baking powder, and salt. Stir in chocolate mixture. Add nuts. Pour into well greased 15½ x 10½ x 1 inch jelly roll pan and spread evenly. Bake at 350° for 22 to 25 minutes or until slight imprint remains when lightly touched with finger. Remove pan to rack and cool.

Meanwhile, combine 6 tablespoons butter, milk and 1 cup sugar in saucepan; stir. Bring to a boil. Boil for 30 seconds. Add chocolate chips. Stir until mixture thickens slightly and cools. Stir in 1 teaspoon vanilla. Spread over cooled brownies. Makes 5 dozen.

Dian Handtke, Branch No. 362, Michigan City, IN

CHOCOLATE BARS

1 c. sugar
½ c. oleo
4 eggs

1 c. Hershey's chocolate syrup
1 Tbsp. vanilla
Nuts

Cream sugar and oleo. Add eggs, one at a time, beating until well blended. Add syrup, vanilla and nuts.

Frosting:

1½ c. sugar
6 Tbsp. milk
5 Tbsp. oleo

1 tsp. vanilla
½ c. milk chocolate chips

Boil sugar, milk and oleo for 30 seconds. Add vanilla and chips. Beat until it holds a peak.

Tillie Buxcel, Branch No. 5985, Midland, SD

BROWNIES

½ c. butter or oleo
1 c. sugar
4 eggs
1 tsp. vanilla

1 can Hershey's chocolate syrup
½ tsp. baking soda
1 c. plus 1 Tbsp. flour
½ c. chopped walnuts

Mix ingredients together until well blended. Bake in a 9x13 inch pan for approximately 25 minutes at 350°.

Frosting: Heat ¾ cup sugar, 3 tablespoons oleo and 4 tablespoons milk. Boil for 30 seconds, then add ¼ cup chocolate chips. When melted and all mixed, pour over brownies.

Betty J. Boggs, Branch No. 1957, Creighton, NE

HERSHEY'S SYRUP BROWNIES

1 c. sugar
½ c. oleo
4 eggs
1 c. plus 1 Tbsp. flour

½ tsp. salt
1 (16 oz.) can Hershey's syrup
1 tsp. vanilla
½ c. nuts

Cream sugar and oleo. Add eggs, one at a time. Add remaining ingredients. Mix and pour into cookie sheet. Bake at 350° for 25 to 30 minutes. Frost while warm.

Icing:

1½ c. sugar
6 Tbsp. milk

6 Tbsp. oleo
½ c. chocolate chips (semi-sweet)

Cook sugar, milk and oleo to full rolling boil. Remove from heat and add chocolate chips. Stir for a few minutes. Frost brownies.

Karen Fritz, Branch No. 3966, Craig, MO

DATE BROWNIES

1 c. graham cracker crumbs
½ tsp. salt
1½ tsp. baking powder
½ lb. dates, cut up
½ c. nuts

½ tsp. vanilla
3 eggs
1 c. brown sugar
Powdered sugar

Beat eggs well. Add brown sugar and vanilla; mix well. Add graham crackers, salt, baking powder, dates, and nuts; mix well. Bake in an 8x11 inch well greased pan at 370° for 25 minutes. Cut into bars and roll in powdered sugar.

Martha Kreutz, Branch No. 3107, Loveland, CO

BROWNIE MIX

4 c. flour
4 tsp. baking powder
4 tsp. salt

8 c. sugar
2½ c. cocoa
2 c. shortening

Mix all ingredients together. Store in airtight container. Makes 16 cups.

For an 8x8 inch pan: For 2 cups of mix, add 2 eggs, 1 teaspoon vanilla, and ⅔ cup chopped nuts (optional). Pour mixture into pan, greased on bottom only. Bake for 22 minutes in a 350° oven.

For a 9x13 inch pan: For 3 cups of mix, add 3 eggs, 1½ teaspoons vanilla, and 1 cup chopped nuts (optional). Pour mixture into pan, greased on bottom only. Bake for 33 minutes in a 350° oven.

Cheryl Schultz, Branch No. 3107, Loveland, CO

CARAMEL BROWNIES

1 (14 oz.) bag caramels
⅔ c. evaporated milk
¾ c. melted butter
1 tsp. vanilla

1 pkg. German chocolate cake mix
1 c. chocolate chips

Combine mix, butter, ⅓ cup of the evaporated milk, and vanilla. Bake half of that mixture for 8 minutes at 350°. Remove and sprinkle chocolate chips on top. Melt together caramels and ⅓ cup of the evaporated milk while mixture is baking. After putting chocolate chips on top of the mixture, pour the melted caramels over them. Crumble remaining cake mixture over this. Top with ½ cup chopped nuts if desired. Bake for 20 minutes at 350°. "Don't overbake."

Mrs. Lucille Riechmann, Branch No. 0356, Dubuque, IA

CARAMEL TURTLE BROWNIES

1 box German chocolate or devil's food cake mix (cake mix without pudding)
⅔ c. evaporated milk, divided

1 c. coarsely chopped nuts
¾ c. margarine or butter, melted
1 (14 oz.) pkg. caramels
1 c. semi-sweet chocolate chips

Use a 9x13x2 inch pan. Preheat oven to 350°. Combine the cake mix, ⅓ cup evaporated milk, margarine or butter, and nuts. Press half of this mixture evenly in bottom of pan. Bake at 350° for about 10 minutes. Melt caramels with other ⅓ cup evaporated milk and set aside. Melt over low heat and stir constantly.

Sprinkle the chocolate chips over the baked cake mix. Pour the melted caramels over this and cover evenly. Drop remaining cake mixture by teaspoons over all and return to oven for 20 minutes more.

These taste better and cut better when completely cooled. These brownies will vanish *fast*.

Mrs. Albert Toberer (Mildred), Branch No. 2803, Buhl, ID

TURTLE CAKE

1 box German chocolate cake mix (Betty Crocker or Duncan Hines)
1 (12 oz.) can Carnation milk
¾ c. melted butter or margarine

1 pkg. Kraft caramels
1 c. chopped pecans
1 (12 oz.) pkg. Nestle semi-sweet chocolate chips

In large bowl, mix together by hand, stirring the "dry" cake mix, ½ cup Carnation milk and ¾ cup melted butter. Spread ½ of mix in an aluminum 9x13 inch greased pan. Bake for 6 to 8 minutes at 350°.

Unwrap caramels and place in Corning Ware glass covered dish and microwave for 30 to 90 seconds (careful they burn) or melt in a double boiler. Add ⅓ cup Carnation and mix well. Pour over baked dough, then sprinkle pecans evenly over melted caramels. Sprinkle chocolate chips evenly over pecans. Spread remaining dough over the top and bake at 350° for 18 to 20 minutes longer.

Bonnie Spoerke, Branch No. 5844, Columbia City, IN

CHOCOLATE CHIP BLOND BROWNIES

1 c. sifted flour
½ tsp. baking powder
⅛ tsp. baking soda
½ tsp. salt
½ c. nuts, chopped

⅓ c. butter or shortening
1 c. packed brown sugar
1 egg
1 tsp. vanilla
1 c. chocolate chips

Sift together flour, baking powder, baking soda, and salt. Add chopped nuts. Mix well and set aside. Melt butter or shortening in saucepan. Remove from heat. Add brown sugar and mix well. Cool slightly. Add egg and vanilla. Blend. Add flour mixture gradually and stir. Spread in greased 9x9x2 inch pan. Sprinkle chocolate chips over top. Bake in a 350° oven for 20 to 25 minutes. Do not overbake. Cool in pan.

Alice Fromm, Branch No. 1683, Hamburg, WI

BLONDE BROWNIES

1 stick oleo
⅓ c. sugar
⅓ c. brown sugar
2 Tbsp. water
1 c. flour
1¼ tsp. baking powder

1 egg
½ c. nuts
1 tsp. vanilla
½ c. coconut
1 (6 oz.) pkg. chocolate chips

Melt oleo in saucepan. Remove from heat. Add sugars, water, flour, and baking powder. Add egg and vanilla; beat well. Add nuts, chips and coconut. Stir lightly to combine. Put into a greased 9x9 inch pan. Bake at 350° for 30 minutes. Do not overbake. Cool in pan. Cut into squares to serve.

Carol Hammerand, Branch No. 1720, Sherrill, IA

PET MILK BROWNIES

1 c. flour
⅓ c. brown sugar
¼ tsp. salt
½ c. shortening
¼ c. Pet milk
1 tsp. vanilla

1 beaten egg yolk
¼ c. Pet milk
1¼ c. brown sugar
½ c. nuts
1 c. coconut

Mix flour, ⅓ cup brown sugar and salt. Work in shortening. Stir in ¼ cup Pet milk and vanilla. Spread in 9 inch square pan. Bake at 400° for 15 minutes. Mix egg yolk, the second ¼ cup Pet milk, the 1¼ cups brown sugar, nuts, and coconut. Spread over baked layer and bake at 350° till set and light brown. Takes about 15 minutes. Don't overbake. Pan doesn't have to be greased.

Ronda Tucker, Branch No. 2512, Ord, NE

ZUCCHINI BROWNIES

3 eggs
2 c. sugar
1 c. oil
2 c. shredded zucchini
2 c. flour
3 tsp. vanilla
1 tsp. baking powder

2 tsp. baking soda
1 tsp. salt
3 tsp. cinnamon
¾ c. dates or raisins (optional)
1½ c. chopped nuts (optional)
1 c. chocolate chips (optional)

1. Mix eggs, sugar, oil, and vanilla.
2. Beat until smooth.
3. Add zucchini and stir.
4. Sift dry ingredients.
5. Add dates and nuts to dry ingredients.
6. Stir together and pour into greased and floured jelly roll or 9x13 inch pan.
7. Bake for 45 minutes at 325°F.

Marion Schmeling, Branch No. 2412, Green Bay, WI

MINT BROWNIES

1 c. sugar
1½ c. butter
4 eggs
1 can Hershey's syrup
1 c. flour
½ tsp. baking powder

2 c. powdered sugar
2 Tbsp. milk
1 tsp. peppermint extract
Dash of green food coloring
6 oz. chocolate chips

Layer 1: Mix well the sugar, ½ cup butter, eggs (beaten), syrup, flour, and baking powder. Bake at 350° for 25 minutes in a greased jelly roll pan. Refrigerate for 20 minutes or until cool.

Layer 2: Mix well the ½ cup butter, powdered sugar, milk, peppermint extract, and food coloring. Spread over layer 1 and refrigerate for 20 minutes.

Layer 3: Melt ½ cup butter and chocolate chips. Pour over layer 2 and spread evenly. Refrigerate until set. Cut into desired size. Will keep well in refrigerator up to a month.

Mavis Schuettpelz, Branch No. 3678, Suring, WI

PRALINE DIVINE BROWNIES

Crust:

¾ c. flour
½ c. firmly packed brown sugar

¼ c. butter or oleo, melted
¾ c. chopped pecans

Heat oven to 350°. Grease a 13x9 inch pan. In small bowl, combine crust ingredients and mix well. Press evenly into bottom of pan.

Brownies:

3 oz. (3 sq.) unsweetened
    chocolate
¾ c. butter or oleo
1½ tsp. vanilla
3 eggs

¾ c. sugar
½ c. firmly packed brown sugar
1¼ c. flour
¾ c. chopped pecans

In medium saucepan over low heat, melt chocolate and butter. Stir constantly till smooth. Remove from heat. Add vanilla, eggs, sugar, and brown sugar. Mix well. Stir in flour and pecans. Mix well. Spread over crust and bake at 350° for 25 to 30 minutes or until set. Cool. Spread 1 can ready to spread coconut pecan frosting for filling over cooled brownies.

Topping:

1 (1 oz.) sq. unsweetened
    chocolate
¼ c. butter or oleo

¼ c. milk
2¼ c. powdered sugar
1 Tbsp. vanilla

In small saucepan over low heat, combine chocolate, butter, and milk. Stir constantly until smooth. Remove from heat; stir in powdered sugar and vanilla until smooth. Pour over filling and spread to cover. Refrigerate for at least 30 minutes, then cut into bars. Store in refrigerator.

Mrs. LaVern (LaVonne) Kuester, Branch No. 2227, Pilger, NE

CHEWY BROWNIES

1 c. sugar
¼ c. shortening
½ tsp. vanilla

2 eggs
4 Tbsp. cocoa
¾ c. flour

Preheat oven to 350°. Grease an 8x8 inch pan. Mix all ingredients in order given. Spread mixture into your greased pan. Bake for 20 minutes. (Do not overbake or these brownies will not be chewy.) Frost with your favorite chocolate frosting. This recipe makes a small batch (about 9 brownies).

Mavis Thompson, Branch 3879, Billings, MT

BROWNIES

2 eggs
1 c. sugar
1 tsp. vanilla
½ c. flour
1 c. chopped walnuts

2 (1 oz.) sq. unsweetened
   chocolate, melted
½ c. melted oleo
⅛ tsp. salt

Grease pan. Beat eggs until thick and lemon colored in medium bowl. Add sugar gradually, beating well after each addition until fluffy. Stir in vanilla, chocolate, and oleo. Fold in flour, salt and ¾ cup nuts. Stir until just blended. Pour into pan. Sprinkle with remaining nuts over top. Bake for 20 minutes in a 350° oven.

Aid Association for Lutherans, Branch No. 6109, Harlan, IA

CHERRY BARS

1 c. margarine
1 c. sugar
3 c. flour
½ tsp. salt

4 eggs
1 tsp. vanilla
1½ tsp. baking powder
1 can cherry pie filling

Cream margarine and sugar; add eggs, one at a time, beating well after each egg. Add vanilla and dry ingredients; mix well. Put half of the batter in greased jelly roll pan. Spoon cherry pie filling over batter. Drop by teaspoon the remaining batter over the pie filling. Spread as much as possible; batter is very stiff. Bake for 25 to 30 minutes in a 350° oven or until done. Drizzle powdered sugar frosting over top while hot.

May use other flavors of fruit pie filling.

Erna C. Boggs, Winnetoon, NE, Branch No. 1957, Creighton, NE

CHERRY BARS

1¼ c. flour
1 tsp. baking powder
¼ tsp. baking soda
¼ tsp. salt
½ c. sugar

½ c. milk
1 egg
1 tsp. vanilla
½ c. oleo
1 (22 oz.) can cherry pie filling

In large bowl, mix flour, baking powder, soda, salt, and sugar. Add egg, milk, vanilla, and oleo. With a spoon, beat till well mixed. Pour into baking pan. In small bowl with fork, combine ½ cup flour, ¼ cup sugar and 2 tablespoons oleo. Mix till coarse. Sprinkle half on top of batter. Spread pie filling over batter. Sprinkle remaining flour mixture on top and bake at 350° for 40 minutes.

Sue Sellmeyer, Branch No. 3966, Craig, MO

SEVEN LAYER BAR

1 stick margarine, melted
1 c. graham cracker crumbs
1 c. coconut
1 (6 oz.) pkg. butterscotch chips

1 (6 oz.) pkg. chocolate chips
1 can condensed sweetened milk
1 c. nuts, chopped

Melt margarine in 9x13 inch pan. Mix in graham cracker crumbs and pat down. Sprinkle coconut and chips over top. Drizzle sweetened milk over top. Sprinkle nuts on top. Bake for 25 to 30 minutes in a 350° oven.

Mrs. Lawrence Greiner, Branch No. 2838, Wilmot, SD

BUTTERSCOTCH BARS

¾ c. all-purpose flour
½ tsp. baking soda
¼ tsp. salt
1 c. brown sugar
½ c. shortening

1 egg
½ tsp. vanilla
1 c. corn flakes
1 c. oatmeal
½ c. chopped nuts

Sift flour, soda and salt. Combine sugar, shortening, egg and vanilla. Beat until creamy. Slowly blend in flour mixture. Stir in corn flakes, oatmeal and nuts. Reserve 1 cup of dough. Spread remaining dough in greased pan.

Butterscotch Filling:

1 (6 oz.) pkg. butterscotch morsels
1 Tbsp. shortening
1 c. finely chopped nuts

⅓ c. sweetened condensed milk
1 tsp. vanilla
¼ tsp. salt

Melt morsels and shortening over hot water. Remove from heat and blend in nuts, milk, vanilla and salt. Spread filling over mixture. Crumble the reserved dough on top.

Colleen Bode, Branch No. 672, Papillion, NE

SEVEN-LAYER COOKIES

1 stick butter or margarine
1½ c. graham cracker crumbs
1 can or 1 c. moist coconut
1 (6 oz.) pkg. butterscotch chips

1 (6 oz.) pkg. chocolate chips
1 c. chopped nuts
1 can sweetened condensed milk
  (Eagle Brand)

Melt butter in 9x13 inch rectangular pan. Layer next 5 ingredients in order listed over melted butter. *Do not mix.* Dribble sweetened condensed milk over all. Bake at 350° for about 25 minutes. These are moist and keep well. Yield: 48 (1 inch) squares.

Erma B. Holl, Branch No. 3383, Indianapolis, IN

SEVEN-LAYER COOKY

1 stick oleo
1 tsp. vanilla
1 c. graham cracker crumbs
1 c. cocoanut

1 (6 oz.) pkg. chocolate chips
1 (6 oz.) pkg. butterscotch chips
1 can Eagle Brand condensed milk
1 c. chopped nuts

Melt stick of oleo in a 9x13 inch pan. Add the vanilla. Add the following in layers: Graham crumbs, cocoanut, chocolate chips, and butterscotch chips. Pour milk over all ingredients and add chopped nuts. Bake at 350° for 30 minutes. Cool and cut into squares.

Myrna Neisius, Branch No. 421, Battle Creek, NE

PINEAPPLE BARS

1 c. flour
1 tsp. salt
1 c. brown sugar, firmly packed

2½ c. quick oatmeal (uncooked)
1 c. oleo (soft)

Sift flour and salt together; add sugar and rolled oats. Add melted oleo and mix well. Place ¾ into a greased 9x13 inch tin. Pat down with your hands. Spread pineapple mix over all and sprinkle remaining oatmeal mix over top. Bake at 350° for 40 to 45 minutes. Cut into bars.

Filling:

¼ c. sugar
1 Tbsp. cornstarch

1 (20 oz.) can crushed pineapple

Cook until thick.

Other fruit can be used in place of the pineapple. It is good with cherries.

Georgiana Mieske, Branch No. 2232, Midland, MI

PINEAPPLE BARS

½ c. butter
½ c. shortening
1 c. sugar
2 c. flour
1 (No. 2) can (20 oz.) crushed
   pineapple

1 c. sugar
2 Tbsp. cornstarch
2 egg yolks

Mix first 4 ingredients as for pie crust. Place ⅔ of mixture on bottom of 9x13 inch pan. Save ⅓ for topping. Mix remaining ingredients in saucepan. Cook over low heat until thick. Spread over crust in pan. Pat remaining crumbs on top and sprinkle with 3 tablespoons uncooked oatmeal over top. Bake in a 350° oven for 20 to 25 minutes.

Delores Ellingson, Branch No. 6817, Cornell, WI

RAISIN BARS

1 c. brown sugar
¾ c. melted margarine
1 tsp. salt
½ tsp. soda in 1 tsp. hot water

1¼ c. oatmeal
1½ c. flour
1 tsp. vanilla

Mix all together. Spread half in bottom of large pan. Pour on Raisin Sauce, then put on rest of crumb mixture. Bake for about 25 minutes at 350°.

Raisin Sauce:

1 c. sugar
1 c. raisins

3 Tbsp. flour
1 c. water

Mix all together and cook until thick.

Edna Leister, Branch No. 1131, Worthington, MN

510

RAISIN BARS

2 c. raisins
2 c. flour
1 tsp. soda
½ tsp. salt
1 tsp. cinnamon
1 tsp. nutmeg

½ tsp. cloves
½ c. butter
1½ c. sugar
2 eggs
½ c. nuts, chopped

Barely cover raisins with boiling water and boil until only 1 tablespoon liquid remains. Cool. Stir together dry ingredients. Cream butter and sugar. Beat in eggs, one at a time. Stir in flour mixture, raisins and nuts. Spread in greased and floured 10x15 inch pan. Bake at 350° until tester comes out clean. Cool for 30 minutes. Cut into bars.

Sally Lundberg, Branch No. 5325, Stratford, IA

MOM'S RAISIN BARS

Combine:

¾ c. oatmeal
1¾ c. flour
1 c. brown sugar

1 tsp. soda
1 c. butter or margarine (I use half of each)

Pat ⅔ of this mixture in a 9x13 inch pan. Bake for 15 minutes at 350°.

For the filling, boil 2 cups raisins, ½ cup water and 1 teaspoon vanilla for 5 minutes. Combine 1 cup sugar and 3 tablespoons cornstarch. Add this to 4 egg yolks along with 1 can Borden's sweetened condensed milk. Add to cooked raisins and cook till thick. Pour filling over baked crust. Sprinkle remaining crumbs on top. Bake for 20 minutes more at 350°. These freeze very well.

Mrs. Arline Schroeder, Branch No. 1131, Worthington, MN

OLD-FASHIONED RAISIN BARS

1 c. seedless raisins
1 c. water
½ c. salad oil
1 c. sugar
1 slightly beaten egg
1¾ c. flour
¼ tsp. salt

1 tsp. soda
1 tsp. cinnamon
1 tsp. nutmeg
1 tsp. allspice
½ tsp. cloves
½ c. chopped nuts (optional)

Combine raisins and water. Bring to boiling. Remove from heat. Stir in salad oil. Cool mixture until lukewarm. Stir in sugar and egg. Mix flour, salt, soda, and spices together. Pour flour mixture into raisin mixture and beat until mixed together. Add nuts. Pour into a 13x9x2 inch pan. Bake at 375° for 20 to 25 minutes. Cool. When cooled, dust with confectioners sugar. Cut into bars. Yield: 2 dozen.

Carole Zilz, Branch No. 5844, Fort Wayne, IN

PECAN PIE BARS

1 pkg. yellow cake mix (reserve ⅔ c.)
½ c. melted oleo
1 egg

Reserve ⅔ cup cake mix for filling. Combine remaining cake mix, melted oleo and egg for crust. Crumble and press in greased 9x13 inch pan. Bake this layer at 350° for 15 to 20 minutes.

Filling:

⅔ c. reserved cake mix
½ c. brown sugar
1½ c. dark corn syrup
1 tsp. vanilla
1 c. chopped pecans

Mix together the reserved cake mix, brown sugar, corn syrup, vanilla, and eggs. Beat for 1 or 2 minutes. Pour filling over baked layer. Sprinkle with pecans. Bake at 350° for 30 to 35 minutes until set. Cut into bars.

Ruby Riedel, Branch No. 3999, Centralia, MO

PECAN BARS

1 box chocolate chip cookie mix
½ c. sugar
¾ c. dark or light corn syrup
1 Tbsp. margarine, melted
2 eggs
1½ c. pecans

Heat oven to 350°. Prepare cookie mix as directed on package, except press evenly in ungreased 13x9x2 inch pan. Bake for 20 minutes. Beat sugar, corn syrup, margarine, and eggs until blended. Stir in pecans. Pour over baked layer. Bake for 25 to 30 minutes until topping is dark golden brown. Loosen edges from sides of pan while warm. Cool and cut into bars. Makes approximately 48 bars.

Jan Faskell, Branch No. 2254, Flat River, MO;

DATE-ORANGE SLICE BARS

Cake:

1 c. brown sugar
¾ c. shortening or margarine
2 eggs
¼ tsp. salt
1 tsp. vanilla
1¾ c. flour
1 tsp. soda, dissolved in 1 Tbsp. hot water
½ c. chopped nuts (optional)

Filling:

1 c. dates
½ c. sugar
2 Tbsp. flour
1 c. hot water

Cream sugar and margarine. Add eggs and salt. Mix in remaining ingredients. Boil filling ingredients until thick. Cool. Spread ½ of dough mixture in greased 9x13 inch pan. Cover with ½ pound candy orange slices, cut into thirds lengthwise.

Spread date mixture over that, then spread last half of dough over filling. Bake at 350° for 35 to 40 minutes. Cool.

Mrs. Donald Kueker, Branch No. 3619, Waverly, IA

ORANGE CANDY BARS

1 lb. orange slices
½ c. butter
4 eggs
½ tsp. salt
½ c. chopped walnuts

6 Tbsp. hot water
2¼ c. brown sugar
2½ c. flour
2 tsp. baking powder
1 tsp. vanilla

Cut orange slices in ⅛ inch pieces and soak overnight in 6 tablespoons hot water. Cream butter and brown sugar. Beat eggs. Add the beaten eggs, flour, salt, and baking powder. Add chopped nuts and vanilla. Add soaked orange slices last. Bake in greased 15½ x 11½ inch pan at 350° for 20 to 30 minutes. Sprinkle with powdered sugar when done. Makes 48.

Delores Sagehorn, Branch No. 2143, Polk, NE

CHOCOLATE-CARAMEL BARS

50 Kraft caramels
⅓ c. evaporated milk
1 box German chocolate cake mix
¾ c. margarine

⅓ c. evaporated milk
1 c. chopped nuts
1 c. chocolate chips

In top of double boiler, melt the caramels and the first ⅓ cup evaporated milk. In a large bowl, combine cake mix, the margarine, second ⅓ cup evaporated milk, and the nuts. Spread half of the dough in the bottom of 13x9 inch pan (greased and floured). Bake for 6 minutes. Sprinkle the chocolate chips on the top of crust. Spread caramel mixture over this combination and the remaining cake mixture on top of that. Bake for 15 more minutes. Refrigerate.

Veloren Osladil, Branch No. 1737, Finlayson, MN

LEMON SQUARES

Crust:

2 c. flour
1 Tbsp. sugar

2 sticks butter, melted

Combine ingredients. Pat the very moist dough into a 12x18 inch cookie sheet with edges or large cake pan. Bake at 350° for 15 minutes. Cool.

Toppings:

1½ c. powdered sugar
16 oz. cream cheese
2 cans Thank You brand lemon pie
   filling

16 oz. Cool Whip
Ground nuts

Cream powdered sugar and cream cheese. Beat until light and fluffy. Spread the lemon filling on top, followed by the Cool Whip. Sprinkle with nuts. Refrigerate for at least 2 hours. Keeps for days.

Arlene Ogg, Branch No. 6940, Harrison, MI

LEMON SQUARES

2 c. flour
½ c. powdered sugar

1 c. butter or oleo (may use half of each)

Mix this part and pat in greased 9x13 inch pan. Bake for about 20 minutes in a 325° to 350° oven.

4 eggs
2 c. sugar
6 Tbsp. lemon juice

4 Tbsp. flour
½ tsp. baking powder

Beat eggs. Add sugar gradually. Add lemon juice, flour and baking powder. Spread over the top of the first mixture. Bake for about 20 or 30 minutes more. When cool, sprinkle with powdered sugar. Cut into bars.

Mrs. Joyce McNeff, Branch No. 2004, Palmer, NE

PUMPKIN BARS

2 c. flour
2 tsp. baking powder
2 tsp. cinnamon
1 tsp. salt
4 eggs

1 (16 oz.) can pumpkin
1½ c. sugar
1 c. oil
1 tsp. baking soda

Mix eggs, pumpkin, sugar, and oil; beat well. Add soda, salt, cinnamon, baking powder, and flour. Mix well. Pour batter into ungreased cookie sheet. Bake at 350° for 25 to 30 minutes.

Marla Voltmer, Branch No. 3966, Craig, MO

PUMPKIN PIE SQUARES

1 c. flour
½ c. quick oatmeal
½ c. brown sugar
½ c. butter
1 (16 oz.) can pumpkin
1 (13 oz.) can evaporated milk
2 eggs, beaten
¾ c. brown sugar

½ tsp. salt
½ tsp. cinnamon
½ tsp. ginger
¼ tsp. cloves
½ c. pecans
½ c. brown sugar
1 Tbsp. butter

Combine flour, oatmeal, brown sugar, and butter; mix until crumbly. Pat in 9x13 inch cake pan. Bake for 15 minutes in a 350° oven. Mix in blender the pumpkin, milk, eggs, brown sugar, salt, cinnamon, ginger, and cloves. Pour over crust and bake for another 15 minutes. Mix the pecans, brown sugar and butter; sprinkle over filling and bake for another 15 minutes. Cool and cut into bars.

Mrs. Melvin Hollatz, Branch No. 1804, Parkers Prairie, MN

YUM YUM BARS

1 c. sugar
1 c. butter or margarine
1 c. graham cracker crumbs
½ c. milk

1 egg, slightly beaten
1 c. coconut
1 c. nuts (optional)

Combine sugar, butter or margarine, graham cracker crumbs, milk, and egg over medium heat until mixture boils. Remove from heat; add coconut and nuts. Line bottom of 9x13 inch pan with a layer of whole graham crackers. Pour cooked mixture over crackers. Place another layer of graham crackers over cooked mixture.

Frosting:

½ c. butter
2 c. powdered sugar

1 tsp. vanilla
1 to 2 tsp. cream

Combine all ingredients and frost bars.

Leona Zander, Branch No. 3619, Waverly, IA

YUMMY BARS

½ c. oleo (soft)
1 c. sugar
1 whole egg
1 tsp. vanilla
2 egg yolks

1¼ c. flour
1 tsp. baking powder
½ tsp. salt
1 c. packed brown sugar
1 c. nuts

Mix thoroughly the first 5 ingredients. Add flour, baking powder, and salt. Put into a 9x13 inch greased cake pan. Beat the egg whites until foamy. Add the brown sugar and beat until stiff and glossy. Fold in the nuts. Spread meringue over dough in pan. Bake for 25 minutes at 375°.

Georgiana Mieske, Branch No. 2232, Midland, MI

RICE KRISPIES CARAMEL BARS

8 c. Rice Krispies
2 c. miniature marshmallows
¾ c. butter

1 can Eagle Brand milk
1 pkg. Kraft caramels

Melt ½ cup butter and 1½ packages marshmallows. Add to Rice Krispies. Spread ½ Rice Krispies mixture on bottom of greased 9x13 inch pan. Put remainder of marshmallows on top of Rice Krispies. Melt caramels, Eagle Brand milk, and ¼ cup butter. Pour over marshmallows. Put remainder of Rice Krispies on top. Refrigerate.

Elaine Briesemeister, Branch No. 3650, Lester Prairie, MN

BUTTERSCOTCH BARS

2 eggs, beaten
1 c. sugar
⅛ tsp. salt
½ tsp. vanilla
¾ c. butter

2 c. marshmallows (small)
2½ c. graham cracker crumbs
1 c. butterscotch bits
3 Tbsp. peanut butter

Combine eggs, sugar, salt, and butter in saucepan. Heat to boiling point. Boil for 2 minutes. Stir constantly. Let cool. Stir in marshmallows and cracker crumbs. Spread into 9x9x2 inch pan. Chill. Melt butterscotch bits and peanut butter at a *low* setting. Add vanilla. Spread over crumb mixture. Refrigerate. Cut into bars when cool. Makes approximately 3 dozen bars.

Note: Have the cracker crumbs crushed before you begin cooking the mixture.

Phyllis Watts, Branch No. 3597, Belle Fourche, SD

CARAMEL LAYERS

2 c. + 2 Tbsp. flour
½ tsp. salt
½ tsp. soda
1 c. packed brown sugar
1½ c. quick oatmeal

1 c. butter
48 caramels
4 Tbsp. cream (or milk)
1 c. chocolate chips

Mix 2 cups flour and dry ingredients with butter. Save back half of the mixture. Press into large cake pan and bake for 10 minutes at 350°.

Melt caramels and cream. Add 4 tablespoons flour and spread over baked layer. Sprinkle chips over top. Pour remaining half of crumb mixture on top and bake again for about 12 minutes. Cut while warm.

If caramel sheets are used, omit 2 tablespoons flour and cream. No need to melt the Wrapples. Double layer of Wrapples are better.

Linda Sedlacek, Branch No. 3107, Loveland, CO

CARAMEL LAYERS

1 c. plus 2 Tbsp. flour
¼ tsp. salt
¼ tsp. baking soda
½ c. firmly packed brown sugar
¾ c. quick cooking rolled oats

½ c. butter
24 caramels
2 Tbsp. cream
½ c. semi-sweet chocolate
    morsels

Combine in mixing bowl 1 cup flour, salt, soda, brown sugar, and rolled oats. Cut in butter until particles are fine. Reserve 1 cup. Press remaining mixture into bottom of greased 8 inch square pan. Bake at 350° for 10 minutes.

Combine caramels and cream in top of double boiler. Cook over boiling water until caramels melt. Blend in 2 tablespoons flour. Spread carefully over base. Sprinkle with chocolate morsels, then reserved crumb mixture. Bake at 350° for 12 to 15 minutes until delicately browned.

Carol Nielsen, Branch No. 4077, Racine, WI

SCOTCHY PEANUT BARS

⅔ c. butter
½ c. firmly packed brown sugar
1⅓ c. flour
1 c. sugar
1 c. light corn syrup

1 (6 oz.) pkg. (1 c.) butterscotch
   morsels
1¼ c. peanut butter
3 c. corn flakes

Cream butter. Add brown sugar and cream well. Blend in flour (mixture may be crumbly). Press into bottom of ungreased 13x9 inch pan. Bake at 350° for 15 to 20 minutes. Combine sugar and corn syrup in medium saucepan. Bring to a boil. Remove from heat. Add butterscotch morsels and peanut butter. Stir until melted. Stir in corn flakes. Spread over base. Cool. Frost.

Nancy Ericksen, Branch No. 4231, Neemeh, WI

PEANUT SQUARES

1 box white or yellow cake mix
1½ lb. shelled or dry roasted,
   unsalted peanuts, *ground* fine

Bake cake as directed. Put in greased 10x15 inch pan. When cool, cut in desired shapes.

Hint: Bake 1 day ahead of icing them, so cake will be easier to handle. *Very good!*

Icing:

½ c. (1 stick) margarine
2 c. (or more) powdered sugar

4 egg yolks

Mix egg yolks with fork. Put in top of *double boiler* along with margarine. Gradually add powdered sugar. Keep icing *hot* in double boiler while icing all 4 sides of cake squares. Immediately roll squares in ground peanuts. Icing must be kept hot and thin. They freeze well.

Lois Meyer, Branch No. 1409, St. Peter, IL

DISAPPEARING PEANUT BUTTER BARS

1 c. chunky peanut butter
½ c. packed brown sugar

1 egg
1 c. butterscotch chips

Preheat oven to 325°. In small bowl, mix peanut butter, brown sugar and egg until well blended. Press evenly in bottom of 8x8 inch pan.

Bake for 20 minutes or until lightly browned. Sprinkle with chips. Cover with foil. Bake for 5 minutes longer. Spread chips evenly over peanut butter layer. Cool pan on wire rack. Cut into 2x1 inch bars. Store in cool place.

Cheryl Schultz, Branch No. 3107, Loveland, CO

PEANUT BUTTER BARS

Melt 2 sticks oleo.

Add:

1 c. peanut butter   1 lb. powdered sugar
1½ c. crushed graham crackers

Mix together and press into ungreased 9x13 inch pan. Melt 1 large package chocolate chips and spread on top. Chill in refrigerator. Cut into squares.

Beverly Harkness, Branch No. 2014, Stillwater, OK

UNBAKED PEANUT BUTTER BARS

¾ c. sugar   1½ c. peanut butter
¾ c. white syrup   3 c. Rice Krispies

Bring sugar and syrup to a boil. Remove from stove. Add peanut butter and Rice Krispies. Press in a greased 9x13 inch pan.

Mrs. Fred Hansen, Branch No. 3420, Sioux City, IA

APPLE BARS

Dough:

1 c. shortening (like Crisco and   1 tsp. salt
    butter)   1 egg yolk and milk to make ¾ c.
2½ c. flour

Filling:

6 c. corn flakes, crushed   2 Tbsp. flour
6 c. apples, sliced   Sprinkle with cinnamon
1½ c. sugar

Roll out half of dough and fit on jelly roll pan. Sprinkle with crushed corn flakes. Cover with top crust. Whip egg white slightly and spread on top crust. Sprinkle with sugar. Bake for 10 minutes in a 400° oven, then for 40 minutes at 350°. Drizzle with powdered sugar frosting. Cut when cool.

Ramona Breitkreutz, Branch No. 1784, Renville, MN

APPLE BARS

Crust:

2½ c. flour   1 egg yolk plus enough milk to
1 Tbsp. sugar   make ½ c.
1 tsp. salt   ⅔ c. soda crackers
1 c. lard or shortening

Filling:

5 c. sliced apples   1 tsp. cinnamon
1½ c. sugar

Frosting:

1 c. powdered sugar   2 tsp. lemon juice

Combine flour, sugar, salt, and shortening. Beat egg yolk and add milk, then mix with other ingredients. Divide in half. Roll ½ dough out to fit on large cookie sheet. Crush soda crackers and sprinkle on crust. Put filling on crust. Cover with top crust. Brush crust with beaten egg white. Bake at 350° for 40 minutes. Frost with frosting.

Florence J. Noess, Branch No. 6384, Java, SD

SOUR CREAM APPLE SQUARES

2 c. flour	½ tsp. salt
2 c. brown sugar	1 c. sour cream
½ c. soft butter	1 tsp. vanilla
½ c. chopped nuts	1 egg
1 to 2 tsp. cinnamon	2 c. apples, chopped
1 tsp. soda	

Combine flour, brown sugar and butter till crumbly. Add nuts. Press 2¾ cups of mixture into ungreased 9x13 inch pan. Add remaining ingredients to the rest of the crumbs and pour over crumb crust. Bake at 350° for 30 to 35 minutes. Serve warm with whipped topping.

Ronda Tucker, Branch No. 2512, Ord, NE

CHOCOLATE CHIP BARS

1 c. shortening	¼ tsp. salt
½ c. white sugar	3 egg yolks
½ c. brown sugar	1 tsp. vanilla

Mix preceding and spread on a greased 9x12 inch pan. Sprinkle chocolate chips over dough. Beat 3 egg whites. Add 1 cup brown sugar. Spread over chocolate chips, then sprinkle 1 cup ground nuts over top. Bake for 25 minutes in a 350° oven. Cut into bars while warm.

Emma Berghoefer (Mrs. Ed), Branch No. 554, Hampton, IA

CHOCOLATE CHIP BARS

2 c. sugar	4 eggs
¼ c. cocoa	1½ c. flour
1 c. melted butter or margarine	1 tsp. salt
2 tsp. vanilla	6 oz. chocolate chips

Grease and flour 9x13 inch pan. Mix sugar and cocoa; add melted butter, then vanilla and eggs. Mix well. Add flour and salt. Sprinkle chocolate chips over top. Bake for 35 minutes at 350°.

Charlene Heck, Branch No. 2714, Ogden, UT

DREAM BARS

First Mixture - Crust:

½ c. butter	1 c. flour
½ c. brown sugar	

Pat crust into a shallow pan (about 8x13 inch). Bake at 375° for 10 minutes.

Second Mixture - Mix:

1 c. brown sugar	½ tsp. baking powder
2 eggs	¼ tsp. salt
1 tsp. vanilla	2 Tbsp. flour
1½ c. coconut	1 c. nuts

Blend second mixture. Pour over previously baked crust. Bake for 20 minutes in a moderate oven. Cool slightly. Cut into bars.

Mrs. Franis Thompson, Mrs. Emma Klebe, Branch No. 1248, Willow City, ND

FROSTED DREAM BARS

½ c. butter	1¼ c. flour
2 Tbsp. brown sugar	

Mix:

1 c. brown sugar	1 c. coconut
¼ tsp. baking powder	2 beaten eggs
1 c. chopped nuts	¼ tsp. salt

Frosting:

¾ c. powdered sugar	1 Tbsp. lemon juice
1 Tbsp. soft butter	

Mix first 3 ingredients and spread in cooky sheet pan. Bake for 5 minutes. Spread egg ingredients over crust and bake for 20 minutes at 350°. Spread with frosting when cool.

Elsie Ringhand, Branch No. 2366, Harlowton, MT

CHERRY BARS

2 c. flour	1 Tbsp. baking powder
1 c. margarine	2 c. brown sugar
2 Tbsp. brown sugar	1 c. nuts
4 eggs	1 c. coconut
½ c. flour	1 (10 oz.) jar maraschino cherries

Mix together 2 cups flour, 1 cup margarine, and 2 tablespoons brown sugar; put in a 9x13 inch pan. Bake for 20 minutes at 350°. Add 4 eggs, beaten. Mix together ½ cup flour, 1 tablespoon baking powder, 2 cups brown sugar, 1 cup nuts, 1 cup coconut, and one 10 ounce jar maraschino cherries; pour over base crust and bake for 20 to 25 minutes at 350°.

For the frosting, mix together powdered sugar, margarine and the reserved cherry juice.

Mrs. Iris Kluever, Branch No. 1131, Worthington, MN

520

CHOCOLATE COVERED CHERRY BARS

½ c. butter
¼ c. sugar
2 Tbsp. cocoa

1¼ c. flour
36 maraschino cherries

Mix cookie ingredients until mixture is in fine particles. Press in bottom of 8x8 inch buttered pan. Bake for 15 minutes at 350°. Cool.

Fondant:

2 tsp. butter
2 c. powdered sugar

2 Tbsp. milk
½ tsp. vanilla

Mix fondant ingredients thoroughly and spread on top cooled baked cookies. Place 36 maraschino cherries (well drained) in 6 evenly spaced rows on top of fondant layer.

Chocolate Glaze:

1 env. no-melt unsweetened
   chocolate

1 Tbsp. melted butter

Mix Chocolate Glaze ingredients. Using a spoon, pour Chocolate Glaze over each cherry. Yield: 36 bars.

Marie Nelson, Branch No. 3715, Cottage Grove, WI

CHERRY DIVINITY BARS

1 c. butter or oleo
½ c. brown sugar
2 c. flour
2 env. Knox gelatine
½ c. water
2 c. granulated sugar

½ c. water
1 tsp. almond extract
1 tsp. vanilla
½ c. chopped nuts
½ c. cut up maraschino cherries
Coconut

Blend oleo, brown sugar and flour with a fork until crumbly. Press into a well buttered pan (10x14 inches). Bake for 10 minutes at 350°.

Sprinkle Knox gelatine over ½ cup water in a large bowl and let stand. Mix sugar and ½ cup water in saucepan. Bring to a boil. Boil for 2 minutes. Add hot sugar mixture slowly to gelatine mixture and *beat, beat, beat.* Beat for at least 10 minutes until stiff like divinity. Add extracts, nuts and maraschino cherries. Mix and pour over cooled crust. Sprinkle with coconut and cut into squares when firm.

Ester Mohr, Branch No. 670, May City, IA

CHEERIOS QUICK BARS

½ c. sugar
½ c. honey or light corn syrup
½ c. peanut butter

3½ c. Cheerios
½ c. salted peanuts

Butter a 9x9x2 inch pan. In large pan, stir together sugar and syrup. Cook and stir just until mixture comes to a good rolling boil. Remove from heat and stir in peanut butter. Pour mixture over cereal and peanuts. Turn into pan. Pat smooth. Cool.

You may double this and put in jelly roll pan.

Linda Meiburg, Branch No. 6715, Rock Rapids, IA

CHOCOLATE MINT STICKS

2 sq. unsweetened chocolate
½ c. margarine
2 eggs
1 c. sugar

¼ tsp. peppermint extract
½ c. flour
Dash of salt
½ c. chopped nuts (optional)

In double boiler, melt margarine and chocolate. Beat eggs separately until frothy and then stir in sugar, chocolate mixture, peppermint extract, flour, salt, and nuts. Mix thoroughly. Bake for 20 to 25 minutes in a 350° oven. Cool when done.

Topping:

2 Tbsp. soft margarine
1 c. sifted powdered sugar

¾ tsp. peppermint extract
1 Tbsp. milk

Work softened margarine into sugar, milk and extract. Spread on cooled, baked batter.

Glaze:

1 sq. unsweetened chocolate

1 Tbsp. margarine

Melt chocolate and margarine in double boiler. Glaze over the topping. Let set till cold. Cut into bars or squares. *Rather rich!*

Ruth Leitch, Branch No. 5844, Avilla, IN

ALMOND PUFF

½ c. margarine, softened
1 c. flour
2 Tbsp. water
½ c. margarine

1 c. water
1 tsp. almond extract
1 c. flour
3 eggs

Glaze:

1½ c. confectioners sugar
2 Tbsp. butter

1½ tsp. almond extract
1 to 2 Tbsp. water

Cut ½ cup margarine into 1 cup flour. Sprinkle 2 tablespoons water over mixture. Mix with fork. Mix into ball and divide in half. On ungreased baking sheet, pat each half into a strip, 12x3 inches and 3 inches apart.

In saucepan, melt ½ cup margarine and 1 cup water to rolling boil. Remove from heat and quickly stir in almond extract and 1 cup flour. Stir vigorously over low heat until mixture forms a ball. Beat in eggs, one at a time, until smooth. Divide in half and spread each half evenly over strip. Bake for 60 minutes or until topping is crisp and brown. Frost with glaze and sprinkle with nuts.

Loretta Smith, Branch No. 2288, Hilton, NY

SALTED NUT BARS

1½ c. flour
½ c. butter

¾ c. brown sugar
¼ tsp. salt

Mix and bake for 10 minutes in a 9x13 inch pan at 350°. Pat in till firm. Spread small can of mixed nuts over the top.

Melt and pour over the nuts:

1 (12 oz.) pkg. butterscotch chips
  (choose a good quality)

2 Tbsp. butter
1 Tbsp. water

Make sure all the nuts are covered completely. Bake at 350° until the mixture just begins to bubble.

Betty N. Kuehl, Branch No. 1292, Selby, SD

FUDGE NUT BARS

1 (6 oz.) chocolate chips
¾ c. Eagle Brand milk
1½ Tbsp. butter
Pinch of salt
2 eggs
¾ c. oleo

1½ c. brown sugar
1 tsp. soda
¾ tsp. salt
2¼ c. quick oatmeal
1¾ c. flour

Mix together chocolate chips, milk, butter, and pinch of salt in bowl. Microwave till chocolate chips are melted. Add ½ cup chopped nuts and 1½ teaspoons vanilla. Blend and set aside.

Cream oleo, sugar and eggs. Add dry ingredients, then oatmeal. Press ⅔ of mixture into greased 9x13 inch pan. Spread chocolate mixture on this and the remaining batter. Bake at 350° for 25 to 30 minutes.

Carolyn Noess, Branch No. 2611, Sac City, IA

FUDGE MELT-AWAYS

½ c. butter, melted
1 egg, beaten
¼ c. sugar
1 tsp. vanilla
1 c. coconut
2 c. crushed graham crackers

½ c. butter
1 Tbsp. milk
2 c. powdered sugar
1 tsp. vanilla
¾ c. peanut butter (crunchy)
1 c. chocolate chips

Mix first 6 ingredients and press into an ungreased 9x13 inch pan. Bake at 350° for 10 minutes. Let cool. Mix well the butter, milk, powdered sugar, and vanilla (next 4 ingredients). Spread over *cooled* graham cracker crust. Melt together peanut butter and chocolate chips. Cool slightly and spread over second layer.

Karen Velgersdyk, Loveland, CO

BUSY DAY BARS

1 c. flour	½ c. butter
5 Tbsp. powdered sugar	Pinch of salt

Mix 4 ingredients as for pie crust. Press into regular 9x13 inch pan. Bake at 350° for 12 minutes.

Filling:

2 eggs, well beaten	½ c. coconut
1½ c. brown sugar	½ c. nuts, chopped
2 Tbsp. flour	1 tsp. vanilla
½ tsp. baking powder	Pinch of salt

Mix and spread over baked warm crust. Return to oven and bake for another 20 minutes.

Frosting:

1 c. powdered sugar	Lemon juice (to spread)

Put on while warm.

Irene Kellner, Branch No. 341, Dorchester, WI

PUMPKIN ROLL

3 eggs	1 tsp. soda
1 c. sugar	¾ c. flour
⅔ c. pumpkin	⅛ tsp. salt
½ tsp. cinnamon	

Line a jelly roll pan or cookie sheet with waxed paper. Coat waxed paper with butter. Pour batter on top. Bake for 10 minutes at 375°. Take from oven and roll up. Cool. When cool, spread with filling and roll again. Freeze and serve frozen.

Filling:

1 (8 oz.) cream cheese	2 Tbsp. butter
1 c. powdered sugar	¾ tsp. vanilla

Whip until smooth.

Edna Rundquist, Branch No. 2810, Stockholm, WI

OATMEAL BARS

Bars:

1 c. quick oatmeal	2 eggs
1¼ c. boiling water	1½ c. white flour
½ c. margarine	1 tsp. soda
1 c. white sugar	½ tsp. salt
1 c. brown sugar	1 tsp. vanilla

Pour boiling water over oatmeal and stir. Let stand for 20 minutes. Mix margarine, sugars, and eggs together. Add flour, soda, salt, and vanilla. Add oatmeal mixture last. Bake in jelly roll pan (10x15 inches) at 350° for 25 minutes. Frost when cool.

Frosting:

½ c. margarine	6 Tbsp. cream
1¼ c. brown sugar	

Boil preceding for 2 minutes. Add 1 teaspoon vanilla. Beat until ready to spread. Sprinkle ½ cup chopped nuts over frosting.

Elsie Schroeder, Branch No. 647, Bordular, ND

CRANBERRY BARS

¾ c. butter	1 tsp. salt
1 c. sugar	2 c. cranberries
1½ c. flour	2 c. sugar
1 c. oatmeal	3 Tbsp. cornstarch
1 tsp. baking powder	½ c. cold water

Mix butter, sugar, flour, oatmeal, baking powder, and salt until crumbly (use a pastry blender). Pat ½ of the mixture into a 13x9 inch pan. Cook the following for 5 minutes: 2 cups cranberries, 2 cups sugar, 3 tablespoons cornstarch, and ½ cup water. Spread over bottom crust. Cover with remaining crumb mixture. Bake for 30 minutes in a 350° oven.

To make Apricot Bars, use the same recipe for the crumbs. In place of the cranberry mixture, spread one 10 ounce jar of apricot jam over the crust.

Mrs. Edna Lohmann, Branch No. 102, Zumbrota, MN

CRANBERRY-DATE BARS

1 (12 oz.) pkg. cranberries	1½ c. brown sugar
1 (8 oz.) pkg. chopped dates	½ tsp. baking soda
1 tsp. vanilla	¼ tsp. salt
2 c. flour	1 c. margarine, melted
2 c. rolled oats	

Make filling in a medium saucepan. Combine cranberries and dates. Cook, covered, over low heat for 15 to 20 minutes till cranberries pop, stirring frequently. Stir in vanilla. Set aside.

In a large mixing bowl, stir together dry ingredients. Stir in margarine till well blended. Pat *half* of the oat mixture on the bottom of a 13x9x2 inch baking pan. Bake in a 350° oven for 8 minutes.

Carefully spread filling over baked oat mixture. Sprinkle remaining oat mixture on top. Pat gently. Bake for 20 to 22 minutes more. Drizzle with Orange Glaze. Cut into bars. Makes 32 bars.

Orange Glaze:

2 c. powdered sugar
½ tsp. vanilla

2 to 3 Tbsp. orange juice

In a medium bowl, stir 2 cups powdered sugar, ½ teaspoon vanilla, and 2 to 3 tablespoons orange juice.

Sharon Alldredge, Branch No. 2785, Santa Maria, CA

MERINGUE TOPS

1 c. butter
½ c. white sugar
1 tsp. vanilla

1 c. brown sugar
2 eggs
1 yolk

Blend these 6 ingredients until light.

Sift dry ingredients:

4 c. sifted flour
2 tsp. baking powder

½ tsp. soda
1 tsp. salt

Add alternately with ½ cup milk. Divide into 4 or 5 parts. Spread dough in Crisco greased, rimmed cookie sheets, ¼ inch thick. Cover with meringue made of 1 egg white (beaten very stiff) and 1 cup brown sugar. Sprinkle top with ⅓ cup chopped nuts. Bake in a slow oven at 325° for about 25 minutes. Cut into small diamonds while warm.

Note: The rest of the dough may be stored in freezer for a later time.

Pauline Fajen, Shirley Kaiser, Branch No. 2470, Lincoln, MO

PUMPKIN CHEESECAKE BARS

1 c. all-purpose flour
⅓ c. packed brown sugar
5 Tbsp. butter, softened
½ c. finely chopped pecans or
    walnuts
1 (8 oz.) pkg. softened cream
    cheese

¾ c. sugar
½ c. solid pack pumpkin
2 eggs, lightly beaten
1½ tsp. cinnamon
1 tsp. ground allspice
1 tsp. vanilla

Combine flour and brown sugar in medium bowl. Cut in butter to make a crumb mixture. Stir in nuts. Set aside ¾ cup mixture for topping. Press remaining mixture into bottom of 8 x 8 x 1½ inch baking pan. Bake in preheated 350°F. oven for 15 minutes. Cool slightly.

Combine cream cheese, sugar, pumpkin, eggs, cinnamon, allspice, and vanilla in large mixer bowl. Blend until smooth. Pour over baked crust. Sprinkle with reserved topping. Bake for an additional 30 to 35 minutes. Cool before cutting into bars. Makes 32 (1 x 2 inch) bar cookies.

Pat Strand, Branch No. 1455, Great Falls, MT

BUTTER PECAN TURTLE BARS

Crust:

2 c. flour
1 c. brown sugar

½ c. softened butter

Mix crust until crumbly. Put into 9x13 inch ungreased pan.

1 c. whole pecan halves

1 c. milk chocolate chips

Sprinkle pecans evenly over crust. Prepare Caramel Layer; pour over pecans. Bake at 350° for 18 to 22 minutes or until Caramel Layer is bubbly. Remove from oven. Sprinkle with chocolate chips. Allow chips to melt slightly. Swirl knife through chips to spread chocolate.

Caramel Layer:

⅔ c. butter

½ c. brown sugar

Cook sugar and butter to a boil. Boil for ½ to 1 minute, stirring constantly.

Marsha Ruesch, Branch No. 5844, Columbia City, IN

ZUCCHINI MUNCHIES

½ c. margarine
1⅓ c. brown sugar
½ tsp. nutmeg
½ tsp. salt
1 tsp. baking soda
1 tsp. cinnamon
1 tsp. ground cloves

1 egg
1 c. zucchini
1½ c. flour
1½ c. oatmeal
½ c. walnuts, crushed
½ c. coconut flakes
½ c. raisins

Cream butter and sugar; add egg and spices. Stir in zucchini, nutmeats, raisins, and oatmeal. Mix till all ingredients are moist. Drop by teaspoon on Pam sprayed cookie sheet. Bake at 350°F. for 10 or 12 minutes or till brown.

Frieda Viola Oblender, Branch No. 736, Bay City, MI

CARAMEL HEAVENLIES

12 double graham crackers
2 c. (4 oz.) miniature
    marshmallows
¾ c. butter
¾ c. firmly packed brown sugar

1 tsp. cinnamon
1 tsp. vanilla extract
1 c. sliced almonds
1 c. flaked coconut

Preheat oven to 350°F. Arrange graham crackers in single layer in a 15½ x 10 ½ inch jelly roll pan. Sprinkle with marshmallows.

In medium saucepan, combine butter, brown sugar and cinnamon. Cook over medium heat, stirring constantly, until sugar is dissolved. Remove from heat and stir in vanilla. Spoon evenly over marshmallows; sprinkle with almonds and coconut. Bake for 12 to 14 minutes or until lightly browned. Cool in pan on wire rack. Cut into 3 inch squares. Cut each square in half to form triangles. Makes about 2½ dozen, about 130 calories each.

To store: Refrigerate in airtight container up to 2 weeks. Or, wrap well; label and date. Freeze up to 3 months.

Debbie Wolff, Branch No. 2085, Atwater, CA

JEWISH COOKIES

½ lb. butter or margarine
3 heaping Tbsp. cocoa
3 eggs
1 c. flour
1¼ c. sugar

1 c. chopped nuts
2 c. coconut
1 can sweetened condensed milk
   (Eagle Brand)

Cream sugar, butter and eggs; add flour, cocoa and nuts. Spread in greased 15 ½ x 10 inch (jelly roll) pan. Bake at 350° for 20 minutes. Remove from oven and spread with mixture of 2 cups coconut and 1 can sweetened condensed milk. Bake for 15 minutes more. Frost while warm with the following.

Frosting:

1 box powdered sugar
3 Tbsp. cocoa
2 Tbsp. butter, softened
2 Tbsp. vegetable shortening
   (Crisco)

1 tsp. vanilla
Milk (enough to spread)

Cut into squares to serve when cool.

Marlene Griffith, Branch No. 1221

CHERRY GELATIN BARS

¾ c. butter or margarine, melted
⅓ c. brown sugar
1½ c. flour
2 pkg. Knox unflavored gelatine
½ c. water
2 c. sugar

½ c. water
½ c. maraschino cherries, drained
   and chopped
½ c. chopped nuts
Coconut

Mix butter, brown sugar and flour until crumbly. Pat in 9x13 inch cake pan. Bake for 10 minutes in a 325° oven. Cool. Dissolve the gelatine in ½ cup of water; set aside. Boil the 2 cups sugar and ½ cup water for 3 minutes. Pour over the gelatine mixture and beat until stiff, about 4 to 5 minutes. Add the maraschino cherries and nuts, then pour over crust. Sprinkle coconut on top if desired. Cool and cut into bars. These bars freeze well.

Mrs. Dean Hollatz, Branch No. 1804, Parkers Prairie, MN

FRUIT BAR BEAUTIES

6 Tbsp. butter or margarine
1½ c. graham cracker crumbs
1 c. shredded coconut
2 c. candied pineapple and
   cherries, cut fine

1 c. cut up dates
1 c. walnuts, coarsely cut
1 (15 oz.) can sweetened
   condensed milk

Melt the butter in a large pan, 15x10x1 inch. Distribute the crumbs in the pan, then sprinkle on the coconut. Put the candied pineapple, dates and cherries evenly on top, then sprinkle in the walnuts. Level and press gently with hands. Lastly, pour the condensed milk evenly over the top. Bake at 350° for 25 to 30 minutes. Cool and cut into bars.

These bars look as good as they taste.

Ruth Just, Branch No. 3866, Audubon, MN

HOLIDAY BARS

¼ c. brown sugar
½ c. margarine

1 c. flour

Mix and pat in 9x13 inch pan.

2 eggs
1 c. brown sugar
¼ c. flour
½ tsp. baking powder

1 tsp. vanilla
1 c. flaked coconut
1 c. chocolate chips

Mix and pour over crust in pan. Top with ½ cup chopped red and green cherries and a few chopped nuts. Bake at 350° for 30 minutes. Cut into squares.

Peanut butter chips or butterscotch chips may be substituted for chocolate chips.

Marion C. Hillmann, Branch No. 2890, Glendora, CA

OATMEAL SNACK BARS

3 c. oatmeal
¼ c. wheat germ
¼ c. sunflower seeds
½ c. sugar
¼ c. honey
¼ c. flour
1¼ sticks margarine or butter,
   softened

½ tsp. salt
1 tsp. vanilla
½ c. nuts
½ c. raisins or chocolate chips
   (may also be added)

Mix all together in large bowl. Have a 9x13x2 inch baking pan, thoroughly buttered or greased and floured. Put the mixture into pan and press down firmly. Bake at 325° for about 30 minutes or until lightly browned. Remove from oven and cool for about 10 minutes (no longer). Cut into squares. *Children just love them!*

Robert Olufs, Branch No. 4928, Kenosha, WI

FUDGE NOUGATS

2 c. sugar
1 c. evaporated milk
1 stick margarine
1 c. chocolate chips
¾ c. flour

1 c. graham cracker crumbs
¾ c. chopped English walnuts
1 tsp. vanilla
45 walnut halves

Combine sugar, milk and margarine in a 3 quart heavy saucepan. Bring to a full rolling boil, stirring constantly. Boil for 10 minutes over medium heat, stirring occasionally. Remove. Blend in remaining ingredients, except walnut halves. Spread in a buttered 8x12 inch baking dish. Immediately top with walnut halves in 5 rows of 9. When cool, cut into 45 squares.

Mrs. Robert Bishop, Branch No. 441, Bloomington, IL

LUSCIOUS APRICOT BARS

⅔ c. dried apricots
½ c. butter
¼ c. sugar
1 c. flour
⅓ c. flour
½ tsp. baking powder

¼ tsp. salt
1 c. brown sugar, packed
2 eggs, well beaten
½ tsp. vanilla
½ c. nuts
Powdered sugar

Cover apricots with water and boil for 10 minutes. Drain. Cool and chop. Mix butter, granulated sugar and 1 cup flour. Pack in 8 inch square greased pan. Bake for 25 minutes. Sift ⅓ cup flour, baking powder and salt. Beat brown sugar into eggs. Add flour mixture. Mix in vanilla, nuts and apricots. Spread over baked layer and bake for 30 minutes. Cool and cut.

Norma McKinnis, Branch No. 2568, Fredericktown, MO

O HENRY BARS

⅔ c. margarine
4 c. uncooked oats
1 c. brown sugar
½ c. light corn syrup

3 tsp. vanilla
1 (6 oz.) pkg. chocolate chips
⅔ c. peanut butter

Cream margarine. Stir in oats, sugar, syrup, and vanilla. Spread mixture in 9x13 inch pan. Bake in a 350° oven for 15 minutes (no longer). Cool. In saucepan, melt chocolate chips and peanut butter. Spread over cooled bars. Refrigerate until cool. Cut into bars. Makes 2 dozen.

Arvalla Schmiege, Branch No. 4374, Chesaning, MI

HEATH BARS

1½ c. brown sugar
¾ c. white sugar
1½ tsp. vanilla
2 eggs

1½ tsp. baking soda
1½ c. buttermilk
5 or 6 Heath bars
¾ c. nuts

Mix first 3 ingredients until like corn meal. Take out ¾ cup crumbs. To rest of crumbs, add rest of ingredients. Put into 9x13 inch greased pan. In other bowl, mix rest of crumbs, chopped Heath bars, and nuts (chopped). Put on top of cake mixture. Bake at 350° for 30 to 40 minutes.

Virginia Heczko, Branch No. 5691, Ironwood, MI

RASPBERRY CREME SQUARES

1¼ c. graham cracker crumbs
¼ c. sugar
½ c. margarine
2 c. powdered sugar
¼ c. margarine, softened

3 oz. cream cheese, softened
½ tsp. vanilla
¼ c. raspberry preserves
1 oz. unsweetened chocolate, melted

In medium bowl, stir all crust ingredients (first 3) together. Press into bottom of 9 inch square pan. Refrigerate for 15 minutes.

In a small mixer bowl, combine all filling ingredients. Beat at medium speed, scraping bowl often, until light and fluffy (3 to 4 minutes). Spread over crust. Spread preserves over filling. Swirl with knife. Drizzle with melted chocolate. Cover and refrigerate until firm (2 to 3 hours). Cut into squares. Store refrigerated. Yield: About 4 dozen.

Marian Beske, Branch No. 1018, Fergus Falls, MN

GOOEY CLUSTERS BARS

1½ c. flour
1½ c. quick cooking oats
1 c. packed brown sugar
¾ tsp. baking soda
¼ tsp. salt
1 egg
½ c. margarine or butter

1 c. flaked coconut
1 (6 oz.) pkg. chocolate chips
1 (12.25 oz.) jar caramel flavored topping
2 c. Clusters cereal
2 Tbsp. margarine or butter

Heat oven to 350°. Grease 13x9x2 inch pan. Mix flour, oats, brown sugar, baking soda, salt, and egg. Stir in ½ cup margarine with fork until mixture is crumbled mixture in pan. Bake for 15 minutes.

Sprinkle with coconut, then with chocolate chips. Drizzle with caramel topping. Mix remaining crumbly mixture and the cereal. Cut 2 tablespoons margarine. Sprinkle over top. Press with fork. Bake until golden. Brown for 20 to 25 minutes. Loosen edges from sides of pan. Cool completely. Cut into bars. Makes 54 bars.

High altitude: Increase first bake time to 17 minutes and second bake time to 25 minutes.

Jane Bach, Branch No. 3107, Loveland, CO

ROCKY ROAD CRISPY BARS

¾ c. chunky peanut butter
⅓ c. light corn syrup
3 Tbsp. sugar
2¼ c. Rice Krispies
1 (12 oz.) pkg. semi-sweet
    chocolate pieces

½ c. light corn syrup
¼ c. sugar
¼ c. margarine
2 c. Rice Krispies
1½ c. small marshmallows
½ c. chopped peanuts

In a medium saucepan, combine peanut butter, ⅓ cup corn syrup and 3 tablespoons sugar. Cook over low heat till peanut butter is melted, stirring constantly. Stir in the 2¼ cups cereal until well coated. Spread the peanut butter-cereal mixture in square 8x8 inch pan, pressing evenly. Set aside.

In the same saucepan, combine chocolate pieces, the remaining corn syrup and sugar, and the margarine. Cook over low heat till chocolate and margarine are melted, stirring constantly. Stir in the 2 cups cereal and marshmallows till well coated. Spread the chocolate-cereal mixture evenly on top of peanut butter-cereal layer. Sprinkle with peanuts. Cool.

Connie Davis, Branch No. 3107, Loveland, CO

MICROWAVE DREAM BARS
(Microwave)

1 c. crushed graham crackers
    (plain)
1 (6 oz.) pkg. chocolate chips
1 (15 oz.) can sweetened
    condensed milk

1 c. coconut
½ c. chopped nuts

Combine all ingredients and place in an 8x8 inch square pan. Bake for 8 minutes in microwave on HIGH, turning ¼ turn every 2 minutes. Cool and cut into bars.

Sharon Geiger, Branch No. 5844, Columbia City, IN

APRICOT BARS
(Microwave)

½ c. butter
1 c. flour
1 c. oats
⅔ c. brown sugar, packed

¾ tsp. ginger
¼ tsp. salt
¾ c. apricot preserves
½ tsp. vanilla

In medium microwavable bowl, heat butter on HIGH for 45 to 60 seconds or until melted. Add flour, oats, brown sugar, ginger, and salt. With fork, mix until crumbly. Reserve 1 cup of topping. Press remaining crumbs in 8x8 inch baking dish. Microwave at 50% for 5 to 6 minutes or until set, rotating dish ¼ turn every 2 minutes.

In small bowl, stir preserves and vanilla until blended. Spread carefully over cooked crust to within ½ inch of edges of dish. Sprinkle reserved crumb mixture over top. Microwave on HIGH for 4 minutes or until topping is set, rotating dish ½ turn every 2 minutes. Remove from oven. Let stand for 5 minutes. Cool completely before cutting.

Cheryl Schultz, Branch No. 3107, Loveland, CO

DIABETIC KNOX-BLOX
(Low calorie)

8 oz. frozen orange juice *(unsweetened)*
3 env. Knox unflavored gelatine

Mix orange juice as directed on can. Put juice in saucepan and sprinkle the 3 envelopes of unflavored gelatine over top. Let stand for 2 minutes. Raise the juice and gelatine to a boil, stirring so gelatine won't clump together. Heat until gelatine is completely dissolved. Put in a 9x9 inch cake pan. Put in refrigerator to set.

Any unsweetened fruit juice will work!

Jeri Manke, Branch No. 5985, Midland, SD

GLAZED OATMEAL CRISPS
(Low calorie)

½ c. butter
1 c. sugar (or less)
1 egg
2 tsp. vanilla
½ tsp. baking powder
Pinch of salt
3 Tbsp. + 1 tsp. flour
1 c. oatmeal

Combine ingredients in order listed. Drop by ½ teaspoon on foil covered cookie sheet (far apart). Bake at 350° for 10 to 12 minutes.

Each cookie contains 33 calories if ½ teaspoon of dough is used.

Marilyn Vogel, Loveland, CO

RITZ CRACKER COOKIES

Crackers
Peanut butter
Almond or chocolate bark

Spread peanut butter between 2 crackers. (Graham crackers are good too.) Make like a sandwich. Melt the almond or chocolate bark in a double boiler. (Have mom help with this.) Dip the cracker sandwiches in the melted bark. Put on a piece of waxed paper to cool.

Doris Ruhs, Branch No. 3107, Loveland, CO

MONSTER COOKIES

12 eggs
2 lb. brown sugar
4 c. white sugar
1 Tbsp. vanilla
1 Tbsp. corn syrup
8 tsp. baking soda

1 lb. margarine
3 lb. peanut butter
18 c. oatmeal
1 lb. chocolate chips
1 lb. M&M's (plain)

In large bowl, beat eggs. Add remaining ingredients in order. Mix thoroughly. Use ice cream scoop to drop on ungreased cookie sheet. Bake at 350° for 12 to 15 minutes.

Myrtle Callies, Branch No. 53, Hartford, WI

NO ROLL WHITE SUGAR COOKIE

1 c. powdered sugar
1 c. sugar
¾ c. Crisco oil
½ c. Crisco
½ c. margarine
1 tsp. salt

1 tsp. baking soda
1 tsp. cream of tartar
1 tsp. vanilla
2 eggs
4 c. flour

Cream first 5 ingredients. Add rest of ingredients and mix well. Drop by teaspoon on ungreased cookie sheet about 1 inch apart. Press down with glass which has been dipped in sugar. Bake at 350° until light brown.

Myrtle Callies, Branch No. 53, Hartford, WI

CHOCOLATE CHIP COOKIES

2 c. shortening (margarine can be
    used)
1 c. white sugar
2 c. brown sugar
4 eggs
2 tsp. vanilla

2 tsp. baking soda
¼ tsp. salt
5 c. flour
1 (12 oz.) pkg. chocolate chips
1 c. nutmeats (walnuts or hickory
    nuts)

Cream shortening and sugars; add eggs and vanilla. Sift together soda, salt and flour; add. Mix in last chips and chopped nutmeats. Bake in a 350° oven for about 12 minutes. Makes 98 cookies.

Viona Buchholz, Branch No. 31, Weyauwega, WI

JOAN'S CHOCOLATE CHIP COOKIES

1½ c. brown sugar
¾ c. white sugar
1 c. shortening
½ c. margarine, softened
2 eggs
¾ tsp. baking powder

1½ tsp. baking soda
1 tsp. salt
3⅓ c. flour
2 tsp. vanilla
½ c. chopped walnuts
Chocolate chips

534

Cream sugars, shortening and margarine. Add vanilla and eggs; mix. Add dry ingredients and mix thoroughly. Add nuts and chips; mix. Roll into balls or drop from spoon onto greased cookie sheets. Bake at 375° for 10 to 12 minutes.

Joan I. Buchhop, Branch No. 1128, Webster City, IA

THE BEST CHOCOLATE CHIP COOKIES

1⅓ c. shortening
1 c. sugar
1 c. brown sugar
2 eggs
2 tsp. vanilla

3 c. flour
1 tsp. salt
1½ tsp. soda
1 (12 oz.) bag chocolate chips

Cream shortening, white sugar and brown sugar. Beat in the eggs. Add vanilla. Mix flour, salt and soda together, then add slowly. Add chocolate chips. Drop on greased cookie sheets by spoonfuls. Bake at 350° for about 8 to 10 minutes.

Jeanette Genthner, Branch No. 5844, Columbia City, IN

CHOCOLATE CHIP COOKIES

1½ c. white sugar
1½ c. brown sugar
2 c. shortening
3 eggs
3 tsp. vanilla

1½ tsp. soda
1½ tsp. salt
5 to 6 c. flour
2 c. chocolate chips

Cream first 3 ingredients. Add eggs and vanilla. Sift soda and salt with flour. Add flour and chocolate chips. Drop on cookie sheet and bake until golden brown. Bake for 10 to 12 minutes at 350°.

Marlys Gronwoldt, Branch No. 3330, Riceville, IA

JUST RIGHT CHOCOLATE CHIP COOKIES

⅔ c. butter
⅔ c. butter flavored solid
   shortening
¾ c. white sugar
¾ c. brown sugar, packed
2 eggs

2 tsp. real vanilla extract
3 c. flour
1 (3½ oz.) pkg. instant vanilla
   pudding mix
1 (12 oz.) pkg. chocolate chips

With mixer, beat shortenings together until fluffy. Add both sugars; beat until well blended. Beat in eggs and vanilla; set aside. In separate bowl, mix together flour, soda, salt, and pudding mix. Gradually add to beaten mixture, stirring well. Stir in chocolate chips. Drop by teaspoonfuls onto ungreased cookie sheet. Bake at 350° for 14 to 18 minutes. (Longer baking time yields a crunchier cookie; less time a chewy one.) Yield: 4 dozen cookies.

Julia Riedel, Branch No. 3107, Loveland, CO

ALMOND FILLED COOKIES

Almond Filling - Mix together:

1 c. finely grated almonds
½ c. sugar

1 tsp. grated lemon peel
1 egg, slightly beaten

Set aside.

Cookie Dough:

2½ c. flour (3 c. if using real
   butter)
1 Tbsp. baking powder
½ c. sugar

1 Tbsp. water
1½ c. butter or margarine
1 tsp. almond extract

Mix and roll out on a floured surface and cut circles like you would for making cut sugar cookies. (I use my biscuit cutter - 2 different diameters). Put the larger circles on a greased cookie sheet and put about a teaspoon of Almond Filling in the center of each circle, then roll out more dough and cut circles that are a little smaller in diameter than the first circles. Put these on top of the filling and seal with a beaten egg. Bake in a 350° oven for about 10 minutes until golden brown.

May put almond slice on each cookie for decoration before baking.

Nelly Straathof, Hersey, MI

WHOLE GRAIN JAM SQUARES

2 c. Quaker Oats (quick or
   old-fashioned)
1¾ c. flour
1 c. butter or margarine
1 c. firmly packed brown sugar

½ c. chopped nuts
1 tsp. cinnamon
¾ tsp. salt
½ tsp. soda
¾ c. preserves or jam

Combine all ingredients, except preserves, in large mixing bowl. Beat at low until crumbly. Reserve 2 cups of mixture; press remaining mixture into bottom of greased 13x9 inch pan. Spread preserves evenly over base. Sprinkle remaining mixture over preserves. Bake in a preheated 350° oven for 25 to 30 minutes or until golden brown. Cool. Cut into squares.

Corry McDowell, Loveland, CO

CHOCOLATE CHIP COOKIES

1 c. white sugar
1 c. brown sugar
1 c. margarine
1 c. cooking oil
1 egg
1 Tbsp. milk

1 tsp. vanilla
1 tsp. salt
1 tsp. soda
4 c. flour
1 (12 oz.) bag chocolate chips
1 c. chopped nuts (optional)

Cream together sugars, margarine and oil, then add egg, milk, salt, soda, and flour. Mix well. Fold in chocolate chips and nuts. Drop by teaspoonfuls on cookie sheet. Bake in a 350° oven for 10 to 12 minutes.

Corry McDowell, Loveland, CO

RITZ CRACKER COOKIES

1 c. dates, chopped
1 c. nuts, chopped
Ritz crackers

1 (14 oz.) can Eagle Brand
sweetened condensed milk

Mix dates and milk in double boiler. Cook until creamy. Remove from heat. Add nuts. Spread mixture onto Ritz crackers. Place on jelly roll pan and bake at 300° for 8 to 10 minutes. Frost with a cream cheese and powdered sugar icing.

These freeze well. May decorate the frosting with maraschino cherries or pecans.

Lois Koch (Mrs. Clifford Koch), Branch No. 1971, Pilger, NE

RITZ CRACKER COOKIES

50 Ritz crackers
1 can sweetened condensed milk

8 oz. dates, cut fine
½ c. nuts, chopped

Combine milk, dates and nuts. Cook over hot water in double boiler until thick. Add ½ teaspoon vanilla. Spread about 1 teaspoon filling on each Ritz cracker. Bake in a 350° oven for 8 minutes. Frost each cookie with frosting.

Frosting:

2 c. powdered sugar
4 oz. cream cheese

½ tsp. vanilla
Milk (to thin)

Spread on each cookie.

Loraine Lohrey, Branch No. 51, Markesan, WI

MOLASSES COOKIES

2 c. sugar
1½ c. shortening
½ c. molasses
2 eggs, well beaten
4 c. flour

2 tsp. ginger
2 tsp. cinnamon
¼ tsp. salt
2 tsp. soda

Mix sugar and shortening. Add eggs and molasses. Sift all dry ingredients together and add to sugar mixture. Drop from teaspoon on greased cookie sheet. Bake at 350° until done.

Mildred Woelfel, Branch No. 4899, Giddings, TX

SOFT MOLASSES COOKIES

1 c. sugar
1 c. lard
1 c. molasses
2 eggs
4½ c. flour

2 tsp. ginger
4 tsp. soda
2 tsp. cinnamon
½ tsp. salt
1 c. hot water

Blend dry ingredients. Mix sugar, lard, eggs, and molasses. Add dry ingredients alternately with hot water. Drop from spoon onto baking sheet. Bake at 375° for 10 minutes.

Norma Pecha, Branch No. 545, Mosinee, WI

MOLASSES COOKIES

¾ c. shortening
1 c. sugar
1 egg
¼ c. molasses
2 c. flour

2 tsp. baking soda
½ tsp. salt
1 tsp. cinnamon
½ tsp. ginger
½ tsp. cloves

Cream shortening and sugar. Add egg and molasses, beating well. Mix together dry ingredients and add to preceding mixture. Mix well. Chill dough. Roll in 1 inch balls, then roll in sugar. Place on greased cookie sheet. Bake at approximately 350° for 8 to 10 minutes. Yield: 6 dozen.

Connie Davis, Branch No. 3107, Loveland, CO

MOM'S MOLASSES COOKIES

2 c. sugar
1½ c. shortening
2 eggs
1 c. molasses
1 c. buttermilk
2 c. flour

2 tsp. soda
¾ tsp. salt
1 tsp. vanilla
1 tsp. cinnamon and 1 tsp. ginger
    (can be added)

Cream sugar and shortening. Add 2 eggs and molasses. Alternate milk and next 4 ingredients. Add more flour (enough to make dough firm enough to roll and cut). Bake at 350°. Watch closely as they burn easy. Makes a large batch and works well for gingerbread boy cookies.

Velma Hornickel, Branch No. 2512, Ord, NE

APPLESAUCE MOLASSES COOKIES

2 c. brown sugar, packed
1 c. white sugar
½ c. lard
1 c. margarine or butter
1 c. molasses
3 eggs
2 tsp. pumpkin pie spice
1 tsp. cinnamon

1 Tbsp. vanilla
2 c. oatmeal
3 tsp. baking powder
3 tsp. baking soda
1 c. raisins
1 c. nuts
1½ c. applesauce
6 c. flour (may need a little more)

Mix together all ingredients and chill overnight. Roll in ball and roll in sugar. Put on cookie sheet. Bake at 350° for 10 minutes. Makes about 8 dozen large size cookies.

Pam Wagner, Branch No. 3425, Morristown, MN

YUMMY SUGAR COOKIES

1 c. powdered sugar
1 c. white sugar
1 c. oleo or butter
1 c. oil
2 beaten eggs

1 tsp. vanilla
¼ tsp. salt
1 tsp. cream of tartar
1 tsp. soda
4 c. plus 2 heaping Tbsp. flour

Mix the sugars, oleo and oil in mixer bowl. Add beaten eggs, vanilla and salt. Mix cream of tartar and soda with the flour; add to first mixture. Roll in a ball or use a No. 40 ice cream dipper. Flatten with a glass dipped in sugar. Bake at 350° for 10 to 15 minutes or just slightly browned. Makes 72 cookies.

Irene Mundt, Branch No. 2143, Polk, NE

CRISP SUGAR COOKIES

1 c. butter
1 c. vegetable oil
1 c. granulated sugar
1 c. powdered sugar
1 tsp. vanilla
2 eggs

1 tsp. soda
4 c. flour
1 tsp. cream of tartar
1 tsp. salt
1 c. nutmeats (if desired)

Preheat oven to 350° to 375°. Cream oil, butter and both sugars. Add vanilla and eggs. Sift dry ingredients. Stir in and blend 1 cup nutmeats if desired. Roll 1 teaspoon dough in ball and roll in granulated sugar. Press down lightly with fork to make design. Bake for 10 to 12 minutes. Makes 8 dozen cookies.

Bernice Sheets, Branch No. 5844, Columbia City, IN

SUGAR COOKIES
(No roll)

1 c. butter
1 c. white sugar
1 c. powdered sugar
2 eggs, well beaten
1 tsp. salt

1 c. salad oil
2 tsp. vanilla
4 c. + 4 Tbsp. flour
1 tsp. soda
1 tsp. cream of tartar

Cream butter and sugars together. Add eggs. Mix well. Add salad oil and vanilla; mix well. Sift together flour, salt, soda, and cream of tartar. Mix and put in cool place for several hours. Put spoonfuls of dough on greased cookie sheet. Press flat with glass dipped in sugar. Bake at 350° for 8 to 10 minutes.

Makes a nice Christmas cookie with glass dipped in colored sugar.

Mrs. Edgar (Hilda) Littleman, Branch No. 1149, Leigh, NE

WORLD'S BEST SUGAR COOKIES

1 c. XXX sugar
1 c. white sugar*
1 c. oleo
1 c. oil
2 eggs

2 Tbsp. vanilla
3 c. flour
1 tsp. soda
¼ tsp. salt (optional)
1 tsp. cream of tartar

Cream sugars, oleo, oil, eggs, and vanilla till light and fluffy. Add sifted dry ingredients. Roll into balls or drop by teaspoon on greased cookie sheet. Flatten with a glass dipped in sugar. Bake at 325° for 8 to 10 minutes. *Very good!*

* Substitute 1 cup brown sugar for variety.

Anita R. Schmidt, Branch No. 2232, Auburn, MI

BEST EVER SUGAR COOKIE

1 c. butter
1 c. shortening
1 c. powdered sugar
1 c. granulated sugar
2 eggs
4 c. flour

1 tsp. cream of tartar
1 tsp. soda
½ tsp. salt
Flavoring (to taste - 1 tsp. vanilla
    and 1 tsp. lemon or almond)

Cream butter, shortening, sugars, and eggs. Add flour sifted with cream of tartar and soda. Blend in flavoring, using 1½ teaspoons or more of your favorite. Roll in small balls in palm of hand. Flatten on cookie sheet with glass with bottom dipped in sugar. Decorate to suit occasion. Bake for 8 to 10 minutes at 350°.

Mrs. Margaret Greiner, Branch No. 2838, Wilmot, SD

SUGAR COOKIES

½ c. butter or margarine
1 c. sugar
1 egg
½ tsp. salt

2 tsp. baking powder
2 c. flour
½ tsp. vanilla

Cream together butter and sugar. Blend in egg. Sift together dry ingredients and add to mixture. Blend in vanilla. Chill dough. Roll out thin and cut with cookie cutters. Bake on lightly greased cookie sheet at 375° for approximately 8 to 9 minutes.

Connie Davis, Branch No. 3107, Loveland, CO

EXTRA CRISP SUGAR COOKIES

1 c. butter or oleo
2 c. sugar
2 eggs
1 c. salad oil
¼ tsp. salt

1 tsp. vanilla
2 tsp. soda
5 c. flour (unsifted)
2 tsp. cream of tartar

Cream butter and sugar. Add eggs, salad oil, salt, and vanilla. Sift flour, soda and cream of tartar into bowl; add to first mixture. Mix until smooth. Drop onto a cookie sheet with a teaspoon or roll into balls and then into granulated sugar. Press down with a fork. Bake for 10 minutes in a 350° oven.

This is a large recipe and they stay nice and crisp when stored.

Donna Giermann, Branch No. 6470, Kiron, IA

SUGAR COOKIES

1 c. shortening	1 c. brown sugar
1 c. white sugar	1 egg
1 tsp. vanilla	Pinch of salt
2 tsp. soda	2 tsp. cream of tartar
2½ c. flour	

Roll in balls the size of walnut. Dip in sugar on one side. Place on baking sheet. Bake at 350° for 10 minutes. Do not flatten. They will crack.

Bernice M. Timian, Branch No. 1412, Corvallis, OR

WHITE SUGAR COOKIES

3 c. flour	1 c. butter or margarine
⅛ tsp. salt	2 eggs
½ tsp. baking powder	1 c. white sugar
½ tsp. baking soda	1 tsp. vanilla

Mix together flour, salt, baking powder, and baking soda with a pastry blender like a pie crust.

In a separate bowl, beat eggs, sugar, and vanilla. Mix the 2 mixtures together. Roll thin; cut and bake in a 350° oven for 8 minutes. Makes about 4 dozen.

Frosting:

4 Tbsp. margarine	Maraschino juice (enough to make
1 c. powdered sugar	creamy) or 1 to 2 tsp. milk

Ramona Unke, Branch No. 1073, Crookston, MN

SUGAR COOKIES

½ c. sugar	1 tsp. salt
1 c. shortening	4 tsp. baking powder
3 eggs	1 tsp. vanilla
4 c. flour	½ tsp. lemon flavoring

Cream sugar and shortening together; add eggs and beat until fluffy. Add flour, salt, baking powder, vanilla, and lemon flavoring. Mix together well. Roll out and cut into desired shapes. Bake at 375° for 10 minutes.

Mildred Bura, Branch No. 2049, Emporia, KS

SNAPPY SUGAR CRISPS

½ c. margarine
¾ c. sugar
1 egg
1 tsp. vanilla

1½ c. sifted flour
¼ tsp. baking powder
½ tsp. salt

Melt margarine in 1 to 1½ quart or larger pan. Add sugar, egg, and vanilla into same pan; beat until fluffy. Blend in dry ingredients and chill dough for 15 to 30 minutes in refrigerator. Bake at 350° for 12 to 15 minutes.

Chocolate Version: Melt ½ cup chocolate chips with margarine

Diamonds: Roll out on floured cookie sheet and mark with pastry wheel or knife. Snap apart after baking.

Roll Cookies: Take out of refrigerator only enough dough as you can handle fast. Roll out and cut shapes with cookie cutter.

Cinnamon Fans: With edge of teaspoon, cut 5 gashes almost to center of 1 inch balls and flatten each section with back of spoon. Sprinkle with cinnamon and sugar.

Refrigerator Cookies: Chill 2 rolls of dough in wax paper. Slice thin, bake, cool, frost and sprinkle.

Else Eickstedt, Branch No. 6083, Lander, WY

SOUR CREAM SUGAR COOKIES

Sift together:

5 c. flour
½ tsp. salt

3 tsp. baking powder
1 tsp. baking soda

Cream together:

1 c. shortening
3 eggs
1 tsp. vanilla

2 c. sour cream
2 c. sugar

Mix together and chill overnight. Roll on floured board and cut out. Bake at 350° until edges turn lightly browned (10 to 12 minutes).

This dough also works well in a cookie press.

Branch No. 628, Farmington, MO

LEMON SUGAR COOKIES

3 c. unsifted flour
2 tsp. baking powder
½ tsp. salt
2 c. sugar
1 c. shortening

2 eggs
¼ c. ReaLemon lemon juice from
    concentrate
Additional sugar

542

Preheat oven to 350°. Stir together flour, baking powder and salt; set aside. In large mixer bowl, beat sugar and shortening until fluffy; beat in eggs. Stir in dry ingredients, then ReaLemon. Mix well. Chill for 2 hours. Shape into 1 ¼ inch balls. Roll in additional sugar. Place 2 inches apart on greased baking sheets; flatten. Bake for 8 to 10 minutes or until lightly browned.

Judy Schmidter, Branch No. 72, Burlington, WI

CHOCOLATE CHIP OATMEAL COOKIES

⅔ c. white sugar
¾ c. brown sugar
1½ c. flour
2 c. oatmeal
1 c. shortening

2 eggs
1 tsp. soda
1 tsp. salt
1 tsp. vanilla
1 (6 oz.) pkg. chocolate chips

Cream shortening and sugars. Add eggs and beat well. Add dry ingredients and vanilla. Add chocolate chips and stir. Drop by teaspoon and bake for 10 to 12 minutes in a 350° oven.

Betty J. Rosvold, Branch No. 239, Brainerd, MN

CHOCOLATE BIT OATMEAL COOKIES

1 c. shortening
¾ c. light brown sugar
¾ c. white sugar
2 eggs
1 tsp. hot water
1 tsp. vanilla

1 (12 oz.) pkg. chocolate bits
2 c. quick oatmeal
1 c. chopped nutmeats (optional)
1½ c. sifted flour
1 tsp. baking soda
½ tsp. salt

Cream shortening and sugar. Add eggs, one at a time, and mix well. Add water and mix well. Add vanilla and mix well. Stir in chocolate bits and oatmeal. Sift flour, salt and soda together; stir into creamed mixture until well mixed. Bake on greased cookie sheet for 8 to 10 minutes at 375°. You can double.

Helen Heine, Branch No. 5124, Alma, MI

COWBOY COOKIES

2 c. sifted flour
½ tsp. baking powder
1 tsp. soda
½ tsp. salt
1 c. shortening (Crisco)
1 c. brown sugar, firmly packed

1 c. granulated sugar
2 eggs
1 tsp. vanilla
2 c. rolled oats ("quick" type)
1 (6 oz.) pkg. semi-sweet
   chocolate chips

Sift together flour, baking powder, soda, and salt; set aside. Blend together shortening, brown sugar and granulated sugar. Add eggs and vanilla. Beat until light and fluffy. Add flour mixture and mix well. Add rolled oats. (Dough will be crumbly.) Drop by teaspoonfuls onto greased cookie sheet. Bake for 15 minutes at 350°F.

Mrs. Helen Genter, Branch No. 283, Leavenworth, KS

BANANA OATMEAL COOKIES

2 c. flour
1 tsp. cinnamon
¼ tsp. nutmeg
½ tsp. salt
1 tsp. baking powder
¼ tsp. baking soda

1 c. sugar
1 c. mashed ripe bananas
2 eggs
1 c. shortening
2 c. rolled oats
1 c. chocolate chips (optional)

Sift together dry ingredients into large mixing bowl. Add shortening, eggs and bananas. Beat until smooth. Fold in oats and chocolate chips. Drop on greased cookie sheet. Bake at 350° for 10 to 15 minutes. These cookies are best if not over-baked.

This is a good way to use the overripe bananas.
Shirley Hoffman, Branch No. 3835, Rolla, ND

BANANA-OATMEAL CHOCOLATE CHIP COOKIES

1¼ c. sifted flour
2½ tsp. baking powder
¾ tsp. salt
⅔ c. shortening
1 c. sugar
2 eggs

1 c. mashed bananas (2 large)
1 tsp. vanilla
2½ c. quick rolled oats
1 (6 oz.) pkg. semi-sweet
   chocolate bits

Sift together flour, baking powder and salt; set aside. Cream shortening and sugar; beat in eggs thoroughly, one at a time, then bananas and vanilla. Add sifted dry ingredients and beat until combined. Stir in rolled oats and chocolate bits. Drop by teaspoon a few inches apart on ungreased cookie sheets. Bake at 375° for 8 to 10 minutes. Makes approximately 4 dozen.
Hollee Milz, Branch No. 2295, Allen Park, MI

CARAMEL OATMEAL COOKIES

2 c. brown sugar
2 c. flour
2 eggs
1 c. melted butter
4 c. oatmeal

1 c. coconut
1 tsp. soda
1 tsp. baking powder
Dash of salt

Melt butter and mix with brown sugar. Add eggs. Dissolve soda in a little water and add. Stir in coconut. Mix baking powder and salt into flour; add. Stir in oatmeal. Drop walnut size portions onto cookie sheet and bake for 10 minutes at 350°.
Kathleen Eschenbacher, Branch No. 2232, Auburn, MI

OATMEAL COOKIES ("THE BEST")

3 eggs, well beaten	2½ c. flour
1 c. raisins	1 tsp. salt
1 tsp. vanilla extract	1 tsp. ground cinnamon
1 c. butter	2 tsp. baking soda
1 c. brown sugar	2 c. oatmeal*
1 c. white sugar	¾ c. chopped pecans

Combine eggs, raisins and vanilla; let stand for 1 hour, covered with plastic wrap. Cream together butter and sugars. Add flour, salt, cinnamon, and soda to sugar mixture. Mix well. Blend in egg-raisin mixture, oatmeal, wheat germ, and chopped nuts. Dough will be stiff. Drop by teaspoons onto ungreased cookie sheets or roll into small balls and flatten slightly on cookie sheet. Bake at 350° for 10 to 12 minutes. Makes 6 dozen.

* Substitute ½ cup wheat germ for more healthful cookies.

Mary Brelfenthim, Branch No. 64, Elkhorn, WI

EMMA'S OATMEAL COOKIES

1 c. sugar	½ c. butter
½ c. shortening	2 eggs
½ tsp. salt	1 tsp. cinnamon
2 c. flour	2 c. oatmeal
1 c. raisins	1 c. nuts, chopped
1 tsp. vanilla	1 tsp. soda

Simmer raisins in water just enough to cover plus 3 tablespoons sugar. Boil until tender. Save ½ cup liquid. Sift flour, salt, and cinnamon. Cream sugar, shortening and butter, then beat in eggs. Add soda to liquid from raisins. Add alternately with dry ingredients. Add raisins and drop by teaspoon on cookie sheet. Bake for 15 minutes at 375°.

Velma Besser, Branch No. 2343, Ogilvie, MN

ICEBOX OATMEAL COOKIES

½ c. butter	1 tsp. soda
½ c. lard	½ tsp. salt
1 c. sugar	1½ c. flour
1 c. brown sugar	½ c. chopped nutmeats
2 eggs, well beaten	3 c. quick cooking oatmeal
1 tsp. vanilla	½ c. shredded coconut

Mix preceding ingredients. Roll into 2 long rolls. Chill in refrigerator. Slice and bake at 350° for about 10 to 15 minutes.

AAL Branch No. 1206, Crosstown, MO

HONEY LEBKUKEN - CHRISTMAS COOKIES

2 c. honey
2 c. sugar
2 eggs
4½ Tbsp. vinegar
1½ Tbsp. soda
¼ lb. almonds

¼ lb. walnuts
¼ lb. citron
½ tsp. cinnamon
½ tsp. cloves
Flour (to stiffen - about 5½ c.)

Mix as ingredients listed. Roll on floured board about ⅛ inch thick and cut into shapes as you prefer (round or oblong).

Frosting:

2 eggs   Powdered sugar (to thicken)

Place a teaspoon of frosting on top of each cookie and bake.

This is my mother's (Louise Leinberger) recipe.

Clara Pfannes, Branch No. 2232, Auburn, MI

LEBKUCHEN

2 c. brown sugar
1 c. white sugar
1½ c. shortening
2 c. molasses
5 or 6 eggs
¾ lb. walnuts, chopped
1 c. mixed fruit
2 lb. raisins, ground

1 lb. dates, ground
1 tsp. vanilla
Anise (optional)
2 tsp. soda
3 tsp. baking powder
1 tsp. salt
½ c. sour cream or ¾ c. sour milk
About 7 c. flour

Let stand overnight in refrigerator. Roll out on floured board about ⅛ inch thick. Beat 1 egg and brush each cookie. Put half of a blanched almond on top of each cookie. Bake in a moderate oven for 10 minutes.

This is my mother-in-law's (Hadwig Pfannes) recipe.

Clara Pfannes, Branch No. 2232, Auburn, MI

HONEY COOKIES

1½ pt. honey
1½ c. brown sugar
Dash of salt
½ tsp. cinnamon

1 c. chopped pecans or almonds
1 tsp. baking powder
Flour (enough for a very stiff
    dough)

Heat honey (but not boiling), then cool a little. Add rest of ingredients and mix well. Roll out on floured board and cut with cookie cutter or place by teaspoonful on greased cookie sheet and flatten with a floured glass. Bake at 325° until golden brown with edges slightly darker. Cookies will be chewy.

History: My great-grandparents, August and Carolin Weiss, operated the first cotton gin operated by steam near Salem, Texas, in Washington County. They were among the first German settlers in that area. Money was scarce; however, there were always bees and native pecans. Consequently, this recipe was a favorite.
Ben H. Scholl, Branch No. 2150, Tomball, TX

GRANDMA'S HONEY COOKIES

1 c. brown sugar	¼ tsp. ginger
1 c. white sugar	½ tsp. cinnamon
2 c. shortening	1 tsp. salt
1 c. honey	2 Tbsp. baking soda
2 c. buttermilk	8 c. flour

Mix all ingredients together and chill in refrigerator. Roll dough for cutout cookies. Bake on greased cookie sheet at 350° for about 10 minutes.
Mrs. June Werth, Branch No. 965, North Tonawanda, NY

HONEY COOKIES

1 c. honey (or ¾ c. honey and ¼ c. molasses)	¼ tsp. salt
	1 tsp. vanilla
1 c. sugar	1 tsp. mace
3 eggs	½ tsp. cloves
2 tsp. soda	3¾ to 4 c. flour

Mix preceding ingredients in the order given. Roll out (not too thin). Bake for 10 to 12 minutes at 350° until golden brown. Frost with powdered sugar frosting.

Can use Christmas cutouts and sprinkle with colored sugar. Can also be eaten unfrosted. A soft, chewy cookie. Do not overbake.
Mildred Melchert, Branch No. 3425, Morristown, MN

NO BAKE CHOCOLATE COOKIES

2 c. sugar	1 tsp. vanilla
½ c. cocoa	3 c. oatmeal
½ c. oleo	½ c. coconut
½ c. milk	½ c. raisins (optional)
½ c. crunchy peanut butter	½ c. walnuts, chopped (optional)

Combine sugar, cocoa, oleo, and milk in heavy saucepan. Bring to a boil over medium heat. Boil for 1 minute. Remove from heat; add peanut butter and vanilla. Mix thoroughly. Add remaining ingredients. Let set for 5 minutes. Drop by teaspoonfuls onto waxed paper. Cool.
Joyce Lidke

CHOCOLATE DROP COOKIES

1½ c. brown sugar
½ c. shortening
2 eggs
½ c. milk
2 c. flour
1 tsp. soda

1 tsp. baking powder
½ tsp. salt
½ tsp. vanilla
1 (1 oz.) sq. unsweetened
   chocolate, melted

Frosting:

3 c. powdered sugar
½ c. milk
¼ c. soft margarine
2 sq. unsweetened chocolate,
   melted

2 tsp. vanilla
½ tsp. salt

Cream together sugar, shortening, and eggs. Add milk and mix, then mix in dry ingredients. Mix in vanilla and chocolate last. Bake on greased pan at 350°. When cool, frost.

Sue Folken, Branch No. 1149, Leigh, NE

CHOCOLATE DROP COOKIES

1 c. sugar
½ c. shortening
1 beaten egg
2 Tbsp. cocoa
¾ c. milk

1 tsp. vanilla
2 c. flour
2 tsp. baking powder
½ c. chopped raisins or nutmeats

Cream together sugar and shortening. Add beaten egg, cocoa, milk, and vanilla; mix together thoroughly. Sift together baking powder and flour; add to mixture. Add raisins or nutmeats and beat well together. Drop by teaspoon on greased cookie sheets. Do not flatten. Bake at 350° for 8 to 10 minutes.

When cool, may be eaten plain or frosted with a chocolate powdered sugar icing. Makes about 4 dozen cookies.

Maxine A. Ernst, Branch No. 2320, Fowler, MI

SOUR CREAM COOKIES

2 eggs
2 c. sugar
1 c. sour cream
1 c. oleo

2 tsp. soda
½ tsp salt
1 Tbsp. vanilla
4 to 4½ c. flour

Cream sugar and oleo. Mix soda and sour cream; add to sugar mixture. Add eggs and vanilla, then flour and salt. Refrigerate overnight or until dough is cold and stiff. Roll out (not too thin) and cut into desired shapes. Bake for 10 minutes at 350°.

These are very good frosted.

Wanda Ogg, Branch No. 6940, Harrison, MI

548

CHRISTMAS WREATH COOKIES

1 c. oleo
1 c. sugar
2 c. flour

½ tsp. salt
2 c. hazelnuts, ground
Red and green candied cherries

Cream oleo. Add sugar. Add nuts. Sift flour and salt; add slowly to creamed mixture and mix well. Dust board with flour; cover dough with wax paper and roll out to ⅛ inch. Cut 1½ inch rings with a small doughnut cutter or a wreath cutter. Lift rings with spatula. Place on greased and lightly floured pans. Place ribbon of meringue (see following for recipe) around ring. Put 1 small piece of red cherry and 2 of green cherries to represent a bow. Bake at 300° for about 12 to 15 minutes. Should be very light in color.

Meringue:

2 egg whites, stiffly beaten

½ c. sugar

Branch No. 5684, Lafayette, IN

GERMAN PEPPERNUTS

2 c. sifted flour
¾ tsp. cardamon
¾ tsp. baking powder
¾ tsp. allspice
¾ tsp. salt
¾ tsp. mace

¾ tsp. soda
¼ tsp. black pepper
⅓ tsp. ground anise seed
1 c. honey
1 egg
3 Tbsp. shortening

Sift dry ingredients; heat the honey. *(Do not boil.)* Add shortening and cool. Beat in the egg; stir in dry ingredients just until blended. Let dough stand to cool for 10 minutes to stiffen enough to handle. Shape into balls. Place on greased cookie sheet (make small balls). Bake at 350° for 12 to 13 minutes. Cool cookies, then frost and store in airtight container for a week to ripen.

Frosting - Combine:

1 egg white
2 tsp. honey

¼ tsp. anise seed

Gradually add ½ cup powdered sugar; beat until smooth.
St. Peter's Ev. Lutheran Church, Moltke Township, Gibbon, MN

DROP PINEAPPLE COOKIES

1 c. brown sugar
½ c. Crisco
2 c. flour
¾ c. drained crushed pineapple

1 c. chopped nuts
1 egg
1 tsp. baking powder
¼ tsp. baking soda

Mix preceding ingredients. Drop cookies by teaspoon on cookie baking sheet. Bake at 350°. Ice cookies while hot with powdered sugar icing.
Edith Graham, Branch No. 5915, Lanse, PA

RAISIN SPICE DROPS

1¼ c. flour
1 tsp. cinnamon
½ tsp. baking soda
½ tsp. salt
¼ tsp. nutmeg
¾ c. margarine, softened
⅔ c. brown sugar, firmly packed

⅔ c. granulated sugar
2 eggs
1 tsp. vanilla
2½ c. Quaker Oats (quick or
old-fashioned, uncooked)
⅔ c. raisins
½ c. chopped nuts

Heat oven to 350°F. Grease cookie sheet. In medium bowl, combine flour, cinnamon, soda, salt, and nutmeg. In large bowl, beat together margarine and sugars until light and fluffy. Blend in eggs and vanilla. Add dry ingredients and mix well. Stir in oats, raisins and nuts. Drop by rounded teaspoonfuls onto prepared cookie sheets. Bake for 8 minutes or until light golden brown. Cool for 1 minute on cookie sheet; remove to wire cooling rack. Makes about 4½ dozen cookies.

Leona Metcalfe, Branch No. 3107, Loveland, CO

GUMDROP COOKIES

1 c. brown sugar
1 c. butter or oleo
3 c. flour
1 c. gumdrops, cut small
¼ tsp. salt
1 tsp. vanilla

1 c. white sugar
3 eggs
1 c. oatmeal
1 tsp. baking soda
½ c. coconut (optional)

Mix all the ingredients together. Drop by spoonful on an ungreased cookie sheet. Bake at 350° for 7 to 10 minutes or until they are golden brown.

I use red and green jellies at Christmas time.

Mary Sebade, Branch No. 6537, Emerson, NE

DATE FILLED COOKIES

½ c. margarine
2 c. brown sugar
2 well beaten eggs
1 tsp. vanilla
3½ c. flour

1 tsp. baking soda
1 tsp. cream of tartar
½ tsp. salt
2 Tbsp. water

Thoroughly cream margarine and sugar. Add eggs and vanilla; beat well. Sift dry ingredients. Add dry ingredients alternately with water to the creamed mixture. Mix well.

Date-Nut Filling:

1 lb. dates, pitted and chopped
½ c. brown sugar

½ c. water
½ to ¾ c. finely chopped nuts

Combine dates, brown sugar and water. Cook until thick. Add nuts.

On a greased cookie sheet, put about 1 teaspoon of mixture for each cookie. Take a spoon and make a small hole, then put about a teaspoon of date mixture on top. Add about a spoon of cookie dough on top. If it isn't covered, that's okay. It will all blend in. Bake at 350° for about 10 minutes or until light brown. Yield: Approximately 5 dozen.

Connie Davis, Branch No. 3107, Loveland, CO

DATE BALLS

1 c. brown sugar	1 c. dates
1 egg	1 c. nuts
½ c. oleo	2 c. Rice Krispies

Mix sugar, egg, dates, and nuts in saucepan; boil until thick. Take from stove and add Rice Krispies. Let stand for a few minutes to cool. Roll into small balls and roll in coconut to cover balls.

Kathleen Eschenbacher, Branch No. 2232, Auburn, MI

DATE STICKS

1 pkg. dates, cut small (1 c.)	1 c. flour
1 c. chopped nuts	1 tsp. baking powder
1 c. sugar	1 tsp. vanilla
1 tsp. salt	1 c. butter
3 eggs, separated	Powdered sugar (to roll cookies in)

Cream butter. Add sugar, egg yolks and dry ingredients. Stir to blend. Add nuts and dates. Beat egg whites stiff. Fold in beaten whites and vanilla. Bake in a greased and floured 8½ x 8½ inch square pan at 350° for 25 minutes. When cool, cut into 1 inch squares and roll in powdered sugar.

These cookies may be baked ahead of time and frozen.

Larry Bernhardt, Branch No. 1995, Hudson, CO

DATE PINWHEELS

1 c. brown sugar	Pinch of salt
1 c. white sugar	1 tsp. soda
1 c. shortening	1 tsp. vanilla
3 eggs, beaten	4 c. flour

Cream sugars and shortening; add 3 beaten eggs. Mix well. Add salt, soda, vanilla, and flour. Mix well. Chill for a couple hours or longer.

Filling:

1 lb. dates, chopped	½ c. water
½ c. sugar	Chopped nuts (optional)

Put chopped dates, sugar and water in saucepan; cook on top of stove until soft and spreadable.

Roll out dough quite thin. Spread with filling and nuts. Roll up like jelly roll. Chill. Slice ¼ inch thick. Bake at 375° for 12 minutes.

Kendra Victor, Branch No. 6537, Emerson, NE

GERMAN FRUITCAKE COOKIES

¾ c. raisins
¾ c. prunes
½ c. candied cherries
½ c. walnuts
½ c. sugar
½ c. butter
½ c. coffee

½ c. Gold Label molasses
2 eggs
1½ tsp. soda
¼ tsp. salt
½ tsp. cinnamon
¼ tsp. nutmeg
3¼ c. sifted flour

Grind together fruits and nuts. Combine sugar, butter, coffee, and molasses in 3 quart saucepan. Simmer for 5 minutes. Cool. Blend in eggs, soda, salt, and spices. Stir in flour and fruit mixture. Chill for at least 4 hours. Shape into 1 inch balls with floured hands. Bake on greased sheets at 350° for 15 to 18 minutes. Dip warm cookies into glaze.

Glaze:

1 c. sugar
½ c. water

¼ tsp. cream of tartar
½ c. sifted powdered sugar

Combine sugar, water and cream of tartar in small saucepan. Boil until clear. Cool and stir in powdered sugar.

Betty Schmidt, Branch No. 483, Lincoln, IL

GIANT FUDGIES

½ c. butter
¾ c. sugar
1 large egg
1 tsp. vanilla
1 c. flour

½ c. cocoa
½ tsp. soda
1 c. chocolate chips
1 c. pecans

Mix butter and sugar until well blended. Add egg and vanilla. Mix cocoa, flour and soda together; add to creamed mixture. Fold into creamed mixture, pecans and chips. Drop by ¼ cup on greased cookie sheet 2 inches apart. Flatten to 3 ½ inch rounds. Bake at 375° for 8 to 10 minutes. Cool.

Donna Phillips, Branch No. 2512, Ord, NE

DOUBLE DUTCH PIZZA COOKIE

¾ c. butter (oleo)
1 c. sugar
1 egg
1 tsp. vanilla
1½ c. flour
¼ c. cocoa

½ tsp. baking soda
¼ tsp. salt
¾ c. M&M's
½ c. nuts
¼ c. miniature marshmallows
¼ c. coconut (optional)

With mixer, cream butter and sugar. Add vanilla and egg. Combine dry ingredients and mix into this mixture. Fold in ½ of the candy and ⅓ cup nuts. Lightly grease pizza pan and cover with foil. Spread dough to within ½ inch of edge. Sprinkle with remaining nuts, candy and marshmallows. Bake for 18 to 20 minutes at 350°. Cool for 10 minutes in pan and then slide onto a plate.

Branch No. 2471, Yankton, SD

SNICKERDOODLE COOKIES

1½ c. sugar
1 c. margarine
2 eggs
¼ tsp. salt

2 tsp. cream of tartar
2¾ c. flour
1 tsp. vanilla
1 tsp. soda

Mix all ingredients together. Shape into balls and roll mixture into a mixture of 2 tablespoons sugar and 2 teaspoons cinnamon. Bake at 400° on ungreased cookie sheet for 10 minutes.

Charmaine Bradley, Branch No. 545, Mosinee, WI

HOLIDAY SURPRISES

1 c. butter
½ c. sifted confectioners sugar
1½ tsp. vanilla
2 c. sifted all-purpose flour

½ tsp. salt
1 c. rolled oats (quick or
     old-fashioned, uncooked)
Candied cherries, pecans or dates

Beat butter until creamy. Gradually beat in sugar. Blend in vanilla. Sift together flour and salt. Add to creamed mixture; mix well. Stir in oats. Shape a small amount of dough to form 1 inch ball around cut candied cherries, pecans or dates.

Place on ungreased cooky sheets. Bake in preheated slow oven (325°F.) for 25 to 30 minutes. While warm, sift confectioners sugar generously over cookies. Makes 4 dozen.

Arlyle Utech, Branch No. 2151, Merrill, WI

CHERRY COCONUT SOUR CREAM DROPS

½ c. margarine
½ c. shortening
1 c. sugar
3 eggs
½ c. sour cream
½ c. chopped nuts

3¼ c. flour
1 tsp. baking powder
½ tsp. soda
1 c. coconut
1 c. chopped, drained maraschino
     cherries*

Cream margarine, shortening and sugar. Add eggs and sour cream. Mix well (may look curdled). Stir in dry ingredients, nuts, coconut, and cherries. Bake in a 350° oven until bottoms are light brown and centers are barely firm to touch. (Do not overbake.)

* A combination of red and green cherries may be used at Christmas time.

Rebecca J. Ault, Branch No. 5433, Newcomerstown, OH

CRANBERRY COOKIES

1 c. sugar
¾ c. packed brown sugar
½ c. softened butter or margarine
¼ c. milk
2 Tbsp. orange juice
1 egg
3 c. flour

1 tsp. baking powder
½ tsp. salt
¼ tsp. baking soda
2½ c. coarsely chopped cranberries
1 c. chopped nuts

Heat oven to 375°. Mix sugars and butter. Stir in milk, orange juice and egg. Stir in remaining ingredients, except Brown Butter Glaze. Drop by rounded teaspoonfuls about 2 inches apart onto greased cookie sheet. Bake until light brown, 10 to 15 minutes. Cool. Spread with glaze. Makes about 5½ dozen cookies.

Brown Butter Glaze:

⅓ c. margarine or butter
2 c. powdered sugar

1½ tsp. vanilla
2 to 4 Tbsp. hot water

Heat butter over low heat until golden brown; cool slightly. Stir in powdered sugar and vanilla. Beat in 2 to 4 tablespoons hot water until smooth and of desired consistency.

Doreen Preuss, Branch No. 5016, Laguna Hills, CA

BUFFALO CHIP COOKIES

1 c. margarine
1 c. shortening
2 c. brown sugar
2 c. sugar
4 eggs
2 tsp. vanilla
4 c. flour

2 tsp. baking powder
2 tsp. soda
2 c. oatmeal
2 c. corn flakes
6 oz. chocolate chips
1 c. coconut
1 c. pecan pieces

Heat oven to 350°. Cream butter, shortening and sugars. Add eggs and vanilla. Add flour, baking powder and soda. Stir in oatmeal, corn flakes, chips, coconut, and nuts. Drop batter 3 inches apart on ungreased cookie sheet. Flatten slightly. Bake for 15 minutes. Makes 30 (5 inch) cookies or around 7 dozen smaller ones.

Branch No. 3207, Mt. Vernon, WA

CRACKER JACK COOKIES

2 sticks (1 c.) butter or margarine,
    softened
1 c. granulated sugar
1 c. lightly packed brown sugar
2 eggs
2 tsp. vanilla

1½ c. unsifted flour
1 tsp. baking powder
1 tsp. soda
2 c. old-fashioned oatmeal
2 c. Rice Krispies
1 c. coconut

Thoroughly cream together butter and sugars. Add eggs and vanilla. Mix well. Sift together flour, baking powder and soda. Combine flour and egg mixture. Add oatmeal, coconut and cereal. Mix well. Drop by heaping teaspoonfuls about 2 inches apart onto a greased baking sheet. Bake at 375° for about 10 minutes. Check in 7 to 8 minutes. Remove from baking sheet immediately. Makes about 6 dozen cookies.

Henrietta Ohlenhopp, Trinity Lutheran, AAL Branch No. 2248, Akron, CO

CHOCOLATE COOKIES

1 (12 oz.) pkg. Nestle chocolate
    chips

1 can Eagle Brand milk
2 c. Grape-Nuts

Melt chocolate chips. Stir in milk and Grape-Nuts. Drop by teaspoonfuls on wax paper. Cool.

Mrs. Shirley Wills, Branch No. 1182, Perryville, MO

CHERRY BALL COOKIES

2 eggs
1 c. sugar
1 tsp. almond

1 c. finely chopped walnuts
1 c. finely chopped coconut
2 jars cherries with stems

Beat eggs well. Add rest. Pour into a greased glass round baking dish. Bake at 350° for 10 minutes. Take out and stir. Bake for another 10 minutes. Take out and stir, then bake again for another 10 minutes. Stir. Have cherries drained (40 to 50). Just cool until can handle; then press a small amount around cherries. Freeze, then dip in chocolate mixture - German chocolate chips and waxes.

Margaret Labe, Branch No. 3339, Esko, MN

SALTED PEANUT COOKIES

1 c. brown sugar
1 c. white sugar
1 c. shortening (do not use
    margarine)
2 eggs
1 c. crushed corn flakes

1 c. salted peanuts
1 c. quick cooking oatmeal
2 c. flour
1 tsp. baking powder
1 tsp. soda
1 tsp. vanilla

Cream sugars with shortening. Add eggs and beat well. Stir in oatmeal, corn flakes, and peanuts. Sift dry ingredients. Add vanilla. Combine. Drop by teaspoon. Bake at 375° for 12 to 15 minutes.

Loraine Grootheius, Branch No. 2714, Ogden, UT

MEXICAN WEDDING RINGS

2 c. flour
½ tsp. salt
¾ c. shortening
¼ c. butter

½ c. powdered sugar
1 Tbsp. almond extract
½ c. chopped nuts

Sift together flour and salt. Cream shortening, butter and powdered sugar. Add dry ingredients to creamed. Blend until smooth. Add almond extract and chopped nuts. Form into 1 inch balls and place on ungreased cookie sheet for 25 minutes at 325°. Allow to cool. Roll in a small amount of powdered sugar.

Diana Stewart, Branch No. 5844, Albion, IN

GLAZED FRESH APPLE COOKIES

1 c. shortening
2⅔ c. brown sugar
2 eggs
2 tsp. soda
1 tsp. cloves
1 tsp. nutmeg
2 tsp. cinnamon

1 tsp. salt
4½ c. flour
1 c. cider
2 c. finely chopped apples (Ida
     Red, Jonathan, etc.)
1 c. raisins
1 to 2 c. nuts, chopped

Sift together flour and spices. Cream shortening and brown sugar. Add eggs, cider and chopped apples. Add dry ingredients. Fold in raisins and nuts. Drop from spoon on greased cookie sheet. Bake for 10 minutes at 375°. Glaze while hot and remove from pan.

Glaze:

1 Tbsp. butter
1½ c. powdered sugar
⅛ tsp. salt

2½ Tbsp. cider
¼ tsp. vanilla

Cream butter, sugar and salt. Stir in cider and vanilla. Can substitute orange juice or milk for cider. Don't use vanilla when using orange juice.

Phyllis Vogtmann, Branch No. 2232, Auburn, MI

PEANUT BUTTER CHOCOLATE CHUNK COOKIES

1 c. chunky peanut butter
2 Tbsp. vegetable oil
2 large eggs (room temperature)
1 (21.5 oz.) box fudge brownie mix
½ c. water

12 oz. milk chocolate, coarsely
     chopped and divided
½ c. unsalted skinless peanuts,
     divided

Preheat oven to 350°. Line a baking sheet with aluminum foil. In a medium bowl, using a hand held mixer set at low speed, beat together the peanut butter and oil for a couple of seconds, just until combined. Add eggs and beat just until combined.

In a large bowl, using a wooden spoon, stir together the brownie mix, peanut butter and water until combined. Stir in all, except for ½ cup milk chocolate and ¼ cup peanuts. One tablespoon at a time, drop the cookie dough onto prepared baking sheet, leaving at least 1 inch between cookies. Adhere several pieces each of the reserved chocolate and peanuts to the top of each cookie. Bake for 12 to 14 minutes.

Doreen Holzhueter, Branch No. 2017, Marshall, WI

CHOCOLATE PEANUT BUTTER COOKIES

½ c. margarine	2 Tbsp. cocoa
¾ c. sugar	¼ tsp. baking powder
2 eggs	2 c. small marshmallows
1 tsp. vanilla	1 c. chocolate chips
¾ c. flour	1 c. peanut butter
½ c. nuts	1½ c. Rice Krispies

Mix all ingredients, except marshmallows, chocolate chips, peanut butter, and Rice Krispies. Put in 13x9 inch pan. Bake at 350° for 15 to 20 minutes. Put marshmallows on top. Bake for 3 minutes. Cool. Melt peanut butter and chocolate. Add Rice Krispies and spread on top. Cool and cut.

Nancy Flowers, Branch No. 3436, Pico Rivera, CA

CREAM WAFERS

1 c. soft butter	2 c. flour
⅓ c. cream	

Mix butter, cream and flour together. Chill thoroughly. Roll ⅓ of dough ⅛ inch thick. Cut with a 1½ inch round cutter. Coat both sides of cookie with sugar. Continue rolling and cutting until all dough has been used. Place on ungreased baking sheet and prick each with a fork 4 times. Bake at 375° for 7 to 9 minutes. When cooled, put together with filling between 2 cookies.

Filling: Blend ¼ cup soft butter with ¾ cup powdered sugar, 1 egg yolk and 1 teaspoon vanilla. Tint with food coloring.

Rita Severinson, Branch No. 6479, Minnewaukan, ND

CINNAMON DROPS

1 c. brown sugar	½ tsp. salt
1 c. white sugar	2½ to 3½ c. flour
1 c. shortening	1 c. cut up dates or raisins
2 eggs	½ c. chopped walnuts
1 tsp. baking soda	

Mix sugar and shortening. Add eggs. Mix well. Add flour. (Start out with 2 cups mixed with the soda and salt. Bake samples until enough flour is added. Dough will be soft.) Add dates and walnuts. Mix ½ cup granulated sugar with 1 teaspoon cinnamon. Drop dough by teaspoonfuls into this mixture. Lift by fork onto slightly greased cookie sheet and bake at 350° till dough mounds and springs back at touch.

Amy Foss, Branch No. 6479, Minnewaukan, ND

LEMONADE COOKIES

1 c. butter
1 c. granulated sugar
2 eggs
3 c. all-purpose flour, sifted
1 tsp. soda

1 (6 oz.) can frozen lemonade
  concentrate (room
  temperature)
Granulated sugar

Cream butter; add sugar. Beat in eggs. Blend in sifted dry ingredients alternately with *only ½ cup* lemonade concentrate. Drop teaspoonfuls onto cooky sheets. Bake at 375° for 8 minutes (about). Brush hot cookies lightly with remaining lemonade concentrate; sprinkle with sugar. Yield: About 10 dozen.

Margaret Richert, Deerfield, WI, Branch No. 2017, Marshall, WI

COCONUT COOKIES

2 c. brown sugar
1 c. shortening
2 eggs
1 tsp. vanilla
1 tsp. coconut flavoring

3½ c. flour
2 tsp. soda
1 tsp. salt
1 c. coconut

Cream sugar and shortening. Beat in eggs and flavorings. By hand, mix in flour and soda. Mix in coconut. Roll into small balls and flatten crisscross with a fork on ungreased cookie sheet. Bake at 350° for about 8 minutes. Yield: 50 to 60 (2 inch) cookies.

Tricia Schellen, Branch No. 1957, Creighton, NE

BUTTER COOKIE

Diabetic:

½ c. butter
3 tsp. Sweet-10
½ tsp. vanilla

1 egg yolk
1 c. flour
Chopped nuts

Not Diabetic:

½ c. butter
¼ c. sugar
½ tsp. vanilla

1 egg yolk
1 c. flour
Chopped nuts

Cream butter and sweetening. Add egg yolk and vanilla. Add flour gradually. At last, roll into small balls and dip in egg white. Roll in chopped nuts. Mash down on cookie sheet. Decorate with half cherry on top. Bake in a 350° oven.

Elsie Lohr, Salem Lutheran Church, Branch No. 389, Affton, MO

GINGER ICEBOX COOKIES

1 c. shortening
1 c. sugar
2 eggs
½ c. molasses
1 tsp. ginger

½ tsp. cinnamon
½ tsp. nutmeg
1 tsp. soda
Pinch of salt
4½ c. flour

Cream shortening and sugar. Add eggs, molasses and dry ingredients. Shape into loaves and let stand overnight in a cool place. Slice and bake in a 350 oven.

Gertrude Krueger, Branch No. 51, Markesan, WI

WALNUT SURPRISE COOKIES

1 egg
1 c. brown sugar, packed
1 tsp. vanilla
½ c. flour

¼ tsp. salt
¼ tsp. soda
¾ c. chopped nuts

Set oven at 350°. Stir together first 3 ingredients. Add next 3 ingredients and mix. Add nuts (walnuts or pecans are best). Spread in 8 inch square pan (batter is thick). Bake at 350° for 18 to 20 minutes.

Cookies will be soft when taken from the oven. Leave in pan until completely cool and then cut into squares.

Yolanda Martin, Breckenridge, OK

FINNISH CHRISTMAS TARTS

3 c. flour
2 tsp. baking powder
1 tsp. salt
1 c. sugar

1 c. lard or shortening
3 to 4 eggs
1 tsp. vanilla

Mix as pie dough. Roll out flat about ¼ inch thick. Cut into 3 inch squares. Cut corners and put in filling of either prunes or raisins. Fold corners to look like pinwheels and sprinkle with sugar. Bake at 350° for 20 to 30 minutes.

Note: Use only cooked and pitted prunes or ground raisins.
Marjorie Johnson, Branch No. 3835, Rolla, ND

BEAR COOKIES

2 c. sugar
2 c. sorghum
1 c. shortening
1 Tbsp. soda
4 eggs, beaten

1 tsp. salt
2 Tbsp. ginger or 1 Tbsp. ginger
    and ½ tsp. anise oil
6½ c. flour (or enough to make
    soft dough)

Mix sugar, sorghum and shortening. Boil together for 5 minutes. Cool and add remaining ingredients. Roll thin for cookie cutouts or make small balls and flatten. Bake on greased cookie sheet at 350° until baked.

This makes great gingerbread bears for Sunday School stockings for Christmas.

Ethel Sanawick, Branch No. 3017, Portland, OR

100 GOOD COOKIES

1 c. white sugar	1 c. coconut
1 c. brown sugar	1 c. ground raisins
1 c. butter	1 tsp. vanilla
1 c. oil	3½ c. flour
1 egg	1 tsp. salt
1 c. Rice Krispies	1 tsp. soda
1 c. oatmeal	1 tsp. cream of tartar

Combine white sugar, brown sugar, butter, oil, and egg. Mix well, using electric mixer. Add Rice Krispies, oatmeal and coconut. Add ground raisins with vanilla. Sift together dry ingredients and fold into the sugar and cereal mixture. Mix very well. Place in refrigerator to chill for an hour or so - even overnight. Drop by teaspoonfuls on ungreased cookie sheet. Flatten dough with a fork. Bake at 350° for about 12 minutes. Cool and enjoy!

Mrs. Irene Blank, Reedsburg, WI, Branch No. 5935, Loganville, WI

POTATO CHIP COOKIES

1 c. shortening	1 c. brown sugar
1 c. white sugar	2 eggs
2 c. flour	½ tsp. salt
1 tsp. soda	1 tsp. vanilla
2 c. potato chips, slightly crushed	1 c. nuts

Cream shortening and sugar. Add eggs and vanilla. Beat well. Add flour, salt, and soda; stir until well mixed. Add potato chips and nuts. Drop onto ungreased cookie sheet and bake for 12 minutes at 350°. Makes approximately 8 dozen.

Helen Petzold Hokett, Branch No. 2205, Granite, OK

MONSTER COOKIES

12 eggs	2 lb. brown sugar
4 c. sugar	1 Tbsp. vanilla
1 Tbsp. syrup	8 tsp. soda
1 Tbsp. salt	1 lb. butter or oleo
3 lb. peanut butter	18 c. oatmeal
1 lb. M&M's candy	1 (12 oz.) pkg. chocolate chips

Mix in dishpan or a very large bowl in order given. Bake at 350°. Drop by large tablespoonful. Bake for 10 to 12 minutes. Cookies will be soft. Allow to cool on cookie sheet.

Betty Oloff, Branch No. 2089, Logan, IA

PEANUT BUTTER BLOSSOMS

1¾ c. flour (all-purpose)
½ c. firmly packed brown sugar
1 tsp. soda
½ c. shortening
1 egg
1 tsp. vanilla

½ c. sugar
½ tsp. salt
½ c. peanut butter
2 Tbsp. milk
48 milk chocolate candy kisses

In large mixer bowl, combine all ingredients, except candy kisses. Blend well at low speed. Shape into balls, using a rounded teaspoonful for each. Roll balls in additional sugar; place on ungreased cookie sheets. Bake at 375° for 10 to 12 minutes. Remove from oven. Top each cookie immediately with candy kiss, pressing down firmly so cookie cracks around edge.

Shirley Ege, Branch No. 771, Elizabeth, IL

SCANDINAVIAN DROPS

½ c. margarine
¼ c. brown sugar, packed
1 egg yolk
1 c. flour

1 egg white, slightly beaten
½ c. chopped pecans
Red or green jelly

Cream margarine. Add sugar gradually. Blend in yolk and flour. Shape into 1 inch balls. Dip in egg white; roll in nuts. Place on greased sheets; make depression in center of each ball. Bake at 300° for 15 minutes. Press down centers again. Bake for 15 to 20 minutes longer. Cool. Fill with jelly.

Mary Schaffer, Loveland, CO

CHOCOLATE TURTLES

2 sq. unsweetened chocolate
½ c. butter
2 eggs
¾ c. sugar

1 c. flour
½ tsp. baking powder
1 tsp. vanilla

Glaze:

2 c. powdered sugar
½ c. cocoa

4 to 6 Tbsp. milk

Melt chocolate and butter. Cool. Beat eggs with sugar. Add flour, baking powder and vanilla. Blend in chocolate mixture. Heat waffle iron to medium heat. Brush with liquid shortening. Drop by teaspoon of dough in middle. Bake for 1 minute. Cool on rack. Frost with glaze.

Sue Folken, Branch No. 1149, Leigh, NE

MELT-IN-MOUTH COOKIES

1 c. shortening
1 c. brown sugar
1 well beaten egg
2 c. flour
½ tsp. salt

½ tsp. soda
½ tsp. cream of tartar
½ c. coconut
½ c. walnuts
1 tsp. vanilla

Sift together dry ingredients. Drop on greased cookie sheet. Press fork dipped in milk.

Mrs. Marion Shelver, Branch No. 2042, Lisbon, ND

SPRINGLE

5 eggs or 1 c. eggs
10 drops of anise oil
1 lb. XXXX sugar (or 4 c. sifted)
1 Tbsp. melted butter or oleo

1 tsp. baking powder
1 tsp. baking soda
2 c. cake flour
2 c. all-purpose flour

Beat eggs until light and fluffy, 20 minutes. While eggs are beating, sift XXXX sugar and flour. After eggs are beaten, fold in 1 tablespoon melted oleo, cooled. Sift 2 cups cake flour, baking powder and baking soda together. Fold in egg mixture. Fold in all-purpose flour. Have on hand 2 cups more flour for rolling.

Roll out on floured board ½ inch thick, then use springle board or springle rolling pin. Set on floured tray in a cool place for 9 to 12 hours or overnight. Bake in a 325°F. oven until straw color. Cool. Store in an air container. To soften, put slice of bread in can every 2 days.

Frieda V. Oblender, Branch No. 736, Bay City, MI

ANISE DROP COOKIES
(Self frosting)

2¼ c. sifted all-purpose flour
½ tsp. baking powder
¼ tsp. salt (or less)
4 eggs

2 c. sugar
½ tsp. anise oil (substitute 1¼ tsp. anise extract)

Sift flour, baking powder, and salt several times. Beat eggs at low speed until frothy, then on medium high for 10 minutes. Beat in 1 tablespoon sugar at a time, using all sugar. Takes about 10 minutes, then at low speed, add dry ingredients slowly. Beat at 15 minutes longer. Blend in anise oil. Make sure to scrape sides of bowl. (Should be thick and creamy white.) Drop by teaspoon onto cookie sheet. Let stand in a cool place or overnight for several hours. Top of cookie should be dry to touch, then bake at 325° for 14 minutes. Makes 12 dozen cookies (size of small half dollar).

Florence Lisko, Branch No. 1400, Arbor Vitae, WI

CHOCOLATE-PEANUT DROP CANDY
(Microwave)

12 oz. chocolate chips   12 oz. Spanish peanuts
12 oz. white almond bark

Melt together in microwave the chocolate chips and almond bark. Stir in the bag of Spanish peanuts. Drop onto cookie sheet to set. Makes a bunch!

Julie Padilla, Branch No. 3107, Loveland, CO

PEANUT BUTTER CUPS

1 c. margarine, melted   1 c. peanut butter
2 c. 10X sugar   12 oz. chocolate chips, melted
1¾ c. crushed graham crackers

Mix together in pan the oleo, confectioners sugar, crushed graham crackers, and peanut butter. Spread in 9x13 inch pan that has been sprayed with *Pam*. Pour melted chocolate chips over top. Chill for 15 to 30 minutes. Cut and serve.

Elizabeth Feldkamp, Branch No. 1061, Saline, MI

REESE'S PEANUT BUTTER CUPS

1 c. peanut butter   1 pkg. graham crackers, crushed
½ c. melted butter   in blender until powdery
2 c. powdered sugar   1 (12 oz.) pkg. chocolate chips

Mix first 4 ingredients with spoon. Spread in a 9x13 inch cake pan. Melt chocolate chips and spread so it covers peanut butter mixture. Cut into squares when chocolate has cooled.

Jamy Manke, Branch No. 5985, Midland, SD

REESE'S PEANUT BUTTER BARS

1½ c. crushed graham crackers   1 (1 lb.) box confectioners sugar
1 c. butter, softened   1 c. crunchy peanut butter

Cream butter and confectioners sugar until light and fluffy. Add peanut butter and crushed graham crackers; stir with spoon. Work until smooth. Press into a buttered 9x13 inch pan.

1 c. chocolate chips   1 Tbsp. peanut butter
1 c. butterscotch chips

Melt chocolate chips, butterscotch chips and peanut butter together. Stir and spread over bars. Cut into squares before chocolate is completely set. Keep refrigerated.

Mary Vander Top, Loveland, CO

PEANUT BUTTER CUPS
(Tastes like Reese's)

3 c. peanut butter
3 c. powdered sugar

1 (12 oz.) bag chocolate chips
1 stick margarine

Mix together in a bowl the peanut butter and powdered sugar. In a small saucepan, melt together the chocolate chips and margarine. Roll peanut butter mixture into walnut size balls. Dip into chocolate mixture and place on waxed paper. Chill.

Jan McLaughlin, Branch No. 3107, Loveland, CO

NEVER FAIL TOFFEE

1 c. white sugar
½ lb. real butter
⅛ tsp. salt

3 Tbsp. water
6 oz. chocolate chips

Combine and cook in heavy pan. Cook on highest heat, stirring constantly until it pulls away from side of pan, turns light brown and starts to smoke. Pour onto buttered cookie sheet. Let cool. Spread on a 6 ounce package of chocolate chips.

Emma Johnston, Branch No. 5844, Churubusco, IN

ENGLISH TOFFEE

2 c. granulated sugar
2 c. butter (not margarine)
¼ tsp. salt
½ lb. semi-sweet chocolate bits or
    grated bar chocolate

1 c. finely ground almonds or
    pecans

Combine sugar, butter and salt in a heavy 3 quart saucepan. Cook at medium heat on range top. Stir constantly until butter melts. Continue to cook, stirring often, until mixture becomes a deep amber color (285°). Pour into a 15x9x1 inch pan or a tray up to 17x13 inches lined with heavy foil.

While toffee is hot, sprinkle chocolate over top and let set for 1 to 2 minutes. Spread chocolate evenly on top with spatula. Press ground nuts into chocolate. Cool for several hours or until set. Break into pieces.

Branch No. 5684, Lafayette, IN

CHOCOLATE TOFFEE

Butter a jelly roll pan. Place whole graham crackers to cover bottom of pan.

Boil for 3 minutes:

1 c. butter
½ c. brown sugar

½ c. chopped pecans

Pour mixture over crackers. Bake at 350° for 8 to 10 minutes. Immediately after removing from oven, place a 6 ounce bag (1 cup) chocolate chips on it. When melted, spread. Cut into small squares when cool.

Cheryl Schultz, Branch No. 3107, Loveland, CO

FONDANT MINT PATTIES

½ c. softened butter or margarine
⅓ c. light corn syrup
½ tsp. salt
1 tsp. peppermint extract

Few drops of red food coloring
1 (1 lb.) box confectioners sugar, sifted

Combine butter or margarine, corn syrup, salt, extract, and food coloring in large mixing bowl. Blend together. Add sugar gradually, stirring until smooth. Knead in remaining sugar with hands. Sprinkle wooden board and rolling pin with confectioners sugar. Roll fondant mixture to ¼ inch thickness. Cut into desired shapes. Makes about 1 pound.

Wintergreen Mint Patties: Substitute wintergreen extract and green food coloring for peppermint extract and red food coloring in preceding recipe.

Alison Ruesch, Branch No. 5844, Columbia City, IN

MINT PATTIES

½ c. oleomargarine or butter
1 egg
1 c. sugar
1 tsp. peppermint extract

1 tsp. soda
1¾ c. flour
2 c. chocolate chips
Paraffin

Beat oleo, sugar and egg together. Combine dry ingredients; add to creamed mixture and mix. Add 1 teaspoon peppermint and mix. Roll in small balls; flatten slightly and place on cooky sheet. Bake at 350° for 10 to 12 minutes. Remove to rack.

In double boiler or microwave, melt chocolate chips and paraffin. Cover baked, cooled cookies and drip on rack.

This is a nice addition to your Christmas goody plate.

Clarice Meyer, Branch No. 2148, Tobias, NE

ENGLISH TOFFEE

1 c. sugar
1 c. butter or oleo
1 Tbsp. corn syrup

3 Tbsp. water
¾ c. chopped almonds or peanuts
1 small chocolate bar, cut fine

Cook sugar, butter or oleo, corn syrup, and water until a few drops tested in cold water crack (290°F.) on candy thermometer. While syrup cooks, chop nuts fine and sprinkle ¾ of them in the bottom of a pie pan. Pour hot syrup over nuts. Sprinkle with finely chopped chocolate bar and top it off with the remaining nuts. When cool, break into chunks.

Clara Schultz, Branch No. 736 Essexville, MI

CHOCOLATE COVERED BONBONS

2 lb. powdered sugar
1 tsp. vanilla
1 can Eagle Brand milk
¼ lb. margarine (room
    temperature)

1 c. chopped pecans
2 (8 oz.) pkg. semi-sweet
    chocolate chips (Nestle only)
¼ lb. paraffin

Mix sugar, vanilla, milk, margarine, and pecans together. Form into balls about the size of a small walnut. Place on cookie sheet and chill. Melt paraffin and chocolate chips in double boiler. Dip the balls in the paraffin mixture and place on waxed paper. Use a toothpick or needle to dip the balls.

Mrs. John (Maxine) Johansen, Branch No. 3365, Rock Springs, WY

PEANUT BUTTER BONBONS

1 c. creamy peanut butter
1 c. powdered sugar
2 Tbsp. soft butter

1 c. chopped nuts
1 c. chocolate chips
1 c. butterscotch chips

Mix butter and sugars; add nuts. Knead to form dough in 1 inch balls. Melt chips. Dip balls into chocolate. Put on waxed paper to dry. Makes 40 pieces.

Belinda Drath, Branch No. 432, Manawa, WI

MICROWAVE PEANUT BRITTLE

1 c. sugar
1 tsp. butter
½ c. light Karo syrup

1½ c. roasted peanuts
1 tsp. baking soda
1 tsp. vanilla

Utensils:

Greased cookie sheet
Large bowl or 1 c. measuring cup

Wooden spoon

Mix together in large microwave safe dish the sugar and corn syrup. Cook on HIGH for 4 minutes. Stir in peanuts and cook for 3 minutes. Stir in butter and vanilla; cook for 1½ minutes. Stir in baking soda till light and foamy. Quickly pour onto lightly greased cookie sheet. Spread evenly. Break into pieces when cool. Makes 1¼ pounds.

Ann Flowers, Branch No. 3436, Pico Rivera, CA

BEST PEANUT BRITTLE

3 c. sugar
½ c. water
2 tsp. baking soda

1 c. light corn syrup
3 c. salted Spanish peanuts

In a heavy saucepan, stir together the sugar, corn syrup and water. Cook over medium heat, stirring constantly, until sugar is dissolved and mixture comes to a boil. Continue cooking, without stirring, until temperature reaches 280° on a candy thermometer or until a small amount of mixture dropped into very cold water separates into threads that are hard, but not brittle (soft crack stage).

Stir in peanuts gradually, so mixture continues to boil. Cook, stirring often and watching closely, until temperature reaches 300° or until a small amount of mixture dropped into very cold water separates into threads which are hard and brittle (hard crack stage).

Remove from heat. Add baking soda; stir in gently, but quickly. This will make it foam. At once, pour candy into 2 greased large cookie sheets, without spreading it with a tool. Cool. Break into pieces. Makes about 2½ pounds.

Carol Nielsen, Branch No. 4077, Racine, WI

PEANUT BRITTLE

1 Tbsp. butter	¼ c. water
1 tsp. soda	1 c. raw peanuts
1 c. sugar	¾ tsp. salt
½ c. white syrup	

Cream and have ready the butter and soda. Mix together sugar, syrup and water. Cook in cast iron skillet. Boil until it forms threads off your spoon. Add peanuts and salt; stir until mixture turns rich tan. Take pan off fire. Stir in butter mixture and pour immediately onto greased cookie sheet.

Ruth Berlin, Branch No. 2311, Saginaw, MI

PEANUT BRITTLE

2 c. sugar	2 Tbsp. butter
1 c. dark Karo syrup	¾ lb. or 2 c. peanuts
½ c. cold water	1 rounded tsp. baking soda

Mix sugar, Karo syrup and cold water. Cook to 242° on candy thermometer. Stir occasionally. Remove from heat; add butter and peanuts. Continue cooking to 292°. Remove from heat and add 1 rounded teaspoonful baking soda. Mix quickly and pour onto buttered pan or pans. Cool slightly and pull until thin. Cool. Break into pieces and store in airtight container.

This candy made and sold every year in early November at Redeemer Lutheran Church annual bazaar.

Redeemer Lutheran Church, Branch No. 1568, Waukegan, IL

BOURBON BALLS

Soak 1 cup chopped pecans in 6 tablespoons whiskey or bourbon overnight or longer. Mix 1 pound plus 3 tablespoons powdered sugar with 1 stick soft oleo. Add nuts and mix well. Refrigerate. Shape into balls and freeze. Dip in dipping chocolate.

When these are done, they look like candy and are like a cream filled chocolate candy.

Gertrude Kummer, Branch No. 3039, Dunlap, IL

BOURBON BALLS
(No bake)

2 c. vanilla wafers, finely ground
2 c. powdered sugar
3 Tbsp. cocoa

2 c. walnuts, finely ground
3 Tbsp. Karo syrup (light)
½ c. bourbon or rum

Mix all ingredients until all is thoroughly mixed. Form into small balls. Roll balls in powdered sugar or finely ground nuts. Store in refrigerator in covered container.

Ella Riebe, Branch No. 5616, Wilton, ND

BUTTER CRUNCH CANDY

1 c. butter (½ lb.)
1 c. sugar
2 tsp. water

1 tsp. light corn syrup
¾ c. chopped walnuts
4 sq. semi-sweet chocolate

Melt butter in 2 quart saucepan over low heat. Remove from heat. Add sugar. With a wooden spoon, stir until well blended. Return to low heat. Stir rapidly until thoroughly mixed and it begins to bubble. Add water and corn syrup; mix well. Put in candy thermometer. Keep heat low. Stirring frequently, cook until thermometer registers 290°F. (brittle stage); takes 15 to 20 minutes.

Remove from heat at once. Sprinkle nuts over surface and mix in quickly. Pour on lightly greased cookie sheet. With spatula, spread ¼ inch thick. Cool to room temperature. As crunch cools, loosen from sheet with spatula 1 or 2 times. Partially melt 2 squares chocolate over boiling water. Remove from water; stir till melted. Spread evenly over crunch. Set aside until firm. Turn over, melt rest of chocolate and spread other side. When firm, break into pieces. Store in tightly covered container in cool place.

Ruth Kriewaldt, Branch No. 3227, Shawano, WI

GLAZED PECANS

1 egg white, slightly beaten
1 to 2 Tbsp. water
½ c. sugar
¼ to ½ tsp. salt

¼ tsp. cinnamon
¼ tsp. cloves
¼ tsp. allspice
1 lb. (4 c.) large pecan halves

Combine all ingredients, except pecan halves. Coat pecans with mixture and place singly on well greased cookie sheet. Bake for 45 minutes at 250°. Remove immediately to prevent sticking. Cool. Store.

Mrs. Arthur L. Harley, Branch No. 1052, South Whitley, IN

SOUR CREAM WHITE FUDGE

2 c. sugar
½ c. sour cream
⅓ c. white corn syrup
2 Tbsp. butter
¼ tsp. salt

2 tsp. vanilla
1 c. coarsely chopped walnuts
¼ c. quartered candied cherries
  (optional)

Combine first 5 ingredients in saucepan; bring to a boil slowly, stirring until sugar dissolves. Boil, without stirring, over medium heat to 236° (soft ball stage). Remove from heat and let stand for 15 minutes. Do not stir. Add flavoring. Beat until mixture starts to lose its gloss (about 8 minutes). Stir in walnuts and cherries; quickly pour into a greased shallow pan. Cool and cut into squares. Makes about 1½ pounds.

Doreen Preuss, Branch No. 5016, Laguna Hills, CA

PEANUT BUTTER BALLS

1 (18 oz.) jar peanut butter
1 stick margarine, softened
1 lb. confectioners sugar

Chocolate (from candy making supply store), melted for dipping

Mix the preceding ingredients with hands. May refrigerate for a short time to make firmer. Roll peanut butter mixture into ¾ to 1 inch balls. Dip into candy making chocolate. Let set in refrigerator for a few minutes; go back over any places that aren't sealed.

Mrs. David Pease, Branch No. 4896, Kalamazoo, MI

HEAVENLY DIVINITY

3 c. granulated sugar
½ c. white syrup
½ c. cold water

2 egg whites
1 tsp. vanilla
Chopped nuts

Mix sugar, syrup and water well; boil to the soft ball stage. Beat eggs and vanilla stiff while syrup is cooking. Pour half of syrup over whites. Boil rest of syrup to hard ball stage and then add to mixture. Fold in nuts. Drop on waxed paper.

Mrs. Margaret Greiner, Branch No. 2838, Wilmot, SD

FUDGEMALLOW CANDY

1 (12 oz.) pkg. semi-sweet
    chocolate pieces
1 c. chunk style peanut butter

4 c. Kraft miniature
    marshmallows

Melt chocolate pieces with peanut butter in saucepan over low heat, stirring until smooth. Fold in marshmallows. Pour into greased 9 inch square pan. Chill until firm. Cut into squares. Makes approximately 2 dozen.

Alison Ruesch, Branch No. 5844, Columbia City, IN

MILNOT MARSHMALLOW FUDGE

1 (13 oz.) can Milnot
4½ c. sugar
½ c. butter or margarine
4½ c. mini marshmallows (or 1
    (13 oz.) jar creme
    marshmallow)

3 c. chocolate chips
2 c. chopped nuts
1 tsp. vanilla

Stir Milnot and sugar together in 4 quart pan. Add marshmallows and butter. Cook over low heat until melted. On medium heat, bring mixture to full boil. Stir for 4 more minutes. Remove from heat. Stir in chocolate chips until melted. Blend in vanilla and nuts. Pour into lightly buttered 9x13x2 inch pan. Cool. Yield: Approximately 5 pounds.

Candy may be refrigerated or frozen once it's set.

Sharon Geiger, Branch No. 5844, Columbia City, IN

CINNAMON HARD CANDY

2 c. sugar
1 c. white corn syrup
½ c. water

¾ tsp. red food coloring
¾ tsp. oil of cinnamon

Cook over medium heat to 295°F. Stir in food coloring and oil of cinnamon. Pour into a buttered pan. The thinner the candy is spread, the easier it will break into interesting irregular shapes. Break as soon as it is possible to handle. Pieces may be sprinkled with powdered sugar for easier handling.

If desired, oil of peppermint and green coloring or oil of cloves (leave clear) could be substituted for red food coloring and oil of cinnamon.

Alison Ruesch, Branch No. 5844, Columbia City, IN

CHRISTMAS HOLLY CANDY

1 stick butter or margarine
32 large marshmallows
1 tsp. green food coloring

4½ c. corn flakes
Cinnamon red hots

Melt butter or margarine and marshmallows together. Stir until smooth. Add in the green food coloring; mix in. Add corn flakes in. Mix until coated. Drop a tablespoon size amount on waxed paper. Drop 2 or 3 red hots on as holly berries. Makes about 2 or 2½ dozen.

Alison Ruesch, Branch No. 5844, Columbia City, IN

COFFEE WALNUTS

1 c. brown sugar
½ c. granulated sugar
½ c. dairy sour cream

1 Tbsp. instant coffee powder
1 tsp. vanilla
2½ c. California walnut halves

In saucepan, combine brown sugar, granulated sugar, sour cream, and coffee powder. Cook and stir till mixture reaches soft ball stage (236°). Remove from heat; add vanilla and walnuts. Gently stir till all nuts are coated. Pour mixture onto buttered large shallow pan or platter. With 2 forks, separate nuts. Cool till set.

Florence Walter, Branch No. 2232, Auburn, MI

MARSHMALLOWS

10 Tbsp. water
2 env. Knox gelatine

10 Tbsp. water
2 c. sugar

Mix water and Knox gelatine; let soak. Boil sugar and water together until it spins a thread. Remove from heat. Add gelatine mixture. Put in large mixing bowl and beat until stiff. Will be white and fluffy. Pour into 9x13 inch buttered pan. Let cool. Cut into squares and wrap in chopped nuts, toasted coconut or colored sugar.

Mathilda Dibbert, Branch No. 2331, Wausa, NE

CORN FLAKES CANDY

1 c. heavy whipping cream
1 c. white corn syrup
1 c. sugar
1 c. peanuts (salted and without
   skins)

1 c. flaked coconut
6 c. corn flakes

Boil cream, white syrup and sugar until it forms a soft ball (should be quite firm). Mix corn flakes, nuts and coconut in a large bowl; pour syrup over and mix. Spread immediately in a buttered 9x13 inch pan and cut into squares or bars as soon as it is set.

Ruth Faszholz, Branch No. 634, Omaha, NE

KIX TREATS

1½ c. sugar
1 c. (less 1 Tbsp.) real butter

2½ c. Kix cereal

In large skillet, heat sugar and butter to boiling; stir constantly (about 10 minutes) or until mixture caramelizes. Remove from heat. Stir in 2½ cups Kix cereal until coated. Turn on ungreased pan. Spread. Break into pieces.

Nancy Ericksen, Branch No. 4231, Neemeh, WI

PRALINE GRAHAMS

40 or 50 plain graham crackers
2 sticks butter
½ c. sugar

1 tsp. vanilla
1½ c. chopped pecans

Place graham crackers in bottom of jelly roll pan. Melt butter and sugar to a boil. Boil for 2 minutes and remove from heat. Add vanilla and pecans. Stir together. Pour over graham crackers. Bake at 350° for 10 minutes. Remove and let cool in pan for 5 to 10 minutes. Remove from pan and break apart or they may start to stick to pan and will not break apart easily.

Dorothy Torbeck, Branch No. 3725, Urbana, IL

VELVEETA CHEESE FUDGE

1 lb. margarine
1 lb. Velveeta cheese
4 lb. powdered sugar

1 c. cocoa
1 tsp. vanilla
1 c. chopped nuts

Melt margarine and cheese over low heat. Sift cocoa and powdered sugar together. Mix with cheese mixture. Add vanilla and nuts. Place in greased 9x13 inch pan. Chill and cut in squares. Makes about 5 pounds.

Aileen Gillam, Branch No. 4845, Youngstown, OH

WHITE PEPPERNUTS

1 qt. white Karo syrup
½ lb. butter
½ lb. lard
3 eggs, well beaten
½ lb. ground nutmeats
½ lb. coconut
1 lb. sugar

½ tsp. cinnamon
½ tsp. cloves
½ tsp. nutmeg
⅔ tsp. baking soda, dissolved in a
    little water
Flour

Let syrup, butter and lard melt together. Add nuts, coconut, sugar, eggs, cinnamon, cloves, nutmeg, and soda in water. Add lots of flour to make a "very stiff" dough. You can't mix this any more with a spoon. Place dough where you can knead in lots of flour. Chill overnight. Roll dough into large ropes, about ¾ inch in diameter. Cut ropes into about ¼ inch slices. Place on greased cooky sheet and bake in 350° oven until golden brown, about 10 to 12 minutes. *Very delicious munching!*

Mrs. Dorothy H. Meyer, Branch No. 5935, Loganville, WI

SALTED PEANUT CHEWS

Crust:

1½ c. flour
⅔ c. brown sugar
½ tsp. baking powder
¼ tsp. soda

½ tsp. salt
½ c. margarine
1 tsp. vanilla
2 egg yolks

In a large bowl, mix all crust ingredients until they make a crumb mixture. Press into a 9x13 inch pan. Bake at 350° for 12 to 15 minutes until a light brown. Immediately sprinkle with 3 cups miniature marshmallows. Return to oven for about 1½ minutes. Cool while preparing topping.

Topping:

⅔ c. corn syrup
¼ c. margarine
1 (12 oz.) pkg. peanut butter chips

2 tsp. vanilla
2 c. salted peanuts
2 c. Rice Krispies

In a large pan, heat corn syrup, margarine and peanut butter chips just until chips are melted and mixture is smooth. (Can be done in microwave.) Stir in peanuts, cereal and vanilla. Spoon warm topping over marshmallows. Spread to cover and chill until firm.

PUDDING CANDY

1 small box regular pudding mix
   (not instant)
½ c. Pet or Carnation milk
   (evaporated)
1 Tbsp. oleo

¼ tsp. vanilla or other flavoring
1 c. salted peanuts or other nuts
   (optional)
1 c. sugar

Mix pudding mix with the evaporated milk and 1 cup sugar. Mix together over medium heat to boiling. Boil for 3 minutes, stirring constantly. Remove from heat and immediately add 1 tablespoon oleo, extract and nuts. Beat the heck out of it till thick and dull. Drop by teaspoon onto wax paper. Add a couple drops of water to loosen if it gets too hard.

Carol Jean Eller, Branch No. 3304, Flushing, MI

CHERRY-ALMOND WHITE FUDGE
(Microwave)

2½ c. sugar
¾ c. sour cream
2 Tbsp. half & half
2 Tbsp. light corn syrup
3 Tbsp. butter or oleo

½ tsp. vanilla
½ tsp. almond extract
½ c. chopped almonds
½ c. chopped maraschino
   cherries, well drained

1. Combine sugar, sour cream, half & half, syrup, and butter in 2 quart glass mix and pour bowl. Mix well.
2. Microwave on (HIGH), uncovered, for 5 to 6 minutes or until mixture boils, stirring once. Stir well and insert microwave candy thermometer.
3. Microwave on (HIGH), uncovered, for 5 to 6 minutes or until thermometer registers 240°. Remove from oven and let stand, without stirring, until 110°, about 2 hours. Add vanilla and almond extract; beat just until mixture begins to lose its gloss. Quickly stir in almonds and cherries. Pour into buttered 8 inch square baking pan. Let stand until firm, about 1 hour. Cut into squares. Makes about 64 (1 inch) pieces.

Carol Jean Eller, Branch No. 3304, Flushing, MI

TURTLES

1 (14 oz.) pkg. caramels (49 to 50
   caramels)
2 Tbsp. evaporated milk

1 Tbsp. butter or margarine
Pecan halves
1 (6 oz.) pkg. chocolate chips

Melt caramels, milk and butter in double boiler. Arrange pecan halves in thirds on buttered baking sheet. Spoon 1 tablespoon caramel mixture over each. Refrigerate, uncovered, for 30 minutes. Melt chocolate chips. Spoon over each to cover.

Sheila Grieser, Branch No. 1265, Creighton, MO

PEANUT BRITTLE

2 c. sugar
1 c. light corn syrup
½ c. water
2 c. raw peanuts

1 rounded tsp. butter
1 tsp. vanilla
1 tsp. baking soda

In large saucepan, combine sugar and water. Cook to hard ball stage. Add peanuts and butter; continue cooking until it browns. Remove from heat; add vanilla and baking soda, mixing well. Spread thinly on two 10x15 inch cookie sheets. When cool, break into serving pieces.

Erna Koelsch, Branch No. 6940, Harrison, MI

CHOCOLATE CREAMS

1 lb. powdered sugar
½ c. margarine

4 Tbsp. whipping cream

Mix preceding ingredients with a mixer. Add any flavoring (maple walnut, coconut or mint) to your own taste. Drop by teaspoon onto powdered sugar for easier handling; roll into balls. Chill for 1 hour. Melt one 12 ounce package chocolate chips, 1 tablespoon butter and a 2 inch square paraffin wax. Mix well. Dip balls into the chocolate mixture, using a fork or spoon to lift balls out. Set on wax paper on cookie sheet. Chill in refrigerator for 1 hour.

Lorraine Graf, Branch No. 1018, Fergus Falls, MN

COCONUT MELTING MOMENTS

½ c. cornstarch
½ c. powdered sugar
1 c. flour

1 c. softened butter or oleo
½ tsp. almond extract
1½ c. flaked coconut

Shape into ½ to 1 inch balls. Roll in coconut and place on ungreased cookie sheet. Flatten with floured fork and bake in a 300° oven for 20 to 30 minutes (don't want them to brown). Makes 3 to 3½ dozen.

Diane Leeds, Branch No. 5325, Colo, IA

Notes

Notes

Miscellaneous

MICROWAVE HINTS

1. Place an open box of hardened brown sugar in the microwave oven with 1 cup hot water. Microwave at high for 1½ to 2 minutes for ½ pound or 2 to 3 minutes for 1 pound.
2. Soften hard ice cream by microwaving at 30% power. One pint will take 15 to 30 seconds; one quart, 30 to 45 seconds; and one-half gallon 45 seconds to one minute.
3. One stick of butter or margarine will soften in 1 minute when microwaved at 20% power.
4. Soften one 8-ounce package of cream cheese by microwaving at 30% power for 2 to 2½ minutes. One 3-ounce package of cream cheese will soften in 1½ to 2 minutes.
5. Thaw frozen orange juice right in the container. Remove the top metal lid. Place the opened container in the microwave and heat on high power 30 seconds for 6 ounces and 45 seconds for 12 ounces.
6. Thaw whipped topping...a 4½ ounce carton will thaw in 1 minute on the defrost setting. Whipped topping should be slightly firm in the center but it will blend well when stirred. Do not overthaw!
7. Soften jello that has set up too hard—perhaps you were to chill it until slightly thickened and forgot it. Heat on a low power setting for a very short time.
8. Dissolve gelatin in the microwave. Measure liquid in a measuring cup, add jello and heat. There will be less stirring to dissolve the gelatin.
9. Heat hot packs in a microwave oven. A wet finger tip towel will take about 25 seconds. It depends on the temperature of the water used to wet the towel.
10. To scald milk, cook 1 cup milk for 2-2½ minutes, stirring once each minute.
11. To make dry bread crumbs, cut 6 slices bread into ½-inch cubes. Microwave in 3-quart casserole 6-7 minutes, or until dry, stirring after 3 minutes. Crush in blender.
12. Refresh stale potato chips, crackers or other snacks of such type by putting a plateful in the microwave oven for about 30-45 seconds. Let stand for 1 minute to crisp. Cereals can also be crisped.
13. Melt almond bark for candy or dipping pretzels. One pound will take about 2 minutes, stirring twice. If it hardens while dipping candy, microwave for a few seconds longer.
14. Nuts will be easier to shell if you place 2 cups of nuts in a 1-quart casserole with 1 cup of water. Cook for 4 to 5 minutes and the nut meats will slip out whole after cracking the shell.
15. When thawing hamburger meat, the outside will many times begin cooking before the meat is completely thawed. Defrost for 3 minutes, then remove the outside portions that have defrosted. Continue defrosting the hamburger, taking off the defrosted outside portions at short intervals.
16. To drain the fat from hamburger while it is cooking in the microwave oven (one pound cooks in 5 minutes on high), cook it in a plastic colander placed inside a casserole dish.
17. Cubed meat and chopped vegetables will cook more evenly if cut uniformly.
18. When baking large cakes, brownies, or moist bars, place a juice glass in the center of the baking dish to prevent a soggy middle and ensure uniform baking throughout.
19. Since cakes and quick breads rise higher in a microwave oven, fill pans just half full of batter.
20. For stamp collectors: place a few drops of water on stamp to be removed from envelope. Heat in the microwave for 20 seconds and the stamp will come right off.
21. Using a round dish instead of a square one eliminates overcooked corners in baking cakes.
22. When preparing chicken in a dish, place meaty pieces around the edges and the bony pieces in the center of the dish.
23. Shaping meatloaf into a ring eliminates undercooked center. A glass set in the center of a dish can serve as the mold.
24. Treat fresh meat cuts for 15 to 20 seconds on high in the microwave oven. This cuts down on meat-spoiling types of bacteria.
25. A crusty coating of chopped walnuts surrounding many microwave-cooked cakes and quick breads enhances the looks and eating quality. Sprinkle a layer of medium finely chopped walnuts evenly onto the bottom and sides of a ring pan or Bundt cake pan. Pour in batter and microwave as recipe directs.
26. Do not salt foods on the surface as it causes dehydration (meats and vegetables) and toughens the food. Salt the meat after you remove it from the oven unless the recipe calls for using salt in the mixture.
27. Heat left-over custard and use it as frosting for a cake.
28. Melt marshmallow creme in the microwave oven. Half of a 7-ounce jar will melt in 35-40 seconds on high. Stir to blend.
29. Toast coconut in the microwave. Watch closely as it browns quickly once it begins to brown. Spread ½ cup coconut in a pie plate and cook for 3-4 minutes, stirring every 30 seconds after 2 minutes.
30. Place a cake dish up on another dish or on a roasting rack if you have difficulty getting the bottom of the cake done. This also works for potatoes and other foods that don't quite get done on the bottom

MISCELLANEOUS

LIFE'S RECIPE

1 c. thoughts
1 c. kind deeds
1 c. consideration for others

2 c. sacrifice for others
3 c. forgiveness
2 c. well beaten faults

Fold in 4 cups prayer and faith. Mix thoroughly and serve with a smile.

Betty J. Boggs, Branch No. 1957, Creighton, NE

RECIPE FOR LOVE

2 c. caring
1 c. giving
Lots of nice things to say
Oodles of smiles
2 c. being near

A dash of kisses
3 *heaping* Tbsp. hugs
½ c. sharing
4 c. patience (may be doubled if
    needed)

Mix together and bake until sweet and tender. Serve daily. Servings: Enough to last forever.

Gretchen Walther, Branch No. 3107, Loveland, CO

HOW TO PRESERVE A HUSBAND

Be careful in your selection. Do not choose too young. When once selected, give your entire thought to preparation for domestic use. Some insist on keeping them in a pickle. Others are constantly getting them in hot water. This makes them so sour, hard and sometimes bitter. Even poor varieties may be made sweet, tender and good by garnishing them with patience, well sweetened with love and seasoned with kisses. Wrap them in a mantle of charity. Keep warm with steady fire of domestic devotion and serve with peaches and cream. Thus prepared, they will keep for years.

Connie Davis, Branch No. 3107, Loveland, CO

WINDOW CLEANER

⅔ alcohol
⅓ water

Coloring (if desired)

SPRAY AND WASH

⅓ c. water
⅓ c. liquid detergent

⅓ c. ammonia

HOLIDAY HOUSE FRAGRANCE

This is an on-the-top-of-the-stove or potpourri pot simmering fragrance *(not edible)*.

Peel from ½ orange
Peel from ½ lemon
1 small cinnamon stick

2 bay leaves
¼ c. whole cloves
1½ qt. water

Combine ingredients and simmer.

Dolores Lund, Branch No. 3107, Loveland, CO

CHILDREN'S PLAY CLAY

3 c. flour
1½ c. salt
6 tsp. cream of tartar
3 c. water

3 Tbsp. oil
Food coloring of choice
½ to 1 tsp. vanilla

Sift dry ingredients into pan. Mix liquids and add color. Blend the fluids into the dry and blend well. Cook over moderate heat, stirring until dough pulls away from pan sides or until it can be squeezed without being sticky. Knead as soon as removed from stove. Store in airtight container.

Sharon Verville, Branch No. 3107, Loveland, CO

SCENTED PLAYDOUGH

2½ c. flour
½ c. salt
2 c. boiling water
1 Tbsp. alum

3 Tbsp. cooking oil
1 to 2 pkg. Kool-Aid (unsweetened
- number of pkg. used will
determine color)

Mix salt, flour, alum, and Kool-Aid together. Add boiling water and stir quickly. Add cooking oil and mix well. When cool enough, use hands. Keeps well in airtight container in refrigerator.

Mona Geidel, Branch No. 3107, Loveland, CO

MODELING CLAY

1 c. flour
1 c. salt
1 Tbsp. alum

About ½ c. water
Food coloring

Add water gradually to just right consistency. Tint desired colors. No cooking required.

Lillian Fairman, Branch No. 3107, Loveland, CO

FINGER PAINTS

½ c. glossy laundry starch
½ c. soap flakes

1½ c. boiling water
1 Tbsp. glycerin

Dissolve starch in small amount of cold water to make a paste. Add boiling water. Cook mixture until it becomes clear, stirring constantly, about 5 minutes. Remove from heat and add the soap flakes, stirring until dissolved. Add glycerin and pour into as many jars as you want colors. Add vegetable colors or calcimine coloring to the mixture in each jar.

This is wonderful, because it does not stain clothes, but washes out.
Lillian Fairman, Branch No. 3107, Loveland, CO

MILLION DOLLAR RELISH

9 qt. cukes (unpeeled), ground
18 large carrots (unpeeled)
6 large green peppers
12 onions (medium size)
3 red peppers (large) or 3 cans
    pimento (large)

9 c. vinegar
12 c. sugar
6 tsp. turmeric
3 tsp. dry mustard
¾ c. salt

Sprinkle salt over cukes. Let set for 1 to 2 hours, then drain. While cukes are soaking in salt, grind carrots, peppers and onions. Mix vinegar, sugar, turmeric, and mustard. Bring mixture (liquids) to boiling point. Add all vegetables. Bring to a boiling point. Boil for 20 minutes. Pour into clean sterilized jars. Seal with lids that have been in hot water. Yields 17 to 20 pints.
Arlene E. Knutson, Branch No. 5616, Tuttle, ND

EASY PERFECT DILL PICKLES

13 to 13½ c. water
1 c. pickling salt

6 to 6¼ c. white vinegar

Boil preceding ingredients for 15 minutes. (This is enough for 9 quarts.) Pack cucumbers in jars with lots of dill. Add 1 tablespoon of sugar to each quart (do not boil sugar). Pour the boiling solution over the cucumbers. Fill to tops of jars and seal tight. Set the jars in boiling water to cover the tops of the jars. Let stand in hot water until cold. These are crisp and do not ferment and stay nice and clear.
Betty J. Boggs, Branch No. 1957, Creighton, NE

SUNSHINE DILL PICKLES

⅓ c. coarse salt (kosher)
1½ tsp. powdered alum
2 c. cider (dark vinegar)
6 c. water
4 to 5 heads dill (or 2 Tbsp. dill
    seed)

2 slices white bread
2 to 4 cloves garlic
Carrot strips and cauliflowerets
Pickles

Small canning pickles, strips or slices can be used.

Mix salt, alum, vinegar, and water together. Boil and partly cool. Place 1 slice of bread in bottom of jar or gallon glass jug. Fill with dill, carrots, cauliflowerets, and pickles, arranging them for color. Fill jar with brine. Top with other bread slice. Put on the lid. Set the jar in the sunshine for 3 days, then refrigerate. These are ready to eat in 3 days. *Very good!*

Anita R. Schmidt, Branch No. 2232, Auburn, MI

GERMAN DILL PICKLES

2 qt. water	1 c. kosher salt
1 qt. white vinegar	Lump of alum
1 clove garlic	Dill

Boil water, vinegar, salt, and alum for 5 minutes. Pack dill and 1 clove garlic into bottom of sterilized jar. Pack pickles and add more dill. Pour hot liquid over pickles and seal.

Erna Koelsch, Branch No. 6940, Harrison, MI

BEET JELLY

Wash beets, then dice into ½ inch squares. Do not peel the beets. Cook until done.

3 c. juice	4 c. sugar
1 pkg. Sure-Jell	1 or 2 pkg. Kool-Aid (raspberry)

Strain beet juice through cloth. Measure juice and Sure-Jell. Let come to a boil. Add 4 cups sugar. Boil until it jells (4 minutes or longer), then add the Kool-Aid. Put into jars and seal.

Mrs. Mary Sahlecker, Branch No. 2042, Milnot, ND

HUCKLEBERRY JELLY

4 c. huckleberry juice	5½ c. sugar
1 (3½ oz.) pkg. dry pectin	

1. Combine berry juice and pectin; bring to a boil, stirring constantly.
2. Add sugar and mix well. Boil at full rolling boil for exactly 2 minutes.
3. Remove from heat. Skim and pour into glasses. Seal with paraffin.

Janelle Reiner, Branch No. 1393, Kalispell, MT

EASY PEACH JELLY

3 c. fresh peaches	3 c. sugar
1 (6 oz.) raspberry jello	

Blend peeled peaches with sugar and jello. Boil for 3 minutes. Remove scum and put in hot jars. Seal

Any flavor jello may be used.

Anna Parsley, Branch No. 2121, Chico, CA

APPLE BUTTER

4 qt. applesauce
8 c. sugar
2 c. vinegar

2 tsp. cinnamon
2 tsp. allspice
2 tsp. cloves

Bake for 3 hours at 350°. Stir once each hour. Makes about 9 pints.

Lois Myers, Branch No. 3651, Chesterland, OH

SURVIVAL FOOD

3 c. dried oatmeal
2 c. powdered sugar
½ c. white sugar
1 (6 oz.) pkg. jello

6 Tbsp. honey
¼ tsp. salt
6 Tbsp. boiling water

Mix together and put in pan. Cut into bars.

Can let dry real well and wrap in plastic and foil. Good for skiers, hunters, etc.

Katherine Fredericksen, Branch No. 1068, Murdo, SD

EGG SUBSTITUTE

8 egg whites
¼ c. nonfat dry milk
1 Tbsp. polyunsaturated vegetable
  oil

7 drops of yellow food coloring

Place egg whites, dry milk, oil, and food coloring into a blender jar. Beat until smooth. Store in a tightly covered jar in refrigerator no more than 1 week. May be frozen if desired.

One-fourth cup egg substitute equals 1 egg. This recipe can be used instead of eggs in baking or in any recipe that calls for beaten eggs and can be used for scrambled eggs and French toast.

Barbara Alsum, Branch No. 3107, Loveland, CO

BASIC SYRUP RECIPE

4 c. juice
1 c. light corn syrup

2 c. sugar

Extract juice from your choice of fruit. Bring to boil all ingredients. Boil for 3 minutes. Pour into hot sterilized jars and seal. Refrigerate when cool. Makes 3½ pints of syrup. Use over pancakes, waffles, French toast, or ice cream.

Variation: When using juice from wild berries, add ¼ cup lemon juice to the ingredients.

Rev. Garland Iseler, Branch No. 2996, Hale, MI

HOMEMADE BUTTER

1 c. buttermilk   1 lb. oleo (margarine)
½ c. vegetable oil

Mix together in mixer or by hand. Add yellow food coloring if desired. Place in covered containers and keep in refrigerator.

This will also freeze for later use. If garlic butter is desired, add garlic salt or powder to taste.

Eleanor Tangeman, Branch No. 4453, Hays, KS

HOMEMADE SWEETENED CONDENSED MILK

1 c. instant nonfat dry milk   ⅔ c. sugar
⅓ c. boiling water   Pinch of salt
3 Tbsp. melted butter or
    margarine

Combine all ingredients in electric blender container. Process until smooth. Remove from blender immediately. This will keep a week or more under refrigeration.

Ruth McDaniel, by Emma J. Wegner, Branch No. 2366, Harlowton, MT

PUSKA

1 qt. milk   ½ tsp. salt
24 eggs

Beat eggs well. Bring milk to boil, then add eggs slowly and keep mixing it at all times till it curdles. Pour into cheesecloth and tie ends so it looks like a cheese ball. Tie ends of cloth over spicket and let drain overnight. In morning, remove cheesecloth and slice to desire needed. Keep refrigerated (bland taste).

Agnes R. Sauers, Branch No. 5196, Monroeville, PA

GOES INTO CHILI SUPPER

"Goes Into Chili:"

15 lb. ground chuck or chopped   onions, and corn (whole
    beef   kernel only), all drained*
An assortment of beans, sauces,
    tomatoes, seasonings,

"Goes into fruit salad:" An assortment of canned fruits and fruit cocktail, bananas, apples, papaya, watermelon, cantaloupe, mangos, coconut, maraschino cherries, etc. (approximately 30 to 40 different or mixed items). Add all ingredients to a large bowl. Mix lightly. Let set for 1 hour to blend flavors. Serve as a side dish to chili.

Take a group of active Branch members and blend them together on a chilly, winter evening. Each must bring a big appetite and their favorite chili ingredient and an addition for the "Goes Into Fruit Salad." Set aside the fruit to be prepared while the chili is simmering. Take the 15 pounds of beef and brown lightly in skillets. Drain.

Place ½ of the browned meat in each of two 4 gallon kettles. Add ½ of the all donated canned ingredients to each kettle. Simmer for 1 to 2 hours and stir often.

Into 1 kettle, add ¼ of the spices. Add the remaining ¾ to the other kettle. (You will have to use good judgment when adding the spices. Make 1 kettle nice and spicy hot and keep 1 kettle mild.) Serve with saltines or oyster crackers and fruit salad. Serves 60 easily.

Note: This is a good fund raiser for Branches who sponsor dinners or suppers. It is called Goes Into because everything goes into it!

* This assortment should be the favorite chili ingredient of the donor. There should be approximately 50 to 60 cans or items to be included.

The Branch (Carol Springer), Branch No. 4582, New Port Richey, FL

Notes

INDEX OF RECIPES

SALADS

SOUPS, SANDWICHES, SAUCES

VEGETABLES

MEATS, POULTRY, SEAFOOD

CASSEROLES AND BREAKFASTS

589

BREADS AND ROLLS

PUDDINGS, PIES, PASTRIES, DESSERTS

CAKES, FILLINGS, FROSTINGS

BARS, COOKIES, CANDIES

MISCELLANEOUS

Notes

Notes

Notes

This Cookbook is a Perfect Gift for Holidays, Weddings, Anniversaries, and Birthdays.

* * * * * * * * * * * *

You may order as many copies of our cookbook as you wish. Drop a line to the address below for more information:

AAL Cookbook
Branch 3107
1101 Hilltop Drive
Loveland, CO 80537

303-667-4506